Violence and Belief in Late Antiquity

DIVINATIONS: REREADING
LATE ANCIENT RELIGION

SERIES EDITORS
Daniel Boyarin, Virginia Burrus, Derek Krueger

A complete list of books in the series is available from the publisher.

Violence and Belief in Late Antiquity

Militant Devotion in Christianity and Islam

Thomas Sizgorich

PENN

University of Pennsylvania Press
Philadelphia

Published by
University of Pennsylvania Press
Philadelphia, Pennsylvania 19104-4112

Printed in the United States of America on acid-free paper

10 9 8 7 6 5 4 3 2 1

Library of Congress Cataloging-in-Publication Data

Sizgorich, Thomas.
Violence and belief in late antiquity : militant devotion in Christianity and Islam / Thomas Sizgorich.
p. cm. — (Divinations: rereading late ancient religion)
Includes bibliographical references and index.
ISBN 978-0-8122-4113-6 (alk. paper)
1. Violence—Religious aspects—Christianity. 2. Violence—Religious aspects—Islam. 3. Martyrdom—Christianity. 4. Martyrdom—Islam. 5. Identity (Psychology)—Religious aspects—Christianity. 6. Identity (Psychology)—Religious aspects—Islam. I. Title.
BT736.15.S57 2009
201'.7633209—dc22 2008017407

For N.A.M. and H.A.D.
Did I find you, or you find me?

CONTENTS

INTRODUCTION 1

CHAPTER ONE
"The Devil Spoke from Scripture": Boundary Maintenance and Communal Integrity in Late Antiquity 21

CHAPTER TWO
"The Living Voice of Kindred Blood": Narrative, Identity, and the Primordial Past 46

CHAPTER THREE
"What Has the Pious in Common with the Impious?" Ambrose, Libanius, and the Problem of Late Antique Religious Violence 81

CHAPTER FOUR
"Are You Christians?" Violence, Ascetics, and Knowing One's Own 108

CHAPTER FIVE
"Horsemen by Day and Monks by Night": Narrative and Community in Islamic Late Antiquity 144

CHAPTER SIX
"The Sword Scrapes Away Transgressions": Ascetic Praxis and Communal Boundaries in Late Antique Islam 168

CHAPTER SEVEN
"Do You Not Fear God?" The Khawārij in Early Islamic Society 196

CHAPTER EIGHT
"This Is a Very Filthy Question, and No One Should Discuss It": The Messy World of Ibn Ḥanbal 231

CONCLUSION 272

LIST OF ABBREVIATIONS 283
NOTES 285
SELECT BIBLIOGRAPHY 367
INDEX 383
ACKNOWLEDGMENTS 397

INTRODUCTION

In the ninth century of the Common Era, the pen of a Christian living in safety very near the heart of Abbasid imperial power scratched out an old and enduring critique of Islam. The Christian, an Iraqi named ʿAmmār al-Baṣrī (d. c. 845 C.E.), charged that as a religion Islam was illegitimate because it had been spread by the sword, whereas Christianity, the one true system of belief, forbade the use of the sword as a means of promulgation of the faith.[1]

It is very likely that in issuing this critique ʿAmmār was responding to certain Muslim communal narratives concerning the birth and early growth of the Islamic *umma*. Among the organizing tenets of these narratives was the belief that the first/seventh-century conquests had been a kind of military miracle in which the will of God was manifested in the lightning conquests of the Persian Sasanian Empire and much of the eastern Roman Empire by ragged Arab armies organized around Muḥammad's revelation. As it was put by the author of an anonymous anti-Christian pamphlet, probably written within a century or so of ʿAmmār's death:

> We set out, barefoot and naked, lacking in every kind of equipment, utterly powerless, deprived in every sort of armament and devoid of all the necessary provisions, to fight the peoples with the most widely extended empires, the peoples that were most manifestly mighty, possessing the most numerous troops, with the most abundant populations and the most imposing domination of the other nations, namely the Persians and the Romans. We went

> to meet them with small abilities and weak forces, and God made us triumph, and gave us possession of their territories.[2]

The Muslim rulers of the former Sasanian domains and much of what had been the most important portions of the Roman east clearly understood the advent of their empire through a narrative of confrontation with and godly victory over the twin terrestrial powers of the late ancient world. This was a narrative in which suffering and death on God's behalf had followed the appearance of a prophet of the God of Abraham and had heralded the advent of a new community of God upon the earth. This was a very old story in the lands of Syria, Mesopotamia, Egypt and North Africa, the territories in which the nascent Muslim *umma* had undergone its formative decades. Indeed, the consequences of violence endured and undertaken in service of God's one community upon the earth had long concerned members of the religious communities arrayed across the landscape of the ancient world.

Similarly, variants of the argument ʿAmmār advanced in his apologetic work, the claim that followers of true religion did not use violence, or at least did not persecute, had echoed in basilicas, churches, monasteries, mosques, and synagogues for centuries.[3] And yet as we shall see in the following chapters, in all of these hallowed spaces there was always a voice willing to answer, and more to the point willing to act, on behalf of the proposition that violence received or undertaken in defense of God's one community upon the earth was in fact virtuous, and indeed the highest of all forms of piety.[4]

Striking indications of the degree to which such attitudes toward violence and piety permeated the imaginative world of late ancient Christians and Muslims sometimes emerge in unexpected places. A Syriac Christian apologetic text written in the later eighth or early ninth century, for example, praises Muḥammad for his willingness to use violence in the service of the one God of Abraham. "Who will not praise, honour and exalt the one who not only fought for God in words, but showed also his zeal for him with the sword?" the Christian hero of the text asks. "[Muḥammad] praised, honoured and exalted those who worshiped God with him, and promised them kingdom, praise and honour from God, both in this world and in the world to come in the Garden. But those who worshipped idols and not God he fought and opposed, and showed to them the torments of hell and of the fire which is never quenched and in which all evildoers burn eventually."[5]

The text presents itself as a dialogue between the *katholikos* Timothy and the caliph al-Mahdi. During their conversation, "Timothy" likens Muḥammad to such Old Testament destroyers of idols and idol worshippers as the prophets Moses and Abraham. It was through Muḥammad and his zeal that God had destroyed two wicked empires, the *katholikos* continues; the first to suffer before Muḥammad's armies was the Sasanian Empire, whose rulers were worshippers of "creatures rather than the Creator." Then the Muslim columns drove from its former domains the Roman Empire, which tolerated wicked Christologies.[6] This Christian iteration of the Islamic *umma*'s own origin narrative is remarkable for a variety of reasons, not least because of the apparent effortlessness with which Muḥammad is rendered here in accordance with models of pious imperial rulership that had been in use within the late antique cultural milieu since the fourth century advent of a self-consciously Christian Roman Empire.

Centuries earlier, for example, while addressing a new imperial sovereign on the occasion of the emperor Theodosius I's death, the bishop Ambrose of Milan recalled the recently deceased emperor in terms strikingly similar to those with which Timothy would centuries later describe Muḥammad; Theodosius, Ambrose said, had been an implacable enemy of idolatry and idolaters, a new Jacob who "put away the idols of the gentiles, whose faith indeed put away all worship of the idols, obliterated all of their ceremonies."[7] Theodosius as a wielder of the sword on God's behalf was an image that stuck among Ambrose's contemporaries and with the generations of literate Christians who came after him. Indeed, Theodosius emerged in the memories of many late ancient Roman Christians as a paragon of intolerant Christian zeal and as a model for emperors who fashioned themselves in accordance with the proposition that the truest test of a Christian ruler's commitment to God and his community was that ruler's willingness to pursue and punish those whom his community took as its enemies.[8]

By the time Ambrose saw Theodosius off the imperial stage in 395, the communities of the late ancient world had for decades felt an abiding fascination for figures who were remarkable for the militant and often aggressive forms their piety took.[9] Most often these were figures whose renunciation of the present world and its concerns located them on the margins of the communities for whom they emerged as exemplars. As they existed in the imaginations of their contemporaries, these were figures that carried within themselves the entire history of the Christian communities of the Roman world, and indeed of the Christian communities that spread across the face of the Persian Empire, and beyond the boundaries of territory controlled by either empire. The ascetic zealots we encounter in many accounts of pious violence emerge in our texts as repositories of all of the qualities recalled by contemporary Christians as characteristic of the steely-eyed defenders of Christianity during storms of persecution, during which a few selfless individuals insisted upon the defining beliefs of their communities and defended them in spite of terrible fear, horrific torture, and finally death. Troublingly, as such zealots went about their work, they adopted as their own the methods, practices, and penchant for violence against which their own communities were recalled to have so bravely defined themselves.

In a nameless Egyptian village, for example, the fifth-century ascetic Macarius of Tkōw led a band of his followers to investigate rumors that a local pagan priest had been sacrificing Christian children to his god. Accusations of child murder had of course been leveled against Christian communities during outbreaks of pagan persecution and had led to acts of official and popular violence against Christians. Now, in a Roman Empire ruled by Christians, Macarius subjected the pagan priest to a process of interrogation concerning the confession-based accusations against him, found him guilty, and burned him alive. He then conducted a pogrom against the remaining pagans in the village, forcing the conversions of some and forcibly expelling the rest.[10]

One of the central questions this book seeks to answer is why such figures so captured the imaginations of the communities of late antiquity. Put another way, the abiding concern of this book is to understand why militant forms of piety and the figures associated with militant and aggressive modes of religiosity became such crucial resources for communal self-fashioning among early Christian and early Muslim communities. This is a difficult problem for a variety of reasons, not least because the view taken of such violence and the individuals who carried it out by members of the communities "represented" by such militants varied greatly. Even as they celebrated pious militants who often violently imposed boundaries between their own communities and the other communities of their world, many late ancient individuals seem to have been quite content to lead lives in which they themselves mixed regularly and intimately with members of other communities. Indeed, most late antique persons, whether they were pagan, Christian, Jewish, or Muslim, seem to have had very little interest in undertaking violence against their neighbors on the behalf of God or anybody else and still less interest in dying as martyrs. And yet, as we shall see, those devout men and women who, in moments of confrontation and conflict, stepped forward and evinced a willingness to kill or suffer on God's behalf occupied a highly charged, privileged position in the imaginations of their contemporaries. Moreover, from the last quarter of the fourth century on, it was militant interpretations of the Christian message and mission that became normative both in imperial Roman policy and in the imaginations of Christian communities arrayed across the landscape of the late antique Mediterranean and Mesopotamia. Later, as the nascent Muslim community sought to define itself in opposition to the other communities of late antiquity, ascetic warriors on God's behalf commanded the imaginations and loomed large in the projects of self-definition of those Muslims who spent their lives in peaceful and urbane coexistence with neighbors, friends, business partners, and relatives representing an array of confessional communities. How can we account for this?

In the chapters that follow, I will argue that if we are to understand the advent of militant piety as a defining feature of late ancient Christianity and Islam, we must look to questions of communal identity and the imaginative structures and historical processes whereby identity is constituted. For simple reasons of chronology, I will address the history of the Christian communities of the later Roman world first. In so doing, I seek to join in a burgeoning discussion among scholars of the later Roman world regarding confessional identity, communal boundaries and the ways in which these coincided with worship-based technologies of the self, social organization and political praxis.

The work of Daniel Boyarin, in particular, has not only consistently underscored the complexities inherent in questions of communal or confessional identity in the later Roman world but also has vividly illustrated that persons situated at various points along a broad and diverse continuum of confessional sites frequently found themselves enthralled with the beliefs and practices of others situated at various points along that continuum. More concretely, Boyarin has shown that rather than two separate and hermetically sealed religious entities, late ancient rabbinic Judaism and Christianity are better understood through the fourth century as ever evolving, mutually influential, and mutually influenced conversations, conversations in whose textual remains the careful reader can still detect a cacophony of competing and often discordant voices. Perhaps most important for the present work is Boyarin's insight that it was through the efforts of individual believers, identifying with distinct but ultimately imagined communities, to delimit and corral these conversations by the imposition of defining boundaries or border lines demarcating Christian from Jewish that the religions of Christianity and Judaism qua religions eventually came into being.

Of particular interest in my own study have been the resources that members of Christian communities had at their disposal as they imagined those communities. Often, as Richard Lim, Éric Rebillard, J. Rebecca Lyman, Mark Vessey, David Brakke, Daniel Boyarin, and Virginia Burrus, among others, have shown, this was accomplished through the elaboration of textual traditions in which Christian intellectuals and churchmen located the bases for orthodox modes of belief and praxis.[11] Meanwhile, Andrew Jacobs has convincingly argued that an increasingly imperial economy of Christian self-definition produced and consumed an imagined Jew and an imagined Jewish past—both of which were inextricably tethered to the lived realities of contemporary Jewish persons and Jewish communities—as resources for the elaboration of the textual and narrative traditions upon which its evolving boundaries depended.[12] Elsewhere, Michael Penn has intriguingly explored the performative role played by kissing among early Christian communities as a means of enacting and policing the boundaries of those imagined communities. The kiss of Christian love, Penn has shown, emerged as a means of inclusion and exclusion and as an emblem for a genre of kinship that resided in the spirit rather than in the flesh.[13]

Other recent research has shown that integral to the process of imagining such bounded communities was the need to conceptualize the character or nature of the Christian community itself. Denise Kimber Buell, for example, has asked, in effect, what models were available to early Christian groups as they conceptualized the communities to which such practices as kissing lent contour. In so doing, Buell has argued that a reelaborated version of classical conceptions of race (*genos, ethnos, laos*) came, through a process Buell calls "ethnic reasoning," to deeply influence the ways in which early Christians conceived of Christianness, and its Others. Aaron Johnson has similarly sought to understand the nature of the Christian communal or national identity as it was envisioned in pointed opposition to Greek ethnicity via processes of "ethnic argumentation" in such early and influential patristic texts as Eusebius's *Praeparatio Evangelica*.[14]

In examining the specific question of militant piety, I have been particularly interested in many of the questions that animate this exceedingly rich constellation of recent research, but I have approached these questions by a rather different route and with a rather different set of questions in mind. What this book shares with these other studies is a concern with the ways in which questions of identity were negotiated in diverse, unstable, and intellectually and culturally fecund spaces, the ways in which these negotiations coincided with the lived social, political, and cultural realities of individuals and communities, and the processes whereby authoritative iterations of the past, interpretations of the present, and projections about the future were produced and articulated. Where the present work diverges from its neighbors in the study of the late ancient world is in the specific components of late ancient political, social, and spiritual economies that it addresses, the breadth of cultural, political, and religious space over which it engages these questions, and the cognitive and cultural engines upon which it focuses as a means of understanding how and why militant piety came to so engage the imaginations of late ancient peoples. More specifically, this book looks to questions of identity and identity production as a means of better understanding the role of violence, whether real and imagined, in the religious and spiritual (and so political, cultural and social) lives of late ancient persons and communities. Within the categories of late ancient persons and communities this book includes not only the exceedingly diverse and far-flung Jewish and Christian communities of the later Roman world but also the Muslim communities of the early Islamic Empire. Key to my analysis of the problem of militant piety in late antiquity are certain recent insights regarding the role of narrative in the articulation of individual and communal identities and the role of narrative in the hermeneutic processes that precede and so often guide cultural, political, and confessional decision making.

For many Christian individuals and communities within the later Roman world, questions of confessional authenticity and legitimacy were articulated, elaborated, and contested in accordance with what were to become core narratives regarding the history of the Christian community within the Roman Empire. Central to these narratives were stories of persecution by, resistance to, and, in the post-Constantine era, eventual triumph over the coercive power of the Roman imperial state. These were tales in which, as they evolved from the second century on, intransigent, godly individuals stood unmoved before proud and confident representatives of Roman imperial power and testified to the truths of their faith. For their courage they were subjected to the most horrific violences of which the Roman imperial edifice was capable and miraculously withstood them. In so doing, these individuals preserved the integrity of their community even as they defended the tenets of the faith that resided, unseen, within their hearts.

This was to become the basis for the defining narrative of Christianity's formative history, a history of desperate defense of an imperiled community by inspired individuals whose capacity and willingness to face terrifying violence preserved the one community of God upon the earth. As we seek to understand the legacy of religious violence within the ongoing history of this community, however, we must ask, as Elizabeth Castelli has recently done, "What does it mean for a group to constitute its identity through the memory of past suffering?"[15]

In seeking an answer to this question, I have drawn upon the work of a number of anthropologists, sociologists, and other scholars dealing with questions of identity. Perhaps most important for this project have been the works of the cultural anthropologist Fredrik Barth, the sociologist Margaret Somers, and the historian and sociologist Ronald Grigor Suny. Much of Barth's best-known work deals with the question of ethnic identity and more specifically, the elements that allow human subjects to inhabit distinct identities as experiential realities. In both his foundational 1969 "Introduction" to *Ethnic Groups and Boundaries* and in his more recent work dealing with the problem of communal boundaries, Barth has illustrated the crucial roles played by social, political, and cultural processes by which difference is described and experienced on the basis of certain ascribed qualities that mark members of a given group as recognizably distinct from nonmembers.[16] Such processes allow for the erection of "communal boundaries" that are understood to circumscribe identity groups, setting each in clear opposition to other identity groups. Moreover, Barth has demonstrated that it is not the specific, "native" cultural forms—modes of dress, kinds of dance, language, modes of production, literary forms—with which identity groups associate themselves or are associated by outsiders that allow and constitute separate identity groups but rather an enduring and renewable discursive system of demarcation on the basis of such ascribed qualities that is carried out at the imagined boundaries of the group by its own members and by members of other groups. Indeed, Barth has noted that the "cultural stuff" traditionally associated with opposed identity groups is often in fact shared by such groups on either side of the communal boundaries that mark opposed groups as self-consciously distinct entities. Moreover, the ascribed qualities that mark individuals as members of such groups may change over time, even though the group itself is understood by contemporary members to have abided continuously down through time as a bounded whole whose integrity has never diminished and whose standards of membership have remained constant.

This mode of experiencing identity as a stable, bounded, and diachronic combination of ascribed characteristics that are innate to all genuine members of a given group is examined at length in Suny's work on post-Soviet Armenia and Azerbaijan and in Clifford Geertz's analysis of certain cultural and political trends in former European colonies in the first years after independence. The term Geertz applies to such modes of reckoning identity—"primordialism"—is derived in turn from Edward Shils's studies of the mentalities of former German soldiers following the Second World War.[17] Suny's studies of primordialism are particularly useful in that they reveal much not only about the functioning of primordialist modes of imagining identity but also about the social and political consequences of primordialism in the emerging states he studies. One of Suny's most important insights concerns the role primordialist discourses play in the ways in which human subjects interpret contemporary events. Suny's work demonstrates that for groups who understand their identity in primordialist terms, recalled events embedded in the defining narratives in accordance with which the group in question imagines its formative past often provide an interpretive grammar through which to make sense of contemporary events.[18]

Indeed, the role of narrative in processes of identity formation and in the interpretation of moment-to-moment experience by human subjects has in recent years become a site of sustained dialogue among scholars working in the fields of psychology, sociology, anthropology, philosophy, and literary criticism. For my work, the studies of Margaret Somers along these lines have proven crucial.[19] Somers, drawing upon the work of Paul Ricoeur and Jerome Bruner, among others, has illustrated the crucial function of narrative forms in the constitution of group and individual identities, and the determinative roles such identity-specific narratives play in the interpretation of the events, personalities, institutions, and cultural forms encountered from moment to moment by human subjects. Individuals, Somers argues, understanding themselves to be "emplotted" in large- and small-scale narratives, most readily find other individuals and groups comprehensible as "characters" within such narratives, with roles to play that are in large measure determined by such elements as the underlying "themes" and "plots" of the narratives in question.[20] Similarly, Somers suggests, "events" become comprehensible to human subjects as "episodes" as they are interpreted through the hermeneutic grammar supplied by the specific narratives in accordance with which those subjects' identities have been constituted. Accordingly, just as individual or communal identity is dependent upon emplotment within certain key narratives of the past, the present and future are also made comprehensible or imaginable via the interpretive possibilities contained within such narratives.

In the later Roman world, as we shall see, the specific readings to which such events as the persecution of Christians, the advent of Constantine, and attacks on the material culture and bodies of pagans, Jews, and heretics were subject frequently depended upon the specific narrative in accordance with which such events were interpreted. Such fourth-century intellectuals as Libanius of Antioch and Ambrose of Milan, for example, drew upon competing narratives of the Roman past as they sought to coax from the emperor Theodosius I certain responses to the violence of militant Christians. In his *Oratio 30*, for example, Libanius articulated a narrative of the Roman past that derived from a centuries-old discourse of Roman imperialism that allowed him to portray the statues and temples currently under attack by Christian militants as material manifestations of the cultural and political traditions in which the capacity of any Roman emperor, Christian or pagan, was rooted.[21]

Ambrose, for his part, evoked a narrative of the Roman past in which the one community of God upon the earth had survived repeated persecution at the hands of Roman imperial officials and had survived only through the strivings of its most committed and godly members.[22] In accordance with this narrative, each and every Christian, whether a small child or the emperor himself, was obliged to "protect" his or her community against its enemies, with whom moments of confrontation or conflict were now understood simply as new episodes within an ancient but enduring story of persecution waged against the Christian community by agents of evil who took many forms. Meanwhile, as we have seen, Christian intellectuals like Ambrose would, during the emperor's lifetime and immediately following his death, craft Theodosius as a militant champion of Christian orthodoxy, and as a model to be emulated by all future Christian Roman rulers.

As the Christian communities of Roman late antiquity defined themselves on the basis of communal boundaries that were, in each case, understood to enclose the one true community of God upon the earth, they articulated local narratives in which those communities were maintained from the primordial beginnings of the community through the protection and preservation of precious revealed truths and via the personal piety, strivings, and sacrifices of its most virtuous members. For contemporary Christians, these narratives were also repositories for the kinds of qualities that were to be expected in all "true" Christians, Christians, that is, who bore all of the creedal and behavioral markings avidly sought through processes of boundary maintenance carried out by, or at the behest of, the intellectual, political, and spiritual leaders of local communities.

The maintenance of such communal boundaries was a particularly complicated task in the later Roman world, in part because, as the research of Daniel Boyarin and others has demonstrated with ever greater clarity, individual members of many communities seem to have imbibed deeply from a rich *koinê* of signs, symbols, narrative forms, holy persons and sites, textual traditions, and strategies of interpretation as they negotiated for themselves questions of divinity, the numinous, salvation, personal piety and holy praxis. It was for this reason, for example, that for centuries after the fabled parting of the ways between Christianity and Rabbinical Judaism, John Chrysostom and other Christian leaders had to insist that real Christians did not get circumcised, attend the feasts and fasts of Passover or visit Jewish shrines to monotheistic heroes revered by Christians and Jews alike, while at the same time Jewish rabbis worried deeply over the attraction the figure of Christ held for members of their own communities, inventing for such individuals the category of the "minim," a rough corollary to the Christian "heretic."[23]

The disciplining of Christian identities that these anxieties inspired required authoritative figures upon which members of discrete Christian communities could rely to discern and enforce the boundaries that set such communities apart from all others. Often, those Christians whose role it was to patrol and defend these communal boundaries were understood by their contemporaries to carry within themselves something of the essential qualities of the heroes celebrated in local Christian foundation stories as communal forebears and patrons, those uncompromising intimates of God, the Christian martyrs. In the later Roman world, the role of stalwart defender of communal truths was frequently taken up by Christian ascetics, whose physical sufferings and spiritual strivings on God's behalf were understood to constitute the basis for a numinous affinity between themselves and their martyr ancestors.

As we shall see, this role frequently put Christian ascetics on the front lines of religious conflict throughout later Roman history and established

Christian monks in the east and the west as archetypical warriors on God's behalf, defenders both of "true religion" and the defining boundaries of various Christian communities. Accordingly, during the latter half of the fourth century and throughout the fifth century, Christian ascetics consistently appear as participants in attacks on the bodies and material culture of pagans, Jews, and those Christians deemed heretics by the communities with which those ascetics identified. By the last decades of the sixth century, we find Christian monks separating by force intimately intermingled Christian and Jewish communities, and, in the context of deadly Christological controversies in Syria, arrayed in ranks opposite heretical Roman imperial armies and dividing orthodox Christians from heretics through spectacular acts of violence.[24]

Notably, it was often Christian ascetics whose violences gave occasion to what would prove defining moments of intentional or unintentional policy making within the Roman world, as when, in the 380s, Theodosius I chose to ignore the destruction of a Jewish synagogue and pagan temples and artworks by Christian militants despite the protests of his Jewish and pagan subjects.[25] Accordingly, although late ancient Christian ascetics were not the primary cause of the religious violences of their age, they emerge in our sources as emblems of that violence and as figures whose role as discerners and defenders of communal boundaries imposed a compelling grammar upon their violence as it was recalled and described by their contemporaries and near contemporaries. It is not surprising, then, that during this period Christian ascetics also became associated with militancy on God's behalf well beyond the borders of the Roman world, so that with the onset of the seventh century, we will find one recently converted Persian noble of ascetic inclination leading mounted raiding parties against impious Roman armies, and the Christian monk embraced as an archetype of militant striving on God's behalf by a new community of Abrahamic monotheists as it imagined and narrated its own past in the cities of Syria and Mesopotamia.[26]

Indeed, in addressing the advent of militant piety in the later Roman world, it has also become possible to understand better the role of militant forms of piety in the formation of the early Islamic community. The early Islamic *umma* took shape within a cultural and religious habitat dominated by the cultural forms, systems of belief and praxis and political traditions that historians of the later Roman and Sasanian empires have come to describe by implied consensus as "late antique." As we shall see, as early Muslim intellectuals undertook the crucial business of articulating a narrative of the primordial Islamic past, they naturally did so in part by elaborating upon certain imaginative forms long native to the communities among which the emerging Muslim polity abided. Central to this process was an ongoing attempt to locate within an emerging Islamic metanarrative the events of the life of the prophet Muḥammad, and the events of the period immediately following his death, when the community he left behind confronted and bested the twin imperial powers of late antiquity.[27] The conquests or *futūḥ* of the Persian Empire and the most important regions of the eastern Roman Empire represented for early Muslim intellectuals a grand drama in which the one God of Abraham had given the long oppressed Muslim *umma* dominion over vast territories and immeasurable wealth via a lightning campaign of military conquest undertaken by bands of ascetic, pious warriors "on the path of God."[28]

As the memory of these events became enshrined in certain privileged narratives of Islamic communal origins in the late first, second, and third centuries after the *hijra*, the qualities recalled to have adorned the Muslim participants in the conquest period—contempt for the present world, utter devotion to God, scrupulously ascetic modes of comportment, fierce determination in the face of worldly imperial power—all came to mark contemporary Muslims as particularly worthy and as exemplars of all that made one "a real Muslim."[29] As we shall see, this was of particular importance in the early Islamic world in part because legitimacy and authority within that world so often depended upon perceived imitation of the example set on earth by Muḥammad and the first members of his community.[30] Who and what "real Muslims" were was a question further complicated by the fact that during its first centuries, the Islamic *umma* lived in constant dialogue with non-Muslim communities and individuals and was itself in the midst of a series of rapid and often traumatic political, cultural, and religious evolutions.

I will argue in the following chapters that as early Muslim scholars struggled to construct a narrative of Islamic origins, they regularly elaborated upon a *koinê* of signs, symbols, and narrative forms with which the other communities of late antiquity had for centuries contested questions of divine revelation, prophetic legitimacy, communal integrity and eruptions of the numinous into the lived experience of individuals and communities and that as they did so they inextricably (and unknowingly) bound their community to a constellation of kindred communities arrayed from Ireland to Yemen and from the Atlantic coast of Iberia to eastern Mesopotamia. One result of this process was that the place of pious violence in the early Islamic imaginary, particularly in the theory and practice of *jihād*, closely depended upon much older models of militancy on God's behalf, so much so in fact that among the earliest discussions we possess of *jihād*, the institution itself is frequently compared by Muslim authors to Christian monasticism, and its practitioners to Christian monks.

Indeed, as the early Muslim *umma* imagined and narrated accounts of a specifically Islamic past, the founding members of that community were constructed as figures of a readily recognizable sort: they were men and women for whom the present world held no allure and whose belief and unswerving faith had led them into conflict with the great powers of their world.[31] These were men and women who refused to be intimidated or bribed into cooperation with the corrupt powers of the present world and whose devotion to God and the world to come manifested itself in a scrupulous asceticism that marked them as it had marked so many other adherents to the revealed truths of Abraham's God. In the first centuries of Islam, pious renunciation emerged as one of the primary markers of heightened piety among Muslim rulers and their subjects, and the idioms of renunciation to which these figures gravitated were those long practiced by the heroes of many non-Muslim communal narratives. These included fasting and the consumption of simple foods, avoidance of worldly power, rejection of material wealth, bouts of weeping, prolonged prayer and lengthy vigils, suspicion of the body and its pleasures and removal of the self from the companionship of other humans.

By the second/eighth century, among the most important exemplars of these "essentially Muslim" characteristics were men like ʿAbd Allāh b. al-Mubārak, an ascetic and traditionalist who spent much of his life on the Muslim frontier with the Roman state, practicing *jihād* even as he composed one of the most influential of all early Muslim texts on the topic. Notably, Ibn al-Mubārak also wrote a similarly important book on the theory and practice of *zuhd* or pious renunciation.[32] In Ibn Mubārak's works we find one of the earliest systematic articulations of the ideals of *jihād*. His thought influenced such crucial Muslim intellectuals as Aḥmad b. Ḥanbal, the founder of one of the four major schools of Islamic jurisprudence, through whom Ibn al-Mubārak's conceptions of *jihād* and renunciation informed generations of piety-minded Muslims as they struggled with questions concerning the kinds of beliefs and behaviors that marked individuals as "real Muslims."[33] Notably, Ibn al-Mubārak's theory of *jihād* and his theory of ascetic praxis or *zuhd* reveal significant overlap, and it is in Ibn al-Mubārak's works on *jihād* and asceticism that we first encounter *ḥadīths* attributed to the prophet Muḥammad likening the practice of *jihād* to the ascetic praxis of Christian monks.[34]

To understand why individuals like Ibn al-Mubārak became exemplars for their city-dwelling contemporaries and descendants, we must look to another text produced in the second/eighth century, that of the Muslim historian al-Azdī, whose history of the conquest of Syria contains a series of vivid and frequently repeated portraits of the earliest Muslim warriors as they confronted the imperial power of Rome and brought forth a new community of God upon the earth. As al-Azdī, his sources, and his contemporaries imagined the foundational Muslim past, they imagined their communal forebears as men like Muʿādh b. Jabal, a poor and determined *mujāhid* who met with Roman imperial officials, spoke for them the truths around which his community had cohered, and called the Romans to observance of those truths. Then, aided by God, Muʿādh and his companions vindicated those truths in bloody confrontation with the Roman army.[35]

Men like Muʿādh occupied a place in the imaginations of Muslims living in the communities produced by the *futūḥ* very much like that occupied by the Christian martyrs in the imaginaries of late ancient Christians; they were figures through whom God had worked his will in the world and made his presence felt in the affairs of the great terrestrial powers of the age.[36] For late ancient Muslims, as for late ancient Christians, the great imperial powers of late antiquity had provided sites in which the organizing truths of local faith communities were tested and vindicated in accord with contemporary understandings of power, the numinous, and the boundaries of the possible.[37] Just as the martyrs had emerged as crucial resources for self-fashioning and the erection of communal boundaries for late ancient Christian communities, now the individuals who carried forth Muḥammad's prophecy and God's will into the lands of the imperial superpowers of late antiquity abided in the imaginary of the early Muslim *umma* as exemplars in whose memory could be located the defining qualities of all real Muslims.

The narratives in which figures like Muʿādh b. Jabal were recalled by al-Azdī and other Muslim authors became for the Muslims what Fred Donner has termed "narratives of Muslim communal origins." It was by articulating these narratives, Donner has shown, that the community of Arab monotheists that had cohered around Muḥammad's revelation became the Muslim *umma*, in the sense that it was through the articulation of a distinct narrative of its own history that the Muslim *umma* advanced specific claims concerning the truth of Muḥammad's revelation, the place of Muḥammad's community in the history of the late ancient world, and the specific character of the community left on earth after Muḥammad returned to God.[38] In this sense, these narratives functioned much as had Christian narratives of the local histories of late ancient Christian communities and particularly those in which such Christian heroes as the martyrs and superstar ascetics performed and embodied the behavioral and personal qualities that marked an individual as an authentic member of the one community of God.[39]

For the Muslim community, as for the Christian community, the character of the foundational narratives in accordance with which individual and communal identities were constituted frequently seems to have determined the ways in which Muslim individuals and communities interpreted the personalities, events, and ideas that surrounded them. Accordingly, the virtues of Muslim leaders were consistently evaluated in accordance with these narratives, as were the actions of their followers. Similarly, relations with other communities were conducted in accordance with the recalled example of the Prophet and his companions. It was for this reason that the central role of violent conflict within the organizing narratives of the Muslim community's privileged renditions of the past posed an enduring series of dilemmas for the late ancient Muslim *umma*, just as it had for the Christian communities of the later Roman world.

For the Muslim community, these dilemmas manifested themselves most acutely in the figure of the Kharijite.[40] Kharijites (Ar. *Khawārij*, s. *Khārijī*) were proponents of certain rigorist interpretations of Islam and members of small, ever more exclusive communities that first appeared in the course of the fourth caliph ʿAlī's civil war with Muʿāwiya. Indeed, the first Kharijites were men who had sided with ʿAlī in the civil war but who came to abandon ʿAlī when he agreed to have his dispute with Muʿāwiya arbitrated by humans rather than settled by God in battle. The men who became the Kharijites are recalled in our sources as figures remarkable for the intensity of their devotion and the flamboyance of their performance of this devotion in acts of ascetic renunciation and regimens of prayer, fasting, and scrupulous observance of religious law as they interpreted it. They were men who understood themselves to stand in the places of previous Muslim martyrs who died in defense of true religion and who avidly sought martyrdom for themselves.[41]

In all of this, the Kharijites were figures that can be said to have embodied all of the virtues recalled by late ancient and early medieval Muslims as having marked the early members of Muḥammad's community as men of God and the participants in the *futūḥ* as warriors fighting in service of the numinous truths around which Muḥammad's community had cohered. Troublingly, however, as they are recalled in the earliest Muslim texts we possess, they were also men who also carried with them a chilling penchant for violence undertaken in God's name. Soon after they left ʿAlī, for example, the first Kharijites encountered the grandson of one of Muḥammad's companions. After questioning him about his attitude to ʿAlī and discovering that he disagreed with them on certain points of belief, they murdered him and then split open the belly of a woman who had been pregnant with his son. Finally, they butchered another group of women traveling with the couple.[42] For the Kharijites, these actions had been taken in accordance with the divine commands issued to men like Muʿādh b. Jabal and the heroes of the conquests; they had found themselves in dialogue with unbelievers who rejected God's word and had brought down upon them God's wrath with placid hearts and steady hands.

Early Muslim authors recalled the Kharijites with a combination of fascination and loathing, crafting them in their texts with minute concern for detail and recounting their exploits in breathless dramatic sequences while at the same time narrating their actions in accordance with a semiotics of profound horror. The Kharijites were acknowledged by these authors to be so seductive in their ascetic virtuosity and steely piety that even their enemies, Umayyad imperial officials among them, savored and were tempted by their glamour.[43] And yet they were also figures whose actions threatened to undo all that the formation of the Muslim umma had accomplished. In the figure of the Kharijite, then, was embodied a seductive danger that resided in the consequences of the Muslim *umma*'s formative narratives and so in the imaginative basis for identity formation within that community. Simply stated, the Muslim *umma*'s narratives of origin recalled the actions of pious, ascetic warriors on the path of God, men who carried with them the truths revealed to Muḥammad, men whose actions shaped the present world in accordance with those truths. In so doing, these men obeyed God's command to reject the pleasures of this world and to strive "on God's path" on behalf of revealed truth, regardless of the power or stature of those with whom this striving brought them into conflict. For Muslims residing within the post-*futūḥ* communities of Syria, Mesopotamia, and Arabia, it was on the basis of the memory of these men that one would craft a genuinely Muslim self.

Within the world inhabited by the early Kharijites, defense of the one community of God upon the earth could still mean struggling on the frontiers of the *dār al-Islām* with external enemies, as did men like Ibn al-Mubārak and other frontier *ghāzī* pietists. Increasingly, however, defense of the true community of Muḥammad had come to mean the defense of that community's behavioral and creedal boundaries from corruption originating within the community itself. This took the form of theological and legal disputes, factional strife, and finally civil wars. Out of the greatest of these, it took also the form of periodic Kharijite rebellions, in which followers of Muḥammad's revelation approached others who also believed themselves to be members of the community founded on that revelation, examined them on the basis of certain beliefs and practices that were understood to mark all real Muslims, and, when those questioned were found wanting, slew them and took possession of their property, as God commanded one must do with all those who heard but resisted his prophet's words and in so doing set themselves outside of the one community of God upon the earth.

Clearly, then, the narratives in accordance with which these later generations of Muslims came to understand the "essential" characteristics of the truest of all Muslims also carried a kind of horrific surplus, a toxic by-product that, when turned back against the Muslim *umma* by Kharijite zealots, posed a danger for the future of that community. In some texts, this danger is signaled by the image of unborn Muslim fetuses, spilled into the world at the moment of their parents' murder, while in others it is suggested by the tendency attributed to the Kharijites to direct their murderous passions at fellow Muslims, while scrupulously seeing to the safety of those Christians and Jews who crossed their paths.[44] This is a danger that early Muslim intellectuals clearly recognized, and it is a danger in reaction to which early Muslim communities articulated unequivocal but not uncomplicated strategies for negotiating questions of communal boundaries and communal belonging without strife or bloodshed.

One of these communities was that which formed around the third/ninth century traditionalist and scholar Aḥmad b. Ḥanbal (d. 241/855). Ibn Ḥanbal was recognized by contemporaries as an authoritative expert on questions of *sunna* or the traditions and sayings of the prophet Muḥammad, and so as a source of authoritative declarations on all aspects of day-to-day life as a Muslim.[45] In time, and particularly in the years after his death, the recalled figure of Ibn Ḥanbal, the extensive corpus of his writings and collections of his *re-*

sponsa to questions concerning such things as acceptable business practices, personal comportment in the presence of non-Muslims, and technical questions related to the practice of *jihād*, became the basis for a self-consciously distinct community of Muslims, one which over time took on the specific contours of the Ḥanbalī *madhhab*.[46] Over time, members of the Ḥanbalī community very consciously defined themselves in opposition to members of other Muslim communities, including various ʿAlid sects, such "heretical" communities as the Murjiʾa, the Nuṣairiyya, the Muʿtazila and the Qadariyya, and, with a special vigor, the Khawārij. At the outset of a monumental Ḥanbalī *ṭabaqāt* text (a kind of biographical dictionary) containing accounts of the lives of the first generations of Ḥanbalī scholars, we find a long section in which orthodox Ḥanbalī beliefs are contrasted with the defining beliefs and practices of other Muslim communities. The longest and most passionate rejection to be found in this section is that issued against the doctrines and practices of the Kharijites, who are described in no uncertain terms as enemies of the Islamic *umma* and failed Muslims in the most crucial sense.[47]

Despite their rejection of the violence excesses of the Kharijites, however, Ibn Ḥanbal and his followers were just as concerned with the maintenance of communal boundaries as were the Khawārij. Indeed, much like the Kharijites, Ibn Ḥanbal was a stern, ascetic, and intransigent champion of his vision of proper Islamic belief and practice.[48] Much of his own authority among Ḥanbalī and non-Ḥanbalī Muslims, for example, stemmed from his willingness to endure torture in defense of his beliefs during the third/ninth-century *miḥna* (often translated as "inquisition") carried out under the Abbasid caliph al-Maʾmūn. Despite this, however, Ibn Ḥanbal clearly understood the excesses of violence committed by the Kharijites and the destabilizing effects of that violence upon the Muslim *umma*, as an exceedingly dangerous threat to the survival of that community. The dilemma Ibn Ḥanbal therefore seems to have faced was how to pursue projects of boundary maintenance within the Muslim *umma* while somehow defusing the potential for violent conflict such projects carried. As we have seen, within the late ancient and early medieval Muslim world, as was true among the Christian communities of the later Roman world, the foundational narratives in accordance with which personal and communal identities were elaborated seem to have frequently enhanced the likelihood of violent conflict around questions of boundary maintenance. Ibn Ḥanbal seems to have taken it as his task to elaborate certain normative modes of Muslim comportment in accordance with which Muslimness might be performed by community members in moment-to-moment interactions with other Muslims and during interactions with non-Muslims. Moreover, Ibn Ḥanbal, uncompromising hardliner though he was, also seems to have sought to set in place a system whereby Muslims could exercise surveillance over the behaviors of other Muslims, intercede when their fellow Muslims seemed to threaten or transgress communal boundaries, and *nonviolently* call them to account through processes of Muslim-to-Muslim interpellation.

In the thought of Ibn Ḥanbal, then, we have one example of the ways in which members of the early Muslim communities sought to negotiate questions of communal identity and defend crucial communal boundaries without recourse to violence. Ibn Ḥanbal's project was only partially successful; in time, Ḥanbalī militants seized control of his memory and waged violent campaigns against Shīʿī Muslims, Christians, Jews, and even Sunnī Muslims whom the Ḥanbalī militants found wanting in their piety. Despite this, however, at the end of antiquity, in early Abbasid Baghdād, we find in Ibn Ḥanbal and the first generations of his followers that rarest breed of late ancient and medieval fundamentalists, those who approached questions of identity and communal belonging through generally peaceable and humane methods, forsaking whatever temptations to violence resided in the narratives in accordance with which they crafted individual and communal selves.

* * *

As the book that follows took its final form, the landscape of the present world seemed filled with indications of the continuing relevance of the questions examined in these chapters. In July 2006, I watched from Rome a conflict in Lebanon in which two narratives of victimhood, martyrdom, and miraculous survival ground out still more of the same on both sides and in the meantime left the lands in which many of the scenes in this book unfold once again soaked in sanctified blood, resounding with the sounds of grief, loss, and horror. In August, from Cambridge and London, I watched as Britain struggled with questions of communal belonging, the memory of violence, and problems of identity and discussed all of these in the language of boundaries and barriers. In September, from Albuquerque, I read the words of a powerful Christian leader repeating much the same indictment of Islam and its prophet as that with which this Introduction begins. Meanwhile, day by day, fundamentalisms great and small devoured Iraq. And so it goes, for now.

CHAPTER ONE

"The Devil Spoke from Scripture": Boundary Maintenance and Communal Integrity in Late Antiquity

RECENT RESEARCH CONCERNING the problem of intercommunal intolerance in the late antique world has proceeded in what would often seem to be divergent directions. On the one hand, it has become readily apparent that where previous generations of scholars were content to find self-evident and impermeable divisions and implacable hostilities between that which was orthodox Christian and that which was pagan, Jewish, or heretical Christian the social and intellectual lives of individuals and communities on the ground were in fact less segregated, their associations and affinities less determined by confessional identity, than contemporary sources were often willing to let on or than most modern authors had been willing to imagine.[1] On the other hand, however, many recent studies have found much to lament concerning the prevalence of intolerance and factional violence among late antique religious communities.[2] The irony, it would seem, is that while our picture of late antiquity has admitted of greater movement across many social and communal boundaries than had previously been imagined, we have continued to find that those same boundaries were increasingly becoming sites for violent confrontation, contestation, and persecution.[3]

Why should this be so? Harold Drake has recently suggested that the question of Christian intolerance in the decades and centuries after the advent of Constantine may be traced to certain political processes that allowed a single, decidedly intolerant vision of the Christian message and mission to emerge as normative. This vision, championed by certain bishops and such Christian intellectuals as the historian and hagiographer Eusebius, insisted upon a Christian emperor's willingness to persecute religious others as the truest test of his faith.[4]

Among the important advances represented by Drake's thesis is that it recognizes that attributing intolerant acts committed by individual Christians, or even whole Christian communities to some essential Christian intolerance not only fails to account for such instances of intolerance historically, but also represents a serious breach of analytical logic. To paraphrase Drake, any Christianity in any time or place is nothing more or less than an *interpretation* of certain sacred texts and traditions of self-fashioning, and any such interpretation takes place in specific historical, cultural, and political circumstances.[5]

It is this recognition which also makes Drake's book an important contribution to the study of identity in the ancient world, and as such it points up one of the most nettlesome difficulties inherent in treating ancient or late ancient identities—in order to do so, one frequently must look past the explanations ancient peoples provide (or seem to provide) for their own behavior, especially insofar as those explanations are contingent upon appeals to what is frequently represented as the "essential nature" of their own identity group.[6]

Such a proposition is often at odds with the historian's training and professional instincts. When a source is so charitable as to tell us what s/he is thinking or why s/he acts as s/he does, we must of course listen. But then what? How, in other words, is one to handle what anthropologists refer to as "identity talk," that is, the discourse which frequently surrounds discussions of a speaking subject's own identity? Such discourse, as described by the ethnographer and anthropologist Ronald Grigor Suny, frequently makes appeal to a verbal and imaginative vocabulary that favors essentialism and reification of current norms.[7] Groups and individuals seldom understand their own identities as contingent, constructed, or subject to elaboration or reinterpretation. Much more common is the belief that one's identity is the sum of some combination of unchanging characteristics which define all *real* members of the group and which are in the present moment as they always have been. These ascribed characteristics often have their bases in some primordial moment of generation, trauma, or revelation, the memory of which has been preserved through historical narratives which recall the formative events and dramas of one's identity group.[8]

Naturally, such reckonings of the qualities that mark one as a real member of an identity group will frequently deny the possibility of defining the essential features of real members in any other way. This may involve processes of negotiation and contestation as dissonant criteria are advanced by individuals and groups claiming to represent the same identity group. In such processes, appeals to the primordial foundations of the community in question will prove of special utility—it is in a community's primordial dramas, enshrined and recalled in historical narratives, that the primordial (and so most essential) qualities or characteristics of those who may claim communal belonging are articulated and demonstrated. Those who may claim to best represent the qualities embodied by the founders of the primordial community, to follow their example in thought and deed, may also claim to represent most exactly those qualities which define real members of the community and which have always defined real members of the community.[9]

It is for this reason that Drake's simple observation—that in fact Christianity is not essentially intolerant, that this (or any) definition of what Christianity "is" or what Christians "must be" is subjective, eminently historical and the product of an observable political process—was so long in coming, and why it gently posed troubling questions regarding the underlying assumptions of much contemporary research on the question of intolerance in the late antique world. One series of definitions forwarded by certain late antique Christians concerning the true and essential character of real Christians, enshrined in communal histories in which they themselves explained the events of their age, the actions of their contemporaries and the character of their community, provided the facts from which generations of modern historians assembled their renderings of the late Roman world and of late Roman Christian intolerance.

So again we face an apparent paradox—late ancient Christians may not have been intolerant by nature, but the Roman Empire ruled by Christian emperors (and one pagan) was increasingly beset by religious controversy and intercommunal violence, this driven by militant and aggressive modes of self-definition accepted within various confessional communities. Drake has located and analyzed the *political* process by which intolerant interpretations of the Christian message and mission came to drive the policy and actions of fourth-century Roman emperors, but it remains to be explained why the militant strains of self-fashioning which underlay this process resonated among late antique Christians (and others) and thus created a necessary constituency for eristic churchmen. The purpose of this and the next two chapters is to examine this process and to suggest something of the attractiveness in the social, cultural, and religious imaginary of the late antique world of figures who could define, declare, and stubbornly defend communal boundaries, thus allowing other members of the community to which those boundaries lent definition to transgress those boundaries as a matter of daily practice.

I will begin this discussion with an examination of the problems inherent in maintaining a distinct, unique communal identity in the late antique world. I will suggest that this problem was especially acute due in part to the semiotic diversity of the imaginative world within which late antique peoples moved, to the multiplicity of signs and symbols with which groups and individuals ordered their world, and to the troubling range of potential readings to which these semiotic elements could be subjected. Within this imaginative *menudo*, there was need of referees, of figures in accordance with which meaning could be circumscribed and the range of possible readings to which especially resonant sites, figures or texts could be narrowed and, ideally, controlled. Furthermore, there was need of resources for self-fashioning among communities and individuals, definitive models in accordance with which identity could be imagined and by reference to which relationships with others could be modeled and crafted.

"It Is for This Reason That I Hate the Jews"

Throughout his eight orations against the Jews, John Chrysostom returns repeatedly to imagery suggesting boundaries and their defense—soldiers in line of battle or stationed along stout city walls, shepherds in the field on guard against wolves, doctors defending patients against infection and disease.[10] The soldiers he narrates must rout their enemies, of course, but must also attend to their own ranks, maintaining their integrity and seeing to their wholeness and well-being.[11] His shepherds must keep ravening wolves from seducing and devouring their flocks. His physicians must cure contagion, driving it from the violated and vulnerable bodies of their patients.[12] Lines of battle, the integrity of the flock, the wholeness and health of the body. The occasion of the sermons was the approach of Passover and of the cycle of fasting and feasting which would accompany it.[13] It was Chrysostom's fear that his parishioners would fast with their Jewish friends and neighbors, that they would then join them in communal meals, and that in so doing, they would compromise their community and put their own souls in peril:[14] "The festivals of the wretched and miserable Jews are about to arrive one after the other with the Feast of Trumpets, the Feast of Tabernacles, the fasts," Chrysostom tells his congregation. "And many of those arrayed among us, claiming to take our part, go to see the sights of the festivals, and they will promiscuously keep the festival and commingle in the observance of the fasts. But now I wish to banish this grievous custom from the church."[15]

For Chrysostom, the allure certain Jewish practices and sites held for members of his congregation represented a special threat. His parishioners clearly respected the antiquity of the ritual and beliefs that they found in the synagogue, and they believed in the efficacy of ritual they encountered there.[16] Moreover, some of Chrysostom's parishioners clearly found individuals and practices within the Jewish community admirable and apparently sought to fashion their own behavior after the example set by these Jews: "I know that many stand in awe of the Jews and even now consider their *politeia* to be holy. It is on this account that I make haste to uproot this deadly opinion."[17] Similarly, for at least some Christians in fourth-century Antioch, Jewish synagogues were sites of dreadful numinous power. Chrysostom recalls, for example, his own experience interfering in a Christian man's attempts to drag a Christian woman into a Jewish temple "and to [force her to] provide an oath about some matters under dispute with him." Chrysostom intercedes, accosting the man and then, after lecturing him, asks him why he chose a synagogue rather than a church for the swearing of the oath. "He said that many people told him that oaths given in that place were more fearsome," Chrysostom recalled. "Over these words I groaned."[18]

During this cycle of sermons, Chrysostom was also at great pains to draw a distinction between proper and improper fasting; that is, between the fasting properly practiced by Christians and that properly (if sinfully) practiced by Jews. Fasting, as is well known, denoted piety and purification across the religious landscape of the late antique world.[19] It was a sign of holy devotion among Christians of ascetic inclination and among all Christians during periods of heightened religious feeling. The same was true for Jews, of course, as well as many pagans, Manichaeans, Gnostics, and others.[20] Fasting was, in other words, a practice shared in common among a spectrum of late antique communities, and it was a practice whose general significance was universally comprehensible among all of those communities even if the specific readings to which it was subject within each discrete community might vary. Indeed, fasting was just the sort of common signifier modern proponents of religious toleration seek to build bridges between religious communities who find themselves at odds—it was, in short, the kind of shared semiotic element which, from one point of view, allows individuals and groups to transcend communal boundaries.

For Chrysostom, however, this was precisely its danger. In warning his flock away from a practice that was, under most circumstances, a mark of piety and religious zeal, he urged his congregation that in this case they must not let the *appearance* of holiness deceive them. "The lawless and unclean fast of the Jews is now at the doors," he began his second sermon against the Jews. "Do not wonder if I called that fast an unclean thing. For a thing done contrary to the will of God, whether it be a sacrifice or a fast, is the most accursed of things."[21] Even that which is seemingly most righteous may be evil when it is done contrary to God's will, he cautioned, while those acts which seem most repugnant may be righteous if God commands them. "Do not say this thing to me, that the Jews are fasting; but show me that it is in accordance with the will of God that they do that thing," he said. "For if it is not, the fast is more unlawful than any drunkenness." Conversely, he continued, "what is done in accordance with the will of God, even if it should seem to be evil, is the best of all things . . . and even if someone kills in accordance with God's will, this killing is better than every sort of philanthropy, while if someone is merciful and behaves humanely contrary to the will of God that mercy is more unholy than any killing. For it is not the nature of things, but rather the decrees of God that makes things good or bad."

Chrysostom reminded his congregation that it was not their place to question the will of God; it was only their place to obey.[22] It is significant here that Chrysostom was, in essence, without a substantive, observable distinction to draw between the fasting practices of the Jews and the fasting that was proper to his own congregation. The difference was, it would seem, the distinction itself, the boundary imposed between this and that, theirs and ours, a boundary which became visible in the form of an interdict whose basis resided, it would seem, in the ineffable will of God.[23] Chillingly, Chrysostom closed this passage with a reference to the famous act of the priest Phinehas, who murdered an Israelite man and a Moabite woman for the transgression of communal boundaries, impaling them as they coupled in a tent. "Phinehas, having killed two people—a man and his wife—in a single moment of time, was honored with the priesthood. Thus not at all did he defile his hands with murder, but rather he made them purer," Chrysostom told his congregation.[24]

The danger represented by Jewish fasting was closely kindred, in Chrysostom's understanding, with the danger posed by the synagogue, and the attractions of the synagogue lamented by Chrysostom were many.[25] Not only were idols shunned within their walls and the Holy Scriptures read there, but an ancient holiness was believed by some among his flock to radiate from the synagogue itself. Indeed, for Chrysostom the menace of the synagogue, with its seductive affinities with Christian holy sites, was far more worrisome than the danger of pagan shrines and temples. While a pagan shrine repelled good Christians, he explained, and no sane Christian would venture there, synagogues were deceptively attractive even to pious Christians. "Where the demons dwell . . . the impiety is notorious and naked," he said. "[That place] would not easily attract or beguile one possessing a chaste mind. But [in the synagogue] are men who say they worship God, and that they turn away in abhorrence from idols, and know and reverence the prophets."[26] In Daphne, Chrysostom complained, some Christians even slept beside the local "synagogue," perhaps in hopes of attaining some spiritual or magical benefit.[27]

As Chrysostom himself suggested, what made the synagogue so intensely holy in the imaginations of some late antique Christians was that it was home to the memory of the prophets, the lingering authority of the Law, the majesty of the ancient priesthood of Israel, the terrible power of the cherubim.[28] Chrysostom's contemporaries knew of these things because they read of them in their own holy texts, and indeed their own holy texts were only comprehensible as the continuation of a much older prophetic metanarrative. The synagogue was thus a venue in which semiotic traces of the primordial dramas in which Chrysostom's community located its own foundational moments lingered, available still within the lived experience of each individual Christian.[29] In this they were much as other outposts of the holy in the late antique landscape, be these martyr shrines or pagan temples. Moreover, recent research has shown that the architectural and decorative motifs found in many late antique synagogues reflected those of contemporary churches (especially where there were large Christian populations) and other non-Jewish buildings.[30]

To counter this troubling semiotic continuity, Chrysostom set about an elaborate refiguring of contemporary Jews as something other than real Jews, and contemporary Judaism as something other than real Judaism. After rehearsing the elaborate rituals by which Aaron was ordained priest, for example, Chrysostom suggested that contemporary Jews were without a legitimate priesthood, without their ancient links to the God they shared with the Christians.[31] Just as Chrysostom insisted that contemporary Jews could not be real Jews because they were not as real Jews once were, so the accoutrements of holiness one might find in the synagogue were poor imitations of now vanished originals. The arks of contemporary Jews, for example, were but sham copies of the first and true Ark, Chrysostom said, without the power to help, but with only the power to harm.[32]

The problem Chrysostom seems to have faced, however, was that clear though such distinctions may have been to him, they were far from obvious to the members of his congregation who still beheld the rituals and holy symbols to be found in and around the synagogue with undisguised awe. Accordingly, the preacher exhorted his congregation's rank and file not to be "childish" in their reverence for Jewish things, and to interpose themselves between these fascinating objects and the less able of their fellow Christians. "Brothers, do not become as children in your minds, but become childlike with regard to your ill qualities (1.*Cor.*14.20)," he said. "And those who wonder at these things, free them from this inopportune anguish, and teach them what is really to be feared and what to be anticipated."

That which was truly to be feared, Chrysostom said, was that errant Christians would destroy the temple of God through visits to the synagogue and by crafting souls that inclined toward Jewish belief and praxis. For Chrysostom, it is clear, the highly charged signs and symbols that Christians and Jews shared in common could disastrously facilitate any such inclination toward Jewish belief and praxis felt by his parishioners. Moreover, the perilous allure of such shared signs and symbols was especially acute in the case of the holy texts wherein resided revealed truths that were precious to those parishioners and to their Jewish friends and neighbors alike.

Accordingly, Chrysostom assured his flock that despite any appearances to the contrary, the fact that the precious books of the prophets were also read and recited in the synagogue meant precisely nothing. Just as fasting was not always holy, he explained, the transcendent and holy truths contained in the common books of the Jews and Christians did not necessarily bestow their blessings to all. Chrysostom cautioned his audience that where these or any other signs were read, by whom they are read and, most importantly, the range of possible meaning assigned to them, determined their capacity to bring God near, to illuminate the speaker and his surroundings. "Do not say to me that the Law and the books of the prophets are laid up in that place," he said. "Those things are not sufficient to make that place holy. For what is the better thing—that the books be stored in a place, or that one speak loud and clear the things that come from the books? Clearly it is to speak loud and clear the things that come from the books, and to comprehend their meanings. Tell me, what about the fact that the devil spoke out loud and clear from the Scriptures? Did this make his mouth holy?"

* * *

In much the same way, Chrysostom said, truth-speaking demons, even when speaking in praise of holy men, were to be shunned. Indeed, Christians had in the past and must in the future "remain averting our faces from them, and hating [the demons]," he said. Similarly, he continued, Christians must also turn their backs on the Jews and hate them as their preacher himself did. The reason Chrysostom loathed the Jews, he explained, was because they not only refused to acknowledge Christ, but they used the trappings of their ancient religion to lure away weak and unsuspecting Christians. "It is because of this that I hate the Jews," he said. "Even now they know the Law, but they hubristically make use of it in their attempts to ensnare the particularly blockheaded [among us]."[33]

The impression created by Chrysostom's sermons against the Jews is frequently one of a man desperately trying to impose what are often rather fine distinctions upon very powerful entities in the imaginary of his congregation. Recasting the valences of universally revered practices or textual representations of transcendent truth is a delicate matter in any circumstance, and this would seem to be all the more so when it is not the validity of such practices and texts themselves that is contested, nor the truths to which they afford access, but instead the capacity of these touchstones of transcendent truth to perform their functions in every circumstance. If one is guided through the dim of the present world by certain beacons left burning by the ancient prophets of an elusive God, the suggestion that some of these beacons may glow with the false fires of error and damnation can cast what might otherwise seem a well-illuminated path to salvation as a disorientating array of potentially meaningless symbols and signs.

The power of such symbols and signs resided in the belief of those who beheld them that they revealed a secret reality that transcended contingency and circumstance, and this was a belief Chrysostom found finally too powerful to overcome. Indeed, long after the last of his eight sermons against the Jews had resounded from his pulpit, such symbols and signs as the synagogue, the Torah, the feasts and fasts of the Jews, and all of the other semiotic elements against which Chrysostom preached in those sermons remained terribly potent in the minds of many members of his congregation, and the readings to which these signs and symbols were subject remained diverse and powerful. By its end, as we shall see, Chrysostom's cycle of sermons proved less a basis for recasting the world and the numinous traces it contained than an incitement to his parishioners to discuss, confess and even contest with one another the boundaries that defined their community, and in so doing to carry the community's boundaries within them, to perform them and perpetually reassert, reaffirm, and remake them.

"One Who Breaks Down a Fence, Let a Snake Bite Him"

Whatever they did or did not accomplish, however, these sermons would certainly seem to beg a series of questions about the character of confessional identity in Antioch in the year 386 C.E., the year in which it is believed they were delivered.[34] Chrysostom was preaching in one of the most important cultural and spiritual centers of the late Roman world, to what we must assume was a fairly sophisticated Christian congregation. This was not a recently converted or isolated population—these were Christian men and women who, if we accept most traditional accounts of the formation of distinctively Christian communities and identities, should have known better than to involve themselves in another community's acts of worship. Indeed, it was this population who had so famously resisted and ridiculed the pagan emperor Julian over his attempts to revive pagan practice in the city (but who so resisted and ridiculed, notably, in the ritual idiom of an ancient pagan festival).[35] Why then should Chrysostom have been obliged to stage a series of eight sermons to remind his congregation of their obligation to keep their distance from the Jews, to forsake their rituals and festival, their traditions and their holy places?

First and foremost, these sermons suggest much about the continued permeability of late antique communal boundaries and, correspondingly, about the need felt by some individuals and communities to assert and preserve such boundaries. On the one hand, we have the very specific vision of community and orthodox Christian identity set forth by Chrysostom. It is a vision dependant upon the careful observance of one's place with regard to other members of one's own community and with regard to individuals belonging to other communities. One's place was to be reckoned less as a geographic location than as an ascribed position in relation to a matrix of identities, events, beliefs, and defining personal qualities, and the communal boundaries Chrysostom championed may be imagined as a series of discursive sites wherein crucial processes of evaluation on the basis of ascribed markers of belonging took place. In his eight sermons against the Jews (and, more to the point, against Christian "Judaizers"), Chrysostom cited a series of practices and acts—among these participation in certain types of ritual fasting and festivals, circumcision, the taking of oaths in temples, seeking divine aid at Jewish holy sites—that he insisted disrupted the processes of ascription that were to take place at the boundaries that he understood to delineate the limits of his community.[36]

As one reads through these sermons, however, it becomes clear that Chrysostom's vision of the Christian community and of the communal identity that he sought to foster was anything but unanimous or even clearly understood among his congregation.[37] The world of Chrysostom's congregation teemed with outposts of the numinous, with options for self-fashioning and with religious practices and modes of belief held in common with members of other communities. Indeed, the social and religious milieu of Chrysostom's Antioch was, it would seem, awash in indeterminate signifiers, holy sites, texts, personages, narratives, individuals, all of them subject to an alarming array of potential readings. Foremost among the tasks Chrysostom adopted for himself in these sermons was that of determining or at the very least narrowing the range of meanings it was possible to ascribe to certain of the locations, practices, and persons at large in his world and the world of his parishioners. This was but a local iteration of a project common to a spectrum of late ancient communities, as we shall see.

In Chrysostom's case, this project was necessitated, it would seem, by social and religious circumstances recently examined at length by Daniel Boyarin. Previous generations of scholarship concerning the question of rabbinic

Judaism's relationship with early Christianity have postulated a complete and early break between two thereafter discrete communities (this usually taking place in the first or second century C.E.). Boyarin has argued that in fact the involvement between Christianity and rabbinic Judaism was much longer and much more complex and productive for both than has previously been recognized.[38]

Boyarin suggests that rather than imagining the relationship between Judaism and early Christianity as that of a parent and offspring as has most often been done, a more plausible and useful metaphor is that of a continuum of practices and identities that ran between two poles. In accordance with this model, on one pole we would find people like Chrysostom, Christians who insisted upon a complete and early break with Judaism, and on the other pole rabbis who similarly insisted upon viewing Christianity as a wholly other religious entity, an arch heresy peeled completely away from orthodox Judaic praxis and thought. Between these poles, however, one would find a spectrum of beliefs and practices in which strictly Christian and Jewish practice and belief would have been difficult to discern, one in which "there could be and would have been social contact, sometimes various forms of common worship, all up and down the continuum of 'Jews' and 'Christians.'"[39]

Other recent research has suggested similarly messy confessional arrays in other outposts of the late ancient world. Since the 1960s Alan Cameron has been at the forefront of a migration from earlier notions of struggles between "pagan and Christian parties" manifested in the intellectual life and literary production of late Roman elites and has demonstrated that classical culture was in fact crucial to the self-definition and social standing of all late Roman elites, regardless of confessional identity.[40] Elsewhere, Harry Maier has shown that as late as the fifth century, Leo the Great was urging his parishioners to exercise surveillance over other members of their community against the adoption of Manichaean practices, and even Augustine discovered Manichaeans among his own North African clergy.[41] In a late ancient Syriac text of uncertain date, meanwhile, a Jew conjured in disputation with a certain Sergius the Stylite comments to the stylite, "I am amazed how . . . there are among you some Christians who associate with us in the Synagogue, and who bring offerings and alms and oil, and at the time of Passover send unleavened bread (and, doubtless, other things also). They are not entirely Christians, and some of our men have said that, if they were truly Christians, they would not associate with us in our synagogue and in our law."[42]

Meanwhile, Christians throughout Syria and Egypt moved in a world in which the dividing line between magic spells and application of holy grace was often a matter of perspective and in which the invocation of minor gods or the casting of spells frequently involved the use of Christian scripture or appeals to Mary, the angels or other mystical personages native to the Christian mythological imaginary.[43]

These realities ill fit the evolving ideas of community and identity which seem to have motivated Chrysostom and many of his contemporaries, however. For these men and women, there was but one community of God upon the earth, this defined by the implications of revelation and human history, rooted in transcendent truth and distinguished from all others by certain sacred boundaries.[44] The contours of these boundaries, their implications, and the imperative for their protection were articulated in the sacred stories and historical narratives though which lived or recalled experience was interpreted and understood and upon which identity was increasingly dependant.

The declaration and defense of communal boundaries was frequently carried on most stridently where contemporaries encountered especially potent semiotic elements whose range of potential readings was contested, and so contested because they provided crucial raw material for claims regarding identity, authority, precedence, and proximity to revealed or reasoned truth. The Melitian church in Egypt, for example, based its claims to be the one "true" church in part upon its possession of martyr relics and seems to have built its own communal boundary on the martyr's remains. The bishop Athanasius, by contrast, strove to undermine the Melitians' claims regarding the relics, even suggesting that the remains that they paraded were not real relics at all. Despite Athanasius's best efforts, however, the martyr remains lofted in Melitian processions intoned profoundly in the imaginary of his congregation.[45]

The Melitians also had their own charismatic ascetics, as did the Arians, and there is some evidence that in fact the Arians claimed for themselves the great Antony, whose memory Athanasius was nevertheless able to capture definitively for the Athanasian church.[46] As David Brakke and others have illustrated, it was the prime role of this literary Antony to define the ideal qualities to be ascribed to all real members of the Athanasian community.[47] Indeed, this Antony recognized heresy and heretics as if by magic and strove zealously to enforce the lines of demarcation that separated his community from Athanasius's rivals. Those of rival communities were to have no claim to the potent array of signs that resided in the figure of Antony or his ascetic colleagues.

Similarly, Julian's attempt in 362 to ban Christians from teaching classical texts may be interpreted as an endeavor to impose a boundary between "true Hellenes" and self-declared Christian outsiders.[48] Like Chrysostom and Athanasius, Julian found the consequences of a common semiotic system troubling and resolved to impose a new and specific range of readings to which those semiotic elements could be subjected. It is both a measure of the folly of this act, and an illustration of the circumstances which prompted it that the Christian intellectual father and son team of Apollinarius and Apollinarius the elder responded by undertaking twin projects to, in the case of the elder Apollinarius, cast the Old Testament as a traditional Greco-Roman epic, and in the case of the younger to fashion the Gospels as Platonic dialogues.[49]

However, although it may be true that "Julian did not . . . prevent Christian children from attending the classes of pagan teachers,"[50] he did succeed in making it necessary for Christians to ponder and contest among themselves the qualities which defined "real" Christians with regard to the ancient classics and in so doing to give life to the boundaries Julian declared through that very discussion. Indeed, "the effect of Julian's efforts was to polarize Christians and pagans, to remove the middle ground that traditional culture had previously provided."[51] It is significant that while the "cultural stuff" on either side of this reaffirmed communal boundary, that is the appreciation and importance of classical culture among pagans and Christians, remained largely unchanged, consciousness of the boundary itself had increased significantly through the processes of contestation and debate Julian's act initiated.[52]

Such policing went on within confessional boundaries as well. Julian famously castigated Cynic philosophers who displeased him, warning them that their behavior blurred the distinctions one could make between them and Christian monks, thus placing the Cynics or suggesting that they might by their own actions find themselves on the wrong side of certain communal boundaries. That the monk, the figure deployed here by Julian, is frequently found on late antique communal boundaries as they are imagined by Christians and non-Christians alike is significant, and this trend will be commented upon at length in a later chapter. Interestingly, Julian went on to argue that the misdeeds of ignorant Cynics, those who practiced their philosophical calling improperly, ruined the reputations of all Cynics, even "real" ones. Julian's efforts at, and even methods of, imposing an ideal form of practice, an orthodoxy by any other name, upon contemporary Cynics, may be read as an analogue to attempts by various Christian intellectuals to discipline and contain Christian ascetic practice.[53]

Among Christians, a troubling diversity of ascetic practice was prompting such churchmen as Athanasius, Jerome, Augustine, and Epiphanius of Salamis to enclose certain styles of asceticism within doctrinal corrals, casting some as orthodox and others as heretical.[54] In his *On the Works of Monks*, for example, Augustine warns that monks who grow their hair long, refuse to work or submit themselves to the authority of monastic communities (and so to bishops) and wander about hawking real or false relics ruin the reputations of "good" monks, or, put another way, make it difficult or impossible for people inside and outside of Christian communities to read the figure of the Christian ascetic.[55]

Julian similarly suggests that some contemporary Cynics adopt the cloak, staff, and wallet of the real Cynic as mere props and that there is no real Cynic beneath them.[56] Like Augustine, he laments the fact that the semiotic elements that suggest piety and godliness in the minds of his contemporaries lend shelter to evil men who adopt these for display, or to camouflage their sins.[57] For Augustine, as for Julian, questions of ascription are key to the critiques to be leveled against their wayward coreligionists—the danger bad monks or errant Cynics represent has to do with their capacity to disrupt the crucial business of knowing one's own, of being able, at the boundaries of one's community, to locate the qualities and characteristics which will determine communal belonging.

Indeed, nothing excited the anxieties of Chrysostom's contemporaries, Christian or not, like the perception of boundary transgression by members of their own communities. In a late antique rabbinical text analyzed by Daniel Boyarin, for example, a rabbi named Elʿazar Ben Dama is bitten by a snake and seeks aid from a Christian acquaintance, much to the chagrin of his uncle, who is also a rabbi. When Ben Dama dies before his Christian friend can arrive and cure him, his uncle rejoices: "Blessed art thou, Ben Dama, for you left in peace, and you did not violate the fence of your colleagues, for anyone who breaks down the fence of the Sages, terrible things happen to him, as it says, 'One who breaks down a fence, let a snake bite him' (Eccl. 10:8)."[58] The irony, as Boyarin points out, is that this narrative may be read to suggest that Ben Dama was bitten by the snake precisely because he had violated his own communal boundaries, enticed by his own curiosity about Christianity.[59]

Ben Dama's uncle would have found a kindred spirit of sorts in Chrysostom as the preacher thundered to his own curious congregation that if, for example, one's Christian friend confided that he visited the Jews to attain magical cures for illnesses, that Christian placed himself in far greater danger than that posed by disease or injury: "I will even put you an extreme case and say that even if they do really cure you, to die is better than to run to the enemies of God and by that means be cured."[60] Chrysostom shared with Ben Dama's uncle the conviction that transgression of communal boundaries, even to save one's own life, cannot be condoned, that death is preferable.

That such stories as these were apparently resonant on either side of the divide upon which they insisted suggests much about why they were told at all. Again, we find that semiotic elements shared in common among distinct "communities"—whether these were stories, texts, holy individuals, or holy sites—are not only incitements to the declaration of communal boundaries, but frequently the imaginative basis for the declaration itself.

"A Stand against Deranged Transgression"

Chrysostom's answer to the problem of boundary transgression within his community was to urge his parishioners to watch the actions of their fellow Christians and to demand that if they were to see them going into a synagogue or joining the Jews in their fasts, they must intervene, forbid them to do so, and command their fellow Christians to do what was right. "To do what was right" was, of course, to shun the Jews and their rituals, to observe the boundaries of the Christian community as Chrysostom envisioned them, and "to show forth an unmixed and unadulterated Christianity, and to flee the evil pastimes and wicked synagogues of the Jews," he said.[61]

Interestingly, Chrysostom would later adopt a similar strategy when urging his congregation to erect another behavioral boundary between themselves and their neighbors. In his homily *Against the Games and Theatres*,[62] Chrysostom urged his congregation that those Christians who fail to keep away from the games and shows should be sought out and chased down, confronted and corrected by their fellow Christians. Here Chrysostom employed the metaphor of hunters and their prey and urged his parishioners to beat the bush for Christians who strayed too close to the Jewish community in their actions, beliefs, or associations. If this did not work, he said, those wayward

Christians must be cast outside of the community. This drastic step was necessary to preserve both the integrity of the community and to avoid the mockery of imaginary Jews and pagans who, Chrysostom said, would ridicule the Christian community were its members to sin by transgressing the communal boundaries upon which he insisted.[63]

Although this homily would be delivered long after the sermons against the Jews (in July 399 to Chrysostom's parishioners in Constantinople), it echoes much of what Chrysostom had preached some thirteen years earlier as he railed against the "Judaizers" of Antioch. In that cycle of sermons, Chrysostom urged all of his parishioners to, in effect, carry the boundaries of the Christian community within them, and in so doing to prevent their friends, wives, husbands, children, and even strangers from falling into sin, and as they did so to "store up riches" for themselves.

To so important a mission did Chrysostom commend his flock in setting them on their friends and neighbors as sentinels that he assured them that if they failed in it not only the Judaizer, but they themselves would face damnation, no matter how numerous their other virtues and good deeds. Conversely, by succeeding in this task, they would have all of their own sins wiped away, and they would become respected within their community, a model Christian to be emulated.[64] The importance of this mission, according to Chrysostom, resided in nullifying the potential breakdown in communal cohesion that the Judaizers represented for the Church. Likening them to heretics, he reminded his congregation that weakness was the product of discord and strife and that strength for any community resided in unity and closed ranks. "A kingdom having fallen into civil war collapses. But two men, bound one to the other, are more unbreakable than a wall," he told his parishioners.[65]

Good Christians sheltered within the walls of their community, Chrysostom said. Outside of those walls lurked beasts intent upon devouring lost souls. Although he might easily have destroyed them, Christ left the beasts prowling outside of the fold of the Church so that Christians would huddle together within it.[66] Chrysostom asserted repeatedly that it was the responsibility of each and every community member to preserve the community, to keep it intact by policing its boundaries and exercising surveillance over his fellows.[67]

As I have noted, Chrysostom used many metaphors for this duty.[68] His parishioners were doctors treating the illness of their Judaizing friends; they were hunters beating the brush for secret Judaizers; they were soldiers, seeing to the loyalty of their fellow troops. Chrysostom declared himself ready to risk his own life in this project, and demanded that his parishioners should be ready to use force if necessary, to enter the homes of strangers, to endure violence themselves, in carrying out this sacred obligation.[69] "Whenever it is necessary for a brother to be set straight, even if it is necessary for one's life to be given freely [in doing so], you must imitate your Lord," he said.[70] "Let every one of you recover one of these brothers with me. Interfere in the affairs of others! Be meddlesome in order that on the coming day we might meet at the assembly by means of much *parrhesia* bearing gifts to God, the most worthy gifts of all, the recovered souls of those having been led astray. Even if it is necessary to be beaten, even if it is necessary to submit to anything else whatever, let us do everything so that we may recover these ones."[71]

Chrysostom compared the mission of correcting wayward Christians favorably with other important acts of piety. It was a deed more righteous than feeding the poor, Chrysostom told his congregation. "The one giving to the poor man alleviated hunger; the one setting a Judaizer straight confounded impiety," he said. "The first one comforted a poor man; the second one made a stand against deranged transgression."[72] Even ascetic practice paled in comparison to the crucial imperative of confronting and reforming Christians who violated communal norms. Instructing his congregation once again to go forth and treat the wounds of their "fallen brothers" with instruction, Chrysostom asked, "What could you do that would be the equal of that? Fasting cannot do as much for you as the salvation of your brother can do, nor can sleeping on the ground, nor all-night vigils, nor anything else."[73]

Nor should this activist concern for communal boundaries be expressed merely in care for one's wayward coreligionists, he added. Rather, Chrysostom suggested that members of his community should also confront the Jews themselves about the participation of Christians in Jewish festivals and fasts. "Let the Jews learn, and let learn also those who pretend to rank themselves among us but who in their minds incline toward the Jews, that we possess a concerned and vigilant zeal for our brothers who have deserted to the Jews," he said. "[In the end], they will give back to us those of us who have gone over to them, no one else will have the heart to go over to them, and the body of the Church will be free from pollution."[74]

Chrysostom thus repeatedly urged members of his congregation to go forth and hunt down members of their community who engaged in the activities he claimed to be unbefitting real Christians. As real Christians themselves, these hunters were to confront boundary transgressors, to hail them as Christians to Christians, and, perhaps most importantly, to compel them to enter into a dialogue concerning their own communal identity and the behavior that properly marked members of their community. Intriguingly, however, as Chrysostom's sermons progress, and particularly in the eighth and final sermon against the Jews, it becomes clear that if Chrysostom's goal had been only to keep his fellow Christians from participating in the Jewish festivals, feasts, and fasts, the cycle of sermons was something of a failure: Christians had feasted. Christians had fasted. Christians had gone to the synagogue. And everybody knew it.

> Let us not be neglectful of our brothers. Let us not go around saying, "How many fasted? How many did they drag away?" But let us take care for those ones. And even if those who fasted are many, do not parade it about, but instead act with brotherly love. Do not hold up as an example the misfortune of the Church, but work to heal it. Don't say to me that many fasted, but set those many straight. I did not squander uselessly such serious words so that you might denounce the many, but that you might make the many few, or rather not even a few, but that you should save even those few. Thus those closing ranks and those shutting down the gossipers and those taking care of those who have fallen down, even if they are many, they easily set these ones straight, and no more of the rumor do they set loose to do harm to others.[75]

Chrysostom's response to what seems to have been widespread Christian participation in the festivals was to insist and to urge his congregation to insist that in fact no such participation had taken place. Remarkably, Chrysostom seems to urge his congregation to lie to those outside of the community who may have seen members of his congregation at the festivals—presumably these will have been Jews—and to then lie to one another about what is clearly a commonly known fact. Moreover, those who speak this commonly known truth are to be "set straight" and silenced.

> If someone says that many fasted, shut him up so that the rumor does not become widely known, and say to that one, "I myself saw no such thing. You've been deceived, man, and lied to. If you know

> about two or three swept away, you say they were many." Shut up the accuser . . . and if it is desirable that the matter not be put about openly, so that it does not become a source of delight for the other side, how much more is it necessary not to disclose it to the general gossip outside [of our community], how much better that it not be disclosed on the outside by us lest the hateful ones rejoice, lest our kindred, learning of this matter, fall down. But the rumor must be shut down and fenced in on all sides. Do not say to me, "I told so-and-so." Restrain what is said yourself. For just as you did not hold out in silence, so that one will not master his own tongue.[76]

How are we to interpret all of this? I would suggest that as he urged his congregation to reprove the transgressions of their fellows, Chrysostom set in place a series of injunctions that functioned to mark and preserve the communal boundaries upon which he insisted, even if these boundaries were in fact routinely transgressed. If, for example, at least some members of his congregation were content to follow his instructions and to hail other members of their community whom they saw entering synagogues or whom they knew to be fasting in observance of Jewish holidays, and in so hailing them compelled them to respond concerning their communal identity by invoking the behavioral bounds Chrysostom has prescribed, Chrysostom's boundaries had thus become a site for the ascriptive processes that were necessary for the illusion (and so the fact) of a bounded community. Clearly, this required the participation of Chrysostom's congregation members in the world outside his church's walls, in the quotidian world of Antioch's streets, markets, and, notably, private homes.

> Let us now make our rounds. Let us be meddlesome and search out those who have fallen. Even if we must enter into the fallen one's home, let us not shrink back from it. If the sinner ["fallen one"] is unknown to you, has nothing to do with you, meddle and interfere. Find some useful friend of his, someone by whom he will be most persuaded, and taking that one with you, go into the fallen one's house. Do not feel ashamed. Do not blush. Sit down and talk with him. Say to him: "Tell me, do you commend the Jews for crucifying Christ, and for now blaspheming against him, and for

> calling him an outlaw?" If the man is a Christian, he will never suffer to say, "I do commend it." Even he has judaized ten thousand times, he will never suffer to say it. But instead he will block up his hearing and say to you: "May it never be! Speak no evil, man!" Then, when you perceive his agreement with you, resume you efforts and say: "Tell me, how can you have dealings with them? How can you take part in their festival? How can you keep the fast with them?"[77]

As they were compelled to contest their own identity at the ascriptive sites Chrysostom had set in place, as they were hailed *as Christians* and compelled to respond (and so made *responsible*, that is, subject to an injunction to respond, to explain themselves)[78] to those criteria *as Christians*, the function of the communal boundary, and the institution of that boundary, proceeded from the very process of contestation itself. Whether the Christian challenged for her perceived participation in the feasts and fasts or for his desire to be circumcised begs forgiveness, defends his/her actions or denies them entirely, that s/he responds *as a member of the bounded community*, and that s/he responds *on the basis of certain ascribed qualities or characteristics* is key. Once s/he has responded to the hail, s/he has acknowledged her/his membership in (responsibility to) the community, and once s/he as accepted the validity of the qualities ascribed to all "real" members of the community and contested his/her own identity on the basis of these, s/he has acknowledged the validity of the community's boundaries as Chrysostom imagines them, whether or not s/he feels that s/he him- or herself has transgressed them. Indeed, if s/he in fact denies that s/he has transgressed them, s/he him- or herself becomes a witness to their authenticity and capacity to authenticate. The only real danger was that s/he would not respond at all. Here Chrysostom urged his congregation to be willing to use force and to be willing to endure violence.

But what of Chrysostom's admonition that his parishioners deny to themselves and to others that the boundaries upon which he insists are routinely transgressed and that in practice transgression of these boundaries did not make the transgressor any less a member of the community? Indeed, transgression of those boundaries seems often to have made of the transgressor a kind of fetishized commodity, a source of riches to be stored up by the Christian who corrected him/her, a newly valued object for her/his having transgressed a charmed threshold.[79] I would suggest two interpretations for this move. The first is that in so fashioning the discourse which surrounds these boundaries, Chrysostom allowed the boundaries themselves to remain both sites of ascription and thoroughly permeable. That is, he allowed them to remain workable boundaries—declared and stubbornly defended while basically independent of whatever "cultural stuff" that was claimed to lie on either side of them and regardless of any migration of ideas and persons across them.[80] In accordance with this strategy, Chrysostom urged his parishioners that they were to insist in their interactions with other members of their community upon the boundaries that their preacher had traced in his sermons and upon the crucial role of those boundaries in defining the community itself, while ignoring, indeed positively denying, that while the bases for those boundaries might *a*scribe an experienced communal reality, they need not *de*scribe the reality they were meant to order.

My second interpretation of this move is that in insisting that his parishioners actively deny a commonly known truth, Chrysostom enlisted them in the preservation of a secret. But what does this mean, especially if the truth on whose behalf Chrysostom conjured this secret was something that everybody already knew? This question must take second place to another: What is a secret? In one sense, it is nothing—it is an empty space that begs for a boundary to make legible the airless pause that abides in anticipation of revelation, to impose a grammar upon this pause, to divide it into a dialectic of knowing and not knowing. But what if the knowing and not knowing are one in the same, as seems to have been the case here? This secret-as-knowing, this "public secret" as the anthropologist Michael Taussig has called it, is the negative space which we must assume in the schema of any discourse. It is the embarrassed silence wherein the power of a menagerie of Foucauldian public scripts, speaking subjects, nascent objects, enunciations qua statements abides, eminent, immanent, and boisterously mute.[81]

The late Roman world was no stranger to such public secrets. In a world in which "violence was endemic and common at all levels of society," and in which often "the nominal guardians of the law were its greatest offenders," this may help to explain the capacity of orators to guide the hand of an emperor or an imperial prefect by standing before him and eloquently lying about his piety, his mercy or his fair-minded love of justice and virtue, and more than that, to do so by telling a lie that everybody knew to be a lie, or more exactly, to be the negative utterance of a truth everybody knew they could not know.[82] Such a speech act was not "a matter of exposure which destroys the secret, but a revelation which does justice to it."[83] Here and elsewhere it also becomes clear that the public secret does not serve any single master but is communal property, the basis for communal acts and processes, and in fact may be the basis for community itself.

In the case of Chrysostom's exhortation to his congregation to lie for their community's sake, the public secret serviced was the negative twin of the string of assertions Chrysostom (and others) made about Christian identity in fourth-century Antioch and about the boundaries at which that identity was tested. As important as knowing what to know about this identity and these boundaries, it would seem, was what one ought to know not to know about them. Crucial among these is the distinction to be drawn, once again, between the ascriptive and descriptive functions of the boundary, and, more specifically, the identity talk in which it was so deeply implicated. Unless we are to deny Chrysostom and his contemporaries the analytical capacity necessary to note that the qualities and behaviors ascribed to members of their community (mostly negatively in these sermons) frequently failed to describe the actual behaviors and qualities Chrysostom himself noted (and denounced) in members of that community, we must account for the fact that Chrysostom claimed with equal fervor that real members of his community did not, for example, participate in Jewish feasts and fasts and that real members of his community *did* participate in such rituals. Both of these are statements of truth, but they are incompatible without something to lubricate their passage against one another, without another truth to smother their dissonance.

In addition to its other functions and qualities as it emerges in Taussig's work and in the work of those with whom he enters into dialogue, secrecy acts as the lubricant that allows human societies to function. But it is also the glue that holds ill-fitting pieces together and the cushion that prevents rending collisions between public scripts and public acts.[84] The public secret Chrysostom commended to his congregation here would seem to have served all of these functions with regard to Chrysostom's project (but not Chrysostom's alone) for the elaboration of communal boundaries and a specific interpretation of Christian identity predicated on narrowly prescribed readings of semiotic elements common to a spectrum of other communities, and so to a spectrum of rival readings. In addition to this, however, and following Taussig, I would note that there is a productive component to this project of knowing what not to know, of dissimulating, of lying and of not only creating a truth, but creating a truth made all the more powerful because it is conjured in the howling void of a public secret.

Anyone can describe a perceived truth, and the task of course becomes easier if the truth one is to describe is commonly acknowledged as a truth or has been frequently discussed as a truth. The act of insisting upon a truth that is commonly known to be false or which describes a circumstance contrary to the perceived experience of the speaker and his/her interlocutors is significantly more complicated. While the act of reporting or repeating a perceived or acknowledged truth may be descriptive or mimetic, to deny such a truth is an act which requires both the effacement of the original truth and the production of a new or countertruth. This is a project that can only be taken on communicatively, and each individual who speaks the new truth while denying the old truth contributes to this process of production/effacement and so to the defining truths of his or her community.

Conclusion

Chrysostom had set before his congregation a strenuous task, one he assumed its members would not be eager to undertake. He asked that they make it their business to interrupt what were widespread practices of personal piety among their fellows and that they insist upon narrowly prescribed (and likely contested) behaviors as the basis of communal belonging. He asked that they do so at the risk of personal shame, the integrity of their personal relationships and even their own physical safety. As he did so, he anticipated that some of them would insist that this was not their place, that there were other Christians better suited to the erection and defense of communal boundaries of the sort Chrysostom demanded. He even foresaw the specific excuse they would offer: "Do not say about yourself, 'I am a worldly man, I have a wife and children; those are the tasks of priests, the tasks of monks,'" he said.[85]

Chrysostom was of course himself a priest, and it is hardly surprising that he would cite others of his office as discerners and enforcers of communal boundaries in the minds of his contemporaries, although it is difficult to know whether many of Chrysostom's fellow priests would have practiced this aspect of their calling as aggressively as Chrysostom did.[86] Monks, on the other hand, frequently appear in our sources as discerners and defenders of communal boundaries, and it has been suggested that it was Chrysostom's experience among the monks of Syria that influenced his own activist interpretation of the priest's role.[87] We will have much more to say about the role of monks in the policing of communal boundaries in Chapter 4. For now it is enough to note that Chrysostom clearly anticipated that the task he repeatedly demanded that his congregation must perform in these sermons, that of patrolling and enforcing communal boundaries, was one his parishioners would interpret as more properly undertaken by monks.

To overcome this, Chrysostom repeatedly commended to his parishioners the example of the Christian martyrs as models after whom they should craft their own attitudes and behavior. For men and women who had no intention of adopting monastic practice or of removing themselves from the world of familial or societal concerns, the martyrs remained crucial resources for self-fashioning as individuals who emerged from teeming urban crowds or anonymous villages to preserve the integrity of their communities in remembered moments of confrontation and persecution. Indeed, it was in the acts of the martyrs that a distinctively Roman Christian communal identity was forged, and the narratives with which those acts were recalled proved crucial as various Christian communities advanced and contested their most important truth claims. It was in the recalled struggles and triumphs of the martyrs that the numinous was understood to have become manifest in the history of the Christian community and to have been certified as such in the fulcrum of Roman juridical ritual. It is to the role of the martyr in late antique strategies of self-fashioning that we will now turn.

CHAPTER TWO

"The Living Voice of Kindred Blood": Narrative, Identity, and the Primordial Past

FROM CHRYSOSTOM'S POINT of view, then, there were certain behaviors and beliefs that served to mark individuals as either inside or outside of the one community of God upon the earth. This was a point of view Chrysostom undoubtedly shared with a good number of his contemporaries.[1] The devil, however, was as always in the details. The operative beliefs were invisible unless manifested by behavior, and the behaviors which marked one as a real Christian (or, indeed, a particularly pious Christian) could be deceptively like those which, according to Chrysostom, marked one as an outsider, as something opposite to a real Christian.

Chrysostom urged his congregation, for example, that they should avoid the fasts of the Jews in the season of Passover (and Easter) not because Christians did not fast (for they did), nor because they did not fast in that particular season (for they did), but because the reasons Jews fasted in that season were *different* from those reasons for which real Christians fasted. Troublingly, however, Chrysostom was up against the semiotic potency fasting carried within his society. Fasting, after all, although a personal act of devotion, was also a social sign, and, moreover, a social sign which stood in for an otherwise invisible referent (that is, the specific reason for which the individual in question fasted). In other words, the act of fasting was, for many of Chrysostom's parishioners, a social symbol that was invested with an affective and imaginative power independent of whatever specific genre of religiosity it expressed.

It is this problem, manifested in a variety of registers, with which Chrysostom so arduously contended in his sermons "Against the Jews."

Take, for example, the problem of "Matrona's Cave" in Daphne. In his sermons against the Jews, Chrysostom rails against Christians who go to the site to spend the night in search of miraculous cures. It is a Jewish site, Chrysostom insists, and not appropriate for real Christians. It is not difficult, however, to understand why Chrysostom's parishioners might have been a bit confused. As Martha Vinson has demonstrated, the site to which Chrysostom refers seems in all probability to have been a shrine to certain local martyrs in which were deposited the earthly remains of four figures from Antioch's communal past. The four martyrs commemorated at "Matrona's" had stood intransigently before worldly power and defied polytheistic error and arrogance on behalf of the God of Abraham. Such sites were common gathering places for Christians around the Roman world, of course.[2]

Indeed, earlier in the fourth century no less a figure than Gregory Nazianzus had established a cult of these particular martyrs in Antioch.[3] The martyrs whose memories were celebrated at "Matrona's" were the Maccabean martyrs, and they were especially problematic as semiotic figures in Antioch because they were revered by more than one community. Vinson has suggested convincingly, for example, that both a Jewish and a Christian shrine to the Maccabean martyrs existed in competition with one another in Antioch.[4] Accordingly, Chrysostom once again found his parishioners perilously drawn to what it must have seemed could only be a holy site for the commemoration of Antioch's glorious monotheistic past but which was in Chrysostom's view nothing other than a space in which communal boundaries dangerously blurred and in which Christians acted like Jews by acting like Christians, a situation which clearly vexed Chrysostom. The wrong martyrs, the wrong feast, the wrong fast—all of these were snares for the faithful and frightful dangers to the integrity of the community.

And these were only the problems one might trace to the system of potent signs and symbols Chrysostom's congregation shared with the Jews of Antioch. The cultural semiotics of the later Roman world teemed with signs and symbols subject to multiple (and, from some points of view, potentially disastrous) readings. Festivals, medicinal cures, love magic, civic ceremonies, art, literature, indeed, the whole historical narrative of the ancient Roman past—all of these things swam in and out of the visual and intellectual grasp of Christians throughout the empire, from the emperor to his officials and functionaries to the elites of the provinces to the peasants of the villages and hamlets of Gaul, Italy, Syria, Egypt, and North Africa.[5] For members of all communities within that world, it was frequently the specific readings to which this shifting lexicon of signs and symbols was subjected that located an individual within the social-political-religious universe of the Roman world.

In what follows, I will draw upon recent work in the fields of anthropology, sociology, and identity studies to try to suggest something of the ways in which members of the Christian communities of the later Roman world went about negotiating the frantic semiotic universe they and their neighbors inhabited. This process involved making "qualitative and lexical distinctions among the infinite variety of events, experiences, characters, institutional promises, and social factors that impinge[d] on [their] lives."[6] Put more simply, members of late Roman Christian communities, like all individuals in all societies, were required to arrange the experiential data which pours in from moment to moment in a manner which made the world they inhabited comprehensible. A growing (and not uncontroversial) body of research in the social and human sciences suggests that human beings undertake such processes in accordance with guiding narratives in which they imagine themselves "emplotted." In the words of the sociologist Margaret Somers, this school of thought suggests that

> people construct identities (however multiple and changing) by locating themselves or being located within a repertoire of emplotted stories; that "experience" is constituted through narratives; that people make sense of what has happened and is happening to them by attempting to assemble or in some way to integrate these happenings within one or more narratives; and that people are guided to act in certain ways, and not others, on the basis of these projections, expectations, and memories derived from a multiplicity but ultimately limited repertoire of available social, public and cultural narratives.[7]

More will be said about the role of narrative in the constitution of identities among individuals and communities of the late Roman world below. First, however, I will begin by outlining the kinds of narratives which one encounters as the members of early Christian groups talked about their communal past. Overwhelmingly, these are stories about persecution, martyrdom, and the triumph of the Christian Church within the Roman world. As is so often the case with narratives of communal origins, these are stories of primordial emergences and tales of sacred boundaries discerned and defended. They are stories in which communal ancestors, embodying the eternal and essential characteristics of all real members of the communities to which they gave birth, blaze forth as exemplars whose image will endure in the memories of their descendants as a model for crafting communal selves.

Recent scholarship treating the problem of late twentieth-century ethnic nationalism and its role in intercommunal conflict has focused upon the function of such "primordial" notions of identity as these narratives seem to have celebrated within late Roman Christian communities. Ronald Grigor Suny, for example, has studied the rise of primordialist narratives of self-fashioning in several former Soviet republics, including Armenia, Azerbaijan, and Georgia, and has traced the effect such narratives have had upon the tenor of intercommunal relations within those republics and across their frontiers. Suny has suggested that a focus upon the kinds of stories with which their groups recall communal pasts and with which they construct communal identities and imagine their relations with other communities, "open . . . up the possibility to locate the potential for conflict in particular constructions of nations, certain national narratives, and styles of discourse."[8] The kinds of stories communities tell about themselves and the kinds of identities constituted in accordance with those narratives may, Suny suggests, be analyzed to better understand the nature of those communities' relations with other groups, the Others in relationship with which they understand themselves to be emplotted.

As communities elaborate narratives of their communal past, for example, members of those communities will interpret contemporary events as further episodes within those narratives. Recast as episodes, these events accordingly accrue meaning within the plot of the narratives in question. In Armenia during the 1990s, for example, certain privileged narratives of the Armenian past emphasized the Armenian genocide of 1915, which was of course committed against the Armenians by certain Turks. As this narrative took hold, contemporary conflicts between Azerbaijanis and Armenians were interpreted through the prism of that narrative, and the Azerbaijanis became Turks in the eyes of many Armenian nationalists. The sentiment behind this narrative shift eventually helped to determine the course taken by post-Soviet Armenian politics and the abandonment of inclusive, tolerant ethnic policies within Armenia.[9]

Similarly, at the outbreak of the genocidal warfare in the former Yugoslavia, much of the Serbian hostility toward Croatia was driven by a tendency among some Serbian nationalists to interpret cotemporary political events in accordance with a narrative of the Serbian past characterized by a discourse of Serbian victimization. The leader of one Serbian paramilitary force, for example, said that while he did not begrudge what he called the "Ustasche" state of Croatia its independence, he darkly warned that he and his fellow Serbs would allow it to contain no Serbian settlements or villages. That, he said, would "dishonor our ancestors and shame our descendants." This same paramilitary leader dubbed his force "Chetniks," and his men wore the uniforms of the dreaded Yugoslav royalist army that had battled both the fascist Ustasche and Communist Partisans during the Second World War.[10] Another Serbian soldier, perched on the hills above the besieged city of Sarajevo, firing a machine gun into the city where he had once been a teacher, understood himself to be protecting Europe from the Turkish invaders who huddled below his guns.[11]

As Suny makes clear, the often violent political dynamics of post-Soviet politics in Armenia-Azerbaijan or the former Yugoslavia "should not be seen as simply the reemergence from slumber of atavistic, repressed or primordial identities and conflicts."[12] Rather, they are the results of specific ways of reckoning communal (in these cases, national) identity, and these specific ways of reckoning identity are tied inexorably to the kinds of narratives with which communities and individuals situate or emplot themselves within their social and political world. Nor are the dynamics Suny isolates unique to the kinds of communities grouped under the rubric "modern state." Within other sorts of bounded identity groupings, whether based upon religious or class identity, political ideology or other rallying points, narrative plays a similarly determinative role in the fashioning of identities and relations within and between bounded groups.[13]

Drawing upon the insights of Suny, Somers and their colleagues I will argue in the following pages that if we are to understand the problem of militant piety in the Roman world after the advent of Constantine, it is crucial to examine the narratives with which the communities of that world recalled the past and with which members of those communities came to imagine themselves emplotted. It was these narratives that would help to determine the ways in which those individuals would interpret the signs and symbols, events and personalities they encountered within their world. And it was in accordance with these narratives that they would read moments of confrontation and conflict, and it was these narratives that would serve late Roman Christians as resources for formulating ethical, moral, and practical responses to the world they perceived.

"Fathers So Great, So Courageous, So Wise"

As John Chrysostom urged his congregation to carry the boundaries of their community within them and to keep watch over their fellow Christians, ensuring that they too remained aware of those boundaries, he had the Council of Nicaea on his side. It was the Council of Nicaea, he reminded his flock, which had decided that the Pasch must not be celebrated on the same day as the Jews celebrated Passover. The celebrations must be kept scrupulously separate, the council had decreed—if 14 Nisan fell upon a Sunday, the Pasch was to be celebrated the next week.[14] In 387, the year of Chrysostom's sermons, Passover had indeed fallen upon a Sunday. Despite the forward planning of the bishops assembled at Nicaea in 325, however, Chrysostom clearly had his hands full keeping Christian and Jewish observances of the Pasch separate.

The date upon which the Pasch was to be celebrated was a point of controversy and confusion every year and in many Christian communities. The coincidence of 14 Nisan and the first day of the week merely added to the confusion.[15] It is not difficult to understand why Chrysostom's parishioners may have been a bit befuddled about precisely when and how they, as real Christians, ought to celebrate the Pasch. As Chrysostom had to concede, Jesus had celebrated Passover with the Jews, and Christians of earlier generations had indeed followed the Jewish calendar in order to determine the date of Easter. Why should the findings of a congregation of mere mortals—whatever their rank within the church—have the authority to overturn such apparently impeccable precedent?[16]

The answer Chrysostom gave his congregation was that the churchmen assembled in Nicaea in 325 were not just any churchmen. They were, rather, martyrs who had endured the horrors of the Great Persecution. As he spoke of the authority of the council and its decrees, Chrysostom located the men who made up the council in what had become an easily recognizable and especially powerful narrative of the Christian communal past.

> Just as champions having set up countless victory monuments and having suffered many wounds, so too at that time, champions of the

> Churches bearing the marks of Christ and able to count many wounds suffered patiently for their confession, came together from every direction. Some could speak of the mines and their suffering in them; others could tell of the confiscation of all that they possessed; others could describe starvation and constant blows. Some could display ribs torn fleshless; some backs pulverized, some eyes dug out, while some could make show of the loss of other body parts for the sake of Christ. The synod as a whole was welded together at that time from these prizefighters, and in good faith they legislated this: to celebrate that festival [Easter] in common and in unison. Moreover, not betraying their faith during those most harsh times, could they act deceitfully about the observance [of Easter]?[17]

The criteria these champions set forth for Christianness did not simply locate an individual inside or outside of the one true community of God; the attitude taken by that individual to the criteria set forth by those men located that individual within a much larger narrative, that of the rise of the Christian community, of its persecution and its eventual triumph, of the process of revelation and salvation in which the martyrs were so intimately implicated.[18] To disregard the criteria set forth by those scarred and battered veterans of the Roman Christian community's primordial traumas was to side with those who attacked the Church, to side with the persecutors of the holy martyrs. "Look what you do when you pass sentence against such great *patres*, such manly and wise *patres*," he says. "For if all of the good things owned by the Pharisee, having condemned the tax collector, were destroyed, what forgiveness will you have, what defense will you make having risen up against such great teachers and friends of God, and these things done so unjustly and with such irrationality?"[19]

For modern students of late antiquity, the narrative to which Chrysostom alluded to authorize the council and its participants is one so well known as to demand a bit of detailed discussion. As it was experienced most intimately throughout the Roman world, it was a narrative of confrontation between truth and error, between individuals and communities to whom certain transcendent truths were revealed and those who denied those truths. It was a story of numinous *irruptions*[20] in the lived experience of the Roman state, irruptions whose authenticity resided in the Roman state's much-proclaimed penchant for seeking out, discerning, and making manifest truth.

Eusebius of Caesarea provides a rather tidy articulation of this narrative in his *Ecclesiastical History*. In Book VIII of that work, for example, the persecutions endured by Christians of the third and early fourth century are rendered in a style that Chrysostom, in the passage cited above, would echo decades later to establish the bona fides of the Council of Nicaea. Before the persecutions, Eusebius says, Christians lived in easy assimilation within Roman society despite earlier periods of persecution, occupying prominent public offices and enjoying both prosperity and power. They lived among non-Christians without fear of persecution, inhabiting the households of the leaders of Roman society, speaking openly and even boldly of their faith. They were tolerated and at peace with their fellow Romans.[21]

This peace, however, which may be read as a dissolution of the crucial communal boundaries between Christian and non-Christian, led to "pride and sloth," to sin and error. "We fell to envy and fierce railing against one another," he says, "warring upon ourselves, so to speak, as occasion offered, with weapons and spears formed from words; and rulers attacked rulers and laity formed factions against laity, while unspeakable hypocrisy and pretence pursued their evil course to the furthest end."[22] Even after the persecutions began, first against those in the army, Eusebius recalls, some, "like some kind of atheists, imagined that our affairs escaped all heed and oversight; we went on adding one wickedness to another; and those accounted our pastors, casting aside the sanctions of the fear of God, were enflamed with mutual contentions, and did nothing else but add to the strifes and threats, the jealousy, enmity and hatred that they used toward one another, claiming with all vehemence the objects of their ambition as if they were a despot's spoils."[23]

Once the persecutions began in earnest, however, those who had made trouble within the Church were brought low and even driven from the fold. Eusebius does not elaborate here, however, because, "it is not our part to describe the melancholy misfortunes in the issue, even as we do not think it proper to hand down to memory their desertions and unnatural conduct before the persecution." Accordingly, Eusebius resolves not to make mention of "those who were tried by the persecution, or . . . made utter shipwreck of their salvation, and by their own free will were plunged in the depths of the billows." Rather, he says, he will tell a story of the time of persecution that will be useful for later generations of Christians.[24]

With the onset of persecution, the Christian community was quickly divided into two groupings, those who would sacrifice and those who would not: "A great many rulers of the churches eagerly endured terrible sufferings, and furnished examples of noble conflicts," he says. "But a multitude of others, benumbed in spirit by fear, were easily weakened at the first onset. Of the rest each one endured different forms of torture. The body of one was scourged with rods. Another was punished with insupportable rackings and scrapings, in which some suffered a miserable death."

Amid the smoke and horror of the persecution, then, the boundaries of the one community of God upon the earth were preserved and protected by the actions of its truest members.[25] The acts of these men and women were recalled in a literary genre whose defining narrative structure underscored the crucial dynamics of the persecution as it abided within the larger narrative of Christianity's formative past. The paradigmatic elements of these smaller narratives repeat regularly through Eusebius's rendition of the tetrarchic persecutions.[26]

In the description of the persecutions that follows, Eusebius tours the empire, recalling the specific martyrs of its various regions and cities. We move from Nicomedia—ground zero of the persecutions—to Tyre in Palestine to Thebais and Alexandria in Egypt to Phrygia to Arabia to Cappadocia to Mesopotamia to Pontus and the city of Antioch. In each of these places we read the names of the martyrs and the horrors they suffered with uniform courage and intransigence. The descriptions of the individual confrontations and deaths of the martyrs literally bleed together as our gaze is drawn from province to province, from city to city. The topography of the Roman world thus becomes a parchment upon which is written a grand narrative of persecution and resistance. This grand narrative is a patchwork of micronarratives, however, assimilating to itself the experiences of local Christian communities and the deaths of local martyrs.[27]

In these micronarratives, a witness to the truths of the Christian community is set in opposition to some representative of Roman imperial power. The witness is asked to perform an act (almost always to sacrifice) with which other individuals perform their membership in a non-Christian community.[28] When the witness refuses, various inducements are advanced; sometimes these are reasoned attempts at persuasion, sometimes they are impassioned appeals to the affective ties between the speaker and the witness, sometimes they are offers of high position or riches, sometimes they are threats. Often these are offered in some combination. When the martyr still refuses, s/he is subjected to tortures, these commonly rendered in pornographic detail.

Miraculously, however, the martyr is able to endure these, and thus defeats the power of the Roman state.[29]

In his own description of the persecution as he addressed his congregation in the days before the Pasch of 387, Chrysostom recalled the persecution with a montage of horrors which closely recalls Eusebius's text: "[There were] frying pans, *katapeltai* [a kind of rack], caldrons, ovens, pits of water, cliffs, the teeth of animals, seas, confiscations [of property], and myriad other tortures not to be mentioned by word nor endured in their action . . . but none of this dissolved the Church, nor did any of it make the Church weaker." That the martyrs endured and the Church survived these trials was a numinous testament to the truths upon which the stripling Christian community was based, he insisted. "And indeed, the wonderful and paradoxical thing is that all of these things were brought about at the beginnings [of the Church]," he said. "The fact that our community was not lessened but even made greater is the miracle transcending all."[30]

For Chrysostom and his contemporaries, it was through the intransigence of the martyrs, their courage and fortitude in defense of their communities, that this miracle manifested itself. For Vincent of Lérins, writing in Gaul in the fifth century, the martyrs had preserved the essential truths upon which the one community of God upon the earth was founded, and they were, in turn, a model in whom contemporary Christians might find resources for crafting Christian selves that mirrored as exactly as possible all of the qualities that marked one as a real Christian. "For who," he asked, "is there who is so perverse of mind that he, though not able to outstrip them, does not wish to follow those whom no force, no threats, no blandishments, not [concern for] life, not [concern for] death, not the imperial palace, not the *satellites*, not the *imperator*, not the *imperium*, not men, not demons, deterred from their defense of the faith of their ancestors (*defensione maiorum fidei*)?" By their sacrifice the martyrs and confessors redeemed their community from the various ravages of the persecution. But they did more: "When at last nearly the entire world was overturned by a savage and sudden storm of heresy, [they] recalled it from new fangled faithlessness to the ancient faith, from the insanity of the new to the ancient right reason, from the blindness of innovation to ancient enlightenment."[31]

The martyrs had preserved the primordial essence of Christianity and kept it from novelty and error. Within the late antique Christian imaginary, the martyrs stood bathed in the ethereal light of revelation, but revelation of a particular kind. They were figures through whom God had worked his good pleasure upon the earth. And yet they were not figures from an unknowable or alien past. The truths they so miraculously manifested were scraped, gouged, and torn from their flesh by the same Roman imperial judiciary that still functioned throughout the Roman world, and that was also crucial to every Roman citizen's understanding of his own place in that world.[32] It was the function of that judiciary to discover truth and to authorize the defining truths of Roman society. This was the function of the Roman judiciary in the time of the persecutions, and it was its function as the Christians of the post-Constantinian era remembered the foundational traumas of their community.[33]

The martyrs were thus Christian men and women who, through their own adherence to all that defined true members of their community, had brought about a moment of divine *irruption*—an emergence and revelation of a transcendent truth. That truth had irradiated them, had permeated them and made them sources of truths that could not be eroded by time, argued away, or effaced by force.

In a world rampant with numinous signs and symbols, holy figures and ways of seeking God, then, the martyrs were figures to which one could look as unchanging models of the qualities and behavioral practices which defined all real Christians. They occupied an unchanging point in a world in which, as Chrysostom's parishioners were discovering in the spring of 387, the perilous allure of powerful and seemingly familiar patterns of worship or holy texts could coax one into the abyss. If, against the well-known power of fasting, the Torah and the example of Christ himself Chrysostom could offer only the counterintuitive fine print in the decision of a church council, the figure of the martyrs could speak with the power of Christianity's organizing narratives, narratives with which Christians of the fourth century had come to imagine their place within their communities, within their society and upon the grand stage of history.

"Does Not the Living Voice of Kindred Blood Call Out to Our Hearts?"

Just as the overarching history of the Christian community within the Roman world was recalled through the narrative of persecution and triumph articulated by Eusebius, throughout the later Roman world, stories describing the suffering and deaths of hometown martyrs—those whose passions were collected by Eusebius into a tapestry of persecution and resistance—were the medium through which local Christian communities recalled their own foundational dramas. These stories resonated with the metanarrative of Christian history which embraced all Christian communities, and yet these were profoundly local stories, the figures they celebrated revered intimately as primordial ancestors whose blood, shed into the soil of the city or town or village in which they died, was the holy seed from which had grown each local community of the universal God. Denise Kimber Buell has written, "Martyr narratives presuppose and play upon the notion that one's identity is embedded in a multiply inflected social network. Through torture and suffering, but also through resituating identity, these texts produce an idea of Christians that applies to both the individual martyr, the witnesses to the martyrs in the narrative, and the reading/hearing community. The texts help to produce a collective identity."[34]

Moreover, the stories of these martyrs' passions were the stories in accordance with which past, present, and future now became comprehensible within the grand narrative of Roman Christianity and with which individual Christians were encouraged to fashion more perfect selves.[35]

When preaching in the Forty Martyrs' hometown of Sebasteia, for example, Gregory of Nyssa did not have to supply his own version of the trial endured by the martyrs. Instead, he asked the congregation to recall and recite their own stories of the martyrs, those that they associated with the history of their city and its place in the grand narrative of Christianity's triumph. As Raymond Van Dam suggests, the stories of the martyrs were perhaps better known to these and other late antique townspeople than those of the Bible. In any case, they were certainly more resonant and more relevant when it came to the distinct identities of local Christian communities.[36]

In fifth-century Gaul, preachers routinely fostered a sense of local communal identity among their parishioners by encouraging a close and even personal identification with local martyrs.[37] In these sermons, some of which are collected in the *Eusebius Gallicanus* corpus, the martyrs are presented as both the founders of the local Christian community and ancestors of the individual Christians residing within that community. The ties between the martyrs of Lyon and the fifth-century residents of that city were primordial ties of kinship and blood. "Does not the living voice of kindred blood call out to our hearts?" the preacher of one of these sermons entreated his congregation.[38]

The blood in question was that which flowed in the veins of the martyrs Epipodius and Alexander and which poured into the soil of Lyon as those "indigenous"[39] martyrs sacrificed themselves as founders of the later Christian community. As Gilian Clark has noted, "To have the blood of the martyrs was equivalent, in modern terms, to having the DNA: human bodies and their reproductive potential were thought to be transformations of blood."[40]

The connection between martyrs, their blood, and a community's native soil was not unique to fifth-century Gaul. As Dennis Trout has detailed in a fascinating study of "the invention of early Christian Rome," the fourth-century Roman bishop Damasus dug into the very soil of the ancient city to reveal to Romans a primordial Christian past, bringing to light the tombs and catacombs of the martyrs.[41] The underground deposits of holy bodies had become "a meandering history exhibit" by the fifth century, a kind of subterranean museum in which Christians could encounter and have interpreted for them the righteous ancestors of their local community.

As Trout notes, past and present "collided abruptly in fourth-century Rome. The collision was the collateral damage of a Constantinian miracle that in a few short years thrust Christianity from persecuted to favored status."[42] The crisis of identity incited among Roman civic elites by this narrative was eased in part, as Trout ably demonstrates, by Damasus's capacity to couch the local implications of that narrative in agreeably classical verse drawn, in some cases word by word, from the works of Augustan-era poets. Thus the acts of the martyrs were commemorated by Damasus in short bits of verse which recalled the triumphalist odes of Horace and Virgil.[43] What Trout describes is a local elaboration upon the grand narrative of the Christian past rendered in an authorizing semiotic *langue de départ* appropriate to the cultural space in which that elaboration took place.

It is significant that it was into the ancient soil of Rome, where so many primordial pasts have resided, that Damasus dug to reveal to the other members of his community their common and heroic ancestors. The holy dead were the long invisible yet potent seeds from which the Christian community of Rome had grown.[44] Significantly, the annual commemoration of the martyrs were not, even in the later fourth century, state *feriae*. That is, unlike other official state holidays which applied to the entire empire, the celebration of the anniversary of the "birthdays" of martyrs remained a private affair, like the familial death rituals within the pagan communities of Rome, "whereby only the *familia* and *collegium* would treat as *feriae* the anniversaries of their special dead."[45] The commemoration of those "special dead" became, as it was for Gregory of Nyssa as he preached in his brother's old see of Caesarea, a kind of family affair writ large. The memory of the martyrs of Rome was thus the special province of the community to which they gave birth, the one true community of God in the Eternal City. That "the one community of God" in the city of Rome was Damasus's own—and not that of the Ursinians (against which Damasus waged bloody urban combat) or any of the other rival Christian groups in fourth-century Rome—Damasus made clear in many of the verse epigrams with which he inscribed the resting places of the martyrs.[46]

Indeed, however else we may interpret Damasus's excavation of the Christian communal past and his stewardship of the memory of the martyrs, these seem to have been integral aspects of a much larger project aimed at establishing his Christian community, the Catholic community of Rome, as the only true offspring of the glorious martyrs. This he accomplished, as M. Sághy has argued, by crafting for himself a space in the imaginary of contemporary Roman Christians through the memories he created of the martyrs.[47] By inscribing their tombs and monuments and monopolizing control of their burial sites, Damasus located himself within the larger narrative of the Christian past I have been describing. As we shall see, Damasus was only one of many Christian communal leaders to adopt such a strategy.

Just as Damasus reordered the history of the Christian community of Rome to suit the needs of its fourth-century present, Paulinus of Milan recalled in his *Life* of Ambrose that one fourth-century Bolognese bishop reached into his own community's subterranean past to retrieve the bodies and memories of local martyrs.[48] He discovered the bodies of Vitalis and Agricola, whose remains "had been buried among the bodies of the Jews, and . . . would not have become known had not the holy martyrs revealed themselves to the bishop of that church."[49] If, as Daniel Boyarin has suggested and the case of Chrysostom's Antioch seems to confirm, Christian bishops of the fourth century still found it necessary to insist upon and reinforce innate distinctions between that which was Jewish and that which was Christian, the recovery of the bodies of distinctly Christian martyrs would have carried a special potency; although the remains of both Jews and Christians may lay within the sacred soil of the community's past, they were remains which could be easily distinguished one from another, discrete, separate, one set of remains ancient and holy, the other simply old.[50]

The bishop Ambrose of Milan used bits of the relics discovered in

Bologna to consecrate a church in Florence. Ambrose had famously also shoveled into the native soil of his own Milan and similarly revealed precious artifacts of that community's primordial past. The bones of two previously unknown or forgotten martyrs, Gervasius and Protasius, emerged from the floor of Ambrose's new basilica, and with their emergence occasioned the consecration of that basilica, giving Ambrose's besieged community a home. In the ground where the martyrs' remains had lain for so long, their holy blood mixed with the earth that supported this new home. With their emergence, they announced their kinship with this one community of Christians, and Ambrose took this as a sign of his community's enduring connection with its forgotten primordial past: "We have found this one thing, in which we seem to excel our ancestors—we have regained the knowledge of the holy martyrs which they let slip."[51]

With this new-old knowledge of his community's foundational past, Ambrose found a pair of models to commend to his congregation as it struggled against the claims of a rival community in Milan, the Arians. "Thanks be to you, lord Jesus, that you have waken up for us the spirits of the holy martyrs in this age when your church needs greater defenses," Ambrose said. "Let all know what sort of defender I require, [those] who are able to defend, but do not wish to attack. These I have acquired for you, *plebs sancta*, who benefit everyone, but harm no one. Such are the defenders I solicit, such are the soldiers I have—that is [I have] not soldiers of the present world, but soldiers of Christ."[52]

The martyrs helped to clarify the nature of the struggle underway in Milan. Just as in Rome there could be but one community of God, there was but one community of God in Milan. It was the community of the martyrs who gave their lives for that same community during the traumas of persecution, and now those martyrs had revealed themselves to their descendants.

Meanwhile, Ambrose's Arian rivals denied that the bones Ambrose had discovered were martyr relics at all. They naturally also disputed the miracles Ambrose claimed that they had performed upon their reemergence, the healings and exorcisms.[53] Enraged, Ambrose assured his congregation that all of this simply demonstrated that the Arians were not simply bad Christians but of another faith altogether and, accordingly, of another lineage. By denying that Ambrose's new martyrs were real martyrs, "[the Arians] demonstrate that the martyrs were of another faith than that which they themselves believe in . . . they do not have the faith which was in [the martyrs], that faith confirmed by the tradition of our forefathers."[54] The Arians were not simply the enemies of Ambrose's community, they were enemies of the martyrs, and if they were enemies of the martyrs, it became rather clear where they fit into the larger narrative of Christian history.

Thus the martyrs of Milan made manifest the sacred boundaries in accordance with which the Ambrosian community was defined and delimited. They themselves were boundaries set in place in the once forgotten but now resurrected past, in moments of confrontation between martyrs and Roman magistrates, in the numinous foundational traumas of Roman Christianity. They were not boundaries subject to choice, argumentation, or negotiation. They were tethered to transcendent truths whose validity would endure even if, like the long hidden bodies of the martyrs, they should become invisible or be denied. While hidden, the martyrs bled in to the sacred soil upon which this community had been founded, their blood connecting heaven with earth, past with present.

Accordingly, the reemergence of the martyrs also had the effect of imposing a kind of grammar upon the events in which Ambrose and his community found themselves enmeshed. The distinctions to be drawn between Ambrose's community and that of the Arians were no longer reducible to theology or Christology, if in fact they had ever been that simple. They had now become manifestations of a much larger, much older, and much more pervasive narrative, one in which the Ambrosian congregation at Milan was now more intimately situated.

The modern reader might conclude that the Arians' refusal to accept Ambrose's newfound martyrs stemmed from the circumstances of their discovery and the fact that they had been previously unknown, both of which are, from one point of view, rather suspicious. In addition to this, however, the discovery of the martyrs, if understood as genuine by members of the Arian community, posed real problems for the Arian leadership as it struggled with the Ambrosian community over the question of which was the real community of Christians. The Arians also revered martyrs, of course, and the appearance of two martyrs from the earth beneath Ambrose's basilica will have provided an attractive kind of capital for the Ambrosian community.

This kind of capital could, for example, produce movements across the boundaries which divided the Ambrosian and Arian communities of Milan. Paulinus of Milan's *Life of Ambrose* tells of one Arian who was "possessed by an unclean spirit" and began to announce publicly that

> They themselves who denied the martyrs or who did not believe in the unity of the Trinity as Ambrose taught were tormented just as he was tormented. But, perplexed by this pronouncement, they who should have been persuaded to do the proper penance by such a confession killed the man, who was submerged in a pond, thus adding murder to faithlessness. Indeed, a fitting necessity brought them to this end. In fact, the holy bishop Ambrose, esteemed as a man of greater humility, stored up the grace granted to him by the Lord and daily grew greater in the sight of God and man by means of faith and love.[55]

One way to read this passage is as a report upon the conversion of a formerly zealous Arian following the discovery of the martyrs, one which carried tragic consequences for the convert. The murder of the man then becomes a rather brutal instance of boundary defense carried out by members of the Arian community of Milan who, in their own zeal, performed an extreme version of the kind of person-to-person policing of communal boundaries John Chrysostom commended to his own parishioners in Antioch.[56] Paulinus seems to suggest that the murder was in part a reaction to the enhanced prestige Ambrose enjoyed following the emergence of the martyrs "when the irreligion of the Arians was diminished."[57] Moreover, another, less violent conversion story follows this episode, in which another former Arian extremist joins the Ambrosian fold.[58] Perhaps a better sense of how all of this looked from the Arian side of things may be gained by turning our gaze south, to the city of Carthage, and to a sermon delivered by Augustine of Hippo in the winter of 397.

The sermon, among those recently discovered by François Dolbeau, was occasioned by an outburst of what Augustine interpreted as disobedience among members of his congregation when some of them challenged a direction he issued about where they ought to stand during the course of one of his sermons.[59] Throughout the sermon we will examine, Augustine dwells upon the problem of telling real martyrs from false martyrs, and the dangers of being deceived by false martyrs like those with which the Donatist church advanced its claims to be the one community of God upon the earth.[60]

The devil first put false gods before men to be adored, Augustine says, but those idols were overthrown thanks to the sacrifices of the martyrs. This is, of course, a version of the narrative with which we have seen other groups of Christians recalling their communal histories above. Now, Augustine told his congregation, the "ancient serpent saw the temples empty and the martyrs honored [and] . . . because he could not make false gods for the Christians, he made false martyrs. But O, you Catholic offspring (*germina*), regard with us those false martyrs as small in rank compared with the true martyrs, and with faithful piety discern what the devil endeavors to mix with venomous deceit."[61]

It was the devil's plan to deceive Christians by offering them a figure so much like those which normally guided Christians to salvation: "He wishes to hide the difference between true martyrs and false martyrs from us; he wishes, lest we discern such things, to put out the eyes of the heart." He urges his congregation that they must not be deceived by things "similar in appearance" (*simili specie*) to the central signs and symbols of their own community. Rather, they must remain alert to what lies beneath such potent figures as the Donatist martyrs and remember precisely why they honor such real martyrs as Vincentius, at whose commemoration the congregation had grown restive the day before. "Behold how great the good they seem to possess and are false!" he cautions. "Yesterday, we listened to the praises of the true martyr, what torments he endured, of what character, how many, how continuous! Let love be lacking, it is folly. For what reason do we praise, for what reason do we herald, for what reason are we joyful, if not because we see in which church, for what faith, how he resisted the king who commanded him?"[62]

As the sermon progresses, Augustine begins an imaginary exchange with the devil concerning his false martyrs. It becomes clear as the sermon develops, however, that the diabolical false martyrs discussed here are in fact those of the Donatist community, and the figure whom Augustine debates is a doubly inscribed foil which may be read as the devil Augustine identifies and a personification of the Donatist community.

> Do you not remember, ancient enemy, he who when he incited his disciples to the glory of suffering said, "*Blessed are they who suffer punishment for the sake of righteousness*?"[63] One phrase remained vigilant against all of your venom, against your double-talking, triple-talking, babble-talking attempts (*bilinguges, trilingues, multilingues ausus*): *for the sake of righteousness (propter iustitiam)*. In view of this phrase, murderers suffer punishment but are not martyrs, adulterers suffer punishment but are not martyrs. For you

make a show of your martyrs: you throw out what they suffered, I ask why they suffered. You laud the penalty, I examine the cause. The cause I examine, I say, the cause I seek. Tell me why he suffered, he whom you toss out to have suffered. For righteousness? Learn this: for this itself is the cause of the martyrs. Punishment does not crown the martyrs, but the cause.[64]

The cause for which the Donatist martyrs were punished, he says, was their refusal to join with their brothers in concord and not, as is true of real martyrs, because they refused to worship idols. The difference, in other words, between this dangerous and deceptively familiar sign, is not the sign itself (that is, the individual who died resisting the powerful of the world while defending the integrity of his or her communal boundaries), but the particular, closely circumscribed readings to which this sign and that which it seems to mimic are to be properly subjected. We have encountered this species of argument before, of course. In Antioch, John Chrysostom advanced such arguments while trying desperately and, it would seem, with no real success, to determine tightly the readings to which certain powerful acts, texts, sights, personages, and other social signs could be read. He did so in order to police his communal boundaries and to make those boundaries relevant to his parishioners by making any movement across them a matter of concern for all members of his community.

Is it possible that Augustine, in the last years of the fourth century, found a similar move necessary in the famously polarized region of North Africa?[65] If so, that he advances such a move by parsing the figure of the martyr is particularly ironic, especially given the fact that it is the Donatist community which has so often been cited for its concern for the maintenance of its communal integrity and for grounding its identity in the memory of the martyrs.[66]

In fact, it would seem that the Donatists were not at all unique in their concern for communal boundaries and the use they made of the figure of the martyr in imagining and policing those boundaries. As we saw above, Ambrose conjured a pair of martyrs for just this purpose in Milan, and Damasus integrated the memory of the martyrs into his own campaign against the other Christian communities of Rome. In Egypt, moreover, the Melitian church claimed to have descended from the martyrs and waged an aggressive campaign in which it, like the Damasian and Ambrosian communities in

Rome and Milan, employed the relics and memories of the martyrs to situate itself within the grand narrative of Christian history.[67] The Melitians' rival, the bishop Athanasius, on the other hand, like Damasus's and Ambrose's respective rivals, and, apparently, Augustine, found himself on the defensive when faced with such potent references to this overarching and increasingly powerful narrative of the Christian past. This was especially so in that the imaginations of many of his parishioners seem to been captured by the claims of the Melitian church, or, as it called itself, the "Church of the Martyrs."[68] It is perhaps not surprising, then, that Athanasius's response to the Melitian situation was to deny that the bodies they paraded through the Egyptian countryside were the remains of martyrs at all.[69]

"The Serpent Does Not Sleep"

Many of the texts upon which I have drawn above were sermons delivered at annual commemorations of the martyrs' passions. These were annual rituals of the kind which the philosopher of religion Mircea Eliade suggests are repeated to evoke "sacred time" and to commemorate some primordial beginning, while the tombs and shrines of the martyrs were what Eliade called "sacred spaces"—sites in which the transcendent divine had broken through into the shifting, contingent world of human subjectivity and historical time. These were sites in which, as Peter Brown and others have repeatedly made clear, humans and the divine communicated; they were "'paradoxical points of passage from one mode of being to another' which is repeatable by man."[70]

For Eliade, Jonathan Z. Smith has written, "repetition is the human mode of articulating absolute Reality. It is expressive of man's 'unquenchable ontological thirst,' his desire to 'found' his existence in 'real existence,' in 'objective reality,' in that which is not 'illusory,' which avoids the 'paralysis' of 'the never-ceasing relativity of purely subjective experiences.'"[71] The ultimate and uncontestable Truth in which to base such ontological surety must reside beyond this world, in that more profound and eternal realm which only occasionally breaks into this shifting, shadowy plane of existence.

It is perhaps a similar desire for freedom from "the never-ceasing relativity of purely subjective experiences" which prompts human communities to fashion their social realities in accordance with what anthropologists and sociologists refer to as "primordialist" discourses concerning identity and the origins of the group to which they belong. As it appears in the work of Ronald Grigor Suny and others, primordialism is the belief in certain essential affinities which tie groups of individuals together as bounded communities across time and space. Such ties may reside in affinities of "blood," "culture," the soil of a group's "homeland," its history or group "spirit."[72] I suggest that for human subjects immersed in social or cultural conditions in which presumed or declared social boundaries are confounded by observed or experienced social realities, primordialism or primordialist discourses for recalling communal pasts may supply a social or cultural equivalent of the kind of firm ontological foundation Eliade suggests "religious man" finds in ritual practice. The social or experiential reality conjured by such discourses is rooted not (or not only) in the transcendent but in the aboriginal past in which those imagined qualities of culture, character, belief and blood which mark all authentic members of the group in question were forged.

Primordialist notions of Armenianness as they are analyzed in Suny's work, for example, hold that Armenians do not choose to be a people but simply *are* a people because they are bound by a shared inheritance from the mythic past, passed down, unchanged, through the trials and persecutions endured by the Armenian people. Real Armenians, according to such notions of identity, share some combination of common, essentially Armenian qualities, and this is true whether the Armenian in question resides in Armenia, Lebanon or the suburbs of Los Angeles. These essential qualities are passed on in one's blood or as part of what are believed to be unchanging cultural traditions uniting contemporary Armenians with an ancient past. This ancient past is, in turn, recalled through a repertoire of closely policed narratives.

As Suny discovered after delivering a paper challenging one such narrative, to question these narratives is not only to risk provoking anger but to find oneself suddenly cast in a role within that narrative. In Suny's case, after delivering a paper which cited archaeological and literary evidence to suggest that the city of Everan had, over time, been home to a diverse population rather than the exclusively Armenian populace ascribed to it by Armenian nationalists, the author found himself emplotted in the role of the "traitor," or "betrayer." Within the history of Armenia as it is recalled in certain privileged narratives, the traitor is a familiar and hated archetype. As he left his talk, members of Suny's audience screamed at him, "You are no Armenian!"[73]

Why the vehemence of this audience's reaction to Suny's talk? To answer this question we must consider the function of the kinds of narratives Suny challenged in his paper and which he desecrated in the eyes of his audience. It is the function of such narratives not simply to recall past events, but, as the sociologist Margaret Somers has argued, to allow human subjects to make sense of the events, personalities, and institutions around them. "[One] crucial element of narrativity is its evaluative criteria," Somers has written. "Evaluation enables us to make qualitative and lexical distinctions among the infinite variety of events, experiences, characters, institutional promises, and social factors that impinge on our lives . . . in the face of a potentially limitless array of social experiences deriving from social contact with events, institutions, and people, the evaluative capacity of emplotment demands and enables *selective appropriation* in constructing narratives."[74]

In other words, such narratives allow human subjects to locate themselves within the world—they allow the ordering of social relations; they clarify ethnical and moral dilemmas; they provide answers to difficult questions and explanations for difficult events. Taking as his example post-Soviet Armenian nationalist identities mediated through such narratives, Suny writes that, "contingent events like the [Armenian] earthquake of December 7, 1988, are 'absorbed into a single historical narrative, which included massacres, genocide, environmental pollution, ethnic violence and state domination.' And even a marginal movement of UFO enthusiasts interpreted the arrival of extraterrestrials through the prism of Armenian national history."[75]

For communities that understand themselves to be imperiled, threatened, or in a state of crisis, narratives of the group's origins may prove crucial in maintaining a sense of communal integrity and for envisioning possibilities for survival. "In telling the story of our becoming, as an individual, a nation, a people, we establish who we are," writes Frances Polletta. "Narratives may be employed strategically to strengthen a collective identity but they also may precede and make possible the development of a coherent community, nation, or collective actor. In periods of actual or potential upheaval, stories maintain the stability of the self and group."[76]

For Edward Said, speaking in an interview with Salman Rushdie, the lack of a stable, authorized narrative of a specifically Palestinian past made it necessary, in the case of attacks by non-Palestinians upon the authenticity of Palestinian cultural forms (specifically a style of dress), to constantly repeat and reiterate certain smaller historical narratives which, in his mind, justified those expressions of Palestinian identity (as well as the ideological programs for which they were a sign) as in fact valid and authentic. Similarly, Said continued, challenges to the legitimacy of the Palestinian cause itself are routinely met with an impassioned recitation of narrative accounts which, from the Palestinian speaker's point of view, validate the claims of Palestinians to the land over which they contend with Israel: "[A charge of illegitimacy] launches you into a tremendous harangue, as you explain to people, 'my mother was born in Nazareth, my father was born in Jerusalem . . .' The interesting thing is that there seems to be nothing in the world which sustains the story: unless you go on telling it, it will just drop and disappear."[77] The greater danger, Said seemed to fear, was that if these specific narratives of the Palestinian past were to disappear or become impossible to recite, so would the reality of a specifically Palestinian identity disappear.

It was perhaps for this reason that Said also worried that the necessary resources for a narrative of the Palestinian past that could sustain a stable Palestinian identity were endangered: "There never seems to be enough time [to constitute a fitting narrative of the Palestinian past], and one always has the impression that one's enemies—in this case the Israelis—are trying to take the archive away," Said said. "The gravest image for me in [the Israeli invasion of Lebanon in] 1982 was of the Israelis shipping out the archives of the Palestinian research center in Beirut to Tel Aviv."[78]

In the modern state, to control the archives is to control a repository of authorizing truths, truths which carry traces (as Said seems to suggest) of a community's primordial beginnings. Archives are, in other words, what the native soil of Rome, Bologna, or Milan was for the Christian communities that resided there in the decades of dramatic change during the fourth century. From the authorizing truths culled from the archives of Beirut or the soil of ancient cities, authoritative narratives of the past may be written or recited, and with these narratives communities may imagine not simply their origins but what it means to be a member of that community in the present moment. It is here that the character of the narratives elaborated matters most for the character of the relationships members of such communities will build with one another and with members of other communities.

Returning to Ronald Grigor Suny's suggestion, cited at the beginning of this chapter, that the character of the narratives with which communities recall their past may help us to understand how and why those communities come into violent conflict with other communities, we may note that one of the most commonly recurring tropes we encounter in communal narratives is that of violent oppression at the hands of a much stronger enemy. For some

Armenians, as we have seen, the memory of the 1915 genocide enshrined in a certain narrative of the Armenian past became a prism through which contemporary conflicts were interpreted. For some Serb nationalists, meanwhile, a narrative of the Serbian past that featured stories of oppression at the hands of Croatian Fascists and Turkish invaders provided an imaginative framework in which contemporary confrontations with Croat nationalists and the Bosnian civilians and militia besieged in Sarajevo were emplotted. During the early 1990s, this was a narrative that for many Serb nationalists rendered acts that were read by much of the world as instances of genocidal aggression as a desperate defense of both Serbia and the rest of Europe from the rebirth of Nazism and the return of the Ottoman Empire.

In the two cases just cited, the narratives of victimization that seem to have authorized greater and lesser acts or policies of aggression toward other communities are neither fanciful nor exaggerated. They reflect real events insofar as they recall the very real murder of very real human beings. The uncomfortable irony here, of course, is that rather than preventing the use of violence against members of other communities, some narratives of remembrance recalling dark moments of brutality and suffering visited upon defenseless and innocent Armenians and Serbs seem to have made it easier for some who imagine their place in the world in accordance with such stories to adopt aggressive and even murderous postures with members of other communities.

Why should this be so? If we take seriously Margaret Somers's suggestion that narratives allow human subjects not just to imagine the past, but to read the present in accordance with the plot of the narrative in question, it becomes clear that as that subject comes to understand him- or herself as emplotted in a given narrative so too will s/he understand others to occupy roles within that narrative. Moreover, if we accept Ronald Grigor Suny's suggestion that narratives of the communal past and primordialist notions of identity are intimately linked, it becomes clear that narratives which stress a "people's" history of victimization will help to produce identity groupings whose members must understand victimhood as one of the essential characteristics of all real members of the group, and indeed as a defining quality of the group itself. Accordingly, when members of identity groups constituted in accordance with narratives in which the memory of persecution and victimization are central find themselves in conflict with other communities, those moments of crisis and confrontation become legible for members of those identity groups as further episodes within a narrative whose plot is one of perpetual confrontation between endangered or victimized self and deadly persecuting Other. Such readings may be made particularly compelling when the individual or group in question embraces a primordialist sense of continuity of the present with the past.

In the letters of the Israeli terrorist Era Rapaport, for example, one encounters a sense of essential, transhistorical affinity with figures from biblical mythology, with Jewish victims of the Shoah and contemporary Jews, all of whom are bound, in Rapaport's estimation, to the soil of Israel. For Rapaport, the individual Jew can only understand the implications of these primordial affinities—the right and indeed obligation of Jews to settle the lands of Palestine, the threats posed by the Arab inhabitants of those lands, the necessity of the settlers in those lands to defend themselves at all costs—if s/he understands him- or herself as situated or emplotted in a specific grand narrative of Jewish history, one which understands the defining experience of "the Jews" as one of victimization, persecution and miraculous survival. Rapaport describes, for example, the feeling he had as he "settled" in Palestine: "A feeling . . . of a people that has been exiled for some 2,000 years. A people that suffered through and triumphed through the worst of what mankind could offer. In 1948, just three years after Hitler and his Nazis wiped out 6,000,000 of us and almost no country in the world was willing to accept us . . . out of all that, one of the greatest miracles of all of modern times occurred—the establishment of the State of Israel. To us, the resettlement of [the Palestinian territories] was a continuation of that step to redemption."[79]

Later, in a letter to a friend from the Tel Mond prison where he was confined for dismembering a Palestinian mayor with a car bomb, Rapaport wrote, "I believe that I hear the voices of the 'choir of the generations,' of all the Jews who walked through these valleys and who climbed to the tops of these mountains, who brought the sacrifices and danced on God's holidays in Shilo. They are in front of us and around us, and God is above us." Jews who chose not to move to the settlements, who confined themselves to the territorial boundaries of Israel or chose to live in New York, "are going to have to answer [to God] why they didn't come here," he says, while he will have to answer for why he was unable to make more of them come.[80]

The Christian communities of the fourth and fifth century also seem to have heard "the voices of the 'choir of the generations'". The narratives these voices recited featured prominently themes of persecution, victimization, and miraculous victory only after appalling hardship and horror. The one true Church was the Church of the martyrs, those voices insisted, and this vision of Christian identity was binding even upon those Christians, like Augustine, who faced creditable accusations of complicity in acts of violence and persecution against their Christian rivals. Indeed, Augustine found it necessary to insist to his congregation that his church—their church—was the one real Church because it, in the present as in the past, suffered persecution: "[L]et nobody say, most beloved brothers, let nobody say—because every one who does say it is fooling himself—that the Church does not suffer persecution because the emperors are Catholic. Let no one say after this that the church does not suffer persecution: It does not suffer the lion, but the Serpent does not sleep."[81]

Real Christians—indeed the truest of all Christians—were those who were persecuted by the enemies of Christ. The ubiquitous narrative of the Christian community's past made this readily clear. Even as this narrative was elaborated by Lactantius and Eusebius after the advent of Constantine to insist that those who persecuted Christians met bad ends, the basic truth remained: In the confrontations of the past between real Christians and non-Christian others, Christians had suffered persecution at the hands of Satan's minions.

It is perhaps a measure of the dependence of fourth-century Christians upon this narrative that the emperor Julian's frequently remarked-upon unwillingness to persecute Christians during his tenure was for some Christians one of the more unsettling and even traumatic aspects of his reign.[82] Gregory Nazianzus's famous *Oratio* 4 put it quite succinctly: Julian was fighting dirty, "denying us the honor of fighting for the faith against tyranny," because he knew the narrative of the Christian past too.[83] This unwillingness to persecute disrupted the ability of Julian's Christian contemporaries to make proper sense of the events of his reign within familiar narratives of Christianity's relations with its adversaries, and it queered the range of possibilities available as Christian individuals and communities formulated responses to the advent of a pagan emperor who would not bring them forcibly before the altars. The fact of Julian's comparative gentleness was not enough to undo these narratives, however, and some Christians did manage to find "martyrdom" during his reign. But these martyrdoms—won by zealots who rushed to the temples to smash idols in contravention of the law or by those who refused to rebuild the pagan structures they had previously destroyed—were only recognizable as such if their actors, events and consequences were read through a rather specific narrative of the Roman past and present.[84]

The implications of this narrative could be particularly tragic when Christian communities found themselves pitted against one another. As we have seen, for example, the Damasian community of fourth-century Rome recalled its past in accordance with the narrative of persecution, martyrdom, and eventual triumph and used that past to establish itself as the one true community of God in the city of Rome. Not surprisingly, perhaps, Damasus's opponents, the community formed around the figure of Damasus's rival Ursinus, had their own version of the confrontation between the two communities. It is preserved in a pamphlet titled *Quae gesta sunt inter Liberium et Felicem episcopos*, which survives in the *Collectio Avellana*.[85] The *Gesta* paints an especially bloody portrait of Damasus's rise to power. Not surprisingly, this story of the Ursinian community's beginnings seems to have been mediated through a narrative of communal oppression and persecution all but indistinguishable from that with which the Damasian community defined itself.

When the bishop Liberius would not consent to the condemnation of Athanasius by the "Arian" emperor Constantius II, he was sent into exile in 355. Although Damasus, then a deacon, and a group of his fellow clerics swore not to have another bishop while Liberius lived and to follow him into exile, Damasus is said to have changed his mind, motivated by ambition. He had always wanted to be a bishop, and now he saw his chance for advancement. He returned to Rome and supported the bishop confirmed in Liberius's place. Eventually Liberius returned and forgave all of the clerics who had "perjured" themselves, including Damasus. When Liberius died, however, Damasus and another Roman cleric, Ursinus, clashed over the succession. The Liberian community split into two factions, and violence soon broke out. Damasus, it is said, hired an army of charioteers and ditch diggers bearing cudgels, swords, and axes and attacked his opponents. The first clash left 160 dead and many mortally wounded. The second clash occurred while the Ursinians were in a cemetery honoring the martyr Agnes. They were set upon by Damasus's troops and butchered.[86]

These are the basics of the Ursinian community's version of its confrontation with Damasus. To understand how these events were mediated through the grand narrative of the Christian communal past, however, it is necessary to attend to the specific ways in which those events were recalled and so subsumed within the plot native to that narrative.

The recollection of these events begins structurally with a formula typically found to begin the *passions* or *acta* of communal martyrs, with the formula "*Temporibus Constantii imperatoris filii Constantini durior orta est persecutio Christianorum ab impiis haereticis Arianis . . .*" [87] Very quickly, we have all of the elements of a martyr narrative before us: Liberius is confronted with an imperial edict from on high which he must disobey in defense of his faith. Augustine, in his own sermon on obedience, articulates nicely the dynamics at play here:

> For what reason do we praise [a martyr], for what reason do we herald, for what reason are we joyful, if not because we see for which church, for what faith, that he resisted the king who commanded him? It is not because he resists the one who orders, but because to comply with the ordering one is a sin; because of this, when something pernicious and sacrilegious is commanded, obedience is not to be called for. Just as it is not faith when something false is believed, so it is not obedience when something injurious is commanded.[88]

Like the martyrs of the past who resisted the call from Roman emperors to sacrifice, Liberius now stood intransigent before the "*persecutio Christianorum ab impiis haereticis Arianis.*" Nor were all Christians up to this moment of truth; as in the history of the persecutions articulated by Eusebius, this moment of *persecutio* was an occasion of self-definition, in which the qualities that defined real Christians were made clear as lesser Christians gave into their fear of the powerful of the world. When Constantius ordered that all the bishops of the empire condemn Athanasius, "because of their fear of the emperor, all of them were tempted to it, and everywhere the high priests condemned him, innocent and untried. But Liberius, the Roman bishop and [other churchmen] refused to give their consent. Therefore they were sent into exile for preserving the faith."[89]

Liberius, then, was cast in the familiar martyr's role, that of the "preserver of the faith." Damasus, by contrast, as he broke with Liberius to remain in Rome during Liberius' exile, was cast in the role of traitor, one of those of whom Eusebius had written "they were shaken by the persecution . . . shipwrecked . . . and by their own will were sunk in the depths of the flood." This theme continued throughout the narrative contained in the *Collectio*; the ugly events of the middle fourth century as two rival Christian communities vied for power in the city of Rome were recast as episodes in a narrative to which both of those communities alluded to explain and understand their past and present. When Damasus later became the rival of this particular narrative's hero, Ursinus, he had already been emplotted in the grand narrative of Christian history—he was one who had failed the test of the martyrs and so set himself outside of the one true community of God upon the earth. As the narrative progressed, he was recast in another familiar role within this narrative, that of persecutor. Particularly telling is the scene conjured in which Damasus' henchmen set upon a group of Ursinians gathered in a cemetery as they commemorated the passion of the martyr Agnes. "The people, fearing God and fatigued by the many persecutions, did not fear the emperor, nor the judges nor even the patron of crimes and murderer Damasus but celebrated the offices of the martyrs without clerics [for their clergy had been exiled]. For this reason while many of the faithful were gathering to Saint Agnes, Damasus, armed with attendants, broke in and struck down many in a disordered mass."[90]

Here we find Damasus set in league with the twin antagonist archetypes of countless martyr narratives, the persecuting emperor and the *judex*, before whom so many martyrs spoke their communal truths and suffered in their defense. Thus for the Christians who identified themselves with the community of Ursinus, who like all late Roman Christians understood their communal past in accordance with a rather specific narrative of persecution and victimization at the hands of pagan emperors and judges, Damasus, a Christian and a contemporary, is recast in the role of persecutor while the founders of their own community, the one true community of God in Rome the are—as they must be—victims and martyrs.

It is, moreover, profoundly significant that this act of violence takes place during the annual commemoration of the martyrdom of one of Rome's founding saints. As Eliade noted, festivals like those commemorating the "birthdays" of the martyrs are cyclical reenactments of primordial beginnings, the "first appearance of reality." In the reenactment of that primordial beginning, that original moment returns. "The festival always takes place in the original time. It is precisely the reintegration of this original and sacred time that differentiates man's behavior *during* the festival from his behavior *before* and *after* the festival. For in many cases the same acts are performed during the festival as during nonfestival periods. But religious man believes that he then lives in *another* time, that he has succeeded in returning to that mythical *illud tempus*."[91]

The events we are shown in this pro-Ursinian account of the attack in the cemetery, then, are not *like* events from the time of the persecution; they *are* events from the time of persecution. In the sacred space created by the commemoration of the saint, a space in which time and existence fold in upon one another and create a point of juncture between the present and the primordial past in what we might call a "primordial present," Damasus and his victims enact the primordial drama of the one real Christian community. The implications of this enactment are simply an inversion of the implication of Damasus's much grander campaign to associate his own community with the legacy of the martyrs.

What we have encountered here is a tendency with which we have met repeatedly in the foregoing pages; as the members of the community gathered around the figure of Ursinus recalled certain formative events of their communal past—and particularly their schism with the Damasian community—they did so within a narrative of Christian history whose plot determined the specific ways in which the events and contingencies of the split with Damasus were interpreted and remembered by members of that community. The conflict with Damasus and his followers was yet another episode of persecution, and Damasus was subsumed into roles which were both necessary and native to that narrative; he becomes first the traitor who in a time of persecution betrays the one community of God and then transforms into the persecuting enemy of the one community of God, taking his place here beside those stars of innumerable *passions* and *acta*, the emperor and the *judex*.

These were not unfamiliar moves. As we have seen, John Chrysostom warned his parishioners that to disobey his application of the findings of the Council of Nicaea was to set themselves against the martyrs, to "condemn" them. To condemn the martyrs was of course to locate themselves within the very narrative Chrysostom had just evoked in gruesome detail to authorize the council and its members. Similarly, the attitude taken by the Arians of Milan to Ambrose's new martyrs made it clear what place they occupied in the grand history of the Christian Church and in the community of Milan—they were enemies of the martyrs and belonged to a faith other than that passed down by the "fathers" of the one real community of God in Milan. For Augustine, the Serpent who persecuted the Church and whom the martyrs bested was yet alive and well and working through the Donatists. It did not matter that the emperors of the Roman world were no longer pagans, but instead (Catholic) Christians whose allegiance Augustine enjoyed. "Let no one say after this that the church does not suffer persecution," he told his congregation. "It does not suffer the lion [that is, in the arena], but the serpent does not sleep."[92]

Against this backdrop, such familiar documents illustrating the growth of religious intolerance and the use Roman state power to coerce belief as Augustine's *Epistle 87* to Januarius, a Donatist official, become comprehensible as part of a pervasive social and religious dynamic, one manifesting itself in many places and under diverse circumstances throughout the Roman world. "You say that you are persecuted while we are killed with clubs and swords by your armed men," Augustine wrote, complaining of the gruesome violences inflicted upon members of his community by the Donatists in an ongoing "persecution." Throughout the letter, Augustine seems incredulous that although they commit violence on behalf of their own community, militant Donatists "claim to be honored as martyrs when they receive the due reward of their deeds."

In the same year, 406 C.E., as he exhorted an imperial official to bring the coercive power of the Roman state to bear upon his own Donatist opponents, Augustine wrote,

> Could there be anything more lamentable as an instance of perversity than for men not only to refuse to be humbled by the correction of their wickedness, but even to claim commendation for their conduct, as is done by the Donatists, when they boast that they are the victims of persecution; either through incredible blindness not knowing, or through inexcusable passion pretending not to know, that men are made martyrs not by the amount of their suffering, but by the cause in which they suffer? . . . And if things which they suffer under this most gentle discipline be compared with those things which they in reckless fury perpetrate, who does not see to which party the name of persecutor really belongs?[93]

Could the Donatists not see, Augustine seems to ask, that the specifics of their acts and the circumstances in which those acts were carried out did not fit the narrative within which they interpreted those acts and the acts of the Catholic authorities who punished them? The modern reader might be tempted to ask whether Augustine himself could really understand his own community as the victim of persecution, guiding as it did the Roman Empire's dreaded penchant of juridical violence to the coercion of its enemies. In each case, however, such suspicions may be misplaced; one's perception of such events and the character of the episodes in which they are recast depends crucially upon the narrative in accordance with which they are emplotted. Such issues as the objective strength or weakness of the individual Christian's community with regard to other communities often mattered less than the character of his or her community's defining narratives in interpreting relations between such communities.

Addressing the famous controversy over the Altar of Victory in the Roman Senate House, for example, Ambrose's letters to the emperor Valentinian II return repeatedly to the time of the persecution. In Ambrose's *Epistle 72* (17), for example, scenes of Christians clustered unwillingly around a pagan altar wreathed in choking sacrificial smoke evoke ugly moments within the defining narrative of the Christian past.[94] Just as in the Ursinian depiction of the slaughter of the faithful during the commemoration of the martyr Agnes's death/birth, time collapses within the ritual space that surrounds the altar. As we have seen, Christians native to communities arrayed around the Roman world were urged by their bishops to fashion their communal selves after the example of the martyr and to defend the boundaries of their communities just as the martyrs had preserved them in the time of persecution. Now, Valentinian too was called upon by Ambrose to take a similar stand with regard to this altar and to preserve his own community, that of the Roman Empire, from the danger represented by that altar.

That Valentinian, though the sovereign of the Roman world, has now changed places with the persecuted Christians of an earlier age Ambrose makes quite clear. "What would you answer to [the reproach of a priest for choosing to allow the return of the altar]? That you have fallen but are a boy? . . . No childhood is allowed in faith, for even children have confessed Christ against their persecutors with fearless mouth."[95] The time of persecution has never ended, even in a moment in which many of the most powerful men in the Roman world are Christians and indeed confer with one another to decide the fate of other communities. Despite the apparent safety and indeed power of Christianity at this moment, however, the choice Valentinian faces in Ambrose's rendering is not whether to allow a religious minority to retain a traditional sign of its faith as part of the public ritual of the Roman world, but, as yet another martyr standing before the altar, whether he will defend his imperiled community.

As Ambrose crafted his argument, the young emperor faced a rather simple choice. As a Christian, he could either take up the defense of his community in the sacral space in which the charged signifier of the altar served as a centerpiece, or he could step into the role of the traitor, despised and lost. As a sovereign, he could either step into the role of the good Christian emperor, a discursive role from the post-Constantinian Christian narrative treated at length recently by Hal Drake, or that of the persecuting emperor, devoid of authority and bound for a bad end.[96] In either case, the specific contemporary question with which he was faced—the restoration of the Altar of Victory—was mediated through the narrative of the Christian communal past we have considered in detail above. The figures, dynamics, and consequences associated with that decision were accordingly recast in terms which, from a detached modern point of view, have very little to do with the actual specifics of the case. Valentinian might easily have found for his pagan subjects without reviving persecution, without forsaking his religion, and even without stepping beyond the policies of previous Christian emperors. Nor did the dilemma as Ambrose framed it reflect (at all) the realities of political power within the world ruled by Valentinian.

What we must remember, however, is that just as we read the events of our own world through the prism of the stories with which we locate ourselves and interpret the events and contingencies of our world, so the social reality of the later Roman world was mediated through a complex of narratives which made it possible to recall not only the past but the present and future as well. This is not to suggest that there were no other ways of imagining the past available to Valentinian or his contemporaries—as we shall see in the next chapter, there were alternatives, and these too made their way into the fourth-century conversation regarding confessional identity, tolerance and intercommunal violence.

What I would emphasize here, however, is that as the Christian communities of the fourth and fifth century imagined and recalled the past in accordance with a common repertoire of narratives, these narratives emplotted not only members of those communities within the grand sweep of Christian (and Roman) history but so emplotted their rivals as well. These narratives made contemporary events comprehensible as further episodes within an ongoing plot in which real Christians (who remained real Christians by preserving the essential, primordial characteristics of their ancestors) found themselves beset by deadly and powerful enemies and were forced to defend their imperiled communities from extinction.

Viewed from within such a plot, moments of intercommunal confrontation and periods of rivalry readily became episodes in which each real Christian had a role to play, and often that role allowed for little in the way of concession or conciliation. It mattered little in such instances that one's rivals also considered themselves Christians, or that it was in fact one's rivals who now faced coercion at the hands of Roman imperial officials, or that the Roman Empire was, as Augustine was forced to admit, administered by members of one's own community or that the individual viewing the world from within this narrative was *himself* sovereign of the Roman empire. As we have seen, under such circumstances, accommodation or compromise imperiled one's place within the one true community of God upon the earth, and indeed the very survival of that community.

Conclusion

The narrative with which I have dealt here at length and which I have suggested returned depressingly to the fore as late Roman Christian communities found themselves at odds with other communities was but one of many narratives available to members of these communities, of course. Other narratives were available in the form of local traditions,[97] the New and Old Testaments[98] and traditional modes of recalling the ancient Hellenic-Roman past. All of these carried implications for emplotting individuals and communities and for the ordering of the contemporary Roman world. All of these could work to situate the same individual in different moments and under different circumstances. As we shall see in the next chapter, for the emperor Theodosius, whose reign is frequently associated with the acceleration of religious intolerance, the question of what to do about militant expressions of piety among members of his own community was framed by two of the leading intellectuals of the age, Ambrose of Milan and Libanius of Antioch, through the use of competing narratives of the Roman past. These competing narratives offered two models of Christian kingship, and two models of Roman rulership. As we shall see in Chapter 4, by the sixth century, elements central to both of these apparently contradictory models of ideal Roman rulership would merge in the imperial ideology of the emperor Justinian.

CHAPTER THREE

"What Has the Pious in Common with the Impious?" Ambrose, Libanius, and the Problem of Late Antique Religious Violence

IN 388 C.E., a band of Christian militants attacked a Jewish synagogue in the city of Callinicum (modern Raqqa, Syria), near the Roman Empire's frontier with Persia, burning it to the ground. The first reaction of the emperor Theodosius to the event was to hold the head of the Christian community of Callinicum responsible for the actions of the militants and to require that he make good the expenses of rebuilding the synagogue. The emperor was dissuaded by the bishop Ambrose of Milan, however, who by letter and sermon convinced Theodosius that he ought not to defend the legal rights of those Roman citizens who now asked for redress against their attackers.[1]

This frequently cited example of what seems to be imperial acquiescence to the rising tide of religious intolerance among Christians toward their Jewish neighbors bears much in common with the episodes of intercommunal aggression and violence we explored in Chapter 2. This is particularly the case as regards the strategies with which Ambrose argued his case before Theodosius. Most familiar, perhaps, is the repertoire of semiotic and narrative forms with which Ambrose worked as he argued that it was not the Jews that Theodosius should be worried about defending but instead his own Christian community.

Ambrose interpreted the events in Callinicum and the potential consequences of Theodosius's decision to redress those events through the narrative of Christian victimization and persecution that we encountered so frequently in Chapter 2. Just as the followers of Ursinus cast their nemesis Damasus in the role of persecuting *judex* as they imagined their communal past, for example, Ambrose warned Theodosius that by insisting upon restitution for the Jews of Callinicum he was in danger of assuming the role of the persecuting emperor, another familiar and despised archetype within the stories with which Christian communities throughout the late antique world recalled their formative pasts and interpreted the events and personalities of their present: "Are you not afraid, lest [the local bishop] oppose your *comes* by means of his words, as will happen? Then he will either have to make him an apostate or a martyr, neither of which is suitable to your reign (*utrumque alienum temporibus tuis*), either of them the same as persecution if he is made either to apostatize or to undergo martyrdom. You see in which direction the outcome of the matter inclines."[2] Throughout his letter to Theodosius, Ambrose adorned such arguments as these with visual images that will have evoked martyr narratives well known to Theodosius. He conjured "rows without number of fettered [members] of the Christian population" under the gaze of falsely accusing Jews, who would lie to imperial officials so that they might see Christians "hidden in darkness . . . smitten with the executioner's axe (*feriantur securibus*), given to the fire, given over to the mines, so that their punishment might not be over quickly,"[3] all of this the result Ambrose foresaw if Theodosius were to insist that the bishop of Callinicum make good the damages caused by the zealots of his community. Elsewhere, Ambrose conjured images of "Christians . . . put to death with a sword, or cudgels, or *plumbei* [leather thongs weighted with lead]"[4] and asked how such things could be explained to his own fellow bishops should they come to pass as a result of Theodosius's efforts to enforce the law.

Although it is likely that Ambrose deployed such troubling imagery in order to evoke the tetrarchic persecutions, by the closing years of the 380s narratives of Christian persecution and triumph had also drafted into service the last of the pagan emperors, Julian, who, whether for reasons of strategy or scruple, famously refused to persecute Christians in the manner of Diocletian, his tetrarchic colleagues, and their imperial predecessors. Despite the comparative tolerance of his policies with regard to his Christian subjects, however, Julian could be convincingly recalled by Christians of Ambrose's generation as a bloodthirsty persecutor or, at the very least, as a facilitator of violence against Christians. In his letter, for example, Ambrose accused Julian of allowing the Jews to burn churches in Gaza, Ascalon, Beirut, Damascus, and Alexandria and of refusing to redress the wrongs thereby committed. These acts of violence by Jews against Christians during the persecution of Julian provided the context in accordance with which Theodosius should ponder the recent events in Callinicum, Ambrose argued.

This narrative of Julian's reign also provided Ambrose with other precedents that complicated the dilemma Theodosius now sought to negotiate. Ambrose suggested that Theodosius's decision was like that faced by a certain imperial *judex* who had, in the time of Julian, overseen the trial of a Christian "who overthrew an altar, disturbed a sacrifice, was condemned by the judge and suffered martyrdom." Intriguingly and perhaps tellingly, this particular *judex* seems not to have been some bloodthirsty pagan, but instead, an unfortunate Christian charged with enforcing Roman law. Having performed his duty under the law by sentencing the Christian zealot to execution, this *judex* was shunned by his community: "Nobody ever considered that *judex* who heard him to be anything but a persecutor; no one deemed him worthy of being associated with, and nobody thought him worthy of a kiss."[5] Ambrose's point seems clear: A Christian *judex*, in enforcing the law on behalf of an apostate emperor, had become an apostate just as the bishop of Callinicum and the local imperial comes must now either disobey Theodosius's commands or themselves become apostates.

Ambrose also suggested to Theodosius that even one wielding imperial power could lose his place in the Christian community by favoring another community over his own. He reminded Theodosius that the usurper Magnus Maximus had once sent an edict to the city of Rome after he heard that a synagogue had been burned, apparently condemning the act.[6] While he shared power with Theodosius and Valentinian II, Maximus had famously presented himself as a fierce defender of orthodoxy (a role in which he had not been accepted by Ambrose). Despite his own orthodox Christian credentials, however, Ambrose says that Maximus's objection to the violence against the Jewish community of Rome marked him as a Jew in the eyes of the Christian people and soon led to a series of disasters on the battlefield. This was a precedent Ambrose suggested Theodosius would do well to avoid. "What has the pious in common with the impious?" Ambrose demanded. "The instances of his unbelief ought to be done away with together with the unbeliever himself. That which injured him, that wherein he who was conquered offended, the conqueror ought not to follow but to condemn."[7]

Throughout his letter, and particularly where he makes reference to the reign of Julian, Ambrose insisted that in the case of Callinicum, it was Christian individuals and the Christian community that were imperiled, that they were always imperiled. If the Jews were given the benefit of law, he argued, they would lie and turn the force of Roman law once again against the Christian Church, as they had against Christ. The Jews despised Roman law, Ambrose said, and yet they now called upon its might to "avenge" them. And in any case, he sneered, "Where were those laws when [the Jews] set fire to the roofs of the sacred basilicas?"

In Ambrose's defense of the violence committed by the militants of Callinicum, apparently at the behest of the bishop of the Christian community there, he mediates the contemporary events at issue through the narratives of remembrance most favored among the Christian communities of his world. For Romans inhabiting spaces of imperial power, and particularly Christian emperors like Theodosius, these narratives could profoundly complicate the fulfillment of one's official duties. As we saw in Chapter 2, members of the empire's various Christian communities now frequently interpreted the social and political realities of their world through the prism of certain crucial communal narratives in which their own Christian forebears matched wills with imperial officials, suffered at the hands of those officials through terrible rounds of official coercion, and finally emerged triumphant, thanks to their intransigence in the face of those who would have destroyed their communities.

The following is one of the countless versions of the discrete saint stories through which this metanarrative of the Christian past now flowed; it is suggestive of the difficulties Roman officials, including the emperor himself, had in enforcing laws against pious Christian zealots.[8] It is the story of the martyr Theodore the Recruit, a Roman soldier who was discovered as a Christian during the time of the emperors Maximianus and Maximinus.[9] During their reign, according to the text, those emperors issued a command that all of their subjects must participate in acts of public worship of the traditional gods; only by doing so could they avoid horrid punishments.[10] Theodore was assigned to "the *legio Marmaritarum* under the command of the *praepositus* Brincas."[11]

When he refused to perform the required acts, he was interrogated gently by the *praepositus* Brincus and the local *ducenarius* Poseidon.[12] After he was released to think the matter over, however, Theodore proceeded to the temple of "the Mother of the Gods" and burned it. He was soon caught, however, and brought before the local judge, one Publius.[13]

The judge, seated on his platform, first questioned Theodore's commanding officer, who replied that he had tried to convince the recruit to comply with the commands of the emperors, but to no avail.[14] Next, the *judex* questioned Theodore himself. He began by asking why Theodore refused to sacrifice and instead burned the goddess. Theodore did not deny his actions, and added, "Of such a sort is your goddess, that fire can burn her." The judge, now angry, concluded that the gentleness of his words had "made [Theodore] bold with regard to *parrhesia*," and ordered Theodore to be beaten. He then threatened Theodore with tortures that would induce his compliance with the orders of the emperors. Theodore answered that he did not fear the judge's tortures, no matter how frightful they might be and that he would not submit. His God would protect him and give him victory in any contest with the judge, he added. The judge now became enraged and dispatched Theodore to a prison cell, where he was to be starved to death.[15]

It is significant to note that the difference between Theodore's refusal to sacrifice to the pagan gods and his destruction of the pagan temple is elided in this story. What is left is Theodore's confrontation with his superiors, the judge, and, remotely, the emperors. It is not difficult to understand how, from the point of view of men and women who fashioned Christian selves in accordance with the model provided by figures like Theodore, the story of Theodore's passion and death provided a template for making sense of events like those which took place in Callinicum, events that were now legible as further episodes within the narrative of persecution and triumph epitomized in Theodore's glorious defiance and death. Nor is it difficult to understand the dilemma faced by Roman officials, like Theodosius, who found themselves in the unenviable position of performing acts seemingly like those of the Roman officials who were forced to respond to Theodore's act of militant piety.

While it is perhaps unsurprising that Julian's refusal to coerce belief violently among Christians did little to spare him the role of persecutor in the interpretations of his reign we encounter in contemporary and later Christian accounts, we have also seen, as in the case of the Ursinian community's depiction of its showdown with Damasus, that *Christian* emperors and bishops could be cast in the role of persecuting *imperator* or *judex* just as readily as the pagan Julian. Now, as Ambrose argued that the Jews and heretics of the Roman world should not enjoy the shelter of Roman law, these narratives once again emerged as central to the processes by which the political, legal, and social realities of the later Roman world were at once interpreted and determined.

As we shall see in this chapter, however, there were other narratives of the distant and recent Roman past available to the empire's intellectual elite, and these narratives too made their way into the ongoing discussion of the roles religion, tolerance, and violent intercommunal aggression were to play within the post-Constantinian Roman world. The most famous articulation of these narratives is preserved in an oration written by the pagan intellectual Libanius two years before the confrontation between Ambrose and Theodosius in Milan over the violence in Callinicum.

Pro Templis

In 386 C.E., Libanius addressed an oration to the emperor Theodosius, urging the emperor to intervene and halt the destruction of pagan temples and holy sites. Libanius's *Oratio 30* assigned responsibility for the campaign against the temples to a cabal of unnamed government officials, and the attacks on the pagan holy sites themselves he described as the work of roving monks.[16] This oration is frequently cited in modern studies of religious violence in the later fourth century. Given the vivid and disturbing imagery with which Libanius described the raids on the temples, this is unsurprising; such imagery resonates conveniently with modern narratives of the advance of an increasingly aggressive strain of Christianity at the end of antiquity.

Less frequently examined, however, is the strategy with which Libanius sought to persuade his emperor that protection of the temples and art treasures of the Syrian cities and countryside represented a crucial imperative. This tendency tends to waste much of the vast potential of this text, because while Libanius's appeal is indeed an exemplum of lush and brazen invective against a particularly militant brand of political Christianity, it is also something more. The oration illustrates the close intersection of communal narratives, individual and institutional identity and political necessity in the later Roman world. Indeed, at the core of the *Oratio 30* is evidence of a struggle over the defining narratives of the Roman world in the last years of the fourth century. At stake in this struggle was the fate of religious tolerance in the political life of the Roman world, and the place of the Roman emperor within that world.

As we noted in the last chapter, a groundswell of recent research produced by scholars active in the fields of sociology, anthropology, literature, psychology, theology and philosophy has emphasized a series of deep interconnections between narrative, identity, and political praxis.[17] Much of this scholarship contends that the centrality of narrative forms to human experience begins with human perception itself. The psychologist Jerome Bruner argues, for example, that human subjects "organize our experience and our memory of human happenings mainly in the form of narrative." That is, the moment-to-moment sensory input that cascades into the mind of the human subject only becomes comprehensible as experience by being organized as a story. This individual experience meshes with social reality as "the narrative mode of *thought*" and "forms of narrative *discourse*" come to inform and support one another. As Bruner puts it, "each enables and gives form to the other, just as the structure of language and the structure of thought become inextricable."[18]

The political and cultural consequences of this process are of course profound. As events become episodes and individuals become characters as they are recast within the plot lines of certain organizing narratives, "our experience of human affairs comes to take the form of the narratives we use in telling about them."[19] The role of narrative in the political life of communities is suggested in Fredric Jameson's discussion of the use that may be made of the Marxist narrative of human history in recasting ancient events as episodes in a recognizable metanarrative in which humanity is still emplotted:

> Only Marxism can give us an adequate account of the essential mystery of the cultural past, which, like Tiresias drinking the blood, is momentarily returned to life and warmth and allowed once more to speak, and to deliver its long-forgotten message in surroundings utterly alien to it. This mystery can be reenacted only if the human adventure is one; only thus . . . can we glimpse the vital claims upon us of such long-dead issues as the seasonal alteration of the economy of a primitive tribe, the passionate disputes about the nature of the Trinity, the conflicting models of the polis or the universal Empire, or, apparently closer to us in time, the dusty parliamentary and journalistic polemics of the nineteenth-century nation states. These matters can recover their original urgency for us only if they are retold within the unity of a

> single great collective story; only if, in however disguised and symbolic a form, they are seen as sharing a single fundamental theme.[20]

Just as events in the ancient past may be recast as episodes within an organizing metanarrative, human subjects who understand themselves to be emplotted in various kinds of narratives also interpret contemporary events in accordance with such narratives. As the sociologist Margaret Somers has argued, "To have some sense of social being in the world requires that lives be more than different series of isolated events or combined variables and attributes. Ontological narratives process events into episodes. People act, or do not act, in part according to how they understand their place in any number of given narratives . . . narrative embeds identities in time and spatial relationships."[21]

That is, narratives not only arrange the past into a comprehensible, plot-derived continuity; they also impose a grammar upon the moment-to-moment experiences and relationships of those whose sense of reality is derived from the arrangement of perception in accordance with those narratives. At this point, the character of the narrative in accordance with which one's identity is constituted becomes crucial to determining the character of one's response to those persons and events with whom or with which one interacts.

Like twentieth-century Marxisms, fourth-century Christianities shared what were in effect permutations of a common pool of organizing narratives. By the 380s, the narrative with which the history of the Christian community within the Roman world was recalled was a narrative that featured at its core the themes of persecution undertaken by the agents of Satan against the faithful of Christ, the defense of the one true community of God upon the earth by its most virtuous members and the eventual triumph of the Christian community over its oppressors.[22] Versions of this narrative were central to Eusebius's and Lactantius's influential renderings of the distant Roman past, while events of the more recent Roman past were interpreted through versions of the same narratives.[23] Among these events were some high-profile attacks upon non-Christians by Christian militants.

One such attack, of course, was that carried out at Callinicum by Christian monks and later defended by the bishop Ambrose. For Ambrose and, as we shall see, Libanius, the social, political and legal consequences of militant expressions of political Christianity depended heavily upon how such events were interpreted by individuals in positions of official power, most notably the Roman emperor himself. Key to the ways in which such acts were interpreted was the character of the narratives within which such events were emplotted as episodes. As Somers and others have suggested, human subjects exist within a matrix of individual, communal, and institutional narratives, and may draw on any of these (or any combination of these) as a means of mediating experience and making decisions. With his *Oratio 30*, Libanius emplotted recent acts of intercommunal violence within a narrative of the Roman past upon which Roman imperial ideology had long depended.

At the heart of this narrative are the story of the evolution within human society from barbarism to civilization and the central role of Rome and Roman imperial identity in this process. According to imperial Roman ideology, Romanization was crucial to the civilizing of the world because it brought a reasoned, organizing impetus to human affairs wherever it went. The first- and second-century moralist and philosophical biographer Plutarch suggested that "time laid the foundation for the Roman state and, with the help of God, so combined and joined together Fortune and Virtue that, by taking the peculiar qualities of each, he might construct for all mankind a Hearth, in truth both holy and beneficent, a steadfast cable, a principle abiding forever, 'an anchorage from the swell and drift,' as Democritus says, amid the shifting conditions of human affairs."

Just as the swirling and disunited atoms of the "ancient times" before the world existed were finally brought into reasoned order to create the earth, Plutarch wrote, so the chaotic terrestrial domains of the world were brought into perfect order by the Roman Empire.[24] This penchant for reasoned mastery of the chaotic principles of the temporal world, whether these originated among the Roman populace or beyond the frontiers of the empire, was central to the claims upon power and authority issued for centuries by members of Rome's ruling class. The capacity to impose reasoned order was and had been the foremost duty of those individuals who led the Roman world as its emperor.

According to Libanius and other Roman writers, then, the story of Roman reason and imperial order was part of a larger history of the emergence of Romano-Hellenic logos and civilization from primordial barbarianism. It was well understood, moreover, that this was a process *sine fine*; it continued into the present, and each member of that empire had a role to play within it. In his panegyric to his home city of Antioch, for example, Libanius refers to the imperial rule of the Romans as a "golden chain" that bound the city.[25] The city itself, in its primeval past, had been as a point of light amid barbarian gloom. This space of reason had taken shape as its founders set in place the material markers of civilization: "One built a temple to Minos, another of Demeter, another of Heracles, and so on. One constructed a theater, another the city hall, another leveled the roads, others brought water by aqueducts, either from the suburbs of the city or from the springs which abound in the old city to the new city. Temple after temple was built, and the greater part of the city consisted of temples, for it was all the same thing; the adornment and protection of the city was bound up with the provision of shrines of the gods."[26]

For Libanius, the temples were just one manifestation—albeit an important one—of the civilizing project undertaken by his city's founding figures, Hellenistic kings who carved out a bastion of reason in the wilds of Asia Minor. Libanius's description of the process of civilizing represented by the foundation of Antioch is, moreover, all but indistinguishable from the civilizing process as it was imagined in Roman imperial narratives, much as the founders of Antioch and their style of rule were all but indistinguishable from Antioch's later Roman rulers. "It seemed that the change of government was merely a change of family," he wrote. "It was as if there was no difference between the founders of the city, and those who had come to control it."[27] Significantly, Libanius refers to this narrative again in his oration in defense of the temples. In that text, he once more traced the emergence of rational Greco-Roman man from the mire of unknowing and cast the first structures they built as emblems of reasoned and civilized life. "The first men who appeared upon the earth" could only raise rough monuments to their gods, he says. But as the advance of reason led humans toward polis life, progress in the necessary *technê* allowed for the construction of cities. Now, Libanius wrote, "after the wall, the beginning of the rest of the physical manifestation [of the city] was by means of a temple and an altar."[28]

Libanius thus casts the temples among the material structures that marked the progress of humankind from the benighted barbarity of precivilization toward reasoned civic life. The role of the Romans within this narrative was, according to Libanius, akin to the role of the founders of his own city; in action the Roman rulers of Antioch had been indistinguishable from the Hellenic kings who fashioned and nurtured the city, providing it with roads, aqueducts, and fortifications. These were also understood to be traditional undertakings for the elites of the Roman Empire, of course, and after Octavian became Augustus individual Roman emperors would also perform such projects as public benefactions. Such undertakings were part and parcel of the emperor's role as protector and provider for the Roman people, and as the first and foremost of Rome's elites. In his grand study of the role of the emperor in the Roman world, for example, Fergus Millar has written that "we can find in Rome, Italy and the provinces examples of temples, public buildings, walls, aqueducts, bridges, and occasionally roads, constructed or repaired 'with his own money' by the emperor. In all these cases it is more than probable, and in the case of roads can be demonstrated, that such payments did not represent a regular responsibility of the emperor, but occasional benefactions conferred by him as demonstrations of liberality, or as a response to immediate needs or requests."[29]

All of these material structures were emblematic of the ordering, civilizing role of the Roman Empire and, in particular, the beneficent aspect of the emperor himself. Like the emperor, moreover, aqueducts, roads, and temples all acquired very specific valences when emplotted within certain privileged narratives of the Roman imperial past and present. These narratives were given early vivid articulation by a number of Roman writers, as Greg Woolf has noted. According to such narratives, Woolf writes, "Primitive Romans had been civilized, just as their destiny was now, in the Elder Pliny's words, 'to gather together the scattered realms and to soften their customs and unite the discordant wild tongues of so many peoples into a common speech so they might understand each other, and to give civilization to mankind (*humanitatem homini*).'"[30]

It was upon such narratives, recalled, articulated and performed in myriad ways, that an ancient lineage of Roman elites had depended as a means of situating themselves within the Roman social and political universe.[31] Polybius (*Historiae* vi.53–55) supplies a particularly vivid description of the social and political use made of narrative by the Romans in his discussion of the "Roman character" as compared to the national characters of the Greeks, the Carthaginians, and others.[32]

After the death of a prominent Roman, Polybius explained, a realistic mask of the dead man was made with great care for the fidelity with which it represented his specific features. At future funerals for members of the man's family, the mask would be worn by surviving family members or by actors who resembled the dead man. His image would thus join a procession of departed family members who were made present via their death masks. Those wearing such masks were attired in the garments appropriate to the station and achievements of the individuals they represented and accompanied by the axes and fasces that announced each dead man's *statio* within the hierarchy of Roman government. So adorned, they would accompany the most recently departed to his funeral and array themselves on ivory chairs upon the Rostra.

After beginning with an initial address specifically concerning the recently departed, the funeral orator would then deliver a lengthy rendition of the defining episodes of the lives of those made present on the Rostra via their death masks. In the presence of the family's surviving members, he would narrate the dead men's accomplishments and honors, beginning with the most ancient of them. Such ceremonies not only reminded the community of the deeds of a long lineage of Roman nobles, Polybius wrote, but also inspired the individual Roman men who attended such funerals to understand themselves as actors within the stories with which both their particular family and the Roman community as a whole recalled a collective past. It was this process of emplotment, Polybius suggests, that instilled a specific sense of *romanitas*, one performed in peace and in war, as soldier and as civilian. Moreover, this narrative-based sense of *romanitas* determined normative relations not only between Roman and non-Roman, but also between Roman citizens and even between Roman father and Roman son.[33]

Foremost among the elites of the Roman world was the emperor himself, and it is therefore unsurprising that emperors seem also to have depended upon a rather similar means of emplotment. As Clifford Ando has noted, for example, in 249 C.E., the emperor Decius issued a series of coins adorned with the images of previous emperors and ordered that Romans throughout the empire offer sacrifices to their ancestral gods, sacrifices that would have been offered in temples in which images representing the ancient lineage of Roman emperors were prominently displayed. "Placed before such a gallery, individuals making their prayers for the eternity of the empire saw the current emperor as one in a series of uniquely capable individuals, whose succession encapsulated and expressed a narrative of stability and strength."[34]

The *statio* of the emperor was in this sense much like the temples and art treasures now under attack throughout the Roman world; it took its range of possible social, political, and cultural meanings from an ancient and abiding narrative of humanity's ascent from benighted unreason toward the light of imperial Roman order.[35] As Somers has suggested, signs that accrue meaning in accordance with their emplotment within narratives do so relationally—that is, the specific valence of any sign within a given narrative depends upon the valences of other signs within the same narrative. It was for this reason, it would seem, that Libanius suggested that the contemporary campaign against the various signs emplotted within one ancient and influential narrative of the Roman past represented a direct threat to the capacity of any emperor—Christian or pagan—to perform his ancient and perpetually evolving roles within his world.

* * *

Libanius began his oration with a brief overview of the approach taken to the question of traditional worship since the time of the first Christian emperor. Upon winning control of the Roman world, he said, Constantine chose to recognize "some other god." Although this resulted in "poverty" in the temples, Libanius said, Constantine "made no change at all to the customs of worship."[36] When Constantine's son took over rulership of the Roman world, however, things changed. "Power passed to [Constantine's] offspring, or one might better say the form of power passed to him, as the capacity to rule belonged to others, those to whom mentorship from early on in his life gave equal power in all things," Libanius lamented. "Then, ruling under the command by others, he was persuaded of unfortunate things, [specifically] that the sacrifices should be no more."[37]

Here Libanius drew a sharp distinction between the self-mastery of Constantine and the weakness of his son's government and assigned the banning of sacrifices to the weakness of the son's personality. Libanius contrasted this weakness with the strength of Constantine, who, during his own competent and self-assured rule, maintained a proper distance between his own, private religious preferences and those of his subjects and his forebears. Libanius went on to recall that although under Valens and Valentinian sacrifice was banned, an exception was made for offerings of incense. Theodosius, he added, has wisely made no further moves against traditional forms of worship. "You have not ordered the temples closed nor have you forbidden anyone to go into them. You have not driven fire or libations or worship with other sorts of incense from the temples or altars," he said.[38]

At the outset of his oration, then, Libanius established a pattern of recent imperial behavior with regard to the temples and suggested a normative imperial attitude toward coercion and interference with traditional cult. Simply stated, Libanius's rendering suggested that strong emperors, emperors in control of themselves and their affairs, do not coerce—it was only an emperor under whom "the capacity to rule belonged to others," who had been compelled to meddle with the public rights of the gods, this by the private, individual whims of those *potentes* who surrounded his throne, and in whose hands the power of the *res publica* had truly resided.[39] Thus, in addition to equating strong, confident leadership with tolerance, Libanius linked coercion with the intrusion into public affairs of invasive, personal interest. Later in his oration, Libanius suggests, albeit subtly, that certain private interests have now once again invaded the public sphere. Despite the sophist's subtlety, however, the troubling implications of this intrusion for the character of Theodosius's reign seem clear enough.

> But nevertheless, if one were to examine this matter closely, this [the phenomenon of temple destructions] is not your affair. Rather, it is the affair of a deceiver befouled with blood, one who is hateful to the gods, a coward and a lover of money, one hostile to the world that received him, one abandoned to the enjoyment of unreasoning fortune and making evil use of his own fortune, acting as a slave to his wife, obliging her in all things, taking his delight in her in all things. She is compelled in all things to comply with the ones who order such things as those, whose proof of their virtue is to live in the attire of mourners, and even better than to live in that type of dress, to live in clothes made by those who weave from sackcloth. Such is the crew that has cheated you, tricked you, brought you under its power and misled you.[40]

Under Theodosius, Libanius claimed, private accumulations of public power in the hands of a man dominated by his wife had resulted in the current outbreak of religious violence. Rather than a manifestation of Theodosius's own policy, the recent violence against the ancient material culture of the empire is interpreted by Libanius as an eruption of private, feminine will. The will of the emperor had been subverted not simply by one of his underlings but by the private agenda of that man's wife. Worse still, the will of this presumptuous woman had been suborned by frenzied Christian ascetics who, as we shall see, Libanius interpreted as loathsome agents of unreason and disorder.[41]

Read in accordance with the narrative of the recent Roman past evoked earlier in his oration by Libanius, these anonymous usurpers of Theodosius's power seem closely kindred with those faceless agents who dominated the notoriously weak-willed Constantius II.[42] Theodosius, in turn, would seem in Libanius's rendering to face the implicit danger of assuming the role of the pathetic Roman sovereign dominated by the private interests of those who serve him. As we have seen, Libanius had suggested that it was only weak-willed emperors who allowed persecution of their subjects at the behest of their courtiers, while strong sovereigns, like Constantine, maintained a respectful boundary between their own beliefs and the beliefs of those they ruled.

Although the individual to whom Libanius traced this intrusion of public interests and belief remains nameless throughout the oration, Petit and others have identified him as the praetorian prefect Maternus Cynegius.[43] This identification seems valid to me, but for our purposes it does not matter whether Libanius had in mind a particular individual or whether he meant to single out Cynegius himself as the object of his scorn. Whoever the individual to whom Libanius refers actually was, he was rendered by the rhetor as a symbol of a very specific brand of political hubris. The individual represented by this figure is less important than the valence the figure itself carried in Roman political thought and in the annals of Roman imperial memory.

Thus, the temple destruction and other episodes of intercommunal violence that had come to characterize the age were, in Libanius's rendering, manifestations of the personal, individualized will of a man whose domestic concerns, signaled here by the sign "wife," had come to dominate his public undertakings. Worse still, these privately motivated instances of intolerance had begun to undermine the concerns of the Roman state generally and Theodosius specifically. If the actions this individual had taken were indeed aimed at illegal acts of pagan sacrifice, the matter should have been handled in accordance with law, Libanius insisted. As matters stood, however, the individual in question had flouted Theodosius's laws and undermined his emperor's authority. "He should not have served the pleasures of his own household," Libanius charged, "nor should he have esteemed as great in importance the opinion of the fugitives from the farms, they who perch in the mountains nattering on about the creator of all things. Instead, he should have esteemed as great in importance your affairs, so that all men might think them fair and worthy of praise.[44]

In this passage and those that precede it, Libanius drew upon a venerable selection of rhetorical tropes culled from Greek and Roman political invective and from familiar narratives of the Roman past. As Kate Cooper has noted, Libanius's rendering of "Cynegius" as slave to his wife Acanthia recalls the imagined immoderation of Marc Antony under the influence of the queen of Egypt: "Acanthia is cast as temptress, a Cleopatra to Cynegius' vile, besotted Antony."[45] In this, "Cynegius" joins not only Antony but also a litany of other vilified Roman and Greek political entities, from Demosthenes' enemy Philocrates to Cataline to the emperor Claudius, all of whom were attacked with gender-charged rhetoric. Because women were so closely associated with the private domestic sphere in Greco-Roman political discourse, to suggest that a man was a slave to his wife's whims was often tantamount to suggesting that, with regard in the eternal tug of war between public duty and private desire that resided in every Roman psyche, such a man was inclined to the private at the expense of the public.[46]

Since the time of the Republic, the intrusion of powerful private interests into the public workings of the *res publica* incited a profound anxiety among theorists of governance and ordinary Romans alike.[47] Private accumulations of power endured as a point of concern for emperors in the third and fourth centuries as well and remained a persistent dilemma into the reign of Justinian and beyond. Indeed, a string of laws issued by later emperors—Diocletian, Constantine, Valens and Valentinian, and Theodosius among them—give voice to the acute unease produced by the capacity of local *potentes* to gather unseemly and even dangerous concentrations of power to themselves.[48]

Given this fact of late Roman political life, the villain Libanius conjures as the ultimate source of the violence connected with political Christianity in the last quarter of the fourth century makes compelling sense; the unnamed figure so often identified as "Cynegius" emerges in Libanius's oration as the ultimate source of imperial behavior that is not only at odds with Theodosius's laws, but subversive of the emperor's own authority. He is a figure of unrestrained personal appetite and ambition, at once historically resonant and frighteningly contemporary in the genre of danger Libanius claims he represents. The invocation of such a figure by Libanius, moreover, indirectly but powerfully suggests troubling implications for the nature of Theodosius's rule.

This is particularly so given the skill with which Libanius emplots Theodosius in a specific narrative of the recent imperial past, much as Ambrose and other Christian authors now routinely emplotted Roman sovereigns they sought to influence within specific narratives of the history of the Christian community within the Roman world. It is not difficult to understand how some Christian Roman emperors, whose individual and communal identities were constituted in accordance with both types of narratives, may have felt themselves pulled at times in opposed directions.

Those directly responsible for the violence Libanius lamented were the monks of Syria. The monks, as Libanius narrated them, lurk in the dark, hidden recesses of the inscrutable countryside until they spill forth across the land to do the bidding of Theodosius's own ministers. The dank caves and dark mountains of the Syrian wilds inhabited by the monks suggested the malignant secrecy and creeping disorder for which the monks themselves were a metaphor. Despite their "artificial pallor," Libanius said, the monks were ravenous in their various appetites. Despite the fact that they extol meekness and self-discipline, he suggested, their true character was revealed in the terrifying frenzy with which they attacked the temples and art treasures of Theodosius's realm.[49]

Nor were the monks merely vandals or overzealous worshipers of Theodosius's god, Libanius insisted. Rather, the "black-robed ones (*melaneimonountes*)" that swept through Theodosius's domain "like raging winter rivers" threatened the material traces that connected contemporary Romans through ties of memory and narrative to civilized humanity's primeval emergence from unreason and barbarism, to the primeval appearance of cities and the growth of civilization.[50] In the time before civilization, Libanius said, primitive men realized the importance of divine good will and built rough idols and crude temples to their gods.

> Then, when the elements necessary for cities appeared, and when the technology necessary for it was completely developed, many cities showed forth on the skirts of the mountain ranges, and many cities showed forth on the plain. In each one, after the wall, the beginning of the rest of the physical manifestation [of the city] was by means of a temple and an altar. For they believed that from such guidance would come the greatest safeguard for themselves against danger. And if you go through the whole of the world that

> the Romans inhabit, you will discover it to be thus in every direction.[51]

It was with the aid of the traditional gods that the Romans spread their *politeia* to the ends of the earth, and throughout Rome's dominion their temples commemorated the advance of Roman *imperium*. Even at the geographic limits of *romanitas*, the temples had aided in the defense of the empire and all that it bestowed. This Libanius insisted they had accomplished with the aid of the numinous and in purely physical terms as well. As an example, the sophist lamented the fate of a recently destroyed temple on the Persian frontier. The temple once protected those who huddled within its sturdy walls at the approach of invading armies. It had also provided, for those who mounted its roof, a strategic view of the surrounding countryside. Within the temple, Libanius adds, one would have encountered magnificent works of artistic expression.[52]

The notion of reasoned order found multiple expressions in the temple; at the furthest end of the Roman world, in the face of Rome's most formidable foe, a citadel of Hellenic grace and Roman strength stood against gales of barbarian unreason.[53] That bastion of imperial *romanitas* was now shattered and in ruins, however, and as Libanius emphasized, the temple's destruction was the work not of Persian armies but instead of Theodosius's own subjects, men who took their orders from Theodosius's own praetorian prefect.

Throughout his oration, Libanius linked all that the temples represented with a series of ideals drawn from Roman political orthodoxy, among them the Roman penchant for ordering and governance and the advance of civilization and culture. These ideas had, by the fourth century, found vivid articulation in contemporary tenets of *paideia*, a system within which central notions of imperial ideology were now located, and to which any claim to imperial *auctoritas* would necessarily appeal.

Clifford Ando has recently explored the role of the imperial Roman "*habitus*" in the shaping of Roman identities among the provincial peoples of the Roman Empire.[54] In so doing, Ando draws intriguingly upon the work of the sociologist Pierre Bourdieu. According to Bourdieu, one of the primary functions of the "orchestration of habitus" is to create an environment in which the cultural features that inform identity tend to reflect, reconfirm, and incite acceptance of certain prevailing social or political conditions. In other words, the function of the *habitus* is, in part, to efface the arbitrariness of certain social and political conditions, and to instill the sense that those conditions are natural or innate. In order to do so, the *habitus* must perform one of the crucial features assigned to cultural systems by the anthropologist Clifford Geertz; that is, it is crucial that the *habitus* feature systems of signs and symbols which act to "provide . . . programs for the institution of the social and psychological processes which shape public behavior." Meanwhile, however, this system of signs and symbols also reflects back to the human subject as natural the social, cultural, and political conditions that produced them. Central to such processes is the role of art as a semiotic cultural system, one that, within a specific culture, "materialize[s] a way of experiencing, [and] bring[s] a particular cast of mind out into the world of objects, where men can look at it."[55] In the late antique cultural milieu within which Libanius thought and wrote, the "way of experiencing . . . [the] particular cast of mind" made manifest by art was one in which the present and future became comprehensible and accrued meaning only through studied reference to the remembered past.

Material manifestations of Romano-Hellenic culture "proclaimed the existence of a common culture that was held to be the distinguishing mark of the diffused governing class of the empire, shared alike by all the notables of each region and by the personnel of the imperial government."[56] The material manifestations of this cultural *koinê*, like the modes of comportment, uses of language and styles of dress that marked Roman elites as members of a bounded group, made the linkage of power and *paideia* eminent in the social and political world of the empire.[57] As crucial components of the later Roman imperial *habitus*, they informed, reflected and reinforced one particular arrangement of political, social and cultural power within the lands ruled by Theodosius and other emperors. As Peter Brown has put it, "The achievements of *paideia* were most widely publicized in the person of the emperor himself . . . [and] it was in terms of an image of supreme, unquestioned power, agreeably saturated with their own values, that notables exercised authority in their own society and judged, controlled, and colluded with the local representatives of the power of the emperor."[58]

As crucial components of the imperial *habitus*, material manifestations of *paideia* culture worked to make the specific arrangements upon which Theodosius or any other Roman emperor relied both visible and invisible; the art treasures and temples of the empire made the power of the emperor visible as public articulations of imperial ideology that imposed a grammar upon the public and private spaces of the Roman world even as they confirmed that the place of Rome and its emperor within their world were innate, natural, and, in a quotidian sense, even unremarkable and thus invisible.

Thus in Libanius's estimation it was not merely marble columns and likenesses of the old gods against which the monks spent their fury, but against material manifestations of the political, historical, and cultural claims of Rome's ruling elites upon the power and authority with which they perform their traditional roles. As an example of the danger posed by the "hubris, drunken frenzy, greed and unwillingness to exercise self-restraint" of the forces of intolerance, Libanius cited the fate not only of ancient temples, but ancient works of art as well.[59] "There was a bronze statue in the city of Beroea in the likeness of the beautiful son of Cleinius," he wrote.

> In it, artistry mimicked nature. The bloom of life was such in it that even those to whom it was available to see every day still had a yearning to see it . . . so then, this statue, O King, so precisely constructed in truth by means of much effort and radiant *psyche*, has been chopped up and done away with. The rabble has distributed among itself the masterpieces of Pheidias.[60] For what blood sacrifices? For what acts of worship in contravention of the laws? In that city [Beroea], even though nobody could say that they were carrying out sacrifices, they chopped Alcibiades, or rather Asclepius, into many pieces, disfiguring the city by means of the acts committed against the statue.[61]

The "hubris, drunken frenzy, greed and unwillingness to exercise self-restraint" of the mob and the forces of coercion generally are contrasted here with the ordered and ordering manifestations of Hellenic culture against which "the rabble" vents its ferocity. The statue of Asclepius, in which truly dwelled the image of Alcibiades (a point to which we will return presently), stood in Libanius's rendering as a representation of human reason's ability to bend or even reproduce the natural world and its elements in accordance with its will; in it, Libanius says, "artistry mimicked nature." The handiwork of the mob was nothing other than its unreasoning violence, with which Libanius contrasted the studied sanity and historical resonance of Pheidias's handiwork. It long abided before its community, crafted by "much effort and radiant *psyche*," as a focal point of polis life. Its destruction was accordingly a desecration of the city itself.[62]

Especially evocative is the image of Alcibiades encased in the statue of the old god, Alcibiades whom Libanius elsewhere depicted as a great aristocratic defender of Hellenic culture whose political enemies allowed their personal hatred to drive them to desecrate public religious icons.[63] We may gain a sense of the resonance borne by this imagery from R. R. R. Smith's description of a late fourth-century or early fifth-century Alcibiades statue recovered from what is believed to have been "a prestigious philosophical school or some kind of place of higher learning" at Aphrodisias. This Alcibiades statue was paired with a portrait of a distinctively Romanized Alexander in "a gallery of cultural heroes," Smith writes.[64] "Alcibiades and Alexander were perhaps the two best-known examples of the philosophical instruction of political leaders—suitable advertisement for any institution of higher learning. They have in common that they were each the most famous pupil of the leading philosopher of their day . . . Alcibiades' career could be seen as a classic archetype for Alexander's."

* * *

Here and throughout his oration, then, Libanius provocatively illustrated the notion that nothing less than the whole history and cultural legacies of Romano-Hellenic civilization resided within the art treasures and temples currently under attack by the agents of militant Christianity. The figure of the emperor, like the figure of Alcibiades/Asclepius, was but a sign within this much larger cultural inheritance. As a sign it was legible only within the tradition to which the temples and art treasures were so intimately bound; it derived its meaning from its emplotment within certain privileged narratives of the past and from its association with a lexicon of kindred signs, symbols, and associations.

Libanius was in every sense an astute and well-connected political player. He chose the arguments and images presented in *Oratio 30* because he had calculated them to motivate his emperor to move against those militant pietists who were currently destroying the temples and art treasures of the ancient world. In a larger sense, however, this oration also suggests a model of leadership that was tethered to the irreducible realities of late fourth-century political life. This was a model of rulership imagined in accordance with privileged narratives of the Roman past and articulated in accordance with the propitiating *koinê* of *paideia*.

Indeed, within the *paideia*-saturated world of later Roman politics, the emperor's authority made implicit reference to and depended upon the remembered past Libanius repeatedly conjures via allusions to the ancient and imperiled statues and temples. Thus the statues and temples made visible a "cast of mind" that was particular to the late Roman world insofar as those figures, like the figure of the emperor himself, accrued meaning in relation to a particular narrative of the Roman past and present. It was frequently the function of the ceremonies performed in the temples, for example, to collapse the expanses of geographic space and temporal distance across which Roman communities imagined ties of kinship and allegiance as a means of experiencing imperial *romanitas*, as Ando has demonstrated.[65] Indispensable to such moments of remembrance and Roman self-identification were both the icon of the emperor and the element of narrative, in accordance with which the semiotic forms of the Roman *habitus*—including the figure of the emperor himself—accrued specific meanings. Accordingly, the art treasures Libanius depicts shattered and strewn on the ground throughout his emperor's realm are material manifestations of the cultural system wherein resided the basis for Theodosius or any emperor's authority and ability to rule.

In the later fourth century certain ancient realities of Roman political life took on new implications. The Roman emperor was all that he ever had been, but he was now subject to new readings by a newly important constituency, and these new readings mattered in new ways. The narrative that located Theodosius within Roman society included acts of persecution and apostasy committed by a cast of imperial actors whose remembered characters were increasingly determined within an evolving Christian discourse concerning persecution, toleration, and the appropriate positioning for Christian Roman emperors with regard to both of these.[66]

Within this evolving Christian discourse, for example, the Roman emperor—even a Christian emperor—was always already a persecutor. Similarly, after Julian, any Christian emperor was always already an apostate, as some bishops were only too happy to remind him should he seem in danger of yielding to those whose notion of good rulership still included toleration and consensus. As we have seen, such readings of the imperial *statio* are often encountered in the letters and orations of the bishop Ambrose, for example, and notably in communications frequently cited by modern scholars of late antiquity in discussions of the increasing willingness of emperors to accede to demands of intolerant Christians.

It should surprise us little, then, that as Libanius joined this discussion concerning the qualities most befitting virtuous Roman sovereignty, he too should address the question of the emperor's historically derived *statio*. The spectrum of cultural and historical ideals that made the imperial *statio* possible, Libanius argued, and that allowed individual Roman men to speak as only a Roman emperor could speak, to act as only a Roman emperor could act and to *be* as only a Roman emperor could be, were given material form in the temples and art treasures then under attack across the Roman world. It was these ideals, and all that had grown from them, that Libanius urged his Christian emperor that he must protect.

Conclusion

Did Libanius manage to convince Theodosius? There is little evidence with which to answer this question, and what evidence we do possess is inconclusive. It has been suggested in some recent scholarship, for example, that a Theodosian law that banned monks from the cities may have been issued in response to the issues raised by Libanius.[67] The law was soon repealed, however, and the tendencies Libanius bemoans in his oration continued beyond the reign of Theodosius. Indeed, whatever the intention or motivation of Theodosius's short-lived law, it may be argued that his specific intentions with regard to militant Christian activism soon came to matter little in the wider history of intercommunal violence in the later Roman world. By the time of his death, Theodosius had himself become a character in an ever-evolving narrative of Christianity's history within the Roman world.

As R. Malcolm Errington has recently demonstrated, for example, the Theodosius who emerges in the writings of contemporary and near-contemporary Christian authors is a Theodosius crafted in accordance with larger narratives of Christianity's triumph over paganism, and orthodoxy's ongoing campaign against heretical error rather than from any specific knowledge of Theodosius's laws or policies with regard to "non-Christians." Only Sozomenos, a lawyer by training, seems to have relied upon actual legal enactments as a resource for his history, and even he seems to have demurred when confronted with popular versions of the recent Roman past that failed to conform to the evidence he culled from his knowledge of Theodosius's legislation. The figure of Theodosius bequeathed to future generations of

Roman Christians, in other words, was crafted as a character in a preexisting narrative of the Christian community's history within the Roman world, and his actions with regard to the problem of religious violence as episodes within the same narrative.[68]

Control of that narrative, which would become crucial to processes of self-fashioning among generations of future Christians and Christian communities, had passed to men like Ambrose. The character of the oration given by Ambrose over the body of Theodosius as it was prepared for its final trip to Constantinople in 395 suggests much about the use these men would make of that narrative. Ambrose painted Theodosius as a smasher of idols and a scourge of heretics, and in the course of the oration he digressed to interpret the story of Helena's journey to the holy land and the discovery of the True Cross as the event that began a reformulation of Roman rulership. Theodosius, in turn, Ambrose cast as a particularly virtuous exponent of that reformulation.

Having found the nails that had fastened Christ's flesh to the cross, Ambrose narrated, Constantine's mother had one of the nails fashioned into a bridle and the other woven into a diadem for her son and his Christian successors. In so doing, Ambrose said, Helena "redeemed" the Roman emperors—the material traces of numinous revelation that Helena pulled from the soil of Jerusalem marked the end of one sort of Roman sovereignty and the beginning of another:

> [T]he beginning of the faith of the emperors is the holy relic which is upon the bridle. From that came the faith whereby persecution ended and devotion to God took its place. Wisely did Helena act, she who placed the cross on the head of sovereigns, that the Cross of Christ might be adored among kings. That was not presumption but piety, since honor was given to our holy redemption. Good, therefore, is the nail of the Roman Empire. It rules the whole world and adorns the brow of princes, that they may be preachers who were accustomed to be persecutors. Rightly is the nail on the head, so that where intelligence is, there may be protection, also.[69]

The nail upon the brow of the Roman emperor was, Ambrose continued, a source of dread for the Jews. It was an emblem of the memory of their persecution of Christ, and a reminder of the fact that those who were persecuted now wielded the vast power of the Roman state. "Now the contest is greater for us," he had an imaginary Jew observe. "Now more furious is the combat against him [that is, Christ]." Immediately, in Ambrose's rendering, this battle against Christ was joined by the Photinians and Arians, the heretical enemies of Ambrose's community (and, we may presume, threats to the community like the Jews).[70] Earlier in his sermon, Ambrose had clearly associated Theodosius with the eradication of pagan religion as well: Theodosius had, he said, like Jacob, "put out of sight the idols of the Gentiles. For his faith removed all worship of images and eradicated all their ceremonies."[71]

The imperial *statio* was, in Ambrose's rendering, fundamentally changed by Helena's discovery of the material traces of Jesus' suffering and death at the hands of the Jews and the Roman state. A relic of the Roman state's first act of anti-Christian persecution was woven inextricably within the symbol of Roman sovereignty to be passed down through generations of Christian Roman rulers. In Ambrose's reckoning, the discovery of the nails and the cross was a turning point in the history of Roman rulership because they would now forever after remain emblems of the persecutor who lived within the Roman emperor's unique *statio*. They would serve, particularly in the form of the bridle, as a check upon the behavior of the emperor. Like the iron of the nail now conjoined with the gold and jewels of the diadem, the base metal of persecution could not be extracted from the diachronic *statio* of the Roman emperor. Moreover, Ambrose seems to suggest, these emblems should also serve as constant reminders, as they do for the Jews he conjures, of Christianity's history of persecution at the hands of its enemies, enemies who were many and varied and who had not ceased to scheme against the one true community of God and its members.

Thus Ambrose took the occasion of Theodosius's death as an opportunity to situate the recently deceased emperor and those emperors who would follow him within a closely managed narrative of the Christian-Roman past. Ambrose stressed Theodosius's role as a defender of the Christian community and as a punisher of its enemies, the list of which seems nevertheless to have grown no shorter during his reign.

Whatever the validity of Libanius's argument concerning Roman rulership, then, and no matter how compelling the narrative of the Roman past he offered Theodosius may have been, Ambrose and men who shared his vision of Christianity's mission and message now took a guiding role in articulating the narratives in accordance with which imperial identities were crafted and with which imperial behavior was frequently managed. As he was emplotted in this evolving narrative of the Christian community's history within the Roman world, moreover, Theodosius became a figure in accordance with which normative imperial behavior would be crafted in the future. Theodosius's reign, as Hal Drake has recently demonstrated at length, represented a crucial step in the evolution of a model of Christian rulership that claimed the willingness of Christian emperors to coerce their non-Christian subjects as the truest test of their faith.[72] And although it was not the last step in this process, the capacity of men like Ambrose and other militant Christians to emplot Theodosius as an avid persecutor of "non-Christians" within the evolving history of their community marked an important milestone in this somber process.

For this reason, it now mattered little whether or not the events at Callinicum or Libanius's pleas had moved Theodosius to briefly ban the monks from the cities; the acts of pious militancy Errington argues that Theodosius "only tolerated" were now subsumed into evolving narratives as a specific and systematic policy of intolerance and coercion—that is, as precisely what Sozomenos, who actually seems to have consulted Theodosius's legislation, apparently believed they were not.[73] However we interpret Theodosius's decisions concerning Callinicum, for example, or his laws concerning the presence of monks in cities, the events of his life were soon transformed through the talent and energy of men like Ambrose into episodes in an increasingly triumphal narrative of Christianity's emergence, formative traumas, and eventual victory over its "enemies."

This process did not mean that the ideals of Roman rulership or the cultural heritage touted by Libanius no longer mattered, however. In the time of Justinian, for example, normative notions of Roman rulership came to incorporate the ideals extolled by Libanius in his oration on the temples—the emperor was to be the protector of his subjects, the defender of his empire, a builder of walls and places of worship, a provider of order and stability—but also those insisted upon by Ambrose. Now, as Procopius detailed the material manifestations of Justinian's power and benevolence, descriptions of fortresses and churches built, restored, and maintained were situated in conjunction with passages recalling Justinian's forceful efforts to root out the worship of the old gods and references to his campaigns to drive theological "error" from his realm.[74]

Procopius opens the same work, however, by describing a magnificent equestrian statue of Justinian dressed "in the manner of Achilles" holding aloft a cross as a weapon of conquest. The semiotic vocabulary on whose behalf Libanius pled was yet alive and well, and it was still crucial to the *statio* of the Roman emperor. What Libanius had not foreseen was the capacity of this *koinê* of signs and symbols to abide in tandem with, and indeed blend with, the genre of aggressive monotheism he so passionately condemned.[75]

CHAPTER FOUR

"Are You Christians?" Violence, Ascetics, and Knowing One's Own

BY THE END of the sixth century, the imperial descendants of Theodosius and the distant offspring of the Syrian monks whose zealotry Libanius lamented in his *Oratio 30* found themselves on opposed sides of a bitter and often violent controversy over the nature of Christ.[1] Central to this controversy, of course, was a contest over the identity of the one true community of God upon this earth. During the decades of the sixth century, the local communities of Syria that opposed the imperial-sponsored genre of orthodoxy that issued from the Council of Chalcedon in 451 recalled their histories through narratives of oppression and persecution, many of which now featured as their stars certain militant and charismatic ascetics whose role it was to defend the behavioral and doctrinal boundaries which set their own communities apart from all others.[2] This was a role kindred with that of the martyr in earlier renditions of the Christian past, and the stories that now recalled the acts of more recent defenders of urgently imperiled communities drew upon much older narratives of persecution and resistance, incorporating now ancient themes, tropes, and aesthetics to mediate contemporary events through the hermeneutic lens afforded by those narratives.[3]

The stories in which these ascetic militants confronted imperial authorities drew upon what was by the middle of the sixth century another well-worn series of traditions, traditions that figured Christian ascetics as characters that controlled, patrolled, and defended the hard edges, the impassable boundaries, of their respective communities.[4] These traditions frequently figure Christian ascetics as zealous and violent warriors on behalf of Christian orthodoxy.[5] Accordingly, during the fifth and sixth centuries, we also encounter a good number of narratives in which Christian ascetics also attack the bodies and material culture of Jews and pagans as well as those of other Christian communities.[6] This phenomenon, which appears in the later fourth century and accelerates thereafter, has often been treated as indicative of the gathering intolerance of the post-Constantinian Roman world.[7] When we examine many such incidents of monastic violence closely, however, it becomes clear that rather than episodes of popular, intercommunal violence waged by opposed and polarized communities, such incidences of militant piety in fact reveal as much about the desire of many later Roman persons and communities to live in peace with their neighbors as they do about the desire of some to prevent such irenic coexistence. Tellingly, however, it is the violence that is remembered rather than the much quieter processes of cooperation, exchange, and harmony that this violence disrupted, however briefly.

When a band of monks raided the pagan sanctuaries at Menouthis in the later fifth century, for example, the immediate cause of the violence was a beating administered to a recent Christian convert by his classmates, who were still pagan and who seem to have grown weary of the new convert's enthusiastic (and apparently very frequent) disparagement of his former religion, including incessant comparisons of the priestess of Isis to a prostitute. The new Christian was eventually rescued by some passing *philoponoi*, members of a Christian guild or confraternity who often took to the streets with clubs in defense of their patron, the bishop of Alexandria.[8]

When there was no enthusiasm for an antipagan pogrom among local imperial officials, including the Prefect Entrexios—whom Zachariah, the author of the text in which this story appears, suspects was secretly a pagan—the outraged student and his supporters sought the aid of local monks, who indeed helped them exact some large-scale vengeance against the pagan temples of the local vicinity. In order to do so, they had to overcome the objections of "those who passed for Christians in Menouthis . . . were weak in their faith to the point that they were enslaved to the money the pagans gave them so that they would not object to the offering of sacrifices to the idols."[9]

Indeed, those who preferred to live with their pagan neighbors in peace, be they imperial officials like Entrexios or the Christian clergy of Menouthis, are often depicted in tales of pious militancy as they are here, as "weak Christians," closet pagans or lovers of money willing to accept bribes to tolerate tolerance. Similar charges were leveled by Mark the Deacon against officials in Gaza as he narrated the Life of the bishop and monk Porphyry, who eventually forcibly converted the population of that Palestinian city, just as John of Ephesus suggested that it was a love of bribes that induced Christians in the environs of Amida to put up with the intermingling of Christians in Jews.[10] In his *Panegyric on Macarius of Tkōw*, Dioscurus of Alexandria claimed that Macarius and a band of Egyptian ascetics murdered a pagan priest and ran other polytheists out of town when local officials who were "money-lovers" did nothing about the ceremonial murder of Christian children by those pagans.[11] This is an accusation we shall encounter repeatedly in this chapter as Christian rigorists try to explain away the willingness of Christian populations to live as one with their pagan, Jewish and heretic neighbors.

In other instances, the spectacle of the violence itself seems to blot out the relative harmony it displaces. Take, for example, the murder by a Christian mob of the pagan philosopher Hypatia of Alexandria in 415, during which the philosopher was hacked apart and her body parts dragged through the streets of her home city before being publicly burned. The horror of this event is frequently taken as a sign to represent ever-darker intercommunal relations in the late Roman world, an emblem of the violence and intolerance that had come to dominate public life in the empire. If we take a slightly broader view, however, we will note that the murder of Hypatia was one of a chain of apparently related events, a sequence that also included the stoning by a band of Christian monks of the local praetorian prefect Orestes, a Christian and, notably, a friend of Hypatia's. Indeed, when we note the fact that both attacks took place within the context of a power struggle between the local bishop—the violent and powerful Cyril—and Orestes, that Hypatia and Orestes were both members of a clique of local pagan and Christian elites who opposed Cyril's power and that our ancient sources are nearly unanimous in attributing Hypatia's murder to her friendship with Orestes and/or the division she was believed to have caused within the Christian community, the murder of the philosopher takes on a very different cast.[12]

But there is more to this incident. When the monks—men "of a very fiery disposition" who had come to the city to fight on Cyril's behalf against the prefect—attacked Orestes, it was a Christian crowd that chased them away, and when the stone thrower was publicly tortured to death, it was the local Christian population that rejected Cyril's bid to elevate the dead monk to the status of martyr. The local Christian population had seen the recent events at close range, and, wrote the fifth century Church historian Socrates Scholasticus, "they knew well that [Ammonius] had suffered the punishment due to his rashness, and that he had not lost his life under torture because he would not deny Christ. And Cyril himself being conscious of this, suffered the recollection of the circumstances to be gradually obliterated by silence."[13] It would seem, then, the violence of 415 in Alexandria was more likely a strike against what was seen as too close a relationship between pagan and Christian within the ranks of Alexandria's elites than a spasm of "popular hate" directed at the polytheist community of Alexandria.[14]

Indeed, as we shall see in this chapter, raids by Christian ascetic warriors for the faith upon communities of religious others may often be interpreted not as manifestations of a generalized or popular intolerance but rather as attempts by Christian rigorists to interrupt what was perceived as a dangerous erosion or obfuscation of communal boundaries. This, of course, was not a new phenomenon, nor were the anxieties produced by this phenomenon specific or unique to the sixth century. Rather, as we have seen, the dilemma posed by the transgression of communal boundaries was one that had deeply concerned John Chrysostom in the fourth century and one with which most all of the communities of the late Roman world struggled in one way or another.

Chrysostom had tried to address this problem by inciting his parishioners to take an active part in confronting one another on the basis of the shared Christian identity, and in so doing to insist upon the behavioral criteria for communal inclusion cited by Chrysostom in his sermons. In so doing, he in effect called upon his flock to contest a specific version of genuine Christianness into existence; it was through a process of contentious Christian-to-Christian interpellation that the communal boundaries that mattered to Chrysostom would come to matter also to his flock. Those boundaries—which plainly were not intrinsic to the experienced Christianness of many of Chrysostom's fellow Antiochene Christians—would become part of the experience of being Christian not through the decisions of some far-away Church council but rather through the person-to-person social interactions of community members themselves.

This was not a task Chrysostom expected his parishioners to relish. It involved policing the behavior of one's friends and neighbors. It demanded the transgression of social norms and the invasion of treasured private spaces, including the home.[15] It was a brand of behavior that went against the social grain of cosmopolitan urban centers and against the decorum that such diverse urban venues demanded.[16] In short it was, as Chrysostom expected his parishioners would point out, a task fit not for men enmeshed in normative social attachments. Instead, it was a job for priests like the preacher who now stood before them authoritatively articulating a version of normative Christian behavior (men, that is, like Chrysostom himself), and, notably, it was a job for Christian ascetics. "I am no priest or monk; I have a wife and children," Chrysostom expected members of his flock to protest. "I am a worldly man, I have a wife and children; those are the tasks of priests, the tasks of monks."[17]

Clearly, for Chrysostom and, presumably, Chrysostom's contemporaries, it was expected that the hard work of patrolling and controlling communal boundaries was to be performed by monks and, unsurprisingly given Chrysostom's position, by the clergy. It was this role, I will suggest in this chapter, that helps to explain the presence of zealous Christian ascetics in so many instances of intercommunal strife in the late Roman world. Indeed, outbursts of such violence involving members of ascetic and monastic communities were part of a very old phenomenon by the sixth century; Christian ascetics—or rather the figure of the Christian ascetic as it abided in the minds of late Roman communities from Ireland to Arabia—had long taken a role in declaring, patrolling, and defending the communal boundaries of Christian communities that believed themselves to be the one true community of God upon the earth.[18] This was a role, moreover, that ensured an enduring place for the monk in the often volatile border region between communal self and other.

The archetypical Christian monk, Antony, was assigned to this post by his hagiographer, the fourth-century Alexandrian bishop Athanasius. As David Brakke has suggested, Athanasius invented Antony in the midst of an attempt to establish his own community as the one true community of Christians in Alexandria.[19] Notably, Athanasius's Melitian rivals seem to have more successfully appropriated for themselves the memory of local martyrs as they advanced their own claims to represent the one true community of descendants from those early Christian martyrs.[20] The Athanasian Antony was, Brakke has suggested, a means of responding to the Melitian monopoly upon the cult of the martyrs in Egypt.[21]

As we meet him in Athanasius's text, Antony is a keen discerner of hidden truths. Perceiving the wickedness and apostasy of the "Melitian schismatics" from the outset, for example, Antony never held communion with them. "And neither toward the Manichaeans nor toward any other heretics did he profess friendship, except to the extent of urging the change to right belief, for he held and taught that friendship and association with them led to injury and destruction of the soul," Antony's Life continues. "So in the same way he abhorred the heresy of the Arians, and he ordered everyone neither to go near them nor to share their erroneous belief."[22] In addition, of course, Antony was always able to see through the devil's attempts at deception and seduction and even instructed his fellow ascetics in the tricky business of telling holy revelation from demonic illusion.[23]

Because of his capacity to tell truth from falsehood and good from evil, the Antony of Athanasius's Life provided a single, dependable fixed point within the world in accordance with which members of the Athanasian community could negotiate the confusing and treacherous doctrinal world around them. With their eyes fixed firmly upon Antony as a beacon of orthodoxy, the faithful of the Athanasian community could seek salvation not by sorting through obscure points of doctrine and theology but by following Antony as an exemplar and by observing the communal boundaries insisted upon by Athanasius and his loyal followers, figures, of course, like Antony.[24]

Athanasius's text tells us, for example, that when the Arians claimed Antony as one of their own, Antony came down from his mountain and disputed the claim, lest other Christians be led astray, and then held forth on the tenets of the true Christian faith.[25] In the sixth century, the Syrian stylite Maro was similarly claimed by local Chalcedonians as one of their own, a claim he denied, just as Theodoret reports that a century before the Syrian ascetic Julian Saba had found it necessary to dispel rumors that he favored the Arian creed lest others fall victim to it.[26] In the first half of the seventh century, the Nestorian bishop Išōʿyahb in Iraq wrote to Mar Ḥnānišōʿ, a respected ascetic of his region, to request that he help head off the "ruin" of the local Christian community when a certain Magian ("one of the persecuting religion") began to win converts among local Christians, who were, Išōʿyahb said, both throwing away their own hope of eternal life and setting a bad example for other Christians.[27]

In the eighth century, living under Muslim rule, the Syrian ascetic Timothy of Kākhushtā corrected a wandering ascetic who had fallen into heretical error by chaining him to his pillar and having two attendants beat the wanderer "with all their might and strength" until he saw the light.[28] Indeed, over a space of centuries, we repeatedly encounter the figure of the monk perched on the boundaries of his community, exemplifying the qualities ascribed to all real members of that community, but also intimately involved in the crucial work of monitoring passage across that boundary—challenging and rebuking those who did not conform, authorizing and admitting those who did.

The sixth-century Syrian ascetic Paul of Antioch, for example, "was earnest and fervent in his zeal from the time of his boyhood, so that from the greatness of his zeal he became stern and harsh, and a rebuker of those who approached religious work sluggishly in any manner."[29] Elsewhere, Socrates Scholasticus reports that the monk Marcianus interceded with a fellow ascetic in a manner that would have no doubt pleased Chrysostom, demanding that an especially old and old-fashioned monk stop celebrating Easter "as previously" and embrace the rules for celebration of the Pasch set down by the council of Nicaea. After the old man would not be convinced, Marcianus "publicly separated himself from communion with him." In time, however, the old man saw the error of his way and repented.[30] Jerome wrote in his Life of the fourth-century ascetic Hilarion that as an old man Hilarion rejected a gift of chickpeas given by a greedy "brother," forbidding members of his community to eat them because he could smell the stink and contagion of avariciousness on them.[31] In a still more explicit instance of boundary defense, Socrates Scholasticus reported that the fourth-century Novatian ascetic and bishop Paul finally caught a Jew who had made a practice of receiving baptism from different Christian sects, each time collecting money for his false conversion. Paul finally saw through the Jew's scheme, however, and prevented his baptism and thus protected his community from contamination.[32]

Three centuries later, the Nestorian monk Rabban Hōrmīzd inspired the Muslim *amīr* of Mosul to convert to Christianity, we are told, by miraculously bringing his son back to life in the name of Christ. Hōrmīzd lacked the vessels necessary to perform the ritual, however, and told the Muslim he would have to wait. A band of Monophysite monks, who had come to console the Arab over the death of his son and whose monastery was nearby, now saw their opportunity. "O my lord the Amīr, behold," one of them said. "Our monastery is provided with everything which is necessary for baptism, and you can be baptized by us just as well as by the hands of Hōrmīzd, because baptism by him or by us is the same thing."

Hōrmīzd predictably disagreed. "O sinful man, the matter is not thus," he said to the Monophysite, "for our baptism and your baptism no more resemble each other than do God and Satan, or light and darkness." To prove it, Hōrmīzd performed an experiment. First he put the son of a Nestorian into the baptismal basin. The holy water stood away from him in two columns. Then he put a Monophysite child into the basin, and the water washed over him. Hōrmīzd explained that the Nestorian boy had already been baptized, whereas the Monophysite boy had not, "for [the Monophysites] do not possess holy baptism, but only an inferior and false one."[33] Despite all appearances (and the claims of those Rabban Hōrmīzd took as his rivals), all baptisms were not the same; it was the role of the ascetic to demonstrate which was the right one, which feast and which fasts were the proper ones, which theology was the correct one, which cure was the acceptable one.

As we saw in a previous chapter, for example, the Egyptian monk and archimandrite Shenoute railed against such acts as tying snake heads, crocodile teeth, and fox claws to parts of one's body as magical cures. He demanded that his fellow Christians make a choice: "If the oracle's sanctuary of demons is useful to you . . . then go there. But if it is the house of God, the Church, that is useful for you, go to it." Shenoute was particularly incensed that after allowing themselves to be anointed with oil and holy water by "enchanters and drug-makers" many Christians then had the same done to themselves again by "elders of the church or even . . . monks!"[34] Shenoute was also believed to excel at ferreting out fake Christians: David Brakke has recently noted an episode in which Shenoute vigorously outed one Gesios, a local Egyptian aristocrat whom Shenoute accused of offering sacrifices to the old gods in the ruin of a burned temple.[35]

The fourth-century hagiographer Sulpicius Severus relates in his *Life of Martin of Tours* that the great militant ascetic was so zealous in his efforts to correct the *pagani* of the Gallic countryside that he mistook a funeral procession for a pagan ceremony and miraculously froze the mourners in their places.[36] Even the "holy fool" Symeon of Emesa took it as his duty to correct Christian adulterers and miraculously shriveled the hand of a Christian juggler in order to make him give up juggling. It seems that in spite of his wicked profession, the juggler in question "had done some good deeds" and so deserved as a Christian to be corrected and so saved.[37]

This duty to "command right and forbid wrong" went beyond matters of

Christology and the fine points of dogma. The monk Telemachus, for example, went to the city of Rome and climbed into the arena in order to stop a gladiatorial combat. His action was not appreciated by the crowd, which subsequently stoned the monk to death. The emperor Honorius was impressed, however, and, Theodoret says, thereafter declared Telemachus a martyr and banned gladiatorial games.[38] This is a rather extreme version of the kind of activism Chrysostom himself had in mind when, in his *Against the games and theatres*,[39] he declared such games to be unfit for Christians, and urged his parishioners that Christians must intercede with their fellow Christians to prevent their attendance at the games, just as he urged that Christians who transgressed their communal boundaries by participating in Jewish feasts and fasts should be confronted and corrected by their fellow Christians.

Public games had in fact long represented a site in which Christians and non-Christians had come together and dissolved into an undifferentiated mass of Roman humanity. This had caused no little anxiety for pietists and rigorists. Long before the fifth century, in fact, such early Christian authors as Tertullian had fretted over the games and railed against the games, warned their fellow Christians away from the games and personally boycotted the games. Despite this, however, in the estimation of Theodoret it took the action of a Telemachus to bring the matter to a head and, Theodoret thought, to a conclusion.[40]

Keeping Christians away from the games seems to have proven a persistent challenge, however. Even as late as the sixth century, for example, Severus of Antioch found it necessary to warn his own congregation away from the spectacles. After citing the prophet Jeremiah as an example of zeal in safeguarding the name of God, he continued,

> But you people—or rather a lot of you, since I don't want to accuse all of you—you go to the spectacle in the hippodrome and to the temple of laughter, or, to give what is perhaps the more fitting name, the temple of lust for prostitution, and the theater given to every luxury. And you say, "From prayers or from the assembly [of the church] we have not fallen away, and as to the spectacles, we will be similarly quiet in them." But have you not heard Paul? He wrote to the Corinthians, "You cannot drink the cup of our lord, and the cup of the demons. You cannot take a place at the table of our lord and a place at the table of the demons."[41]

For Severus, it would seem, there was more to the issue of Christian attendance at the games and spectacles than the way in which individual Christians comported themselves while in the theater; there was also the larger problem inherent in the intermixing of Christians with members of other communities and participating in their festivals, thus the potential for blurring the behavioral lines of demarcation that set Christians apart from non-Christians. Moreover, it seems clear that as Severus addressed his Antiochene congregation, he, like his predecessor John Chrysostom, found himself attempting to control communal boundaries on the basis of normative behaviors that were anything but self-evident in the minds of his parishioners.

As Jacob of Serugh preached to his own skeptical flock against the games, probably in the late fifth century, he anticipated the arguments that members of his congregation might offer in defense of their attendance at the theater: "'It is a show,' they would say, 'not paganism . . . I am baptized even as you, and I confess one Lord; and I know that the mimings which belong to the spectacles are false. I do not go out that I may believe, but I go that I may laugh . . . what shall I lose on account of this?'" To this, Jacob asked his congregation, "Who can bathe in mud without being soiled?" For Jacob as for Chrysostom and Severus, the issue was the pollution to which Christians subjected themselves at the games and in the theater.[42]

It was in such circumstances that monks quite frequently stepped in to draw a line. The monk Hypatius had done something very like this in the year 434–35. When he heard that the Olympic games were to be held in that year, he immediately resolved to forbid the local magistrate, one Leontius, to give them. He then gathered a party of his fellow monks, saying to them, "If there are any who cringe from dying for Christ, let them not come with me." When they made their way to the house of the local bishop, Eulalius, the bishop asked what all of the commotion was about. Hypatius responded, "I know that idolatry must return with the Olympic games, close to us and to the holy church of God, and I've decided to go the theater tomorrow and to die, rather than allow that this happen."

The bishop, however, suggested that there was no call for such drastic action, asking him, "Are you absolutely compelled to die, even if nobody is making us sacrifice? Since you're a monk, keep yourself in repose and stay calm. This affair is my concern." Hypatius sensed that the bishop missed the point: "Since this is your affair and you aren't concerned about it, I—seeing the Lord outraged by those who attempt this thing [and] the Christian people ensnared in their ignorance, returning themselves to the worship of idols—I have come to affirm solemnly to your holiness that tomorrow, when the prefect presides over the games, I will intervene with a group of monks, I will pull the prefect down from on high in his seat, and I will die for Christ, rather than permit, while I live, that this thing should take place."[43]

When the prefect Leontius heard that Hypatius had gathered a group of monks to oppose him, he canceled the games, claiming to be ill.[44] Hypatius's hagiographer, Callinicus, who records these events, makes the point of Hypatius's actions clear: Through a man named Eusebius, whom God sent to Hypatius, the monk learned "that [the Olympics] were the summit of idolatrous madness, and for Christians an occasion of slipping and falling."[45] It was Hypatius's duty, as Callinicus saw it, to prevent this, to prevent Christians from losing themselves in the dangerously promiscuous social milieu the games seem to have represented to him.

"Do You Know That Him Who Destroys the Wall, the Serpent Will Bite?"

As we have seen, then, late Roman Christian ascetics were assigned by their contemporaries the task of locating and declaring what could easily be confusing, if crucial, aspects of their respective communal boundaries. Monks were especially well equipped to perform this function. Those individuals who became monks, as we meet them in the hagiographical literature of their age, are those Christians who drew ever tighter boundaries around themselves, sealing themselves into an ever smaller community of real Christians within which salvation was possible. It is this tendency, for example, that accounts for the often-repeated trope in which a particularly pious ascetic cuts himself off first from the company of ordinary Roman society and then from Christian society generally, retreating into the desert or into a monastic institution. In such stories, the ascetic then often erects and enforces a line between himself and his fellow ascetics, drawing a boundary around himself within which resides an ever-smaller community.[46] This community often eventually becomes a community of the great man or woman him- or herself and a few disciples, within which the numinous power of revelation remains ever present and within which contact with that power never fades into the remembered past but instead remains ever present, ever accessible.[47]

The view of the world such stories suggest—one in which the single true community of God upon the earth is maintained through the imposition of tightly regimented and closely enforced communal boundaries—was articulated not only in texts about Christian ascetics but also in the texts produced by those ascetics. In his sermons and letters, for example, the fifth-century Egyptian archimandrite Besa rebuked an elderly member of his monastic community for leaving the confines of the monastery to aid his birth sons, who it seems had been arrested or were in danger of arrest. He wrote of the act as one by which the ascetic in question, one Matthew, had "forsaken the community of [his] fathers." It was those fathers—presumably men like Besa's predecessor Shenoute—who had instituted and observed the communal boundaries Matthew had now transgressed in an effort to help his sons. As the descendants of those great men, Besa says, it is the responsibility of each member of the community to maintain that community against all temptations and dangers, so that the community itself might endure: "If everyone decides . . . as you did, weakly, to take foreignness to their hearts, who will dwell with all of his companions? Unless our fathers had persevered in their constancy, where were we to find them that we might dwell with them? But now our fathers perfected their constancy and went to God. If we ourselves are like them, many will profit through us, but if we turn back and renounce our constancy, many will be lost because of us and stumble."[48]

Matthew had confused his family of flesh and blood for his real family, and in so doing he had forsaken the one true community of God and the salvation it bestowed. "For many of the brethren amongst us did not waver in their constancy towards God when their sons or their brothers departed from us [i.e., died], since they knew that they would not find a son beside them, or a daughter, of any of those related to them by the flesh, in the time of their need, when they came into the hands of Christ."[49]

Matthew's act was not one of idolatry, it should be noted, nor had he adopted heretical views of the nature of Christ or even visited a synagogue. Rather, he had transgressed the physical and imagined boundaries that separated his community from all of the other Christian communities of his world. He had moved physically into the outside world without the permission of his community. In another sermon of rebuke, Besa seems to chastise another monk who left the monastery without permission, redistributing certain loaves of bread designated as offerings. Notably, Besa assigns this monk a new lineage, now the he has betrayed the fathers of the White Monastery community (presumably previous generations of leaders, like Besa's predecessor Shenoute):

> You do not understand that as it was in the case of your father Judas, who fell upon his face, burst asunder and all his bowels gushed out, so it is in your case, God and his Christ having revealed the wickedness which you have perpetrated, which no man knows, because your works are his. That man is a thief and a sinner in everything, a stealer of that which is cast into the bag. So are you, taking the loaves of offering, giving them to whomsoever you wish to give, covertly, without restraint and without asking. You did not consider and you did not reflect that it is a fearful thing to come into the hands of the living God. Moreover you did not remember that it is a fearful thing to expect the judgment and the fierceness of the fire which will devour the adversaries. Who are the adversaries of whom mention is made except those who do evil and transgress the commandment like you and all those who resemble you, in the way in which you did not reflect before going into a town, or house, or strange community?[50]

Like the uncle of Elʿazar Ben Dama, the rabbi we encountered in Chapter 1 who rejoiced at his nephew's death because he died before a Christian could intervene to save him, Besa drew upon Ecclesiastes 10:8 as an expression of the danger of boundary transgression as he lambasted the errant monk: "Do you know that him who destroys the wall, the serpent will bite?" he asked.[51] Although the community that the errant monk entered was presumably Christian—Besa would scarcely have missed an opportunity to raise the specter of idolatry or Judaizing were it not—it was nevertheless a community alien to his own. After a litany of abuse leveled at the monk, Besa said, "In the place to which you went, they do not mock you thus and despise you, unless their heart is unlike yours. They still also blaspheme the name of God and despise the name of our fathers after it had already been told to us, 'On no account, then, let the name of God be blasphemed because of us,'[52] and the name of our father be despised because of our ignorance."[53] It was presumably concern over the effects of mixing with such alien communities that led the leaders of the White Monastery to forbid its members to trade with outsiders, much as, as we shall see, in another context Syrian Christians were rebuked for participating in trade with Jews.[54]

Nor does this concern for communal integrity seem to have been unique to the White Monastery Besa oversaw. In a study of the traditions surrounding a supposed vision experienced by Pachomius, for example, James Goehring has noted that the oldest of these traditions, that which is preserved in a Bohairic Coptic version of Pachomius's Life, in fact served as the seed for later versions of the Pachomian vision.[55] This version of Pachomius's vision described a procession of monks, "the entire congregation of the community," traveling together through the dark, clinging to one another. "Our father Pachomius watched how they proceeded," the tradition continues. "If one of them let go [of the others] he would get lost in the dark with all those who were following him."[56] Indeed, some of the monks do leave the collective to follow an errant monk and are lost.

Goehring suggests that this most basic element of a tradition recalling a Pachomian vision in fact represents "a particular vision dealing with a specific problem in the Pachomian community" which was subsequently subjected "to a reinterpretation of that vision in terms of a later understanding of heresy," probably in the post-Chalcedonian period.[57] The "specific problem" with which the vision deals is clearly one of communal cohesion and, it would seem, the illusions and deceptions that could coax members of the Pachomian community beyond its boundaries.

As Goehring's article makes clear, however, this sense of communal boundaries and the dangers associated with their transgression in monastic thought lent itself quite easily to a later rhetoric of Christological controversy as Christian identity was contested on the basis of theological theory and praxis. By the sixth century, for example, the Egyptian monastery of Epiphanius at Thebes stood as a metaphor not only for the textualization of Christian ascetics and for their association with the Christological and theological controversies of the age but also for the processes of boundary-sensitive discernment on the basis of ascribed qualities and beliefs with which Christian ascetics were so closely associated.[58]

The monastery was a popular pilgrimage site for sixth-century Christians.[59] Built in an abandoned pharaonic tomb system, the monastery seems to have been structured so that as the visitor approached and entered the monastery and moved toward the cell of its founder and star, Epiphanius, s/he passed a series of doctrinal texts painted upon the interior walls of the monastic hive.[60] These texts laid out a series of doctrinal positions, indicating what beliefs were acceptable for members of the one real community of God and which were not. They set forth guidelines for knowing on the basis of profession who should be accepted as one's kindred and who should be rejected and scorned. They warned of the dangers of following false doctrines and heeding the teachings of false prophets, likening these to a "sycamore . . . splitting a rock," and urged the faithful to "Shut thy door [. . .] and be far from these," to "receive not the seed [. . .] thou shall destroy thy faith."[61]

Accordingly, the "passages" through which one moved to find nearness to the numinous presence of Epiphanius were material manifestations of communal boundaries as described by Fredrik Barth and others; they were sites in which individuals might be evaluated against certain ascribed criteria for inclusion within a given community. They were points of both exclusion and inclusion and sites at which each visitor who could read them (or who had them explained to her/him) could carry out a private process of internal interrogation, testing his/her identity against those laid out within the texts upon the walls. Did s/he believe in accordance with the texts? Whatever her/his answer to this question, the texts, arrayed as a kind of screen before the numinous center of the monastery (that is, the figure or space of "the prophet" Epiphanius himself), demanded that the visitor draw a line of inclusion/exclusion between her-/himself and the Others that this internally conjured boundary evoked. Enclosed within that boundary was the community within which the visitor experienced belonging and within which the figure of Epiphanius made the numinous present, authorizing the community itself.[62]

Because the texts themselves are written in Greek, Syriac, and Coptic, it is clear that they were intended for a diverse readership. Accordingly, it is likely that the theological detail contained within them was just one of many legible layers of meaning that resided in them. Interestingly, the texts themselves are consistently ascribed to and authorized by the community at Thebes's "fathers"; Athanasius, Severus of Antioch, Damianus of Alexandria, and Cyril of Alexandria are all evoked, usually at the outset of the texts where the beginning of the inscription is still discernable.[63] In Besa's letters and sermons as well, the fathers of the community of the White Monastery, men like Athanasius and Shenoute, are frequently cited as authorities in accordance with whose words membership within the community and normative standards of behavior marking one as a member of that community may be discerned.[64] Like Epiphanius himself, Shenoute and other Egyptian monastic figures were referred to by monastic writers as "prophets," figures whose connection with the divine was sufficient to serve as the basis for a community of the saved and whose personal example was sufficient to lead the members of that community through a world of confusion and peril toward the one truth that would matter on the day of judgment.[65]

The binary simplicity of monastic notions of community and identity clearly held great fascination for Christians who passed their lives within the baffling complexity of cities like Chrysostom's Antioch. As imagined, what we might (for lack of a better term) call "ascetic space" was space cleared of the confusing clutter and ambiguities that bedeviled questions of identity in the cities—the contingency and vanity of the present world was shaken off, and exempla culled from remembrance of the words, deeds, and personality of communal fathers (whether martyr or monastic) led one toward a peaceful and glorious future. "By the fourth century," Peter Brown has written, "the desert was already a landscape of the mind, created by the interplay of powerful antitheses and associated even then with ancient legends. In the vast hush of Sinai, the people of Israel had lived for forty years in the presence of God, in a state of suspended animation, it was believed, not unlike that ascribed to the great ascetics."[66]

In Milan and Rome and Jerusalem, the primordial past lay buried within the sacred soil, waiting to be discovered in order that it might emerge and impose order in the often chaotic world most Christian men and women inhabited day by day. Within the ascetic communities of the later Roman world, by contrast, the primordial past resided within the numinous space created by the ascetic. Like the bones and bodies of martyrs secreted in the sacred soil of local communities, these ascetic communities and those who belonged to them were abiding resources of transcendent certitude for the Christian selves fashioned in quiet and mundane ways from Ireland to Arabia. "The myth of the desert simply touched humdrum and uncomfortable practices, that were widespread in the Christian churches, with the stillness of eternity," Brown writes. "It was good to think that, somewhere to one side of settled society, a few Christians lived this way, at every moment and for all their lives."[67]

Indeed, in a world in which an ever-growing body of research suggests the boundaries upon which communal identity was dependant were transgressed and confounded as a matter of daily practice, it was vital that somewhere, somehow, those boundaries were permanently preserved and maintained. Ascetic space was accordingly an imaginative space in which late Roman Christians could believe that an essentially pure strain of Christianness abided, perpetually illuminated by the presence of the numinous and incessantly verified by a constant enactment of the suffering of the martyrs.

Of Monks and Martyrs

As Phillip Rousseau, Michael Gaddis, and others have shown, the literature that grew up around monks and monastic praxis seems to suggest that the figure of the monk was kindred with the martyr in the minds of late antique people in several ways, and there is evidence that many ascetics took the martyrs as models to be emulated.[68] Monks frequently took up residence in martyrs' shrines and near martyrs' graves, for example, and as he gave birth to the textually bound monk, Athanasius emphasized the martyr lineage of Antony, his archetypical ascetic.[69]

That the monk played a role closely kindred with that of the martyr in the imaginary of late Roman Christians is made especially clear in the deployment of certain motifs common to both martyr literature and the Lives of various ascetic superstars. One of these is especially telling: what one might describe as the obsessive attention paid to the size, type, gravity, and horror of the physical wounds inflicted upon the martyrs during their labors. This is a particular feature of martyr literature in all its forms, from Prudentius's poetic Latin renderings of the martyrs' passions to the much simpler Coptic and Syriac stories detailing the suffering of the saints.[70] In these stories we see, in pornographic detail, brains pouring forth from the nostrils of a savagely beaten martyr "like milk," the glimmer of bone showing through ravaged flesh and rendered fat "oozing forth and flow[ing] upon the ground" from the martyr's burning body.[71]

Why is this mode of presentation of the martyr's wounds so common in late Roman hagiography? This is a particularly compelling question when the point of such stories is to elucidate the spiritual qualities of the martyr in question and to make clear his or her proximity to God, an agenda that is concerned not with the corporeal, which this mode of presentation emphasizes, but instead with the immaterial and essentially invisible qualities of the soul. I would suggest, following the insights of Linda Williams's studies of the aesthetics of modern pornography, that this graphic and lingering attention to the wounds and physical sufferings of the martyrs represents an attempt to make visible that which is by definition invisible—that is the numinous proximity of the divine and the working of God in the lived experience of the Christian community upon the earth.

Williams has noted that the obsessive close-ups of human body parts, the detailed and studied visual appropriation of bodies, particularly female bodies, during sexual congress, represents an attempt to make visible that which is by normative standards invisible—the female orgasm. By deploying an unblinking, apparently unmediated visual catalogue of the physical truths of sex, it is the aim of the pornographic gaze to capture, appropriate and make available an invisible but highly fetishized phenomenon, female sexual pleasure. The invisibility of this object is made all the more conspicuous by the easily pictured spectacle of male arousal and pleasure, a pleasure which, while normative, is made unremarkable because of its overt nature.[72]

In the highly contentious world of late Roman religion, as we have seen, many communities claimed possession of transcendent truth and cited the possession of transcendent truth as the enduring basis of the community itself. As Christian communities established themselves, they faced an unending process of contestation and debate, first with Jews and pagans, later with other Christian communities. As we have seen, the martyrs proved central to these processes, for it was through their actions and by their memory that these communities recalled primordial moments of revelation in which defining truths were set out and made manifest in the world of men.

But how was one to verify these truths? As I suggested in Chapter 2, this was a task performed for the Christian community in large measure by the truth-producing machinery of the Roman juridical apparatus and in particular by its technologies of pain and punishment. As Synesius, a Christian of the early fifth century, put it, "torturers are terribly clever at refuting pretense, and they have invented claws with the force of scientific syllogisms, so that whatever is revealed when they hold power is truth itself." Torture cleared away reasoned attempts to dissimulate or to lie. It left only truth in its wake.[73]

This aspect of Roman imperial ideology left its imprint on the aesthetics of late Roman Christian literature. Indeed, no less an authority than the Coptic ascetic and archimandrite Shenoute, considered the graphic depiction of the martyr's suffering as a sure way of telling "true" martyr stories from "false ones." As Peter Brown has written, "To Shenoute . . . it was easy to distinguish between authentic and unauthentic accounts of the martyrs. Any account that did not recount how the martyr had died under great torments, that did not report that the martyr's eyes had been torn out, that the martyr's body had not been chopped limb from limb, that did not describe how scorching fires had been applied to the martyr's sides . . . such an account could not be authentic: it was a *martyros nnoudj*, an account of a martyr based on lies."[74]

The truth-value of martyr stories, then, resided in their pornographic depictions of the suffering of the martyr and was to be verified by attention to the detail in which the wounds and torments of the martyr were depicted. But precisely what element of the story did the hyperrealistic, detailed, and graphic depiction of the wounds of the martyr allow the hearer to verify? The central point of the story itself, of course, is the presence of God and his attendance and support of the martyr in his or her moment of (presumably) agonizing ordeal. It was this numinous presence that both allowed the martyr to endure such gruesome tortures and underlay the organizing truths of the communities who later recalled such scenes. The martyr Theodore, for example, told the judge who interrogated him that he did not fear tortures, because he could see his God there, present although invisible to the judge and ready to ransom him from those tortures.[75]

It suggests much about the role of the monk in late Roman society that this strategy reemerges in the depiction of the ascetic labors of the monks and their effects on the bodies of those who performed them. Hilarion's ascetic labors brought upon him, Jerome tells us, a "spread of scabby, desiccated mange" that covered his shriveled body.[76] Elsewhere, we are treated to very vivid depictions of the ulcerated and rotted flesh of the feet of Daniel the Stylite and the thighs and knees of the younger Symeon the Stylite, for example, and even to a description of the worms that had infested Daniel's tortured flesh.[77] John of Ephesus shows us the bloody footprints left behind as the Syrian wanderer Mare stumbled frostbitten through the snow and the pus that dripped from the coarse and soil-blackened skin of Thomas the Armenian's own legs and feet: "His feet were like charred columns, being thick and black, until after ten years they used to discharge a large quantity of matter, and were as if they were not his, since he was smitten with severe ulcers, and would not concern himself even to wash off that discharge, and to apply a poultice."[78] In other texts, we are shown in gory detail the palm-leaf cords that worked their way into the flesh of both Symeon the elder and Symeon the younger.[79] And as the figure of the monk and the figure of the martyr blended back into one another as the Christological controversies of the post-Constantinian world raged, we see the eyeball of the monk Samuel of Kalamun knocked out by a lead-weighted leather thong swung at him by a Chalcedonian imperial Roman official, and we see its burst remains hang by its stalk against his cheek.[80]

Like the martyrs, it was the numinous power of God that allowed the monks to endure such agonies and injuries. Accordingly, such ascetics should be read as figures through whom the primordial moments of *irruption* we encountered in Chapter 2 associated with the trials and triumphs of the martyrs remained present in the world and with it perpetual access to the defining truths around which late antique Christian communities were organized. Thus the monks, as doubles for the martyrs, provided constant resources for self-fashioning. Their unending proximity to the eternal and transcendent truths that animated the martyrs made of them stable, unchanging sources for navigating the shifting and perilous semiotic world in which late Roman Christians found themselves. All of this made monks ideal figures for the discernment, policing, and enforcement of communal boundaries.

Of Monks and Monsters

This was, of course, a job to be carried out by a figure at home in the liminal spaces of the late Roman imaginary. Indeed, as they existed in the minds of their contemporaries, monks were themselves thoroughly marginal figures, ever wedged between the opposed binaries with which the Romans had always ordered their world. As the Life of the younger Symeon the Stylite made explicit, for example, ascetics were to be viewed as figures who patrolled the boundary between heaven and earth,[81] while in terms of the mental geography of the later Roman world, ascetics frequently situated themselves or were imagined by contemporaries and later Christians to have situated themselves between the settled lands of civilization and the desert wilds.[82] Whether in desert retreats or in the towns and cities of the empire, they were always out of place, always alien to their surroundings.[83] They caused dread and apprehension among the city-dwelling humans they encountered, and they even made the monsters who inhabited the desert wastes uneasy.[84]

Ascetics frequently made their homes in the taboo spaces of civilized men, the demon-infested necropoleis or abandoned temples on the edges of cities and towns, and as we have seen, monks even united life and death within their own bodies.[85] Symeon the younger and Daniel the Stylite, for example, were literally both dead and alive, their souls miraculously continuing to inhabit bodies even as they rotted and decomposed.[86] The Syrian monk Abbi described himself simply as a "dead man."[87] Some ascetics, notably the "harlot" or "transvestite" saints Pelagia and Mary of Egypt, came to embody both maleness and femaleness even as they also embodied worldly pleasure and ascetic rigor, the sins of the flesh and purity of soul.[88] Holy fools like Symeon of Edessa were also miraculous moral hybrids, embodying both the virtue they secretly commanded and the decadence they secretly forbade but publicly performed. Meanwhile, as David Brakke has noted, the black-skinned superstar monk Moses the Ethiopian may be usefully read against the ubiquitous "Ethiopian demons" of late ancient hagiography as an embodiment of the opposites that were joined so imperfectly but so powerfully in the figure of the monk.[89]

Moreover, despite their depiction in hagiographical literature as keen discerners of orthodoxy, James Goehring has demonstrated that in fact Christian ascetics frequently cared little for the specifics of Christological and theological doctrine and that monastic communities could and did contain ascetics of opposed doctrinal views. Indeed, it is clear even from hagiographical sources that monks were also viewed suspiciously as potential bearers of heresy. We also know that some and perhaps many Egyptian monks were well familiar with magical rites and rituals and that such monasteries as that of Epiphanius at Thebes contained, in addition to strict theological tracts, recipes for spells to be cast employing bits of mummies to be used with certain "'names of power' and similar utterances juxtaposed with the Persons of the Trinity." Other magical recipes found at the monastery also call for the use of bat's blood and waxen figures.[90] Monks were alternately extolled by Christians as paragons of virtue and denounced as committers of crimes and slaves to vice, as the epitome of philosophical reason and as bearers of barbarian unreason.[91] Indeed, Michael Gaddis has described succinctly the dread and loathing ascetics provoked in late Roman Christians even as they became objects of reverence and indeed points of enduring surety in an uncertain and deceptive world.[92] In the minds of these contemporaries, ascetics incorporated all that lay on either side of the boundaries it was their function to locate, impose, and defend.

In this way monks were akin to monsters as Michel Foucault defined them long ago, creatures that should not exist but do.[93] As the work of Jeffrey Jerome Cohen suggests, such "monstrous" figures are frequently to be found patrolling crucial sites of demarcation and boundaries, particularly those that give shape to the social and cultural life of the society that produces them. Such monsters impossibly embody all of the oppositions to which they give rise and between which they impose a boundary.

Monsters appear in moments of "category crisis" as a wholly alien third-option supplement to those native to binary hermeneutic systems, confounding familiar categories of the possible or knowable, particularly as regards problems of identity.[94] Monstrous figures tend to abide on the edges of the knowable or the familiar and serve as a warning, a *monstrum*, against moving beyond those edges.[95] They can serve this function in part because they are, in their unnerving similarity/alterity, an embodiment of all that is at stake with regard to the observance of boundaries. One can locate in them that which is precious on this side of the boundary in question and that which is loathsome and dreadful—abject in Kristeva's sense—on the other side of the boundary.[96] It is this blending of the familiar and the frisson-inducing awful that gives the monster its unique charge and that allows it to perform its crucial function of marking and patrolling divisions and frontiers.[97] As Foucault put it,

> The notion of the monster is essentially a juridical notion—juridical, of course, in the large sense of the term, because that which defines the monster is the fact that he is, in his very existence and in his form, not only a violation of the laws of society, but also a violation of the laws of nature. He is, in a double register, a violation of the laws of existence itself . . . the monster appears as a phenomenon at once extreme and extremely rare. He is the limit, he is the point of turning away from the law, and he is, at the same time, the exception that can only be found in cases that are particularly extreme. Let us say that the monster is that which combines the impossible and the forbidden.[98]

The monk, as imagined in later Roman society, was an especially potent figure precisely because of his capacity to subvert the laws of society and the laws of nature; the laws of society he violated not only in the strict sense of this term, although as Peter Brown and others have noted, this too was certainly the case, but also all of Roman society's less formal but no less binding strictures, those of public comportment, familial duty, social obligation and status performance, among others.[99] The laws of nature he violated by his celibacy, his active or passive abuse of his body and his penchant for miraculously suspending the rules of the physical world. Because of his capacity for violation of society's laws, the monk could intercede with the powerful of the world and speak brazenly to them, correct wayward Christians without worry of giving offense or earning enmity, set himself apart from the day-to-day worries of the world, and, as we have seen, act violently in contravention of Roman law in order to police communal boundaries.[100]

Indeed, violence is immanent in all that makes of the monk a privileged entity in his world: violence against normative social behavior, violence against normative legal strictures, violence against the normative ways of being in one's body. Much the same may be said of the martyr, who by his actions subverted Roman juridical discourse and violated the most basic rules of the body. It was the immanent violence of the transgression of the ordering possibilities of the later Roman world that imbued the spectacle of the martyr's passion with the glow of the numinous.

It should not surprise us, then, that the monk, like the martyr, should have been viewed by his contemporaries with a mix of awe, dread, and reverence—these are, as Rudolph Otto argued long ago, typical reactions to the perceived presence of the numinous, the uncanny presence of the divine in human experience.[101] Monks were familiar presences who made possible the vital presence of the wholly other within the world of human experience. Because of their monstrous capacity to conjoin familiarity/alterity in their person, monks became points in which the primordial (but otherwise absent) past and the shifting and confusing (but ready-to-hand and compelling) present also touched. Hence, for Christian communities and individuals struggling with the question of what it meant to be a Christian or the problem of the kinds of behaviors and qualities that marked one as an authentic member of the one true community of God upon the earth, the monk as monster, abiding on the frontier between here and there, now and then, they and we, became an invaluable resource for fashioning one's self and knowing one's own.

Christian ascetics of the late Roman world did not only perform this function as exemplars, however. Rather, as we shall see, it was frequently the role of Christian monks to demonstrate precisely where the boundaries of true Christianness were. This was a role in which the monks' penchant for violence would frequently play a decisive role.

"Something Alien and Barbarous"

One sixth-century Syrian monk made something of a career of violently intervening in situations in which communal boundaries had become dangerously blurred. John of Ephesus tells this monk's story as part of his *Lives of the Eastern Saints*.[102] His name was Sergius, the "zealous" disciple of another, older ascetic named Simeon, who was himself a hermit. When Chalcedonian imperial officials came to the town in which Sergius had his cell, they tried to reason with him about the "orthodox" creed. They spoke to him "softly and gently," praising the bishop who was head of Sergius's community while talking up the Chalcedonian creed, urging Sergius, "there is nothing wrong, but agree and accept." Given the fact that this bit of cajoling on the part of the Roman officials comes amid descriptions of the cruelties to which the "real Christians" of Syria were subjected for refusing to communicate with the "heretics," the structure of this narrative has much in common with the martyr narratives we have encountered in previous chapters. Predictably, Sergius rebukes the officials, and they turn him out of his cell and out of the town. Sergius promises that they have not heard the last of the matter.

Soon thereafter, Sergius makes good on his promise. It seems that it was local practice for both Chalcedonian and non-Chalcedonian Christians to attend services together. "The whole city was there . . . listening to the preacher (because those who were orthodox also used to be present in the congregation during the hearing of the service and the lessons of the preacher, only without communicating). Then suddenly there appeared at the door a vision, something alien and barbarous (*nukrāyā w-barbabrāyā meddem*); and everyone was startled when they saw a form that was not their own (*skemā d-law dilhūm*), an anchorite coming in, clad in a patchwork of rags made of sackcloth, and carrying his cross on his shoulder."[103]

Sergius made his way silently to the chancel, the congregation watching in stunned silence and awaiting some kind of sermon from him. Instead, "on reaching the third step, where the preacher was standing, [Sergius] flung out his hand and seized him by the neck and grasped him tightly." Sergius rebuked the preacher and then "he swung his hand around and gave him a buffet, and distorted his mouth; and he seized him and shook him down. And [Sergius] himself sprang up and stood in his place at the top of the chancel-steps and said, 'Cursed are the renegades, cursed are the persecutors, cursed is the synod of Chalcedon, and whoever assents to it. Cursed is every soul that receives the oblation from you and assents to your opinion unless he repents.'"[104]

Immediately where there had been one congregation there were immediately two communities, incensed at one another, "some threatening, some expressing indignation, some crying, 'This man is a teacher of error, let him be arrested,' and some crying, 'Let no man lay hands upon him and die'".[105] With the community in a riotous uproar, the local officials politely asked to be allowed a private interview with the monk in the vestry. Once there, they beat him savagely and bound him. Then they sent him to a monastery in Armenia in which Chalcedonian monks tortured their rivals. Sergius soon escaped, however, jumping out of a third-story window to continue his career.[106]

This story combines several elements we have traced through the previous chapters in an intriguing manner. The efforts of Roman imperial officials to introduce the Chalcedonian creed to the Christian communities of Syria and the acts of coercion that accompanied these efforts are interpreted in accordance with the much older narratives of persecution and resistance we encountered repeatedly in Chapters 2 and 3. Just before Sergius leaves to attack the rival cleric, for example, an older ascetic warns him to look after his own safety. Sergius is not dissuaded, but says, "I for my part am prepared for suffering, and I will contend until death with the renegades who malign God, and fire will not frighten me, nor sword, nor scourgings, nor rakes," thus rehearsing a litany of the weapons commonly deployed against martyrs.[107]

Sergius's violence against the rival cleric is accordingly to be read through the prism of narratives of persecution and resistance. More interesting, however, is the scene in which that violence takes place; it is in the presence of the entire (non-Chalcedonian) Christian community, gathered, apparently quite willingly, with the "heretics" of their city to hear the Chalcedonian cleric preach. The scene, as John of Ephesus describes it, is rather irenic. Suddenly, however, a bizarre and rather frightening figure intrudes upon this scene, and through an act of exemplary violence makes immediately manifest the rightful boundaries between the one true community of God and the "heretical" others amongst whom they were apparently rather content to worship their God.

In so doing, Sergius has interceded and interrupted this perilous commingling of communities. We need not assume that the members of these two communities then segregated themselves from one another, or that the town was then wracked with intercommunal rioting. Rather, through Sergius's declaration and violent iteration of the proper communal boundary, awareness of that boundary and whatever it might mean for members of each community was awakened or simply preserved, and individuals from either side of that boundary might carry on the daily business of transgressing it at will.

The Church historian Socrates, for example, included in his account of the destruction of the Serapeion information that he, a Christian who wrote glowingly of ascetics and even the Alexandrian bishop Theophilus, who was responsible for the Serapeion's destruction, gathered from two of his pagan teachers, one of whom revealed that he had killed Christians during the rioting that went before the temple's fall.[108] If we accept a model of intercommunal violence that holds that members of communities set violently at odds must thereafter view members of rival communities with fear or enmity, this exchange between Christian student and militant pagan teacher should never have taken place, nor should a self-consciously Christian historian include the account of a militant pagan in his grand history of the rise of the Christian Roman empire.

Nor should we imagine that such interventions always succeeded in driving a wedge between perilously commingled communities, as another episode from the Life of Severus the zealot suggests. At the outset of his ascetic career, Severus found himself in a local war against the Jewish population of the village in which he built his cell. "Because there were many Jews in that village, and they went about with great freedom (*parrhesia*), he carried on a continuous contest against them," the text explains, "and every day he used to contend against them as with slayers of God, being fervent in the love of his Lord, and gnashing his teeth, and saying: 'These crucifiers of the Son of God should not be allowed to live at all"; and he used to upbraid Christians who had dealings with them in the way of taking and giving."[109]

When Sergius led a band of his followers to burn the synagogue of the Jews, however, the local Christian community turned on him. That the local Christians would support the Jews John attributes to their desire for the gold of the Jews, suggesting that it was simple greed that prompted local Christians to oppose intercommunal violence, an accusation we will encounter again. Once the synagogue was destroyed, however, Sergius and his band quickly replaced it with a martyr's chapel, apparently checkmating any effort to rebuild the synagogue on that spot. The Jews, in response, burned the cells of Sergius and his followers who, in their turn, burned the synagogue the Jews were rebuilding on another site.[110]

Although he did not succeed in setting the Jewish and Christian communities against one another, Sergius's action and the response it demanded made an issue of communal identity in a manner that could not be ignored. Just as Chrysostom had urged his own parishioners to do, Sergius had scolded Christians who had dealings with the Jews before he burned down the synagogue. The issue was the freedom with which Jews moved in a Christian community, and, clearly, the freedom with which Christians of that community interacted with their Jewish neighbors. While the Christians of the area may have been put off by Sergius's behavior, just as, for example, pagan intellectuals had been appalled by the emperor Julian's ban on Christians teaching the classics, the issue of identity had been raised in a manner whose memory would remain long after the local synagogue had been rebuilt.

And Sergius went still further. By building a martyr chapel on the site of the synagogue, Sergius drew yet another line: in order to rebuild on the original site of the synagogue, local Christian authorities would have to authorize the destruction of a structure holy to Christians. Having violently made local Christians and Jews aware of the proper communal boundaries separating them, he now dared the Christians to step across that line. As is clear from John's narrative, the Christians declined to do so.

"Tell Me, My Sons, Are You Christians or Jews?"

Sometime in the sixth century, another of the distant descendants of the monks Libanius described in his oration in defense of Syria's temples emerged from the mountain wilds, where he abided "like an animal" (*badmutā d-hayyutā*), and entered a tiny and isolated town and "went among humans" or "into the dwelling place of humans."[111] Within that settlement, each dwelling was situated miles from the nearest neighbor. The monk, although he himself spent most of each year wandering the wilds of the Syrian mountains, wondered at the isolation of this village. When he asked the villagers about their style of life, they explained that they simply lived as their fathers had.[112]

The condition of the small community grew more unsettling for the ascetic visitor when he inquired about the religious life of its members. When he asked the men of the area how they were able to meet to hear the scriptures read and take communion, they laughed at him and asked what benefit the taking of communion would be to them. John of Ephesus, in whose collection of ascetic biographies the story occurs, recorded the reaction of the ascetic, one Simeon the Mountaineer: "When the blessed man heard these words, his bones shook from his fright and his tears gushed out, and he said to them: 'Tell me, my sons, are you Christians or Jews (*atton krestyānē aw yudāyē*)?'"[113] The men insisted that they were Christians and took umbrage at the suggestion that they might be Jews. Simeon said, "And, if you are Christians, how is it that you have mocked at God . . . how is it that you were not frightened to perform with your tongues the acts of pagans and Jews, when you say that you are Christians?" The men confessed that they had never seen the gospels or had communion and that they were ignorant of all of these things because "we live on these mountains like animals."[114]

Simeon soon understands that these men are indeed "like animals (*ayk d-huyyutē*)" and, in fact, worse than pagans. "What pagan is there, or what worshipers of creation, who for so long a period of time would neglect to pay honor to the object of his worship, and would not always worship that which is reckoned by him as God?" he asks. "These men neither worship God like Christians, nor honor something else like pagans; and they are apostates against the one and against the other."[115] At another village "on the same frontier" he found a church that had fallen into disuse, and its Christian inhabitants equally ignorant of Christian dogma and praxis. Gradually, Simeon induced them to "meet together every first day of the week, keeping themselves from blasphemy and from fornication, and from murder." Those guilty of grave crimes were to be separated from the reborn Christian community, "and they were set apart as Pagans and Jews."[116]

Simeon thereafter continued hunting down errant Christians in the region, "converting them afresh, as if from paganism, and thus he used to gather them all together like wild animals."[117] After a time he began secretly to learn which of his parishioners had children. Finally, promising the children presents, he coaxed them into the temple of his god, where a confederate was waiting with a razor. He then closed the doors and divided the ninety children into two groups, sending the larger of the two groups into another room so they would not see what was to happen to the thirty he had chosen. He then took the thirty boys and girls to the altar and consecrated them to his god, tonsuring them. The distress of the children's parents upon discovering what Simeon had done is quite vivid in the text: "When the news arrived, the women assembled with lamentations, crying, 'Alas, what has taken place and what has befallen us?'" The old man simply laughed at them, however, and when two sets of parents insisted upon taking their children back, the old man pronounced a death sentence on their children.[118]

When the children died, their parents crept back to the old man in terror and begged his forgiveness. Thereafter, "if the old man wished to tonsure anyone, there was none who presumed to speak; and thenceforth whoever pleased him he would mark and take away without impediment." Meanwhile, Simeon instructed his small community in proper Christian praxis and dogma, "and they trembled to commit any breach of order, lest the old man should hear it and separate them from the fellowship of men, or that he should curse them." We are told that the children Simeon stole from their parents grew up to honor him, "and he was a law and a judge of that country, and every matter that was in need of reform was referred to him."[119]

We should note here that there is from the beginning of John of Ephesus's narration of Simeon's acts an apparent affinity drawn between Simeon and the villagers he encounters—he and they are both "animal-like." Indeed, whereas over time the animal-like qualities of the villagers are dispelled by Simeon's instruction in proper Christian belief and praxis, Simeon himself remains "like a beast" throughout the story or, more exactly, he remains as a disturbing amalgam of human and animal qualities. It would seem that it is Simeon's capacity to embody that which he would dispel from this Christian community that allows him to perform this crucial step in the fashioning of a Christian community. This a point to which we will return later in this chapter.

In this anonymous mountain town, then, Simeon the Mountaineer had performed what we frequently encounter as one of the essential roles of the Christian ascetic in late Roman society: encountering a "Christian" community whose confessional identity is from his point of view ambiguous and disordered, Simeon imposes upon that community a clearly articulated and rigorously bounded sense of its own Christian identity, this predicated upon and performed through strictly prescribed and enforced behavioral norms. As he emerges in this and countless other late Roman texts, the figure of the Christian monk is one through whom those qualities, practices and exclusions that mark any individual as a "real Christian" become readily clear.[120] He is, moreover, a figure whose function it is to declare and defend the boundaries that enclose the one community of God upon the earth.

But he is also a figure whose work is inflected with a kind of terrifying violence. Indeed, although it is a story told to celebrate the godly virtue of Simeon, it is nevertheless a deeply unsettling tale. Although it is true that the sensibilities of reading audiences change over time and across cultural distance, we need only read John Chrysostom's accounts of the horror of Antioch's Christians at the notion of their own children joining monastic orders, to see that "losing" one's children to the monastic life was indeed a traumatic prospect for Syrians of the late Roman world.[121] But this is not the truly frightening part of the story of Simeon and the mountain peasants he took as his flock. Instead, the really unnerving aspect of this story is something best discerned through comparison with another tale of ascetic zeal set in a rural hamlet, this one in upper Egypt.

In that Egyptian village, it was said, Christian children were lured into a certain pagan temple with the promise of presents of bread and food. They were then trapped, secluded, and butchered. Their blood was poured out at the altar of the god of that temple, and their intestines were made into harp strings. Their bodies were then burned, and the ashes were used, together with music played on the harps strung with the children's gut, to uncover hidden treasure. Local authorities allowed this to continue "since all the leaders of the district were money lovers." But when this was discovered by local Christian ascetics, we are told, the village was purged of pagans, the priest of the temple burned alive. Christians then took up residence in the houses of the pagans cleansed from the village. This is the story of the ascetic Macarius of Tkōw and his cleansing of one Egyptian village.[122]

In the story of Macarius and his campaign of what we might term "confessional cleansing" of this anonymous Egyptian village, we encounter another aspect of the figure of the late Roman ascetic warrior for the faith, this one kindred with those noted above: Macarius discovers a monstrous practice in which Christians, through their unknowing, innocent trust of outsiders, and more specifically their willingness to transgress their own communal boundaries and enter the holy space of another community, are literally consumed by a foreign community. In discerning this situation and interceding with violence, he ends the intermingling of pagan and Christian, this symbolized by the performance of pagan ceremony and magic by means of the bodies of the slain Christian children, and purges the village of the contagion of paganism by the murder of the priest and the exodus or conversion of the pagan population.

What is puzzling about these texts, however, is not the affinities between Simeon and Macarius, but those between Simeon and the pagan priest. In the story of Macarius's cleansing of the village, the pagans of the Egyptian countryside are transformed into monstrous child-killers, apparently to justify the violences committed against them by Macarius and his band. In the story of the monk's tonsuring of the Syrian children, however, a number of the chilling components from the other story seem to peek out from behind the formal elements of the narrative: A stranger—described at the outset of his story as "like an animal (*ba-dmutā d-ḥayyutā*)"—comes into a tiny mountain settlement from outside and gains the trust of the community.[123] Then he, like the pagan priest incinerated by Macarius and his band, uses that trust to coax local Christian children away from their parents with the promise of gifts. Once he has them in his power, he closes himself within the church with the children and, with a razor, transforms their bodies in order that they might now serve his god. As he does so, the children themselves can only cry or stand in frightened silence.

All of this hints at a deep and disturbing affinity between the figure of Simeon, whom we are repeatedly reminded we ought to admire in the text that describes his actions, and that of the monstrous pagan priest, who is evoked to demonstrate the dangers of paganism, and particularly paganism that entices Christians into its sphere. This affinity may be traced to the role that each of these figures is assigned to play in the literature in which it appears: they mark a perilous frontier. The pagan priest and the Christian monk alike bring danger and doom to Christians (signaled in each text by the sign of dead Christian children) who do not recognize him for what he is.[124] Each is a figure tinged with power and dread, but the pagan priest is a rather flat and one-dimensional figure while the monk, whether configured as the child-stealing Simeon or the avenging Macarius, is inflected also with piety, grace, and numinous power. Accordingly, if the pagan priest is a human that commits terrifying acts against Christian children, the monk emerges in the literature of the late Roman world as a figure that incorporates both a penchant for chilling savagery and world-saving loving-kindness. In this sense, it is the monk, rather than the pagan priest, who meets the eye of the reader as most truly monstrous.

In another text recalling the Christological conflicts of the Syrian east in the time of Justinian, we find another sort of domesticated monster called forth from a local monastery and deployed by pro-Chalcedonian imperial forces against the "orthodox" community of Syria. In his campaign of terror against the anti-Chalcedonian communities around Amida, the pro-Chalcedonian bishop Abraham b. Kayli is said by one Syrian chronicler to have dispatched the lepers resident in a monastery outside the city to purge his community of "heretics" just as Macarius and his band had purged one Egyptian village of its hapless pagan population. Like Macarius and his band, Bar Kayli burned a rival priest alive, and then dispersed his monastic monsters through the local community to purge it of unbelief.

Alongside "shaven monks, called there 'troops' [sent] to stay in the houses of the believers . . . [who] did what the barbarians would never recognize at all (as legitimate)" and "barbarian forces themselves," Bar Kayli "took a band (of lepers) as many as they were in a monastery of lepers located outside the city, called 'Mār Romanus.' He sent them and let them dwell in the house of a believer. The latter [was] compelled to leave his house and to flee."[125] The lepers, "a more hideous sight than the dead placed in the grave," would spread pus and their diseased blood throughout the believer's house, and "roll in their beds, filling them with stinking pus and turning them abhorrent. They even put on their beautiful [garments], plundering and taking over whatever pleased them. And there was no one to re[strain] and stop them."[126]

After this, the owners of the houses were of course unable to return to them, and were purged from their former community. The author of the chronicle makes the monstrousness of the lepers clear, describing in almost obsessive detail their "hideous appearance, full of terror . . . their disfigured faces and their body, wholly putrid and rotten, producing an abominable stink . . . hands . . . putrid and dripping blood and pus."[127]

If we ask how this episode might have looked from the pro-Chalcedonian side of the boundary imposed and enforced by the lepers, we may read the figure of the leper as that abject sign which embodies the loathsome alterity that resides on the further side of the boundary he now institutes and protects. His monstrous contagion mirrors the monstrous contagion of heresy, and it is precisely his loathsome alterity that makes him capable of rooting out the loathsome alterity he displaces.[128] That the lepers put on the clothes of those whose houses they entered and befouled seems significant in this regard; how must it feel to see a monster put on one's clothes? How again must it feel to witness a monster wearing the garments of one's neighbor?

From the point of view of the author of the chronicle itself, the leper is a more vivid double for the "shaven monks" who terrorize the "orthodox" community of Syria, whose excesses are worse even than what one would expect from barbarians. Like such ascetic superstars as Daniel the Stylite and Symeon the Stylite the Younger, the leper carries both death and life within his putrid and rotting skin. Lepers, like monks, are frequently depicted in Byzantine art as figures enclosed in long, black robes. That monks and lepers, both normally secluded in monasteries, are assigned the same task here—that is to go forth and enforce divisions between Christian communities—says as much about the perceived role of the monk within his society as it does about the leper.

That the notion of contagion and death terrifyingly joined to life could take the monk as its sign seems suggested from another passage in the same Syrian chronicle. During a time of plague, people began to believe that plague came in the form of figures attired in monastic garments. Like those Christians who ran from the horrifying sight of the lepers, local Christians now fled at the approach of monks:

> Therefore, whenever a monk or a cleric appeared, people used to howl at him and run away, thinking that he was himself the death that destroyed him. Thus the erroneous belief that death came in the form of the tonsured ones spread. It occurred mainly among the simple and common people of the city, to the point that it became difficult for a monk to be seen on the street. When they saw one, they would fall over each other in flight, pushing and shouting, "Why is he coming here? We belong to the mother of God, we belong to such and such a martyr, we belong to such and such an apostle!" Thus even after that time and until the end of two years, this erroneous belief remained among a few.[129]

If the monk and the leper are presented in the above texts as kindred monsters, (barely) domesticated in order to patrol crucial communal boundaries, they were not alone in the late Roman imaginary. Among the Christian martyrs (themselves monstrous in their capacity to resist all of the ordering truths of their world for the purpose of announcing a still higher one) we encounter monsters of classical contours. Saint Christopher, for example, a dog-headed former cannibal from the geographical margins of the world, was said to have adopted Christianity and stood before the imperial authority of the Romans in valiant defense of his faith:

> Again the most wicked king ordered that Christopher be brought to him, and he said to him, "Reprobus, why have you desired such doctrine? Why have you displayed such great madness? So now, compromise while you are away from the tortures, and offer sacrifice to the great gods. But if you do not, by the great gods I will make an evil end of you." However, Christ's martyr replied, "Inventor of every wickedness, disciple of the devil, partner in eternal damnation, you have already been told that I neither compromise with, nor sacrifice to, those who are called gods by you. I hold firm to the God who made me."[130]

The Ethiopic Martyrdom of Saint Mercurius tells the tale of two dog-headed cannibals who were captured in hunters' nets. "Their heads were horrible," the texts tells us, "and the hair thereof was like unto the manes of horses, and their teeth were like unto the teeth of lions, their eyes were like fire, their hands and feet were like a rod of iron, and nails were like unto the claws of lions."[131] After devouring one of the hunters, they spare his son, who eventually leads them to civilization, tames them with the taste of figs, wine, and bread, and brings about their conversion to Christianity. When they are dispatched with some fellow Christians as soldiers, they defend their fellow Christians from lions and other wild beasts. Once again we find that the domesticated monster is uniquely capable of defending from the very alterity he embodies.[132]

Ammianus Marcellinus knew this well. In his classicizing history of the events of the fourth century, he recalled another showdown between domesticated monster and menacing Other at one of the most precious boundaries of the Roman world, the walls of the imperial capital Constantinople. Following the disaster at Adrianople, at which the emperor Valens was killed and the Roman army obliterated, the Gothic army marched against the heart of the Roman world. Waiting for them there were Arab tribesmen, Roman allies to be sure, but a nevertheless frightening and alien presence whose capacity to defend the Roman world resided in their monstrous alterity. "The contest was long and obstinate, and both sides separated on equal terms," Ammianus wrote. "But the Oriental troop had the advantage from a strange event, never witnessed before. For one of their number, a man with long hair and naked except for a loin cloth, uttering hoarse and dismal cries, with drawn dagger, rushed into the thick of the Gothic Army, and after killing a man applied his lips to the throat and sucked the blood that poured out. The barbarians, terrified by this strange and monstrous sight (*quo monstroso miraculo*), after that did not show their usual self confidence."[133]

In the imaginary of late Roman Christians and pagans alike, the monk emerged repeatedly as yet another of these domesticated monsters. The troublesome implications of this relationship come to the fore in unexpected places. Daniel Caner has recently explored very profitably the interconnection of urban elites and their ascetic clients. The ascetics brought to their patrons a touch of the numinous, but they also caused no little unease in the cities in which they gathered. The key to the ability of Christian ascetics to play their privileged roles in the social and religious life of the later Roman world was their profound alterity. It was this privileged difference that the erudite fifth-century ascetic Nilus of Ancyra worried his town-dwelling ascetic contemporaries were eroding and undermining with their incessant begging and hustling on the streets of Ancyra. He advised his fellow monks to retreat to the caves and mountains where, in the past, their monastic forebears had lived the lives of "real monks." As it was, "those who once taught self-restraint are now driven out as corruptors of cities, as if they were cursed with leprosy. A person might put more trust in brigands or burglars than in those who adopt the monastic life, reckoning it easier to guard against open mischief than against credentials that have been contrived for ambush."[134]

If this was indeed the way in which Nilus's Christian contemporaries viewed the bands of monks moving through their cities, they will have shared in many respects the pagan views of ascetic bands that rolled across the countryside of Antioch decades before. It was the foreignness of Syria's ascetics that Libanius had emphasized as he bemoaned their insidious effects upon the ordering cultural traditions of Roman society, and like Nilus's Christian contemporaries, he seems to have imagined the monks as something akin to brigands and bandits, stealing out of the caves and shadowy recesses of the Syrian hills to plunder and destroy.[135]

Nilus's pagan contemporary Eunapius thought the monks more monstrous still, like beings that seemed to be men but who were in fact bestial and indeed "swinish." He likened one of their more violent leaders, the Alexandrian bishop Theophilus, to Eurymedon, "who ruled over the overweening

Giants."[136] It was the violent disorder of the Giants, their bid to overthrow the gods, the destruction they wrought through their frenzy and their monstrous appearance that classically educated late Roman men and women imagined when they thought of the Giants.[137]

More than a century after Eunapius wrote, a detachment of Roman soldiers sent to enforce Chalcedonian orthodoxy arrived in the environs of Amida, on the upper Tigris River, where they were confronted by an army of monks, marshaled in ranks before them on the field. It is perhaps unsurprising that they did not see men arrayed against them. "When the Roman army went in and saw the extended rows (of monks) standing one after another . . . God cast fear over them and they appeared to them as giants. They departed and started to say to each other: 'Let us avoid fighting with these for if one of them takes a staff he will wound twenty of us!'"[138]

Later, however, the Roman troops returned, "equipped as for combat" to look for the monkish army. It had vanished. In time, however, another monkish army would appear in Syria, and it would not melt away before the force of Roman arms. Rather, it would make manifest new prophetic truths in the territories it would call *bilād al-Shām*.

CHAPTER FIVE

"Horsemen by Day and Monks by Night": Narrative and Community in Islamic Late Antiquity

DURING THE CENTURY or so after the *hijra* OF 622 C.E.,[1] monotheistic Arab armies conquered the Syrian, Egyptian, and North African territories of the Roman Empire, and completely overran the Persian Sasanian Empire in Mesopotamia. Later, the Visigothic kingdom of Iberia was destroyed and its territories absorbed into the new Arab commonwealth. The coming of these armed Arab monotheists to the lands outside of Arabia was preceded by the advent of an Arab prophet of the God of Abraham, although the connection between these two events is anything but clear.[2] What *is* clear, however, is that the conquests left in their wake not only a landscape dotted with émigré Arab monotheist settlements but also an often tenuously united confessional community knit together from many smaller social and political groups. It was a community that seems to have felt strongly the imperative to define itself and that faced the immediate need to explain to its own members and to its neighbors how and why the landscape of the present world had come to change so rapidly. This process of explanation took place within the context of a growing imperial self-awareness on the part of Arab Muslims, as well as during a period of profound cultural fluidity and fecundity that manifested itself notably in the hermeneutic resources at the disposal of those who now imagined and interpreted a Muslim past and in so doing articulated the earliest "narratives of Islamic origins."

While it is tempting to understand the advent of Islam within "the world of late antiquity" as a cataclysmic break with the classical and late classical past, to do so is in many ways to radically misinterpret the social, political, and cultural processes that accompanied Islam's emergence and to ignore the character of the early Islamic *umma* or community as it was understood by its own members. Indeed, although a new revelation had given birth to a new community, that community went about the complex process of inventing itself as a cultural, social, and political entity side by side with the very communities whose struggles for self-definition we have traced through the preceding pages. Moreover, this process of Muslim self-definition was clearly carried on in intimate dialogue with other late ancient confessional communities. The coming chapters will repeatedly return to the traces this process left upon the Muslim community's formative narratives, the anxieties these traces provoked and the strategies with which these anxieties were eased, if never wholly relieved.

Indeed, in what follows, the dangerously charged affinities between members of self-consciously distinct communities that we have repeatedly encountered in the preceding chapters and the corresponding desire of some members of those communities to impose delimiting boundaries will recur as one of the defining social and political motifs in the history of the late ancient Muslim *umma*. Indicative of the complexity of the world in which these affinities manifested themselves, however, is the fact that the maintenance of communal boundaries was often undertaken by members of the early Muslim *umma* with discursive and narratological resources that themselves reflected the very cultural affinities they were meant to contain, bound, and, if possible, efface. One result of this, as we shall see in this chapter, was that the very signs, symbols, and narrative forms that were deployed by Muslim intellectuals to narrate the emergence of a self-consciously distinct community of God in fact had the effect of binding succeeding generations of Muslims to the other communities of late antiquity and their descendents via a shared semiotic vocabulary, shared moral ideals, and shared strategies of communal self-fashioning. Notable among these was the role of militant forms of piety in the programs of communal self-definition undertaken by Christian and Muslim communities alike. Key to this common mode of crafting communal selves was a closely kindred semiotic and narrative tradition in accordance with which the Muslim and Christian communities of late antiquity recalled their respective pasts. It is with this tendency that we will begin.

"*Narratives of Islamic Origins*": New Directions

Once the Muslim conquests had begun in 633, shortly after the death of the prophet Muḥammad, they seem to have taken on a momentum all their own. When the momentum of the conquest had slackened after c. 750 C.E., however, the Arab communities newly settled in the conquered territories of Syria and Mesopotamia found that they had a lot of explaining to do.[3]

First was the need to explain how the events of the conquest era had happened and to understand them for what they had become, the basis of a new political community and the foundation for a vast empire. Second was the need to explain the conquests as a consequence of Muḥammad's prophecy and thus the basis for a new monotheistic faith community, this despite the fact that if the Prophet foresaw the conquests, he never said so. These things had to be explained within the "community of believers" and to those who stood beyond its evolving boundaries. It was in explaining these things that one late antique faith community among many others became the Muslim polity or *umma*.[4]

The stories the Arabs told in these years about the events and personalities of the *futūḥ* period (literally the "opening" of the conquered lands) have come down to us in the works of the great compilers and early historians, those of al-Ṭabarī, Ibn Aʿtham, al-Azdī, and others. They are collected as short narrative segments called *akhbār* (sing. *khabar*), and incorporated into larger, hybrid compositions centered upon battle accounts rendered in what seems to be a very traditional Arabic style. As they appear in these larger compositions, however, these *akhbār* are set in juxtaposition to narratives in which ascetic, pious Muslim warriors confront and best proud and powerful representatives of Roman and Persian imperial might. The linkage of these two types of narrative works to contextualize the events of the conquest period within an evolving Muslim metanarrative.

It has been frequently suggested that these early Muslim historical narratives are unlike any other of the ancient or medieval world and that they thus represent a uniquely Muslim mode of historiography. In one sense, this it true. Structurally, they bear little in common with the works of the classicizing historians of the late antique world or with those of the chronographers and Church historians who succeeded them.[5] And yet these were not the sorts of texts with which the local communities of Syria, Egypt, and Mesopotamia reckoned their histories by the first/seventh century. Instead, the histories of local communities flowed through the remembered deeds of holy personages, monks, and martyrs, wonder workers and zealous defenders of the faith.

When we recognize that the narratives of remembrance which mattered in the late Roman world familiar to members of pre- and postconquest Arab communities were not those of the classicizing historians or Church chroniclers but rather those of hagiographers and pious storytellers, the ways in which the *akhbār* collected by the first Arab historians were fashioned into Muslim communal histories become more comprehensible. The juxtaposition of pious monotheistic topoi with traditional Arab battle narratives one finds in these *akhbār* represents an essentially Muslim mode of historiography only insofar as the category "Muslim" was itself constructed through the elaboration of a set of historical narratives which I want to suggest are best understood as hybrid texts composed in part of semiotic elements held in common among a spectrum of late antique monotheistic faith communities.

In asserting the authenticity of Muḥammad's revelation, for example, several early Muslim narratives depict the Prophet recognized first by Christian monks. In so doing, these narratives deploy a figure, the monk, which had been recognized and acknowledged for more than four centuries in communities of variant confessional alignment as a discerner of truth and godliness to support truth claims crucial to early Muslim programs of communal self-fashioning.[6] By elaborating locally upon a common set of late antique narratives to declare its unique character and destiny, the nascent Muslim community bound itself to a much wider universe of communities whose own histories were conjured from the same spectrum of images, ideas, and claims to exclusive, transcendent truth.[7]

I focus this chapter, then, upon the place of the early Islamic community within the world of late antiquity. In so doing, I hope that I may offer an alternative to the frequent tendency to treat Islam, often by simple omission, as somehow discrete from the world in which it took shape, and as something essentially other from its inception. Despite some recent and very worthy attempts to initiate scholarly study of early Islam within its late antique milieu, synthetic studies of early Islam as an organic part of the late antique cultural and religious *oikoumenê* have been slow to appear.[8] This has been due to a series of factors, prime among them the divergent historiographic traditions of each field, to which certain linguistic obstacles are crucial if subsidiary.

The study of the early history of Islam is and has long been dominated by the problem of the available source material.[9] The earliest sources we have for the advent of Islam date to roughly a century to a century and a half after the events they purport to describe. Moreover, those sources went through a long and largely invisible process of oral transmission and redaction before and after they were first set down in writing.[10] This has made the production of a factual representation of the very early Islamic past exceedingly problematic, whether undertaken by medieval Muslim scholars or the great Western Orientalists of the nineteenth and early twentieth century.[11] The positivist inclinations of the latter frequently prompted them to adopt the strategies and tactics of the former, closely scrutinizing individual reports or traditions (*khabar* or *ḥadīth*) to determine their value as resources for fashioning historical accounts of the early Islamic world "*wie es eigentlich gewesen war*."[12]

The attitudes assumed by later twentieth-century historians regarding the early Arabic literary sources have ranged from guarded optimism to deep skepticism to outright pessimism. In the 1970s and '80s a series of radically skeptical evaluations of the historical worth of all early Muslim texts (including the Qur'ān) ignited a chain of sharp exchanges concerning the possibility of factual representations of the early Islamic past based upon those documents. Stubborn debate concerning the validity of the methodologies and conclusions advanced in these works—principally those of John Wansbrough, Patricia Crone, and Michael Cook—has continued to the present.[13]

Meanwhile, increasingly sophisticated analyses of the rhetorical and discursive forms manifested in early Islamic texts have begun to appear, and with them has come a more profound understanding of the ways in which early Muslims imagined and recalled a specifically Islamic past.[14] This, in turn, has led to new theories regarding the historical process whereby the early community of believers came to understand itself as a single, bounded Muslim community. Especially notable among these has been Fred Donner's seminal *Narratives of Islamic Origins: The Beginnings of Islamic Historical Writing*, which attempts to account for the advent of early Muslim historical texts as a process of communal self-definition undertaken as the early community of believers debated problems of prophecy and dogma internally and with other communities of monotheists.[15]

I wish to join this discussion by reasking a question which frequently recurs in Donner's book—why do such narratives look as they do and not some other way?—but to do so while remaining alert to the character of the communal narratives native to the milieu in which those early Islamic narratives took shape. The aim of this study is not to recover what actually happened during the first centuries after the *hijra* but to illuminate, however slightly, the ways in which Muslims of the first three centuries after the *hijra* drew upon the semiotic *koinê* they shared with the communities around them to cast certain crucial events of the first/seventh-century Arab conquests as episodes within a specifically Muslim narrative.

Borderlands

As the early Muslims began to articulate the narratives with which they would assert the truth claims most central to their communal identity, they did so across a cultural borderland. By the term "borderland," I mean a space in which no one cultural or political force is able to exercise uncontested hegemony and in which one is likely to encounter discursive economies that incorporate (but do not necessarily assimilate) the influences of various cultural traditions and political interests. Borderlands are thus often home to hybrids, entities that combine some or all available influences in distinct, often alarming ways. A hybrid incorporates and embodies the tensions of ungovernable and so irresolvable self-other dichotomies confined in a single entity, be it biological, textual, or economic.[16]

In the eastern lands of the Roman world at the start of the seventh century, decades of war with the Persian empire, constantly shifting front lines, the accelerating alienation brought on by Christological controversy, and the general erosion of centralized Greek-Byzantine cultural influence had left the lands of Syria and Mesopotamia liminal and continuously contested, even when firmly in the grasp of one or the other competing armies.[17] Local economies of power, authority, and prestige developed, and the vivid local, cultural, and confessional particularities so indicative of the late antique world accordingly asserted themselves all the more strongly. With the advent of the Arab armies, another religious, cultural, and political force joined this seething exchange, but the coming of the Arabs did little in the seventh century to establish the sort of cultural hegemony the Romans and Greeks had enjoyed (at least ostensibly) through the preceding centuries.[18]

Long before the advent of the Arab armies the Syro-Mesopotamia steppe was a contested space in which pastoralists and farmers, ascetics and merchants mingled and "were joined by a network of symbioses."[19] In the border regions across which the Persian and Byzantine imperial powers asserted themselves militarily and diplomatically, Zoroastrians, Jews, polytheists, and Christians of various confessional stripes also advanced and contested communal truths touching the nature of the numinous.[20] Even such putative outposts of Roman cultural resistance or political exclusion as the limes forts arrayed along the frontier seem to have functioned most often as points of mingling and coordination between settled and nomadic peoples, Byzantines or Romanized Syrians and Arabs or Nabateans, Christians, Jews, and pagans.[21]

Among the structures over which these imperial tides washed were those in accordance with which religious/municipal communities reckoned their history, asserted their identity, and articulated their relationships with their god. As Elizabeth Key Fowden has recently illustrated, a host of holy personages, martyred saints, and pious ascetics alike, loomed large in the imaginative landscape of not only Hellenized Christians, but Arabs allied with both the Byzantines and the Sasanians, and even among Persian Zoroastrians themselves. These figures, while conjured from the Christian tradition, resonated with individuals and communities aligned with other confessional identities across the sixth- and seventh-century Syrian steppe. These individuals and communities no doubt read such figures differently than did those who maintained their cults and who enunciated official versions of their passions, lives, and miracles but nevertheless understood them as powerful, revered personae who somehow united lived experience with the numinous, the day-to-day world with that other, more real world in which resided the unbounded power of transcendent Truth.[22]

The attraction of such figures as Sergius, a martyr saint whose cult was exceedingly popular in the frontier regions separating the Byzantine and Persian empires, is suggested by the reports of Theophylact Simocatta that the Zoroastrian Persian king Khusrau II offered the saint dedicatory offerings after winning back his domain with Roman help in 591 and again after his wife conceived a child.[23] Meanwhile, the sanctuary of Symeon the Stylite in Syria routinely attracted members of both monotheistic and pagan Bedouin tribes,[24] and the cult of Sergius was central to the bishop Ahudemmeh's mission to convert Arab tribes. Such seems to have been the cult's impact on the imaginations of the tribesmen (and hence its political importance) that when Ahudemmeh's shrine to Sergius was burned by Christian rivals, Khusrau ostentatiously rebuilt it, although the bishop himself died in the King of Kings' prison after converting a Persian prince.[25]

This pattern repeated itself through the late antique world and continued in the Islamic period—locations and symbols (pious mounted warriors, for example) retained imaginative functions and continued to serve similar roles in the lives of communities and individuals, even after their original significance or specific sign value had been reelaborated.[26] Recent archaeological evidence has suggested that this process continued into the early Islamic period. Many early mosques in the Negev highlands, for example, incorporated elements of Nabatean stele cult practices, and their dispersion through the Golan region suggests both that their spread was gradual and that locations of mosque building were on or near traditional stele cult sites.[27]

The borderlands of Syria and Mesopotamia bred hybrid places of worship and hybrid objects of worship. They also housed individuals and communities who exploited their liminal status and who engaged in economies of various sorts (those of prestige, wealth, power, and so on) that existed independent of the great powers between which they abided. The borderlands were a seedbed for cultural fusion as well, and in the arena they provided signs and symbols made up yet another fluid and promiscuous economy in which ideas and truth claims were negotiated and elaborated. This takes dynamic visual form in one of the most frequently remarked upon architectural and decorative sites from the early Islamic period, the Dome of the Rock.

Why the first/seventh-century Umayyad caliph ʿAbd al-Malik built the Dome of the Rock has been the subject of intense debate among modern scholars, but it seems, in part, to have been intended to counter the theological claims of the Christian community in Jerusalem and to announce Islam as an imperial presence.[28] In order to issue the kinds of statements the Dome seems to have been intended to make, so Oleg Grabar has argued, its builders drew upon a spectrum of contemporary architectural and decorative motifs, most of which had found earlier use in Byzantine martyr shrines and other buildings. Modern readers might think it paradoxical that a Muslim leader should draw on the cultural traditions of his rivals to articulate his and his community's claims to ascendancy and the possession of unique truth.

Yet such an assumption presupposes that individuals in any given period of history or cultural space have recourse to an unlimited array of signs and symbols with which to articulate such claims. In fact they do not. In any time and under any cultural conditions, individuals and communities must articulate ideas in accordance with recognized sets of signs and symbols. Why they choose the specific signs and symbols they do may be interesting and often relevant but is just now beside the point—the point is that when ʿAbd al-Malik or any other early Muslim chose to articulate claims about his community, he necessarily had recourse to a vocabulary of signs and symbols which resonated with those who were to read them, be they members of his own community or members of other communities.

Grabar's study of the semiotic use of common resonances in space, structure, and design and the multivalent specific readings to which these were subject, what he terms "common themes that differed in their specific associations," led to his insistence that artistic merit may transcend and evade the parochial specifics assigned to it in any given historical moment and so serve the needs of those who come to it as long as its forms have a place within a recognized semiotic system.[29]

I want to suggest that the new, specific associations Grabar understands ʿAbd al-Malik to have assigned to certain elements native to a very old, widely comprehensible semiotic system are emblematic too of the fusion of cultural expression one finds in early Muslim historical narratives. Tarif Khalidi identifies the component elements of this fusion as "Muslim and tribal" expressions which were conjoined in the early Muslim historiographic traditions. Fred Donner sees them in much the same way, describing them as expressions of "piety" and tribal pride, the elements around which he suggests the early community of believers cohered. The tribal aspects of these narratives bear much in common with pre-Islamic poetry, for example, which celebrated the actions in battle of tribal members and whose possession fell to the family and tribal groups of those whose actions they celebrate.[30]

Donner has further suggested that as the postconquest community of believers sought to define an identity for itself, one distinct from the other monotheistic faith communities among which it resided, it did so on the basis of Muḥammad's prophetic status. Thus, it was in the truth of Muḥammad's revelation that the nascent Muslim community had its basis, and it was the truth of this revelation which the communities with whom the early Muslims came into contact would most want to contest. For these reasons, understanding the conquests as an indisputable proof of Muḥammad's authority as a prophet and the truth of his revelation became crucial.[31]

But there was a problem. Muḥammad seems never to have given what one scholar has called the "prophetic stamp of approval" to the conquests—the Prophet died before they were properly underway and seems not to have clearly foreseen them.[32] How, then, was the early Muslim community to frame the conquest period, for themselves and for others, as a manifestation of divine will and as a proof of holy revelation?

In early Islamic historical narratives, the so-called "tribal" components represented the stories, passed on orally, which had survived (or which were believed to have survived) from the time of the conquest. These told what happened during the conquests. The "pious" elements of these narratives, on the other hand, gave the "how" and "why" of the conquests and provided a new way to read the traditional "tribal" components of the narratives.[33] While "tribal" *akhbār* might recall, for example, a specific warrior or tribal group's decision to attack a group of Persian war elephants because to do so is to tempt "a most painful death," this act becomes a specifically Muslim act and carries significance within a specifically Muslim narrative because it is contextualized by other parts of the text in which it appears. In those parts of the text ascetic, pious witnesses to the truth of Muḥammad's revelation meet and defy the Persian nobles at whose behest those terrifying war elephants take the field.[34] These witnesses to Muḥammad's revelation stand before representatives of worldly power and articulate the defining truth claims of their community. I want to suggest that in so doing, they make the events which surround them comprehensible as episodes in a much larger, specifically Muslim narrative.

Early Muslim Tradition and Late Antiquity

This, of course, raises a question. If the "tribal" aspects of the early Muslim histories represented an older, pre-Islamic medium of remembrance, what was the basis for the "pious" aspects of the stories that would eventually define and lend contour to the Islamic polity? From what vocabulary of signs and associations did they derive? This is a crucial question in that it was these "pious" components of the earliest specifically Muslim communal narratives that made the early histories of the conquests comprehensible as stories about the validity of Muḥammad's prophetic mission and message. Moreover, such early narratives of remembrance and the exempla culled from them would provide important resources for self-fashioning to generations of later Muslims.

Long before the Arabs who settled in Syria and Mesopotamia began to collect tribal war stories and pious tales into communal narratives, the Arabs of the Ḥijāz and Jazīra clearly recognized the spiritual power ascribed to such figures as the martyr Sergius or the pillar saints of the Syrian countryside, although the specific readings to which such signs were subject had always been diverse and open-ended. Indeed, such figures were signs which could be ascribed any number of specific meanings and could be incorporated into the communal narratives of various communities. Just as rival Christian communities could and frequently did issue competing claims about the legitimacy of their own communities grounded in imagined lineage from the same early martyrs or in the approval of the same all-seeing, all-knowing ascetics, so it was possible for all of the various peoples who encountered such symbols to incorporate them into their own communal narratives.[35]

This process continued as the early community of believers told the stories that would provide the basis for the constitution of an Islamic community and Muslim identity. To better understand how this process took place and to make sense of the hybrid narratives with which the Muslim communal past was constituted, we will return once again to the work of the sociologist Margaret Somers.[36]

Simply stated, Somers has suggested that it is frequently the case that individuals develop an understanding of their own place in the cosmos by imagining themselves as actors in an ongoing narrative, one that by its nature links the present to an earlier series of events, all of which become comprehensible, as do contemporary events, in relationship to one another. Thus "events" become "episodes" in that the possible range of interpretation for any discrete event is dependant upon that event's imagined relationship with a constellation of other "episodes." Somers continues,

> Another crucial element of narrativity is its *evaluative criteria*. Evaluation enables us to make qualitative and lexical distinctions among the infinite variety of events, experiences, characters, institutional promises, and social factors that impinge on our lives . . . in the face of a potentially limitless array of social experiences deriving from social contact with events, institutions,

> and people, the evaluative capacity of emplotment demands and enables *selective appropriation* in constructing narratives. A plot must be thematic. The primacy of this narrative theme or competing themes determines how events are processed and what criteria will be used to prioritize events and render meaning to them [original emphasis].[37]

In the premodern Mediterranean and Near East, every community was, first and foremost, a religious institution.[38] Consequently, one important theme in accordance with which communal identity and communal narratives of the late antique or early Islamic world would be fashioned was one that we might render as "community of God (or of the gods)."[39] One of the defining features of the late antique world, moreover, was that this theme was restated as "the one community of God (or the gods)." This tendency becomes ominously visible in tetrarchic legislation against Manichaeism and Christianity, for example, and took many forms thereafter.[40] Throughout the period of anti-Christian persecution, and accelerating after the advent of Constantine, this theme cast certain events of Christianity's confrontations with the Roman state as episodes in a plot which saw discrete instances of persecution interpreted as so many truth tests during which the validity of Christian belief was made manifest by the strivings of certain godly men and women.

This one true community of God theme remained the basis for narratives of communal self-fashioning as an ever-proliferating array of Christian communities advanced and contested communal truth claims vis-à-vis other Christian communities. Instances of inter-communal violence were now understood as further episodes in plots belonging to communal narratives stretching back to Christ's persecution and crucifixion and the persecution and deaths of the martyrs. Because many communities shared narratives that were, in effect, variations on the same basic plot, a common pool of semiotic elements served in the articulation of those narratives.

This semiotic system prominently featured superstar ascetics and tortured martyrs, all of whom exemplified the power of the numinous in narratives that detailed the experiences of such men in confrontation with representatives of worldly power.[41] This vocabulary of signs and symbols was one with which, again, members of various late antique confessional groupings were familiar and whose power they acknowledged in various ways.

Moreover, such figures as the martyr and the ascetic fighter for the faith were most frequently deployed in narratives which worked to set the enunciating community apart from all others and in narratives marshalling events from the lived experience of that community as episodes in a plot which sought to establish that community as the "one true community of God."[42]

As the postconquest Arab community of believers imagined its own communal past and in so doing articulated narratives recasting events from its communal past as episodes in a plot which sought to establish itself as the one true community of God, it did not do so in a cultural, social, or ontological vacuum. Rather, it did so amid a cacophony of late antique communal narratives concerning the problems of prophecy, numinous revelation, and transcendent truth, narratives with which, as I shall demonstrate below, early Muslims were intimately familiar. Thus, there should be little surprise that the figures and dynamics with which monotheistic communities contested communal boundaries and questions of identity should find roles to play as first/seventh- and second/eighth-century Arab communities now elaborated their own claims concerning prophecy, proximity to the numinous and transcendent truth (and in so doing composed those famously hybrid communal narratives).

"There Was a Monk by the Name of Bahira"

The hybrid character of early Muslim historical narratives is exemplified especially well in traditions recorded by the Muslim historians al-Ṭabarī, al-Azdī, and Ibn ʿAsākir.[43] In these narratives Arab tribesmen undertake acts of martial valor and demonstrate warrior virtue, recalling traditional or pre-Islamic poetry motifs. Meanwhile, the ascetic character ascribed to these warriors adorns such narratives with the meaning they were to carry within broader Muslim communal discourses which looked to the conquests as irrevocable proofs of the truth claims of Muḥammad's followers.[44] Before moving on to these texts, however, let us first examine a series of passages which establish the familiarity of early Muslims with the late antique semiotic vocabulary I have been discussing.

In these stories, early Muslims offered as proof of Muḥammad's prophetic status and mission stories in which the Prophet is recognized as such not by those who would soon follow him but rather by a charismatic Christian ascetic. This was an accustomed role for the monk in the literatures of late antique peoples from Persia to Ireland. In the semiotic world of these peoples, the monk was a figure whose ability to discern more profound realities was taken for granted and whose capacity to discern truth from falsehood and good from evil was tied ultimately to his proximity to the numinous.[45]

The monk Baḥīrā figures in both Christian and Muslim traditions regarding the Prophet and is the subject of a series of traditions in Ibn Isḥāq's *Sīra*, the first extant biography of Muḥammad.[46] In this tradition, Muḥammad attaches himself to a caravan going to Syria with his uncle, Abū Ṭalib. When the caravan reaches Busra,

> [T]hey stopped near Baḥīrā's cell, [and] he made for them a great feast. And this, so they allege, was because of something he saw while he was in his cell. They allege that in his cell he saw the apostle of God in the caravan while they approached, and [he saw] a cloud overshadowing [Muḥammad] amidst the troop. Then they came and stopped in the shade of a tree near the monk, and [Baḥīrā] looked at the cloud when it overshadowed the tree, and the branches of the tree bent over the apostle of God until he was shaded beneath it. And when he saw that, Baḥīrā came out of his cell and ordered that the food be arranged. Then he sent to them and he said "I have made for you a feast, O kinsmen of Quraysh, and I would like all of you to attend."

The Arabs are shocked by the sudden hospitality of the monk but accept his food. They leave Muḥammad to guard their merchandise, but the monk insists that he also come and eat. After the meal, he questions Muḥammad regarding his dreams and habits and compares these with what he knows of prophets. He inspects Muḥammad's body and finds the mark of prophecy between his shoulder blades. The monk warns Abu Ṭālib to protect and hide the boy from the Jews, because if they recognize him they will hurt him.[47] A number of similar stories about the role of monks in the early career of Muḥammad are to be found elsewhere in Ibn Isḥāq's *Sīra*.[48]

Interestingly, Muslim tradition records the role of monks in another would-be Arab prophet's career, and again the monks take on the role of gatekeepers and discerners of truth. In this case, however, they recognize a pious man of the Arabs as just that, but as something less than a prophet. ʿUmayya

b. Abī al-Ṣalt, an Arab poet, became aware of rumors that there was to be an Arab monotheistic prophet and approached a group of monks for recognition. Ultimately, his is disappointed when a monk discerns his "companions" as jinn rather than angels.[49]

The recognition of Muḥammad as a prophet by Christian monks may be read as an elaboration upon an important theme in Christian hagiography, suggesting that Christian monks retained in the imaginations of early Muslims at least one of the qualities with which they were constructed in late antique Christian narratives. The fact that monks retained this function in the imaginations of Muslims suggests that they served in the borderlands milieu of first/seventh- and second/eighth-century Syria as a symbol which could be read, like the architectural and decorative motifs of the Dome of the Rock, free of specific, parochial significance and as a free-floating signifier that could take up residence in a variety of discourses.

"Monks by Night, Horsemen by Day": Making Mujahidun

That first/seventh-, second/eighth- and third/ninth-century Arabs were well familiar not just with the hagiographical archetypes of the late antique world but with the texts in which those archetypes did their discursive work is made clear in several Arabic Muslim texts from the period.[50] As Gordon Newby has noted, for example, there is what amounts to an abbreviated Christian saint's life in the *Sīra* of Muḥammad,[51] and a version of the same story reappears in al-Ṭabarī's monumental *Ta'rīkh*.[52] In this story,[53] a wandering "ascetic and zealous fighter for the faith" named Faymiyūn is featured in a narrative which traces his journey from one master to another, through a career of wonder-working and eventually flight from town to town as he evades the crowds which gather to see him.[54]

The Muslim Arab authors whose works featured such narratives also seem to have understood the function of these narratives in describing the foundational dramas of various monotheistic communities. Muḥammad's biographer Ibn Isḥāq and al-Ṭabarī, the great historian of the early Islamic world, both record a tale told by the Christian community in the southern Arabian city of Najrān about the coming of monotheism to their city and thence to the rest of Arabia.[55] Like millions of other late antique monotheists throughout the Mediterranean basin and across Mesopotamia, the Christians of Najrān recalled the genesis of their community with stories prominently featuring pious ascetics and the drama of martyrdom. The narratives preserved by al-Ṭabarī and Ibn Isḥāq describe the actions of a wandering Christian ascetic figure (whom al-Ṭabarī identifies as "Faymiyūn"), who, upon arrival in Najrān, instructs the son of a local notable in his faith. The boy (inevitably) comes into conflict with the local king but miraculously resists all of the king's attempts to punish and torture him. The boy, ʿAbd Allāh b. al-Thāmir, insists that the king accept his view of God as single and alone. The king does so, strikes ʿAbd Allāh on the head, killing him, and then himself drops dead.[56]

In these stories as preserved in the works of Ibn Isḥāq and al-Ṭabarī, the figure of the martyr and the figure of the ascetic are linked, and each performs essentially the same functions that it does in contemporary Christian literature. Each is identified with the founding of a monotheistic faith community in Najrān, and indeed in Arabia more generally, and with the maintenance of that community's boundaries. Such stories as these, told to explain the birth of the Christian community in Najrān, were repeated in innumerable communities to describe the foundational deeds and dramas of those communities, and it was among such communities and necessarily in dialogue with such communities that the early Muslim *umma* imagined its own origins as a monotheistic polity.

Al-Ṭabarī's *Taʾrīkh* preserves another late antique saint story which was frequently deployed as a communal narrative. In it, the martyr George destroys a persecuting king's idols.[57] The figures associated with the destruction of idols and their homes in Christian hagiographical polemic were in fact typically militant ascetics.[58] Despite the trend current among some scholars of late antiquity to paint the ascetics of late antiquity as benevolent and gentle spiritual fathers, Christian ascetics were widely imagined by their contemporaries, Christian and non-Christian alike, to be volatile and often violent, "zealous fighters of the faith."[59] This is the description we find in the hagiographical text transmitted by al-Ṭabarī, that of the ascetic Christian ambassador to Najrān, Faymiyūn, and it echoes descriptions of monks that evolved during the Christological controversies of the fifth and sixth centuries.[60] Monks were figures charged with maintaining and enforcing boundaries between communities and occasionally launching attacks against religious others when many or most elements of their host community seem to have been content to live in peace.

Christian monks appear in several Muslim traditions linked with the idea of martyrdom, militant guardianship of true religion, and what may best be described as orthodoxy or correct monotheistic practice. In a useful 1989 article, for example, Sara Sviri[61] cites a passage from the *Nawādir al-uṣūl* of al-Ḥakīm al-Tirmidhī (d. c. 300/912) which clearly links Christian ascetics with the question of martyrdom and persecution—they originated as those who would not fall into line with a heretical reading of the gospel.[62] The passage also contains latent apologetic elements which recall strategies with which Christianity's archetypal hagiographical texts were constructed. It suggests that real Christian holy men—the original anchorites, stylites and wandering "sarabaite" ascetics who first objected to the corruption of Jesus' faith—later accepted Muḥammad and his mission. Christian ascetics of al-Tirmidhī's time who rejected Muḥammad and his revelation could accordingly be dismissed as representative of a later, fallen brand of monastic pretender.[63]

Thus the figure of the pious Christian ascetic emerges in early Muslim tradition as evolved from those who discerned and rejected heresy and the worldly power which supported it. In so doing, the monk preserved the true religion of Jesus while it was corrupted by the powerful of the world.[64] In the recognition and rejection of tainted monotheism, the monk plays much the same role here as had the Christian martyrs when faced with polytheistic idolatry. The monk as an emblem of militancy and ascetic piety joined in the person of a communal vanguard reemerges in early Islamic descriptions of *jihād* and those who waged it.

In his third/ninth-century *ʿUyūn al-akhbār*, for example, Ibn Qutayba (d. 276/889), records the following story. A Muslim traveler recalled that he once met a monk with huge bags under his eyes from his constant weeping. When he asked the monk why he was weeping, the monk expressed despair at the fact that the end of his life was nearing and he had not yet accomplished his spiritual goals. When he passed by the site of the monk's cell some time later, the Muslim asked about the monk. He was told that "he had become a Muslim and gone raiding and had been killed in the lands of the Romans."[65]

Composed in a still earlier period, the second/eighth-century Muslim historian al-Azdī's *Ta'rīkh futūḥ al-Shām* (History of the Conquest of Syria) contains the story of an Arab Christian ascetic *(nāsik)* who was traveling with the Roman army in Syria as it encountered the Muslim armies. The Roman commander sent the ascetic among the Muslims. When he returned, he reported that: "I come to you from a people staying up through the night praying and remaining abstinent during the day, commanding the right and forbidding the wrong, monks by night, lions by day. Should their king steal, they cut off his hand, and if he commits adultery they stone him."[66]

In this passage, the Christian ascetic dispatched among a band of *mujāhidūn* immediately recognizes a kinship between himself and the Muslim warriors he meets. They, like Christian monks, represent the hard edge of their community. By the eighth/second century, when this story was finally set down in writing, Christian ascetics had in fact long "commanded the right and forbidden the wrong" within their own communities, correcting Roman emperors and even stoning Roman officials as they imposed and enforced communal boundaries and normative behaviors.[67] Versions of this story are also included by al-Ṭabarī and Ibn ʿAsākir in their histories, although in these the warriors are described as "horsemen by day and monks by night," as reborn hybrids who embody Arab identities of the *jāhiliyya* past and the prophetic present, at once both mounted raider and ascetic monotheist.[68] Meanwhile, the Arabic life of Stephen of Mar Sabas describes the second/eighth-century Christian ascetic hero of the work as "like a brave horseman who fights to receive a crown from the king" [11.11] and "like a horseman brave and bold."[69]

Perhaps the most striking indication of the ways in which the early Muslims understood the figure of the monk comes from a pair of prophetic traditions recorded by ʿAbd Allāh b. al-Mubārak (d. 181/797) in his *Kitāb al-jihād* regarding monastic practice. The first of these is, "Every community has its monasticism, the monasticism of my community is *jihād* for the sake of God," and the second is "Roving monasticism was mentioned in front of the Prophet: The Prophet said: 'God gave us in its stead *jihād* on His path and the *takbīr* [the act of shouting "God is Greatest!"] on every hill.'"[70]

Some scholars have suggested that these traditions reveal negative attitude among early Muslims toward celibacy and radical ascetic practices, and there do seem to be other traditions which specifically address the question of celibacy and extreme asceticism.[71] But these traditions may also be read in tandem with other traditions comparing *mujāhidūn* to monks to suggest that early Muslims identified the figure of the monk as a model of militant piety, one in which devotion to internal and external struggle were linked with devotion to God and zealous defense of one's faith community.

Much is made, in fact, of the asceticism of the early Muslim *mujāhidūn* and their leaders. On the eve of Qādisiyya, for example, al-Ṭabarī has the caliph ʿUmar b. al-Khaṭṭāb (d. 23/644) say to his troops, "God has provided for everything a door, and for every door a key; the door of justice is reflection and its key is *zuhd* [asceticism or pious renunciation] . . . *zuhd* is taking what is due from everyone who owes it and giving what is due to anyone who has a right to it. Do not grant favor to anyone in this matter . . . I am between you and God, and nobody is between me and Him."[72]

ʿUmar was in fact frequently cited by early Muslims as a paragon of ascetic virtue. In his *Kitāb al-zuhd* or *Book of Asceticism*, for example, the prominent third/ninth-century traditionalist Aḥmad b. Ḥanbal recorded traditions in which ʿUmar frets over the corrupting influence of material worth, muttering of donations of wealth to the piously poor community, "By God, this offers a people nothing but it casts them into antagonism and antipathy," or of a set of fancy silverware captured in the early conquests, "I esteem more a leather mat used as a table cloth . . . [this] adorns the crowd with a love of covetousness."[73] At his own table, ʿUmar was remembered to have subsisted on bread, salt and water, the accustomed diet of generations of Christian monks.[74]

Al-Ṭabarī's rendering of ʿUmar's exhortation to the assembled *mujāhidūn* suggests a model of *zuhd* which coincides nicely with the description of Muslim warriors al-Azdī puts into the mouth of the Christian ascetic sent into the Muslim camp in Syria. The centrality assigned to *zuhd* in ʿUmar's address to his warriors designates ascetic moderation as a core value attributed to the warriors who were remembered to have conquered the world's proud and decadent temporal powers. It was this ascetic ethos which made these men recognizable actors in a narrative about revelation and its consequences in human affairs.

In his own history of the conquest of Syria, for example, al-Azdī sets a pious Muslim warrior named Muʿādh b. Jabal in juxtaposition to a delegation of Romans dispatched, apparently, to find out how the empire might buy off the Arab raiders in the early days of the conquest. A translator explains to the Muslim that the Roman officials, who sit upon pillows and cushions arranged upon fine rugs, will be offended if he does not sit while conversing with them. Muʿādh informs them that to sit with them on their carpets and cushions, and so to partake with them in the pleasures of this world, is antithetical to the ethos of his community. "[These things] are an adornment of the present world, but God has induced [in us] a loathing [*zahhada*] of the present world and its deception, and he has rebuked and forbidden covetousness and extravagance in it. And so I shall sit right here upon the earth, and having spoken to me you may then be on your way."[75]

Another series of such episodes is to be found in al-Ṭabarī's account of the crucial battle of Qādisiyya.[76] In these, pious, ascetic Muslim warriors rebuff offers of bribes and attempts at truce, lecture proud and powerful Persian officials and, when the Persians try to overawe them with a display of wealth, slash at their silken pillows and ride their horses upon their fine carpets.[77] In one exchange with a poor and pious Arab warrior, the Persian commander Rustam recounts the Persian Empire's long relationship with the Arabs and hints at some sort of truce. His Arab interlocutor, however, has different ideas. "We did not come to you looking for things of this world," he says. "Our desire and aspiration is the hereafter. In the past those of us who came to you were obedient to you, they humbled themselves before you, and sought what was in your hands." Those days are gone forever, he explains, swept away by the implications of Muḥammad's revelation.[78]

In tandem with the *akhbār* passed on by the tribes whose members fought at Qādisiyya and elsewhere, then, are those stories sampled above, in which pious, ascetic warriors confront representatives of Persian power, making clear that with the divine revelation they represent, worldly power arrangements are to change. Structurally, these narratives bear much in common with certain ubiquitous martyr narratives, versions of which eventually found a home in the texts of al-Ṭabarī and Ibn Isḥāq. In these, a comparatively powerless individual, a "witness,"[79] confronts a representative of terrestrial power, insisting upon the terms of the revelation around which his or her community has cohered. An attempt is made by the representative of worldly power to restore the status quo, but this attempt is rejected by the witness. Often, some sort of bribe is offered but is roughly rebuffed and the witness insists upon pressing the claims of his or her new revelation. A contest ensues and the witness emerges triumphant, thus clearly manifesting the will of God.[80]

In this sort of narrative, in both its Muslim and Christian permutation, historical contingency has been recalled within a prophetic metanarrative and so recast with specific implications regarding the truth claims of each community. In the case of early Christianity, periods of persecution constituted a remembered fact and had to be interpreted in a literary form which would frame the suffering and deaths of the witnesses to Jesus' revelation and, more particularly the ability of the witnesses to endure that suffering, as a proof of divine intercession on behalf of those witnesses. In Muslim narratives, traditional battle narratives describe the military events of the conquest, whose results Muslims living in Syria, Mesopotamia, Egypt, and North Africa could see every day.[81] In order to contextualize the conquest period, however, and to allow it to play the role assigned to it within the evolving truth claims of the community of believers, there was need for some sort of framing device which would bracket the tribal battle narratives which recalled the events of the conquest period clearly within a prophetic framework and so determine the range of possible readings to which they were subject.

Accordingly, as the early Muslim communities recalled the events of the conquest period as episodes in a larger narrative of revelation and prophetic truth, they too imagined scenes in which pious and resolute witnesses to the truth around which their own community cohered stood in confrontation with representatives of worldly power. As they did, the battlefield exploits recalled in tribal or family histories took on an otherworldly glow: they were no longer simply acts of bravery and Bedouin élan. They were manifestations of God's good pleasure on earth and proofs of the truth of Muḥammad's revelation. They were, in short, the basis for a new community of God.

Conclusion

In an important discussion of the place of early Islam within the world of late antiquity, Peter Brown has written that "[t]he sense of the past which was achieved through the creation of [an Arabic historical] tradition tacitly excluded all outsiders to Arabia. Jews, Christians, Persians and East Romans were allotted 'walk-on parts,' but little more. The immensely rich but inward-looking Arabic historical tradition virtually ignored the intimacy and complexity of the relations between the Arabs and the other cultures of the Near East . . . this has to be recovered from other, non-Arabic sources."[82]

In one sense Brown is quite right. Early Muslim texts are indeed remarkably inward looking, even (perhaps especially) when they make mention of non-Muslims. Nor do they frequently make explicit mention of the "intimacy and complexity" of the relationships many early Muslims maintained with non-Muslims. Despite this, however, the notion that Arabic Muslim historical sources do not or cannot convey the interconnectedness of the early Islamic community with the non-Muslim communities among which it took shape depends finally upon how we read those texts, how closely we listen to what they say, and, perhaps most importantly, how alert we remain to the ways in which they say what they say.

Clifford Geertz has famously described the semiotic elements about which this chapter has so much to say as "extrinsic source[s] of information" that function much like a kind of cultural "DNA" in that they are both "models of" and "models for" social reality. In other words, such clusters of symbols as I have been discussing may be deployed to describe or explain the world in terms that are comprehensible to human subjects and to help human subjects then fashion individual and communal selves in accordance with the reality they perceive.[83]

If we take seriously Geertz's notion of signs and clusters of signs as so many strands of cultural "DNA," certain "familial" affinities between the early Islamic community and the other communities of late antiquity become immediately clear. But it is also clear that the early Muslim texts in which traces of those affinities appear are not "genetic" (or generic) copies of the kinds of texts with which the Christian communities of Syria or Egypt had reckoned their own histories. They are, instead, texts of hybrid lineage, part *jāhiliyya*-style Bedouin war narrative, part pious tale in the late antique tradition. It was the union of these two traditions of remembrance, the commingling of two vocabularies of signs that created a specifically Muslim mode of recalling the past. Around this and other specifically Muslim literary genres there in turn evolved specifically Muslim technologies for the evaluation and authorization of narratives and texts, specifically Muslim modes of authority and ways of knowing which were bound to those texts and specifically Muslim ways of reading and redeploying what were now specifically Muslim signs, despite whatever previous readings to which those signs might have been subject.[84]

Just as the signs contained within these specifically Muslim texts helped to provide models of the events of the conquests which fit the needs of a specifically Muslim narrative, the ways in which the conquests and the men who participated in them were imagined provided models for crafting communal identities for generations of later Muslims. In the eighth/second century, for example, as the Muslim historian al-Azdī composed his history of the deeds of the early *mujāhidūn*, men who were like "monks by night and lions by day," ʿAbd Allāh b. al-Mubārak lived his life in daily imitation of those early Muslim warriors. Ibn al-Mubārak was a *ghāzī*, a "raider" who practiced *jihād* on the Islamic world's frontier with Byzantium. He was also a noted ascetic and scholar. In the two works for which he is best known, his *Kitāb al-jihād* and *Kitāb al-zuhd*, Ibn al-Mubārak set forth a doctrine of *jihād* which insisted that it was the ascetic piety of the individual warrior alone which made war against the infidel holy in the eyes of God.[85] In both his work on asceticism and his treatise on *jihād*, for example, Ibn al-Mubārak included the prophetic utterances cited above equating monasticism with the practice of *jihād*.

Among Ibn al-Mubārak's admirers was Aḥmad b. Ḥanbal (d. 241/855), a renowned Baghdādī scholar and the eponymous founder of one of the four principal schools of Islamic jurisprudence. Ibn Ḥanbal's son Ṣāliḥ recalled that Ibn Ḥanbal had desired to study with Ibn al-Mubārak but that the famous ascetic warrior had died before he could.[86] Nevertheless, Ibn Ḥanbal's own *Kitāb al-zuhd* celebrated the ascetic piety of such conquest era warriors as Muʿādh b. Jabal, the *mujāhid* who would neither sit with the Roman officials nor accept their bribes, and the caliph ʿUmar.[87] It was such figures, of course, after whom Ibn al-Mubārak and his *ghāzī* colleagues had modeled themselves. Pious renunciation was, accordingly, a crucial aspect of the Muslim self fashioned by Ibn Ḥanbal. Aḥmad's son Ṣāliḥ, in turn, emphasized his father's ascetic morality and intransigence in the face of worldly power as he composed his father's biography.[88] In so doing Ṣāliḥ of course crafted an image of himself based in part upon the qualities he chose to recall in his father.[89]

Ṣāliḥ b. Aḥmad b. Ḥanbal's biography of his father is in some ways a more intimate version of the processes I have tried to elucidate here and an example of the success of those processes in producing a distinct and specifically Muslim culture, yet one intimately linked to a much wider world. All that the early Muslims themselves claimed to be new about their community was Muḥammad's revelation and its consequences. The baffling task of explaining those consequences was left to men and women who were not prophets, however, and who necessarily drew upon their environment for potent signs and symbols to make the consequences of Muḥammad's revelation comprehensible for themselves and their descendants. The birth and early growth of the Muslim community within a late antique cultural milieu did nothing to undermine the evolution of a distinctively Islamic cultural tradition. Rather, the tradition begun within that milieu would prove so powerful as to recast ancient signs and symbols as uniquely its own.

This blend of militancy and ascetic praxis would not prove unproblematic for the early Islamic community, however. Rather, as we shall see in the next chapter, the role of ascetic, militant piety in standard narrations of the Muslim past would carry profound consequences for the character of the spiritual, social, and political life of this newest late antique community of God. In time, the potential for discord, disunity, and bloodshed that resided in the volatile mix of revelation, ascetic rigor, and an evolving mythology of righteous raiding would demand a quieter, more manageable means of making useful in the daily lives of ordinary Muslims the determined renunciation and steely-eyed piety that imbued the figure of the primordial *mujāhid* with such profound imaginative power.

CHAPTER SIX

"The Sword Scrapes Away Transgressions": Ascetic Praxis and Communal Boundaries in Late Antique Islam

Said the judge . . . men of god and men of war have strange affinities.[1]

THE NARRATIVES OF Muslim communal origins articulated by al-Azdī, Ibn Isḥāq, and other early Muslim authors repeatedly emphasized the unflinching ascetic virtue of the first Muslims, particularly as these first Muslims came into conflict with the great powers of late antiquity during the opening days of the *futūḥ*. These early Muslim *mujāhidūn*, men like Khālid b. al-Walīd and Muʿādh b. Jabal, soon became models for self-fashioning not only among Muslims like the second/eighth-century frontier *ghāzī* ʿAbd Allāh b. al-Mubārak but also among settled city-dwellers in such decidedly worldly urban centers as Damascus and Baghdād. Much as the desert-dwelling Christian monks of late antiquity had become for their less overtly spiritual contemporaries paragons of an idealized and genuine Christianness, now the world-renouncing *mujāhid*, fasting and praying in Tarsus in preparation for war with the Romans or gazing longingly from a frontier *ribāṭ* (rather like a monastery for traveling ascetics, mystics, pilgrims, or *mujāhidūn*) across the Anatolian borderlands at the *dār al-ḥarb* or "abode of war" and its promise of martyrdom "on the path of God," became for his citified Muslim contemporaries an embodiment of a pure and primordial strain of Islam, one modeled upon figures emplotted in the foundational narratives of their community.[2]

We have seen that as the very early Muslim *umma* articulated those foundational narratives, its members frequently drew upon a universally legible late antique semiotic system to construct a history of the conquest period that made the events of that period comprehensible within a late antique prophetic metanarrative. So constituted, those narratives recalled the men who conducted the conquests as hybrid raider-ascetics, warrior monks who combined Bedouin élan with ascetic rigor and piety. One effect of this process was that the moral and behavioral ideals inscribed in the heroes of Christian and Muslim communal narratives were not only close matches for one another but were also signaled by closely kindred casts of characters, all of which were animated within texts structured in accordance with a remarkably similar set of narrative forms. However different the metanarratives in service of which these Muslim and Christian signs, symbols, and narrative forms were evoked, the specific notions of ideal devotional piety, the forms that that piety ought to take, and the ways in which that piety was legible in the actions of individual worshippers was to become equally central to the confessional self-fashioning of particularly conscientious and observant Muslims and Christians alike.

Thus pious renunciation or asceticism emerges in our earliest Muslim sources as a characteristic that marked certain Muslims and Christians alike as men and women of God. This quality, called "*zuhd*" in Arabic, was notable not only among heroic *futūḥ*-era *mujāhidūn* or frontier *ghāzīs* (a "raider" or frontier warrior practicing *jihād*) but also among such early leaders of the Muslim *umma* as the caliph ʿUmar, such early heroes of the *ʿulamāʾ* as Aḥmad b. Ḥanbal and a number of lesser-known pietists and their pupils. The specific forms that early Muslim *zuhd* took were often indistinguishable from the *zuhd* of Christian ascetics, and indeed many early Muslim *zuhhād* (sing. *zāhid*, practitioners of *zuhd*) were said to have learned ascetic praxis in exchanges with Christian monks.

Over time, and by the second/eighth century at the latest, this seems to have provoked certain anxieties within the Muslim community. This anxiety grew from the paradoxical role ascetic praxis had come to play in at once imposing and obscuring the communal boundaries that were to set the Muslim *umma* in opposition to all other communities. On the one hand, pious and otherworldly scorn for the enticements of the present world was believed to have been a marker of particularly accomplished Muslims from the beginnings of Islam. Think, for example, of the shabby but inspired Muslim warriors who confronted the proud imperial functionaries in early conquest narratives and in so doing not only rejected their demands for obedience but also scorned their offers of gifts and promises of wealth and prestige. These, from the point of view of the second/eighth- and third/ninth-century Muslims who imagined them, were figures that embodied all of the qualities that most befitted real Muslims.

Troublingly, however, by the time our earliest Muslim texts were produced, some Muslims had begun to note that while rejection of the present world might be commended to them by the example of these primordial heroes, the specific forms that such rejection took could often uncomfortably mirror the behaviors of those exemplary non-Muslims, the Christian monks. Now, the gaunt, cloaked pietist who padded through town freshly returned from the scorching frontiers of the known world was less immediately legible than he should have been; he might be a Muslim *mujāhid* cut from the cloth of Islam's *futūḥ*-era heroes and so a resource for confident Muslim self-fashioning, but he might also be a Christian monk, ready to lead Muslim men and women astray with his example. Perhaps more troublingly still, he might turn out to be a brother or son or friend of those Muslims who beheld him, resplendent in his godly tatters, and yet now a stranger, an ambiguous figure whose specific communal identity had been scoured away by the rigors of renunciation in God's name. Neither properly Muslim nor properly Christian in the eyes of some of their contemporaries, such figures seem to have represented for these contemporaries a genre of danger closely akin to that which John Chrysostom detected in those of his parishioners who sought nearness to their God via "Jewish" rituals, holy sites, and holy personages. Such Muslims represented, in short, a perilous blurring of those boundaries that gave shape and experiential weight to the nascent Muslim *umma*.

The origin of this perceived peril seems to have resided in the *koinê* of ascetic praxis to which the very devout tended to subject themselves, irrespective of their specific confessional identity. The threat represented by this tendency seems to have been felt most acutely by the Muslim community; after all, throughout the first two centuries of Islam, it was this community rather than its deeply entrenched neighbors that faced the very real prospect of absorption by the communities it now ruled. The response that the Muslim *umma* seems to have formulated to this threat depended upon the place of the doctrine and practice of *jihād* within early Islam's defining metanarrative, although not in a manner that the reader might expect.

* * *

While the origins of Muslim mysticism and the advent of the various Sufi schools have attracted much scholarly attention through the years, the question of the origins of Muslim asceticism as an aspect of Muslim religious identity has attracted considerably less, and what attention asceticism has garnered has been concerned ultimately with its role in the formation of the mystic movement. This is especially troubling in that asceticism clearly became crucial to early Muslim strategies of self-fashioning, serving as the basis for what one scholar has referred to an "Islamic moral imagination," while mysticism, although influential, was to become the vocation of a comparative few.[3]

Indeed, the origins of a specifically Muslim range of ascetic expression have been mostly taken for granted. This is problematic in that the specific acts of asceticism, the moral content (or sign value) of those acts, and the role of ascetics in early Muslim society seem all but indistinguishable from those of a spectrum of late antique faith communities. What made the various forms of renunciation scholars have consistently labeled as indicative of Muslim asceticism Muslim at all? This question becomes more urgent when we recognize that many early Muslims not only associated various forms of renunciation with Muslimness, but also acknowledged heightened proficiency in ascetic praxis as a mark of communal authority.[4]

The role of ascetic praxis in the elaboration of a specifically Muslim "moral imagination" was inextricably linked to the elaboration of normative behavioral traits that inscribed individuals as members of the Muslim *umma*. Although not every Muslim was an ascetic, just as not every late ancient Christian was a monk, certain Muslims whose social persona was defined through an ethos of detachment from the concerns of the present world became, over time, both models of ideal Islamic virtue for their contemporaries and descendents, and, frequently, discerners and defenders of the behavioral, doctrinal, and social boundaries that were understood to enclosed the Muslim *umma*. The apparent paradox we have begun to identify, however, is that the theory and practice of ascetic renunciation in accordance with which these privileged figures were crafted was, in itself, without substantive difference from the theory and practice of ascetic renunciation observable among the early *umma*'s non-Muslim contemporaries. In other words, the visible manifestations of the ascetic praxis upon which the early Muslim *umma* depended as a means of self-definition and self-differentiation were very often indistinguishable from the patterns of ascetic renunciation that flowed back and forth across (indeed seemingly in defiance of) the very communal boundaries to whose constitution they were so crucial.

In examining this apparent paradox and its consequences, we will return once again to the work of the anthropologist Fredrik Barth, in particular to his suggestion that in considering the formation and maintenance over time of identity groupings, it is frequently the case that focusing upon the cultural traditions, practices, or belief systems which communal boundaries are said to enclose may be deceptive in that the traditions, practices, or beliefs which are claimed to characterize a certain group may shift over time while the claimed identity of the group remains constant.[5] Barth demonstrates that such traditions, practices, or beliefs may be shared in common with persons or communities that, on the basis of tradition, practice, or belief would seem to be contiguous with the "in group" but which are in fact considered to constitute an "out group." More productive, Barth argues, is to note where and how boundaries are drawn and maintained between groups, because it is here that the dynamics of identity are played out.[6]

With Barth's insights in mind, we will ask in the first part of this chapter how it was that certain ascetic behaviors shared in common with other communities eventually came to inscribe Muslims as members of one specific community and distinguish them from members of all other communities. A series of incidents from the literature surrounding the early Muslim ascetic Ibrāhīm b. Adham, who it is believed died in the later eighth/second century, will help to illustrate this problem.[7]

Ibn Ḥibbān's rather dry fourth/tenth-century biographical notice for Ibrāhīm b. Adham lays out the basics of his life: Ibrāhīm b. Adham b. Mansūr Abū Isḥaq was born in Balkh (about 20 km northwest of modern Mazari Sharif in Afghanistan) and migrated to Baghdād. He then went to Syria to seek pure *ḥalāl* (righteous living in accordance with Islamic law). There he became a *ghāzī* and was posted as a warrior "persevering in extreme piety and hard striving with adherence to *zahāda* (renunciation or asceticism)" in performing acts of worship until he died raiding in the lands of the Romans.[8]

The Ibn Adham who became important to later Muslims, however, was the Ibn Adham of legend.[9] This Ibn Adham was distinguished by his hard-striving asceticism, his compassion, and his penchant for the miraculous.[10] Among narratives detailing the doings of late antique holy folk of all confessional stripes, conversion narratives are crucial for establishing both the character of the protagonist and the distance that his initial encounter with the numinous puts between himself and the mundane world (of which the reader is of course a part). There are several narratives detailing Ibrāhīm's conversion experiences, of which versions of the following are perhaps the most frequently cited.

One day the young aristocrat is out hunting on his horse, when a disembodied voice calls out to him, "O Ibrāhīm, you were not created for this, nor were you commanded to this!" The voice repeats the admonition twice more, prompting Ibrāhīm to renounce his life of privilege and become a wandering ascetic seeking a pure Muslim life. Eventually, he takes employment in an orchard. One day, the orchard's owner asks Ibrāhīm to pick out a ripe pomegranate, but he is unable to do so. Surprised, the man asks him, "O keeper of the orchard, since such and such a time you have been in our orchard eating of our fruits and our pomegranates, but you do not know the sweet from the sour?" To which Ibn Adham replies, "By God, I do not eat any of your fruit, and no, I don't know the sweet from the sour!" People from the local community learn that there is an accomplished ascetic in the neighborhood and so pester him with their admiration that he has to flee the area.[11]

This narrative is intriguing for a variety of reasons. As David Braund and, more recently, Joel Thomas Walker, have noted, the association of royalty with hunting in societies subject to Persian cultural influence makes the hunt a prime venue for the conversion of nobles native to those societies. It is on the hunt, where the king is most regal, that he may be most dramatically humbled by the overawing power of God and then duly called to true religion. The narratives of the conversions to Christianity of the fourth-century Georgian king Mayrian, for example, and the Sasanian noble Mar Qardagh both center upon miraculous events that take place while the protagonist is on the hunt. They, like Ibrāhīm, are humbled by their encounters with the numinous and soon thereafter undergo spiritual transformations.[12]

Frequent also in late antique hagiography are scenes set in gardens located in strange or unlikely places, or in which the monk is as a stranger, a topos which in Christian literature alludes to the creation of a "new Adam" who has, through his strivings and obedience, undone the sins of the first Adam. The suggestion in this text seems to be that through his ascetic virtue and by remembering the duties of a servant, Ibrāhīm has preserved his Paradise unsullied.[13] Similarly common in late antique hagiography is the topos in which a young noble leaves home in search of enlightenment and travels from one teacher to another in search of purer forms of ascetic practice.[14] Also common is the figure of the exemplary ascetic who, upon discovery of his holiness by the masses, flees their admiration. Indeed, these latter two tropes are featured prominently in Christian saints' lives that are inserted into the works of such Muslim authors as Ibn Isḥāq and Ṭabarī.[15]

Taken by themselves, however, the inclusion of these topoi in this narrative only suggest that it is a text which would have been comprehensible across various late antique communal boundaries; it is a text that elaborates upon a set of signs and symbols comprehensible in a spectrum of late antique communities. Another pair of narratives describing the deeds of Ibn Adham, however, may suggest something more.

Yet another topos common to late antique saints' lives is that of a meeting between a young or would-be ascetic and a holy man whose example inspires the novice to undertake the ascetic life or to press on more zealously with such a life already undertaken.[16] In the collections of narratives detailing the deeds of Ibn Adham, two are especially noteworthy. In the first of these Ibn Adham learns from an old Christian ascetic, who eats just one chickpea every day, about the practice of fasting. The old monk named Abū Simʿān (Symeon) explains the rationale for his asceticism thus: "Whenever my soul grows weary from worship, I recall the Hour of Judgment, and I endure striving for a year for the sake of the glory of that hour. And so endure the striving of an hour for the sake of the glory of eternity, O Ḥanīfī!"[17]

It is implicit in this passage that Ibn Adham is inspired by the example of the monk, who serves as an exemplar of the sort of strenuous renunciation for which Ibn Adham was to become known. This, then, is a literary rendering of what is suggested structurally by the deployment of commonly comprehensible topoi in the conversion narrative just discussed—Ibn Adham, as sign and literary figure, is to be understood as participating in a semiotic universe in which Christian monks carry resonances that may be described as very much akin to his own. This is not to suggest that Ibn Adham is a Christian monk, of course. Rather, he is to be understood as a keen embodiment of virtues prized by his own community. Clearly, however, the virtues of which he is representative are not distinctly Muslim, nor do they by themselves inscribe individuals as members of any specific community. This becomes clearer in a second narrative.

> Ibrāhīm b. Adham said . . . "I passed by a monk in his cell, and the cell was on a pillar, and the pillar was on the top of a mountain, and whenever the wind blew, the cell would lean. I called to him and said, 'O monk!' And he did not answer me. So again, I called to him, and he did not answer me. And I said, for the third time, 'By he who enclosed you in your cell, will you not answer me?' His head came out from his cell and . . . I said, 'O monk, you are not a monk. Nay, rather, the monk is whoever fears his Lord' [a play, it would seem, upon the root *rāʾ-hāʾ-bāʾ*, from which both the verb *rahiba*, "fear" and the substantive *rāhib*, "monk" are derived]. I said, "What are you?" He said, "I am a jailer, imprisoning the beast of beasts." I said, 'What is it?' He said, 'My tongue is a ravenous beast. If I were to neglect it, it would tear people apart. O Ḥanīfī, for God's sake ascetics [*ʿubbād*] are deaf with regard to hearing, and silent with regard to speaking, and blind with regard to sight . . . They are plucked along by the winds of conviction until they take anchor along the shores of sincere devotion. By God, ascetics rub their eyes through the night in sleeplessness, and if you were to see them in the night when the eyes of men are sleeping, they would be tending to their endurance . . . O Ḥanīfī, make use of their path!' I said, 'Are you in accord with Islam? [that is, Are you a Muslim?]' He said, 'I do not know our religion to be unlike Islam, although the Messiah [Jesus] was entrusted to us . . . your religion is a new one.'"[18]

This narrative seems to confirm that the qualities and practices that identify Ibn Adham as an exemplarily pious Muslim—those qualities and practices, indeed, to which the monk exhorts him—cannot be called essentially Muslim. As if to underscore this point, Ibn Adham, after listening to the monk exhort him to withdrawal, silence, and vigil, feels the need to inquire regarding his confessional alignment. Is this man a Muslim, Ibn Adham wants to know. The answer the monk gives is particularly telling, lightly effacing, as it seems to, the significance of each ascetic's specific confessional identity and suggesting, as this and the preceding narratives also seem to, a shared identity based in ascetic practice rather than dogma.

The question of confessional identity is sometimes so subsidiary to ascetic practice as to become moot, as seems to be the case in some other stories of Ibn Adham's encounters with various ascetics. In one of these, for example, he describes the activities of an ascetic he encountered in the "mountains of Alexandria," a region renowned for its vast array of Christian ascetic communities.[19] Ibrāhīm tries to imitate the rigor of this ascetic, but fails. "As I took up his place, I tried [to meet his standard] but I was not equal to it."[20]

This ascetic is described rather ambiguously using the term *ʿābid* [pl. *ʿubbād*], a term also used by the Christian monks in Muslim texts to refer to their coreligionists. C.-A. Keller has recently suggested that frequently such references in texts describing encounters between well-known Muslim ascetics and *ʿubbād* should be read as encounters with "Christian or Gnostic" ascetics.[21] While it seems somewhat hasty to read all such references in this way, we might more cautiously conclude that in such narratives as these, there is an ambiguity in the confessional identity of such figures that does little to undermine their sign value. In other words, that the confessional identity of such figures is indeterminate is less important than the unambiguous character of their ascetic accomplishment, a semiotic element that may be read independent of any specific confessional coloring. Many such ambiguous figures are to be found in reports concerning other second/eighth- and third/ninth-century ascetics, notably, as Keller points out, Dhū al-Nūn.[22]

Such encounters as these narratives describe, those that take place between members of various confessional communities who, because of their shared ascetic vocation, could be described with such generic terms as *ʿābid*, were not without precedent in the late antique world. As James Goehring has shown, despite the frequent late antique literary construction of Christian ascetics as divinely inspired experts in the discernment and defense of orthodoxy, the ascetics who occupied the orthodox monastic communities of Egypt sometimes included those whose Christology was decidedly heterodox according to the standards of the Church hierarchy and were occasionally members of Manichean and Gnostic sects. Goehring has suggested convincingly that even ascetics whose confessional communities were bitterly at odds with one another found a kind of spiritual *koinê* in their shared ascetic practice.[23]

In addition to the intercommunal contacts Goehring has discerned among ascetics, late antique holy men became symbols that resonated in a variety of cultural registers and as such attracted admirers not only from within their own communities but from other communities as well. Daniel the Stylite, for example, famously attracted non-Christian Arab tribesmen as well as diverse crowds of admirers while the saints' shrines attended by ascetics throughout the late antique world were, as Elizabeth Key Fowden has recently shown, points of intercultural, interconfessional exchange, attracting visitors and patrons from a diverse range of communities.[24] Elsewhere, Muhammad Qasim Zaman has recently demonstrated that the funerals of such figures frequently put on display their capacity to capture the imaginations and admiration of individuals and groups beyond their immediate community. He cites the funeral of the ascetic churchman Basil of Caesarea at which Gregory Nazianzus writes, "A contest arose between our people and outsiders, pagans, Jews, strangers as to who should lament the more and thereby gain the greater benefit."[25] Zaman might have added the description of the bishop Ambrose of Milan's funeral written by his biographer/hagiographer Paulinus, which was likewise attended by "not only Christians, but also Jews and pagans."[26]

Similar intercommunal appeal becomes evident in the reports of the funerals of some Muslims of ascetic tendencies in the eighth and ninth centuries. Aḥmad b. Ḥanbal's funeral, for example, was attended by Christians, Jews and Zoroastrians as well as a multitude of Muslims. Al-Awzāʿī, a legal scholar who took up the role of local protector, a role recognizable in such men as Libanius and, as Zaman notes, other late antique holy men, was buried after a procession which included Jews, and members of two Christian factions (the "Copts" and the "Christians") as well as Muslims.[27] Zaman also notes what he interprets as a hint of unease in the report of the Jews and Christians who accompanied al-Awzāʿī's body to burial: "On the one hand, it is a mark of the dead man's status that *everybody* wants to join in; but, on the other hand, and from the perspective of later Muslims at least, such participation also threatens to blur religious boundaries" [Zaman's emphasis].[28]

Plainly, then, while it might be desirable that the virtues of the moral and religious paragons of one's community be recognized beyond the confines of the community, such recognition was only possible on the basis of a shared semiotic vocabulary, and such shared recognitions might well promote slippage in the very boundaries upon which communal identity depends. Asceticism constituted a system of ideas and ideals that resonated across a spectrum of late antique communities. As Ibn Adham, blinded momentarily by the brilliance of his Christian interlocutor's ascetic *ʿilm* ("wisdom/understanding") loses track of the old renunciant's confessional identity, the possibility seems to suggest itself that in such a situation even a pious Muslim might well lose track of his *own* identity. Such a possibility seems to have occurred, at any rate, to later Muslims imagining the disorderly amalgamation of identities that saw al-Awzāʿī to his grave. Indeed, during his lifetime Ibn Ḥanbal himself had much to say regarding the necessity of maintaining strict boundaries between Muslims and others in life and death and in the charged spaces of funeral processions and burials.[29]

Traces of the unease felt by some Muslims concerning the blurring of communal boundaries around questions of ascetic practice may be found in a variety of second/eighth- and third/ninth-century Muslim texts. There exists a body of *ḥadīths* in such early Muslim texts as Ibn Saʿd's *Kitāb al-ṭabaqāt al-kabīr*, for example, that address the issue of fasting or the adoption of ascetic affectations associated with Christian monks that may reasonably be read, following Ignaz Goldziher, as antimonastic in character.[30] Although the specific basis for the objections raised to ascetic behaviors in these traditions is not always clear, there is a significant body of antimonastic traditions in which it would seem that the trouble some Muslims saw with ascetic behavior was its potential to blur the boundaries between Muslim and non-Muslim. In these traditions, it is often the Prophet himself who is evoked to insist upon the behavioral boundaries (in the guise of *sunna* or the recalled, normative traditions of the Prophet) that demarcate Muslim from non-Muslim.

In a passage from the *tafsīr* (a work of Qur'ānic exegesis) of Muqātil b. Sulaymān (d. 150/767), for example, a group of particularly pious Muslims decide that each of them would "cut off his penis and dress himself in monastic garb, and . . . build cells and become monks in them and live separately." The angel Gabriel comes to Muḥammad, however, and tells him of their plan. The Prophet goes to the wife of one of the men and tells her, "When your husband comes, tell him that he is not of my people whoever does not follow my *sunna* . . . [and] this is our *sunna*: Clothes, food and women. Let your husband know this—whoever detests my *sunna* is not of my people."[31]

Making much the same point is a brief passage from Ibn Qutayba's third/ninth-century *ʿUyūn al-akhbār*, which runs: "About ʿAkkāf b. Wadāʿa it was said that the Prophet said to him: 'O ʿAkkāf, do you have a woman?' He said, 'No.' And [Muḥammad] said, 'Then you are of the brothers of Satan! If you are of the monks of the Christians, then betake yourself to them. But if you are one of us, our *sunna* is marriage.'"[32]

Amounting to the same series of ideas is one prophetic *ḥadīth* from Aḥmad b. Ḥanbal's third/ninth-century *Musnad*. In it the Prophet questions the young man named ʿAkkāf b. Bashir al-Tammiyya about his ascetic habits:

> The Prophet said to him, "Do you not have a wife?" He said, "No." He said, "No concubine?" He said, "No." He said, "Are you well off as regards property?" He said, "I am well off as regards property." [Muḥammad] said, "In that case you are among the most faithless of devils! If you were a Christian you would be one of their monks. Our *sunna* is marriage. Your sin is your celibacy, a contemptible one. Your death is your celibacy. Do you practice what is Satan's with Satan? Everyone who is pious is stronger [in his piety] with a pious woman. Are your married friends not pure, free from the guilt of fornication? Let this inspire you, O ʿAkkāf!"[33]

The maintenance of communal boundaries would seem to be at issue in each of these passages. In each case, the piety of members of Muḥammad's community is expressed in an idiom that plainly makes sense within a late antique cultural milieu—that is, rigorous ascetic practice. These passages seem to suggest, however, that with these expressions of piety, both these individuals and those around them have become subject to the disorientating slippage that Ibn Adham has experienced in his encounter with the monk, and the question he poses, "Are you a Muslim?" or more literally, "Are you in accord with Islam?" has now been posed to ascetically minded Muslims by the founder of the faith.

The marks of inclusion stressed in both of these narratives, and in many of the other "antimonastic" *ḥadīths* from Ibn Saʿd's text, emphasize the question of marriage and secondarily attend to alimentary practices and styles of dress and comportment. If it was these issues upon which membership in the Muslim community would depend, there could be no peace with those of the community whose piety tended to ascetic expression—this because the areas of life to which these issues attend, namely familial ties to the community, commensality, and social prestige, were the issues around which ascetics defined themselves in opposition to their fellows, and it is in that opposition that they paradoxically became exemplars and as such resources for communal self-fashioning.[34] Nor could it be expected that asceticism would just go away or radically change its forms—it was in the very vocabulary of forms that were now cited as troubling by the Muslim community that the imaginative power of asceticism resided. Moreover, it seems clear that from an early date, asceticism had and would continue to exercise a profound hold over the imagination of those Muslims most interested in defining the true community of the faithful.[35]

If the forms of asceticism were not likely to change, or if they would be without value within a late antique cultural milieu were they to change, it became necessary to understand ascetic practice in its familiar forms as relevant to the Muslim community in some primordial sense. There was need, in other words, to connect asceticism to the Islamic community's foundational past so that it might have a recognizable and manageable place in defining its present. Crucial to understanding this process are a pair of *ḥadīths* to be found in ʿAbd Allāh b. al-Mubārak's *Kitāb al-jihād* (Book of Jihād). They are among the most frequently cited antimonastic *ḥadīths* in the early Muslim corpus. While there may indeed be an antiascetic charge to these *ḥadīths*, however, I will suggest that in fact they also function to tell us much about the conjunction of ascetic modes of piety in early Islam with the practice of *jihād*. The *ḥadīths* in question are as follows.

> Every community has its monasticism, and the monasticism of my community is *jihād* on the path of God.[36]

> Wandering monasticism was mentioned in the presence of the Prophet of God, and the messenger of God said, "God gave us in its place *jihād* on the path of God and the *takbīr* from every hill."[37]

One key to understanding the importance of these *ḥadīths* is to understand something of the author of the work in which they appear. Ibn al-Mubārak was a frontier warrior and a noted ascetic.[38] He was also a noted traditionalist and scholar. In addition to his *Kitāb al-jihād*, he was the author of a *Kitāb al-zuhd* (The Book of Renunciation or Book of Asceticism). Both his treatise on *jihād* and his work on *zuhd* lay particular emphasis upon the internal qualities of the individual worshipper.

The renunciation of worldly concerns, which manifests itself as purity of intention, is a recurrent theme in each work. Crucial to this form of renunciation is the diminution of individual ego, which was in turn common to most strains of late antique asceticism.[39] In the books of Ibn al-Mubārak, this diminution of the individual self is given a role both in the soteriological concerns of the individual and in the crafting of his community. His status within his community, reckoned both terrestrially and cosmologically, is to be imagined as an inverted image of his investment in the present world and its concerns. "This world is a copy of the next one—it is as a man who has two wives, and if he satisfies one of them, he will embitter the other," Ibn al-Mubārak counsels his reader in the *Kitāb al-zuhd*.[40] Those who lived for the next world were to be exemplars in this one, a proposition which could turn the world upside down: One of Ibn al-Mubārak's companions said: "I asked Ibn al-Mubārak, 'Who are the kings?' He said, 'The ascetics.' I said, 'Who are the riff raff?' He said, 'A rich man and his companions.' I said, 'Who are the lowly?' He said, 'Those supporting themselves by means of their religion.'"[41]

There is much in Ibn al-Mubārak's ascetical work that would have found consensus in any late antique ascetic community. "The present world is the paradise of the infidel, and the prison of the faithful man," he assures his reader. "And just as a man who was in prison leaves it and turns around in the world and stretches his arms, [so it is when] the faithful man escapes [the present world]."[42] The present world was full of evils to be endured and temptations to be bested. The truly pious man would leave it all behind and see to the care of his soul. Even the companionship of pious men could become burdensome.

One of Ibn al-Mubārak's companions remembered, for example, that while in the Silk Road oasis city of Merv, Ibn al-Mubārak lived in a large house and had constant visitors. When he moved to al-Kūfa in Iraq, however, he had a small house and few visitors. "And I said to him, 'O Abu ʿAbd al-Raḥman, do you not feel lonely here compared to [when you lived] in Merv?' He said, 'Rather I fled from Merv . . . and I love what is here [although] I see you loathing it on my behalf . . . [for] in Merv there was no instruction except [the people] coming to me for it, and no question except people questioning Ibn al-Mubārak. Here I have respite from that.'"[43] Such sentiments could be given a finer point: "I find nearness to God away from most people," Ibn al-Mubārak told one of his companions. "When someone flees the masses, it is like you would flee from the lion. May you hold fast to your religion and may your striving bring peace to you."[44]

The necessity of flight from the corrupting influences of the crowd and the desire for a solitude in which the believer could perfect his soul emerge as recurrent themes in Ibn al-Mubārak's ascetical compilation. It was in opposition to the material concerns of the community at large that the truly pious man was to define himself. "The people of property eat and we eat. They drink and we drink. They wear clothes and we wear clothes. They ride horses and we ride horses," runs one passage. "Their superabundance of property they gaze upon, and we gaze upon it with them; its reckoning is to their disadvantage, and we are free from it."[45]

If one could cut oneself off from the corrupting concerns of the world, one might begin the rigorous process of remaking oneself from the inside out and in so doing make oneself deserving of God's mercy. This process involved familiar ascetic ritual—Ibn al-Mubārak was famous for his fasting, for example—but at the heart of this process was an obedience and renunciation focused upon a diminution and eventual annihilation of the individual will.[46]

It was in this way that the individual believer might become closer to God. Ibn al-Mubārak commented once to his companions that those whose home was in the present world tended to leave it without ever having tasted the sweetest of its pleasures. When someone asked what exactly this pleasure was, Ibn al-Mubarak replied, "Knowledge of God, powerful and exalted."[47] This answer would not have surprised Ibn Adham or his Christian counterparts. Above all, it was the worshipper's will that must be mastered and laid before his God, humbled and pure, and the complexion of his will manifested in the purity of his intention. As Michael Bonner has noted, it is the intention of the individual worshiper which for Ibn al-Mubārak allows for a true appraisal of the merits of his actions, especially with regard to those undertaken during *jihād*, but it was only through ascetic practice that pure intention could be crafted.[48]

It is around the question of purity of will that one begins to encounter significant overlap between the doctrine of *jihād* and the practice of asceticism in Ibn al-Mubārak's thinking. This overlap is visible in the following two passages, the first of which appears in Ibn al-Mubārak's *Kitāb al-jihād*, and the second of which is from his *Kitāb al-zuhd.*

> The killed are three men: A faithful man striving with his person and his property on the path of God until he meets the enemy, fighting until he is killed. This *shahīd* is the most favored in the tent of God, under his throne. The prophets are not preferred to him except with regard to the status of [their] prophethood. [Then there is] a faithful man peeling himself from misdeeds and sin,

striving with his person and his property on the path of God, until he meets the enemy and is killed. This is a cleansing, scraping away his misdeeds and transgressions—for the sword scrapes away sin—and he enters paradise by whatever gate he pleases. And there are eight doors to paradise, and seven doors to Hell, and each one is lower [than the others]. And a hypocritical man strives with his person and his property on the path of God until he is killed. This one is in Hell, for the sword does not scrape away hypocrisy.[49]

[A traditionalist] said . . . "I heard the Prophet of God say, 'When it is resurrection day, God will manifest himself to his servants so that he may pass judgment among them, and the whole community will be on its knees. First summoned shall be the man who knows the Qur'ān by heart and God the Exalted will say to him, "My servant! Has not what I revealed to my Prophet instructed you?" And he will say, "Yes, O Lord." And God will say, "What then do you know of what I taught you?" The man will say, "O Lord, I am subsumed in it day and night." And God shall say, "You lie." And the angels shall say to him, "You lie. Nay, rather, you want it said, 'So and so is a reciter of the Qur'ān,' and so it was said. But go away, for you have no place among us today." Then a possessor of property will be sent down and God will say to him, "My servant! Have I not pampered you? Have I not given preference to you? Have I not been generous to you?" And the man will turn to him and say, "Yes, O Lord." And God will say, "What then do you know of what I sent down to you?" And he shall say, "O Lord, I was a source of mercy, and I gave alms and I gave and I gave." And God shall say, "You lie." And the angels shall say to him, "You lie. Nay rather, you desired that it be said, 'So and so is generous,' and this was said. But go away, for there is nothing for you among us this day." And a man who had been killed will be sent forth, and God shall say, "My servant! Why were you killed?" And the man shall say, "O Lord, for you I was killed, on your path." And God the Most High will say, "You lie." And the angels will say to him, "You lie. Nay, rather, you desired it should be said, 'So and so is courageous,' and so it was said. But go away, for there is no place for you among us today."'"[50]

In the second of these passages, intention as a function of individual will comes distinctly to the fore. Each man brought before God and his angels has accomplished an outward act of piety prior to his death, but in each case this outward act was in fact a manifestation of ego rather than sincere piety. In the narrative that precedes it, identical deaths on the path of God have dramatically different results due to the differences implicit in the internal landscapes of the individual worshipers whose deaths bring them to the doors of paradise.

Read in tandem, these passages suggest that in these texts the intersection of *jihād* and ascetic practice has much to do with asceticism's perceived capacity to prepare the individual Muslim to craft his inner life in such a manner that his actions in life might resonate as expressions of his absolute subjection to his community and his God. Each act of piety mentioned above, the recitation of the Qur'ān, the giving of alms, or the participation in *jihād*, is meaningless if the individual who performs these acts has not subdued his will and made of himself a constant sincere *ʿābid*. To extend such ideas to the lives of everyday Muslims will not have been difficult.

In this alone, however, ascetic practice had not become exclusively Muslim. The late antique Christian monastic experience,[51] as described by John Cassian and others,[52] began with a series of steps by which the self was humbled and by which the initiate submitted himself to the authority of the monastery and its leadership. In so doing, he began a process of subject formation which would, ideally, leave the monk shorn of his individual will.[53]

The initiate then entered a period of assessment during which individuals unable to "vanquish [their] own desires" were weeded out and expelled.[54] He was confined to a cell, forbidden to leave without the direct permission of his superior, even to "satisfy the common and natural needs."[55] A fifth-century Persian monastery called for a year spent in the monastery before a priest or deacon was allowed to assume monastic garments.[56] Through this confinement novice monks "carry out without any discussion everything that is ordered by [their superiors], just as though they were commanded by God in heaven, so that sometimes impossible things are commanded of them, and undertake them with a faith and devotion so great that they devote all of their effort to execute and accomplish them, without any hesitation of the heart; such is their reverence for their superiors that they do not think about whether the thing that is ordered is an impossibility."[57]

As regards the elimination of the personal will, Ibn al-Mubārak could not have asked any more of his companions.[58] Ascetic practice had become crucial to the business of *jihād* as Ibn al-Mubārak imagined it in the middle decades of the second/eighth century because it was understood to prepare the individual Muslim to undertake his strivings with a pure soul and pristine intentions. Asceticism, then, made *jihād* a venue in which acts of martial valor or conquest (or simple raiding, theft, or murder) could be reinscribed as acts of piety and as moments of communion with the numinous. Its association with *jihād*, in turn, made of asceticism a distinctly Muslim expression of piety, especially as the early Muslim community elaborated historical narratives that constructed the conquest period as a series of martial miracles which manifested God's judgment and good pleasure.[59]

To understand how the second part of this process worked, that is, how ascetic piety was imagined to have made Islam, and how in turn an Islamic asceticism was made, it will serve us well to return to the *ḥadīths* with which we began this section, those which contain the Prophet's proclamations regarding *jihād* and monasticism. "Every community has its monasticism, and the monasticism of my community is *jihād* on the path of God."[60] What precisely is the claim being made here? As I argued in the previous chapter, the early Muslim community seems to have understood the history and function of monasticism within Christian society fairly well, so well in fact that in composing the early histories of their own community, Muslims were quite able to elaborate certain claims regarding monks and monasticism to their own ends.

In the imaginative world of late antique Christianity, monasticism provided a venue in which the community's primordial past remained present, and moments of numinous revelation remained perpetually available and yet properly alien.[61] The strivings of Christian ascetics, and more to the point their capacity to endure those strivings, made available the moments around which the post-Constantinian Christian world cohered, those in which pious and determined witnesses to the truths of the faith made those truths manifest in the fulcrum of Roman justice. The grisly texts that retailed in pornographic detail the bodily ravages to which martyrs were subjected resonated with the presence of the divine—trials and tortures produced truth in the Roman world, and the truth of the martyr was the strength of his God flowing through him in the moment of his death.[62]

For Christian monks, this death was spread over years—so Daniel the Styilite could stand atop his column literally both dead and alive, worms already greedily partaking of his flesh as it fell away from his bones—but it was the presence of God, as much for the monk as the martyr, which made this lingering life/death possible. Around the monks of late antiquity time collapsed. The striving and triumphs of the persecution-era martyrs became present again and continuously available, as did the world-changing intrusion of the numinous which their lives and deaths betokened. Meanwhile, the otherwise unyielding boundaries between this world and the next melted to so many strands of translucent gauze, so that miracles and visions, numinous revelations and angelic visitations flooded in around the men of the monasteries.

Monasticism, then, became an imaginative space in which the primordial dramas of various late antique faith communities were reenacted and in which moments of numinous intrusion into the history of the community itself were made continuously available. In such circumstances, the primordial identities of the communities to which these dramas were imagined to have given birth were reaffirmed (or reinvented) by the men who now stood in for the vanished martyrs and whose strivings were to become the basis for communal ethical, moral and behavioral ideals.[63] The ideals so elaborated in the monastic venue were utterly indisputable as resources for communal self-fashioning, arising as they did from the reemergence and repetition of the community's primordial drama, this illuminated in turn by what was only to be understood as the incursion into human affairs of the one true God, whose will became manifest in the triumph of the martyrs over their persecutors.[64]

The early Muslims clearly understood the link between the early Christian martyrs and the monks of the later period.[65] They seem also to have understood quite well the role of Christian monks in establishing and maintaining communal standards of piety and sometimes imagined monastic communities as sanctuaries in which the truth of Jesus' revelation was preserved while in the outside it was distorted and lost.[66] While the identification in early *ḥadīths* of *jihād* as the Muslim community's own form of (or substitute for) monasticism may be read as yet another of the boundary-sensitive traditions discussed previously, a survey of some narratives included by Ibn al-Mubārak in his *Kitāb al-jihād* suggests that these traditions should perhaps be taken more seriously than they have been previously and that they may in fact suggest something of the way in which a specifically Muslim asceticism evolved.

The narratives included by Ibn al-Mubārak in his work evoke *jihād* as an institution in which the Muslim communal past, and particularly that of the conquest or preconquest period, merges with the lived present of his *ghāzī* companions.[67] The narratives themselves drift in time, located (and barely so) only by the presence of the Prophet or his companions. They seldom make reference to specific events which would confine them in an unrecoverable past, but instead describe situations and events which, in their timeless narration, collapse the present into the past and conjure a past resonant with the present. This is particularly the case as regards the reams of *ḥadīths* contained within the work, crafted as they are in notoriously flat and ahistorical phrasing, but this tendency comes into especially sharp focus in the *akhbār* also assembled in the work. The following illustrates this well.

The Prophet one day turned to his companions and asked for a volunteer for a particularly dangerous mission. The man expresses his zeal and then leaves to prepare for his mission. "And the messenger of God said, 'Whoever wants to see a man preparing his eternal green place for the morrow, let him look upon this man.' And he rushed away to his people, bidding them farewell, and his women took hold of his garment and said, 'O Abū al-Sabuʿ, you are leaving us, and you will perish.' And he gently pulled away his garment until he left them behind, and then he turned back to them and said, 'The day of resurrection is promised to you.' And then he was killed."[68]

The events described in this *khabar* hang indeterminately suspended in time, and the presence of the Prophet does more to authorize the ideas contained within it than to locate it in any specific time or place. Moreover, this narrative suggests much about the character of early formulations of *jihād* and their affinities with Christian monasticism. The warrior featured here is, as the antimonastic *ḥadīths* cited above would demand, married and may be counted as part of a familial unit. But his renunciation of these bonds in the service of Muḥammad's revelation is at the heart of this narrative. As Peter Brown has shown, it was the renunciation of those communal bonds which kept one from God which truly drove much Christian monasticism, and it was less from the temptations of the flesh and tyranny of appetites than those of the family and social responsibility that many Christian ascetics fled. To defeat these, in Christian monasticism as in Muslim *jihād*, was to become a worthy and devoted servant of one's God.

To defeat these, however, was to undo the bonds of one's traditional society. In late antique Christian society, this frequently meant the dissolution of family wealth, or the end of long lines of aristocratic breeding. In the case of late antique notions of *jihād*, this meant that the lives and welfare of one's own family were to become subsidiary to one's responsibilities on the path of

God. This could be a complicated proposition, despite the zeal of the individual worshiper.

In a passage from Ibn al-Mubārak's work on *jihād*, for example, a dream reveals that a *mujāhid*, Abū al-Ṣahbā' is to receive "two martyrdoms." Abū al-Ṣahbā' happily interprets this to mean that he and has son will both be martyred. When his band is overrun by the Turks, however, he wavers: "'O my son,' he said, '[Go] to your mother.' And [Abū al-Ṣahbā''s son] said, 'O my father, you desire good for yourself, but you order me to withdraw. By God you are better to my mother than to me.'"[69] Abū al-Ṣahbā' sees the light and he and his son attack the Turks. Father and son are predictably martyred shortly hereafter.

This passage suggests something of the limits of devotion and brings us back to the question of intention and individual ego. At the suggestion that Abū al-Ṣahbā' and his son will both become martyrs, Abū al-Ṣahbā' is clearly quite proud. But when his own death and the annihilation of his family come upon him, he hesitates, corrected by the piety of his son. Here, once again, it is the individual ego that threatens to come between the individual believer and the purity of intention which will win him salvation. It was one thing to know that "death is a gift to the faithful"[70] as Ibn al-Mubārak exhorted his reader but quite another to put such an ethic into practice if one were still attached to the world.

In one especially intriguing passage of Ibn al-Mubārak's work we encounter an individual who has apparently overcome such attachments, and he represents a type of ascetic warrior who will reemerge frequently in later Muslim narratives recalling the conquest period. In the passage, a young Muslim is invited by a friend to witness the behavior of a certain Kufan whose actions are apparently considered to constitute something of a spectacle. As they catch sight of him, the man is haranguing a group of Muslims as they move along a road. The two young men follow the figure, clad all in rags, to the local mosque, in which he moves off by himself and performs many prostrations. He then comes before the congregation and scolds them for their lack of zeal. "In this mosque there are three parties huddled," he says. "The faithful who have wisdom, the faithful who have no wisdom and the hypocrites." He then called the assembled Muslims to *jihād*, likening the practice of *jihād* to the soothing rain. Concluding, he begs, "O God, bestow upon me martyrdom, with its joy surpassing its pain, and its terror surpassed by its peace.'"

The man soon thereafter leads a group of *ghāzī* against the infidel, and the young men accompany him.[71] In this figure once again ascetic and warrior are melded, and in his ragged apparel and single-minded devotion, this militant charismatic represents what was to become a recognizable type in the narratives evolving during Ibn al-Mubārak's lifetime concerning the opening of the lands of the new Islamic empire, a series of events that had come to be understood not only as the primordial drama of the Muslim world, which indeed it was, but also as a series of military miracles which spectacularly manifested the will of God in the affairs of men, apparently confirming not only Muḥammad's revelation but the very basis of the community it invented. Take, for example, the following narrative, which appears in the grand history of al-Ṭabarī. It describes one of the men who defeated the forces of the Persian shah at the battle of Qādisiyya.

> [The Arab] came in on a hairy, short-legged mare, having with him a polished sword whose scabbard was made of shabby cloth. His spear was bound with a strap of sinew, and he had a shield made of cowhide, whose exterior was of bright color, like a thick, round loaf of bread . . . his coat was the cover of a camel, in which he made a hole, used it as a shield, and tied to his waist with a bark of reeds. He was the hairiest of the Arabs, and he tied to his head a piece of cloth which was the girth of a camel. On his head he had four locks of hair which protruded like horns of a goat.[72]

Upon entering the presence of the Persians, the Arab refuses to dismount, rides onto their carpets, and slashes their pillows. Approaching the Persian commander Rustam, he pokes more holes in the Persian carpets and cushions. He is asked why he fights, and he replies that his community has been sent by God to spread Islam and to "fulfill the promise of God." Rustam asks, "What is the promise of God?" and the Arab answers, "Paradise for him who dies while fighting those who have refused [to embrace Islam] and victory for him who survives."

As we have seen, the caliph ʿUmar I was remembered to have exhorted the early *mujāhidūn* who set out for raids against the imperial powers of late antiquity to embrace an ethos of pious renunciation as the basis for their struggles against the powerful of the present world.[73] In addition to the ascetic piety to which he exhorted his troops, however, ʿUmar was remembered to have himself been a paragon of ascetic moderation. Shortly before his death, for example, he is remembered in a series of *akhbār* to have been found by a messenger reporting from the front serving food to the local people, personally directing the distribution of meat. Offered captured gems, he leaps up and exclaims, "May God never fill ʿUmar's belly again [if I accept this]!" and orders them turned over to "the Muslims."

In variant forms of this passage, ʿUmar is consistently depicted partaking of rough food. "When I was pushed into his presence, he told me to sit down. I did so among the people nearest [to him]," runs one version. "There was some rough food—even the food I had with me was better!" Eventually, one of ʿUmar's wives serves her husband and his visitor a meal of bread, olive oil, and "unground salt." In another passage, the messenger is served a draft of the barley meal beverage ʿUmar is drinking.[74]

By the period during which the narratives which would find their way into al-Ṭabarī's work were elaborated, that is during the second/eighth and third/ninth centuries, ascetic ethical and moral behavior had been long recognized among Muslims as a marker of elevated piety. Chase Robinson has noted, for example, that in the imaginations of such first/seventh-century Khārijī warriors as Sāliḥ b. Musarriḥ and those non-Khawārij who served as generational audiences for their displays of fanaticism/piety/rebellion, ascetic piety wedded to militant activism resonated with evolving communal narratives.[75] And even if the narratives collected by al-Ṭabarī or the other Muslim historians upon which Robinson depends are tainted by the intrusion of later attitudes, the recent publication of an especially early Khārijī text seems to confirm that from a very early stage in the development of the Muslim community, renunciation and ascetic piety were considered markers of religious excellence among some (and probably many) Muslims.[76]

But if ascetic piety and practice were useful in telling greater and lesser Muslims apart, it was less useful when it came to telling especially pious Muslims from especially pious people belonging to other communities and was thus problematic as a resource for communal self-fashioning. Despite this, however, there can scarcely have been any doubt that asceticism would play a role in Muslim self-fashioning—it was, after all, one of the most powerful imaginative presences in the cultural milieu in which Islam took shape and a crucial element in contesting questions of prophecy and revelation. The question was how common modes of ascetic practice would function to inscribe Muslim individuals and their community as discrete and indeed unique in the messy world of late antique monotheism.

At the same time the embryonic Muslim community was pondering questions of piety in accordance with the semiotics of asceticism, the conquest period and the narratives that made it and its consequences comprehensible within a prophetic metanarrative were also evolving. As Fred Donner has shown, it was through the elaboration of "narratives of origin" that the nascent Muslim community sought to set itself apart from other late antique monotheistic faith communities.[77] In elaborating such narratives, the early Islamic community naturally drew upon a currency of signs and symbols common to many late antique communities, among these the figure of the militant martyr/ascetic, who was by the seventh century a veteran of countless rounds of contestation concerning prophecy and community.[78]

As a consequence, the men who conducted the campaigns of the conquest period were remembered to have been pious, ascetic warriors, "horsemen during the day and monks at night," as one *khabar* put it.[79] By the eighth and ninth centuries, pious men were gathering on the Syrian frontier and striving in imitation of the figures now imagined to have conquered the lands of the Romans and Persians in service of Muḥammad's revelation. Just as ascetic piety allowed the victories of the *mujāhidūn* at Qādisiyya and al-Yarmūk to be read as miraculous manifestations of the will of God, it was now the ascetic piety and pure intentions of the individual *ghāzī* that transformed his actions into zealous and righteous striving *fī sabīl Allāh* (or *jihād* on the path of God), and it was this that would be rewarded in the next world. Ascetic piety was thus accorded a place within the foundational narratives of the Muslim community, a home in the practice of *jihād* and a resonance unique to the Muslim community.[80]

The generations of Muslim ascetics and, increasingly, mystics, who followed Ibn Adham and Ibn al-Mubārak through emulation of their lives and modes of piety were exceedingly diverse in their range of practice. Some, men like the famous early Baghdādī ascetic and mystic Sarī al-Saqaṭī (d. 867), for example, still spent al least part of their life as practitioners of *jihād*.[81] Sarī, however, is far more notable for the gentle, increasingly mystical, and thoroughly urban character of his life.[82]

As had so many late antique holy men before him, Sarī's journey toward ascetic and mystical enlightenment was marked by well-defined stages rendered in rather formulaic ways by his biographers. Early in his career, for example, Sarī found himself, as had so many of his holy man predecessors, in the presence of a master ascetic whose example would change his life. Like

Ibrāhīm b. Adham during his encounters with Christian monks, Sarī now found a figure to emulate, a standard of ascetic praxis to which he might aspire. Sarī said,

> I left Baghdad seeking a hospice for ascetics so that I might remain abstinent in it during Rajab, Shaʿbān and Ramadhān, and on my way I encountered . . . one of the great ascetics. When I ate my first meal at the end of Ramadhān, I had with me crushed salt and bread, and I said [to him], "Come, may God have mercy upon you." And he said, "Your salt is ground and you have with you all sorts of food. You shall not pass through and you shall not enter the gardens of the beloved." I looked at a provision sack he had with him in which was some barley mush. He ate from it, and I asked him, "What introduced you to this?" He said, "I count whatever is in the mouth against seventy hymns, and I have not tasted bread for forty years." And when the [other] ascetics joined us, I said, "Might I keep spiritual counsel with you?" He said, "God willing, yes."[83]

At a glance, it might be suggested that we have here the same problem we encountered at the outset of this chapter, illustrated in narratives concerning the deeds of Ibrāhīm b. Adham. Each of these passages is rife with topoi at home in the hagiographical traditions of a spectrum of late antique communities. Indeed, even the details of ascetic practice referred to here, such dietary staples as bread and salt, for example, were well known centuries before among the Christian ascetics of Syria. Julian Saba, for example, ate a diet of barley bread and salt,[84] as did the prototypical Christian ascetic, Antony.[85]

As we have seen, however, there were now other associations for the ascetic details of these narratives, associations that bound the figures sketched within them to the evolving history of the Muslim community. The unground salt Sarī's ascetic teacher favors to his pupil's ground salt and the saturated barley he carries with him once also adorned the table of the famously pious ʿUmar, nourishing him during the conquest of the Persian empire, as we saw in the narrative cited above. Whether or not the reader knows this specific reference is unimportant—the point is that as universal acts of ascetic zeal were accorded a place within the narratives of community that would eventually be enshrined in the works of the great compilers, they became for

Muslims potential markers of communal belonging despite whatever other readings to which they might also be subject.

Sarī represents a series of transitions—his life span crosses what is widely recognized as the boundary between the "late antique" world and the medieval world, for example, and in his generation a shift from asceticism to mysticism has been detected by some scholars.[86] Furthermore, in Sarī we find a figure who straddles two realms of ascetic practice. Sarī, like Ibrāhīm b. Adham and Ibn al-Mubārak, abided for a time on the frontier, waging *jihād*,[87] but he is remembered primarily as an urban figure whose strivings included such traditional ascetic practices as fasting but also took the form of such distinctively social actions as charity and teaching.[88]

Indicative of the new milieu in which Sarī is situated is another story from his early career as an ascetic. "[Sarī said] 'I praised God once, asking His pardon, and this praising lasted 30 years.' It was asked, 'How is this?' He said, 'I had a shop, and in it commodities, and there was a fire in our *sūq*, and it was reported to me, and I headed out to learn news of my shop, and I met a man and he said, "Rejoice, for your shop is safe!" and I said, "Praise God!" Then I reflected and I understood my mistake."[89]

Sarī's mistake was to rejoice over the safety of his shop before he knew whether there had been injury to other members of his community. Concern for community and purity of intention are understood to drive Sarī's action with the same fervor that they drove Ibn al-Mubārak and his companions, but rather than in raiding or bloodshed, Sarī frequently expresses the yield of his ascetic ethos in quiet acts of kindness. The following passages are illustrative of this tendency.

> A slave girl passed by Sarī carrying a container with something in it. It fell from her hand and broke, and Sarī took something from his shop and gave it to her for free. Maʿrūf al-Karkhī marveled at what he had done, and he said, "God has made the present world hateful to you."[90]

> Sarī said . . . "I turned away from holiday prayers and I saw an unkempt child with Maʿrūf al-Karkhī, and I said, 'Who is this?' And he said, 'I saw two children playing, and this one a bystander, downcast, and I asked him why he didn't play, and he said, "I am an orphan."' Sarī said, 'I said to him, "What do you think you will

do with him?"' He said, 'I shall gather palm pits for him so that he may buy walnuts with them and be happy.' And I said to him, 'Hand him over to me and I shall change his situation.' And he said to me, 'You will?' and I said, 'Yes.' He said, 'Take him and may God make your heart free from want, for you put the present world in order!'"[91]

The present world is perhaps no less hateful for Sarī than for his ascetic predecessors, but the self fashioned in accord with the ascetic moral imagination he has inherited from them is a social self. In Sarī we find an emblematic figure heralding an ethic of renunciation which has become a marker of communal identity. In him we find an ethical paragon who has emerged as a viable source of attributes for projects of self-fashioning among Muslims who would not spend their lives on the frontier waging *jihād*, nor in flight from the busy world of their fellow Muslims. He still fulfills many of the roles of the late antique holy man,[92] but does so at much closer range, as a figure as accessible as the shops of the *sūq* or as one's next-door neighbor.

This Sarī's ancestors were men like Ibrāhīm b. Adham, whose school Sarī joined after his conversion to asceticism, and Ibn al-Mubārak. In this intellectual and spiritual lineage he was not alone. Other Muslims, Aḥmad Ibn Ḥanbal, for example, lived all of their lives in cities, engaged in quotidian routines of family, scholarship, and communal affairs. Despite this, Ibn Ḥanbal's life and character were inflected with a distinctively ascetic moral sense, and he counted among his heroes Ibn al-Mubārak.[93]

For Ibn Ḥanbal and his contemporaries, there was no question but that ascetic virtue was a thoroughly Muslim virtue. Ibn Ḥanbal, in his own work on *zuhd*, cited examples of the asceticism of the companions of the Prophet as well as of the *mujāhidūn* after whom Ibn al-Mubārak had pattered himself.[94] And although the association of ascetic renunciation with the outward practice of *jihād* in the period of the conquests had lent a specifically Muslim connotation to ascetic practices shared among a spectrum of late antique communities, the necessity of that association did not long persist. Now, for many Muslims, one's daily striving on the path of God increasingly turned inward, toward the production of a more perfect Muslim self, and did so through acts of selfless compassion, kindness, and charity. This genre of early Muslim piety may be interpreted as one consequence of early Muslim participation in late ancient modes of devotion and the elaboration by members of the early Muslim *umma* upon a late antique *koinê* of signs, symbols, and narrative forms. The models of piety, shared in common with countless other local communities arrayed across the Mediterranean and Mesopotamia, with which the early Muslim *umma* imagined its monkish forbearers, now manifested themselves in the mildness, benevolence, and gentleness of men like Sarī al-Saqaṭī and in the scrupulous moral and ethical praxis of men like Aḥmad b. Ḥanbal.

Sadly, this was not the only consequence of Islam's foundational narratives for the early history of the Muslim community. As had been true for the Christian communities of late antiquity, the formative narratives with which early Muslims recalled the past and interpreted the present also seem to have carried with them a certain deadly surplus. In the cases of Christian and Muslim communities alike, this surplus lurked in the memory of the violence inherent in the tests endured by each of the nascent communities of God as it confronted and bested the terrestrial powers of the regions in which it emerged. As we shall see, traces of the menace posed by this surplus as it was interpreted by our early Muslim sources emerge in a wide variety of texts, but nowhere more starkly than in the works of the early historians of the Muslim world as they recalled the deeds and personalities of the Khawārij, Muslim men and women who embodied both the best that Islam had to offer and a species of horror that threatened to undo all that Muḥammad's revelation had brought forth upon the Earth. It is to the figure of the Khawārij as it emerges in our very early Muslim sources and to the troubling genre of militant piety that they represented that we shall now turn.

CHAPTER SEVEN

"Do You Not Fear God?" The Khawārij in Early Islamic Society

SOMETIME IN THE year 37/657-58, a group of Muslim pietists encountered the son of one of the companions of the Prophet on a road leading from the city of Baṣra in Iraq. They asked the man, whose name was ʿAbd Allāh b. Khabbāb, what he thought of the Prophet's son-in-law, ʿAlī b. Abī Ṭālib (d. 661). He replied that ʿAlī was "Commander of the Faithful and Imām of the Muslims." To this he added that his father had passed on to him something Muḥammad had said during his time on earth. The Prophet had predicted, he said, that a great upheaval (*fitna*) would arise among the people sometime in the future, during which the hearts of men would die, and the faithful would become unbelievers and unbelievers would be taken as the faithful.[1] Another version of this story reports that the son of Muḥammad's companion recalled that his father told him that the Prophet predicted that "there will be an upheaval (*fitna*) [in which] the shirker will be better than the upright one, and the slanderer will be better than the striving one." When matters came to this, his father had advised him, "be ʿAbd Allāh the killed one rather than ʿAbd Allāh the killer [or 'a servant of God who is killed rather than a servant of God who kills']."[2]

After Ibn Khabbāb delivered the *ḥadīth* passed down to him by his father, al-Balādhurī tells us, he and his pregnant *umm walad* (literally his "baby's mama," that is, a slave who had become pregnant with her master's child) were seized and bound by the pietists they had encountered on the road, men who believed that they alone preserved among them the one true community of God upon the earth. Ibn Khabbāb and his *umm walad* were resting with their captors under a date palm when a date fell from the tree. One of the pietists picked up the date and put it into his mouth. One of the man's companion's forbade him to do so, saying, "Without [having paid] its price, and without [having paid] its cost?" The man plucked the date from his own mouth and began to sharpen his sword. Then a pig that belonged to a *dhimmī* (a protected non-Muslim) wandered by, and the pietist killed it. His companion again objected, and the man sought out its owner and paid recompense for the animal. Observing this, Ibn Khabbāb said, "If indeed you are righteous men [as] I see and hear, I am safe from every evil among you."[3]

Ibn Khabbāb had spoken either ill-advisedly or too soon, however, for his captors now took him and laid him down by a stream and "butchered him over the carcass of the pig." Then, "they seized his woman and ripped open her belly, and she said, 'Do you not fear God?'" Then they killed three women who had been traveling with the couple.[4]

The men who killed Ibn Khabbāb, his *umm walad*, and their companions were members of a group of Muslims known as the Khawārij, "those who went out," men who had chosen rebellion and murder as the only way to preserve the one true community of God upon the earth.[5] The first Khawārij were those Muslims who had sided with ʿAlī in his struggle with the Qurayshī governor of Syria Muʿāwiya b. Abī Sufyān (d. 680) over leadership of the Muslim *umma* but who had abandoned ʿAlī when he agreed (at the insistence of his troops, many of whom later became Khawārij) to have his dispute with Muʿāwiya arbitrated by humans rather than adjudicated by God in battle.[6] Although the first Kharijite rebel groups would be put down decisively by ʿAlī (who would in turn be murdered in revenge by a Khārijī assassin), other groups of dissident pietists would rebel against the Umayyad and Abbasid caliphates, whom the Khawārij regarded as the corrupt temporal rulers of the Muslim *umma*. Meanwhile, these flamboyant monk-horsemen hybrids would enforce their own rigorist criteria for inclusion within the Muslim community with doctrinal rigor, raiding, and murder.

"There Is Nothing Between You and Us But the Sword"

A sense of the character of the very early Khārijī movement may be had from the following passage from al-Balādhurī's third/ninth-century *Ansāb al-ashrāf*.

After the initial break with his rigorist followers who were in the process of becoming the Khawārij, ʿAlī, who was in a hurry to finish up his conflict with Muʿāwiya and so was disposed to let things lie with the rebels, tried to coax the hardliners back into his coalition. Meeting with a group of potential rebels in the city of al-Kūfa, ʿAlī tried to reassure his former followers.

> And ʿAlī said, "We are not holding back from them the *fay'*, nor are the mosques inaccessible to them, nor will we disturb them so long as they do not shed blood and as long at they take hold of nothing that is forbidden [to them]" . . . And ʿAlī went to Ḥurqūṣ b. Zuhayr, Shurayḥ b. Awfā al-ʿAbsī, Farwa b. Nawfal al-Ashjaʿī, ʿAbd Allah b. Shajara al-Sulamī, Ḥamza b. Sinān al-Asadī and ʿAbd Allāh b. Wahb al-Rāsibī, who was called Dhū al-Thafīnāt ["Possessor of Calluses"] because of the marks on his face and his hands [left] by his bowing in prayer, for they were like the calluses of the camel. And he asked [ʿAlī] that he not dispatch Abū Mūsā [the arbitrator agreed to by ʿAlī at the insistence of many of those who now opposed him as Khawārij][7] so that they might go to Syria, but [ʿAlī] refused. So [Dhū al-Thafīnāt] said, "We departed the group over an issue whose violation is not permitted [or whose invalidation is not possible]." And they departed to ʿAbd Allāh Ibn Wahb's dwelling immediately . . . and they recalled the wounding of their companions at Ṣiffīn . . . and [they said,] "whoever is content with the arbitrators commits unbelief, as does anyone who absolves ʿAlī" . . . And they discussed candidates for leadership [of their band], but none of them accepted it until Dhū al-Thafīnāt ʿAbd Allāh b. Wahb al-Rāsibī accepted it. And he said, "By God, I do not take it from pleasure in the present world, and I will not renounce it for fear of death."[8]

Later, when ʿAlī once again attempted rapprochement with them and asked them to help him in his war with Muʿāwiya, their reply was even less ambiguous. "It is not allowed to us that we help you as *imām*, for you are an unbeliever until you bear witness against yourself with regard to unbelief and you repent just as we did," they said. "For you did not stand up for God, rather you stood up for yourself." Having heard this answer, we are told, ʿAlī "gave up on them" and decided to set out for his confrontation without the help of the Khawārij, who for their part set out "massacring the people in their path."[9]

Another tradition had ʿAlī summoning the Khawārij back to communion with his community after the murder of Ibn Khabbāb and others, requesting them to

> "Surrender to us the killers of Ibn Khabbāb, my messenger and the women so that I might execute them. Then I shall leave you to make myself rid of the commander of the people of the West [i.e. Muʿāwiya] . . ." And they replied to him, "There is nothing between you and us but the sword unless you acknowledge unbelief and you repent." And ʿAlī said, "After my *jihād* with the Prophet of God, and my faith, I should bear witness against myself for unbelief? <I shall be lost and not one of those following the rightly guided>." Then he said . . . "I bear witness that I am a helper more praiseworthy than anyone who doubts in God. I am rightly guided."[10]

This would not be the last conference between ʿAlī and the Khawārij, however, nor the last meeting between his followers and the rigorist schismatics. Indeed, the best accounts we possess for the events surrounding the first *fitna*, those of al-Balādhurī and al-Ṭabarī, recall a series of dialogues and confrontations between ʿAlī, his followers, and the Khawārij. After initial attempts at arbitration had broken down, for example, ʿAlī tried once again to reason with the Khawārij before meeting them in battle with his troops. In their reply, as it is recorded by al-Balādhurī, the reader is provided with a glimpse of the way in which the Arab pietists who now confronted the terrestrial power of their world envisioned that confrontation and a sense of the character of the narrative in which the Khawārij imagined themselves emplotted.

> [ʿAlī] wrote to them: "Now then . . . you are of those who separate themselves from their religion, and are a faction after God has accepted their covenant about the community and united your hearts in obedience <that you are like those who became disunited and squabble among themselves after indisputable evidence has come to them>."[11] And he summoned them to piety toward God

> and righteousness and observance of the truth. And ʿAbd Allāh b. Wahb al-Rāsibī said, <“God does not alter what is with a people until they change what is with themselves>[12] . . . You arrived at Ṣiffīn other than a hypocrite and not weak, not making yourself vulgar in a manner that brought gratification to your Lord. But when the enemy put up a defense and the pious died . . . those who did not possess understanding in true religion surrounded you and there was no longing for *jihād* among the like of al-Ashʿath b. Qays and his companions and they sought to make you commit an error with the result that you put your trust in the present world when copies of the Qur'ān (*maṣāḥif*)[13] were raised before you as a ruse, hastening to those who sought to make you commit an error. And we too erred in that way, but then God, in his mercy, set us aright with regard to him. And you chose an arbiter with regard to God's Book and yourself, and you were distrustful of your religion, and strayed from it, and your enemy and his misdeeds are upon you. Not at all, O ʿAlī b. Abī Ṭālib! <You all entertained wicked thoughts, and you are a lost people>[14] . . . Repent to God and affirm your sin, and if you do so we will be your hand against your enemy. But if you refuse, then God will decide between us." [The narrators] said: Qays b. Saʿd b. ʿUbāda went out to them and called to them, "O servants of God, come to us per our request and pounce upon our enemies and your enemies together." And ʿAbd Allāh b. Shajura al-Sulamī said to him, "Truth has enlightened us, and we will never follow you unless you bring us a caliph like ʿUmar." And he said, "By God, we do not know of anyone in this world the like of ʿUmar unless it is our master." And ʿAlī said to them, "Obstinacy and quarreling has overcome you, and you follow your desires and you are Satan's equivalent. I warn you that you will be found in the morning thrown down along the course of this canal." And he did not leave them, but he preached and called to them, and when he saw no yielding among them [he arranged his forces for battle].[15]

How will these events have looked to the parties bound to them, both as frightened and angry participants in the events themselves and as Muslims of later generations whose political and social worlds were remembered to have been forever altered, as these exemplars of the early community's primordial past clashed over the volatile mix of revelation and worldly power? What resources did these Muslims have with which to make sense of these events? How, in other words, did these events become the kinds of episodes al-Balādhurī, al-Ṭabarī, and their informants came to inscribe within the rapidly evolving narrative of early Islamic history?

Beyond these questions lurk still larger and more difficult ones. Prime among these is that of the interconnection of Islam's narratives of origin, Muslim communal identity, and pious violence. This question is intimately related to the problem I explored in Chapters 1–4 of this book within the context of the pre-Islamic, late Roman world. Within that world, I have suggested, problems of communal identity, communal boundaries, narrative, and intercommunal violence existed within a web of interdependence that also included regular transgression of communal boundaries and identities that were fluid, locally negotiated, and contingent. Within that world, moreover, we have seen that peaceful coexistence and intercommunal exchange was the norm rather than an exception. What then of the early Islamic world?

We have seen that as the early Muslims imagined their communal past, they drew upon a series of figures and narratives that were also crucial to the imaginary of other late antique communities. Accordingly, such behaviors as pious renunciation, the obligation to confront and correct sin and the sinful, and intransigence before representatives of worldly power became vitally important to the performance of Muslimness insofar as that performance was predicated upon imitation of the earliest Muslims as they were now recalled to have been. These were those devoted monotheists who accompanied Muḥammad during the trials and struggles of the early community of believers and those believers who participated in the military miracle of the *futūḥ* and in so doing participated in a numinous manifestation of God's will upon the earth.

Indeed, as I have demonstrated elsewhere, many early Muslims believed that God had commended to them such late ancient Christian heroes as the sixth-century martyrs of Najrān as models of intransigence in the face of worldly power and in defense of monotheist truth.[16] Similarly, the institution of *jihād* was thought of as a Muslim analog to the Christian institution of monasticism, and the earliest practitioners of *jihād* were imagined on the model of Christian monks. Through the evolution of specifically Muslim historical narratives, however, ascetic rigor and intransigence in the face of worldly might became distinctively Muslim qualities, whatever other connotations they may have previously carried. Now the fact that the outer qualities that marked one as an exemplary Muslim might also mark one as an exemplary member of other communities mattered little in that all of those qualities could be traced to a specifically Muslim lineage, conjured within a specifically Muslim narrative of the past, present, and future.

We have also seen, however, that the narratives with which Christians of the later Roman world reckoned their communal pasts carried a series of troubling implications for how individual Christians and whole Christian communities might imagine the possibilities for their interactions with contemporaries. Drawing upon the work of Margaret Somers and others, I have suggested that Christians who imagined themselves emplotted in narratives that prominently featured stories of Christian victimization and eventual triumph over the enemies of their communities and their God in some circumstances seem only to have been capable of interpreting contemporary events as further episodes within such narratives. This was particularly problematic when such Christian communities found themselves involved in conflicts with other communities, whether these communities were Christian, Jewish, or pagan. In such circumstances, these communities tended to interpret their conflict as yet another episode of persecution at the hands of an enemy determined to annihilate the one community of God upon the earth. Accordingly, as genuine Christians, it was the duty of members of such imperiled communities to defend themselves, often aggressively. Moreover, it was antithetical to the sense of genuine Christianness engendered by imitation of the early Christian martyrs that members of these communities should compromise or seek consensus with their enemies. Rather, it was their duty to defend the boundaries and essential truths in accordance with which their communities had cohered at the cost of everything else.

As we attempt to understand the Khawārij and, more importantly, the broader range of phenomena the Khawārij represented within the larger Islamic world, it is necessary to ask whether the narratives with which the early Islamic community reckoned its own past carried similarly grim implications for the social and political life of the early Islamic *umma*. This is a question that may be pursued at two levels. On the one hand, one may ask, as scholars of the early Islamic world have long done, what the appearance of the Khawārij meant for the history of Islam and Islamic civilization. This is clearly an important question, and it has produced much engaging scholarship. On the other hand, however, one might also ask how and where the Khawārij fit into a larger analysis of the period of human history they inhabited; that is, how do they fit within the currents of religion, politics, and culture that flow over and around such events as the Arab conquests of Syria and Mesopotamia or the advent of a new monotheistic prophet within the late ancient world?

"Praise God Who Made Our Community Command Right, Forbid Wrong and Destroy Sin"

Let us take the first of these questions first. In al-Ṭabarī and al-Balādhurī's depiction of the emergence of the Khawārij and indeed in their depictions of later Khārijī rebellions, we encounter a series of dialogues in which members of Khārijī groups confront ʿAlī or other bearers of centralized power and engage them in disputes. In these scenes, the representatives of caliphal power try to reason with the pious militants before them, and attempt to induce them to compromise, to return to a certain *status quo ante*. The Khawārij featured in these scenes are serenely contemptuous of the worldly power of those whom they confront. They have numinous truth on their side and indeed numinous truth that has redeemed them from error. Those who call them to obedience have placed their faith in the present world, and it is in the present world only that their power resides. According to the Khawārij, it was the duty of all real Muslims to confront such representatives of corrupt worldly might and to fight them.

> [Khirrīt b. Rāshid] said to [ʿAlī], "By God, I do not bless your command and I will not pray behind you." And ʿAlī said, "May your mother be bereft of you! For you disobeyed your lord and violated your pledge, and you will only harm yourself. But why would you do that?" He said, "Because you chose [people rather than] the Book as an arbitrator and you were too weak for the truth (*ḍaʿufta ʿan al-haqq*) when things got serious and you put your trust with the group that does wrong. And I am an avenger visiting you and visiting them."[17]

Later, as he called other Muslims to his cause, Khirrīt b. Rāshid framed the reasons for his revolt in this way: "This house [ʿAlī and the ruling house of Islam] is exalted among the unknowing. The sublime in character is exalted in Islam, but those ones transgress that which is *ḥarām* [forbidden] to them. And if a group is themselves evil, then the rightly guided ones, the delightful of mankind, fight with them. They have caused corruption upon the Earth, and this house regards that which is *ḥarām* as permissible. But we are restrained, and so let the people chose an *imām* for themselves."[18]

* * *

The foremost concern of Khirrīt b. Rāshid and his early Kharijite colleagues was, it would seem, the integrity of the one community of God upon the earth that collected around the truths revealed to Muḥammad. For Muslims of the first centuries of Islam, the integrity of that community depended upon imitation of the behavior of the individuals who were now remembered to have been present at the founding of the community and who observed for themselves the personal example of the Prophet. The basis of membership within the early Muslim *umma* was, accordingly, a mimetic performance of the community's privileged narratives. In an exchange between one Khārijī group and ʿAlī, there is what seems to be a very condensed version of one such narrative. In it, one encounters a falling away from the primordial, essentially Muslim virtues embodied by Abū Bakr and ʿUmar. In the rendering found in al-Balādhurī's text, this virtue has much to do with preserving the behavioral patterns upon which Muslimness was dependent.

> God dispatched Muḥammad with the truth, and he became responsible to God as a supporter just as he imparted his messages. Then he took him to his mercy and [God] set up in command after him Abū Bakr because of [his] tenacious clinging to the religion of God that you saw with your own eyes, preferring [God's] good will until the command of his Lord came to him. Then ʿUmar followed him. You are aware of what his way of life was; a rebuker did not reproach him. As his certification he received the seal of God [i.e., martyrdom]. Then there was [also] the command of ʿUthmān, until a group, having traveled to him, killed him because he preferred pleasure and transgressed the judgment of God.[19] Then God appointed you successor over his worshipers, and the faithful acknowledged you . . . because of your kinship with the Prophet and your precedence in Islam.[20]

In this narration, Muḥammad brought revelation to his community, and with that revelation came responsibility, but for Muḥammad, God's prophet, that responsibility was directly to God. The appearance of Abū Bakr, however, seems to sign the advent of social responsibility in accordance with this revelation; the narrator emphasizes that ʿAlī saw Abū Bakr "with [his] own eyes," and Abū Bakr is thus evoked in the gaze of ʿAlī (and by extension other members of the early community of believers) as an exemplum available to his fellow Muslims. The virtue of which Abū Bakr is sign and exemplar is, in turn, his unswerving defense of God's religion. It was this that made him an especially virtuous Muslim, and, according the Khārijī ideology, a suitable leader for the one community of God.

ʿAlī also had before him the example of the famously pious ʿUmar. Despite this, he, like ʿUthmān, ignored the example provided by the second caliph. Like Abū Bakr, it was ʿUmar's determined willingness to defend his community through his behavior that made him a virtuous leader of the Muslim *umma.* In ʿUmar we may sense more fully the social (and political) implications of this willingness, however. ʿUmar was not "reproached by a rebuker." His example was irreproachable, and ʿUmar himself was storied for his willingness to intervene forcefully—sometimes even violently—to correct erring members of his community. Here is articulated what was by the time Balādhurī wrote one of the crucial duties of a pious Muslim and particularly the leader of the umma itself; a good Muslim must protect his community not only from threats posed from without but also those issuing from within. In the case of ʿUmar, this was sometimes achieved, for example, by beating wayward Muslims.[21] But this was the duty of all Muslims, enjoined upon them as the obligation to "command right and forbid wrong" (*al-amr bi-ʾl-maʿrūf wa-ʾl-nahy ʿan al-munkar*).[22]

We will explore the act of commanding and forbidding in detail later in this chapter and in the next. For now, however, it is enough to note that a willingness to command and forbid was one of the qualities ascribed to *futūḥ*-era mujāhidūn by al-Azdī, Ibn Aʿtham, Ibn ʿAsākir, and Ibn Qutayba, among others. In a passage cited in Chapter 5, for example, the second/eighth-century historian al-Azdī includes a passage in which an Arab Christian *nāsik* or ascetic returns from the camp of a group of Muslim warriors somewhere in Syria and reports to the leader of the Roman army: "I come to you from a people staying up through the night praying, and remaining abstinent during the day, commanding the right and forbidding the wrong, monks by night, lions by day. Should their king steal, they cut off his hand, and if he commits adultery they stone him. And their passion is righteous and their following of it is for the sake of devotion."[23]

Another second/eighth-century text, the *Kitāb al-siyar* of Abū Isḥāq al-Fazārī, refers to the penchant of both Abū Bakr and ʿUmar for commanding and forbidding.[24] ʿUmar's preference for stern and sometimes violent enforcement of communal behavioral norms figures prominently in another Khārijī narration of the early Muslim past very similar to that cited above. In this narration, which appears in the *Taʾrīkh Mawṣil* of Abū Zakariyyāʾ Yazīd b. Muḥammad al-Azdī (d. 334/946) and is attributed to the Khārijī leader Abū Ḥamza al-Khārijī, ʿUmar is remembered to have "comported himself in accordance with the *sīra* of his master [Muḥammad], collected property and gave donations, collected [and tended] the people during the month of Ramadhān, and dealt eighty lashes for wine [drinking] and raided the enemy in their own lands."[25] This depiction of the early heroes of the Muslim world bears much in common with many of the descriptions one encounters of the Khawārij and their actions. Muslim sources stress their ascetic rigor even as they condemn the uses to which that rigor was put. Al-Balādhurī, for example, includes the following brief portrait of one first/seventh-century Khārijī band, in which the author provides a rather vivid sense of the militant and ascetic character ascribed to them.

> The foremost personalities (*wujūh*) of the Khawārij gathered with ʿAbd Allāh b. Wahb al-Rāsibī and he made an address to them, and he called them to the commanding of right and the forbidding of wrong, (*al-amr bi-ʾl-maʿrūf wa-ʾl-nahy ʿan al-munkar*) and the speaking of truth, but he was fervent and he was injurious, and he said: "Go out with us as an assembly of our brothers, from this village, whose people belong to the unjust one. Let some [of us] go to the *sawād*, some to the mountain districts that are uninformed regarding these loathsome innovations [or Let some [of us] go to the *sawād*, some to the mountain districts condemning these loathsome innovations]. Then Ḥurqūs b. Zuhayr got up and he held forth, and they discussed as an assembly, rebuking the present world and calling for its abandonment, and for earnestness in seeking truth and rejection of innovation and oppression.[26]

In another scene from al-Azdī's *Futūḥ*, the famous conquest-era commander Khālid b. al-Walīd is featured in dialogue with the Roman commander "Bāhān." Khālid, although a controversial figure within the broader Islamic tradition, is presented in al-Azdī's text as an idealized Muslim warrior, "striving on the path of God" during the heady opening days of the *futūḥ* era. A sense of the lengths to which Khālid b. al-Walīd was willing to go in defense of his community and its integrity may be gained from certain traditions in which he was recalled to have killed a Christian woman who spoke ill of the Prophet.[27] The scene al-Azdī records is revealing of the centrality accorded to the role of commanding and forbidding to the figure of the *futūḥ*-era *mujāhid* as he was later recalled, but it also suggests much about how comparatively mainstream Khārijī notions of proper Muslim rulership actually were.

> Bāhān said, "Praise God, who made our prophet the most excellent of the prophets, and our king the most excellent of the kings and our community the superior of the communities." And when he came to this place, Khālid spoke to the translator and . . . he said, "Praise God who made us faithful to our prophet *and* your prophet and to the assembly of the prophets, and who made the *amīr* we appoint as head of our affairs a man like each one. Were he to allege that he was a king over us, we would remove him on our own authority and we do not think that he is better than any man of the Muslims, except that he is more reverent and pure in the eyes of God. And praise God who made our community command the right and forbid the wrong and to destroy sin and to apologize to God for it and to know God and his boundary, and not to associate anything else with him."[28]

"They Are the Excepted of God, Under the Throne, Girded with Swords"

Knowing what to make of such apparent similarities in the actions and behavior of the early *mujāhidūn* and those of the Khawārij is complicated by several factors. The first of these is that trying to discern the outlook and attitudes of any Muslims of the first century and a half after the *hijra* is an undertaking immeasurably complicated by the character of the sources we possess. When dealing with such groups as the Khawārij, however, the inherent difficulties faced by historians of the early Islamic world, discussed briefly in Chapter 5, are exacerbated by the fact that the Khawārij were viewed by the authors of the texts that describe them as representative of non-normative behaviors and deviant beliefs.

It is necessary, then, that one proceed with a good deal of caution in approaching the texts of al-Ṭabarī and al-Balādhurī as sources for Khārijī history. What these sources can tell us, of course, is what the informants of al-Ṭabarī and al-Balādhurī and other early Islamic authors thought of the Khawārij, how they imagined them and what they believed motivated them. What these texts seem to reveal, in this sense, is that the Khawārij were imagined, perhaps by those around them, most certainly those who recalled them sometime later, as figures who, whatever else the reader might make of them, possessed many of the qualities that early Muslims believed marked one as a genuine Muslim. That is, they were figures who were imagined to have acted in accordance with the example set for them by members of the early community of believers, particularly as those members participated in the military miracles that announced the truth of Muḥammad's prophetic mission.

Given this, it is unsurprising, for example, that the Khawārij ethos, as it is represented in such texts, has much in common with that of the militant renunciants who, by the early second/eighth century, were gathering on the Syrian frontier with Byzantium to practice *jihād*. Among these *ghāzī* was ʿAbd Allāh b. al-Mubārak. As I have noted, Ibn al-Mubārak's treatises on *jihād* and *zuhd*, particularly when read in tandem, prescribe a way of zealous striving on the path of God that combined well-worn forms of late antique ascetic praxis with the practice of raiding rather in the tradition of pre-Islamic Arabian heroes. For Ibn al-Mubārak and his peers, renunciation of the present world served as a means of purifying the individual's inner self, of purging the ego and making of oneself a pure vessel for the enactment of God's command. The culmination of a life spent in this manner was, of course, martyrdom on God's behalf.

We have seen, for example, that in his *Kitāb al-jihād*, Ibn al-Mubārak recalled the story of one mujāhid and his son, who, when their party was overrun by the Turks "on the path of God," steeled themselves for martyrdom, the highest aspiration of any *ghāzī*.[29] The *Kitāb al-jihād* in fact contains numerous *akhbār* and *aḥādīth* exalting martyrdom on the raid. Typical of these is the following. "Saʿīd b. Jabīr said, in his sermon '[He is destroyed in the heavens or on earth except he whom God wills].' He said, 'They are the martyrs. They are the excepted of God, under the throne, girded with swords.'"[30] Muḥammad was said to have listed first among those whom God loves the *ghāzī* who fights until "he is killed or God kills on his behalf."[31] Elsewhere in the text, when the caliph ʿUmar was addressed by a Bedouin as "the best of the people," he replied that in fact the best of the people was the man who takes his camel herd, sells it and uses the receipts to go raiding, putting himself "between the Muslims and their enemies."[32] There can be little doubt, then, that Ibn al-Mubārak would have been impressed with the commitment of Muʿādh b. Juwayn, a Khārijī in the time of Muʿāwiya, as Umayyad forces finally bore down upon him: "We are indeed small in number, but let us carry out *jihād* against our enemies! And let us fight whoever of them fights us! And then let us be martyred!"[33]

Very similar was the attitude of the Khārijī rebel Ḍaḥḥāk b. Qays, as he confronted an overwhelming Umayyad force sent against him in A.H. 128. The larger force hailed him, "By God, since Islam has been there has never been gathered for an issuer of a summons this sight [i.e., a spectacle of the sort made by the assembled Umayyad troops]. But you delay this beginning, so let your cavalry and your infantry and your horsemen come across!" [Ḍaḥḥāk] said, "All I have in this present world of yours is this desire—just that this tyrant should be destroyed. And I am made over to God, and will act upon [the tyrant] until God decides between us and them." Ḍaḥḥāk is killed in battle shortly thereafter, presumably much as he will have wished.[34]

Indeed, the early Khawārij are reported to have developed something of a cult of their own martyrs. As he "went out" in 42/662–63, Ḥayyān b. Ẓabyān recited a poem that began, "My friend, I have neither solace nor composure . . . after the victims at al-Nahr," recalling the Khawārij martyrs killed at the battle of the Canal fought and lost by the first Khawārij against ʿAlī's troops in 37/658.[35] Meanwhile, those of Khārijī sympathies would motivate themselves for renewed rebellion by "reminding each other of the dignity of their brothers at al-Nahrawān, seeing that in staying put was deceit and defection, and in *jihād* against the *ahl al-qibla* (non-Khārījī Muslims) was excellence and the hereafter."[36] In the year 76/695–96, as he went out against the Umayyad rulers of the Jazīra, Ṣāliḥ b. Musarriḥ and his companions were said by al-Balādhurī to have made a pilgrimage to Nahrawān, "and prayed at the death site of their colleagues, and [Ṣāliḥ] said, 'O God, let us be numbered with them, for they suffered for their obedience to you.'"[37] Ṣāliḥ's companion and successor Shabīb b. Yazīd, also went to Nahrawān, "and he and his companions stood at the tomb of those killed by ʿAlī b. Abī Ṭālib, and asked their forgiveness" during their own rebellion.[38] In the late seventh century, the Ṣufriyya Khārijī sect would trace their communal lineage through a series of earlier Khawārij back to two of the martyrs of Nahrawān, Dhū Thafīnāt and Ḥurqūṣ b. Zuhayr.[39] Nor would the Ṣufriyya go out without first stopping at the tomb of Ṣāliḥ b. Musarriḥ to cut their hair, as Chase Robinson has noted.[40] Abū Bilāl Mirdās b. Udayya, a Muslim of quietist Khārijī views, was finally prompted to violent rebellion by the sight of the body of a Khārijī woman named Baljāʾ, whom he had warned that she was wanted by the local governor, ʿUbayd Allāh b. Ziyād. She was all but unconcerned with this news. "[Baljāʾ said] 'If he seizes me then he shall have a difficult time with me, and as for me, I do not wish men to sin on my account.' And ʿUbayd Allāh found her and he brought her to the *sūq*, and [there] he lopped off her hands and feet and cast her down. And Abū Bilāl passed by her, and he said, 'Who is that?' They said, 'It is Baljāʾ,' and he stood over her and he looked at her, and he bit his beard.'"[41]

When Abū Bilāl's small force was wiped out and its leader killed by Umayyad forces, the leader of those forces was assassinated by the Khārijī ʿAbīda b. Hilāl upon his return to the city.[42] ʿAbīda proclaimed himself in verse a follower of the "religion of Abū Bilāl" and rebelled in the memory of a martyr who had taken up arms following the example of a previous Khārijī martyr.[43]

The profound desire for martyrdom one encounters in both the work of Ibn al-Mubārak and in early medieval depictions of the Khawārij is only one expression of a more profound ethos of renunciation as a means of purifying oneself in preparation to serve God in all things. We have seen, in Chapter 6, how for the *ghāzī* of the Syrian frontier, *jihād* was understood as dependant upon a purity of intention that was linked inextricably to a diminution of the worldly appetites of the individual worshipper. This was best achieved, Ibn al-Mubārak and those who followed him believed, through ascetic practice and through a "going out" from among the public spaces of the Muslim world, in which the concerns of the world might so easily encroach upon proper care for one's soul.

Even for those pious Muslims who strove to perfect themselves while subsumed in the quotidian life of such bustling Muslim cities as Baghdād, men like Aḥmad b. Ḥanbal, removal to the frontiers of the world as a means of spiritual perfection was the ideal. "The raid is better than the *ribāṭ*," he said, referring to communal sites of ascetic retreat and once again underscoring the interconnection of asceticism and *jihād* in the early Islamic imaginary.[44] *Jihād* was also better than the profoundly revered obligation to seek knowledge, he said, adding "*jihād* has no equal."45 Asked whether a man whose family was in al-Dīnabūr while he was raiding from Tarsus on the Byzantine frontier should bring his dependants to Tarsus, Ibn Ḥanbal had replied, "No, abstaining with regard to them is better."[46] To another questioner, who asked him about an old man who wanted to go raiding on the frontier but who was hindered by those around him who insisted that he could not go because he had not performed the Ḥajj, Ibn Ḥanbal said, "Let him go raiding. No harm done! And if God sets him at liberty, he may then perform the Ḥajj. We see nothing wrong with raiding before the Ḥajj."[47]

And yet removal to the frontier was not the end in and of itself in the view of Ibn Ḥanbal; rather, the duty of God's good servant was to confront the enemies of God where he found them. In still another question put to him concerning the practice of *jihād*, for example, Ibn Ḥanbal was asked about the man who wished to go to Tarsus to fight the Romans while Turks occupied his home region. He replied by reciting a Qur'ānic verse: "[O believers, fight the unbelievers around you].[48] It is not for anyone that he go from his own land while the enemy is in it, and fight someone other than them. Let him fight in defense of his lands, and drive away the enemies of God."[49] He was even said to have faulted Ibn al-Mubārak for going to Tarsus to fight, presumably because there were enemies of the *umma* to be found closer to Ibn al-Mubārak's home in the city of Merv.[50]

Clearly then, the combination of ideals embodied by the frontier warriors of the first centuries of Islam, those of ascetic renunciation of the present world bound to a penchant for violent activism, were not ideals at home only on the geographical boundaries of the *dār al-Islām*. The narratives in accordance with which the early community of believers articulated a sense of its past and in so doing imagined the qualities that marked all real members of that community were narratives in which pious, ascetic Arab warriors confronted, fought, and defeated the proud and decadent powers of this world. Accordingly, those raider-ascetic hybrids, modeled on the men who had confronted the representatives of Roman and Persian imperial power in the time of the conquests, were exemplary models of a kind of virtue that was ideally at home wherever Muslims dwelled.

For this reason, the authentic Muslimness of any individual could, ideally, be traced to that individual's willingness to violently confront God's enemies wherever he found them. If he found them on the frontiers of the Muslim world, all was well. But if he found them dwelling next door or in the home of the caliph, the integrity of the Muslim community could be endangered by the very efforts of its most pious members to defend its integrity, a duty that seems to have been enjoined upon Muslims by Muḥammad himself.

"Woe to You! Have You Ever Heard of Men Killing Women?"

The great Muslim historians of the third/ninth and fourth/tenth centuries crafted the Khawārij who appear in their works in such a manner that quietly underscores this dilemma. Al-Ṭabarī, for example, included in his *Ta'rīkh* the text of what is purported to be a letter from the late seventh-century Khārijī leader Ṣāliḥ b. Musarriḥ to his companions. The letter articulates a blend of ascetic renunciation and militant activism very much in accord with the brand of *jihād* championed by Ibn al-Mubārak, his companions and his admirers.[51] In the *Ta'rīkh*, Ṣāliḥ is described as "an ascetic man (*rajul nāsik*), a humble man (*mukhabit*), pale of face and a *ṣ'āhib al-'ibāda* ("one of the pious folk")." This passage continues:

> And [the companions of Qabīṣa b. ʿAbd al-Raḥmān] asked him to send a letter to them, and he did . . . [It said,] "Praise God, who made the heavens and the earth and who put in place the darkness and the lights. Then those who disbelieve in their lord deviated. O God, we shall not deviate from you . . . and we shall serve only you. Truth and command are yours, and you help and you harm and the future is yours. We bear witness that Muḥammad is your servant, whom you deemed pure, and your messenger, whom you selected and with whom you were content for the conveyance of your message and sincere advice (*naṣīha*) for your servants. We bear witness that he has conveyed the message, and given sincere advice to the *umma* and called it to the truth. He stood up for justice, and

> protected true religion and practiced *jihād* against the polytheists until God took him to him, may God bless him and grant him salvation. I commend to you all the fear of God, renunciation (*zuhd*) in the present world and craving for the next world, frequent remembrance of death, separation from the deviators and love for the faithful. Renunciation (*zahāda*) in the present world awakens desire for what is with God, and drains the body for obedience to God. The frequent remembrance of death causes the worshiper to pray fervently to him and surrender to him. Separating from the deviators is obligatory for the faithful. God said in his Book, <never pray over any of them, nor stand at his tomb, for they disbelieve in God and his prophet and they died. They strayed from the proper course>.[52] And love of the faithful is as a means by which the generosity of God might be granted, and God will grant us his mercy and his paradise. You all are of the sincere, enduring ones (*al-ṣādiqīn al-ṣābirīn*)."[53]

In al-Ṭabarī's rendering, Ṣāliḥ then goes on to articulate a narrative of the recent Muslim past very much like that which al-Balādhurī had put into the mouth of ʿAbd Allāh b. Wahb al-Rābisī a generation earlier as he sparred with ʿAlī. It becomes clear, then, in the rendering of the Khawārij that we encounter in the works of al-Balādhurī, al-Ṭabarī, and their informants, that whatever the actual motivations or worldview of those who "went out" against the early caliphs, they were recalled to personify many of the most intensely valued qualities of both the early *mujāhidūn*, and also the ascetic warrior *ghāzīs* who were, by the eighth century, helping to define for all Muslims what it meant to be a real Muslim. They were otherworldly, uncompromising, selfless, valiant, and fierce. Most important, they took it as their primary duty to confront all that threatened the integrity of their community, particularly that which threatened the character of Islam from within. As the *ghāzī* warriors of the Syrian frontier inhabited the geographical marches of the Islamic world, the Khawārij, at least in intention, patrolled the in many ways more crucial boundaries that gave practical contour and experiential weight to the Islamic *umma*.

For the Muslims of the first centuries after the *hijra*, the key to genuine Islam, in belief and in practice, resided in studied imitation of the founders of that community. It would seem that the Khawārij, as did so many of their contemporaries, took very seriously this obligation to perform this primordialist doctrine as a matter of daily practice. In fact, however, we cannot know what the Khawārij of the first/seventh century intended with anything approaching certainty, and even for the second/eighth century we must rely upon such tantalizing but ultimately limited sources as the recently published Ibāḍī *Sīra* of Ibn Dhakwān.[54] What one can glean from such sources as al-Ṭabarī and al-Balādhurī's texts, however, is evidence of what would seem to have been an exceedingly troubling dilemma for Muslims of the first few centuries A.H. The problem may be stated thus: The Khawārij undeniably embodied all that early Muslim society valued most. And yet they were also monstrous figures whose murderous zeal seems to have threatened to undo all that Muḥammad, as prophet and communal leader, had accomplished according to the narrative of the birth and growth of the Muslim community as it was evolving during those years.

In the Khawārij we encounter a community personified, on the one hand, by men like Ṣāliḥ b. Musarriḥ, a "pale-faced" and gaunt ascetic, a man who would "not raise his head because of his pious reticence," and Dhū al-Thafīnāt, a man whose *nom de guerre* derived from the "marks of the *sujūd* (prostrations performed during prayer) on his forehead and his nose and his hands and his knees, [which] were comparable with the calluses of a camel"; an individual, that is, whose incessant prostrations during prayer had left thick calluses on his face, knees, and hands.[55] The piety of these men was literally inscribed across their faces and legible in their battered and neglected bodies. Their reputation for ascetic virtue was such that even the Christian author of the *Zuqnīn Chronicle* included in his work the observation that when Muslims went out in rebellion as Khawārij, they gave up their wives and all of their possessions.[56] Although he does not draw a parallel to monasticism, he does ascribe an act of renunciation very like that undertaken by Christians entering monasteries to Muslims "going out" as Khawārij (and in fact does so incorrectly).[57] The individuals Khārijī rebellions attracted may be sensed from the following passage, from the *Kamīl* of al-Mubarrad:

> Wāṣil b. ʿAṭāʾ Abū Ḥudhayqa [and a group of companions] went out to [a group of Khawārij], and the [Khawārij] said, "Who are you and your companions?" He said, "Unbelievers (*mushrikūn*) seeking what is best so that they might honor the *kalām* of God and know his laws/boundaries (*ḥudūd*)." They said, "We have

> recompense for you." He said, "Then teach us." And they began teaching them their opinions and he said, "I and anyone who is with me agree [with your opinions]." They said, "Then throw your weight behind those around you, for we are your brothers," [Wāṣil b. ʿAṭāʾ] said, "That is not [proper] for you. God said, <Anyone from the *mushrikūn* seeking refuge among you, grant it until he has heard the *kalām* of God, then give him shelter>.[58] And so supply us with shelter." And each of them looked at the others and then they said, "You are entitled to that." And they traveled with their group until they brought them to their place of shelter.[59]

Those to whom Khārijī dogma appealed, it would seem, were individuals of thoroughly rigid, literalist, and fearless character, individuals who would not hesitate to command and forbid their new and deadly "brothers," calling them up short and reminding them of their duty in accordance with *sunna*. The Khawārij, as strictly observant pietists, accepted the rebuke and complied with the demand of their new colleagues.

And yet the Khawārij were also figures recalled to have performed as a matter of course acts much like those with which we began this chapter; they were men (and, notably, women) who were readily willing to murder self-confessed Muslims whom they encountered as travelers on the road, willing to butcher the son of one of Muḥammad's companions, willing to disembowel a woman pregnant with that man's child. Similar acts were committed by other Khawārij groups. These bands slaughtered Muslim travelers, massacred families, butchered the feeble minded, hacked off the heads of women, and made no distinction in accordance with the ages of their victims, murdering "women, children and babies," slaughtering the very old and the very young alike.[60] The public spaces of the Muslim world became sites of sudden massacres as the Khawārij attacked non-Khārijī Muslims without warning, as al-Malaṭī (d. ca. 333/944) recalled: "As for the first sect of Khārijites, they are the *Muḥakkima* who used to go out with their swords into the markets while people would stand around not realizing what was happening; they would shout 'no judgment except God's!' and plunge their swords into whoever they could reach and go on killing till they were killed."[61]

In the city of Madāʾin, a band of Khawārij "ripped open the bellies of pregnant women" and slaughtered people of all ages. One of their victims, a woman named Bunāna b. Abī Yazīd b. ʿĀṣim al-Azdī who "had read the

Qur'ān" said to her killers, "Woe to you! Have you ever heard of men killing women? Woe unto you! You kill someone who stretches out no hand against you, wishes you no harm, and has no power to help herself."[62] All of these actions were affronts to acceptable behavior, even in war against non-Muslim enemies. Abū Isḥāq al-Fazārī (d. 186), a *ghāzī*/scholar like Ibn al-Mubārak, included in his own work on righteous warfare a vehement prohibition of the killing of children said to have issued from the lips of Muḥammad himself. "You do not kill children, you do not kill children, you do not kill children!" the Prophet warned his followers.[63] Especially abhorrent to Muslim contemporaries seems to have been the chilling practice of splitting open pregnant women, an act repeatedly attributed to the Khawārij. After the murder of ʿAbd Allāh Ibn Khabāb and his pregnant *umm walad*, one of ʿAlī's deputies is said to have asked the Khawārij incredulously if the root of their objection to ʿAlī would be found in the womb of a woman.[64] Although Khārijī factions eventually came to disagree over the legitimacy of such behavior, which was part of a practice known as *istiʿrāḍ*, and such quietist Khārijī sects as the Ibāḍiyya would eventually deny that the first Khawārij had engaged it at all, our sources for very early Khawārij history repeatedly insist that they did.[65]

The bonds of Islamic identity were no protection in these encounters as the Khawārij pounced upon their victims and hacked away with their swords, although Christians and Jews were scrupulously left alive and were often the only witnesses left to tell the tale. In 37/657–58, for example, just after the split between ʿAlī and those who would compose the first faction of Khawārij, ʿAlī received a letter from one of his deputies. It read:

> A Jew tumbled in to us and reported to us that horsemen approached a village called Niffar from the direction of al-Kūfa, and they met in it a man from the people of this village who was named Zadhān Frūkh. They asked him about his religion, and he said, "I am a Muslim." Then they asked him about the Commander of the Faithful, and he said, "[He is] *imām*, and [he is] my guide," so they pounced upon him with their swords. Then they asked the Jew about his religion, and he said, "I am a Jew," and they cleared his path. So he came to us and reported to us this story.[66]

In the time of Muʿāwiya, Sahm b. Ghālib al-Hujaymī went out against the governors of al-Baṣra on two occasions, the first time killing three Muslims after an argument about whether or not he and his companions were indeed Muslims. Later, with the arrival of a new governor, he and some companions rebelled again, this time killing those they met on the road. But when they encountered a group of Jews on the road "he left them alone, and instead seized Saʿd, a *mawlā* of Qudāma b. Maẓʿūn . . . and killed him."[67] After a Khārijī raid on one community, during which a man named Simāk b. Yazīd, who was "touched with madness," was butchered, along with a number of his neighbors and his daughter, who pled for her father's life, it was a Christian slave woman, whom the Khawārij spared, that reported the events.[68]

As we ponder what to make of such reports, it will perhaps aid us to note the emergence within the divergent narrations of Khārijī behavior sampled here a series of "topoi" of the kind Albrecht Noth noted in his own studies of the early Muslim histories of the conquest period. These "topoi," Noth suggested, were recurrent stories and figures deployed by such Muslim authors as al-Ṭabarī and al-Balādhurī to structure their narratives of the conquest period. Often, Noth suggested, such topoi were deployed when there was need for an account of an event but no real information about the event was available. This did not mean that such events could not become what Somers would call "episodes," however. In Noth's estimation, certain stock topoi could be deployed in such circumstances to narrate the Muslim past, regardless of the factual content of those topoi.[69]

In the histories of the Khawārij authored by al-Balādhurī, al-Ṭabarī and other early Muslim authors, a series of recognizable topoi also emerge. More than once, for example, the Khawārij are alleged to have ripped open the abdomens of pregnant women. These were in turn instances of a much broader topos associated with the Khawārij, that of violence toward women and children. This topos in turn is closely related to another frequent topos associated with reportage of Khārijī violence, that in which women, within mere moments of their deaths at the hands of the Khawārij, speak boldly to their attackers and condemn the outrage they commit. One of the best known instances of this topos is that cited at the beginning of this chapter, in which Ibn Khabbāb's *umm walad* asked her murderers, "Do you not fear God?"[70]

I have noted already the frequent occurrence of scenes in which the Khawārij are set in opposition to representatives of caliphal power, and I have also noted several of the many instances in which the ascetic piety of the Khawārij is exemplified by the words and deeds of various Khawārij groups and individuals. The brand of asceticism stressed by the authors of these texts is recognizable as that which we might describe as specifically Muslim in that it entails a late antique *koinê* of ascetic praxis read through a particular narrative of the Muslim past and deployed as the practice of *jihād* as it was theorized and performed by such early Muslim warrior-scholars as the *ghāzī* Ibn al-Mubārak. The effect of this topos is to imbue the Khārijī actors in these episodes with a rather homogenous but instantly recognizable ascetic ethos. The same may be said for the motivations for rebellion articulated by these actors. I have noted, for example, that al-Ṭabarī and al-Balādhurī attribute to different Khārijī leaders operating in different periods what are in effect the same speeches. In each case, closely matched narrations of the recent Muslim past, phrased in what is often identical language, are put into the mouths of the Khārijī leaders in order to conjure the world view of different men, rebelling under different circumstances.[71]

The presence of these topoi in the textual sources we have for the history of the Khawārij within the early Muslim world should, as Noth suggested long ago, give us some pause before we treat the texts in which they appear as instances of strict reportage of the events they purport to recall. It is, of course, possible that the reports contained in the works of al-Balādhurī, al-Ṭabarī, and other early medieval Muslim authors do indeed merely pass on "factual" accounts of actions and words of the early Khawārij, and that the apparent uniformity in the behavior and rhetoric of the Khawārij is the result of a cohesive and conscious continuity from one Khārijī rebellion to the next. In this case, the recurrence of certain apparent topoi in these texts would represent not an attempt by later authors to reconstruct the personalities and events of the early Khārijī rebellions from a repertoire of stock figures, plots and speeches, but rather so many reflections of behavioral patterns consciously crafted in accordance with a Khārijī idiom of rebellion. It is equally possible, however, and perhaps more probable, that the extant sources for the actions and beliefs of the early Khawārij represent a blend of factual information about the events of the early Khawārij rebellions and attempts to reconstruct the worldview, motivation, and ethos of the early Khawārij themselves. Indeed, this would seem to be the view taken by a number of prominent scholars in recent articles and monographs treating the Khawārij and their times, among them Chase Robinson and Patricia Crone and Fritz Zimmermann.[72]

As is so often true of early Islamic history, however, it is ultimately impossible to know how closely extant accounts accord with what actually happened. What one can analyze, of course, is the collection of images, ideas, and stories the early Muslim sources were drawn to as they assembled their narratives; that is, one can trace the pattern of representation that emerges as authors like al-Balādhurī and al-Ṭabarī recalled the Khawārij. Whether they are based upon "hard fact" or crafted from a tool kit of stock tales and speeches inherited by these authors, the accounts we have represent records of the kinds of images and ideas that drew the attention of these authors as they worked and that they chose as a means of explaining the Khawārij and what they represented. It is in this sense that their use of topoi does not obscure some objective first/seventh- or second/eighth-century truth, but instead may help to reveal the way in which the Khawārij as a phenomenon were imagined and interpreted by non-Khawārij Muslims. This, ideally, will help illuminate how the problem of militant piety was understood within the late antique Muslim *umma*.

As we have seen, our early sources for the Khawārij, particularly al-Balādhurī and al-Ṭabarī, present the Khawārij as individuals who acted in close accordance with a system of values that crystallized in the ideology of *jihād* set forth by men like Ibn al-Mubārak; that is, they act with a purity of intention and pious rigor that manifests itself in ascetic praxis before, during, and after they engage in actual combat. This becomes particularly clear when the Khārijī ethos of rebellion is set in juxtaposition with those of such figures as the first/seventh-century ʿAlid rebel al-Mukhtār b. Abī ʿUbayd (d. 67/687), who, as his movement collapses, confesses in al-Ṭabarī's text that he only rebelled out of a sense of personal ambition when he saw the Umayyad empire being divided up among rival insurgents.[73] The version of al-Mukhtār's rebellion recorded by Dīnawarī is even more damning of al-Mukhtār and his motives. When a companion exclaims, "Abū Isḥāq, people think you undertook this enterprise as a matter of religion," al-Mukhtār replies, "No, by my life it was only to seek [the goods of] this world."[74] Whatever else the Khawārij are as they are rendered in the histories of the early Islamic world, they are pure in their intentions; the slaughter they wrought was committed with no care for gain and with sincere hope for the next world as opposed to the present one. In this, they fought pure *jihād* as Ibn al-Mubārak and his colleagues theorized it, their monstrous acts carried out as demonstrations of unblemished personal piety. The reader's attention is drawn to this difficult paradox repeatedly in all of the sources consulted above by the deployment of topoi demonstrating the ascetic rigor and studied Khārijī devotion to *sunna* and Qurʾān.

As al-Ṭabarī, al-Balādhurī and other early Muslim historians marshaled scenes and images with which to narrate the early Khārijī rebellions, the topos of the confrontation between the earnest, pious and ascetic Khārijī warriors cannot but recall the topos deployed by early Islamic historians of the *futūḥ* period in which the early *mujāhidūn* called Roman and Persian imperial officials to Islam, rejected attempts to negotiate, and insisted upon the communal truths it was their duty to defend. If, as I have suggested, this topos was descended in part from the martyr narratives of late antique Christian communities, with the Khawārij it now returned to its roots. In al-Balādhurī's text, for example, a captured Khārijī is brought before Umayyad officials in the time of Muʿāwiya. The caliph sends a letter instructing his officials, "'If he bears witness that I am caliph, then let him go . . . The officials came to the man and said to him, 'Bear witness that Muʿāwiya is caliph and that he is commander of the faithful.' And he said, 'I bear witness that God is truth, and that the hour is approaching, no doubt about it.' And he said, 'You are indeed a madman (*majnūn*) . . . do you bear witness to what I said to you?' He said, 'I bear witness that [my tribe] is most noble . . .' And a man from Banū Ḥilāl . . . said, 'Give me his blood to drink.' And he said, 'Help yourself.' And he killed him."[75]

Just was the early *mujāhidūn* emerge in the texts of al-Ṭabarī and al-Azdī as hybrid monk-horsemen, here this Khārijī witness stands as an emblem of rigorous monotheistic piety fused with Arab tribal identity; he will not acknowledge the temporal power of the imperial master of his world, and as a means of bringing about his martyrdom he draws upon tribal rivalry to coax his interrogators into killing him. In so doing, he is just one of many Khawārij conjured in our sources grimly rejecting the attempts of the imperial power of their age to make them compromise on their interpretation of Muḥammad's revelation and its consequences for the nature of power and community within their world. Like Muʿādh b. Jabal or Khālid b. al-Walīd rebuffing the diplomatic advances of Roman officials and insisting upon conversion, *jizya*, or war, men like Dhū al-Thafināt and Ṣāliḥ b. Musarriḥ insisted that the powerful of their world either acknowledge God's truth or fight them to the death.

Whether these men understood themselves emplotted within the narrative of Islamic history I have traced through the last three chapters is of course impossible to know. We may note, however, that as al-Ṭabarī, al-Balādhurī, and other early Muslim authors wrote the Khawārij into the history of the Islamic world, they did so by casting them in scenes rendered in a manner very like that which was used to sketch *futūḥ*-era Muslim heroes. This is particularly true as the Khawārij are set in opposition to representatives of caliphal power.

In ʿAbd Allāh b. Wahb's late second/eighth-century *ḥadīth* collection, for example, there appears the following story. A number of Khawārij rebelled during the time of ʿUmar II b. ʿAbd al-ʿAzīz (d. 720), who wrote to them, calling them back to the community, to the truth, and to the *sunna*. Finally, he reminded them that they were but a small, weak group, to which they responded by citing the Qur'ānic *Sūrat al-anfāl, aya* 26: "As for your mentioning our fewness and weakness, God said of the companions of the Messanger of God, upon whom Peace, <Remember when you were few, oppressed in the land and fearful that the people (*al-nās*) would snatch you up, and he sheltered and supported you with his aid>."[76] This verse frequently appears in early *tafsīr* works glossed as a reference to either the struggles of Muḥammad's community against the power of Quraysh, or as a reference to the *futūḥ*-era struggle with the Persian and Roman empires.[77] In whichever sense it is meant here, it clearly makes reference to the struggles waged by the founders of the Muslim *umma* against oppressive representatives of worldly might, precisely the role, that is, in which the Muslim authorities against whom this particular band of Khawārij waged their rebellion are cast.

The notion of the Khawārij as self-conscious opponents of corrupt worldly power even played a part in ʿAlī's overtures to them as he attempted to win them back to his side. In al-Ṭabarī's *Ta'rīkh*, ʿAlī is portrayed as interpreting his struggle with Muʿāwiya through the prism of the *futūḥ* narrative for the benefit of the Khawārij. "By God if [Muʿāwiya and his followers] were to have charge over you, they would treat you like Chosroes and Heraclius," he warned the militants, referring to the archetypical Persian king of kings and Roman emperor, the heads of the imperial powers overthrown during the first heady days of the *futūḥ* period. It was he himself, ʿAlī urged the rebel pietists, who represented true Islam, and by following him they might resist men who were the equivalent of the very Roman and Persian tyrants dispelled by the followers of Abū Bakr and ʿUmar. If they failed to follow him, on the other hand, those worldly tyrants would once again hold sway over the lives of the Arabs.[78]

Indeed, that the Khawārij represented for these authors an attempt to maintain or return to the primordial essence of *futūḥ*-era Islam is made clear by the character of the narratives Dhū al-Thafināt and Ṣāliḥ b. Musarriḥ are said to recite by al-Balādhurī and al-Ṭabarī as explanations for their rebellion. As Chase Robinson has written, "According to the vision of Ṣāliḥ b. Musarriḥ, to embrace *shārī* Khārijism was to reassert a primeval, conquest-era Muslim identity that had been abandoned by the Umayyads."[79] Robinson also notes, with Brünnow and others, that the Khawārij differed little from other Muslims in their basic system of belief. Neither, one might add, were they unique or even distinct with regard to their sense that the primeval forms of Muslimness enshrined in their communal narratives had been betrayed and required redemption.[80]

Real Muslims, the Khawārij declared, and particularly legitimate leaders of the Muslim *umma*, defended the integrity of Islam from within through a combination of piety and intransigence with regard to innovation.[81] "Bring us a caliph like ʿUmar," they demanded. It was in imitation of the behavior of such men that real Islam might be maintained through mimetic daily practice, and it was such men alone who could rightly lead the one community of God upon the earth. There was no ʿUmar to bring them, however; the choice was ʿAlī or Muʿāwiya, and the Khawārij chose neither. Instead, they went out from among their former companions and allies, taking the one true community of God with them they believed, illuminated with the unadulterated word of God and enacted in strict accordance with *sunna*. That the primordial essence of the Islamic *umma* should be so maintained was not the desire of the Khawārij alone, of course. Muslims of the second/eighth and third/ninth centuries, for example, readily acknowledged the authority of men like Ibn al-Mubārak, who preserved primordial Muslimness on the frontiers of the Roman world in the practice of raiding combined with pious renunciation.[82]

In the estimation of these authors, then, it would seem that the kind of militant piety the Khawārij represented was in fact one exceedingly destructive consequence of the formative narratives of the late antique Muslim community; the horrifying violence of the Khawārij was in this sense little other than one defining aspect of Muslimness turned back against the Muslim *umma*, much as one Umayyad governor reported to his caliph that "the fury of the Khawārij turned back on them" when one Khārijī group divided against itself over issues of doctrinal purity.[83] Much as some Christians of fourth-, fifth-, and sixth-century Rome, Egypt, Syria, and North Africa found themselves bound by the narrative bases for their local and cosmic communal identities to cycles of violence and persecution, so now some Muslims found themselves caught in a perpetual reenactment of the struggle and bloodshed of their own foundational narratives. For the Muslims of the seventh, eighth and ninth centuries, as for the Christians of an earlier era, the potential implications of these dilemmas were unending tragedy, bloodshed, and communal dissolution.

This danger is signaled in these texts by the figure of butchered women and children, and most especially by the sign of the pregnant woman slit open, spilling her child, and, presumably, the future of the Muslim *umma* out into a very violent world. This sign is particularly poignant in the case of the murdered consort and child of Ibn Khabbāb, himself the offspring of one of Muḥammad's companions. The violence represented by the Khawārij, it would seem, was a threat to the security and future survival of the Muslim *umma*. That the Khawārij themselves never represented a valid threat to the survival of the *umma* or the regimes that ruled it through their actions is less important than the danger represented by their particular application of a set of values and ideals shared in common among their Muslim contemporaries, these derived, of course, from an evolving narrative of the Islamic past.

The perversity of this inversion, this turning in of the militant piety that had become central to Muslim communal narratives, is underscored by the propensity of the Khawārij to slaughter Muslims while leaving alive Christians and Jews. When he was informed of such an event, ʿAlī is said to have written back to his official, "I have taken note of what you have said about the band that passed by you and slaughtered the pious Muslim while the transgressing infidel had security with them. They are a people whom Satan has seduced."[84] It was with policing of Muslim identity that the Khawārij were concerned, and on the rare occasion that their wrath turned against non-Muslims, it was over issues of boundary transgression. Just before murdering ʿAlī outside a mosque in al-Kūfa in the year 40/660-61, for example, the Khārijī Ibn Muljam is reported to have seen a funeral pass by in which Christians and Muslims were walking together. The funeral was for a Christian man, Abjar, whose son, Ḥajjār, was now a Muslim. The militant recited a poem:

If Ḥajjār b. Abjar is (really) a Muslim,
the bier of Abjar would have been kept away from him;
But if Ḥajjār b. Abjar is an infidel,

then this sort of infidelity is not inappropriate.
Do you accept this—that a priest and a Muslim are
together before a bier? Shameful spectacle!
If it were not for what I intend to do, I would scatter their
company with a sword
polished, burnished, shining and drawn from its scabbard.
But my intention with that (sword) is as an instrument of access to
God or this man (ʿAlī).
Take it or leave it.[85]

In an alternate version of this episode, recorded by al-Dīnawari, Ibn Muljam's words are more blunt: "I would have indiscriminately massacred them (*istaʿraḍtuhum*) with my sword."[86] Ibn Muljam's concern for the imposition and maintenance of the proper boundaries between Muslim and Christian (even if they were also father and son) reflects what would seem to be the central concern of most Khārijī activities—the declaration and defense of crucial divisions that were to demarcate the one true community of God upon the earth from all other communities. This is particularly apparent, for example, as one consults the second/eighth-century Khārijī *Sīra* of Sālim b. Dhakwān, a member of the quietist Ibāḍī subsect of the Khawārij. Within the text, which is in essence a statement of faith, the author is careful to distinguish his own sect from all other Khawārij subsects on matters of doctrine and praxis. Ibn Dhakwān's *Sīra* enumerates the differences, for example, between the Ibāḍiyya and the extremist Azāriqa, Najadāt, and other Khārijī sects on such questions as whether it is permissible to indiscriminately kill women and children or whether a Khārijī Muslim is justified in taking the property of Muslims who do not accept his particular version of Khārijī dogma. The statement of faith also draws distinctions between the author's community and Murjiʾites, the Fatana and those Muslims who, from the Ibāḍī point of view, had fallen away from Islam in its pure, pre-*fitna* form.

Indeed, one of the intriguing characteristics among the early Khawārij is their tendency to draw ever tighter boundaries around themselves, excluding those who had set themselves outside of the one true community of God upon the earth whether through sin or by false belief or by failing to display the proper level of zeal in opposing the transgressions of the imperfect Muslims around them.[87] Each boundary required a new act of *barāʾa* or dissociation from those around them, a new *hijra* from what had now become the *dār al-kufr*, the abode of unbelief.[88] To undertake *barā'a* in this way, the Khawārij believed, was to follow the example of Muḥammad and the primordial Muslim *umma*. As Ibn Dhakwān put it, "In Muḥammad's time, God's judgment on those who failed to respond to his call was that those who adhered to Islam and made it their religion must disown those who (failed to) do so until they acknowledged Islam."[89]

For the Khawārij communities contained within the ever-shrinking boundaries produced by the obligation of *barā'a*, a world already filled with enemies and with strangers became more perilous and more hateful with every new split, and the tragedy of Ṣiffīn was replayed repeatedly as new episodes within the sad and violent Khārijī narrative of Muslim history. Clearly, upon this model, the *dār al-Islām* could only ever be a perpetually collapsing edifice, bringing disappointment, death, and horror to those dwelling within its walls. Indeed, even for the Shīʿa, for whom dissociation was a crucial aspect of communal identity, the Khārijī penchant for dissociation was despised as an example of how measures necessary to maintain one's community as distinct and discrete could be taken too far. The Shīʿa imam al-Bāqir is reported to have scolded a group of his followers who too zealously practiced *barā'a*, "What business do you have dissociating from one another? You behave like the Khārijīs who have defined their doctrine so narrowly that they dissociate from one another."[90] The world the Khawārij created for themselves and for those around them in this manner was in many ways like the pre-Islamic "time of ignorance" or *jāhiliyya* described by early Muslim warriors as they narrated the pre-Islamic Arab past to Roman generals and Persian kings: It was a world in which only distrust and fear could rule, a world in which the norm was a state of all-against-all warfare, and in which lasting bonds of community, peace, security, and prosperity would be unknown.[91]

"What Does a She-Wolf Birth Except a Wolf?"

> *How can the righteous be certain that his peace of mind is not error itself, since it differs in no way from the peace of mind of him that is in error? If pious devotion is an index of peace of mind in both cases, who shows more devotion than the monk in his cell, the Khārijite that sacrifices his life, etc?*
>
> —al-Jāḥiẓ[92]

In recent monographs, Michael Morony and Chase Robinson have each asked, in effect, how the Khawārij fit into their extra-Islamic, late antique milieu. Morony in particular has noted certain specific similarities between the "militant asceticism" of Mesopotamian Jews and Christians as practiced in ostracism and excommunication, and extremist attitudes toward apostasy among Magians.[93] He moreover noted that the ascetic sentiments expressed by Khawārij like Ṣāliḥ b. Musarriḥ were common to many communities in late antique Iraq, just as the concept of selling one's worldly happiness in return for salvation was well known in Jewish and Christian communities.[94]

Morony is quite cautious as he tries to situate the Khawārij within their larger cultural and religious milieu, however. In discussing the concept of dying for God as a metaphor for the renunciation of worldly concerns, for example, he draws a careful distinction between the spiritual war advocated by such Syrian Christians as Isaac of Nineveh and unflinching militancy of individuals like Ṣāliḥ or Shabīb b. Yazīd.[95] In his own discussion of the possibility of understanding the Khawārij as part of a more pervasive "Late Antique" milieu, Robinson is more reticent still. Although he concedes that "some of [the] message" of such ascetic rebels as Ṣāliḥ and his companions "no doubt struck familiar chords among local Christians," he nevertheless concludes that "Ṣāliḥ fits a Late Antique pattern only as much as Muḥammad does." That is, in Robinson's estimation, very little or not at all.[96]

Although it is not entirely clear what Robinson means by a "late antique pattern," I suggest that if we draw back from our focus upon the individuals and groups identified as Khawārij in our sources and consider their actions and ideologies as they were recalled by our early Arabic sources, a pattern recognizable beyond the confines of the Islamic community does indeed seem to emerge.

Whether or not they imagined themselves to act in the tradition of Muḥammad, his companions, and the warriors of the early *futūḥ* era, the Khawārij were certainly patterned after the model of these men as they were written into the history of the Islamic world. Part of the basis for that model, in turn, seems to have been a narrative of the early Islamic past articulated in accordance with a late antique vocabulary of signs and symbols shared in common among a network of communities strewn through the world in which Islam was taking shape. The aspects most frequently stressed by Muslim sources in describing the character of the Khawārij, moreover—those of pious renunciation, an avid concern for the defense of their communal boundaries, a fervent desire for martyrdom in defense of the community those boundaries enclosed—were qualities with which the early *mujāhidūn* were invested as they were assigned roles within the evolving narrative of the Islamic *umma*'s primordial moments.

We has seen throughout the previous pages that in the early Muslim imaginary, these early Muslims and the institution of *jihād* as a form of devotional praxis had been understood as kindred with other forms and practitioners of ascetic praxis and rigorous striving on God's behalf, particularly those of the Christian monks and martyrs. As I have noted repeatedly, monks were closely associated in very early Muslim literature with martyrdom and striving in defense of monotheistic truth, and monastic practice was cited as an analog for *jihād* in prophetic *aḥādīth* circulated by no less an authority than Ibn al-Mubārak. Meanwhile, the earliest Muslim warriors were described repeatedly by early Muslim authors as "like monks by night and horsemen by day." For Ibn Qutayba, for example, conversion to Islam, raiding and martyrdom on the path of God simply amounted to an extension and fulfillment of one Christian monk's life of monastic rigor.

In this sense, whatever outward similarities the Khawārij might have born to the militant Christian pietists of their time, we need not imagine horizontal influences between discrete groups of rigorist monotheists; rather, the role of the Khawārij within their own society, that of zealous and often murderous defenders of the primordial character of the Islamic *umma* (as they imagined it to be), may be traced on the one hand to the specific narrative within which they were emplotted (either by later Muslim authors or by their own accord) and on the other to the role of ascetic rigor within the larger cultural milieu within which that narrative was articulated and elaborated.

The Khawārij, like Christian monks and like the *ghāzī* frontiersmen of the second/eighth century, were figures in whom the numinous past remained present and available and through whom it made its (sometimes awful) presence felt in the world. Through their retreat from the fallen communities of the rapidly changing Muslim world, they sought to hold at bay the decadence and worldly sin that had begun to creep in and to contaminate the one community of God upon the earth. It is tempting to believe that the Khawārij were imagined in this way only among themselves and perhaps among a few of the non-Muslims whom they famously impressed. But there is a good deal of evidence to suggest that in tandem with the horror elicited by their acts, the Khawārij also excited the imaginations of those who recalled or imagined their exploits. This is not difficult to understand. Khārijī renunciation of self, strict adherence to the Word of God (as they interpreted it), and particularly their unwillingness to compromise with the powerful of their world clearly spoke profoundly to Muslims who rejected their methods but who empathized with their disillusion, their outraged piety, and their anxiety at the notion that the crucial link between themselves and numinous moment of Muḥammad's revelation might be lost through human frailty. That this link could only be retained through studied and rigorous adherence to the *sunna* of the Prophet and the behavioral exempla of his primordial community very few of the early Khawārij's contemporaries doubted.

The seductiveness of the Khārijī idiom as it was imagined by Muslim authors may be gauged from the care with which authors like al-Ṭabarī crafted such figures as Dhū al-Thafināt and Ṣāliḥ b. Musarriḥ, who was, as Chase Robinson has pointed out, actually something of a flop as an insurgent. Particularly noteworthy in this regard is the frankly breathless relish with which al-Ṭabarī and other authors recount the exploits of such Khārijī rebels as Shabīb b. Yazīd.[97] Shabīb, as he appears in the works of these authors, is a thoroughly romantic figure, a trickster saint and monk-raider hero of larger-than-life proportions.[98] He is pitted against the Umayyad governor al-Ḥajjāj, a figure whose overbearing and violent nature is made clear by al-Ṭabarī's depiction of his arrival in al-Kūfa in the year 75/694, soon after which he begins lopping off the heads of Muslims who do not wish to fight the Khawārij.[99] Sketched in opposition to such a man, al-Ṭabarī's Shabīb, for all of his own violence, is easily legible as a paragon of primordial Muslim virtue.

Indeed, even Shabīb's mother, Jahīza, whom Shabīb took with him on his campaign against the Umayyads, is rendered by al-Ṭabarī as an exemplum of pious monotheist intransigence. She was said by al-Ṭabarī to have been captured as a young woman in a *ghāzī* raid on Roman territory and purchased by Shabīb's father. The man had initially tried to force the young (presumably Christian) woman to convert to Islam by beating her, but she had only become more adamant in her faith. After the birth of her son, however, she converted out of love for Shabīb's father. She reportedly experienced a vision in which fire shot out from her vagina, announcing Shabīb's future career (and the manner of his death, by drowning).[100] Al-Balādhurī tells us that at the end of her son's campaign, she finally went down fighting fiercely. A poem recited about her ran: "Umm Shabīb gave birth to Shabīb / What does a she-wolf birth except a wolf?"[101]

It is particularly intriguing that Jahīza was imagined to have been a strident and brazen defender of her faith before her conversion to Islam, of which she then became an equally militant champion, rather on the model of Ibn Qutayba's monk/*mujāhid*. Among Shabīb's other followers, we are told, was a woman captured by al-Ḥajjāj at the final defeat of Shabīb's band, whereupon she was brought before the governor. He greeted her, "O enemy of God, praise God who killed your son, your brother and your husband," to which she replied, "Yes, praise God who placed them in paradise, and who has delayed me behind them." As she began to proclaim the tenets of her faith to al-Ḥajjāj, she would not raise her head (rather after the fashion of Ṣāliḥ b. Musarriḥ), to which the governor commanded her, "Raise your head and look at me!" She replied, "I certainly would be loath to look upon one whom God does not look upon," whereupon the governor ordered her killed. "And she said, '*Lā ḥukma illā lillah*!' ('There is no judgment but God's!')[102] until she died."[103] For men and women raised on stories of showdowns between intransigent and ascetic Muslim warriors who sneered at their former imperial masters, or on tales of the Christian martyrs of Najrān in their role as the Qur'ānic "People of the Trench" defying overbearing and worldly kings, such tales must have made exceptionally complicated reading.

The potential allure of the Khawārij and their ideas, so our sources tell us, could even ensnare those who hunted them. When another captured Khārijī woman was brought before al-Ḥajjāj, she simply ignored him. His *mawlā*, a man named Yazīd b. Abī Muslim, secretly sympathized with the Khawārij, but was trying to hide this from his master. When the Khārijī woman would not respond to al-Ḥajjāj, Yazīd said to her, "Woe to you, the *amīr* is talking to you!" To which she responded "The woe is to you, O sinful denier," employing a term the Khawārij used to disparage those who shared their views but sought to hide them.[104]

Not even the ruler of the Umayyad Empire was thought to be immune to the seductive charge of the Khawārij, it would seem. The caliph ʿAbd al-Malik was remembered to have questioned a captured Khārijī, who would not cooperate with his interrogators but who explained in fluent, learned and seductive terms the basis of his community's *qawm* and *madhhab*. Finally, he insulted the Caliph, suggesting that he was alienated from the truth. When his captors began to torture him, however, ʿAbd al-Malik wept uncontrollably, for he could not stand to see a man of such quality treated so harshly. He rescinded the Khārijī's death sentence, and instead had him imprisoned.

Later, he apologized for even this, and explained to the man that he would not have bothered him at all if he had not feared that something like the admiration and sympathy that stirred in his own breast for the Khārijī might drive the less perfect Muslims he ruled to deadly error.[105]

The dilemma represented by the Khawārij, then, was not easily resolved by Muslims of the first centuries after the *hijra*, nor was the dilemma itself limited to the actions and ideology of those who identified themselves as members of Khārijī communities. Insofar as we can observe the birth and growth of discrete Muslim communities, it is a process carried forth in accordance with permutations of an Islamic metanarrative grounded in the recollection of Muḥammad's emergence as a prophet, his formation of the primeval *umma*, the *hijra*, the conquest of Arabia, and the post-Muḥammad period of conquest. The bases for the discrete Muslim identities that were now developing—those we might call Khārijī, proto-Sunnī and proto-Shīʿī, among others—were in effect variant readings of this Islamic metanarrative. As disparate Islamic narratives evolved, so too did self-consciously separate Muslim communities. What would seem to outsiders relatively minor variations in the plot of these narratives, or in the valences accorded to certain personalities and events carried profound consequences for those whose identities were dependant upon such narratives.

Meanwhile, Muslims found themselves living on intimate terms with non-Muslims throughout the *dār al-Islām*. As Peter Brown has noted, the Muslim historical tradition does not tend to make frequent mention of the non-Muslim inhabitants of this world or of the relationships that formed between Muslims and non-Muslims.[106] As we shall see in the next and final chapter, however, there are ways of recovering not only the complexity and diversity of the *dār al-Islām* but also the means by which Muslims maintained stable and dependable communal boundaries within that world without frequent or systematic recourse to violence against religious others. In so doing, we shall examine the processes of communal self-fashioning that made of the followers of the *madhhab* of Aḥmad b. Ḥanbal a self-consciously discrete and self-contained community within the greater Muslim *umma*.

CHAPTER EIGHT

"This Is a Very Filthy Question, and No One Should Discuss It": The Messy World of Ibn Ḥanbal

ONE DAY IN the eighth century, we are told, a monk bishop was walking down a road in the region of Margā, in Mesopotamia. He came upon a camel herder, facing the east, singing a complicated hymn. Amazed, he approached the man to ask him where he had learned the hymn. The man answered him in Arabic, however, pretending not to understand his question. When the monk cast himself onto the ground and vowed not to rise until he got some answers, the man said in Arabic, "Get up, monk. What is there between you and me? Go in peace from my place." The monk would not relent, however, and finally the camel herder agreed to tell his tale.

He said he had been a Nestorian bishop forty years before but had been captured by a raiding party of Muslims and had been given the duty of tending camels. When the monk heard this, he immediately offered to raise money to pay for the former bishop's freedom. The camel herder told the monk not to bother, he found his way of life satisfactory, and, he added, if he had wanted to run off or buy his freedom at any time in the previous forty years, he had had plenty of chances. His contentment had in part to do with the relationship he enjoyed with the Muslims who owned him. "For forty years I have been as thou seest me, and our Lord hath protected me from all evil, and [the Arabs] have accounted me as one of their elders and as one of their brethren, because they found me upright and obedient. And I have received from them no compulsion to sin in any way."[1]

In the same era, another Christian traveler was taken ill in the Holy Land. One of those traveling with him to see the holy sights in Palestine was a particularly zealous Muslim. When the Christian traveler grew more desperately ill, he was taken to a monastery. The Muslim went with him and, having witnessed the cure, we are told, he then converted.[2] The capacity of Christian monks to cure the sick is associated with many conversion stories in this period, in fact, whether it is the Muslim governor of Mosul who was said to have been converted to Christianity by the cure of his son, or the monastery of monks who were converted to Islām when a Muslim who was ill and who had decided to go to the monks for a cure did so by riding a lion to the monastery.[3]

Not all of these stories hinged upon acts of conversion, however. Sometime in the ninth century, for example, a Muslim man was said to have set out from Persia to bring his son to the Palestinian enclosure of a Christian monk so that the ascetic might cure the boy. On the road to the monk's home, however, things went wrong. The man was robbed, his son was kidnapped and the man was told that in any case the Christian wonderworker would probably have insisted that he give up his Islamic faith and adopt Christianity in order that his son might be cured.

When he arrived at the monk's cell, however, he discovered something very different. God would cure his son and return all that the man had lost, the monk said. Moreover, although he knew that the man had been told that he should expect the monk to try to convert him, the monk assured him that God did not require this of him; his faith and his piety were pleasing to God, and this was enough to bring down God's mercy upon the sick little boy, wherever he was, and his unfortunate father. "God compels no one," the monk assured him. When the man returned home, he found his son cured and all of his lost property returned.[4] Muslims and monks had a long history of mutual toleration. A century before, on the Syrian frontier with Byzantium, the Muslim *ghāzī*/scholar al-Fazārī had included in his work on the religious rules of warfare a pair of long entries forbidding the harming of Christian monks by Muslim raiders.[5]

Meanwhile, in Egypt, the anti-Chalcedonian archbishop of Alexandria, Isaac, enjoyed such a cordial relationship with the Muslim *amīr* of the city, ʿAbd al-ʿAzīz, that, we are told, certain malicious Muslims talked the *amīr* into forbidding Isaac to cross himself when he came to dine at the *amīr*'s table on pain of death. Arriving for dinner, the bishop's hagiographer tells us, the bishop received the *amīr*'s command and then asked if the *amīr* preferred that he sit at the place across the table from him, to the left, to the right or right in front of him, gesturing with his hand to each position (and in the process making the sign of the cross). The *amīr* was fooled, but his deputies were not. When they informed the *amīr* about the Christian's trick, however, the *amīr* was simply charmed.[6] The anecdote answers what seems to have been a perceived need to emphasize to the reader that although the bishop's relationship with the *amīr* was very close, it was not *too* comfortable and carried the threat of persecution despite the fact that the bishop clearly made a habit of dining with his infidel governor.[7]

All of these anecdotes are taken from Christian hagiographical texts written in lands under Muslim rule in the decades and centuries immediately following the *futūḥ*. One would certainly expect that such texts, in which we encounter frequent reports detailing incessant and sometimes bloody conflict between opposed Christian factions, would contain complaints of persecution at the hands of the new Muslim masters of Syria, Iraq, and Egypt, were there much at all to report.[8] Similar texts produced during the fifth and sixth centuries, for example, vividly relate the enormities inflicted upon the anti-Chalcedonian communities of the eastern empire by Roman imperial forces. Indeed, in the same texts in which we encounter reports of pacific relations between local Muslim and Christian communities and between Christian religious leaders and Muslim governmental figures, we also encounter residual traces of the loathing with which such Roman emperors as Heraclius and Justinian were recalled by the Christians of those communities, this due of course to the policies of religious persecution pursued by those sovereigns within the lands eventually subsumed into the *dār al-Islām*.[9]

The relative toleration with which non-Muslims were treated by their Muslim conquerors in the decades and centuries after the *futūḥ* is particularly remarkable given the character of intercommunal relations while the lands of Syria, Egypt, and Mesopotamia were still part of a Christian empire.[10] In this final chapter, I will ask what might account for this level of relative toleration within the Muslim empire. This tolerance is all the more notable given the potential for militancy and violence around questions of Muslim communal identity which we explored in the previous chapter. The vast majority of Muslims rejected the kind of violent pursuit of primordial Islamic identity that is characteristic of Khārijī theory and praxis, however, even as they shared with the Khawārij a basic narrative of the Islamic past and an urgent sense that the primordial essence of Islam, as exemplified in the example of the Prophet and his companions, required strict defense.

As we shall see, although the metanarrative of the Muslim communal past within which the Khawārij imagined themselves emplotted was shared with a spectrum of other Muslim communities, the specific reading to which that metanarrative was subject varied from community to community. This, predictably, carried implications for the ways in which Muslim communal identity, normative political behavior, and even the soteriological role of the Prophet himself were imagined within the discrete Muslim communities that now emerged. Not incidentally, these new communities also possessed distinct modes of performing Muslim identity and tending the boundaries that set their communities apart from all others. As we shall see, this was a complicated and delicate task within the world these emerging Muslim communities inhabited.

"He Was Tortured for God, and He Suffered Patiently"

Among the Muslim communities that rejected the Khawārij and their beliefs was that formed around the figure of Aḥmad Ibn Ḥanbal (d. 241/855).[11] In Ibn Abī Yaʿlā's *ṭabaqāt* work, which recalls the lives, deeds, and words of the first generations of followers of Ibn Ḥanbal's *madhhab* (pl. *madhāhib*),[12] there is a detailed refutation of the methods and beliefs of the Khawārij. The passage occurs very near the beginning of the work itself and is part of a more comprehensive series of distinctions drawn between Ḥanbalī beliefs and those groups of Muslims the Ḥanbalīs believed to have strayed from the defining truths of the one community of God on the earth, among them the Murjiʾa, the Nuṣayriyya, the Muʿtazila, and the Qadariyya. In its form and function, it may be read on the analogy of the passages leading into the Monastery of Epiphanius at Thebes; it is a textual site in which the ascribed beliefs of members of the Ḥanbalī community might be weighed against those of the reader. This, of course, provided an occasion for pondering one's identity, for affirming one's sense of belonging to the community formed around the figure of Ibn Ḥanbal, or for sensing one's variance with the normative beliefs and practices of that community.

Although the beliefs and practices of several groups are discussed in contrast to those that mark the contours of Ḥanbalī identity, it is the Khawārij who are discussed in the most detail and whose doctrine is most stridently rejected.

> As for the Khawārij, they passed through the religion, and they separated themselves from the community, and they wandered away from Islām, and they isolated themselves from the community and they strayed from the path, and they rebelled against the government (*al-sulṭān*); they took the sword against the *umma*; they made the blood of the *umma* permissible, as well as their possessions; they treat as an enemy anyone who disagrees with them . . . They dissociate themselves from them, and they reproach them with unbelief and enormities. They think their contentiousness in the legal prescriptions of Islām is proper . . . and they say whoever tells lies or commits a few or many sins, he must die without repentance, and he is in Hell, abiding forever, deathless.[13]

This passage continues to list such Khārijī beliefs as the impermissibility of prayer in shoes or the wiping off of shoes as a means of preprayer purification, concluding, "they do not recognize that the government has any claim on their obedience, nor that Quraysh has any claim upon the caliphate, and in many things they are opposed to Islām and its people." The Ḥanbalīs, by contrast, are people of tradition, those who follow the *sunna* and teaching of a lineage of scholars and pious men all the way back to Muḥammad, to the primordial origins of the one community of God. Adherence with prescribed Ḥanbalī praxis and such touchstones of Ḥanbalī belief as the uncreatedness of the Qur'ān in turn marked one as a member of that community.[14]

Prior even to the doctrine that defined the Ḥanbalī *madhhab*, however, there was the figure of Ibn Ḥanbal himself. The Ḥanbalī community looked to Aḥmad not only as an authority whose *ʿilm* was indisputably sound but also as a figure who was personally favored by God and who could accordingly intervene on behalf of those who remained true to his memory and his teachings. One member of the Ḥanbalī community recalled that in a dream he saw "one of the *ahl al-ḥadīth* (*ḥadīth* scholars)" who had died sometime before. The dreamer asked the man what God had done with him when he had come to him after death. The departed *ḥadīth* scholar said, "He forgave me." When he was asked why he was forgiven, he said, "For my love of Ibn Ḥanbal." His interlocutor noted, "You are at rest, and you smile," and the dead man agreed, "I am at rest and in happiness."[15]

A rather similar story helps to clarify the basis of Ibn Ḥanbal's apparent intercessory power with God. Sometime after Ibn Ḥanbal's death, we are told, another Ḥanbalī saw the great man in a dream. He too asked the dead man what God did with him after his death. Ibn Ḥanbal's answer is revealing: "He forgave me, and then he said, 'O Aḥmad, were you tortured for me?' And I said, 'Yes, O Lord.' And [God] said, 'O Aḥmad, this is my face. Look at it, for I reveal it to you to gaze upon.'"[16] Even before his death, however, there were signs that Ibn Ḥanbal had a special relationship with the numinous. Once, for example, a mysterious man showed up to a gathering of Aḥmad and his companions and announced to him that he was directed in a dream to seek out Ibn Ḥanbal in a distant land and report to him that "God is pleased with you, and the angels of his heaven and his faith are pleased with you." Equally remarkable from the point of view of the narrator was the fact that the man then left without even asking about *ḥadīth* or posing any kind of legal "issue or problem" for the great man to solve.[17] On another occasion, it was recalled by his son Ṣāliḥ b. Aḥmad b. Ḥanbal (d. 265/878), a wandering ascetic came to Aḥmad from a great distance to engage him in a discussion of asceticism.

The torture Ibn Ḥanbal endured on God's behalf took place during his *miḥna* interrogation. The *miḥna* of the caliph al-Maʾmūn, which is commonly referred to in English as "the Inquisition," began in 218/833. Its cause and purpose has been debated by scholars, but the immediate issue over which Ibn Ḥanbal was interrogated was the createdness of the Qurʾān.[18] To paraphrase the letter of al-Maʾmūn that announced the start of the *miḥna*, as it is preserved in the history of al-Ṭabarī, those who conducted the *miḥna* were to question local legal and religious authorities about whether there was a time when the Qurʾān was not.[19] The *miḥna* of al-Maʾmūn has been interpreted by modern historians as a struggle between speculative theologians and scholars of *ḥadīth* and as an attempt to centralize religious authority in the person of the caliph. Among medieval Muslims, however, the narrative of the *miḥna* that gained currency emphasized first and foremost Ibn Ḥanbal's intransigence before his interrogators.[20] This was a narrative first articulated by two men who were contemporaries and relatives of Ibn Ḥanbal, his son Ṣāliḥ, whose biography of Aḥmad we have briefly encountered already, and that of

Ḥanbal b. Isḥāq b. Ḥanbal (d. 273/886-87), Aḥmad's cousin.[21] It was this narrative and Aḥmad's emplotment within it that established Aḥmad as an indisputable authority and resource for the fashioning of authentically Muslim selves, much as the fathers of the Council of Nicaea were authorized by their status as martyrs of the Great Persecution of the late third and early fourth centuries.[22]

Ibn Ḥanbal's capacity and willingness to endure the pain inflicted upon him during his interrogation was remembered by later generations of Ḥanbalīs (as well as many non-Ḥanbalī Muslims) as an exemplary act of witnessing in defense of his community's crucial truths. Through Ibn Ḥanbal's intransigence in the face of the powerful of his world, the boundaries of the one community of God upon the earth had been preserved; Ibn Ḥanbal would not consent to the error represented by the false beliefs propagated by his interrogators but instead stood up fearlessly in defense of Muḥammad's revelation and the defining traditions of his primordial community. "[Ibn Ḥanbal] was tortured for God, and he suffered patiently," members of the Ḥanbalī community later recalled. "For God's book he was a helper, and he stood up on behalf of the *sunna* of the Prophet, . . . He did not fear what was threatened, and he was not a coward when he was cautioned, he expounded truthfully, and he spoke with truthful candor."[23] The specific character of this "truthful candor" may be gauged from one passage from the account of Ibn Ḥanbal's interrogation as it was recorded by Ḥanbal Ibn Isḥāq b. Ḥanbal. During one of his interviews with the caliph al-Muʿtaṣim and his theological advisors, Ibn Ḥanbal declared on the issue of the createdness of the Qurʾān, "The Qurʾān is the *ʿilm* of God, and whoever maintains that the *ʿilm* of God is created has committed unbelief." The implications of this statement were clear to his interrogators, one of whom said to the caliph, "O Commander of the Faithful, he called us infidels, and he called you an infidel!"[24] Elsewhere in the Isḥāq's account, Ibn Ḥanbal made clear precisely the stakes over which he and his fellow resisters were contending. "[ʿAbd Allāh] said, 'I asked Abū ʿAbd Allāh, "To what are you all summoned?"' He said, 'We are summoned to unbelief in God.'"[25]

Accordingly, Ibn Ḥanbal was, in the estimation of members of his community, "an authoritative source of knowledge (*ḥujja*) between God and his servants in his lands."[26] His defense of the Muslim *umma*'s communal integrity was in turn read through now familiar narratives of the Islamic past: "God supported the religion with two men possessing no equal: Abū Bakr al-Ṣadīq in the time of the *Ridda*, and Aḥmad Ibn Ḥanbal in the time of the *miḥna*," later generations of Ḥanbalīs claimed, drawing an analogy to Abū Bakr's defeat of the rebellion of certain Arab tribes after the death of the Prophet, an act of stalwart intransigence that it was believed preserved the community from the onset of error and disbelief.[27]

Ibn Ḥanbal's defense of "real Islam" was not limited to his suffering during the *miḥna*, however. After the *miḥna* had come to an end and the much more tolerant al-Mutawakkil ruled the Abbasid world, for example, Ibn Ḥanbal systematically rejected attempts by the caliph to bestow upon him and his family various kinds of gifts and stipends.[28] During a period of compulsory caliphal service, for example, Ibn Ḥanbal was barracked in a luxurious house commandeered by the government. Although he agreed to stay in the house, he refused to eat the sumptuous meals sent to him by the caliph and fasted rather than partake of the luxuries bestowed by the imperial power that ruled his world. His fasting went on so long that his body grew weak and he became very ill. When the caliph dispatched a doctor to cure Ibn Ḥanbal, the doctor soon returned to the caliph and reported that it was not an illness that had taken Ibn Ḥanbal's health, but rather his piety.[29] Eventually, Ibn Ḥanbal agreed to take some food—a mush made of barley (*sawīq*).[30] The significance of this choice of food may be gauged from the fact that it was a kind of barley mash that the anchorite and ascetic virtuoso ʿAlī al-Kharjānī consumed as he shamed Ibn Ḥanbal's Baghdādī contemporary Sarī al-Saqaṭī for the extravagance of his own meal of bread and ground salt.[31]

In order to better understand the meaning of Ibn Ḥanbal's act, it will be useful to consider the following anecdote, taken from the tenth-century text known as the *Kitāb adab al-ghurabāʾ*, attributed to Abū l-Farajal-Iṣfahānī, in which are collected literary graffiti from around the early Islamic world.[32] In this text, the caliph al-Mutawakkil, traveling in Syria, stops in a Christian monastery. Marveling at the sumptuous beauty of his surroundings, including the young men and women who flit about the ground, he soon becomes smitten with one of the young women who dwells there, the daughter of one of the monks. The girl, whose name is Saʿānīn, brings him simple food, but he rejects it in favor of "his own food," which consists of various forms of meat. Soon, the girl's father brings al-Mutawakkil's party communion wine, and they begin to drink. As she becomes intoxicated, the girl begins to sing, and al-Mutawakkil is transported. He eventually marries her after she converts to Islam.[33]

Whether this story is true or not is beside the point. What matters is that this was the way in which Muslims of the third and fourth/ninth and tenth centuries imagined not only al-Mutawakkil but also the bearers of worldly power generally. From the point of view of pietists like Ibn Ḥanbal, this story may only be read as an account of damnable boundary transgression. Taking place in a site which stood as an emblem for Christianity and moreover the world of "those who were before" the Muslims, it is a tale in which the foremost representative of worldly power within the Muslim world, the caliph al-Mutawakkil, performs a series of acts that flout the behavioral boundaries upon which Muslims relied to distinguish members of their community from members of the communities that surrounded them; he enters a markedly Christian space from love of its splendor and richness; he drinks wine, something definitively un-Muslim; he listens to music, also something definitively non-Muslim according the ascetic moral imagination so central to the mode of Muslim self-fashioning embraced by Ibn Ḥanbal and his companions; he seduces a Christian girl in the presence of her monk father, and, it would seem, with the man's pandering complicity.[34] In the process, al-Mutawakkil rejects the simple fare native to the diet of the monastery's inmates, a diet that we have seen was shared by such icons of Muslim piety as ʿUmar. In essence, then, al-Mutawakkil has transgressed most of the behavioral barriers that set Muslim individuals apart from non-Muslims.

Despite this, of course, al-Mutawakkil remains a Muslim. According to Ṣāliḥ b. Aḥmad's *sīra* of his father, however, Ibn Ḥanbal drew a distinction between "Muslims" and "believers" (*mu'minūn*), between "Islam" and "belief (*īmān*)." For Ibn Ḥanbal, Islam was a "general" condition, whereas belief was a specific condition. Belief was the combination of the internal processes of Islam—knowledge of holy texts, for example—with directed action undertaken in combination with that knowledge: "Faith is knowledge and active confession," as he put it. Accordingly, belief was a higher condition than simple Islam, and the believer (*mu'min*) was more accomplished and refined in religion and spiritual matters than the Muslim. Ibn Ḥanbal said that "Faith is intention in Islam, and a man who commits adultery goes out from faith to Islam."[35] This was a distinction Ibn Ḥanbal traced to the Prophet himself. Accordingly, in Ibn Ḥanbal's social cosmology, those who were Believers as well as Muslims represented a community within a community, an elite among followers of Muḥammad's revelation.[36] Here the thinking of Ibn Ḥanbal seems to reveal some of the influence of the *ghāzī* scholars he so admired; the difference between a Believer and a base-model Muslim was one of intention, he suggests, and Ibn al-Mubārak and Ibn Isḥāq al-Fazāri are cited as sources of the tradition, "Faith is word and deed."[37]

For this reason, as we read of al-Mutawakkil's attempts to bestow unto Ibn Ḥanbal and his family gifts and worldly pleasures like the diverse and sumptuous foods Ibn Ḥanbal rejected at the cost of his health and, as Nimrod Hurvitz has noted, his relationship with his family, we should understand these as Ibn Ḥanbal apparently understood them, as attempts to entice him beyond the boundaries of his true community, that of those who "believed," and into the abandonment of the primordial character of Islam and its defining truths.[38] In this they bore crucial affinities with the trial Ibn Ḥanbal endured during the *miḥna*: just before he was repeatedly flogged into unconsciousness, for example, one of his interrogators said to him, "O Aḥmad, I feel pity for you. Just comply with me. I wish I had not come to know you—God! God!—by your blood and your soul. I truly pity you as I would pity my own son Hārūn, so comply with me." Here and elsewhere, Ibn Ḥanbal's interrogators expressed compassion and even admiration for him and tried to present opportunities for him to avoid the torture that awaited him.[39] Despite this, however, Ibn Ḥanbal, like those Muslim heroes of the *futūḥ* who found themselves in confrontation with imperial powers who would have preferred to reach some kind of negotiated settlement with the steely-eyed pietists whom they encountered, insisted upon the truths of his faith as he understood them. He repeated a version of what Cooperson has called Ibn Ḥanbal's "creed" during his ordeal—that his adversaries could not bring any evidence from either the "Book of God or the *sunna* of the Prophet of God" in support of their claims.[40] Now his interrogator exploded. "God curse you!" he exclaimed. "I had hoped you would comply with me." Ibn Ḥanbal was ordered seized and stripped. Then his inquisitors called for the tools of torture.[41]

As we have seen, the narrative of the Islamic empire's advent during the *futūḥ*, like the narratives recalling the formative dramas of other late antique communities, was peopled with intransigent and determined witnesses on behalf of revealed truths whose defense animated those stories, and whose validity was tested against the violence and temptations of the imperial powers of the age. Ibn Ḥanbal, as he was recalled by his son, his cousin, and the generations of admirers that followed them, was yet another ascetic and intransigent bearer of authentic Islam set in opposition to the powerful of his world as he endured the violence of al-Ma'mūn and al-Muʿtaṣim, and the temptations of al-Mutawakkil.[42]

Ibn Ḥanbal accordingly abided in the imaginary of early Muslims as a figure who embodied all of the stubborn piety and dour intransigence of those idealized members of Muḥammad's primordial community of Muslims. For this reason, he seems to have emerged as a figure rather like the high-profile ascetics of Roman late antiquity around whom communities formed as contemporaries found in them an exemplar of all of the qualities that marked one as a genuine member of the one true community of God upon the earth. Just as in an earlier era some particularly accomplished ascetics seemed to preserve the essential qualities of those ideal Christians, the early martyrs, through whose rigorous example God made the validity of Christian belief known in the world, now Ibn Ḥanbal stood before his contemporaries as a repository of all that defined genuine Muslimness, a figure whose renunciation, piety, and zeal matched all that those around him knew of such *futūḥ*-era Muslims as Abū Bakr and ʿUmar. He was, moreover, a figure in relation to whom one could effectively orient oneself within the often-confusing world of the Abbasid *dār al-Islām*. Indeed, the attitude one took to the memory of Ibn Ḥanbal located one either inside or outside of the one community of God upon the earth, in the estimation of some of his admirers: "[al-Rabīʿ b. Sulaymān said] al-Shāfiʿī said, 'Any who loathes Aḥmad b. Ḥanbal is an unbeliever.' And I said, 'You apply the name of unbeliever to him?' He said, 'Yes. Anyone who loathes Ibn Ḥanbal opposes the *sunna*, and whoever opposes the *sunna* is opposed [*qaṣada*] to the companions, and whoever is opposed to the companions is hateful to the Prophet, and whoever is hateful to the Prophet disbelieves in God the Sublime.'"[43] Reasoning of this sort had the advantage of rendering a complicated and often confusing world considerably simpler.

It is little surprise then that as Muslims of the third/ninth century and later periods sought to define what it meant to be a true Muslim and to mark out and defend the behavioral boundaries that made of the Muslim *umma* a discrete and distinct community, they turned to Ibn Ḥanbal as a living and recalled resource for the fashioning of Muslim selves.

"This Is a Filthy Question, and One Must Not Discuss It!"

Muslims of the ninth century approached Ibn Ḥanbal for answers to questions about many things. He answered queries about whether it was permissible to use bits of mouse and frog meat as fishing bait, for example. Although this question clearly disturbed him—"They *do* that?" he asked—he was nevertheless able to provide guidance for his questioner.[44] He provided opinions on such matters as the relative propriety of raiding on the Byzantine frontier using another's property, what one should do in the event that one discovered wine in the house of a friend, and whether a man could compel his Christian or Jewish wife to wash.[45] He gave advice concerning the division of spoils (including captives) taken on *ghāzī* raids and the delicate question of what one should do if one were in the presence of a non-Muslim when he sneezed.[46]

But there was one question that Ibn Ḥanbal refused to answer and that he forbade to be discussed, although it is clear from Abū Bakr al-Khallāl's *Kitāb ahl al-milal*, where it appears as the first of all questions concerning the proper way of comporting oneself with regard to non-Muslims, the question came up quite a bit. From one point of view, the question was a comparatively simple one:

> I asked Abū ʿAbd Allāh [i.e., Aḥmad] whether there were Christians and Jews among the *umma* of Muḥammad. And he became enraged, and he said, "This is a filthy question, and one must not discuss it!" I said, "Then should I forbid anyone who speaks about this?" He said, "This is a very filthy question, and no one should discuss it." And Abū ʿAbd Allāh censured anyone who discussed it.

> [A man] asked Abū ʿAbd Allāh about the Jews and the Christians of the *umma* of Muḥammad, and he became enraged and he said, "Does a Muslim say this?" Or he said something like this.

> Muḥammad b. Abī Hārūn and Muḥammad b. Jaʿfar reported to me that Abū Ḥārith reported to them, and one of them tossed out to the other, "I asked Abū ʿAbd Allāh about the Jews and the Christians of the *umma* of Muḥammad; were there any or not? For a group of people dispute about this." And [Ibn Ḥanbal] said, "What is this?!" rejecting the question and growing angry. I said, "There is someone here saying this." [Ibn Ḥanbal] said, "Let us summon him and let him change his spots." I said, "Should we rebuke and refute what they say?" He said, "Yes, and the rebuke and the refutation should [each] be a sharp one."[47]

When another group asked him once again about the presence of Christians and Jews in Muḥammad's primordial *umma* and asked whether Muḥammad would intercede on behalf of Christians and Jews on Judgment Day, Aḥmad said he would not. When one of them quoted the line, "The prophets speak to all the people," Aḥmad snapped, "Who says so? Christians and Jews?"[48]

Why did this question provoke such a reaction from Ibn Ḥanbal? Why was this question so distasteful, so dangerous, perhaps, that it could not even be discussed? And why did it so compel the imagination of those who came to Ibn Ḥanbal for answers to the questions that worried or intrigued or excited them? In order to suggest an answer these questions, we will briefly turn our attention to what al-Khallāl's *Kitāb ahl al-milal* reveals about the complexity of the social world inhabited by Ibn Ḥanbal and his peers.

We might best begin by recalling once again Peter Brown's comment, cited in Chapters 5 and 7, that the early Islamic historical tradition tends to ignore interactions between Muslims and non-Muslims in the lands of the Islamic empire. Brown suggests that it is to the works of non-Muslim authors that we must turn in order to gain any understanding of the interpenetration of the lives of Muslims and non-Muslims within the early Islamic world. The stories with which this chapter began are illustrative of this means of overcoming the silence of Islamic historical sources regarding the diversity and complexity of the social, political, and cultural spaces of this world. They are also illustrative of the inherent limitations of these sources, however. As hagiographical texts, they may be suspected of employing Muslim figures as mere props against which the heroes of such texts may define themselves, for example. Against such objections we may argue that even if these texts do not reflect objectively real or discrete events, they reveal much about how contemporaries imagined their relationship with Muslims and other groups of Christians, and as such may tell us much about the experiential realities of those who produced them even if they tell us less than we might like about the facts on the ground in eighth- and ninth-century Iraq, Syria, and Egypt. Happily, however, we do not have to rely upon these texts alone to gather an understanding of the complexity of the early Muslim empire and of the intimacy with which Muslim and non-Muslim coexisted within that world.

Abū Bakr al-Khallāl is generally recognized as the figure most directly responsible for the formation of a formal *madhhab* around the teaching of Ibn Ḥanbal in the decades and centuries after Ibn Ḥanbal's death.[49] A member of the second generation of Ḥanbalīs, al-Khallāl collected and reported thousands of answers given by Ibn Ḥanbal to the various questions put to him regarding the behavior proper to Muslim men and women. Although his great collection of these *responsa*, his *Jāmiʿ*, has been lost as a complete work, sections of it have been discovered and recently published. One section of the *Jāmiʿ*, that which deals with the proper modes of Muslim comportment with members of other religious communities, has been mentioned in passing in this and other chapters. Here it will serve as a means to illustrate the degree to which Muslim and non-Muslim lives were interwoven within the greater *dār al-Islām*.[50] As we will see, this was a world within which the maintenance of communal boundaries necessarily became a matter of daily praxis and an integral component of performing Muslim identity for those who followed the authoritative advice issued by Ibn Ḥanbal and his followers.

"How Are You, Christian?" or "How Are You, Jew?"

Among those who came to Ibn Ḥanbal with questions about how they ought to interact with their Christian, Jewish, and Magian neighbors, relatives, business partners, slaves, and friends were those who wondered what one ought to make of Jews and Christians who said that Muḥammad had been "a prophet of God."[51] Were such people still Christians and Jews, or had they become Muslims? Was it acceptable to leave a copy of the Qurʾān with a non-Muslim?[52] And what about the permissibility of a Muslim man teaching a Magian boy passages from the Qurʾān or teaching a Christian boy to pray for Muḥammad?[53] What was to be done about a monk who spoke ill of Muḥammad?[54] Was it wrong for a Muslim to witness Christian religious festivals?[55] Was it acceptable to call a non-Muslim by his *kunya*, which might be construed as a sign of intimacy?[56] Could one shake hands with non-Muslims?[57]

These questions and hundreds like them fill the pages of al-Khallāl's collection of Ibn Ḥanbal's responses on such matters, the *Kitāb ahl al-milal*. That there was need for answers to such questions suggests much about the intimacy with which Muslim and non-Muslim intermingled within Ibn Ḥanbal's society. These questions and the responses Ibn Ḥanbal gave to them also offer tantalizing evidence of the anxieties experienced by individuals inhabiting that world over where the boundaries of their community began and ended.[58]

Through these questions and answers we gain fleeting glimpses of quotidian scenes that confound the image of rigidly segregated Muslim and non-Muslim social, political, and religious spheres.

The images these *responsa* conjure—a Muslim man tutoring a young Magian in the holy text of Islām or a Christian boy uttering prayers for the prophet of the Arabs, perhaps growing into one of the Christian men who accepted Muḥammad as a prophet and yet himself remained a Christian—suggest that the holy signs and symbols of the Muslims had accrued numinous meaning for some ninth-century Christians and Jews just as in an earlier period Christian and Jewish signs and symbols had taken up residence in a specifically Muslim imaginary and accrued specifically Muslim meanings through their deployment within a specifically Muslim narrative. Indeed, Ibn Ḥanbal himself is said by his son Ṣāliḥ to have been mourned by massive crowds of Christians, Jews, and Magians, while another tradition claims that many Christians and Jews converted to Islām on the day of his death.[59]

Certain Christian texts of the period seem to bear traces of their authors' familiarity with what were now specifically Muslim narratives. Just as early Muslims seem to have drawn upon the figure of the monk to imagine the founders of their empire, for example, as Christians abiding within that empire constructed the heroes of their own communities, they incorporated specifically Muslim semiotic elements fashioned through the processes we explored in Chapter 5. As we saw in that chapter, for example, one of the earliest appearances of the figure of the monk in Muslim literature is in Ibn Isḥāq's *sīra* of Muḥammad. In that text, the Christian monk Baḥīrā recognizes Muḥammad as a prophet when, as a boy, he is brought to Syria with a caravan led by his uncle, Abū Ṭālib. This is a story repeated in various permutations throughout early Muslim literature.

Intriguingly, the hero of the late eighth-/early ninth-century life of the Christian ascetic Stephen of Mar Sabas seems to have undergone a very similar kind of recognition when he, like Muḥammad, traveled to Syria on business with his uncle. In that story, Stephen is serving food to a community of monks when he is recognized by the monastic veteran as a future monastic superstar.[60] Whether the author of this text had some version of the Baḥīrā story in mind as he wrote is impossible to know. We do know, however, that Baḥīrā was a figure well known to non-Muslims, so the apparent similarity may well be more than coincidence.[61] What does seem clear is that for Christians and Muslims alike writing in Arabic in the decades and centuries after the *futūḥ*, the way in which one authorized a communal hero varied very little. That is, the assumptions members of each community carried with them about the place of the numinous in the world, the ways in which it manifested itself, and the figures with which it was associated seem to have been drawn from what we might call a common "late antique *doxa*."[62]

We also noted in Chapter 5 that early Muslim authors frequently described the men who participated in the conquests as "like monks by night and horsemen by day." By the eighth and ninth century, Christians had begun to enunciate very similar descriptions of their own communal heroes. As I noted in Chapter 5, for example, the Arabic life of Stephen of Mar Sabas describes the eighth century Christian ascetic hero of the work as "like a brave horseman who fights to receive a crown from the king" and "like a horseman brave and bold."[63] Like their Muslim neighbors, then, Christians of the post-conquest age seem to have conjured their own hybrid monk/horseman as exemplars of piety and zeal. Stephen, it should be noted, understood the duty of monks "to strive on the [patriarch's] behalf with all our power and all our soul— even to the point of shedding our blood."[64]

Elsewhere, in the martyrdom of the Arab Christian Rawḥ al-Qurayshī, who was recalled to have been killed under the Abbasid caliph Hārūn al-Rashīd in 183/799, the martyr is depicted as a former Muslim *ghāzī* who converted to Christianity after miraculous encounters with a mounted warrior saint, St. Theodore. As we saw in Chapter 3, Theodore had effectively blurred the line between martyrdom and militancy during his own martyrdom. In the first of the miracles by which he is converted, Rawḥ, who had previously taken part in raids on Byzantine territory and engaged in vandalism of Christian churches, becomes agitated by the image of the mounted warrior Theodore he encounters in a church. He fires an arrow at the image, but it comes back at him and hits his hand. It is as though he has attacked a mirror and has wounded himself through the attempt to efface the uncomfortable affinities with the figure who will become his spiritual patron.[65]

The mimetic character of this episode is especially apparent when we consider the way in which mounted Muslim warriors like Rawḥ were constructed within the Islamic imaginary and within the defining narratives of their community. The interconnection of Rawḥ's *ghāzī* past, Muslim communal narratives, and his final role as a martyr of the Christian community emerges even more starkly when Rawḥ, like both his Christian martyr ancestors and his Muslim *mujāhid* forebears, is brought into confrontation with a representative of worldly power in the person of Hārūn al-Rashīd. During their encounter, the caliph concludes that it is only poverty that has driven Rawḥ to take the stand that has brought him into conflict with the rulers of his world, and the caliph offers him riches if he will recant. In so doing, the Muslim caliph is cast in a familiar role from the Muslim *futūḥ* histories we have encountered at various points throughout the preceding chapters—that of Persian shah or Roman general, concluding that it is poverty that has driven the Arabs to rebel against his authority and that they can be placated with a handout.[66] Within the Muslim histories of the conquest period, this topos may be read as evolved from Christian martyr literature (as I argued in Chapter 5). If this is a legitimate reading, this text may be read as this late antique topos coming full circle.

Meanwhile, just as students of Ibn Ḥanbal authorized their *shaykh* by recalling him in opposition with the rulers of their world and through tales in which certain numinous truths about him were revealed through dreams, the followers and admirers of the Arab Christian intellectual Ḥunayn b. Isḥāq, who emerged as a prominent figure in the transmission of Greek learning into Arabic and who was one of the recipients of the caliph al-Maʾmūn's patronage at the famous Bayt al-Ḥikma in Baghdād, followed a rather similar course.[67] One such story, cited by Michael Cooperson in his study of Ḥunayn's purported autobiography, describes a dream had by al-Maʾmūn, in which the caliph "saw a vision of a dignified and splendid man sitting enthroned in the caliphal audience room. Told that the man was Aristotle, he asked him a series of questions about the good." In response to the dream, al-Maʾmūn summons Ḥunayn because of his skill as a translator, acquired during journeys back and forth across the Byzantine frontier. The caliph gives the Christian Arab the duty of translating Greek philosophical works into Greek.[68]

Later, however, Ḥunayn and the caliph came into conflict. He was accused of sacrilege after being tricked into spitting upon a Christian icon, the stories go, and was punished by the caliph with torture and imprisonment at the behest of Christian authorities. Although the cause of the downfall of Ḥunayn is obscure, Cooperson argues that it may be traced in part to the scholar's intimate—and independent—relationship with powerful Muslims of his world and the unease this seems to have caused the Christian religious authorities of the Abbasid world. The purported words of Ḥunayn himself seem to hint at this. "All men of culture—regardless of religious affiliation—

love me and take part and treat me with honor, and receive what I teach them with gratitude, and reward me with many favors," Ḥunayn is supposed to have written. "But as for those Christian doctors, most of whom learned from me, and whom I watched grow up—it is they who cry for my blood, even though they could never manage without me!"[69]

As Cooperson notes, the ordeal endured by Ḥunayn during his own small *miḥna* recalls in its character and its presentation that Ibn Ḥanbal bore during his own period of detainment and torture at the hands of al-Ma'mūn and his successor al-Muʿtaṣim. Moreover, Ḥunayn's ordeal comes to an end when the caliph has another dream vision, this time in which Jesus comes to him accompanied by Ḥunayn (rather as Ibn Ḥanbal was seen by one of his followers in a dream walking down a path hand in hand with the Prophet), and in which the Messiah asks the caliph to release the illustrious cultural broker.[70] Once again, then, it would seem that for Christians of the Abbasid world, the deployment of tropes and signs shared in common with their Muslim neighbors had become a means of constructing memories of their own communal heroes.[71]

In addition to the profound intermingling of Muslim and non-Muslim lives in the ninth century, then, it would seem that Muslims and non-Muslims also shared a *koinê* of signs and narratives with which to imagine relations between humans and the divine and with which to discuss, contest, and celebrate the consequences and implications of those relations. As we saw in Chapter 1, however, a similar *koinê* of signs and narratives, shared among the Christians and Jews of John Chrysostom's Antioch, proved the basis of a deep unease for Chrysostom and many of his contemporaries. Indeed, the essay *al-Radd ʿalā al-naṣārā* (Against the Christians) by the Iraqi Muslim author al-Jāḥiẓ (d. c. 255/868–69), gives voice to a variety of anxieties which recall Chrysostom's sermons against the Jews.[72] The basis for these anxieties seems to have been in part what was perceived as an excessive familiarity among Muslims and Christians with one another's holy texts and sacred symbols. He says that Christians have made an unpleasant habit of "pick[ing] up on [certain Qur'ānic verses] and used them to bend the ears of the rabble" and confusing simple-minded Muslims, for example, and cites one set of verses in particular, *Sūrat al-Mā'ida* (5) 80-85, that Christians liked to use. These verses run as follows:

80. You can see among you many of them
Allying themselves with the infidels.

Vile it was what they sent ahead of them,
So that God's indignation came upon them;
And torment will they suffer in eternity.
81. If they had believed
in God and the Prophet and what had been revealed to him,
they would never have held them as allies;
and many among them are transgressors.
82. You will find the Jews and idolaters
most excessive in hatred of those who believe;
and the closest in love to the faithful
are the people who say: "We are the followers of Christ,"
because there are priests and monks among them,
and they are not arrogant.
83. For when they listen to what has been revealed
to this Apostle, you can see their eyes brim over with tears
at the truth they recognize, and say:
"O Lord, we believe; put us down
among those who bear witness (to the truth),
84. And why should we not believe in God
and what has come down to us of the truth?
And we hope to be admitted to our Lord
Among those who are upright and do good?"
85. God will reward them for saying so
with gardens where streams flow by,
where they will live forever.
This is the recompense for those who do good.[73]

In addition to "twisting" the meanings as such Qur'ānic passages, al-Jāḥiẓ says, Christians also have the disagreeable habit of picking up "on any contradictory aspects of our traditions, weak chains of transmission and ambiguous verses in the Qur'ān. Then they corner the weak minded of the brethren—who know little about heretical sophistry and damned atheism—and start putting questions to them." In so doing, "they provoke doubt among rational men and perplex the simple folk."[74] The result is that Christians have led many Muslims astray, not just into an interest in Christianity, al-Jāḥiẓ says, but also into involvement in "Manichaeism, obscure sects of Zoroastrianism and all sorts of other -isms."[75] The Christians and their familiarity with

Muslim texts—*ḥadīth* traditions as well as the Qur'ān, according to al-Jāḥiẓ—had the effect of creating disorder within the Muslim *umma* and enticing Muslims across their own communal boundaries. Many of the Muslims executed for heresy, he points out darkly, were children of Christian parents.[76]

A good deal of the essay is devoted to explaining why Muslims find Christians to be so intriguing, or at least more attractive as a group than the Jews. The answers al-Jāḥiẓ suggests run from the historical—Jews and Arabs lived in close proximity in Arabia before the advent of Islam, and so share an enmity that can only come from profound intimacy[77]—to the aesthetic—the Jews are particularly ugly, he says, because their xenophobic marriage practices have left them inbred[78]—to the socioeconomic—the Christians are rich and highly placed in Muslim society.[79] Christian women frequently bear the children of powerful Muslims, he says. Muslims also hold the cultural traditions associated with the Christians in high esteem, he says, particularly those of the Greek and Roman scientists and philosophers, men like Aristotle, Galen, Ptolemy, and Euclid. What his fellow Muslims do not realize, he adds, is that these men were neither Byzantine nor Christian, but instead members of another culture whose heritage contemporary Christians unjustly usurped as a source of undeserved cultural capital.[80]

The combination of the prominent positions held by Christians in Abbasid society and the cultural prestige they claim for themselves has resulted, al-Jāḥiẓ says, in an inordinate fondness of Muslims for Christians. This, in turn, has led to what he seems to interpret as especially troubling blurring of the proper markers of Christianness and Muslimness.

> As regards influence, power and position in society, we all know that Christians ride pedigree horses, hold riding tournaments and play polo. They comb their forelocks fashionably and dress sharply in double-breasted tunics tailored from blended fabrics. They even employ bodyguards. They call themselves good Muslim names like Hassan, Husayn, 'Abbās, Fadhl and 'Ali. About the only names left which they have not appropriated are Muhammad and Abū'l-Qāsim. Many Christians have stopped wearing the obligatory waistband or have taken to wearing it under their tunics. Many of their grandees are too proud to pay the poll-tax, although it is well within their means. They exchange insults and blows with Muslims.

Muslim judges are lenient in such cases, al-Jāḥiẓ says, and protect Christians with the same care they would a Muslim! Christians have even gotten away with calling the virtue of Muḥammad's mother into question by pointing out that she was not a Muslim.[81] Whatever the indignity suffered by Muḥammad's mother, however, it seems clear that the real problem in al-Jāḥiẓ's estimation is the disappearance of any means of distinguishing Christian from Muslim, whether by name, by appearance, or by their treatment under the law.

The essay then moves on to a short apologia with regard to contested points of doctrine, theology, and mythology over which his Christian and Muslim contemporaries debate. In al-Jāḥiẓ's brief opening tirade, however, we gain yet another indication of the depth of the fluency possessed by Christians living in Muslim society with regard to Muslim scripture and *ḥadīth* literature. More than this, however, we have an articulation of the rather sharp anxiety felt by one Muslim member of third/ninth-century Baghdādī society regarding what he clearly perceived as undependable boundaries between Muslim and Christian. The Christians, as al-Jāḥiẓ describes them, have taken to violating a series of behavioral obligations enjoined upon them by the so-called "Ordinances of ʿUmar."[82] These rules of comportment for non-Muslims forbade the riding of horses, the bearing of weapons (as bodyguards presumably would), fighting with Muslims, and changing their style of dress from what it had been before the conquest period. Non-Muslims were to "cut their hair from the front" presumably disallowing fashionable forelocks, and were to wear the belt or sash al-Jāḥiẓ says many of them had now abandoned or hidden. As Albrecht Noth has demonstrated, all of these rules were instituted to make Muslims and non-Muslims instantly recognizable from one another.[83] By grouping these behaviors as he does, it would seem that al-Jāḥiẓ is underscoring the flouting of these behavioral restrictions by Christians as one key basis for his hostility toward them. Particularly worrisome seems to have been the tendency of "the rabble" to lose track of their own Muslim identities as they were drawn to Christians through a shared interest in certain texts, narratives, and ways of imagining the numinous.

This can only call to mind the anxieties experienced by John Chrysostom as he contemplated the approach of Passover and the likelihood that members of his Christian community would soon lose themselves in the seductive ceremony and semiotic confusion represented by the Jewish festivals. Chrysostom's reaction to this dilemma was to incite his parishioners to carry the boundaries of their community within them, and to perform them by summoning their fellow Christians to proper Christian behavior, and forbidding transgression of the normative communal boundaries upon which their preacher so vehemently insisted. Like Chrysostom, as we shall see, Muslims of the early centuries of Islam seem also to have experienced a profound desire to institute and maintain certain communal boundaries demarking their own communities from all others, be they Muslim, Christian, Jewish, or Magian. In what follows, we shall trace the efforts of one Islamic community to do just this.

M. J. Kister and, as I have briefly noted above, Albrecht Noth have both noted the efforts taken by early Muslims to remain distinct in appearance from their non-Muslim neighbors.[84] It was important, Noth has written, that Muslim and non-Muslim be able to recognize one another immediately in the street if Islam were to remain a separate religion.[85] The rules for non-Muslim comportment Noth cites—such restrictions as a ban on dying grey hair and beards in the Arab fashion and a ban upon riding horses—were crucial for creating a kind of semiotic grammar in the shared public spaces of the lands taken under Muslim rule. The effacement of this grammar clearly provoked al-Jāḥiẓ, as we have seen.

The *responsa* of Ibn Ḥanbal, however, underscore the fact that the issue of boundary maintenance went far beyond the organization of public spaces—it played out in the intimate spaces of the early Islamic empire as well and was indeed a problem necessarily negotiated at the level of the individual Muslim and as a matter of daily practice and comportment. Normative standards of dress and grooming could mark one outwardly as Muslim or non-Muslim, but for those Muslims who interacted intimately with Christians, Jews, and Magians in their daily lives, it would seem that more than prohibitions concerning the dying of beards or obligations enjoining the continuation of pre-Islamic styles of dress for non-Muslims were necessary to maintain the crucial boundaries that gave Muslim, Christian, or Jewish identity experiential weight.[86] These Muslims shared with their non-Muslim contemporaries a spectrum of holy stories, holy symbols, and holy personages. Moreover, it would seem, in addition to the fact that Muslims and non-Muslims alike now relied upon certain universally legible narrative forms with which to make sense of experience and with which to fashion identities, Muslims and non-Muslims were also bound to one another at the level of family, and so through a series of personal and familial obligations, narratives, affective ties, and economic and social constraints.

As Ibn Ḥanbal's *responsa* make clear, the intermingling of Muslim and non-Muslim, as well as the potential for anxiety-inducing ambiguity about these categories, came about in a variety of ways. On the one hand, it becomes clear in the *Kitāb ahl al-milal*, that many families contained both Muslim and non-Muslim. There was, for example, the sticky problem of what was to be done if a Magian's daughter converted to Islam and wanted to perform the Ḥajj. If she had no Muslim guardians, could her father take her on the Ḥajj? No, Ibn Ḥanbal replied, "He does not believe in accord with her."[87] There was also the question of whether a newly converted Muslim woman should be allowed to stay with her Magian father. Ibn Ḥanbal allowed that they could be separated if it was feared that the father would sleep with his daughter or commit violence against her.[88] Nor could Jewish, Christian, or Magian fathers arrange marriages for their daughters once they had converted to Islam. Ibn Ḥanbal seems even to have been ambivalent about whether an impoverished Muslim woman should accept the financial support of her non-Muslim father for the expenses associated with a wedding.[89]

Then there was the problem of what to do with Christians, Jews, and Magians who accompanied Muslim raiding groups in the lands of the Romans, and fought alongside them against the enemies of Islam. Were they entitled to a share of the booty? Yes, Ibn Ḥanbal said, but a small one. And the practice itself made him uneasy. It was best not to seek help from non-Muslims, he said. Indeed, he admitted that scholars disagreed on the matter, and cited a prophetic *ḥadīth* in which Muḥammad said, "Do not seek the aid of *mushrikūn* against the *mushrikūn*."[90] Despite this prophetic admonition, however, from these *responsa* it becomes clear that among the *ghāzī* bands that raided Roman territory, and which included ascetic/scholar/warriors who were perfecting the ideology of *jihād* and, not incidentally, providing citified Muslims like Ibn Ḥanbal with a model of real Muslimness, were sometimes also included Christians, Magians, and Jews.[91]

There was also the complicated problem of Christian or Jewish captives taken in raiding expeditions. Should these be forced to convert to Islam? No, said Ibn Ḥanbal. This had been forbidden by God and his Prophet.[92] But what if some of the captives were children? If their parents were taken with them, Ibn Ḥanbal said, they remained with their parents in their religion. If they were taken without parents, however, they could be compelled to Islam and thus presumably accorded a place (albeit a subservient one) within the Muslim *umma*.[93] The institution of raiding also demanded rulings about the treatment of Jewish or Christian slave girls, marriage to Christian women, the bearing of children to Muslim masters of Christian slaves by Christian slave mothers, and the status of such children.[94]

In response to this messy social milieu, Ibn Ḥanbal's answers to the questions put to him on such matters recommend a wide variety of ways of performing Muslimness as a matter of daily practice. First and foremost, he himself was recalled to have adopted outward gestures clearly undertaken to maintain a performed boundary between Muslim and non-Muslim. Ibn Ḥanbal was said to have hidden his eyes whenever he happened upon a Christian, for example, because he did not want to look upon one who, in his estimation, "slandered God or lied about him."[95] He told those around him that it was not pleasing to him that a Muslim should visit the home of a non-Muslim, although as we shall see below, there were circumstances under which it was acceptable. If one found it necessary to visit a sick Christian neighbor, he said, one should go no further than the front door and express one's sentiments from there. One editor of al-Khallāl's *Kitāb ahl al-milal* explains that this action (and Ibn Ḥanbal's recommendation of it) should be interpreted as the imposition of a barrier between Muslim and Christian on the basis of their religious differences.[96]

This principle extended even to brief encounters on the street with members of other communities. In response to a question about whether a Muslim encountering a group of Christians in the road should greet them with a salutation of "peace," Ibn Ḥanbal replied that the Muslim should not do so, and that even if he were to do so that the Christians should not reply, "and peace unto you."[97] Interestingly, Ibn Ḥanbal also instructed his interlocutors to avoid non-Arabs, who, he said, "do not love the Arabs, who do not appreciate their precedence, and to whom there is heresy, hypocrisy and controversy." Although Ibn Ḥanbal did himself once meet a *dhimmī* with a greeting of "peace," it was only because he did not know the man was a *dhimmī*.[98]

Ibn Ḥanbal insisted that this was the way of Muḥammad's primordial *umma*, which of course itself contained no Christians or Jews. He said, for example, that when Muḥammad met someone of another religion, he would not sit with him, and when he passed a Jew or a Christian in the street he would say, "'How are you, Christian?' or 'How are you, Jew?'" That is, he would acknowledge them and greet them civilly but would not greet them as he would greet a Muslim, with the salutation "*salām*" or "peace."[99] Moreover, even in the act of greeting non-Muslims, he maintained the distinction between Muslim and non-Muslim, marking the individual he addressed as "Christian" or "Jew" even as he asked after his wellbeing. Ibn Ḥanbal seems to have found in this a kind of model for ordering interactions between Muslim and non-Muslim.

"Islam Is the Word, Faith Is the Deed"

As we have seen, for Ibn Ḥanbal and those who followed his lead, membership within the elect of the Islamic community, the community within a community of those Ibn Ḥanbal called "believers" or "faithful ones" was dependent upon a blending of belief and practice, understanding with action. "Islam is different from faith (*īmān*)," he said, "Islam is the word (*qawl*), faith is the deed."[100] Those who denied that belief must manifest itself in action, such communities as the Murji'a, for example, were among the worst of the unbelievers, Ibn Ḥanbal taught his own community: "[Theirs] is the most wicked of doctrines, and it makes one lose his way and sends him from the true path."[101]

On this point many of the Khawārij would have readily agreed. The Azāriqa, for example, who were particularly zealous Khawārij, considered those who would not actively "go out" from the "abode of unbelief" were themselves unbelievers, and their blood and property were accordingly licit.[102] And yet the ways in which the Khawārij put their own beliefs into action were forbidden to the Ḥanbalīs. Rebellion against the leadership of the Muslim empire was strictly prohibited, for example, and Ibn Ḥanbal instructed his companions to avoid those who expressed pro-Khārijī sentiments. "If it is said that the Khārijī strives earnestly when he goes out, [and that] the Commander of the Faithful is wretched," he said, "this statement is a wicked, vile and evil one." Moreover, he continued, if anyone said, "It was ʿAlī who was the real Khārijī" this statement too was wretched, and Ibn Ḥanbal advised that upon hearing it one should "take refuge in God from the transgression of proper boundaries."[103]

The stance taken to contemporary and earlier "commanders of the faithful" also set the Ḥanbalīs in opposition to other Muslim communities. In contrast to the views of the Shīʿa, for example, the Ḥanbalīs taught that the first four caliphs were to be honored, their example followed and their memory protected. Anyone who set ʿAlī above ʿUthmān, for example (presumably a Shīʿī), was "founding a heresy," Ibn Ḥanbal said, and he urged his followers to remind such people that the companions of the Prophet "gave ʿUthmān precedence."[104]

Not only were the founders of the Muslim *umma* to be revered, but contemporary rulers were to be obeyed. The community had seen good leaders and bad leaders, pious leaders and impious leaders, Ibn Ḥanbal said, but the piety or impiety of the head of the Muslim *umma* had no bearing on the prohibition of active rebellion against Muslim state authority. "Obedience to whomever God puts in charge is your commandment," he was remembered to have said.

> And you shall not pull away from obedience to him, and you shall resist rebelling against him with your sword until God makes for you an opening and an escape. And you shall not rebel against the government (*sulṭān*), but you shall listen and you shall obey and you shall not violate a pledge of allegiance (*baiʿa*). Whoever does that, he is a heretic (*mubtadiʿ*) transgressing the boundaries of the community. If the government gives you a command, and it is rebellious toward God, then you must not follow it actively, but nor is it for you to rebel against [the government], and you are not to hold back what is due to it . . . You shall not aid in a *fitna* by means of hand or tongue, but rather hold back your hand and tongue, and your passion, by God.[105]

Nor was one free to declare the blood of one's fellow Muslims licit simply because one disagreed with them, as is clear from the negative example of the Khawārij, and from Ibn Ḥanbal's various *responsa* regarding the commanding of right and forbidding of wrong: Asked about the practice of commanding and forbidding "with the hand," Ibn Ḥanbal prescribed "gentleness (*al-rifq*)" and said that commanding with the hand was intended simply to separate the sinner from the sin, just as he demonstrated when he physically intervened to stop two boys from fighting in the street.[106]

And yet the fact remained that in Ibn Ḥanbal's estimation membership in the one true community of God, that which abided in faith, combining understanding with action, depended upon putting one's faith into daily practice, and that this meant resisting evil wherever one encountered it. This, in turn, entailed actively making the boundaries of the Muslim community a component of the moment-to-moment social reality of life within the *dār al-Islām*. Troublingly, however, it was a similar project that had repeatedly created around generations of Khārijī rebels an aura of conjoined romance and horror. This had been a project, moreover, undertaken in conjunction with a narrative recollection of the Islamic past the Khawārij shared with Ibn Ḥanbal and his contemporaries. Complicating matters still further was the social character of the world in which Ibn Ḥanbal, his contemporaries, and his followers negotiated matters of Muslim identity, the potentially bewildering complexity of which is suggested by the questions to which Ibn Ḥanbal was called upon to respond.

The potential for violence connected with boundary issues within this world was very real. Recall, for example, the attitude taken by Ibn Muljam, the Khārijī who murdered ʿAlī in 40/660–61, to the funeral procession in which Muslim and Christian walked side by side. Had he not more important matters to attend to, he was remembered to have said, he would have "indiscriminately massacred" those accompanying the body of the dead man. Simeon the Syrian zealot who attacked the pro-Chalcedonian preacher as he addressed a mixed congregation and who burned the synagogue of the local Jewish congregation whose members mixed too easily with Christians would have understood this impulse. Indeed, as we have seen, the history of late antique religious violence is replete with acts of violence undertaken to impose boundaries blurred by simple curiosity, commerce, shared sets of semiotic devices, or ancient cultural patterns in confrontation with new ways of reckoning identity, as well as other common aspects of human behavior. Moreover, as we have seen, it frequently fell to individuals like Ibn Ḥanbal to impose and defend the boundaries endangered by such processes, often because they were reckoned by those around them to represent repositories of the essential qualities possessed by those figures that populated the foundational narratives of the communities to which they belonged.

For Muslims of Ibn Ḥanbal's era, the evolving metanarrative of the Muslim *umma*'s advent, from besieged community to world power via a process of numinous military conquest conducted by pious and fierce warriors on God's behalf, had produced a kind of horrific excess in the Khārijī phenomenon. Particularly horrific was the character of the violence with which the Khawārij were associated. More than the predictable if deadly results of raiding, political rivalry, or tribal warfare, the violence associated with the Khawārij was violence that undid the constraints and transgressed the limits that Muslims believed set the post-Prophetic Muslim age apart from the desperate and dismal days of the *jāhiliyya* or "time of ignorance," in which life had been brief and brutal and in which lasting bonds of brotherly community were impossible and unknown.

Although the path of the Khawārij was forsaken by Ibn Ḥanbal, his followers, and most of their contemporaries, the world had become no simpler since the days of Ṣiffīn and al-Nahrwān. Indeed, the very scene that enraged Ibn Muljam the day he killed ʿAlī was also a concern for Ibn Ḥanbal, his contemporaries, and those who came after them. This is made clear by the fact that numerous *responsa* to the question of proper Muslim comportment at non-Muslim funerals, particularly when the departed was a non-Muslim relative, were collected by al-Khallāl into a section of his *Kitāb ahl al-milal* called the *Kitāb al-janāʾiz* (Book of Funeral Processions). A brief examination of these *responsa* will shed light on the means devised by the Ḥanbalī community for the maintenance of "believerness" within a world beset with occasions for transgression and betrayal of the boundaries that made of their community an experiential reality.

The *Kitāb al-janāʾiz* deals generally with the care to be provided for the dead. Within Islamic society, there was of course a formidable body of knowledge concerning the care to be given to the dead, the proper behavior during mourning, and the rites of burial.[107] The questions to which Ibn Ḥanbal was asked to respond in the entries arranged by al-Khallāl in the *Kitāb al-janāʾiz* dealt with the complexities that arose when death visited Christians, Jews, or Magians traveling in the company of Muslims, or when mother and son or father and son were members of self-consciously distinct communities and yet were obliged to care for one another in one last gesture of filial piety and affection. As it is accommodated in most human societies, death brings an occasion for definition and self-fashioning on the parts of the living, and the care afforded to the dead is a means of articulating the essential truths around which communities adhere. As such, funerals are charged social and cultural spaces in which issues of identity must be negotiated with precision.[108]

The section begins not with a question about death, however, but rather with an inquiry about visiting. If a man has a Christian relation, the questioner asks, it is permissible to visit his non-Muslim relative? Ibn Ḥanbal said that it was. When it was asked, apparently with some disbelief, "A *Christian*?" Ibn Ḥanbal replied, "I do not expect that God would become angry with his servants." When he was asked again, "He may visit a *Christian* or a *Jew*?" Ibn

Ḥanbal said, "Did the Prophet not visit with a Jew and call him to Islam?"[109] This was in fact the catch in Ibn Ḥanbal's willingness that Muslims should visit their Christian or Jewish relations or neighbors—they could do so, but only so long as they did so with the intention of calling them to Islam. It was acceptable for a Muslim to visit "one of the *mushrikūn*" for example, "if he believes that if he presents Islam to him, he will be amenable."[110] A related question is posed regarding whether one may visit a sick Christian neighbor.[111]

This cluster of *responsa* begins, then, with the problem of crossing communal boundaries, of social interactions between members of self-consciously distinct communities. It deals, moreover, with certain inherent tensions that will have derived from competing communal identities, those of the family, those of the neighborhood, and those of confessional community (and all that these will have entailed). One did not stop being a member of one community merely by becoming the member of another, of course. One did not stop being the son of a Jew or a Christian merely because one had embraced the revelation of Muḥammad. And yet it is easy to understand how the ties between father and son, between neighbors or between friends—whether these were shared family narratives, neighborhood interests or personal loyalties—might tend to obscure the crucial boundaries that demarcated one community from another and that necessarily resided in the behavior and beliefs of each member of those communities. Not only was the safety of the individual community member's soul imperiled in such moments, members of such communities believed, but indeed the integrity of the community itself was threatened.

Despite the perceived dangers inherent in contact between members of distinct communities, however, members of these communities could not be expected to forsake their relationships with non-Muslims. Indeed, it is clear just from Ibn Ḥanbal's *responsa* that Muslims of his time had Christian mothers, Jewish fathers, Magian neighbors, non-Muslim comrades on raiding expeditions against the enemies of Islam, non-Muslim partners in business, Christian slaves, Christian lovers, Jewish clients, and Magian students.[112] What is more, these were not uncommon kinds of relations between Muslim and non-Muslim; indeed, they seem to have been so common as to require involved reflection and informed decisions in order to regulate them. The intimacy of Muslim and non-Muslim ran from the battlefields of the Syrian frontier to the *ṣūqs*, bedrooms, and birthing spaces of the Muslim world. Clearly, then, there was pressing need of a systematic way of maintaining genuine Muslimness amidst all of this cultural clutter.

What Ibn Ḥanbal and, more to the point, those Ḥanbalīs like al-Khallāl who came after him and arranged his *responsa* into a usable corpus, seem to have come up with was a system of accommodating all of the promiscuous comings and goings of social life within the Muslim world while allowing believers to carry the boundaries that defined their communities within them and to perform them even as they joined their non-Muslim friends and neighbors in the intimate bustle of daily life.

A number of the *responsa* collected in the *Kitāb al-janā'iz* deal with what Muslims who have been traveling with a Christian or a Magian ought to do if the non-Muslim dies, and there is no one of his faith about to perform the requisite death rituals on his behalf. Should the Muslims wash him? Should they bury him? Should they pray over him? Ibn Ḥanbal said in response that although they could bury him, Muslims should not wash unbelievers.[113] "There is no objection to interring them," Ibn Ḥanbal said, but added, "Do not pray over them; do not deviate from the straight path on their behalf! The Prophet commanded ʿAlī that he should commit Abū Ṭālib to the ground, and he was a polytheist."[114] Ibn Ḥanbal explained that if the Muslims did not bury unaccompanied unbelievers when they died among the Muslims, the Muslims themselves might suffer because of it.[115]

In such cases, it was merely a matter of saving the community itself from the potential danger of an unburied corpse, although it was crucial that one not make the mistake of praying over the dead of another community. There was Qur'ānic basis for this reading—Muḥammad himself had been scolded by God for praying over nonbelievers—but other communities of Muslims argued that it was the Prophet alone, and not other Muslims, who was debarred from praying over the dead of other communities.[116] For the Ḥanbalīs, however, the boundary between believer and unbeliever was to be maintained even when only Muslims were left above ground, and even when the departed was likely a stranger. There were, of course, much more complicated problems associated with the death of a Christian or Jew and the proper Muslim response to this, particularly when the Christian or Jew in question was bound to the Muslim via ties of kinship or local community.

Could, for example, a Muslim follow the funeral procession of a "polytheist" (*mushrik*)? Yes, said Ibn Ḥanbal, adding, "follow what al-Ḥārith b. Abī Rabīʿa did. He was witnessing his mother's funeral procession, and he stood to the side and did not dig, that he should be cursed."[117] That is, he attended the funeral, but he separated himself as he did so. He did not participate in the moving of earth, which would presumably have involved other members of his mother's community. Instead, he stood aloof, present but separate from the burial ritual itself. Similar advice is given in other *aḥādīth*.[118] Asked about the Muslim son of a Jew who has died, and how the Muslim son should behave with regard to his father's funeral, Ibn Ḥanbal said that he should follow the instruction of the caliph ʿUmar: "Let him mount his riding animal and go ahead of the funeral procession, and let him not follow it. And when they are ready to bury him, let him circle back." ʿUmar's advice, seconded by Ibn Ḥanbal, once again allowed the Muslim to participate in his father's funeral, and yet to do so while maintaining a crucial distance between himself and the other mourners.[119]

A *ḥadīth* known to Ibn Ḥanbal that is quoted in this section seems to further clarify the point of this behavior. A member of Muḥammad's *umma* had come to him and reported that his mother, a Christian, had died, and that he wanted to attend to her. "The Prophet said to him, 'Mount your riding animal and go ahead of [the funeral procession], for if you ride and you are ahead of it you will not be in its company.'"[120] That is, the man will participate in the funeral procession and yet remain apart from it. Similarly, the Muslim son of a non-Muslim father may help to take stewardship of some of his father's affairs so that (or until) he is buried, as well, although the washing of the body should be left to members of his father's own *umma*.[121] Likewise, a Christian mother's Christian friends should take care of her and wrap her in her shroud. Her son should not stand over her grave and pray but should stand aside as her Christian brethren cry for her.[122] Here, once again is emphasized the theme of attendance upon the burial rite of what has become a foreign community while maintaining a distance. Moreover, a number of *responsa* from another of al-Khallal's Ibn Ḥanbal collections forbid Muslims the practice of lamenting or crying over the departed. In one of these, it is described as a *jāhilī* behavior, and in another as disobedient to God. If one summoned to wash a body encounters Muslims engaging in such behavior, Ibn Ḥanbal says, he should "forbid them."[123] Read against this background, the distinction here between the lamenting Christians and the forbearing Muslim son is even more dramatic.

It is perhaps not surprising that al-Khallāl included in this chapter questions dealing with consolations exchanged between Muslims and non-Muslims. When he was asked about how one should console non-Muslims, Ibn Ḥanbal replied either, "I don't know what to tell you" or "I can't remember what I heard about that." On another occasion, when he was asked how one ought to console a Christian, he said, "I don't know. Why console him?" Other sources were more helpful. One reported hearing a Muslim comfort a Christian by saying, "May God give you strength and patience." Another man suggested consoling People of the Book by saying, "May God make plentiful your property and your children, and may he make your life long." Another Muslim suggested that one might try, "Whatever happens to you is for the best."[124] When he was asked how a Muslim should react when a non-Muslim consoled him, Ibn Ḥanbal simply hung his head for a time and finally said, "I don't know anything about that."[125]

It would seem, then, that from the point of view of Ibn Ḥanbal, there was no good way to console a Christian or by a Jew and no particularly commendable way to respond if a Christian or Jew offered words of commiseration. This is not especially surprising. The suggestions for consoling a Christian or a Jew offered by other traditionalists, after all, are predicated upon the shared monotheist belief of both Muslim and Jew or Muslim and Christian. Indeed, one can hardly imagine an effective way of offering sympathy while maintaining the observance of the boundaries upon which Ibn Ḥanbal seems to have insisted in all else. Those expressions of sympathy that are set forth would be as appropriate for a Muslim as for a Jew or a Christian. The second and fifth forms of the verb *ʿazā* as they are used in these *aḥādīth* denote shared sentiment, common suffering, or conjoined pain. The expression of such sentiments does not lend itself to the declaration of boundaries between persons or between communities.

Throughout al-Khallāl's *Kitāb al-janāʾiz* one encounters a recurrent theme: the tendency to accommodate quotidian intermingling of Muslims and non-Muslims by maintaining in the Muslim subject a studied awareness of his or her own identity and by insisting that that identity be performed as an aspect of any interaction with non Muslims. This theme recurs throughout Ibn Ḥanbal's *responsa* dealing with Muslim/non-Muslim interactions. But what was to happen if the authoritative prescriptions contained within these *responsa* were ignored? There are hints within the *Kitāb ahl al-milal*, to be sure—Ibn Ḥanbal's admonition that believers must issue sharp and stern rebukes to those who dare to pose the question of non-Muslim members of the primordial *umma*, for example—but in the context of funerals and the problem of boundary transgression, the best evidence we have comes from another collection of Ibn Ḥanbal *responsa*, that collected by in Isḥāq b. Ibrāhīm b.

Hāniʾ al-Nīsābūrī (d. 275/888–89). In that work, Ibn Ḥanbal is asked about the carrying of palm fronds (*jarīd*, glossed in the text as *saʿaf al-nakhl*) in funeral processions. Ibn Ḥanbal responds, "If someone sees the family of the deceased doing that, he may follow the bier, and pray over it, but he should command [the family members] and forbid them, and say, 'This is loathsome (*makrūh*).'"[126]

The presence of palm fronds at a funeral would tend to suggest Christian influence, which would explain the strong reaction to their presence by Ibn Ḥanbal. His admonition to "command and forbid" the family members of the deceased must be read as a single small outpost in a much larger and more pervasive Ḥanbalī program of "commanding and forbidding" recently studied at great length by Michael Cook.[127]

In his study of Ibn Ḥanbal's doctrine of commanding and forbidding as it is recalled in al-Khallāl's work, Cook notes that the practice was to be performed by Muslims with regard to other Muslims—commanding and forbidding Christians or Jews seldom comes up, and where it does it is discouraged. The issues over which commanding and forbidding is enjoined—most typically the playing of musical instruments or the possession, drinking or production of alcohol—were among the primary behavioral traits that were understood to set Muslim apart from non-Muslim. Other matters over which one was compelled to command and forbid—the proper performance of prayer, for example—were also issues in accordance with which Muslims distinguished themselves from non-Muslims, as M. J. Kister has shown.[128] And while it is of course possible that the practice of commanding and forbidding could be extended to non-Muslims, Ibn Ḥanbal's *responsa* seem overwhelmingly concerned with how the practice ought to apply to interactions among Muslims. Frequently, then, the basis for the act of commanding and forbidding as Ibn Ḥanbal seems to have imagined it was the perceived transgression of the behavioral boundaries that distinguished Muslim from non-Muslim.

Whoever was to be commanded and forbidden, moreover, there were very clear limits on the lengths to which the act was to be taken in practice, as Cook points out repeatedly. Commanding and forbidding is not to be performed if the individual fears violence at the hands of the one he would command and forbid, for example, or if the offender in question is armed. If one is repeatedly ignored by the offending party, one might speak harshly to the wrongdoer but it was often best to simply leave the wrongdoer to his or her own devices. Hence Ibn Ḥanbal prescribed three kinds of commanding—that to be done with the heart, that with the tongue and that with the hand. The hand was to be used to separate the offender from, for example, the individual with whom he is sinning. Objects may be attacked, but people were to be treated gently. The tongue was the preferred mode of commanding and forbidding, and this was to be done civilly if possible. Finally, when conditions did not allow any other kind of action, commanding and forbidding in the heart were enjoined upon the believer. Cook notes also the practice seems to have been imagined to apply only to the home areas of the Ḥanbalīs:

> [A]bsent is any tendency [in the practice as revealed in al-Khallāl's text] for Ḥanbalites to go looking for trouble in other parts of town. There is no indication that they were attempting to carry out the duty in quarters where the population might have been even less sympathetic to their values. They do not seek out Muʿtazilite preachers to revile and assault, or go raiding the brothels, or interfere with the pleasurable activities of the military or political elite. This is hardly surprising. Ḥanbalites as they appear in these responsa are ill-equipped to confront the immoral majority; they can hardly hope to dominate their own streets, let alone those of others.[129]

In fact, one might well wonder if the point of commanding and forbidding as Ibn Ḥanbal imagined it had to do with "dominating" anything. Given the limits placed upon the practice of commanding and forbidding by Ibn Ḥanbal, all of which seem intended to mitigate the chance of violent social conflict, it seems doubtful whether the point of commanding and forbidding was to change the exterior environment in which the Ḥanbalīs lived. It would seem rather that commanding and forbidding served as a means for members of Ibn Ḥanbal's community of "believers" to perform daily their self-consciously distinct identity, one calling the other to account, demanding that the other respond as a believer or as a Muslim, but always on the basis of the markers of Muslimness that were the starting point for commanding and forbidding as Ibn Ḥanbal imagined them. Even when it was too dangerous to issue such a call, it was necessary for the believer to note the transgression in his or her heart and to condemn it, performing an invisible yet potent act of evaluation, moral or ethical response, and, accordingly, communal self-identification.

As we have noted, Ibn Ḥanbal's imagined community of believers, a pious elite living in the midst of many lesser Muslims, was predicated upon the joining of religious knowledge with active application of that knowledge. Commanding and forbidding fellow Muslims in the manner prescribed by Ibn Ḥanbal seems to have been a means of joining religious understanding to daily practice and a means of doing so in a way that called upon the believer him- or herself to confront transgression of the boundaries set in place by God for Muḥammad's community. This was to be a quiet duty, performed in small ways, in brief social interactions, in which shared communal identity was evoked and reaffirmed through a means very much like that John Chrysostom had tried to set in place among his Antiochene congregations centuries before: the ascribed behaviors that marked one as a member of the Ḥanbalī community, or as a member of the Islamic community, were to be evoked as members of that community (or those communities) observed one another's behavior and, when necessary, objected to that behavior on the basis of the praxis ascribed as essential to membership within that community. In a social world in which Ḥanbalīs lived intimately with Muslims of other communities as well as non-Muslims, this will have served as a means of constantly affirming and reaffirming membership in the community that cohered around the figure of Aḥmad Ibn Ḥanbal.

The act of commanding and forbidding undertaken in support of the behavioral prescriptions set forth by Ibn Ḥanbal with regard to interactions with non-Muslims will have been simply another application of the practice as it seems frequently to have been undertaken; that is as a means of policing communal boundaries and evoking communal membership for both the individual commanding or forbidding and the individual addressed. If we briefly consider once again the scene that so enraged Ibn Muljam, ʿAlī's Khārijī assassin, we will see how this will have worked. Remember that the occasion was the funeral of a Christian man whose son had become a Muslim. During the funeral the sight of Muslim and Christian walking together drew the considerable ire of the Khārijī, as it might other Muslims, even if the result was not as murderous as that Ibn Muljam threatened.

In the event that a member of Ibn Ḥanbal's community's Christian father died, that Ḥanbalī individual would have a specific means of fulfilling his duties within the funeral ceremonies. In so doing, however, he will have had a means of performing his identity that will have prevented the spectacle of boundary transgression that many Muslims seem to have been determined to avoid, as Kister and Noth have shown. He would, ideally, participate in the funeral procession, seeing his father to his grave. He would keep himself apart from the Christian mourners, however, both spatially and behaviorally. He would leave the duties of washing the body and prayer over the grave to his father's community, and he would set himself apart from the Christians both by riding a horse—a specifically Muslim prerogative—and by riding ahead of the procession.

In so doing, he will have, through his own behavior, consciously performed his identity and maintained a boundary between himself and his fellow mourners. To the outside observer as well, there will have been a good number of indicators that he as an individual was in no danger of becoming subsumed within his father's community through shared bonds of grief and ritual. Accordingly, in both the experience of the individual himself and in the perception of those who might observe him, a boundary was maintained between the Muslim son and his father's Christian community, even (or particularly) in the identity-charged social space of the funeral.[130] If, however, a Muslim observer took issue with this Muslim son's actions and he chose to command and forbid the young man, the communal identity of both will have been reaffirmed whether the young man responded positively or negatively, as long as he responded on the basis of the ascribed behavioral norms of his community.

In any case, there was within Ibn Ḥanbal's prescriptions a means of accommodating such potentially volatile situations as a multicommunal funeral while avoiding anxiety-inciting ambiguity over questions of identity, or the blurring of communal boundaries. As the cultural anthropologist Fredrik Barth has suggested, such boundaries, built into the social relations of individuals identifying themselves as members of distinct communities, may function much as might a fence or wall between two neighbors. The division marks a boundary but also accommodates communication and interaction by providing a dependable grammar for such interactions. Such boundary markers make interactions predictable, and because they are predictable, they may also tend to be safer. Barth refers to such boundary markers as "affordances": "For a simple illustration . . . reflect for a moment on the scene of two English neighbours, conversing over the garden fence. The territorial boundary of their properties separates them but it gives shape to their interaction in a way that I suspect positively enables it, since it frames and defines the nature of the opportunity. Thanks to that boundary, the conversation can proceed in a more carefree and relaxed way, and be elaborated and pursued with less risk of other entanglements—a consideration that may loom large in the role performances of neighbours."[131]

Within Islamic society of Ibn Ḥanbal's time, it was becoming ever more difficult to pick out Christian from Muslim on the basis of appearance, knowledge of Islam, cultural literacy, social positioning, access to power, and even, if we are to believe al-Jāḥiẓ, treatment under the law. It is perhaps not surprising then that there also seems to have been very keen interest over such questions as whether there had been Christians and Jews within Muḥammad's primordial community and how exactly one was supposed to define who and what a Muslim was. This will have become a particularly urgent question when it is clear that a number of Christians, Jews and even Magians were reading Muslim texts and conversing knowledgably about the Qur'ān and *ḥadīth*. Some non-Muslims, according to Ibn Ḥanbal's *responsa*, were even praying for Muḥammad and acknowledging him as a prophet of God.

For those members of Ibn Ḥanbal's community who were concerned to maintain the distinctions that set them in opposition to all other communities, and in so doing retain the boundaries that they believed enclosed God's chosen community upon the earth, Ibn Ḥanbal's behavioral prescriptions offered a means of bringing with them something closely akin to Barth's "garden fence" as they ventured out into the world. They were not left on their own to struggle through each interaction with those who stood outside of their community, negotiating crucial performances of their identity in a perilous ad hoc manner. Nor were they left open to the arbitrary assessment of others of their behavior in such situations. Rather, such prescriptions as Ibn Ḥanbal set forth made such interactions predictable and easily evaluated. Moreover, as non-Muslims came to understand the content and intention of such prescriptions, which I must believe they did, interactions with Muslims also became more structured and so more predictable.

Interestingly, however, Barth notes that once such boundaries are set in place, they become subject to the adaptive qualities of those whose lives they order. A national border may appear as a boundary or an obstruction to those who depend upon it to define their territorial domain, for example, but that border looks very different to a smuggler, for example, or to asylum seekers. For such persons, that boundary offers a means of profit or a portal to escape. In the texts we have consulted in this chapter, there are hints of such approaches to the boundaries established within Abbasid society to distinguish Muslim from non-Muslim.

Recall, for example, that al-Jāḥiẓ insists that the highly placed and prosperous Christians of his society openly flout the rules set in place within Muslim society to mark the inferior status of non-Muslims: They ride horses (indeed, very fine horses) in contravention of what were by al-Jāḥiẓ's time very old rules against such behavior by non-Muslims.[132] They refuse to wear the distinctive sash that marks them as Christians, or they hide it under a tunic. They take "Muslim names."[133] They refuse to pay the *jizya*, one of the foremost markers of non-Muslimness and the object of much discussion in al-Khallāl's *Kitāb ahl al-milal.*[134] It is significant that al-Jāḥiẓ emphasizes that these rich Christians refuse to pay the tax not because they lack the means, but because they are "too proud." Finally, Christians dare to beat Muslims, he says, something expressly forbidden in Muslim-*dhimmī* relations, apparently from a very early period.[135]

In al-Jāḥiẓ's essay, all of these behaviors are interpreted as evidence of the exalted status within Abbasid society of the Christian individuals who perform them. Indeed, it would seem that this was precisely the point of these gestures—that the boundaries set in place to mark Muslim from inferior non-Muslim had become "affordances" that allowed elite Christians to announce their status via their transgression. In this way, these boundaries—so vehemently insisted upon by individuals as distinct (and of opposed religious views) as al-Jāḥiẓ and Ibn Ḥanbal[136]—became for Abbasid Christians much like what national boundaries are for smugglers: socially and religiously charged barriers whose subversion became a means of accumulating social capital.

Something very similar might also be suggested about Muslim behavior around these communal boundaries. We have noted, for example, that the caliph Mutawakkil, as an exemplar of the Abbasid power elite's uppermost stratum, was imagined to have entered a Christian monastery in order to partake in a series of pleasures that transgressed normative Muslim behaviors as they were imagined by individuals like Ibn Ḥanbal, a man whose approval Mutawakkil courted by attempting to share with him and members of his family the sumptuous benefits of Abbasid power and wealth. In fact the association among Muslims with transgressive pleasures enjoyed in monasteries was something of a trope in Abbasid *adab* literature.[137] The *Kitāb adab al-ghurabā'* contains a number of other vignettes in which the pleasures that mark an individual as among the sophisticated and privileged of Abbasid society are specifically associated with the transgression of these boundaries.[138]

In one of these, a group of (presumably elite) Muslims gathers at "the monastery of al-Thaʿālib to watch the Christians gather there and to drink by the Yazegerd Canal, which flows by the gate of the monastery."

> While we were walking around the monastery, accompanied by a group of the sons of Christian secretaries and (other young men) of theirs, we saw a young woman with a face like an inscribed dinar, as the saying goes, who was swaying like a branch of basil in the breeze of the north wind. She stretched out her hand to Abū 'l-Fatḥ, saying "Sir, come and read the poetry written on the wall of the martyrion." We went with her, filled with a pleasure in her and her grace and sweetness of diction that only God knows. When we entered the room, she pointed, unbarring a forearm like silver, to a place where somebody had written the following:
>
> She went out on the day of her feast,
> Dressed as a nun,
> And captivated with her haughty walk
> Everyone coming and going.
> For her misery I saw her
> On the feast of the Thaʿālib monastery,
> Swaying among women,
> A buxom girl among buxom girls,
> In whose midst she was like the full moon
> Surrounded by stars.

The Muslim visitors to the monastery realize that she is the girl described in the poem, and one of them eventually writes his own poem about her, which begins,

> A slender girl of bewitching looks passed by us
> [in the monastery]
> brought out from her seclusion by the monks,
> to glorify the religion as living proof of it . . .

The girl and one of the Muslims soon undertake a liaison.[139] Here, as in the story of Mutawakkil's sensuous monastery visit we examined above, the seduction of a Christian girl is not just the seduction of a Christian girl;

rather, it is the consummation of a certain genre of boundary-transgressing indulgence, one represented by the monastery, the wine, and the poetic celebration of luxuriant decadence. The girls are notably either, in one case, a monk's daughter or, in the other, a nun. They are not simple peasant girls or prostitutes. Rather, they stand as personifications of Christianness, as exoticized emblems of refined and alluring alterity who function not only as a means of exquisite sensual indulgence but also as a means of elite male self-fashioning. In this sense, they find male counterparts in the Christian sons of secretaries with whom the Muslim revelers spend the afternoon. They may also be read as equivalent to the Christian intellectuals and scholars patronized by al-Ma'mūn, men like the Christian cultural broker Ḥunayn and his colleagues. Read in tandem with al-Jāḥiẓ's apparent contention that Christians are shown preference by powerful Muslims within Abbasid society at the expense of ordinary Muslims, these texts would seem to suggest that for elite Muslims as well as for elite Christians, transgressing the normative boundaries between Muslim and Christian, of which Ibn Ḥanbal's prescriptions represent a particularly notable articulation, was a means of announcing exalted status and a means of accumulating and displaying cultural capital in opposition to others of their community.[140]

Conclusion

It would seem, then, that Ibn Ḥanbal provided his contemporaries not only with a means of erecting and maintaining communal boundaries rooted in the imagined primordial character of Muḥammad's *umma* but also with a normative standard of behavior that could function as a boundary or border in the sense that Barth has recently suggested. That is, Ibn Ḥanbal personified a definition of Muslimness that loomed large in the imaginary of his contemporaries not simply as a barrier, but also as a seemingly stable standard of Muslimness against which it was possible to define or refine one's relationship to other Muslims. This was particularly so, it would seem, in matters of status, class, and wealth. As tolerance for, patronage of and social contact with non-Muslims and particularly Christians became recognized as a mark of status, it is hardly surprising that the question of communal boundaries, upon which this economy depended, became ever more a matter of concern not just for men like Ibn Ḥanbal, but also for men like al-Jāḥiẓ.

Despite the fact that he was undeniably cranky and, as Nimrod Hurvitz has shown, rigorist to the point of damaging his familial relations over matters he regarded as questions of virtue and vice, Ibn Ḥanbal's theory of communal boundaries and their defense was not one that lent itself to violence, rebellion, or riot. This, at least, is the picture that emerges of his ideology and praxis as it appears in the texts we have surveyed in the foregoing pages, particularly in the *responsa* collections compiled by al-Khallāl.[141]

Despite this, however, the Ḥanbalī *madhhab* was to be associated in the centuries after his death with increasingly aggressive acts of intolerance, riot, and bloodshed led by such figures as the infamous Ḥanbalī preacher al-Barbaharī (d. 329/941).[142] The violence of Ḥanbalī militants in these years would be visited upon rival Muslim communities, Christian communities, and those whom puritanical Ḥanbalīs deemed to be sinners, men and women unrelated by blood walking together in the street, for example.[143] Now the figure of Ibn Ḥanbal was reread in new contexts, his ideas interpreted and reinterpreted more rigidly, their application undertaken more violently. In the modern period, the intransigent Muslim pietist would become remembered as the intellectual and spiritual ancestor of Wahhābism, a brand of fundamentalist Islamic revivalism that would capture the imaginations of individuals who found themselves subsumed in an era in which once again it seems the boundaries that order the present world and ensure the next have become blurred, broken, and perilously unstable. What is notable about the most recent permutations of Ibn Ḥanbal's thought is that their rigidity and vehemence make the *responsa* and their "affordances" recorded and transmitted by al-Khallāl seem by comparison graceful, gentle and remarkably generous in spirit.[144]

CONCLUSION

IN MANY WAYS, this book ends where it began. It began, in Chapter 1, with John Chrysostom's anxieties concerning what he understood as the perilous transgression by members of his community of the behavioral standards that marked one as a genuine Christian. In response to this anxiety, I suggested, Chrysostom urged his parishioners to make certain behavioral boundaries a matter of their daily practice and a component of their social relations with their fellow Christians. In essence, they were to exercise surveillance over one another, and to "command and forbid" any member of their community whom they suspected of transgressing those boundaries by becoming too intimate with the Jews or by participating in what Chrysostom understood as specifically Jewish rites, festivals, and other forms of religious observance.

The anxiety Chrysostom attempted to address in this way was one we have encountered as the basis of various acts of intercommunal aggression and violence within the late antique world. This anxiety may be traced to the need felt by human subjects in various social and cultural circumstances to maintain a stable sense of individual and communal identity within unstable social spaces. This phenomenon is much commented upon in recent anthropological and sociological literature, and I have drawn upon a cross-section of this literature to theorize the social dynamics that seem to have resided at the root of the intercommunal violence associated with the post-Constantinian Roman world. In particular, the insights of Fredrik Barth have led me to examine the issue of communal boundaries and their role in lending experiential weight to the communal identities of persons living and acting as part of self-consciously bounded groups. Barth's primary insight is that it is these boundaries, rather than the cultural stuff those boundaries are believed to enclose, that define identity groupings. That is, it is the maintenance of a sense of boundedness that makes a discrete group and not, as is often supposed, the imagined attributes of those who make up the group. This in turn requires the implementation of imagined structures with which a given identity group may be enclosed. In the periods and cultural spaces treated by this book, as in most periods and cultural spaces, these structures tend to manifest themselves in the realms of discourse, praxis, and dogma. The maintenance of these enclosures is carried out through strategies and cultural forms specific to and effective within the imaginative spaces in which those enclosures are meant to act as communal boundaries.

The cultural specificity of the ways in which these boundaries are imagined and instituted depends closely upon the narratives in accordance with which identity is imagined within the groups whose communal extent such boundaries are meant to trace. Drawing upon the work of Margaret Somers, I have suggested that it is through narrative that the specific attributes to be sought during processes of boundary maintenance are articulated; what marks one as a real member of the community in question, and so which qualities or behavioral traits should be insisted upon by those who patrol communal boundaries, are frequently exemplified in certain narratives privileged by that community. As we have seen, those narratives that recall the primordial origins of the community in question are particularly powerful in this respect. In such narratives, I have suggested, communal ancestors are understood to embody the essential qualities of all real members of the community. Accordingly, their recalled personal qualities and actions serve as both patterns for self-fashioning and as the bases for contesting membership within the community itself.

Somers has also suggested that as individuals and communities constitute identities in accordance with such narratives, they come to understand themselves as emplotted within versions of those narratives; that is, as they imagine the past as a story at whose center is a plot that leads from a foundational drama toward the present and then on to a foreseen telos, events in the past and present accrue meaning as they are imagined as episodes in that plot. The character of past and present episodes is in turn determined by the character of the theme in accordance with which the plot in question is cast.

Accordingly, sociologists, philosophers, and anthropologists have suggested, narratives play a crucial role in assigning meaning to the contingencies of existence within the natural, social, and political world. This dynamic carries very real implications for individuals living in groups and for groups living with one another. As Somers and Ronald Grigor Suny have suggested, the relations of individuals and communities with other individuals and communities may be deeply affected by the character of the narratives within which they understand themselves to be emplotted.

I have suggested that this facet of identity formation carried grave consequences for many communities within the late Roman world. Many Christian communities, for example, seem to have read contemporary events through a narrative of persecution and survival that had become central to Roman Christian modes of self-fashioning. These recalled the periods of pre-Constantinian persecution and the capacity of the community to survive these as a numinous manifestation of God's will in the affairs of the Roman Empire.

Accordingly, members of these communities looked upon the martyrs whose actions were recalled in these stories as exemplars upon whose model one might best fashion a genuinely Christian self. Tragically, however, as these communities found themselves at odds with other communities, whether these were Christian, Jewish, or pagan, they seem to have consistently interpreted these conflicts as further episodes within a metanarrative of persecution and resistance. Accordingly, many Christian individuals understood themselves in such circumstances as besieged defenders of holy truths, duty bound to defend those truths at any cost. Understood in this way, moments of conflict with other communities became legible as new episodes in an ancient cycle of persecution, in which the survival of the one true community of God upon the earth depended upon the capacity of true Christians for intransigence and, increasingly, active or even violent resistance.

This tendency to interpret contemporary conflict through narratives recalling Christianity's history of persecution and resistance paradoxically helped to produce, on the one hand, high-profile acts of grass-roots violence undertaken by local Christian zealots, and on the other increasingly coercive behavior on the part of Christian Roman imperial officials. It should be clearly noted, however, that these processes were carried out despite what seems to have been the determination on the parts of most members of late Roman society to live in peace with their neighbors, whatever their confessional identity. Indeed, it was the tendency of members of all of these communities to freely transgress their respective communal boundaries that I have found frequently provoked the violent actions of local militants.

Many of the most frequently noted instances of intercommunal violence in the later Roman world may be read as attempts by Christian rigorists to defend or reiterate crucial communal boundaries that, in their view, had become dangerously obscured or were too freely transgressed. This work frequently fell to ascetics, figures who were associated from their earliest appearance within the late Roman imaginary with the preservation of the most essential qualities to be found in real Christians. This was a role inherited from the Christian martyrs and performed now by individuals who were understood to bear the burden of discerning and enforcing the doctrinal and behavioral boundaries that preserved various Christian communities as self-consciously discrete communities.

Often, it was this role that brought these individuals into conflict with members of other communities. During the Christological conflicts of the fourth century, monks themselves began to play crucial roles in the narratives of local Christian communities as zealous (and sometimes violent) defenders of the truths upon which those communities were founded. These ascetics were particularly well suited to this role because they were understood as figures who maintained the numinous link between their communities and the divine. Because of their close association with this most elemental source of legitimacy, they were read as preservers of the qualities most befitting genuine members of those communities. These were complicated roles, and these ascetic warriors for the faith were looked upon with a mix of awe and dread by their contemporaries, Christian and non-Christian alike.

This long process established a lexicon of signs, symbols, narratives and associations that might be described as essentially late antique in that it was this semiotic brew that united a constellation of communities otherwise separated by language, culture, and dogma across a geographic expanse stretching from Ireland to Yemen. During the seventh century, a community of Arab monotheists joined this constellation of communities, and its members began to tell stories of their own about revelation and the sacred foundations of their community. As they did so, it was natural that they should participate in the system of universally comprehensible signs and symbols current in the world in which they settled.

Fred Donner has argued quite convincingly that as the early Islamic community came into being as a self-consciously distinct polity, its members began to imagine and articulate narratives of the foundational events of the extra-Arabian Muslim *umma*. Particularly pressing was the need for a means of explaining the conquests as a sign of God's approval of Muḥammad, his revelation, and his community. Inhabiting a world in which narratives of the numinous foundations of local and transregional communities had long occupied the imaginations of their new neighbors and subjects, the Muslims seem to have imbibed a late antique *koinê* of signs, symbols and narratives they encountered within the world settled by Arab *muhājirūn* in the decades and centuries after the *futūḥ* period.

With this semiotic *koinê* seems also to have come certain resources for imagining the founders of the Islamic community. These figures were rendered in accordance with the model of the pious, zealous communal defender, whether this individual was a martyr or a monk. Embedded in these figures and stories, however, was a certain recipe for imagining the character of relations between real members of the communities they founded and others, whether these were possessors of worldly power, deviant members of their own communities, or members of other communities.

In one of its versions, this recipe envisioned confrontation, conflict, and victory for the zealot as an expression of divine approval. As early Muslim warrior scholars articulated a theory of ascetic, militant piety or "*jihād*" on the frontier with Byzantium, they incorporated an ascetic ethos that recalled the heroes of the conquest period, heroes who are repeatedly described in early Muslim sources as kindred in spirit and praxis with Christian ascetics. It is little surprise, then, that as Muslims of the first centuries after the *hijra* described the institution of *jihād*, they called it the "monasticism of the Muslims."

This model of militant piety was put into practice from a very early period not only against the external enemies of Islam but also against self-identified Muslims who failed to meet the behavioral ideals of other Muslims. As we have seen, for example, the first/seventh-century Khawārij were remembered to have taken the frequent role of late antique ascetic militants—defense of communal boundaries—to horrifying extremes as they indiscriminately murdered self-confessed Muslims who disagreed with them.

The Khawārij undertook this role as a result of their reading of the evolving narrative of the Islamic past. Troublingly, their reading of this narrative seems to have differed very little from that of most Muslims. That is, the Khawārij seem to have put into practice a version of piety fashioned in accordance with the narrative of the Islamic past embraced by their contemporaries and those generations of Muslims who came after them. This carried potentially grave implications for the Islamic community; if real Muslims were those who, like the early *mujāhidūn*, were willing to violently confront those whose actions they considered transgressive of normative communal behaviors, the Muslim *umma* faced the danger of incessant factional violence of the sort endured by late Roman Christian communities.

This dilemma is underscored by the fact that the Khawārij, for all the horror they provoked with their actions, were also recalled as figures who embodied the ideals of their community; they were selfless, ascetic, tough, and exceedingly pious. With very few exceptions, they were doubles for the frontier raider heroes to whom many city-dwelling Muslims now looked as preservers of the essential qualities of the members of Muḥammad's primordial *umma*, men and women upon whom Muslims of all communities sought to pattern themselves. This, of course, presented the Muslim *umma* with a profound problem.

Among the Muslim communities that contended with the problem represented by the Khawārij was that which adhered around the figure of Aḥmad Ibn Ḥanbal. With Ibn Ḥanbal we encounter a conception of community that opposed a small, select community of believers within the larger Muslim *umma* to the mass of Muslims who fell short of the ideals embodied by the members of Muḥammad's primordial *umma*. According to Ibn Ḥanbal, this division was based upon the capacity of believers to put their Islamic understanding into effective practice, a notion that would have made compelling sense to the Khawārij.

Ibn Ḥanbal, however, like most of contemporaries, vehemently rejected the behavior of the Khawārij, even as he closely adhered to what we know of their vision of the very early Islamic past and their notions of pious praxis. What is crucial about Ibn Ḥanbal is that although there was much in his understanding of Muslim identity that might have led him and his contemporaries into violent confrontation with those whom they regarded as poor Muslims in the manner of the Khawārij, he represents a decision taken by the vast majority of Muslims that the Khārijī path was to be rejected. The problem he faced was how a believer was to perform the crucial work of putting faith into practice, particularly as this related to the defense of the boundaries of real Islam.

As we have seen, Muslims of Ibn Ḥanbal's generation had inherited an idiom for the reckoning of communal identity that had been long shared in common among a constellation of late antique communities. Militant piety wed to ascetic praxis was one of the defining elements of this idiom. It had been taken up with relish both on the Byzantine frontier among theorists of *jihād* and by the Khawārij as they were recalled by later Muslim historians. Ibn Ḥanbal also participated in this tradition. He had no doubt that it was the duty of the believer to confront error and evil where he found it and to make of himself a bulwark in defense of his community.

He imbibed this ethos from such *ghāzī* heroes as Ibn al-Mubārak, and had put it into practice during his own confrontation with the great powers of his world. In so doing, he acted out the implications of the late antique semiotic *koinê* in accordance with which his community's formative narratives had been founded. It was within these narratives that the means for fashioning specifically Muslim selves resided, and it was in accordance with these narratives that the self so fashioned would read the events of his or her world. It was within this matrix of semiotic elements and the narratives through which they were animated that the community of Ibn Ḥanbal was bound to the other communities of late antiquity.

This is not to suggest that Ibn Ḥanbal or his contemporaries necessarily conceived of any innate affinity between the Muslim *umma* the communities of Christians and Jews that surrounded them. Although it is exceedingly doubtful that Ibn Ḥanbal had in mind the specific example of the *aṣḥāb al-ukhdūd* as he confronted his interrogators during the *miḥna*, for example, or that his son or cousin had the Christian martyrs of Najrān in mind as they composed their accounts of his trials, Ibn Ḥanbal was the product of a cultural milieu in which the proper behavior of a faithful monotheist faced with exhortation to sin or error was understood and articulated through the recitation of such stories within his own community just as it was in Christian communities. In other words, a common set of assumptions, beliefs, and expectations about the relationship between properly pious monotheists and the powerful of the world connected Ibn Ḥanbal's community with communities arrayed across a vast geographical and chronological range, and, more importantly, across multiple communal boundaries. This shared set of assumptions and associations manifested itself, at one level, in the capacity of identical stories to express these shared assumptions and associations, even when recited be members of self-consciously distinct communities.

These stories, and more importantly the attitudes and beliefs that they articulated and which made them comprehensible, confirmed and reflected certain assumptions about the way the world worked. Accordingly, they may be read as traces of Geertz's "cultural DNA." The markings of this cultural coding are visible in the attitude taken by Ibn Ḥanbal to his *miḥna*, but perhaps more importantly in the narrative of the *miḥna* crafted by those who recalled it and those who imagined the figure of Ibn Ḥanbal in accordance with this narrative.

It was simply another aspect of this cultural inheritance that insisted that defense of communal boundaries must manifest itself in activist militancy. This found a specifically Islamic expression in the institution of *jihād* insofar as *jihād* combined a late antique ethos of renunciation, retreat, and zealous service on behalf of God and community with a frontier raiding culture mediated through privileged narratives of the Islamic *umma*'s foundational past. And yet when it came to how this ethos should be manifested in the public spaces of the urban Islamic society, individuals like Ibn Ḥanbal and, as we have seen, Sarī al-Saqaṭī, faced the difficult task of reelaborating upon the received tradition in order to craft Muslim selves at home in social circumstances distinguished by their diversity and the weaknesses of ordinary human beings.

Sarī managed this by putting into practice the ascetic renunciation of ego so valued by practitioners of *jihād* through concern for other members of his community and through acts of kindness toward the vulnerable and weak. As Ibn Ḥanbal theorized the problem of the believer's role in defending the boundaries of his community, he articulated a system of praxis in accordance with which the individual believer might stand daily in defense of his community and his communal identity but need not soil himself with the blood of fellow Muslims or those who stood beyond his community's boundaries.

I have suggested that Ibn Ḥanbal accomplished this in a manner that would have made compelling sense to John Chrysostom. For Ibn Ḥanbal, it was the duty of the believer to carry within him the behavioral boundaries of his community and to observe these through closely circumscribed modes of comportment with other Muslims and with non-Muslims. With Muslims, instances of boundary transgression were to be noted and rebuked, either verbally, in an act that would amount to hailing the offending Muslim on the basis of their shared Islamic identity, or with the heart. By rebuking with his heart but not with his tongue, the believer in question performed an invisible but no doubt powerful act of self-fashioning, condemning what he saw on the basis of the behavioral boundaries that marked him as a true member of the one community of God upon the earth. Only very rarely, according to Ibn Ḥanbal, should the believer physically intervene to prevent transgression of proper Muslim behavior, and even then it should be done "gently."

In the case of interactions with non-Muslims, Ibn Ḥanbal elaborated importantly upon a much older body of thought regarding the proper relations between Muslim and non-Muslim. He seems to have believed that Muslims and non-Muslims would inevitably have very intimate business with one another but that Muslims must at all times remain conscious of, and indeed perform, their own distinct, communal identity. His prescriptions for Muslim interactions with non-Muslims represent an attempt to animate this theory as a mode of practice. He did not, like Chrysostom, demand that members of his community caught associating with Jews (or Christians or Magians) must be hauled before him to be lectured and rebuked. Rather, he set in place a series of what Barth has called "affordances," usable boundaries which seem to have structured Muslim relations with non-Muslims, making them predictable and, it would seem, safer.

Ibn Ḥanbal did not invent this approach to intercommunal relations; the implementation and preservation of communal boundaries had been (or were believed to have been) a central part of Muslim interactions with non-Muslims since the time of the conquests, as Kister and Noth have ably demonstrated. What he did do was elaborate importantly upon a much older tradition as a means of negotiating what was, in the third/ninth century, becoming an ever-more complicated social, political, and cultural milieu in the imperial center of Baghdād. Perhaps most importantly for the purposes of this study, however, Ibn Ḥanbal stands not as an emblem of toleration, or even as the founder of any lasting path or ideology of toleration. Rather, he is remarkable as a figure who reminds us that whatever the power of narrative to fashion identities, the ways in which human subjects respond to those narratives remains a matter of subjective choice.

Ibn Ḥanbal worked within the same received Islamic narratives as the militants of his own and previous generations. He shared with those militants many of their ideals concerning the role of the individual Muslim in defending his community and his responsibility to confront evil where he found it. He was stern and even rigid. He was remembered to have endured violence on behalf of his understanding of transcendent truth, and he approved wholeheartedly of the practice of *jihād* on the frontiers of the Muslim world. But as regarded relations among Muslims living within the *dār al-Islām*, and between those Muslims and their non-Muslim subjects, he seems consciously to have sought a means of applying the dictates of these narratives in a way that will have allowed, and even facilitated, peaceful coexistence. The communal boundaries the faithful individual was obliged to defend were to be policed from the inside out; their defense was a matter of constant awareness of one's own identity and the nonviolent reiteration of the identity of others through prescribed modes of comportment. Physical violence against other persons had little place in this process as Ibn Ḥanbal imagined it.

Once again, Ibn Ḥanbal did not invent this means of Muslim coexistence with non-Muslims, but through his *responsa*, given and received at the end of antiquity, we do have a priceless window onto the world inhabited by the scholar and his contemporaries and a close study in the ways in which that world was negotiated by Ibn Ḥanbal and many other Muslims.

That other Muslims had embraced the principles upon which Ibn Ḥanbal elaborated in his *responsa* is illustrated in one final story of communal boundaries, opposed identity groups, and factional violence. The story also suggests much about the benefits enjoyed by all inhabitants of the Islamic empire when such principles as Ibn Ḥanbal articulated were enacted as a means of resolving disputes and avoiding or ending intercommunal violence.

In the year 727 C.E., the Christian community of Aleppo split into two opposed factions. In part because these opposed factions were obliged to share the same church, they soon came into violent conflict with one another. In order to resolve this problem peacefully, the Muslim *amīr* of the city came up with a very simple solution. He had a wooden barrier built in the church and assigned one community to each side of the barrier. Now, the *amīr* seems to have believed, the two communities could share the church structure peacefully, together within the church but separate nonetheless. Given what we have seen of the strategies many Muslims embraced for the fashioning of a shared social universe in which communal boundaries were nonetheless preserved and protected, the *amīr*'s solution makes compelling sense.

It didn't work. During the services performed by the clergy of each community, we are told, its rival community would try to interrupt the liturgy by raising a clamor. This, predictably, produced frustration and aggression on the parts of both parties, and the violent attacks against the members of each community by partisans of the other continued.

Finally, the *amīr* had had enough. His solution was even simpler than the first, and yet it retained what seems to have been the theoretical core of the first. He allowed the opposed Christian communities to remain separate, but he decided that they would hold services together. The distinct identities of each community would be performed during communion, when the priest of each community would give communion to members of his own community while the leader of the opposed community would do the same a few feet away. To ensure order, he dispatched armed Muslim soldiers to oversee the process. In time, the two communities reunited, reconciled, and lived in peace.[1] The ancient world had come to an end, but the dilemma faced by the Christian communities of Aleppo and the *amīr* who sought to give them peace would incessantly reemerge in search of new and more lasting solutions.

ABBREVIATIONS

AJP	*American Journal of Philology*
CCSL	*Corpus Christianorum Series Latina*
BASOR	*Bulletin of the American Schools of Oriental Research*
BSOAS	*Bulletin of the School of Oriental and African Studies*
CSCO	*Corpus Scriptorum Christianorum Orientalium*
CSEL	*Corpus Scriptorum Ecclesiasticorum Latinorum*
EI^2	H. A. R. Gibb, ed., *Encyclopedia of Islam*, 2nd ed., 9 vols. (Leiden, 1960–)
GRBS	*Greek, Roman and Byzantine Studies*
IJMES	*International Journal of Middle Eastern Studies*
JAOS	*Journal of the American Oriental Society*
JECS	*Journal of Early Christian Studies*
JHS	*Journal of Hellenic Studies*
JMEMS	*Journal of Medieval and Early Modern Studies*
JNES	*Journal of Near Eastern Studies*
JRA	*Journal of Roman Archaeology*
JRS	*Journal of Roman Studies*
JSAI	*Jerusalem Studies in Arabic and Islam*
JSS	*Journal of Semitic Studies*
JTS	*Journal of Theological Studies*
NPNF	P. Schaff and H. Wace (eds.), *A Select Library of Nicene and Post-Nicene Fathers of the Christian Church* (New York, 1892)
PG	J.-P. Minge (ed.), *Patrologia cursus completus. Series graeca* (Paris, 1857–66)
PL	J.-P. Minge (ed.), *Patrologia cursus completus. Series latina* (Paris, 1844–1902)
PO	*Patrologia Orientalis*

SC	*Sources chrétiennes*
SI	*Studia Islamica*
SP	*Studia Patristica*
TAPA	*Transactions of the American Philological Association*
VC	*Vigiliae Christianae*

NOTES

INTRODUCTION

1. ʿAmmār al-Baṣrī, *Kitāb al-burhān*, ed. Mishal Hayek, in *ʿAmmār al-Baṣrī: Apologie et controverses* (Beirut, 1977), 32–33. This critique appears, for example, in the seventh-century *Doctrina Jacobi Nuper Baptizati*, 5.16.11, ed. and French trans. Vincent Déroche, *Travaux et Mémoirés* 11 (1991): 209: Here a former Jew recalls that when he asked an elderly and learned Jew about the prophet who had appeared among the Saracens, the old man replied, "He is a false [prophet]. For do prophets come with a sword and war chariot?"

2. See the edition of this pamphlet, with French translation, of Dominique Sourdel, "Un pamphlet Musulman anonyme d'époque 'Abbāside contre les Chrétiens," *Revue des études islamiques* 34 (1966): 1–33, here 33.

3. See H. A. Drake, *Constantine and the Bishops: The Politics of Intolerance* (Baltimore, 2000), 429–31, 249–50. See also P. S. Davies, "The Origin and Purpose of the Persecution of A.D. 303," *JTS* 40 (1981): 66–94, esp. 84–85.

4. See most recently Michael Gaddis, *There Is No Crime for Those Who Have Christ: Religious Violence in the Christian Roman Empire* (Berkeley, 2005).

5. "The Apology of Timothy the Patriarch before the Caliph Mahdi," Syriac text ed. and trans. A. Mingana, *Woodbrooke Studies* 2 (1928): 1–162, here, 61–62. See also the Arabic version, ed. Hans Putman, *L'Église et L'Islam sous Timothée I (780–823)* (Beirut, 1986), 32–33 (#162–68).

6. "The Apology of Timothy," ed. and trans. Mingana, 62.

7. Ambrose, *De obitu Theodosii* 4, ed. and trans. Mary Dolorosa Mannix, *Sancti Ambrosii Oratio de Obitu Theodosii* (Washington, D.C., 1925), 47.

8. R. Malcolm Errington, "Christian Accounts of the Religious Legislation of Theodosius I," *Klio* 79 (1997): 398–443; R. Malcolm Errington, "Church and State in the First Years of Theodosius I," *Chiron* 29 (1998): 21–72; Drake, *Constantine and the Bishops*, 441ff.; Peter Brown, *Power and Persuasion in Late Antiquity: Towards a Christian Empire* (Madison, 1992), 109.

9. See Gaddis, *No Crime*; Drake, *Constantine and the Bishops*, 409–11; Brown, *Power*

and Persuasion, 105–8. See now David Brakke, *Demons and the Making of the Monk: Spiritual Combat in Early Christianity* (Cambridge, Mass., 2006), 214–26.

10. Dioscurus, *A Panegyric on Macarius, Bishop of Tkōw*, 5.2, ed. and trans. D. W. Johnson (Louvain, 1980), CSCO 416 (Copt. 42), 20–30. Coptic text CSCO 415 (Copt. 41), 30–40.

11. See, as examples, Daniel Boyarin and Virginia Burrus, "Hybridity as Subversion of Orthodoxy? Jews and Christians in Late Antiquity," *Social Compass* 52 (2005): 431–41; Richard Lim, *Public Disputation, Power, and Social Order in Late Antiquity* (Berkeley, 1995); Éric Rebillard, "A New Style of Argument in Christian Polemic: Augustine and the Use of Patristic Citations," *JECS* 8 (2000): 559–78. J. Rebecca Lyman, "The Making of a Heretic: The Life of Origin in Epiphanius *Panarion* 64," *SP* 31 (1997): 445–51; Mark Vessey, "The Forging of Orthodoxy in Latin Christian Literature: A Case Study," *JECS* 4 (1996): 495–513.

12. Andrew S. Jacobs, *Remains of the Jews: The Holy Land and Christian Empire in Late Antiquity* (Stanford, 2004).

13. See Michael Philip Penn, *Kissing Christians: Ritual and Community in the Late Ancient Church* (Philadelphia, 2005), 91–119.

14. See Denise Kimber Buell, *Making Christians: Clement of Alexandria and the Rhetoric of Legitimacy* (Princeton, 1999), 35–51; Denise Kimber Buell, *Why This New Race: Ethnic Reasoning in Early Christianity* (New York, 2005); Aaron Johnson, "Identity, Descent and Polemic: Ethnic Argumentation in Eusebius' *Praeparatio Evangelica*," *JECS* 12 (2004): 23–56; Aaron Johnson, "Greek Ethnicity in Eusebius' *Praeparatio Evangelica*," *AJP* 128 (2007): 95–118; Aaron P. Johnson, *Ethnicity and Argument in Eusebius'* Praeparatio evangelica (Oxford, 2006).

15. Elizabeth A. Castelli, *Martyrdom and Memory: Early Christian Culture Making* (New York, 2004), 10.

16. See Fredrik Barth, "Introduction," in Fredrik Barth (ed.), *Ethnic Groups and Boundaries: The Social Organization of Cultural Difference* (Boston, 1969), 15–38. Barth's own notion of boundaries has recently been restated in his "Boundaries and Connections," in Anthony P. Cohen (ed.), *Signifying Identities: Anthropological Perspectives on Boundaries and Contested Values* (London, 2001), 17–36.

17. Clifford Geertz, "The Integrative Revolution: Primordial Sentiments and Civil Politics in the New States," in Clifford Geertz, *The Interpretation of Cultures* (New York, 1973), 255–310; Edward Shils, "Primordial, Personal, Sacred and Civil Ties," *British Journal of Sociology* 8 (1957): 130–45.

18. Ronald Grigor Suny, "Constructing Primordialism: Old Histories for New Nations," *Journal of Modern History* 71 (2001): 862–96; Ronald Grigor Suny, "Provisional Stabilities: The Politics of Identities in Post-Soviet Eurasia," *International Security* 24.3 (2000): 139–78.

19. Margaret R. Somers, "The Narrative Constitution of Identity: A Relationship and Network Approach," *Theory and Society* 23.5 (1994): 605–60. See also Francesca Polleta,

"Contending Stories: Narrative in Social Movements," *Qualitative Sociology* 21 (1998): 419–46; Francesca Polleta, "'It Was Like a Fever . . .': Narrative and Identity in Social Protest," *Social Problems* 45 (1998): 137–59; Lewis P. Hinchman and Sandra Hinchman, *Memory, Identity, Community: The Idea of Narrative in the Human Sciences* (Albany, 1997); Paul Ricoeur, *Time and Narrative*, 3 vols. (Chicago, 1984–88); Martin Kreiswirth, "Merely Telling Stories? Narrative and Knowledge in the Human Sciences," *Poetics Today* 21 (2000): 293–318; David Wood (ed.), *On Paul Ricoeur: Narrative and Interpretation* (London, 1991); Jerome Bruner, "The Narrative Construction of Reality," *Critical Inquiry* 18 (1991): 1–21; Hayden White, "The Value of Narrativity in the Representation of Reality," in *On Narrative*, ed. W. J. Thomas Mitchell (Chicago, 1981), 1–23.

20. The role of narrative in the constitution of individual identities has recently been the topic of sharp debate between scholars who accept the role of narrative in the formation of individual selves and those who argue that the process of self-creation is in fact "episodic," that is, the product of recollected significant "episodes" that are not united by an organizing narrative. Following Somers, I would suggest that "episodes" emerge from events only through the medium of narrative; that is, discrete life events take on the thematic meanings necessary to be reckoned as "episodes" only if they are understood within some sort of organizing and narrated history of the self and of the events/episodes themselves. In the case of communities, moreover, the communicative processes upon which any experience of communal belonging or communal identity depends refer by necessity to some sort of sustained, communally articulated narrative of continuity from moment to moment, year to year and generation to generation. For the narrative vs. episode debate, see Paul John Eakin, "What Are We Reading When We Read Autobiography?" *Narrative* 12 (2004): 121–32; George Butte, "I Know That I Know That I Know: Reflections on Paul John Eakin's 'What Are We Reading When We Read Autobiography?'" *Narrative* 13 (2005): 299–306; James Phelan, "Who's Here? Thoughts on Narrative Identity and Narrative Imperialism," *Narrative* 13 (2005): 205–10; Paul John Eakin, "Selfhood, Autobiography, and Interdisciplinary Inquiry: A Reply to George Butte," *Narrative* 13 (2005): 307–11; Galen Strawson, "Against Narrativity," *Ratio* 17 (2004): 428–52; Paul John Eakin, "Narrative Identity and Narrative Imperialism: A Response to Galen Strawson and James Phelan," *Narrative* 14 (2006): 180–87.

21. See *Oratio* 30, ed. Richard Foerster, *Libanii Opera*, 12 vols. (Leipzig, 1903–27 [1963]), 3.80–118.

22. Ambrose, *epp.* 40, 41 (PL 16.1148–60, 1160–69). See also Paulinus of Milan, *Vita Ambrosii* 22–23, ed. and trans. Mary Simplicia Kaniecka, *Vita Sancti Ambrosii* (Washington, D.C., 1928), 62–65.

23. See Daniel Boyarin, *Border Lines: The Partition of Judeo-Christianity* (Philadelphia, 2004). See also Daniel Boyarin, *Dying for God: Martyrdom and the Making of Christianity and Judaism* (Stanford, 1999).

24. See Gaddis, *No Crime*, ch. 5, 6. See also Timothy E. Gregory, *Vox Populi: Popular Opinion and Violence in the Religious Controversies of the Fifth Century A.D.* (Cincinnati,

1979); Raymond Van Dam, "From Paganism to Christianity in Late Antique Gaza," *Viator 16* (1985): 1–20; Garth Fowden, "Bishops and Temples in the Eastern Roman Empire A.D. 320–435," *JTS* n.s. 29 (1979): 53–78.

25. See Drake, *Constantine and the Bishops*, 436–40.

26. See now Joel Thomas Walker, *The Legend of Mar Qardagh: Narrative and Christian Heroism in Late Antique Iraq* (Berkeley, 2006).

27. See Fred M. Donner, *Narratives of Islamic Origins: The Beginnings of Islamic Historical Writing* (Princeton, 1998); Nadia Maria El Cheikh, *Byzantium Viewed by the Arabs* (Cambridge, Mass., 2004), ch. 1.

28. See Donner, *Narratives of Islamic Origins*, 174–82; Chase F. Robinson, *Empire and Elites after the Muslim Conquest: The Transformation of Northern Mesopotamia* (Cambridge, 2000); El Cheikh, *Byzantium Viewed by the Arabs*, 34–54, 204–14; Albrecht Noth and Lawrence Conrad, *The Early Arabic Historical Tradition* (Princeton, 1994), 111ff.; David Cook, "Muslim Apocalyptic and *Jihād*," *JSAI* 20 (1996): 66–105, esp. 81.

29. See Cook, "Muslim Apocalyptic and *Jihād*," 102.

30. See Donner, *Narratives of Islamic Origins*, 40–46, 112–22.

31. See Thomas Sizgorich, "Narrative and Community in Islamic Late Antiquity," *Past & Present* 185 (2004): 9–42.

32. For Ibn al-Mubārak, see Michael Bonner, *Aristocratic Violence and Holy War: Studies in the Jihad and the Arab-Byzantine Frontier* (New Haven, 1996), 119–34.

33. For Ibn Ḥanbal and the Ḥanbalīs, see Nimrod Hurvitz, "From Scholarly Circles to Mass Movements: The Formation of Legal Communities in Islamic Societies," *American Historical Review* 103 (2003): 985–1008; Nimrod Hurvitz, "Schools of Law and Historical Context: Re-Examining the Formation of the Ḥanbalī Madhhab," *Islamic Law and Society* 7 (2000): 37–64; Nimrod Hurvitz, *The Formation of Hanbalism: Piety into Power* (London, 2002); Nimrod Hurvitz, "Biographies and Mild Asceticism: A Study in Muslim Moral Imagination," *SI* 85 (1997): 41–65; Henri Laoust, "Le Hanbalisme sous le califat de Bagdad," *Revue des études islamiques* 27 (1959): 67–128, esp. 69–74; Henri Laoust, "Les premières professions de foi hanbalites," in *Mélanges Louis Massignon* (Damascus, 1957), 3.7–34; Henri Laoust, *La profession de foi d'Ibn Baṭṭa* (Damascus, 1958); Michael Cooperson, *Classical Arabic Biography: The Heirs of the Prophet in the Age of Ma'mūn* (Cambridge, 2000), ch. 4; Christopher Melchert, *The Formation of the Sunni Schools of Law: 9th–10th Centuries C.E.* (Leiden, 1997), ch. 7; Christopher Melchert, "The Hanabila and the Early Sufis," *Arabica* 48 (2001): 352–67; Susan A. Spectorsky, "Aḥmad Ibn Ḥanbal's Fiqh," *JAOS* 102 (1982): 461–65; Ira M. Lapidus, "The Separation of State and Religion in the Development of Early Islamic Society," *IJMES* 6 (1975): 363–85, esp. 378–85; George Makdisi, "The Significance of the Sunni Schools of Law in Islamic Religious History," *IJMES* 10 (1979): 1–8; Michael Cook, *Commanding Right and Forbidding Wrong in Islamic Thought* (Cambridge, 2000), ch. 5. Scott C. Lucas, *Constructive Critics, Ḥadīth Literature and the Articulation of Sunnī Islam: The Legacy of the Generation of Ibn Saʿd, Ibn Maʿīn, and Ibn Ḥanbal* (Leiden, 2004), passim and esp. 192–217.

34. See, for example, on monks and *jihād*, Sizgorich, "Narrative and Community," 29–38. For conquest-era *mujāhidūn* compared to monks, see, for example, Muḥammad b. ʿAbd Allāh al-Azdī al-Baṣrī, *Taʾrīkh futūḥ al-Shām*, ed. ʿAbd al-Munʿim ʿAbd Allāh ʿĀmir (Cairo, 1970), 211; Abū Jaʿfar Muḥammad b. Jarīr al-Ṭabarī, *Taʾrīkh al-rasul wa-al mulūk*, ed. M. J. de Goeje et al., 15 vols. (Leiden, 1887–1901), I. 2125–26, trans. Blankinship, *History of al-Ṭabarī* 11, 126–27; I. 2395, trans. Friedmann, *History of al-Ṭabarī* 12, 181–82; Ibn ʿAsākir, *Taʾrīkh madīnat Dimashq*, ed. ʿUmar b. Gharāma al-ʿAmrawī and ʿAlī Shīrī, 80 vols. (Beirut, 1995–2001), 2.95–96. For *jihād* as "the monasticism of the Muslims" in prophetic *aḥādīth*, see ʿAbd Allāh b. al-Mubārak, *Kitāb al-jihād*, ed. Nazīh Ḥammād (Beirut, 1978), #15–17; ʿAbd Allāh b. al-Mubārak, *Kitāb al-zuhd wa-ʾl-raqāʾiq*, ed. Ḥabīb al-Raḥmān al-Aʿzamī (Beirut, 1970), #840, 845. See also Ibn Qutayba, *ʿUyūn al-akhbār*, ed. Aḥmad Zakī ʿAdawī, 4 vols. (Cairo, 1973 [1925]), 2.297, cited and translated by Suleiman A. Mourad, "Christian Monks in Islamic Literature: A Preliminary Report on Some Arabic *Apophthegmata Patrum*," *Bulletin of the Royal Institute for Inter-Faith Studies* 6 (2004): 90.

35. See al-Azdī, *Taʾrīkh futūḥ al-Shām*, ed. ʿĀmir, 115–17. Al-Azdī's *Futūḥ al-Shām* is believed to be one of the oldest Muslim historical sources we have for the conquest period. On this text, see Suleiman Mourad, "On Early Islamic Historiography: Abu Ismāʿīl al-Azdī and his *Futūḥ al-Shām*," *JAOS* 120 (2000): 577–93; Lawrence I. Conrad, "Al-Azdī's History of the Arab Conquests in Bilād al-Shām: Some Historiographical Observations," in Muhammad Adnan Bakhit (ed.), *Proceedings of the Second Symposium on the History of Bilād al-Shām During the Early Islamic Period Up to 40 AH/640 AD* (Amman, 1987), 1.28–62; Robert Hoyland, "Arabic, Syriac and Greek Historiography in the First Abbasid Century: An Inquiry into Inter-Cultural Traffic," *ARAM Periodical* 3 (1991): 211–33, esp. 223–33.

36. See Sizgorich, "Narrative and Community," 26–38.

37. See El Cheikh, *Byzantium Viewed by the Arabs*, 21–71.

38. See Donner, *Narratives of Islamic Origins*, 112–18.

39. Sizgorich, "Narrative and Community," 23–38.

40. For the Khawārij, see Rudolf Ernst Brünnow, *Die Charidschiten unter den ersten Omayyaden* (Leiden, 1884); Julius Wellhausen, *The Religio-Political Factions in Early Islam*, trans. R. C. Ostle and S. M. Walzer (Amsterdam, 1975); Patricia Crone, "The First Century Concept of Higra," *Arabica* 41 (1994): 352–87; Gerald R. Hawting, "The Significance of the Slogan *Lā Ḥukma Illā Lillāh* and the References to *Ḥudūd* in the Traditions About the Fitna and the Murder of ʿUthmān," *BSOAS* 41 (1978): 453–63; Uri Rubin, *Between Bible and Qurʾān: The Children of Israel and the Islamic Self-image* (Princeton, 1999); Patricia Crone, "A Statement by the Najdiyya Kharijites on the Dispensability of the Imamate," *SI* 88 (1998): 55–76; Patricia Crone, "'Even an Ethiopian Slave': The Transformation of a Sunni Tradition," *BSOAS* 57 (1994): 59–67; Patricia Crone, *God's Rule: Government and Islam* (New York, 2004), ch. 5; Michael Cook, "'Anan and Islam': the Origins of Karaite Scripturalism," *JSAI* 9 (1987): 161–82; Bogdan Skladanek, "The Kharijites in Iran I: Division into Sects," *Rocznik Orientalistyczny* 44.1 (1985): 65–92; Jeffery T. Kenney, "The Emer-

gence of the Khawarij: Religion and the Social Order in Early Islam," *Jusur* 5 (1998): 3–20; Jeffrey T. Kenney, "Heterodoxy and Culture: The Legacy of the Khawarij in Islamic History" (Ph.D. diss., University of California, Santa Barbara, 1991); Keith Lewinstein, "Making and Unmaking a Sect: The Heresiographers and the Sufriyya," *SI* 76 (1992): 75–96; Keith Lewinstein, "Notes on Eastern Hanafite Heresiography," *JAOS* 114.4 (1994): 583–98; Keith Lewinstein, "The Azariqa in Islamic Heresiography," *BSOAS* 54 (1991): 251–68; Khalid Yahya Blankinship, *The End of the Jihad State: The Reign of Hisham ibn 'Abd al-Malik and the Collapse of the Umayyads* (Albany, 1994); Martin Hinds, "Kufan Political Alignments in the Mid-Seventh Century A.D.," *IJMES* 2 (1971): 346–67 reprinted in Patricia Crone, Jere Bacherach, and Lawrence I. Conrad (eds.), *Studies in Early Islamic History* (Princeton, 1996); Robinson, *Empire and Elites*, 114–26; C. E. Bosworth, *Sistan Under the Arabs, From the Conquest to the Rise of the Saffarids (30–250/651/864)* (Rome, 1968), 37ff., 90; Michael G. Morony, *Iraq after the Muslim Conquest* (Princeton, 1984), 468–78.

41. See Robinson, *Empire and Elites*, 113–14.

42. Al-Balādhurī, *Ansāb al-ashraf*, II ed. Wilfred Madelung (Beirut, 2003), 325–26 (#679); al-Balādhurī, *Ansāb al-ashrāf*, II 328 (#680). See al-Ṭabarī, *Ta'rīkh*, I. 3337–39, trans. G. R. Hawting, *The History of al-Ṭabarī* 17: *The First Civil War* (Albany, 1996), 123–25; Abū al-ʿAbbās Muḥammad b. Yazīd al-Mubarrad, *Kamīl fī al-lugha*, ed. W. Wright, 2 vols. (Leipzig, 1892 [Hildesheim, 1992]), 560; al-Baghdādī, *Al-farq bayna al-firaq*, ed. Muḥammad Muḥī al-Dīn ʿAbd al-Ḥamīd (Cairo, n.d.), 76–77.

43. See, for example, al-Mubarrad, *Kamīl fī al-lugha*, ed. W. Wright, 572–73.

44. See, for example, al-Balādhurī, *Ansāb al-ashrāf*, II 364–65 (#719); al-Ṭabarī, *Ta'rīkh*, I. 3424, trans. Hawting, *The History of al-Ṭabarī* 17, 177.

45. See Cooperson, *Classical Arabic Biography*, ch. 4; Hurvitz, *The Formation of Ḥanbalism*, passim.

46. See Hurvitz, "From Scholarly Circles to Mass Movements"; Hurvitz, "Schools of Law and Historical Context."

47. See Ibn Abī Yaʿlā, *Ṭabaqāt al-fuqahā al-Ḥanābila*, ed. ʿAlī Muḥammad ʿUmar, 2 vols. (Cairo, 1998), 1.61–62.

48. See Hurvitz, "Biographies of Mild Asceticism," passim.

CHAPTER ONE

1. See, among others, Alan Cameron, "The Roman Friends of Ammianus," *JRS* 54 (1964): 15–28; Alan Cameron, "The Date and Identity of Macrobius," *JRS* 56 (1966): 25–38; Alan Cameron, "Paganism and Literature in Late Fourth Century Rome," in Alan Cameron and Manfred Fuhrmann (eds.), *Christianisme et formes littéraires de l'Antiquité tardive en Occident: Huit exposés suivis de discussions* (Geneva, 1977): 1–40; James O'Donnell, "The Demise of Paganism," *Traditio* 35 (1979): 44–88; Averil Cameron "Education and Literary Culture," in Averil Cameron and Peter Garnsey (eds.), *The Cambridge Ancient*

History, vol. 13: *The Late Empire, A.D. 337–425* (Cambridge, 1998), 665–707; Clifford Ando, "The Palladium and the Pentateuch: Towards a Sacred Topography of the Later Roman Empire," *Phoenix* 55 (2001): 369–406; Peter Brown, *Authority and the Sacred: Aspects of the Christianization of the Roman World* (Cambridge, 1995), 27–54; Peter Brown, *Power and Persuasion in Late Antiquity*; Naomi Janowitz, "Rethinking Jewish Identity in Late Antiquity," in Mitchell and Greatrex, *Ethnicity and Culture in Late Antiquity*, 205–19; James Goehring, "Monastic Diversity and Ideological Boundaries in Fourth Century Egypt," *JECS* 5 (1997): 61–83; David Brakke, "Origins and Authenticity: Studying the Reception of Greek and Roman Spiritual Traditions in Early Christian Monasticism," in David Brakke, Anders-Christian Jacobsen, and Jörg Ulrich (eds.), *Beyond Reception: Mutual Influence between Antique Religion, Judaism, and Early Christianity* (Frankfurt am Main, 2006), 175–89; Boyarin, *Dying for God*, 1–21; Elizabeth Key Fowden, *The Barbarian Plain: Saint Sergius Between Rome and Iran* (Berkeley, 1999); Stephen Mitchell, "The Cult of Theos Hypsistos between Pagans, Jews, and Christians," in M. Frede and Polymnia Athanassiadi (eds.), *Pagan Monotheism in Late Antiquity* (Oxford, 1999), 81–148; Scott Bradbury, "Julian's Pagan Revival and the Decline of Blood Sacrifice," *Phoenix* 49 (1995): 331–56. Recent studies downplaying the desire of ordinary pagans and Christians to engage members of other communities violently include Neil McLynn, "The Fourth-Century *Taurobolium*," *Phoenix* 50 (1996): 312–30; Neil McLynn, "Christian Controversy and Violence in the Fourth Century," *Kodai* 3 (1992): 15–44.

2. Important recent examples include Brown, *Authority and the Sacred*; Peter Brown, "St. Augustine's Attitude to Religious Coercion," *JRS* 54 (1964): 108–16; Drake, *Constantine and the Bishops*; H. A. Drake, "Lambs into Lions: Explaining Early Christian Intolerance," *Past and Present* 153 (1996): 3–36; Gaddis, *No Crime*; Ramsay MacMullen, *Christianity and Paganism in the Fourth to Eighth Centuries* (New Haven, 1997); Ramsay MacMullen, *Christianizing the Roman Empire A.D. 100–400* (New Haven, 1984); David Frankfurter, "Things Unbefitting Christians: Violence and Christianization in Fifth-Century Panopolis," *JECS* 8 (2000): 273–95; Gregory, *Vox Populi*; Polymnia Athanassiadi, "Persecution and Response in Late Paganism: The Evidence of Damascius," *JHS* 113 (1993): 123–45; Frank Trombley, "Religious Transition in Sixth-Century Syria," *Byzantinische Forschungen* 20 (1994): 153–95; Tessa Rajak, "Talking at Trypho: Christian Apologetic as Anti-Judaism in Justin's *Dialogue with Trypho the Jew*," in M. Edwards, M. Goodman, and S. Price (eds.), *Apologetics in the Roman Empire: Pagans, Jews, and Christians* (Oxford, 1999), 59–80; Richard Lim, "Religious and Social Disorder in Late Antiquity," *Historia* 44 (1995): 204–31; K. Holum, "Identity and the Late Antique City: The Case of Caesarea," in H. Lapin (ed.), *Religious and Ethnic Communities in Later Roman Palestine* (Bethesda, 1998), 157–77; H. Lapin, "Introduction," in H. Lapin (ed.), *Religious and Ethnic Communities*, 1–28.

3. The concept of boundaries with which I am working here was first articulated in Fredrik Barth's protean "Introduction," in Barth (ed.), *Ethnic Groups and Boundaries*. Barth's own notion of boundaries has recently been reformulated in his "Boundaries and

Connections," in Cohen (ed.), *Signifying Identities*, 17–36. Barth's 1969 article has proven crucial for many important discussions of ancient and late ancient identity issues, including John Hall's *Ethnic Identity in Greek Antiquity* (Cambridge, 2000), esp. Hall's "Introduction" and Sacha Stern's *Jewish Identity in Early Rabbinic Writings* (Leiden, 1994). Although Hall and Stern each take issue with Barth's conclusions, his methodology and general thesis frequently loom large in those authors' works.

4. Drake, *Constantine and the Bishops*, ch. 10.

5. For the "constructedness" of various kinds of identities, see Hall, *Ethnic Identity*, "Introduction" and passim.

6. For a concise and useful discussion of essentializing identity discourses, see Somers, "The Narrative Constitution of Identity," esp. 607–12.

7. Suny, "Constructing Primordialism: Old Histories for New Nations"; Suny, "Provisional Stabilities." For foundational statements of the problem, see Shils, "Primordial, Personal, Sacred and Civil Ties"; Geertz, "The Integrative Revolution," in Geertz, *The Interpretation of Cultures*, 255–310. For late antiquity, see Richard Miles, "Introduction: Constructing Identities in Late Antiquity," in Richard Miles (ed.), *Constructing Identities in Late Antiquity* (London, 1999), 1–17.

8. In addressing the question of identity here and throughout this chapter, I have tried to remain mindful of the admonitions set forth in Rogers Brubaker and Frederik Cooper, "Beyond 'Identity,'" *Theory and Society* 29 (2000): 1–47.

9. Denise Kimber Buell has fruitfully examined the ways in which second-century Christian communities thought, wrote, and contested about questions of identity and communal belonging, and did so through essentialist discourses of descent, kinship relations, and "procreative imagery." Meanwhile, Michael Phillip Penn has examined the role of the ritual kiss in "inscribing and reinforcing social boundaries" and has, in so doing, intriguingly underscored the role of boundary institution and defense as a means of defining Christianness among early Christians and Christian communities. See Buell, *Making Christians*, 95–106; Buell, *Why This New Race?*; Penn, *Kissing Christians*, 91–119, here 92.

10. *Adversus Judaeos orationes*, PG 48:843–942 (hereafter *AJ*). These sermons were treated at length in R. L. Wilken, *John Chrysostom and the Jews: Rhetoric and Reality in the Late 4th Century* (Berkeley, 1983). While Wilken supplies a wealth of historical and cultural background and subtle insights against which to read these sermons, his interpretation of their general implications and his analysis of Chrysostom's intentions in delivering them assume a model of Jewish and Christian relations which has recently been called into question by Daniel Boyarin. For Wilken, Jews and Christians are, in Antioch, two objectively separate groups, and therefore it is the actions of Christians who mix freely with Jews which must be accounted for rather than the efforts of Chrysostom to stop such practices. I want to suggest that in so proceeding, Wilken has quite understandably bought into Chrysostom's convincing and very refined strain of identity talk and so into the identity categories upon which Chrysostom insists throughout the sermons. Troublingly, however, he has done so without asking whether those categories in fact reflect the lived reality of

Chrysostom's congregation. Why Chrysostom should have to insist so strenuously upon these identity categories and upon their exclusivity and rigid parameters is a question which goes largely unasked in Wilken's study. If, as Boyarin has suggested, what we are seeing throughout the late antique world and indeed into Chrysostom's era is an ongoing conversation which unites Judaism and Christianity within a continuum of belief and practice, these sermons beg a series of questions not only about competing ways of imagining Christian identity in fourth-century Antioch but also about the strategies employed by Chrysostom toward the articulation of a discrete and bounded Christian community and identity. It is these questions with which this part of this chapter is concerned. For an illustration of the implications of Boyarin's recent work, compare, for example, Wilken's discussion of "Judaizing Christians" and "Jewish Christians" (68–79) with Boyarin's discussion of the same question in Boyarin, *Dying for God*, 1–21. See now Boyarin, *Border Lines*, passim. See also Charlotte Elisheva Fonrobert, "Jewish Christians, Judaizers, and Christian Anti-Judaism," in Virginia Burrus (ed.), *Late Ancient Christianity* (Minneapolis, 2005), 234–54. See also Wayne Meeks and Robert Wilkens, *Jews and Christians in Antioch* (Missoula, 1978); J. N. D. Kelly, *Golden Mouth: John Chrysostom Ascetic, Preacher, Bishop* (Ithaca, 1995), 2–10, 63–66. Translated sources include Wendy Mayer and Pauline Allen, *John Chrysostom* (New York, 2000); Gilbert Dagron, "Judaïser," *Travaux et Mémoirés* 11 (1991): 359–80; M. S. Taylor, *Anti-Judaism and Early Christian Identity* (Leiden, 1995). J. H. W. G. Liebeschuetz, *Antioch: City and Imperial Administration in the Later Roman Empire* (Oxford, 1972). On Chrysostom's preaching and conceptions of community, see now Aideen H. Hartney, *John Chrysostom and the Transformation of the City* (Oxford, 2004). For an English translation of the sermons, see Paul W. Harkins, *Saint John Chrysostom: Discourses Against Judaizing Christians* (Washington, D.C., 1977).

11. For Chrysostom's use of military metaphors in invective attacks, see Wilken, *John Chrysostom and the Jews*, 110. Obviously, the specific connotations of the military metaphor deployed in each situation are crucial to understanding the specific point to be made with it. As will be seen below, the frequent use of military metaphors for the acts of martyrs Wilken cites is of special interest here.

12. Wilken, *John Chrysostom and the Jews*, 116–20.

13. Wilken, *John Chrysostom and the Jews*, 66–68, 75–58. For the participation of Antioch's Christians in "pagan" New Year's celebrations and Chrysostom's condemnation of the festivals and instructions to his parishioners to stay away from these, see Maud Gleason, "Festive Satire: Julian's *Misopogon* and the New Year at Antioch," *JRS* 76 (1986): 106–19 and esp. 110. Participation in Jewish festivals and the calendar in accordance with which they were celebrated had long been sites of Jewish communal boundary maintenance as well. See Stern, *Jewish Identity*, 77–79.

14. For the definitive discussion of the concept of "Judaizing" in the ancient and late ancient world, see Shaye J. D. Cohen, *The Beginnings of Jewishness: Boundaries, Varieties, Uncertainties* (Berkeley, 1999), 175–98.

15. *AJ* 1.1.5.

16. Hence *AJ* 1.3.1 [PG 48.844–45]; cf. *AJ* 1.3.7. [PG 48.848]. See also Fonrobert, "Jewish Christians, Judaizers, and Christian Anti-Judaism," 238–40. Cf. Wilken, *John Chrysostom and the Jews*, 66–94.

17. *AJ* 1.3.1 [PG 48.844–45].

18. *AJ* 1.3.4–5 [PG 48.847–48].

19. Peter Brown "Asceticism: Pagan and Christian," in *CAH* 13; Peter Brown, *The Body and Society: Men, Women and Sexual Renunciation in Early Christianity* (New York, 1988), 201–22. See now Eliezer Diamond, *Holy Men and Hunger Artists: Fasting and Asceticism in Rabbinic Culture* (Oxford, 2003).

20. For Manichaeans, see S. N. C. Lieu, "The Self-Identity of Manichaeans in the Roman East," *Mediterranean Archaeology* 11 (1998): 205–27; J. BeDuhn, "Regimen for Salvation: Medical Models in Manichaean Asceticism" *Semeia* 58 (1992): 109–26; For pagans, see Garth Fowden, "The Pagan Holy Man in Late Antique Society," *JHS* 102 (1982): 33–59; J. N. Bremmer, "Symbols of Marginality from Early Pythagoreans to Late Antique Monks," *Greece & Rome* 39 (1992): 205–14; A. Henrichs, "Mani and the Babylonian Baptists: A Historical Confrontation," *Harvard Studies in Classical Philology* 77 (1973): 23–59. For the importance of fasting among rabbinical Jews, see, for example, the uses of fasting alluded to in Naomi Janowitz, "Rabbis and Their Opponents: The Construction of the 'Min' in Rabbinic Anecdotes," *JECS* 6 (1998): 449–62.

21. *AJ* 2.1.1 [PG 48.857].

22. *AJ* 4.1.6–2.6 [PG 48.873].

23. This is a distinction also made on the basis of narrative-based notions of identity and the historical narratives articulated in accordance with these. This is an issue to be taken up in the next chapter.

24. *AJ* 4.2.6 [PG 48.874]. The murders committed by Phinehas (Num. 25) occur in the context of a more generalized outbreak of communal boundary transgression—Israelite men have begun sleeping with Moabite women and the women began to invite the men to the sacrifices performed to their gods. Eventually the Israelite men begin to sacrifice to the foreign gods as well. Moses eventually declares Phinehas's act righteous because it reaffirmed Israelite communal boundaries and appeased the Hebrew God. Cf. Stern, *Jewish Identity*, 166 for the exaltation of Phinehas's murders among Jewish rabbis as instances of righteous violence and particularly for a brief analysis of an exceedingly gory Midrashic passage treating the Numbers passage cited above. See also John J. Collins, "The Zeal of Phinehas: The Bible and the Legitimation of Violence," *Journal of Biblical Literature* (2003): 3–21. I am indebted to Hugh Horan for bringing this article to my attention.

25. For the synagogue in late antiquity, see the articles collected in Lee I. Levine (ed.), *The Synagogue in Late Antiquity* (Philadelphia, 1987), esp. 159–81.

26. *AJ* 1.6.3 [PG 48.851–52].

27. *AJ* 1.6.2–3 [PG 48.851–52]. The site to which Chrysostom makes reference here, "Matrona's," seems to have been not a synagogue but in fact a Jewish shrine for the Maccabean martyrs, which sat near the famous shrine to Apollo. Here again, members of

Chrysostom's congregation will have found themselves confronted with an outpost of the holy which will have resonated with the semiotic system with which the orthodox Christian community of Antioch imagined its own history, particularly after Gregory Nazianzus's invention of the Maccabean martyrs as signs with which to recall its time of trials under Julian. See M. Vinson, "Gregory Nazianzen's *Homily 15* and the Genesis of the Christian Cult of the Maccabean Martyrs," *Byzantion* 64 (1994): 166–92, esp. 183–84, notes 54–56. Cf. Tessa Rajak, "Dying for the Law: The Martyr's Portrait in Jewish-Greek Literature," in M. J. Edwards and S. Swain (eds.), *Portraits: Biographical Representation in the Greek and Latin Literature of the Roman Empire* (Oxford, 1997), 40–67. And even in centers of Christian community, supposed bits and pieces of the bodies of the Hebrew prophets to whom Chrysostom makes reference were making their way into local churches and martyr shrines to be adored and to mark out local sites of numinous power. Thus local Christian communities understood themselves to have been founded, as Andrew Jacobs has recently put it, "on the remains of a Jew." Andrew Jacobs, "The Remains of a Jew: Imperial Christian Identity in the Late Ancient Holy Land," *JMEMS* 33 (2003): 23–45. See now Christine Shepardson, "Controlling Contested Places: John Chrysostom's *Adversus Iudaeos* Homilies and the Spatial Politics of Religious Controversy," *JECS* 15 (2007): 483–516.

28. See Wilken, *John Chrysostom and the Jews*, 66–94. See now Jacobs, *Remains of the Jew*.

29. See Smith, *To Take Place*; Miruchi "Place of Ritual in Our Time."

30. The insides of many synagogues were becoming less and less unlike churches, so D. Milson, "Ecclesiastical Furniture in Late Antique Synagogue," in Mitchell and Greatrex, *Identity in Late Antiquity*, 221–40. For a later period, see S. Fine, "'Chancel' Screens in Late Antique Palestinian Synagogues: A Source from the Cairo Genizah," in H. Lapin (ed.), *Religious and Ethnic Communities in Later Roman Palestine*, 67–85. For the creep of "pagan" decorative motifs into synagogues, see Sacha Stern, "Pagan Images in Late Antique Synagogues," in Mitchell and Greatrex, *Identity in Late Antiquity*, 241–52.

31. *AJ* 6.5.9 [PG 48.912].

32. *AJ* 6.6.6–7.2 [PG 48.914].

33. *AJ* 6.6.11 [PG 48.914].

34. Mayer and Allen, *John Chrysostom*, 148–50.

35. Gleason, "Festive Satire," passim.

36. Chrysostom did not, of course, invent these as markers of communal belonging. All of these had been important practices for the ascription of Jewish identity among rabbinical Jews for centuries. For the problem of early Jewish communal boundaries generally see Cohen, *The Beginnings of Jewishness*. See also Judith Lieu, "'Impregnable Ramparts and Walls of Iron': Boundary and Identity in Early 'Judaism' and 'Christianity,'" *New Testament Studies* 48 (2002): 297–313; Tessa Rajak, "The Jewish Community and Its Boundaries," in Judith Lieu, John North, and Tessa Rajak (eds.), *The Jews among Pagans and Christians in the Roman Empire* (London, 1992), 9–28. For festivals, see Stern, *Jewish Identity*, 56–59, 77–78, 80, 151–52, 165–66, 221–25; Gary G. Porton, *Goyim: Gentiles and Israelites in*

Mishna-Tosefta (Atlanta, 1988), 140–71, 205–20, 236–46. For the important but changing significance of temples and synagogues, see A. Kerkeslager, "Jewish Pilgrimage and Jewish Identity in Hellenistic and Early Roman Egypt," in D. Frankfurter (ed.), *Pilgrimage and Holy Space in Late Antique Egypt* (Leiden, 1998), 99–225; Shaye Cohen, "Pagan and Christian Evidence on the Ancient Synagogue," in L. Levine (ed.), *Synagogue*, 159–81. For circumcision, see Stern, *Jewish Identity*, 3–6, 229–32; Porton, *Goyim*, 164–71, 232–35; Cohen, *Beginnings of Jewishness*, 183–93, 214–21.

37. For Jews who similarly ignored the communal boundaries insisted upon by rabbis and the view of such Jews among rabbis, see Stern, *Jewish Identity*, 114–38.

38. Boyarin, *Dying for God*, 6ff.

39. Boyarin, *Dying for God*, 10. See now Boyarin, *Border Lines*.

40. See Alan Cameron, "The Roman Friends of Ammianus"; Alan Cameron, "The Date and Identity of Macrobius"; Alan Cameron, "Paganism and Literature"; Averil Cameron, "Education and Literary Culture"; Ando, "The Palladium and the Pentateuch," esp. 371–73.

41. See, for example, with regard to the confessional mix to be found in late antique monasteries, those supposed seed-beds of "orthodoxy," Goehring, "Monastic Diversity." For new studies which question such constructions as "Jewish Christianity" and instead suggest a continuum of what Boyarin has called "Judeo-Christian" practice and belief, see Fonrobert, "The Didascalia Apostolorum"; Becker, "Anti-Judaism and Care for the Poor." For the conspicuous lack of any central church authority in the city of Rome before Constantine, see now Bill Leadbetter, "Constantine and the Bishop: The Roman Church in the Early Fourth Century," *Journal of Religious History* 26 (2002): 1–14. See also note 1 above.

42. Sargis Istunaya de-Gusit, *The Disputation of Sergius the Stylite against a Jew* XXII, ed. and trans. Allison Peter Hayman, CSCO 338 (Syr 52) 73–74; CSCO 339 (Syr 153) (Louvain, 1973), 72. The Syriac text has been dated variously to the sixth and to the eighth or early ninth century. See CSCO 339, 1–6.

43. See David Frankfurter, "The Perils of Love: Magic and Counter Magic in Coptic Egypt," *Journal of the History of Sexuality* 10 (2001): 480–500; David Frankfurter, "Collections of Recipes: Introduction," in Marvin Meyer and Richard Smith (eds.), *Ancient Christian Magic: Coptic Texts of Ritual Power* (San Francisco, 1994), 259–62; David Frankfurter, *Religion in Roman Egypt: Assimilation and Resistance* (Princeton, 1998), 257–64. See Shaul Shaked, "Popular Religion in Sasanian Babylonia," *JSAI* 21 (1997): 103–17, esp. 105–6 for Jewish, Christian, Zoroastrian, Mandean and pagan use of prayer bowls. And one wonders what these Church fathers would have made of the finds recently made in the Egyptian monastery of another Epiphanius, a sixth-century monk and archimandrite. Although the walls of his complex were painted with selections from properly Monophysite (and so orthodox by local reckoning) tracts, the monk and his community seem to have worked charms and spells using such ingredients as bits of scripture mixed with pieces of ancient mummies, thus significantly blurring the lines between holy healing and traditional magic.

See L. S. B. MacCoull, "Prophethood, Texts, and Artifacts: The Monastery of Epiphanius," *GRBS* 39 (1998): 307–24.

44. For the involvement of women in such projects, see, for example, Mark the Deacon, *The Life of Porphyry of Gaza*, 40 for the (perhaps fictional) efforts of the empress Eudoxia on behalf of the eradication of paganism in Gaza, and the perhaps more historical report regarding John Chrysostom's female patrons by Theodoret in his *Ecclesiastical History* 5.29 (trans. B. Jackson, NPNF ser. 2, vol. 3): "On receiving information that Phoenicia was still suffering from the madness of the demons' rites, John got together certain monks who were fired with divine zeal, armed them with imperial edicts and dispatched them against the idols' shrines. The money which was required to pay the craftsmen and their assistants who were engaged in the work of destruction was not taken by John from imperial resources, but he persuaded certain wealthy and faithful women to make liberal contributions, pointing out to them how great would be the blessings their generosity would win."

45. David Brakke, "'Outside the Places, Within the Truth': Athanasius of Alexandria and the Localization of the Holy," in Frankfurter, *Pilgrimage*, 445–81 and esp. 465–67.

46. See James Goehring, "The Dark Side of Landscape: Ideology and Power in the Christian Myth of the Desert," *JMEMS* 33.3 (2003): 437–51. For the suggestion that Antony was claimed by Arians, see Robert C. Gregg and Dennis Groh, *Early Arianism: A View of Salvation* (Philadelphia, 1981), 135ff.

47. David Brakke, *Athanasius and the Politics of Asceticism* (Oxford, 1995), passim.

48. Julian *Epistle* 61, ed. J. Bidez, *L'empereur Julien: Oeuvres Complètes*, 2 vols. in 4 parts (Paris, 1924), 1.2 72–75. For Julian more generally, see Polymnia Athanassiadi-Fowden, *Julian and Hellenism: An Intellectual Biography* (Oxford, 1981); Vasiliki Limberis, "'Religion' as the Cipher for Identity: The Cases of Emperor Julian, Libanius and Gregory Nazianzus," *Harvard Theological Review* 93 (2000): 373–400.

49. Raymond Van Dam, *Empire of Snow: Roman Rule and Greek Culture in Cappadocia* (Philadelphia, 2002), 196ff.; Socrates Scholasticus, *Historia Ecclesiastica* 3.16, ed. and French trans. Pierre Périchon and Pierre Maraval, *Socrate de Constantinople, Histoire Ecclésiastique*, 2 vols. (SC 477, 493) (Paris, 2004–5), 2.308–17, English trans. A. C. Zenos, NPNF ser. 2, vol. 2. All references are to this translation. Sozomenos, *HE* 5.18, trans. Chester D. Hartranft, NPNF ser. 2, vol. 2. All references are to this translation. See also Stern, *Jewish Identity*, 176–81 for Jewish anxieties over the problem of "Greek Wisdom."

50. Drake, *Constantine and the Bishops*, 434–36.

51. Drake, *Constantine and the Bishops*, 436.

52. See now Susanna Elm, "Hellenism and Historiography: Gregory of Nazianzus and Julian in Dialogue," *JMEMS* 33 (2003): 493–515 for a discussion of the effects of Julian's move on the thinking of Gregory of Nazianzus with regard to the proper relationship between Hellenic culture and Christianity.

53. Julian *Or.* 7.18.224a.

54. By far, the most impressive studies of this phenomenon are those collected in

James Goehring, *Ascetics, Society and the Desert: Studies in Early Egyptian Monasticism* (Harrisburg, Pa., 1999); J. Rebecca Lyman, "Ascetics and Bishops: Epiphanius on Orthodoxy," in Susanna Elm, Éric Rebillard, and Antonella Romano (eds.), *Orthodoxie, Christianisme, Histoire/Orthodoxy, Christianity, History* (Rome, 2000), 149–61; Virginia Burrus, *The Making of a Heretic: Gender, Authority, and the Priscillianist Controversy* (Berkeley, 2005); Goehring, "Monastic Diversity"; Phillip Rousseau, "Orthodoxy and the Cenobite," *SP* 30 (1997): 239–56; Daniel Caner, "Notions of 'Strict Discipline' and Apostolic Tradition in Early Definitions of Orthodox Monasticism," in Elm, Rebillard, and Romano, *Orthodoxie, Christianisme, Histoire*, 23–34; Susanna Elm, "*Virgins of God*": *The Making of Asceticism in Late Antiquity* (Oxford, 1994), 150–91, 347–74; David Hunter, "Rereading the Jovianist Controversy: Asceticism and Clerical Authority in Late Ancient Christianity," *JMEMS* 33 (2003): 453–70. For heresy in general, see A. Le Boulluec, *La notion d'hérésie dans la littérature grecque IIe–IIIe siècles*, 2 vols. (Paris, 1985). Cf. Elm, Rebillard, and Romano, passim; Rebecca Lyman, "2002 NAPS Presidential Address: Hellenism and Heresy," *JECS* 11 (2003): 209–22; Averil Cameron, "How to Read Heresiology," *JMEMS* 33 (2003): 471–92.

55. Augustine, *De opere monachorum* 36, ed. Joseph Zycha, CSEL 41 (Leipzig, 1906), 585–86.

56. Julian 7.5.210b–7.18.224a–d. See Margarethe Billerbeck, "The Ideal Cynic from Epictetus to Julian," in R. Bracht Branham, Marie-Odile Goulet-Cazé, (eds.), *The Cynics: The Cynic Movement in Antiquity and its Legacy* (Berkeley, 1996), 205–21.

57. Augustine, *De opere monachorum* 36, ed. Zycha, CSEL 41, 585–86.

58. Boyarin, *Dying for God*, 34, citing M. S. Zuckermandel (ed.), *Tosephta: Based on the Erfurt and Vienna Codices, with Lieberman, Saul*, "Supplement" to the *Tosephta* (in Hebrew) (Jersusalem, 1937), 227. Boyarin interestingly interprets this text to suggest that the snakebite itself is the result of prior associations by Ben Dama with Christians, and his death (in which he slips away without having "broken down fences" is a kind of rehabilitation (34ff.). Cf. Stern, *Jewish Identity*, 105–35, 52–79, 139–94 for a vivid discussion of the various and clearly quite compelling anxieties concerning boundary transgression, apostasy, heresy, intercommunal sexual contacts and other forms of pollution by repulsive communal others as they are manifested in rabbinical writings.

59. Boyarin, *Dying for God*, 34ff. Cf. Stern, *Jewish Identity*, 140 for rabbinical texts featuring pious Jews who would rather "be martyred" than mix with Gentiles.

60. *AJ* 8.5.4 [PG 48.935].

61. *AJ* 5.12.12 [PG 48.904]. Chrysostom elsewhere exhorts members of his congregations to exercise surveillance over one another and to compel compliance with communal norms (see, for example, his sermon "To Those Who Had Not Attended the Assembly," 1–2), though throughout this cycle of sermons Chrysostom returns repeatedly to this admonition, and the individual parishioner's duty to police his or her fellow Christian's behavior, and to "command and forbid" on issues of communal boundary transgression becomes the cycle's organizing theme.

62. PG 56.263–70, trans. Allen and Mayer, *John Chrysostom*, 118–25.

63. PG 56.268–9, trans. Allen and Mayer, *John Chrysostom*, 123–24.

64. *AJ* 8.4.4 [PG 48.933]. For interceding Christians as respected in their community, see *AJ* 8.7.6 [PG 48.938].

65. *AJ* 3.1.3 [PG 48.861–62]; *AJ* 3.1.6 [PG 48.863]. Cf. Boyarin, *Border Lines*, 37–73.

66. *AJ* 3.1.7 [PG 48.863].

67. For similar arguments made by Jewish rabbis concerning the *Minim*, see Stern, *Jewish Identity*, 109–12.

68. Many of the same metaphors would recur in his homily against the theaters and games. See, for example, PG 56.268–70, trans. Allen and Mayer, *John Chrysostom*, 123–25, where Chrysostom conjures hunting imagery, healing imagery, and the metaphor of the shepherd, all of them deployed to suggest the defense of communal boundaries.

69. Risking his own life: *AJ* 1.4.8 [PG 48.849]. Using force: *AJ* 1.4.5 [PG 48.849]. Suffering violence: *AJ* 4.7.9 [PG 48.882]. Willingness to lay down life: *AJ* 4.7.3 [PG 48.881]. Going into homes: *AJ* 8.5.2 [PG 48.934]. Christians seeking Christians like hunters and fishermen: *AJ* 2.1.4–5 [PG 48.857–58]. Christian soldiers like Roman soldiers in the field, with severe penalty for preferring enemy to fellow soldiers: *AJ* 1.4.9 [PG 48.849]. See also *AJ* 4.3.5 [PG 48.875].

70. *AJ* 4.7.3 [PG 48.881].

71. *AJ* 4.7.9 [PG 48.882]. See also *AJ* 4.7.11 [PG 48.882].

72. *AJ* 6.7.9 [PG 48.916].

73. *AJ* 8.4.3 [PG 48.933].

74. *AJ* 7.6.10 [PG 48.927–28].

75. *AJ* 8.4.5–9 [PG 48.933–34].

76. *AJ* 8.4.5–10 [PG 48.933–34].

77. *AJ* 8.5.2–4 [PG 48.934].

78. For responsibility and its role in the formation of religion out of "demonic" revelation, see Jacques Derrida, *The Gift of Death* (Chicago, 1995), 3.

79. For the fetish as a concept which was invented and evolved in "unstable spaces" and, more specifically, in conjunction with the frequent transgression of boundaries and borders, see William Pietz, "The Problem of the Fetish, I," *Res* 9 (1985): 5–17; William Pietz, "The Problem of the Fetish, II," *Res* 13 (1987): 23–45; William Pietz, "The Problem of the Fetish, IIIa," *Res* 16 (1988): 105–23. See also Patricia Spyer, "Introduction," in Patricia Spyer (ed.), *Border Fetishisms: Material Objects in Unstable Spaces* (New York, 1998), 1–11.

80. On the desirability of communal boundaries which may be both strenuously and strategically insisted upon and generally transgressed, see David Nirenberg, *Communities of Violence: Persecution of Minorities in the Middle Ages* (Princeton, 1996). For the independence of boundaries with regard to the "cultural stuff" they are said to contain, see Barth, "Introduction," 15.

81. Michael Taussig, *Defacement: The Public Secret and the Labor of the Negative*

(Stanford, 1999) passim and esp. 2–3: "Yet what if the truth is not so much a secret as a *public* secret, as in the case with most important social knowledge, *knowing what not to know?* . . . For are not shared secrets the basis of our social institutions, the workplace, the market, the family, and the state? Is not such public secrecy the most interesting, the most powerful, the most mischievous and ubiquitous form of socially active knowledge there is? What we call doctrine, ideology, consciousness, beliefs, values and even discourse, pale into sociological insignificance and philosophical banality by comparison: for it is the task and life force of the public secret to maintain that verge where the secret is not destroyed through exposure, but subject to a quite different sort of revelation that does justice to it."

82. For the character of Roman power relations in the fourth century, see Van Dam, *Kingdom of Snow*, 122–25. For the classic treatment of the public secret in Roman imperial politics, see Andrew Wallace-Hadrill, "Civilis-Princeps: Between Citizen and King," *JRS* 72 (1982): 32–48.

83. Taussig, *Defacement*, 2.

84. Taussig, *Defacement*, 49–77.

85. *AJ* 8.4.1 [PG 48.932].

86. Chrysostom's penchant for disciplining his community seems, for example, to have been considered remarkable by Theodoret: "When the great John had received the tiller of the Church, he boldly convicted certain wrong doers, made seasonable exhortations to the emperor and empress, and admonished the clergy to live according to the laws laid down. Transgressors against these laws he forbade to approach the churches, urging that they who showed no desire to live the life of true priests ought not to enjoy priestly honor. He acted with this care for the church not only in Constantinople, but throughout the whole of Thrace, which is divided into six provinces, and likewise of Asia, which is governed by eleven governors. Pontica too, which has a like number of rulers with Asia, was happily brought by him under the same discipline" (*Ecclesiastical History* 5.28: trans. B. Jackson, NPNF ser. 2, vol. 3). For a comparably kindred role for monks and martyrs in the defense of Antioch's Christian community, see Chrysostom's 17th Homily on the Statues (PG 49.171–80; translation Allen and Mayer, *John Chrysostom*, 104–17).

87. See Andrea Sterk, *Renouncing the World Yet Leading the Church: The Monk Bishop in Late Antiquity* (Berkeley, 2004), ch. 6.

CHAPTER TWO

1. And near contemporaries. See, for example, the Coptic preacher and archimandrite Shenoute railing against the "pagan" practices of Christians in Egypt, such acts as tying snakes' heads, crocodile teeth, and fox claws to parts of their bodies as magical cures. He, like Chrysostom, demands that his parishioners make a choice: "If the oracle's sanctuary of demons is useful to you . . . then go there. But if it is the house of God, the Church, that is useful for you, go to it." See Richard Valantasis (ed.), *Religions of Late Antiquity in*

Practice (Princeton, 2000), 475 for David Frankfurter's translation of this and another Shenoutean tirade about such boundary-blurring behavior.

2. Vinson, "Genesis of the Christian Cult of the Maccabean Martyrs," passim.

3. Vinson, "Genesis of the Christian Cult of the Maccabean Martyrs," passim.

4. Vinson, "Genesis of the Christian Cult of the Maccabean Martyrs," 185–86.

5. The literature on the shared semiotic world of the late Roman world is prodigious and growing, see, among others, Daniel Boyarin, "'Semantic Differences,' or, 'Judaism'/'Christianity,'" in Adam H. Becker and Annette Yoshiko Reed (eds.), *The Ways That Never Parted: Jews and Christians in Late Antiquity and the Early Middle Ages* (Tübingen, 2003), 65–86; Robin Cormack, "The Visual Arts"; Drake, *Constantine and the Bishops*; Frankfurter, *Religion in Roman Egypt*; Gleason, "Festive Satire"; Rebecca Lyman, "The Politics of Passing: Justin Martyr's Conversion as a Problem of 'Hellenization,'" in Kenneth Mills and Anthony Grafton (eds.), *Conversion in Late Antiquity and the Early Middle Ages: Seeing and Believing* (Rochester, 2003), 36–60; Michael Maas, "Roman History and Christian Ideology in Justinianic Reform Legislation," *Dumbarton Oaks Papers* 40 (1986): 17–31; Michael Maas, *John Lydus and the Roman Past* (London, 1992); Stern, "Pagan Images"; Susan Walker, "Painted Hellenes: Mummy Portraits from Late Roman Egypt," in Simon Swain and Mark Edwards (eds.), *Approaching Late Antiquity: The Transformation from the Early to the Late Empire* (Oxford, 2003), 310–26; Alan Cameron, "Poetry and Literary Culture in Late Antiquity," in Swain and Edwards (eds.), *Approaching Late Antiquity*, 327–54; Mark Edwards, "Pagan and Christian Monotheism in the Age of Constantine," in Swain and Edwards, (eds.), *Approaching Late Antiquity*, 211–34. Milson, "Ecclesiastical Furniture in Late Antique Synagogue"; Fine, "'Chancel' Screens."

6. Somers, "The Narrative Constitution of Identity," 617; Polleta, "Contending Stories"; Polleta, "'It was Like a Fever . . .'"; Ricoeur, *Time and Narrative*, vol. 1, ch. 2; Kreisworth, "Merely Telling Stories"; Bruner, "The Narrative Construction of Reality"; White, "The Value of Narrativity." For some recent applications of theoretical models developed in the study of modern ethnic or nationalist sentiment, see, for example, Denise Kimber Buell, "Race and Universality in Early Christianity," *JECS* 10 (2002): 429–68; Denise Kimber Buell, "Rethinking the Relevance of Race for Early Christian Self-Definition," *Harvard Theological Review* 94 (2001): 449–76; Vasiliki Limberis, "'Religion' as the Cipher for Identity"; Johnson, "Identity, Descent, and Polemic."

7. Somers, "Narrative Constitution of Identity," 613–14. See also Polletta, "Contending Stories," esp. 419–26.

8. Ronald Grigor Suny, "Provisional Stabilities," esp. 146.

9. Suny, "Provisional Stabilities," 157.

10. Marcus Tanner, *Croatia: A Nation Forged in War* (New Haven, 1997), 247. Serbian fears regarding Croatian nationalism were stoked by the adoption of some Croat nationalists—notable among them Franjo Truðman—of apologist attitudes toward the horrors perpetrated by the Ustasche against Serbian civilians, as well as such anti-fascist Croatian victims as the "December Victims," a group of Croatian intellectuals hanged by the Us-

tasche in December of 1943. It is now estimated that of the 1,027,000 people killed during the Second World War in Yugoslavia, 530,000 were Serbs. For rehabilitation of the Ustashe by some Croatian nationalists in the early 1990s, see Alex J. Bellamy, *The Formation of Croatian National Identity: A Centuries-old Dream* (Manchester, UK, 2003), ch. 4, esp. 65–71. For the Yugoslav death toll during WWII, see Arnold Suffan, "Yugoslavianism Versus Serbian, Croatian, and Slovene Nationalism: Political, Ideological, and Cultural Causes of the Rise and Fall of Yugoslavia," in Norman M. Naimark and Holly Case (eds.), *Yugoslavia and Its Historians: Understanding the Balkan Wars of the 1990s* (Stanford, 2003), 116–39, esp. 129–30.

11. David Reiff, *Slaughterhouse: Bosnia and the Failure of the West* (London, 1995), 103. See also Ivan Čolovic, *Politics of Identity in Serbia: Essays in Political Anthropology* (New York, 2002).

12. Suny, "Provisional Stabilities," 176.

13. See, for example, Margaret R. Somers, "Narrativity, Narrative Identity and Social Action: Rethinking English Working-Class Formation," *Social Science History* 16 (1992): 591–629; Polleta, "Contending Stories"; Peter S. Bearman and Katherine Stovel, "Becoming a Nazi: A Model for Narrative Networks," *Poetics* 27 (2000): 69–90.

14. Wilken, *John Chrysostom and the Jews*, 76.

15. Wilken, *John Chrysostom and the Jews*, 75–79.

16. For earlier Christian practices, see *AJ* 3.3.1 [PG 48.864–65]. For the precedent of Christ keeping the Pasch with the Jews, being circumcised, keeping the Sabbath, observing festival days and eating unleavened bread, see *AJ* 3.3.9 [PG 48.866].

17. *AJ* 3.3.4 [PG 48.865]. For Chrysostom and the martyrs, see Gus George Christo, *Martyrdom According to John Chrysostom: "To Live is Christ, To Die is Gain"* (New York, 1997). See also William Tabbernee, "Eusebius' 'Theology of Persecution': As Seen in the Various Editions of His Church History," *JECS* 5 (1997): 319–34; Drake, *Constantine and the Bishops*, 356–80; Averil Cameron, "Eusebius of Caesarea and the Rethinking of History," in Emilio Gabba (ed.), *Tria Corda: Scritti in onore di Arnaldo Momigliano* (Como, 1983), 71–88. For important recent treatments of the Christian Martyrs, see Glen Bowersock, *Martyrdom and Rome* (Cambridge, 1995); Buell, *Why This New Race*, 52–62; Brent Shaw, "Judicial Nightmares and Christian Memory," *JECS* 11 (2003): 533–63; Maud Gleason, "Truth Contests and Talking Corpses," in James I. Porter (ed.), *Constructions of the Classical Body* (Ann Arbor, 1999), 287–313; Lucy Grig, "Torture and Truth in Late Antique Martyrology," *Early Medieval Europe* 11 (2002): 321–36; Carlin A. Barton, "Savage Miracles: The Redemption of Lost Honor in Roman Society and the Sacrament of the Gladiator and the Martyr," *Representations* 45 (1994): 41–71; Boyarin, *Dying for God*; Daniel Boyarin, "'Language Inscribed by History on the Bodies of Living Beings': Midrash and Martyrdom," *Representations* 25 (1989): 139–51; Daniel Boyarin, "Martyrdom and the Making of Christianity and Judaism," *JECS* 6 (1998): 577–627; Drake, *Constantine and the Bishops*, 84–85, 98–103; Markus, *The End of Ancient Christianity*, 92–95, 142–51; Peter Brown, *The Cult of the Saints: Its Rise and Function in Latin Christianity* (Chicago, 1981); Peter Brown,

"Enjoying the Saints in Late Antiquity," *Early Medieval Europe* 9 (2000): 1–19; Theodore Baumeister, *Martyr Invictus: Der Martyrer als Sinnbild der Erlösung in der Legende und im Kult der frühen koptischen Kirche* (Münster, 1972); Gillian Clark, "Bodies and Blood: Late Antique Debate on Martyrdom, Virginity and Resurrection," in Dominic Montserrat (ed.), *Changing Bodies, Changing Meanings: Studies on the Human Body in Antiquity* (New York, 1998), 99–115; Gillian Clark, "Victricius of Rouen: *Praising the Saints*," *JECS* 7 (1999): 365–99; Gillian Clark, "Translating Relics: Victricius of Rouen and Fourth Century Debate," *Early Medieval Europe* 10 (2001): 161–76; David G. Hunter, "Vigilantius of Calagurris and Victricius of Rouen: Ascetics, Relics, and Clerics in Late Roman Gaul," *JECS* 7 (1999): 401–30; Jill Ross, "Dynamic Bodies and Martyrs' Bodies in Prudentius' *Peristephanon*," *JECS* 3 (1995): 325–55; Brent D. Shaw, "Body/Power/Identity: Passions of the Martyrs," *JECS* 4 (1996): 269–312; Brent D. Shaw, "The Passion of Perpetua," *Past & Present* 139 (1993): 3–45; Terry Wilfong, "Reading the Disjointed Body in Coptic," in Montserrat, *Changing Bodies, Changing Meanings*, 116–36; Gaddis, *No Crime*, ch. 1; Carole Straw, "Settling Scores: Eschatology in the Church of the Martyrs," in Caroline Walker Bynum and Paul Freedman (eds.), *Last Things: Death and the Apocalypse in the Middle Ages* (Philadelphia, 2000), 21–40; Alan Thacker, "*Loca Sanctorum*: The Significance of Place in the Study of the Saints," in Alan Thacker and Richard Sharpe (eds.), *Local Saints and Local Churches in the Early Medieval West* (Oxford, 2002), 1–43; Alan Thacker, "The Making of a Local Saint," in Thacker and Sharpe, *Local Saints*, 45–73.

18. For a rather similar use of the council by Athanasius, see Virginia Burrus, *Begotten Not Made: Conceiving Manhood in Late Antiquity* (Stanford, 2000), 66–69; See also Boyarin, *Border Lines*, 194–97.

19. John Chrysostom, *AJ* 3.3.5 [PG 48.865]. For Rabbinical Jewish uses of imagined genealogies of fathers and the pronouncements of those fathers as resources for communal boundaries, see Boyarin, *Border Lines*, 76–86.

20. The term is Mircea Eliade's. See his *Aspets de mythe* (Paris, 1963), 15, cited by Jonathan Z. Smith, "The Wobbling Pivot," in Jonathan Z. Smith, *Map Is Not Territory: Studies in the History of Religion* (Chicago, 1993), 88–103.

21. Eusebius, *Historia Ecclesiastica* 8.1.2–3 ed. and trans. J. E. L. Oulton and H. J. Lawlor, *Eusebius: The Ecclesiastical History*, 2 vols. (Cambridge, Mass., 1932 [2000]), 250–53. I have used this translation throughout.

22. Eusebius, *HE*, 8.1.7. ed. and trans. Oulton and Lawlor, 250–53.

23. Eusebius, *HE*, 8.1.8. ed. and trans. Oulton and Lawlor, 254–55.

24. Eusebius, *HE*, 8.2.2–3. ed. and trans. Oulton and Lawlor, 256–57.

25. Although, as Eusebius notes, it was sometimes unclear even to contemporaries precisely who these individuals were: "One man was brought to the abominable and unholy sacrifices by the violence of others who pressed around him, and dismissed as if he had sacrificed, even though he had not; another who did not so much as approach or touch any accursed thing, when others had said that he has sacrificed, went away bearing the false accusation in silence." See Eusebius, *HE*, 8.3.2. ed. and trans. Oulton and Lawlor, 258–59.

26. For the role of narrative in making large, traumatic events comprehensible within a plot and therefore imbuing them with meaning, see Polletta, "Contending Stories," 419–26; For the role of communal boundaries in questions of identity, see Barth, "Introduction" and Barth, "Boundaries and Connections."

27. For the sacred topographies of the Roman world, see, among others, Ando, "The Palladium and the Pentateuch"; Jas Elsner, "The *Itinerarium Burdigalense*: Politics and Salvation in the Geography of Constantine's Empire," *JRS* 90 (2000): 181–95; Michelle Salzman, "The Christianization of Sacred Time and Space," in W. V. Harris (ed.), *The Transformations of* Urbs Roma *in Late Antiquity* (Journal of Roman Archaeology Supplement 33) (Portsmouth, R.I., 1999), 123–34; Markus, *End of Ancient Christianity*.

28. Clifford Ando, *Imperial Ideology and Provincial Loyalty in the Roman Empire* (Berkeley, 2000), 206–9, 385–98.

29. For the pornographic character of some late ancient martyr accounts, see Virginia Burrus, "Reading Agnes: The Rhetoric of Gender in Ambrose and Prudentius," *JECS* 3 (1995): 25–46. For the aesthetics of martyr literature, see, among others, Anne-Marie Palmer, *Prudentius on the Martyrs* (Oxford, 1989); Martha Malamud, *A Poetics of Transformation: Prudentius and Classical Mythology* (Ithaca, 1989); Michael Roberts, *Poetry and the Cult of the Martyrs: The "Liber Peristephanon" of Prudentius* (Ann Arbor, 1993); Ross, "Dynamic Writing"; Catherine Conybeare, "The Ambiguous Laughter of Saint Laurence," *JECS* 10 (2002): 175–202.

30. *AJ* 5.2.8–9 [PG 48.885–86]. For *katapeltai*, see E. A. Sophocles, *Greek Lexicon of the Roman and Byzantine Periods* (Cambridge, 1914), 642, sub *katapeltês*.

31. Vincent of Lerins, *Commonitorium*. 5.13. ed. Adolph Jülicher, *Vincenz von Lerinum, Commonitorium pro Catholicae fidei antiquitate et universitate adversus profanas omnium haereticorum novitiates* (Freiburg and Leipzig, 1895), 6–7.

32. Ando, *Imperial Ideology and Provincial Loyalty*, ch. 4.

33. See Shaw, "Judicial Nightmares and Christian Memory." See also Gleason, "Truth Contests and Talking Corpses"; Grig, "Torture and Truth in Late Antique Martyrology."

34. Buell, *Why This New Race*, 52.

35. Those towns with no martyrs of their own adopted martyrs whose stories then became their own. Preaching a sermon in Caesarea on the Forty Martyrs, for example, Basil of Caesarea subtly elided certain specifics of the episode in which those martyrs gave up their lives on behalf of their community—the names, places, and other details of their passions were muted so that, as Raymond Van Dam argues, "[the Forty] could be adopted by his audience in Caesarea as members of their city and their own patrons." For martyrs as models for self-fashioning see, for example, the sermon of an anonymous fourth- or fifth-century preacher from Gaul: After describing the suffering and death of the martyr Genesius, the anonymous preacher exhorted his congregation, "Therefore, most beloved, let us admire these [martyrs] in this way, that we remember them to have been human. I say, let us admire them in this way, that we recognize that they were like us, that they, like us, lived under the fragility of the flesh. And on this accord, let us fol-

low, as much as we are able, their faith. Let us pursue the virtue of soul with which, rejecting the worldly and the ephemeral, they carried forth the power of the king to the heavens. They conquered the agonies of the flesh; let us conquer the passions of our hearts and our habits. They triumphed over torture; let us triumph over our vices. They shuddered at sacrifice to demons; let us shudder at malice, envy, disparagement and accusations as much as we detest profane sacrifices so that, among the disputes, errors and persecutions against virtue of this world, we may prove ourselves to be martyrs." "Homilia LVI Homilia [De natale] Sancti Genesii" 8 = *Eusebius Gallicanus* 51.8. *Eusebius 'Gallicanus': Collectio Homiliarum*, Fr. Glorie (ed.) (CCSL 51a) (Tournholt, 1971), 654. For Basil, see Raymond Van Dam, *Becoming Christian: The Conversion of Roman Cappadocia* (Philadelphia, 2003), 139–41.

36. Van Dam, *Becoming Christian*, 149.

37. Lisa Bailey, "Building Urban Christian Communities: Sermons on Local Saints in the Eusebius Gallicanus Collection," *Early Medieval Europe* 12 (2003): 1–24.

38. "Homilia LV Homilia de Sanctis Martyribus Ephypodio et Alexandro" 6 = Eusebius Gallicanus 55.6. (*CCSL* 51a) 640 cited by Bailey, "Building Urban Christian Communities," 8.

39. The cult of these two saints is described in the sermon as "*indigenarum martyrum cultus*." Eusebius Gallicanus 55.1 cited by Bailey, "Building Urban Christian Communities," 1.

40. Gillian Clark, "Victricius of Rouen: *Praising the Saints*," 370; Gillian Clark, "Bodies and Blood," in Montserrat, *Changing Bodies, Changing Meanings*.

41. Dennis Trout, "Damasus and the Invention of Early Christian Rome," *JMEMS* 33 (2003): 517–36. For the city of Rome more generally in this period, see John Curran, *Pagan City and Christian Capital: Rome in the Fourth Century* (Oxford, 2000), 116–57; Bertrand Lançon, *Rome in Late Antiquity: Everyday Life and Urban Change, A.D. 312–609*, trans. Antonia Nevill (New York, 2000); Harry O. Maier, "Topography of Heresy and Dissent in Late Fourth Century Rome," *Historia* 44 (1995): 231–49; Dennis Trout, *Paulinus of Nola: Life, Letters and Poems* (Berkeley, 1999), 33–47; McLynn, "Christian Controversy and Violence in the Fourth Century"; Frederico Marazzi, "Rome in Transition: Economic and Political Change in the Fourth and Fifth Centuries," in Julia M. H. Smith, *Early Medieval Rome and the Christian West: Essays in Honour of Donald A. Bullough* (Leiden, 2000), 21–41.

42. For the role of narrative in the social integration of such events as the conversion of Constantine, see Polletta, "Contending Stories," 422–24.

43. Trout, "Damasus."

44. For a modern corollary, see Čolovic, *Politics of Identity in Serbia*, 36: "For the image of the nation as fatherland, that second bloodstream, the one that flows through the soil, is more important because, together with the dust and bones of the forebears, which the soil preserves, it completes the image of the fatherland as a gigantic grave . . . the territory of the nation-fatherland stretches as far as the graves of the forebears, while the peripheral graves have the role of boundary markers."

45. Richard Lim, "People as Power: Games, Munificence, and Contested Topography," in W. V. Harris (ed.), *The Transformations of* Urbs Roma *in Late Antiquity* (Portsmouth, R.I., 1999), 267–81. For a forth or fifth century explanation of "birthday" as a term describing the anniversary of a martyr's death, see "Homilia LVI Homilia [De natale] Sancti Genesii" 1 = *Eusebius Gallicanus* 51.1. (*CCSL* 51a), 651.

46. M. Sághy, "*Scinditur in partes populus*: Pope Damasus and the Martyrs of Rome," *Early Medieval Europe* 9 (2000): 273–87. For Damasus and the martyrs, see Jean Guyon, "Damase et l'illustration des martyrs: Les accents de la dévotion et l'enjeu d'une pastorale," in Mathijs Lamberigts and Peter Van Deun (eds.), *Martyrium in Multidisciplinary Perspective: Memorial Louis Reekmans* (Leuven, 1995), 157–77; See also the articles collected in Pontifico Istituto di Archaologia Cristiana (ed.), *Saecularia Damasiana: Atti del Convegno Internazionale per il XVI Centenario della Morte di Papa Damaso I (11–12–384—10/12–12–1984)* (Vatican City, 1986).

47. Sághy, "Damasus and the Martyrs of Rome," 279–87.

48. For Ambrose generally, see Neil McLynn, *Ambrose of Milan: Church and Court in a Christian Capital* (Berkeley, 1994). For Ambrose and the cult of the saints, see also Jean-Michel Spieser, "Ambrose's Foundations at Milan and the Question of Martyria," in Jean-Michel Spieser, *Urban and Religious Spaces in Late Antiquity and Early Byzantium* (Aldershot, 2001), VII; Thacker, "*Loca Sanctorum*," esp. 5–12.

49. Paulinus of Milan, *Vita Ambrosii* 29.1. ed. Kaniecka, 70–71.

50. For the uses made of the "remains of Jews" within Christian imperial discourse, see Jacobs, *Remains of the Jews*.

51. Ambrose, *ep*. 77.11. (ep. 22.11), ed. Zelzer, CSEL 82.1:133.

52. Ambrose, *ep*. 77.10. (ep. 22.10), ed. Zelzer, CSEL 82.1:132–33.

53. Paulinus of Milan, *Vita Ambrosii* 14–18. ed. Kaniecka, 52–59. For a sense of the ways in which Milan's Arian community organized itself and negotiated its changing fortunes, see Harry O. Maier, "Private Space as the Social Context of Arianism in Ambrose's Milan," *JTS* 45 (1994): 72–93.

54. Ambrose, *ep*. 77.19. (ep. 22.19), ed. Zelzer, CSEL 82.1:138.

55. Paulinus of Milan, *Vita Ambrosii* 16. ed. Kaniecka, 54–57.

56. See, for example, John Chrysostom. *AJ* 2, passim [PG 48.857–62]. Augustine, *ep*. 88.6 gives and account of a Catholic presbyter who had abandoned the Donatist church and who was thereafter captured, tortured, publicly humiliated, and held captive by members of his former community.

57. Paulinus of Milan, *Vita Ambrosii* 14. ed. Kaniecka, 52–55.

58 Paulinus of Milan, *Vita Ambrosii* 17. ed. Kaniecka, 56–57.

59. Augustine, *De oboedientia* = F. Dolbeau, "Nouveaux sermons du saint Augustin pour la conversion des païens et des donatists (III)," *Revue des Études Augustiniennes*, 32 (1992): 50–79. For Augustine and the martyrs, see Maureen A. Tilley, *The Bible in Christian North Africa: The Donatist World* (Minneapolis, 1997). For Augustine and the Donatists, see Peter Brown, "Religious Coercion in the Later Roman Empire: The Case of

North Africa," *History* 48 (1963): 83–101; Peter Brown, "St. Augustine's Attitude to Religious Coercion"; Peter Brown, *Augustine: A Biography* (Berkeley, 1967); Maureen Tilley, "Understanding Augustine Misunderstanding Tyconius," *SP* 27 (1993): 405–8.

60. For the Donatists in general, see Tilley, *The Bible in Christian North Africa*; Maureen A. Tilley, "Sustaining Donatist Self-Identity: From the Church If the Martyrs to the *Collecta* of the Desert," *JECS* 5 (1997): 21–35; W. C. H. Frend, *The Donatist Church: A Movement of Protest in Roman North Africa* (Oxford, 1952); Drake, *Constantine and the Bishops*, 212–29; Peter Brown, "St. Augustine's Attitude to Religious Coercion"; Gaddis, *No Crime*, 103–30. For an important correction to much previous scholarship on the militant Donatist pietists known as the Circumcellions, including Gaddis, see Brent D. Shaw, "Bad Boys: Circumcellions and Fictive Violence," in H. A. Drake and Emily Albu (eds.), *Violence in Late Antiquity: Perceptions and Practices* (Aldershot, 2006), 179–96; Brent D. Shaw, "Who Were the Circumcellions?" in A. H. Merrills (ed.), *Vandals, Romans and Berbers: New Perspectives on Late Antique Africa* (London, 2004), 227–58.

61. Augustine, *de obedientia* 16.

62. Augustine, *de obedientia* 13.

63. Mt. 5.10; a passage, notably, hurled at Augustine by the Donatist Petilian. See *Contra litteras Petiliani* 2.71, ed. M Petschenig, CSEL 52 (Leipzig, 1909), 101–2; Drake, *Constantine and the Bishops*, 416–17.

64. Augustine, *de obedientia* 17. Elsewhere, Augustine similarly argued, as Michael Gaddis has noted, that although Donatist Circumcellions destroyed pagan idols like "real Christians," they did so in the wrong way. Rather than doing so with the power of the Roman state on their side, they did so on their own, impetuously. When they were killed by the pagans whose idols they destroyed, Augustine reasoned, not only had they failed to achieve martyrdom (because they had undertaken their act of iconoclasm for the wrong reasons) but they had actually aided and abetted idolatry by giving themselves over as sacrificial victims to the pagans. See Gaddis, *No Crime*, 115–16. See Augustine, *Contra Gaudentium* 1.28, ed. M. Petschenig, CSEL 52 (Leipzig, 1910), 231–32.

65. See, among others, Brown, *Augustine of Hippo*, 217–27.

66. See Tilley, *The Bible in Christian North Africa*, esp. 53–76, 130–74; Maureen A. Tilley, "Introduction," in Maureen A. Tilley, *Donatist Martyr Stories: The Church in Conflict in Roman North Africa* (Liverpool, 1997); W. H. C. Frend, *Martyrdom and Persecution*, 220–21, 410ff. Cf. Brown, *Augustine of Hippo*, 217–18.

67. Brakke, "Outside the Places," 465–67.

68. The Melitians, like the Donatists, were rigorists with regard to those deemed to have become *traditores* during the persecutions. See Eusebius, *Life of Constantine*, introduction, translation, and notes by Averil Cameron and Stuart George Hall (Oxford, 2000), 249.

69. Brakke, "Outside the Places," 465–67.

70. J. Z. Smith, "The Wobbling Pivot," 94–95, citing Mircea Eliade, *The Sacred and the Profane* (New York, 1959), 26–27. See, for example, Brown, *Cult of the Saints*. For the role of ritual in late antique and early medieval society, see Frans Theuws, "Introduction:

Rituals in Transforming Societies," in Frans Theuws and Janet Nelson (eds.), *Rituals of Power: From Late Antiquity to the Early Middle Ages* (Leiden, 2000), 1–13.

71. Smith, "The Wobbling Pivot," 92.

72. Early and influential works on primordialism include Clifford Geertz, "The Integrative Revolution: Primordial Sentiments and Civil Politics in the New States," in Geertz, *The Interpretation of Cultures*, 255–310; Shils, "Primordial, Personal, Sacred and Civil Ties." For primordialism as an aspect of ancient communal identity, see, for example, Josiah Ober, *Mass and Elites in Democratic Athens: Rhetoric, Ideology and the Power of the People* (Princeton, 1989), 261–66. Ober does not use the term "primordialism," but instead discusses the role of the concept of "autochthony" in Athenian political ideology.

73. Suny, "Constructing Primordialism," 864. See also Suny, "Constructing Primordialism," 894 for the role of the traitor in Armenian national narratives.

74. Somers "Narrative Constitution," 617 (original emphasis).

75. Suny, "Constructing Primordialism," 890–91, quoting Stephanie Platz, "Pasts and Futures: Space, History, and Armenian Identity: 1988–1994" (Ph.D. diss., University of Chicago, 1996), 8. In the fourth century, contemporary local events which ostensibly had little to do with religious persecution seem sometimes to have been read into local narratives of persecution and martyrdom. Ammianus Marcellinus (*Res gestae* 17.7.5–6: trans. Rolfe) reports, for example, that after a former imperial *agens in rebus* named Diodorus and "three attendants of the deputy-governor of Italy" were executed at the command of the emperor Valentinian after finding themselves on the losing side of a legal struggle with a local general, the men were remembered and revered at the place where they were buried, which was called "Ad Innocentis." The following passage makes it all but certain that this was an instance of martyr adoration as Ammianus supplies another brief story in which Valentinian is advised to show mercy to condemned prisoners because if they are executed "the Christian religion will honor [them] as martyrs (that is to say, as beloved of God)."

76. Polletta, "Contending Stories," 423.

77. Salman Rushdie, *Imaginary Homelands: Essays and Criticism 1981–1991* (London, 1992), 178.

78. Rushdie, *Imaginary Homelands*, 179.

79. Era Rapaport, *Letters from Tel Mond Prison: An Israeli Settler Defends His Act of Terror*, ed. William B. Helreich (New York, 1996), 80–81. See also 79–85, 87–86, 95–100, 103–18, 136–37, 208, 251–54. Cf. Suny, "Constructing Primordialism," 894: "[The national narrative of the Armenians] is replete with invasions and massacres, with near disappearances, culminating in the genocide in the early twentieth century. Yet they have survived!"

80. Rapaport, *Letters from Tel Mond Prison*, 270–73.

81. Augustine, *de obedientia* 25.

82. For Julian's dealing with his Christian subjects and Christian views of Julian, see Drake *Constantine and the Bishops*, 316, 340, 433–37; Gaddis, *No Crime*, 90–96; Glen Bowersock, *Julian the Apostate* (Cambridge, 1978), 79–93.

83. Gregory Nazianzus, *Or.* 4.57, ed. and French trans. Jean Bernardi, *Gregoire de*

Nazianze, Discours 4–5 Contre Julien (SC 309) (Paris, 1983), 162–65; See also Socrates Scholasticus, *Historia Ecclesiastica* 3.12, ed. and French trans. Périchon and Maraval, 2.298–301. Each cited by Gaddis, *No Crime*, 92 n. 67; Sozomenos *HE* 5.5.

84. Under other circumstances, similar actions leading to the deaths of the (Donatist) iconoclasts involved would be read by no less an authority as Augustine as "false martyrdoms."

85. *Collectio Avellana* I.1.1–14, ed. O. Guenther, *CSEL* 35 (Vienna, 1895).

86. *Collectio Avellana* I.1.1–14. Cf. Jerome *Chronicon* 2382; Ammianus Marcellinus, *Res gestae* 27.3.2. See Sághy, "Damasus and the Martyrs of Rome," 281 for Damasus's later appropriation of the site of Agnes's tomb and the massacre of Ursinus's supporters.

87. See Alan Dearn, "The *Passio S. Typasii Veterani* as a Catholic Construction of the Past," *VC* 55 (2001): 88. This formula was often used in Greek-language martyr stories as well. See, for example, "SS. Ionae et Barachisii: Martyrum in Perside," *Analecta Bollandeana* 22 (1903): 345–407, esp. 396.

88. Augustine, *de obedientia* 13.

89. *Collectio Avellana* I.1.1. Liberius later reversed himself, a fact that is glossed over in this text. As Michael Gaddis has noted (*No Crime*, 69 n. 3), the surviving text of the letter from Liberius explaining this decision is "frequently interrupted by the bitter denunciations of a later copyist, inserting remarks such as 'This is an Arian falsehood!' and 'Anathema to you, prevaricating Liberius!'"

90. *Collectio Avellana* I.1.12–14.

91. Eliade, *The Sacred and the Profane*, 85 [original emphasis]. For a kindred reading of the Ara Pacis, see John Elsner, "Cult and Sculpture: Sacrifice in the *Ara Pacis Augustae*," *JRS* 81 (1991): 50–61, esp. 54–55.

92. Augustine, *de obedientia* 25.

93. Augustine, ep. 139.2, ed. Goldbacher, CSEL 34.419–20, English trans. NPNF Series 1, vol.1.

94. For this episode, see Glen W. Bowersock, "From Emperor to Bishop: The Self-Conscious Transformation of Political Power in the Fourth Century A.D.," *Classical Philology* 81 (1986): 298–307; Willy Evenepoel, "Ambrose vs. Symmachus: Christians and Pagans in A.D. 384," *Ancient Society* 29 (1998–99): 283–306; Kirsten Groß-Albenhausen, *Imperator christianissimus: Der christliche Kaiser bei Ambrosius und Johannes Chrysostomus* (Frankfurt am Main, 1999), 63–78; Drake, *Constantine and the Bishops*, 403.

95. Ambrose, *ep.* 72.15 (ep. 17.15.), ed. Michaela Zelzer, *Sancti Ambrosi Opera, Pars X: Epistulae et Acta* CSEL 82 (Vienna, 1990), 18–19. Trans. H. de Romestin et al., NPNF ser. 2, vol. 10. As an emperor, he would ideally step into another role in the narratives of the age, that of the pious Christian emperor, a role fulfilled in Ambrose's rendering by Valentinian's father and brother. Failing this, he would find himself cast in the role of the apostate (the figure of Julian has already been subtly evoked), or the persecuting emperor, compelling Christians to sacrifice at the altars.

96. See Drake, *Constantine and the Bishops*, 140–46, 384–92.

97. See, for example, Libanius, *Oratio* 11, trans. A. F. Norman, *Antioch as a Center of Hellenic Culture as Observed by Libanius* (Liverpool, 2000), 3–65.

98. See, for example, Tilley, *The Bible in Christian North Africa*, and Tilley, "Sustaining Donatist Self-Identity" for Donatist uses of Old Testament narrative in projects of self-fashioning. See McLynn, *Ambrose of Milan*, ch. 7, for Ambrose's elaboration upon Old Testament narratives in his dealings with the emperor Theodosius.

CHAPTER THREE

1. See Ambrose, *Epp*. 40, 41 (*epp*. 1, 1.a), ed. Michael Zelzer, *Sancti Ambrosi Opera, Pars X: Epistulae et Acta* CSEL 82.3 (Vienna, 1982), 145–77; Paulinus, *Vita Ambrosii* 7. For this incident, see Drake, *Constantine and the Bishops*, 409–10, 444–45; Brown, *Power and Persuasion*, 108–9, 115; Brown, *Authority and the Sacred*, 49–50; McLynn, *Ambrose of Milan*, 298–309; Gaddis, *No Crime*, 194–98.

2. Ambrose, *ep*. 40.7 (ep. 1), ed. Zelzer, CSEL 82.3: 165–66.

3. Ambrose, *ep*. 40.19 (ep. 1), ed. Zelzer, CSEL 82.3: 171.

4. Ambrose, *ep*. 40.29 (ep. 1), ed. Zelzer, CSEL 82.3: 175–76.

5. Ambrose, *ep*. 40.17 (ep. 1), ed. Zelzer, CSEL 82.3: 170. For the kiss as a mark of communal inclusion among late antique Christians, see Penn, "Performing Family"; Penn, *Kissing Christians*.

6. Ambrose, *ep*. 40.7–9 (ep. 1), ed. Zelzer, CSEL 82.3: 165–67. Maximus, who held power 383–88, was defeated and killed by Theodosius at Aquileia. See A. H. M. Jones, *The Later Roman Empire 284–602: A Social, Economic and Administrative Survey* (Baltimore, 1964), 158–59. Theodosius had had much in common with Maximus, so much so in fact that the panegyrist Pacatus clearly found himself at some pains to efface the relationship between the two men and their families, which had been quite close. See Pacatus, *Panegyricus* 24, trans. and notes by C. E. V. Nixon, *Pacatus: Panegyric to the Emperor Theodosius* (Liverpool, 1987), 35–36, 75 n. 80.

7. Ambrose, *ep*. 40.23 (ep. 1), ed. Zelzer, CSEL 82.3: 173–74.

8. For this phenomenon more generally, see Gaddis, *No Crime*, ch. 1.

9. *The Martyrdom of Saint Theodore* 1, ed. Hippolyte Delehaye, *Les légends grecques des saints militaries* (New York, 1975), 127–50, here 136. I cite this text as an illustration of the ways in which the role of the martyr in late Roman society was imagined, rather than as evidence concerning "what actually happened" during the trial and martyrdom of any particular Christian martyr.

10. *Martyrdom of Saint Theodore* 1, ed. Delehaye, 127.

11. *Martyrdom of Saint Theodore* 1, ed. Delehaye, 127.

12. *Martyrdom of Saint Theodore* 2, ed. Delehaye, 128.

13. *Martyrdom of Saint Theodore* 3, ed. Delehaye, 129.

14. *Martyrdom of Saint Theodore* 3, ed. Delehaye, 129.

15. *Martyrdom of Saint Theodore* 4, ed. Delehaye, 129–30.

16. *Oratio* 30, ed. Richard Foerster, *Libanii Opera*, 12 vols. (Leipzig, 1903–27 [1963]), 3.80–118.

17. In addition to the works cited elsewhere in this chapter, see Polleta, "Contending Stories"; Polleta, "'It Was Like a Fever . . .'"; Hinchman and Hinchman, *Memory, Identity, Community*; Ricoeur, *Time and Narrative*; Kreiswirth, "Merely Telling Stories? Narrative and Knowledge in the Human Sciences" *Poetics Today* 21 (2000): 293–318; David Wood, *On Paul Ricoeur*; Bruner, "The Narrative Construction of Reality"; White, "The Value of Narrativity in the Representation of Reality."

18. Bruner, "The Narrative Construction of Reality," 4–5 (original emphasis).

19. Bruner, "The Narrative Construction of Reality," 5.

20. Fredric Jameson, *The Political Unconscious: Narrative as a Socially Symbolic Act* (Ithaca, 1981), 19.

21. Somers, "The Narrative Constitution of Identity," 618.

22. See Eusebius, *Historia Ecclesiastica* VII, ed. Wilhelm Dindorf, *Eusebii Caesariensis Opera*, 4 vols. (Leipzig, 1867–90), 4.297–348. For the local elaborations upon this narrative, see for example, John Chrysostom, *Adversus Judaeos orationes* 5.2.8–9 (PG 48:885–86.). See also Raymond Van Dam, *Becoming Christian: The Conversion of Roman Cappadocia* (Philadelphia, 2003).

23. Drake, *Constantine and the Bishops*, 355–60; Van Dam, *Becoming Christian*, 82–156.

24. Plutarch, *Moralia*, 317 a-c, ed. and trans. Frank Cole Babbitt, *Plutarch's Moralia*, 15 vols. (Cambridge, MA, 1936 [1962]), 4.324–27.

25. Libanius, *Or.* 11.129. ed. Foerster, *Libanii Opera*, 1.476–77. For the historical background of the Roman acquisition of Antioch and its environs, see the commentary on the *Antiochikos* by Georgios Fatouros and Tilman Krischer, *Antiochikos (or. XI): Zur heidnischen Renaissance in der Spätantike* (Berlin, 1992), 182–87.

26. Libanius, *Or.* 11.124–25, ed. Foerster, *Libanii Opera*, 1.478–79. Trans. A. F. Norman, *Antioch as a Centre of Hellenic Culture as Observed by Libanius* (Liverpool, 2000), 30.

27. Libanius, *Or.* 11.130, ed. Foerster, *Libanii Opera*, 1.479. Trans. Norman, *Antioch as a Centre of Hellenic Culture*, 32.

28. Libanius, *Or.* 30.5, ed. Foerster, *Libanii Opera*, 3.90. Cf. Vitruvius, *De architectura* 2.1, ed. Valentine Rose, *Vitruvii de architectura* (Leipzig, 1899), 30–36.

29. See Fergus Millar, *The Emperor in the Roman World (31 B.C.-A.D. 337)* (Ithaca, 1977 [1992]), 192. See also Andrew Wallace-Hadrill, "The Roman Revolution and Material Culture," in Fergus Millar and Adalberto Giovannini (eds.), *La révolution romaine après Ronald Syme, bilans et perspectives: Sept exposés suivis de discussions Vandoeuvres-Genève, 6–10 septembre 1999*, Entretiens sur l'antiquite classique XLVI (Geneva, 2000), 283–321.

30. Greg Woolf, "Becoming Roman, Staying Greek: Culture, Identity and the Civilizing Process in the Roman East," *Proceedings of the Cambridge Philological Society* 40 (1994): 116–43, here 119.

31. See Greg Woolf, *Becoming Roman: The Origins of Provincial Civilization in Gaul* (Cambridge, 1998), 55–56.

32. Polybius, *Historiae*, ed. Theodore Buettner-Wobst, *Polybii Historiae*, 5 vols. (Stuttgart, 1882), 2.303–6.

33. Polybius, *Historiae*, 6.54, ed. Theodore Buettner-Wobst, *Polybii Historiae*, 2.304.18–22.

34. Ando, *Imperial Ideology and Provincial Loyalty*, 209.

35. In this usage of the term "*statio*" I follow David S. Potter's suggestion concerning the use of the term to signal the juridical and imaginative space of the *princeps* in Roman society. See David S. Potter, "Political Theory in the *Senatus Consultum Pisonianum*," *AJP* 120 (1999): 71, 78–79.

36. Libanius, *Or*. 30.6. ed. Foerster, *Libanii Opera*, 3.90.

37. Libanius, *Or*. 30.7. ed. Foerster, *Libanii Opera*, 3.90–1.

38. Libanius, *Or*. 30.8. ed. Foerster, *Libanii Opera*, 3.91. For Constantine's attitude with regard to traditional religion, see John Curran, "Constantine and the Ancient Cults of Rome: The Legal Evidence," *Greece & Rome* 1 (1996): 68–80; See also David Hunt, "Christianizing the Roman Empire: The Evidence of the Code," in Jill Harries and Ian Wood (eds.), *The Theodosian Code: Studies in the Imperial Law of Late Antiquity* (London, 1993), 143–57; Michelle Salzman, "*Superstitio* in the Codex Theodosianus and the Persecution of Pagans," *VC* 41 (1987): 172–88.

39. Libanius, *Or*. 30.7, ed. Foerster, *Libanii Opera*, 3.90–91.

40. Libanius, *Or*. 30.46, ed. Foerster, *Libanii Opera*, 3.112–13.

41. There is some evidence that Theodosius shared this view of the monks. See Ambrose ep. 41.27 (PL 16.1168c). See also Drake, *Constantine and the Bishops*, 409–10.

42. See Ammianus Marcellinus, *Res gestae*, 21.16.16, ed. and trans. J. C. Rolfe, *Ammianus Marcellinus*, 3 vols. (Cambridge, Mass., 1940 [1972]), 2.182–83. "He was to an excessive degree under the influence of his wives, and the shrill-voiced eunuchs, and certain of the court officials, who applauded his every word, and listened for his 'yes' or 'no' in order to be able to agree with him." See also Jones, *The Later Roman Empire*, 127, 568.

43. Paul Petit, "Sur la Date du *Pro Templis,*" *Byzantion* 21 (1954): 295–309; Kate Cooper, "Insinuations of Womanly Influence: An Aspect of the Christianization of the Roman Aristocracy," *JRS* 82 (1992): 161; Van Dam, "From Paganism to Christianity," 15; Fowden, "Bishops and Temples."

44. Libanius, *Or*. 30.48, ed. Foerster, *Libanii Opera*, 3.114.

45. Cooper, "Insinuations of Womanly Influence," 161. The wife of "Cynegius" is also depicted by Libanius as a source of political and cultural pollution within the empire, thus fulfilling another feminine role in the estimation of ancient Greek intellectuals. See Anne Carson, "Dirt and Pollution: The Phenomenology of Female Pollution in Antiquity," in *Constructions of the Classical Body*, ed. James I. Porter (Ann Arbor, 1999), 77–100.

46. See, for example, Cicero, *Philippics* 3.10, ed. Albert Curtis Clark, *M. Tullii Ciceronis Orationes*, 6 vol. (Oxford, 1901 [1989]), 2.160 in which the "spinning rooms" (*qua-*

silla), a feminine space within Mark Antony's home, are the scene in which gold plundered from the empire is weighed. As Treggiari makes clear (see next note), this feminine space is equated by Cicero with Mark Antony's violent acquisitiveness, which is deemed to exceed even that of Tarquinius. This tendency in Antony's character, is further contrasted by Cicero with the collective, communal interests of the Populus Romanus: *una in domo omnes quorum intererat totum imperium populi Romani nundinabantur* ("in a single house, every one of those who took part were selling the entire empire of the *Populus Romanus*"). For Philocrates and Demosthenes' invective against him, see James N. Davidson, *Courtesans and Fishcakes: The Consuming Passions of Classical Athens* (London, 1997), 115, 156.

47. Susan Treggiari, "*Leges Sine Moribus,*" *Ancient History Bulletin* 8 (1994): 86–98; Susan Treggiari, "Home and Forum: Cicero Between 'Public' and 'Private,'" *TAPA* 128 (1998): 1–25; Andrew Riggsby, "'Public' and 'Private' in Roman Culture: The Case of the Cubiculum," *JRA* 10 (1997): 36–56. See, for example, Livy, on the abuses of the *decemvirs, Ab urbe condita*, 3.36–37, ed. Robert Seymour Conway, *Titi Livi ab urbe condita*, 5 vols. (Oxford, 1914). As further examples, see, among many other such instances in Cicero's corpus, *Pro T. Annio Milone* 87–89, ed. Albert Curtis Clark, *M. Tullii Ciceronis Orationes*, 2.36–37; *In Pisonem* 27–30, ed. R. G. M. Nisbet, *M. Tulli Ciceronis, In Calpurnium Pisonem Oratio* (Oxford, 1961 [1975]), 16–18.

48. J. Schlumberger, "*Potentes* and *Potentia* in the Social Thought of Late Antiquity," in Frank M. Clover and R. Stephen Humphreys (eds.), *Tradition and Innovation in Late Antiquity* (Madison, 1989), 89–104; See also J. S. Richardson, "*Imperium Romanum*: Empire and the Language of Power," *JRS* 81 (1991): 1–12.

49. See Daniel Caner, *Wandering, Begging Monks, Spiritual Authority and the Promotion of Monasticism in Late Antiquity* (Berkeley, 2002) for Christian perceptions of apostolic monastic wanderers. See also Philip Rousseau, *Ascetics, Authority and the Church* (Oxford, 1978), 169–234. See also Brown, *Power and Persuasion*, 106: "[The monk Macedonius] confronted the commissioners with a brusque courage so alien that it seemed to carry the awesome force of the Holy Spirit."

50. For monks described as "black-robed ones (*melaneimonountes*)" see Libanius, *Or.* 30.8, ed. Foerster, *Libanii Opera*, 3.91–92. Aeschylus uses a kindred term to refer to the Erinyes in his *Eumenides* (line 370) "And the proud thoughts of men, that flaunt themselves full high under the heavens, they waste away and dwindle in dishonour 'neath the earth at our sable-stoled (*melaneimosin*) assault and the vengeful rhythm of our feet." Herbert Weir Smyth (ed. and trans.), *Aeschylus*, 2 vols. (Cambridge, Mass., 1922), 2.304–5. For the progress of the monks through the Syrian countryside described as like that of "raging winter rivers" see Libanius, *Or.* 30.9, ed. Foerster, *Libanii Opera*, 3.92.

51. Libanius, *Or.* 30.4–5, ed. Foerster, *Libanii Opera*, 3.89–90.

52. Libanius, *Or.* 30.45, ed. Foerster, *Libanii Opera*, 3.112–13.

53. Libanius, *Or.* 30.44–45, ed. Foerster, *Libanii Opera*, 3.111–12.

54. See Ando, *Imperial Ideology*, ch. 2, esp. 21–42.

55. Clifford Geertz, "Art as a Cultural System," in Clifford Geertz, *Local Knowledge: Further Essays in Interpretive Anthropology* (New York, 1983), 99.

56. Brown, *Power and Persuasion*, 36. See also Ando, *Imperial Ideology*, 209–15.

57. See Maud Gleason, *Making Men: Sophists and Self-presentation in Ancient Rome* (Princeton, 1995), 53–81; Brown, *Power and Persuasion*, esp. 41–47, 58–61.

58. Brown, *Power and Persuasion*, 58. See also Drake, *Constantine and the Bishops*, 63.

59. Libanius, *Or.* 30.21, ed. Foerster, *Libanii Opera*, 3.99. The allusion to "drunken frenzy" may be explained by the fact that Libanius has just hinted darkly that the days and in particular the nights of the monks are spent in something less savory than isolated contemplation of transcendent truth and had earlier in his oration (*Or.* 30.8) suggested that their drinking feats were prodigious.

60. At *Or.* 30.21.12 (*Libanii Opera*, ed. Foerster, 3.99.12), Foerster suggests *polloi* for *pollai*.

61. Libanius, *Or.* 30.22, ed. Foerster, *Libanii Opera*, 3.98–99.

62. See also Libanius, *Or.* 30.42, ed. Foerster, *Libanii Opera*, 3.110–11.

63. Libanius, *Declamation* 1.136–38, ed. Foerster, *Libanii Opera*, 5.90–93. Trans. D. A. Russell, *Libanius: Imaginary Speeches A Selection of Declamations* (London, 1996), 47–48.

64. R. R. R. Smith, "Late Roman Philosopher Portraits From Aphrodisias," *JRS* 80 (1990): 127–55, here 139. Elsewhere, the emperor Julian's *Caesars* (316b) makes clear that Alexander was himself understood as an early archetype of the Roman *princeps*, as the work includes Alexander in a procession of Roman emperors who pass in review before the assembled Olympian gods.

65. Ando, *Imperial Ideology*, 207–9. See also John Elsner, "Cult and Sculpture," 54, where the author argues that the Ara Pacis "was not an untypical Roman templum in its layout and structure" and that within the Ara compound, scenes which depicted previous sacrifices reflected the sacrifices currently being made during each new ritual, thus recalling the countless prior performances of the same ritual, performed for the same ends, and in anticipation of future ritual performances (like the one now being performed and like the ones the ritual now being performed anticipates). See also Susan L. Mizruchi, "The Place of Ritual in Our Time," in Susan L. Mizruchi (ed.), *Religion and Cultural Studies* (Princeton, 2001), 56–79, here 56: "Ritual acts express an unbridgeable gap—a chasm—between what is sought or aspired to and the historical present. Ritual actors are always at a loss in relation to some prior moment."

66. See, for example, Lactantius, *De mortibus persecutorum*, passim, ed. and trans. J. L. Creed, *Lactantius: De Mortibus Persecutorum* (Oxford, 1984). See also Eusebius's reproduction of Constantine's "Oration to the Assembly of the Saints," at Eusebius, *Constantini imperatoris oratio ad coetum sanctorum*, 23–26, ed. I. A. Heikel, *Eusebius Werke, Band 1: Über das Leben Constantins. Constantins Rede an die heilige Versammlung. Tricennatsrede an Constantin Die griechischen christlichen Schriftsteller* 7. (Leipzig, 1902): 151–92. See also H. A. Drake, "'Compare Our Religion with Your Own': Constantine's Concept of Chris-

tianity in the 'Oration to the Saints,'" conference paper delivered at the 2003 Oxford Patristics Conference, Oxford, England.

67. Drake, *Constantine and the Bishops*, 409–10. The law in question, cited by Drake, is *CTh.* 10.3.1 [390]. It was repealed by *CTh.* 10.3.2 [392]. See also Gaddis, *No Crime*, 233.

68. See Errington, "Christian Accounts of the Religious Legislation of Theodosius I"; Errington, "Church and State in the First Years of Theodosius I."

69. Ambrose, *de obitu Theodosii* 47–48, ed. Mannix, 61.

70. Ambrose, *de obitu Theodosii* 49, ed. Mannix, 61–62.

71. Ambrose, *de obitu Theodosii* 4, ed. Mannix, 47.

72. Drake, *Constantine and the Bishops*, passim.

73. See Errington, "Christian Accounts of the Religious Legislation of Theodosius I," 435.

74. In North Africa, for example, the Gabaditani, who were "exceedingly addicted to what is called the Greek form of atheism, [Justinian] . . . made into zealous Christians. He also walled the city of Sabrathan [the modern Tripoli Vecchia] where he also built a very noteworthy church." Procopius, *Buildings* 6.4.12–13, ed. and trans. H. B. Dewing, *Procopius*, 7 vols. (Cambridge, Mass., 1961 [1940]), 7.376–77. Also in North Africa, Procopius says, there were two cities, both called Augila. "They are both ancient cities whose inhabitants have preserved the practices of antiquity," he says. "They were all suffering from the disease of polytheism up to this day." Justinian, however, changed all that. "In that place there have been from ancient times shrines dedicated to Ammon and to Alexander the Macedonian. The natives actually used to make sacrifices to them even up to the reign of Justinian. But the emperor has now made a provision, not alone for the safety of the persons of his subjects, but he has also made it his concern to save their souls, and thus he has cared in every way for the people living there. Indeed, he has taught them the doctrine of the true faith, making the whole population Christians and bringing about a transformation of their polluted ancestral customs. Moreover he built for them a church of the Theotokos to be a guardian of the safety of the cities and of the true faith," Procopius, *Buildings* 6.2.15–20, trans. H. B. Dewing, *Procopius*, 7.368–69. For a brief but concise account of Justinian's religious policies, see Michael Maas, *Exegesis and Empire in the Early Byzantine Mediterranean* (Tübingen, 2003).

75. See Michael Maas, *John Lydus and the Roman Past: Antiquarianism in the Age of Justinian* (New York, 1992); Averil Cameron, *Procopius and the Sixth Century* (London, 1985 [1996]).

CHAPTER FOUR

1. W. H. C. Frend, *The Rise of the Monophysite Movement: Chapters in the History of the Church in the Fifth and Sixth Centuries* (Cambridge, 1972); Maas, *Exegesis and Empire*,

42–60; Susan Ashbrook Harvey, *Asceticism and Society in Crisis: John of Ephesus and the Lives of the Eastern Saints* (Berkeley, 1990); Nina Garsoïan and Robert Thompson, *East of Byzantium: Syria and Armenia in the Formative Period* (Washington, D.C., 1982); P. T. R. Gray, *The Defense of Chalcedon in the East (451–553)* (Leiden, 1979); Gregory, *Vox Populi*; Ernst Honigmann, *Évêques et évêchés monophysites d'Asie antérieure au VIe siècle*, CSCO 127/Sub. 2 (Louvain, 1951); Arthur Vööbus, *History of Asceticism in the Syrian Orient: A Contribution to the History of Culture in the Near East*, 3 vols., CSCO 184, 197, 500 (Louvain, 1958–88); Arthur Vööbus, "The Origin of the Monophysite Church in Syria and Mesopotamia," *Church History* 42 (1973): 19–27; Olivier Hendriks, "L'activité apostolique du monachisme monophysite et nestorien," *Proche Orient Chrétien* 10 (1960): 3–25, 97–113; Morony, *Iraq after the Muslim Conquest*, 346–83; Leslie S. B. MacCoull, "'When Justinian Was Upsetting the World': A Note on Soldiers and Religious Coercion in Sixth Century Egypt," in T. S. Miller and J. Nesbitt (eds.), *Peace and War in Byzantium: Essays in Honor of George T. Dennis, S.J.* (Washington, D.C., 1995), 106–13; Mark Whittow, *The Making of Byzantium, 600–1025* (Berkeley, 1996), 42–46; David Johnson, "Anti-Chalcedonian Polemics in Coptic Texts, 451–641," in Birger A. Pearson and James E. Goehring (eds.), *The Roots of Egyptian Monasticism* (Philadelphia, 1986), 216–34; Sebastian Brock, "The Christology of the Church of the East in the Synods of the Fifth and Sixth Centuries," in George Dion Dragas (ed.), *Askum, Thyateira: A Festschrift for Archbishop Methodios* (London, 1985), 125–42 (reprinted in Sebastian Brock, *Studies in Syriac Christianity* [Hampshire, 1992], ch. 12); Sebastian Brock, "The Conversion with the Syrian Orthodox under Justinian (532)" *Orientalia Christiana Periodica* 97 (Rome, 1981), 87–121 (reprinted in Brock, *Studies in Syriac Christianity*, ch. 13).

2. Frend, *Rise of the Monophysite Movement*, ch. 7; Harvey, *Asceticism and Society in Crisis*, 61–68, 84–87, 106–7.

3. See, for example, *Zuqnīn Chronicle*, 57–67, trans. Amir Harrak, *The Chronicle of Zuqnīn: Parts III and IV A.D. 488–775* (Toronto, 1999). On this and the Syriac chronicle tradition, see Witold Witakowski, *The Syriac Chronicle of Pseudo-Dionysius of Tel-Maḥrē* (Uppsala, 1987).

4. Christian ascetics have of course generated one of the most prodigious bodies of scholarship in the historiographic corpus treating the later Roman world. The following is intended only as a representative sampling of recent work. See, among many others, Brakke, *Demons and the Making of the Monk*; Peter Brown, "The Rise and Function of the Holy Man in Late Antiquity," *JRS* 61 (1971): 80–101; Peter Brown, "The Saint as Exemplar in Late Antiquity," *Representations* 12 (1983): 1–25; Peter Brown, "The Holy Man," in Cameron et al. (eds.), *The Cambridge Ancient History XIV*; Brakke, *Athanasius and the Politics of Asceticism*; Frankfurter, "Stylites and *Phallobates*"; Elm, *Virgins of God*; Goehring, *Ascetics, Society, and the Desert*; Goehring, "The Dark Side of Landscape"; Philip Rousseau, *Ascetics, Authority, and the Church in the Age of Jerome and Cassian* (Oxford, 1978); Philip Rousseau, *Pachomius: The Making of a Community in Fourth Century Egypt* (Berkeley, 1985); Philip Rousseau, "The Spiritual Authority of the 'Monk-Bishop': Eastern Elements

in Some Western Hagiography of the Fourth and Fifth Centuries," *JTS* n.s. 23 (1971): 381–419; Philip Rousseau, "Orthodoxy and the Coenobite," *SP* 30 (1995): 241–58; Philip Rousseau, "Eccentrics and Coenobites in the Late Roman East," *Byzantinische Forschungen* 24 (1997): 35–50; Caner, *Wandering, Begging Monks*; Sterk, *Renouncing the World Yet Leading the Church*; Sebastian Brock, "Early Syrian Asceticism," *Numen* 20 (1973): 1–19; Averil Cameron, "On Defining the Holy Man," in James Howard-Johnston and Paul Anthony Hayward, *The Cult of Saints in Late Antiquity and the Middle Ages: Essays on the Contribution of Peter Brown* (Oxford, 1999), 27–43.

5. See, for example, *The Zuqnīn Chronicle*, 63, where a Chalcedonian bishop is said to have called his monks "troops" as he deployed them for the persecution of local anti-Chalcedonians. See also John Wortley, "Military Elements in Psychphelitic Tales and Sayings," in Miller and Nesbitt, *Peace and War in Byzantium*, 89–105. For this phenomenon more generally, see Fowden, "Bishops and Temples in the Eastern Roman Empire"; Gregory, *Vox Populi*; Gaddis, *No Crime*; Hendriks, "L'activité apostolique du monachisme monophysite et nestorien."

6. See, for example, John of Ephesus, *Lives of the Eastern Saints*, ed. and trans. E. W. Brooks, *PO* 17, 18, 19 (Paris, 1923–25 [Turnhout, 1974]), here *Lives*, 43, ed. and trans. Brooks, *PO* 18, 659–60; *The Life of Alexander the Sleepless*, 9, trans. Daniel Caner, *Wandering, Begging Monks*, 256; *Life of Symeon the Stylite the Younger*, 161, 164, ed. and trans. Paul van den Ven, Subsidia Hagiographica 32 (Brussels, 1962); Sulpicius Severus, *Vita S. Martini*, 12–15, ed. and French trans. Jacques Fontaine, *Vie de Saint Martin*, 3 vols. (SC 133–35) (Paris, 1967), 1.278–87; *Life of Saint Nicholas*, 15–20, ed. and trans. Ihor Ševčenko and Nancy Patterson Ševčenko, *The Life of Saint Nicholas of Sion* (Brookline, Mass., 1984), 34–41; Zachariah Scholasticus, *Life of Severus*, ed. and French trans. Kugener, 29–33; Besa, *Life of Shenoute*, 83–84; *Histoire de Barḥadbešabba ʿArbaïa* XII, ed. and French trans. F. Nau, *PO* 23.2 (Paris, 1932), 252–55; See also Trombley, "Religious Transition."

7. See, among others, MacMullen, *Christianizing the Roman Empire*; Brown, *Authority and the Sacred*, 50–51; Gaddis, *No Crime*; Maria Dzielska, *Hypatia of Alexandria*, trans. F. Lyra (Cambridge, Mass., 1995).

8. For the *Philoponoi*, see Christopher Haas, *Alexandria in Late Antiquity: Topography and Social Conflict* (Baltimore, 1997), 238–40; E. Wipszycka, "Les confréries dans la vie religieuse de l'Égypte chrétienne," in *Proceedings of the Twelfth International Congress of Papyrology* (Toronto, 1970), 511–25; P. J. Sijpesteijn, "New Light on the *Philoponoi*," *Aegyptus* 69 (1989): 95–99, cited by Haas.

9. Zachariah Scholasticus, *Life of Severus*, ed. and French trans. Kugener, 29–31.

10. See, for example, Mark the Deacon, *Life of Porphyry*, 27, ed. and trans. Henri Gregoire and M. A. Kugener (Paris, 1930); John of Ephesus, *Lives of the Eastern Saints*, 5, ed. and trans. Brooks, 90–93; cf. the popular suspicion of bribery as an explanation for perceived leniency during the sixth-century antipagan pogrom in Antioch, John of Ephesus, *Ecclesiastical History*, 3.30. See also Van Dam, "From Paganism to Christianity at Late Antique Gaza," 13–17.

11. Dioscurus, *A Panegyric on Macarius, Bishop of Tkōw*, 5.2, ed. and trans. Johnson, CSCO 416 (Copt. 42), CSCO 415 (Copt. 41), 23.

12. Sources for Hypatia's murder, all cited by Dzielska: Socrates, *Historia Ecclesiastica*, 7.13–15, ed. Günther Christian Hansen, *Sokrates Kirchengeschichte* (Berlin, 1995), 357–61; John of Nikiou, *Chronicle*, 84.87–103, trans. R. H. Charles, *The Chronicle of John, Bishp of Nikiu* (Oxford, 1916), 100–102; Damascius, *Life of Isidore*, ed. C. Zintzen (*Damascii Vitae Isidori Reliquiae*) (Hildesheim, 1967). See also Haas, *Alexandria in Late Antiquity*, 307–16; Brown, *Power and Persuasion*, 115–17.

13. Socrates, *Historia Ecclesiastica*, 7.14, ed. Hansen, 359–60.

14. See Dzielska, *Hypatia of Alexandria*, ch. 3.

15. Brown, *Power and Persuasion*, ch. 2.

16. Brown, *Power and Persuasion*, ch. 2.

17. *AJ* 8.4.1. PG 48.932.

18. For the function of boundary maintenance, and its role in communal identities, see Barth, "Introduction."

19. Brakke, *Athanasius and the Politics of Asceticism*, 135–38, ch. 4.

20. Brakke, "'Outside the Places, Within the Truth,'" 445–81 and esp. 465–67.

21. Brakke, "'Outside the Places, Within the Truth'"; Brakke, *Athanasius and the Politics of Asceticism*, ch. 3, 4.

22. Athanasius, *Vita Antonii* 68, trans. Robert C. Gregg, *Athanasius: Life of Anthony and the Letter to Marcellinus* (New York, 1980). All translations of this text are by Gregg unless otherwise noted. See also *Vita Antonii*, 91.

23. Athanasius, *Vita Antonii*, 22–43.

24. Brakke, *Athanasius and the Politics of Asceticism*, 135–38, ch. 4.

25. Gregg and Groh have in fact argued forcefully that the Arians may also have claimed Antony for their own community, and Brakke has demonstrated that before Athanasius built a relationship with the monastic communities around Alexandria, these communities seem to have taken little interest in doctrinal matters, a point underscored by the recent work of James Goehring. See Brakke, *Athanasius and the Politics of Asceticism*, ch. 2, 3; Goehring, *Ascetics, City and the Desert*, ch. 10.

26. Theodoret, *Historia Religiosa* 2.16–18, ed. and French trans. Pierre Canivet and Alice Leroy-Molinghen, *Théodoret de Cyr, Histoire des Moines de Syrie: Histoire Philothée*, 2 vols. (SC 234 & 257) (Paris, 1977–79), 1.230–39. Maro: John of Ephesus, *Lives of the Eastern Saints*, 1.98.

27. Išōʿyahb Patriarch III, *Liber Epistularum*, IV, ed. and Latin trans. Rubens Duval, CSCO 64.2 (Syr. 11) (1905), 9–10; CSCO 64.1 (Syr. 12) (Paris, 1905), 5–6.

28. *The Life of Timothy of Kākhushtā*, Saidnaya Version, 45, ed. and trans. John C. Lamoreaux and Cyril Cairala, *PO* 48.4 (Turnhout, 2000), 604–9.

29. John of Ephesus, *Lives of the Eastern Saints*, 46, ed. and trans. Brooks, *PO* 18, 672.

30. Theodoret, *Historia Religiosa*, 3.17, ed. and French trans. Canivet and Leroy–Molinghen, 1.278–81.

31. Jerome, *Vita s. Hilarionis*, 28.

32. Socrates, *Historia Ecclesiastica*, 7.17, ed. Hansen, 362.

33. Rabban Mār Simon, *The History of Rabban Hōrmīzd*, 11–12, trans. E. A. Wallis Budge, *The Histories of Rabban Hōrmīzd the Persian and Rabban Bar-ʿIdtā* (London, 1902 [Piscataway, N.J., 2003]), 101–6. I have adapted Budge's translation slightly. See also *Life of Symeon the Stylite the Younger*, 132–35, ed. and trans. van den Ven, where Symeon refuses to sanction the celebration of the Eucharist in the presence of heretics, and 157–65, where he confronts directly and through prayer the "unbelief" of various communities in and around Antioch.

34. Translated in Valantasis, *Religions of Late Antiquity in Practice*, 475. See also Brakke, *Demons and the Making of the Monk*, ch. 5, esp. 100–113.

35. Brakke, *Demons and the Making of the Monk*, 97–98.

36. Sulpicius Severus, *Vita S. Martini*, 12, ed. and French trans. Fontaine, 1.278–83.

37. Leontius of Neapolis, *Life of Symeon the Holy Fool*, 149–50, trans. Kreuger, 154–55.

38. Theodoret, *Historia Ecclesiastica*, 5.26. See Gaddis, *No Crime*, 204–6.

39. PG 56.263–70. Translated in Allen and Mayer, *John Chrysostom*, 118–25.

40. See, for example, Tertullian, *de spectaculis* 21. See also Jerome, *Vita s. Hilarionis*, 2 for the ascetic virtuoso Hilarion's rejection of the "insanity of the circus, the gore of the arena, the transgression of the theater . . ."

41. Severus of Antioch, *Homily XVI*, ed. and French trans. Rubens Duval, *PO* 4.1 (Paris, 1906), 45–47. I have preferred my own translation of the Syriac version of Severus's homily to Duval's French rendering here. The passage cited by Severus is 1 Corinthians 10:21. Cf. the Nestorian *Histoire de Barḥadbešabba ʿArbaïa* XII, ed. and French trans. Nau, 257–59, where the theater shows are depicted as a festival in which, "as a matter of antique custom, the whole *chora* of the city unites not for the purpose of seeing the play, or to hear the voice of the singer—for the great racket of those gathered blots out the singer, and those who are accustomed to act cannot act because of the great racket. This is because all of the people with a single voice invoke the demon himself." On one occasion, the text says, the crowd chanted in unison for blessings from "the master of the gods," but instead got a nasty plague, which was eventually cured through the intervention of Gregory of Neocaesarea (Thaumaturgus). Here, the individual and communal identities of discrete members of the crowd, whatever those identities might have been, were subsumed in the space of the theater into "a single voice" raised in praise of the old god. It is perhaps unsurprising that for some Christians, opposed to such promiscuous intermingling of Christians with non-Christians, the theater became a venue for contagion, itself a familiar metaphor for boundary transgression and pollution.

42. Jacob of Serugh, *Homily 5*, trans. C. Moss, "Jacob of Serugh's Homilies on the Spectacles of the Theater," *Le Museon* 48 (1935): 87–112.

43. Callinicus, *Vita Hypatii*, 33, trans. A. J. Festugière, *Les moines d'Orient*, 4 vols. (Paris, 1961–65), 2.57–58.

44. Callinicus, *Vita Hypatii*, 33, trans. Festugière, *Les moines d'Orient*, 2.57–58.

45. Callinicus, *Vita Hypatii* 33, trans. Festugière, *Les moines d'Orient*, 2.58.

46. See, for example, the Arabic version of the Life of Saint Samuel, text and translation in A. Alcock, "The Arabic Life of Anbā Samawīʾl of Qalamūn," *Le Muséon* 109 (1996): 321–36, esp. 327–31; Paphnutius, *Life of Onnophrius*, passim, Coptic text ed. and English trans. E. A. Wallis Budge, *Coptic Texts*, 4.205–24, 455–73; Leontius of Neapolis, *Life of Symeon the Fool* I–II, trans. Derek Krueger, *Symeon the Holy Fool: Leontius's* Life *and the Late Antique City* (Berkeley, 1996), 134–48. Also see Krueger's ch. 3 for a discussion of late antique hagiographical topology.

47. See, for example, *Histories of the Monks in the Egyptian Desert*, English trans. E. A. Wallis Budge, *Coptic Texts*, 5.954–55.

48. Besa, *To Matthew*, 5.6–7, ed. and trans. K. H. Kühn, *Letters and Sermons of Besa*, 2 vols., CSCO 22 (Louvain, 1956), 2.91. I have adapted Kühn's translation here. For the Coptic, see 1.94–95.

49. Besa, *To Matthew*, 5.4, trans. Kühn.

50. Besa, *To an erring monk*, 2.4, trans. Kühn.

51. Besa, *To an erring monk*, 3.4, trans. Kühn. Cf. Boyarin, *Dying for God*, 34. In the narrative analyzed by Boyarin, when the rabbi Ben Dama dies before his Christian friend can arrive and cure him, his uncle rejoices: "Blessed art thou, Ben Dama, for you left in peace, and you did not violate the fence of your colleagues, for anyone who breaks down the fence of the Sages, terrible things happen to him, as it says, 'One who breaks down a fence, let a snake bite him' (Eccl. 10:8)." M. S. Zuckermandel (ed.), *Tosephta: Based on the Erfurt and Vienna Codices, with Lieberman, Saul, "Supplement" to the Tosephta* (in Hebrew) (Jerusalem, 1937), 227.

52. Cf. Is. 52:5.

53. Besa, *To an erring monk*, 5.1, trans. Kühn.

54. In the sermon "To the Brethren on Maintaining Unity" (X.7) for example, Besa asks, "Is it not a great sin that you buy and sell with the laymen, contrary to the judgment of your fathers who take care of you? It is especially laid down by our fathers from the beginning that men shall not buy and sell contrary to the rules of judgment." Trans. Kühn.

55. James E. Goehring, "Pachomius' Vision of Heresy: The Development of a Pachomian Tradition," in James E. Goehring, *Ascetics, Society and the Desert: Studies in Early Egyptian Monasticism* (Harrisburg, Pa., 1999), 137–61.

56. Translated by Goehring, *Ascetics, Society and the Desert*, 144.

57. Goehring, "Pachomius' Vision of Heresy," in *Ascetics, Society and the Desert*, 150–51.

58. H. E. Winlock, W. E. Crum, and Hugh G. Evelyn White, *The Monastery of Epiphanius at Thebes*, 2 vols. (New York, 1926 [New York, 1973]).

59. See MacCoull, "Prophethood, Texts, and Artifacts."

60. Winlock, Crum, and White, *The Monastery of Epiphanius*, 1.29–31, II Appendix I. MacCoull, "Prophethood, Texts, and Artifacts," 307–14.

61. "Inscription C" in Winlock, Crum, and White, *The Monastery of Epiphanius*, 2.337.

62. See MacCoull, "Prophethood, Texts, and Artifacts," 307–14. For Epiphanius as a "prophetic figure," see 308–10. For Christian monks as prophets see David Frankfurter, "Introduction: Approaches to Coptic Pilgrimage," in Frankfurter (ed.), *Pilgrimage and Holy Space in Late Antique Egypt*, 1–48, esp. 24–26; Frankfurter, "Syncretism and the Holy Man," esp. 344–52; Frankfurter, *Religion in Roman Egypt*, 186–97, ch. 5.

63. See Inscriptions A, D, and fragments a. b., in Winlock, Crum, and White, *The Monastery of Epiphanius*, II Appendix I.

64. See, for example, Besa, Fragment 1 ("On Vigilance"), 5; Besa, Fragment 6 ("On Strife in the Community") passim; Besa, Fragment 12 ("Reproofs and Monastic Rules"), 9; Besa, Fragment 18 ("To Sinful Nuns"), 2.

65. See, for example, Besa, Fragment 38 ("A Catechesis Commemorating Shenoute"). For Epiphanius, see the letter addressed to "Abba Epiphanius, the prophet and anchorite," Winlock, Crum, and White, *The Monastery of Epiphanius*, 2.29–31 and note 20. For other Egyptian ascetics remembered as prophets, see also MacCoull, "Prophethood, Texts, and Artifacts," 311–12. See now Brakke, *Demons and the Making of the Monk*, ch. 5.

66. Brown, "Asceticism Christian and Pagan," in Cameron et al. (eds.), *Cambridge Ancient History* XIII, 614.

67. Brown, "Asceticism Christian and Pagan," 617.

68. Rousseau, *Pachomius*, 122–24; Gaddis, *No Crime*, ch. 2; Brakke, *Athanasius and the Politics of Asceticism*, 223–24; Harvey, *Asceticism and Society in Crisis*, 9–12; M. A. Tilley, "The Ascetic Body and the (Un)Making of the World of the Martyr," *Journal of the American Academy of Religion* 59 (1991): 467–79; Harvey, "Sense of a Stylite," 380; Athanasius, *Vita Antonii*, 46–47.

69. See Brakke, *Athanasius and the Politics of Asceticism*, 135–38, ch. 4; Caner, *Wandering, Begging Monks*, 229–30.

70. For Prudentius, see Palmer, *Prudentius on the Martyrs*; Malamud, *A Poetics of Transformation*; Roberts, *Poetry and the Cult of the Martyrs*; Ross, "Dynamic Writing and Martyr's Bodies"; Conybeare, "The Ambiguous Laughter of Saint Laurence." For Coptic martyr narratives, see, for example, Terry Wilfong, "Reading the Disjointed Body in Coptic: From Physical Modification to Textual Fragmentation," in Dominic Montserrat (ed.), *Changing Bodies, Changing Meanings: Studies in the Human Body in Antiquity* (London, 1998), 116–36; J. Horn, *Studien zu den Märtyrern des nordlichen Oberägyptens. I Märtyrerverehrung und Märtyrerlegende im Werk des Schenute* (Wiesbaden, 1986); Baumeister, *Martyr Invictus*.

71. For brains pouring forth like milk and bones poking through flesh, see *The Martyrdom and Miracles of Saint George of Cappadocia: Oriental Text Series I*, trans. E. A. Wallis Budge (London, 1888), 289. For rendered fat running from a seventh-century anti-Chalcedonian bishop tortured under Heraclius, see Sāwirūs b. al-Muqaffaʿ, *History of*

the Patriarchs of Alexandria, part I, chapter 14, ed. and trans. B. Evetts, *PO* 1.4 (Paris, 1948); 5.1 (Paris, 1947), 491.

72. Linda Williams, *Hard Core: Power, Pleasure and the "Frenzy of the Visible"* (Berkeley, 1989), esp. 48–57.

73. Synesius, *ep.* 43.155–61, ed. and French trans. Antonio Garzya and Denis Roques, *Synésios de Cyrène, Correspondance: Lettres I–LXIII*, 3 vols. (Paris, 2000), 2.63, cited and translated by Maud Gleason, "Talking Bodies and Truth Contests," 305; Shaw, "Juridical Nightmares and Christian Memory," esp. 552–63; duBois, *Torture and Truth*, ch. 5; Shaw, "Body/Power/Identity: Passions of the Martyrs," 269–312; Shaw, "Judicial Nightmares and Christian Memory"; Grig, "Torture and Truth in Late Antique Martyrology"; Ramsay MacMillan, "Judicial Savagery in the Roman Empire," *Chiron* 16 (1986): 147–66.

74. Brown, "Enjoying the Saints," 7. See also Thomas J. Heffernan, *Sacred Biography: Saints and Their Biographers in the Middle Ages* (Oxford, 1988), 58.

75. *Martyrdom of Saint Theodore* 4, ed. Delehaye, 130.

76. Jerome, *Vita s. Hilarionis*, 11.

77. *Life of Daniel the Stylite*, 98, trans. Elizabeth Dawes and Norman H. Baynes in *Three Byzantine Saints: Contemporary Biographies Translated from the Greek* (Oxford, 1948 [Crestwood, N.Y., 1977, 1996]), 68–69; *Life of Symeon the Stylite the Younger*, 31, ed. and trans. Paul van den Ven. For the phenomenon of holy pain such as these ascetics inflicted upon themselves, see Ariel Glucklich, "Sacred Pain and the Phenomenal Self," *HTR* 91 (1998): 389–412; Ariel Glucklich, "Self and Sacrifice: A Phenomenological Psychology of Sacred Pain," *HTR* 92 (1999): 479–506.

78. For Mare's bloody feet, see John of Ephesus, *Lives of the Eastern Saints*, 36, trans. Brooks, *PO* 18, 628. For Thomas the Armenian, see John of Ephesus, *Lives of the Eastern Saints*, 21, *PO* 17, 291.

79. Theodoret, *Historia Religiosa* 26.5, ed. and French trans. Canivet and Leroy-Molinghen, 2.166–67; *Life of Symeon the Stylite the Younger* 26, ed. and trans. van den Ven.

80. Isaac the Presbyter, *Life of Samuel of Kalamun*, 7, ed. and trans. Anthony Alcock, *The Life of Samuel of Kalamun by Isaac the Presbyter* (Warminster, England, 1983), 81.

81. *Life of Symeon the Stylite the Younger*, ed. and trans. Paul van den Ven. Cf. John of Ephesus, *Lives of the Eastern Saints*, 44, ed. and trans. Brooks, 663, where the stylite Zʿura is described as having spent years "on a column between earth and heaven."

82. Goehring, *Ascetics, Society and the Desert*, 80–81. Goehring very usefully emphasizes that ascetic practice was topographically quite diverse, but that in the imaginary of late antique peoples, asceticism was properly practiced in an alien setting, indeed *the* alien setting for the settled peoples of the Roman world, the desert. See *Ascetics, Society and the Desert*, ch. 4, 5, 6.

83. Caner, *Wandering, Begging Monks*, 199–205 and passim; Goehring, *Ascetics, Society and the Desert*, ch. 4.

84. See the *Life of Alexander the Sleepless*, trans. Caner, 34; Jerome, *Life of Paul*, 8. See

Paul B. Harvey, "Saints and Satyrs: Jerome the Scholar at Work," *Athenaeum* 86 (1998): 35–56, esp. his translation 37–38.

85. See Athanasius, *Vita Antonii*, 8–10; *History of the Monks of Egypt*, 5; MacCoull, "Prophethood, Texts, Artifacts," 308; Goehring, *Ascetics, Society and the Desert*, ch. 4, esp. 94–95.

86. *Life of Daniel the Stylite*, 98, trans. Dawes and Baynes, 68–69; *Life of Symeon the Stylite the Younger*, 31, ed. and trans. Paul van den Ven.

87. John of Ephesus, *Lives of the Eastern Saints*, 14, ed. and trans. Brooks, *PO* 17, 216.

88. See, for example, *The Life of Pelagia of Antioch*, Syriac text ed. J. Gildemeister, *Acta sanctae Pelagiae syriace* (Bonn, 1879); trans. Sebastian P. Brock and Susan Ashbrook Harvey, in *Holy Women of the Syrian Orient* (Berkeley, 1987), 40–62; trans. A. Guillaumont, "La version syriaque," in *Pélagie la Pénitente, Metamorphoses d'une légende*, vol. 1, *Les texts et leur histoire* (Paris, 1984), 287–315; *The Life of St. Mary/Marinos*, Syriac version ed. F. Nau, *Revue de l'Orient Chrétien* 6 (1901): 283–89; Latin version ed. L. Clugnet *Revue de l'Orient Chrétien* 6 (1901): 357–78; trans. Nicholas Constans in Alice-Mary Talbot (ed.), *Holy Women of Byzantium: Ten Saints' Lives in English Translation* (Washington, D.C., 1996), 1–12; *The Life of Mary of Egypt*, PG 87:3697–726; trans. Maria Kouli, in *Holy Women of Byzantium*, 65–93; *Life of Hilaria*, ed. J. Drescher, in *Three Coptic Legends* (Cairo, 1947); Wilfong, "Reading the Disjointed Body in Coptic," 116–36. For recent studies of these texts, see Stephan J. Davis, "Crossed Texts, Crossed Sex: Intertextuality and Gender in Early Christian Legends of Holy Women Disguised as Men," *JECS* 10 (2002): 1–36; Virginia Burrus, *The Sex Lives of Saints: An Erotics of Ancient Hagiography* (Philadelphia, 2004), 128–59; Patricia Cox Miller, "Is There a Harlot in This Text? Hagiography and the Grotesque," *JMEMS* 33 (2003): 419–35; Evelyn Patlagean, "L'histoire de la femme désguisée en moine et l'évolution de la sainteté féminine a Byzance," *Studi Medievali*, ser. 3, 17 (1976): 597–623; Harvey, *Asceticism and Society in Crisis*, 115–16; Wayne E. Meeks, "The Image of the Androgyne: Some Uses of Symbol in Earliest Christianity," *History of Religions* 13 (1973–74): 165–208; J. Anson, "The Female Transvestite in Early Monasticism: The Origin and Development of a Motif," *Viator* 5 (1974): 1–32; Susan Ashbrook Harvey, "Women in Early Byzantine Hagiography: Reversing the Story," in Linda Coon et al. (eds.), *"That Gentle Strength": Historical Perspectives on Women in Christianity* (Charlottesville, 1990), 36–59; Elizabeth Castelli, "'I Will Make Mary Male': Pieties of the Body and Gender Transformation of Christian Women in Late Antiquity," in Julia Epstein and Kristina Straub (eds.), *Body Guards: The Cultural Politics of Gender Ambiguity* (New York, 1991), 29–49.

89. See the various episodes described at Leontius of Neapolis, *Life of Symeon the Holy Fool*, IV, trans. Krueger, 150–71. For Moses, see Brakke, *Demons and the Making of the Monk*, 157–81.

90. MacCoull, "Prophethood, Texts, and Artifacts," 318; Frankfurter, *Religion in Roman Egypt*, 270–73.

91. See Athanasius, *Life of Saint Antony*, 72–80; Synesius, *Dion*, 12; Brown, *Power and Persuasion*, 123; Drake, *Constantine and the Bishops*, 410–11.

92. Gaddis, *No Crime*, ch. 6, esp. 208–20, 249–50.

93. Michel Foucault, *Les anormaux: Cours au Collège de France (1974–1975)*, (Paris, 1999), 51.

94. See Jeffrey Jerome Cohen, "Monster Theory: Seven Theses," in Jeffrey Jerome Cohen (ed.), *Monster Theory* (Minneapolis, 1996), 3–25.

95. Cohen, "Monster Theory," 12–16.

96. See Julia Kristeva, *Powers of Horror: An Essay on Abjection*, trans. Leon S. Roudiez (New York, 1982), 1–17.

97. Cohen, "Monster Theory," 4–16.

98. Foucault, *Les anormaux*, 51.

99. Brown, *Power and Persuasion*, 107–8; Brown, *Authority and the Sacred*, 50–51, Gaddis, *No Crime*; Drake, *Constantine and the Bishops*, 409–18; Van Dam, "From Paganism to Christianity at Late Antique Gaza," 8–13, 17–20.

100. See, in particular, Brown, "The Rise and Function of the Holy Man," passim; Brown, *Power and Persuasion*, 14, 27, 105–7, 143, 153–57; Drake, *Constantine and the Bishops*, 409–15.

101. See Rudolf Otto, *The Idea of the Holy: An Inquiry into the Non-Rational Factor in the Idea of the Divine and its Relation to the Rational*, trans. John W. Harvey (Oxford, 1923 [1958]), 1–24; Derrida, *The Gift of Death*, ch. 2, 3.

102. John of Ephesus, *Lives of the Eastern Saints*, 5, ed. and trans. Brooks, 84–111.

103. John of Ephesus, *Lives of the Eastern Saints*, 5, 102. I have adapted Brooks's translation.

104. John of Ephesus, *Lives of the Eastern Saints*, 5, ed. and trans. Brooks, 102–3.

105. John of Ephesus, *Lives of the Eastern Saints*, 5, ed. and trans. Brooks, 103.

106. John of Ephesus, *Lives of the Eastern Saints*, 5, ed. and trans. Brooks, 103–6.

107. John of Ephesus, *Lives of the Eastern Saints*, 5, ed. and trans. Brooks, 101.

108. Socrates, *Historia Ecclesiastica*, 5.16, ed. Hansen, 290.

109. John of Ephesus, *Lives of the Eastern Saints*, 5, ed. and trans. Brooks, 90. Harvey, *Asceticism and Society in Crisis*, 53–54; J. B. Segal, "The Jews of North Mesopotamia Before the Rise of Islam," in J. M. Grintz and J. Liver, *Sefer Segal* (Jerusalem, 1964) 32–63, cited by Harvey.

110. John of Ephesus, *Lives of the Eastern Saints*, 5, ed. and trans. Brooks, 90–93.

111. John of Ephesus, *Lives of the Eastern Saints*, 16, ed. Brooks, 229–47; "like an animal," 229; "went among humans" or "into the dwelling place of humans," 231–32. Harvey, *Asceticism and Society in Crisis*, 94–99.

112. John of Ephesus, *Lives of the Eastern Saints*, 16, ed. and trans. Brooks, 233.

113. John of Ephesus, *Lives of the Eastern Saints*, 16, ed. and trans. Brooks, 234.

114. John of Ephesus, *Lives of the Eastern Saints*, 16, ed. and trans. Brooks, 234–35.

115. John of Ephesus, *Lives of the Eastern Saints*, 16, ed. and trans. Brooks, 235–36.

116. John of Ephesus, *Lives of the Eastern Saints*, 16, ed. and trans. Brooks, 240–41.

117. John of Ephesus, *Lives of the Eastern Saints*, 16, ed. and trans. Brooks, 241–42.

118. John of Ephesus, *Lives of the Eastern Saints*, 16, ed. and trans. Brooks, 242–46.

119. John of Ephesus, *Lives of the Eastern Saints*, 16, ed. and trans. E. W. Brooks, *PO* 17.1 (Turnhout, 1974), 229–47.

120. Brown, "Saint as Exemplar," passim.

121. See John Chrysostom, "Against the Opponents of the Monastic Life," trans. D. Hunter, *A Comparison between a King and a Monk; Against the Opponents of the Monastic Life: Two Treatises* (Lewiston, N.Y., 1988), 77–176.

122. Dioscurus, *A Panegyric on Macarius, Bishop of Tkōw*, 5, ed. and trans. D. W. Johnson, 2 vols. CSCO 416 (Copt. 42), CSCO 415 (Copt. 41), (Louvain, 1980), 416:20–30. Coptic text 415:30–40.

123. See John Block Friedman, *The Monstrous Races in Medieval Art and Thought* (Cambridge, Mass., 1980), 195–96; Cohen, "Monster Theory," 12–16; Steven Baker, *Picturing the Beast: Animals, Identity, and Representation* (Manchester, 1993), cited by Cohen; Kristeva, *Powers of Horror*, 4, 15.

124. Cf. John of Ephesus, *Ecclesiastical History*, 3.29, where, during a strange bout of antipagan persecution, in which most of the accused seem to have been prominent Christians, including a number of high-ranking churchmen and their associates, the provincial governor and procurator Anatolius, the patriarch of Antioch Gregory and Eulogius, who was to become the archbishop of Alexandria. Anatolius, Gregory and Eulogius were accused of having participated in a pagan ceremony at Daphne during which a child was sacrificed. This accusation, made under torture by Anatolius's secretary, "filled the populace with horror and amazement, and various cries were raised, and the cathedral closed, while Gregory could not venture to leave his palace, nor could the liturgy be celebrated." Trans. R. Payne Smith, 213. A local imperial official also seems to have been among the victims of another, especially ghastly bit of antipagan persecution in the last years of the sixth century and the first years of the seventh under the emperor Maurice, during which those suspects who resisted conversion to Christianity were cut asunder and their limbs hung up in public view. See *The Chronicle of Michael the Syrian*, ed. and trans. Jean Baptiste Chabot (*Chronique du Michel le Syrien patriarche jacobite d'Antioche [1166–1199]*), 4 vols. (Paris, 1899–1924), IV 388, II 375–6; *Chronicle of 1234*, ed. and trans. Jean-Baptiste Chabot (*Chronicon anonymum ad annum 1234*), Syriac text CSCO 81 (Syr. 36) (Louvain, 1953), 1.214–15, Latin trans. CSCO 109 (Syr. 56) (Louvain, 1952), 1.168–69, cited by Sebastian Brock, "A Syriac Collection of Prophecies of the Pagan Philosophers," in *Orientalia Lovaniensia Periodica* 14 (1983): 209, reprinted in Sebastian Brock, *Studies in Syriac Christianity* (Aldershot, 1992), ch. 7.

125. *Zuqnīn Chronicle*, trans. Harrak (*The Chronicle of Zuqnīn: Parts III and IV A.D. 488–775*), 63 [37].

126. *Zuqnīn Chronicle*, trans. Harrak (*The Chronicle of Zuqnīn: Parts III and IV A.D. 488–775*), 63–64 [38].

127. *Zuqnīn Chronicle*, trans. Harrak (*The Chronicle of Zuqnīn: Parts III and IV A.D. 488–775*), 63 [37].

128. See Kristeva, *Powers of Horror*, 101–12. For heresy as contagion, see Rebecca Lyman, "Ascetics and Bishops: Epiphanius on Orthodoxy," in Elm, Rebillard, and Romano, *Orthodoxy, Christianity, History*, 149–61.

129. *Zuqnīn Chronicle*, trans. Harrak (*The Chronicle of Zuqnīn: Parts III and IV A.D. 488–775*), 113 [109–10]. It is intriguing to note here that even as an object of dread, the monk remained a figure that incited a declaration of communal identity.

130. See *The Passion of Saint Christopher* (BHL 1764). See also *The Passion of Saint Christopher*, 16, trans. David Woods, *Military Martyrs*, http://www.ucc.ie/milmart/BHL1764.html, where Christopher's example led one of his fellow martyrs to put her zeal to work in a brief flurry of idol destruction. After pretending that she would yield to the demands of the emperor and his magistrates, that she would sacrifice, the woman is led before the statues of the gods: "The priests said, 'Repent, and the great god Jupiter will take pity on you.' Laughing she replied, 'I will ask them not to take pity on my sin.' And saying this she took her belt, and tied her handkerchief about the statue of Jupiter, and pulling it towards her, she threw the statue down. It was immediately smashed to pieces as fine as sand. Then she ran to Apollo and said, 'These gods are not awake, but sleep, so they do not hear their personal servants.' In a similar manner she tied her belt to this statue, and threw it down. It was broken into three pieces. The result was that all who were watching cried out, 'The audacity of the woman who does not fear such statues!' And she said to Hercules, 'Get going, if you are a god, so that I do not destroy you.' And she jumped up, grabbed the idol with her hands, and threw it down. She said to the people standing by, 'Call the doctors, and let them cure your gods.'"

131. *Martyrdom of Saint Mercurius*, trans. Budge, *Coptic Martyrdoms*, 5.1161–62.

132. *Martyrdom of Saint Mercurius*, trans. Budge, *Coptic Martyrdoms*, 5.1161–69.

133. Ammianus Marcellinus, *Res gestae*, 31.16.5–6, trans. J. C. Rolfe, 3.501–3; For discussions of this incident, see David Woods, "Ammianus and the Blood-Sucking Saracen," in *Pleiades Setting: Essays for Pat Cronin on His 65th Birthday* (Cork, 2002), 127–45; David Woods, "The Saracen Defenders of Constantinople in 378," *GRBS* 37 (1996): 259–79.

134. Nilus of Ancyra, *De mon*, ex. 9 (PG 79.729AB), trans. Caner, *Wandering, Begging Monks*, 180–81.

135. See Libanius, *Oratio* 30.

136. Eunapius, *Lives of the Philosophers*, 472, ed. and trans. Wilmer. C. Wright, *Philostratus and Eunapius: Lives of the Sophists* (Cambridge, Mass., 1921 [1961]), 421–23. Eunapius is quoting Homer, *Odyssey*, 7.59.

137. See Jeffrey Jerome Cohen, *Of Giants: Sex, Monsters and the Middle Ages* (Minneapolis, 1999).

138. *Zuqnīn Chronicle*, trans. Harrak (*The Chronicle of Zuqnīn: Parts III and IV A.D. 488–775*), 65–66.

CHAPTER FIVE

1. The *hijra* was the migration, in 622 C.E., of Muḥammad and his persecuted community from Mecca to the city of Yathrib, later called "Medina." The *hijra* marks the traditional beginning of the Muslim era. For its role in Islamic chronology, see Donner, *Narratives of Islamic Origins*, ch. 10, esp. 230–39.

2. See Fred McGraw Donner, *The Early Islamic Conquests* (Princeton, 1981), 5–9.

3. See Donner, *Early Islamic Conquests*; Morony, *Iraq After the Muslim Conquest*; Walter Kaegi, *Byzantium and the Early Islamic Conquests* (Chicago, 1992).

4. Fred Donner has recently and very importantly explored the genesis of the early Islamic historical record, taking it as his task to "situate the beginnings of historical writing in the Islamic community in its proper historical context, and to provide some basis for understanding why the narratives of Islamic origin we have before us look the way they do." Donner, *Narratives of Islamic Origins*, 275. It is the purpose of the present study to further situate these early Islamic communal narratives not only in their historical context but within their late ancient cultural and religious context as well. For a detailed critique of Donner, see Amikam Elad, "Community of Believers of 'Holy Men' and 'Saints' or Community of Muslims? The Rise and Development of Early Muslim Historiography," *JSS* 47 (2002): 241–308.

5. R. Stephen Humphreys, "Qur'anic Myth and Narrative Structure in Early Islamic Historiography," in Frank M. Clover and R. Stephen Humphreys (eds.), *Tradition and Innovation in Late Antiquity* (Madison 1989), 271–90, esp. 272–73. "When these scholars set about reconstructing the history of early Islam, what historiographic models were available to them? Plainly, they did not draw on the resources of late Roman culture—either the profane political tradition represented my Ammianus Marcellinus and Procopius or the ecclesiastical chronicle tradition."

6. The broad range of communities within which such figures as the monk were recognized is suggested, for example, by the inclusion of one version of this narrative in a recently translated Samaritan chronicle which seems to have been written within Islam's first century. In addition, the monk most frequently named in Muslim narratives as the first person to recognize Muḥammad as a prophet, one Baḥīrā, also appears in several Christian narratives, albeit frequently identified as a "heretic." See Milka Levy-Rubin, *The Continuatio of the Samaritan Chronicle of Abū l-Fatḥ al-Sāmirī al-Danafī* (Princeton, 2002), 46. Levy-Rubin also cites versions of the Baḥīrā story that appear in Jewish texts.

7. It was such local elaborations upon commonly held semiotic systems that exemplified late antique religiosity, whether situated in Syria, Egypt, Gaul, Armenia, Ireland, or Mesopotamia. See, among many others, Frankfurter, *Religion in Roman Egypt*; Brown, *Power and Persuasion in Late Antiquity*; Peter Brown, *The Rise of Western Christendom: Triumph and Diversity, A.D. 200–1000*, 2nd ed. (Oxford, 2003); Lisa Bitel, *Isle of the Saints: Monastic Settlement and Christian Community in Early Ireland* (Ithaca, 1990); Joseph Falaky

Nagy, *Conversing with Angels and Ancients: Literary Myths in Medieval Ireland* (Ithaca, 1997); Sebastian Brock, *Syriac Perspectives on Late Antiquity* (London, 1984). For Armenia, see Nina Garsoïan, *Church and Culture in Early Medieval Armenia* (London, 1999); Nina Garsoïan, *Armenia between Byzantium and the Sasanians* (Aldershot, 1985).

8. The Studies in Late Antiquity and Early Islam series edited by Averil Cameron and Lawrence I. Conrad is the most important resource for the investigation of early Islam and its late antique milieu, although until the present no truly synthetic study of the early Islamic community as part of the late antique *oikoumenê* has appeared even in that series. See, for example, the very useful and frequently admirable contributions in Averil Cameron and Lawrence I. Conrad (eds.), *The Byzantine and Early Islamic Near East: Problems in the Literary Source Material* (Princeton, 1992). For other explorations of the question of late antiquity's links with the early Islamic period, see, among others, Morony, *Iraq after the Muslim Conquest*; Peter Brown, "Late Antiquity and Islam: Parallels and Contrasts," in Barbara Daly Metcalf (ed.), *Moral Conduct and Authority: The Place of Adab in South Asian Islam* (Berkeley, 1984); Brown, *Rise of Western Christendom*, 12, 13; Frank Clover and R. Stephen Humphreys, "Introduction," in Clover and Humphreys, *Tradition and Innovation*; Pierre Canivet and Jean-Paul Rey-Coquais (eds.), *La Syrie de Byzance à l'Islam VIIe–VIIIe siècles: Actes de Colloque international Lyon-Maison de l'Orient méditerranéen Paris—Institut de Monde Arabe 11–15 Septembe 1990* (Damascus, 1992); Garth Fowden, *Empire to Commonwealth: Consequences of Monotheism in Late Antiquity* (Princeton, 1993); Michael G. Morony, "Economic Boundaries? Late Antiquity and Early Islam," *Journal of the Economic and Social History of the Orient* 47 (2004): 166–94.

9. See R. Stephen Humphreys, *Islamic History: A Framework for Inquiry* (Princeton, 1991), ch. 3, Chase F. Robinson, "The Study of Islamic Historiography: A Progress Report," *Journal of the Royal Asiatic Society* III.7.2 (1997): 199–227.

10. The literature surrounding these processes is vast. The following is meant only as a representative sampling of the field. Michael Cook, "The Opponents of Writing of Tradition in Early Islam," *Arabica* 44 (1997): 437–530; G. Schoeler, "Writing and Publishing on the Use and Function of Writing in the First Centuries of Islam," *Arabica* 44, (1997): 423–35; cf. a longer, German-language version of the same article, G. Schoeler, "Schreiben und Veröffentlichen: Zu Verwendung und Funktion der Schrift in den ersten islamischen Jahrhunderten," *Der Islam* 69 (1992): 1–43; cf. Gahan Osman, "Oral vs. Written Transmission: The case of al-Ṭabarī and Ibn Saʿd," *Arabica* 48 (2001): 66–80; Stefan Leder, "Authorship and Transmission in Unauthored Literature: The Akhbar Attributed to Haytham Ibn ʿAdi" *Oriens* 31 (1988): 67–81; Michael Lecker, "The Death of the Prophet Muhammad's Father: Did Wāqidī Invent Some of the Evidence?" *Zeitschrift der Deutschen Morgenlandischen Gesellschaft* 145 (1995): 9–27; Michael Lecker, "Wāqidī's Account of the Status of the Jews of Medina: A Study of a Combined Report," *JNES* 54 (1995): 15–32; For these problems as they relate to prophetic tradition and *ḥadīth* collections, see Joseph Schacht, *The Origins of Muhammadan Jurisprudence* (Oxford, 1979); Harald Motzki, *Die Anfänge der islamischen Jurisprudenz: ihre Entwicklung in Mekka bis zur Mitte des 2./8. Jahrhunderts*

(Stuttgart, 1991); Harald Motzki, "The Musannaf of ʿAbd al-Razzaq al-Sanʿani as a Source of Authentic Ahadith of the First Century A.H.," *JNES* l (1991): 1–21; G. H. A. Juynboll, *Muslim Tradition: Studies in Chronology, Provenance, and Authorship of Early Hadith* (Cambridge, 1983); M. J. Kister, *Society and Religion from Jāhiliyya to Islam* (London, 1990).

11. Humphreys, "Early Historical Tradition and the First Islamic Polity," in Humphreys, *Islamic History*.

12. Often the assessment of a given body of material was based upon the reputation of the first- or second-century Muslim traditionalist to whom it was attributed. It was also a central and quite valid concern of these scholars to detect and correct for the influence of later political or religious agendas or ideologies upon the statements or stories attributed to earlier figures. See M. J. de Goeje, *Mémoire sur la conquête de la Syrie* (Leiden, 1900); Julius Wellhausen, *Prolegomena zur ältesten Geschichte des Islams* in his *Skitzen und Vorarbeiten* VI (Berlin, 1899); Julius Wellhausen, *Das arabische Reich und sein Sturz* (Berlin, 1902) translated as *The Arab Kingdom and Its Fall* (Calcutta, 1927); Leone Caetani, *Annali dell'Islam* 10 vols. (Milan, 1907), vol. 2; Ignaz Goldziher, *Muhammedanische Studien*, 2 vols. (Halle, 1889–90), translated as *Muslim Studies*, 2 vols. (Oxford, 1971). See also Fred Donner, "Introduction," in Donner, *Narratives of Islamic Origins*. One classic debate concerning the reliability of certain early Muslim reports and the credibility of the traditionalist to whom they were attributed is that which has persisted concerning the traditionalist Sayf b. ʿUmar, one of al-Ṭabarī's important informants. For early and decidedly negative assessments of Sayf as a source of facts, see above works. For more recent reassessments of Sayf as a source, see R. S. Humphreys, "The Odd Couple: al-Ṭabarī and Sayf ibn ʿUmar," in Lawrence Conrad (ed.), *History and Historiography in Early Islamic Times* (Princeton, forthcoming); Ella Landau-Tasseron, "Sayf Ibn ʿUmar in Medieval and Modern Scholarship," *Der Islam* 67 (1990): 1–26.

13. For examples of the guardedly optimistic approach, see Donner, *The Early Islamic Conquests*; Morony, *Iraq after the Muslim Conquest*; Robinson, *Empire and Elites*; Chase F. Robinson, "The Conquest of Khuzistan: a Historiographical Reassessment," *BSOAS* 67 (2004): 14–39; Albrecht Noth, "*Futūḥ*-history and *Futūḥ*-historiography: The Muslim Conquest of Damascus," *al-Qantara* 10 (1989): 453–62. For skeptical and pessimistic views, see principally John E. Wansbrough, *The Sectarian Milieu: Content and Composition of Islamic Salvation History* (Oxford, 1978); John E. Wansbrough, *Quranic Studies: Sources and Methods of Scriptural Interpretation* (Oxford, 1977); Patricia Crone and Michael Cook, *Hagarism: The Making of the Islamic World* (Cambridge, 1977); Patricia Crone, *Slaves on Horses: The Evolution of the Islamic Polity* (Cambridge, 1980); Patricia Crone, *Meccan Trade and the Rise of Islam* (Princeton, 1987); Lawrence I. Conrad, "The Conquest of Arwad: A Source Critical Study in the Historiography of the Early Medieval Near East," in Averil Cameron and Lawrence I. Conrad (eds.), *The Byzantine and Early Islamic Near East: Problems in the Literary Source Material* (Princeton, 1992), 317–401; Lawrence I. Conrad, "Theophanes and the Arabic Historical Tradition: Some Indications of Intercultural Transmission," *Byzantinische Forschungen* 15 (1988): 1–44, G. R. Hawting, *The Idea of*

Idolatry and the Emergence of Islam: From Polemic to History (Cambridge, 1999). For reactions to these, see R. B. Serjeant, "Meccan Trade and the Rise of Islam: Misconceptions and Flawed Polemics," *JAOS* 110 (1990): 472–86; Donner, "Introduction," in Donner, *Narratives of Islamic Origins*; Andrew Rippin, "Literary Analysis of *Qur'ān, Tafsīr* and *Sīra*: The Methodologies of John Wansbrough," in Richard C. Martin (ed.), *Approaches to Islam in Religious Studies* (Oxford, 2001), 151–63; Judith Koren and Yehuda D. Nevo, "Methodological Approaches to Islamic Studies," *Der Islam* 68 (1991): 87–107.

14. See, among others, Humphreys, "Qur'anic Myth and Narrative Structure"; Robinson, *Empire and Elites*; Uri Rubin, *Between Bible and Qur'ān: the Children of Israel and the Islamic Self-image* (Princeton, 1999); Uri Rubin, *The Eye of the Beholder: The Life of Muḥammad as Viewed by the Early Muslims: A Textual Analysis* (Princeton, 1995); Albrecht Noth and Lawrence Conrad, *The Early Arabic Historical Tradition* (Princeton, 1994); Tayeb El-Hibri, *Reinterpreting Islamic Historiography: Hārūn al-Rashīd and the Narrative of the ʿAbbāsid Caliphate* (Cambridge, 1999).

15. Donner, *Narratives of Islamic Origins*, esp. 149–53.

16. See Jeffrey Jerome Cohen, "Introduction: Midcolonial" and "Hybrids, Monsters, Borderlands: The Bodies of Gerald of Wales," in Jeffrey Jerome Cohen (ed.), *The Postcolonial Middle Ages* (New York, 2000), 1–17, 85–104.

17. See, among others, John Haldon, *Byzantium in the Seventh Century: The Transformation of a Culture* (Cambridge, 1997).

18. Fowden, *The Barbarian Plain*, 3; C. Edmund Bosworth, "Byzantium and the Syrian Frontier in the Early Abbasid Period," in M. A. Bakhit (ed.), *Bilad al-Sham During the ʿAbbasid Period (132A.H./A.D. 170–451A.H./A.D. 1059) Proceedings of the Fifth International Conference on the History of Bilad al-Sham* (Amman, 1991), 54–62; Hans J. W. Drijvers, "Christians, Jews and Muslims in Northern Mesopotamia in Early Islamic Times: The Gospel of the Twelve Apostles and Related Texts," in Canivet and Rey-Coquais, *Syrie de Byzance à l'Islam*, 67–74; T. Bianquis, "L'Islam entre Byzance et les Sassanides," in Canivet and Rey-Coquais, *Syrie de Byzance à l'Islam*, 281–90; Irfan Shahid, "Ghassanid and Umayyad Structures: A Case of Byzance après Byzance," in Canivet and Rey-Coquais, *Syrie de Byzance à l'Islam*, 299–308; Hugh Kennedy, "The Last Century of Byzantine Syria," *Byzantinische Forschungen* 10 (1985): 141–83; Mordechai Haiman, "Agriculture and Nomad-State Relations in the Negev Desert in the Byzantine and Early Islamic Periods," *BASOR* 297 (1995): 29–53; A. Shboul and A. Walmsley, "Identity and Self-image in Syria-Palestine in the Transition from Byzantine to Early Islamic Rule: Arab Christians and Muslims," *Mediterranean Archaeology* 11 (1998): 255–87.

19. Fowden, *Barbarian Plain*, 3.

20. The sixth-century author John of Ephesus reported, for example, that in the neighborhood of Amida (modern Diyarbakār) Zoroastrian priests would weigh the theological arguments of opposed Christian communities and decide for one side or the other. See John of Ephesus, *Lives of the Eastern Saints* 10, ed. and trans. Brooks, *PO* 17.1, 137–58. Cf. Trombley, "Religious Transition in Sixth-Century Syria."

21. Haiman "Nomad-State Relations," 46.

22. Fowden, *Barbarian Plain*, 4–5. On the attraction this more profound reality, see Smith, *Map Is Not Territory*.

23. Theophylact Simocatta, *Historia Universalis*, 5.1ff. See Fowden, *Barbarian Plain*, 135ff.

24. Theodoret, *Historia Religiosa*, 16.13-16, ed. and French trans. Canivet and Leroy-Molinghen, 2.190–97.

25. Fowden, *Barbarian Plain*, 128. See also Irfan Shahid, *Byzantium and the Arabs in the Sixth Century* (Dumbarton Oaks, 1995), 1.2, 842–43, 854–55; on Arab devotion to Sergius, see Shahid, *Byzantium and the Arabs*, 949ff. See the *Life of Ahoudemmeh* 29, ed. and French trans. F. Nau *PO* 3.1 (Paris, 1905), 29.

26. See, for example, David Frankfurter, "Stylites and Phallobates: Pillar Religions in Late Antique Syria," *VC* 44 (1990): 168–98. See also Brown, *Authority and the Sacred*, ch. 3. For similar phenomena in Egypt, see David Frankfurter, "Syncretism and the Holy Man in Late Antique Egypt," *JECS* 11 (2003): 339–85.

27. See Gideon Avni, "Early Mosques in the Negev Highlands: New Archeological Evidence on Islamic Penetration of Southern Palestine," *BASOR* 294 (1994): 83–100, esp. 95: "Echoes of the early stele cult can be found in both the mosques and the adjacent settlements. In several mosques, the mihrab niche is constructed of large standing stones reminiscent of stelea. The mosque in Nahal Oded has no niche, and a stone slab instead. Another stele-like monument with a paved area in front can be seen at a cult site in a nearby settlement."

28. See Oleg Grabar, *The Shape of the Holy: Early Islamic Jerusalem* (Princeton, 1997), 170ff. Oleg Grabar, "The Meaning of the Dome on the Rock," in Marilyn Chiat and Kathryn Reyerson (eds.), *The Medieval Mediterranean* (St. Cloud, 1988); R. Shani "The Iconography of the Dome of the Rock," *JSAI* 23 (1999): 158–89, for a concise summary of the trajectory of Grabar and his interlocutors' thought regarding the Dome. For the Dome and Jerusalem generally treated in an especially helpful diachronic fashion, see Julian Raby and Jeremy Johns, *Bayt al-Maqdis: ʿAbd al-Malik's Jerusalem*, 2 vols. (Oxford, 1992).

29. See n. 28 above. Cf. Geertz, *The Interpretation of Cultures*, 99: "The signs or sign elements . . . that make up a semiotic system . . . are ideationally connected to the society in which they are found . . . they are . . . not illustrations of conceptions already in force, but conceptions themselves that seek—or for which people seek—a meaningful place in a repertoire of other documents, equally primary."

30. Donner, *Narratives of Islamic Origins*, 104–11, 178–80. Structurally and in spirit, these narratives bear much in common with tribal war narratives issued by ancient Greek heroes or nineteenth-century Sioux and Cheyenne warriors. H. David Brumble, *American Indian Autobiography* (Berkeley, 1988), 29–30, 49–51. Cf. H. David Brumble, "The Gang-banger Autobiography of Monster Kody (aka Sanyika Shakur) and Warrior Literature," *American Literary History* 12 (2000): 158–86.

31. Donner, *Narratives of Islamic Origins*, ch. 5, esp. 149–54. See also Robert G.

Hoyland, "The Content and Context of Early Arabic Inscriptions," *JSAI* 21 (1997): 108–41, esp. 84–85.

32. Cook, "Muslim Apocalyptic and *Jihād*," 66–105.

33. For the union of these two kinds of narrative, see Donner, *Narratives of Islamic Origins*, 203–19; Tarif Khalidi, *Arabic Historical Thought in the Classical Period* (Cambridge, 1994); Abd al-Aziz al-Duri, *Rise of Historical Writing among the Arabs* (Princeton, 1983); Noth and Lawrence, *Early Arabic Historical Tradition*. See also Brumble, "Gangbanger Autobiography," 158–86. For the various problems associated with the early Islamic historical tradition, see n. 9–14 above. Non-specialists will appreciate the concise discussions available in Humphreys, *Islamic History*, ch. 2, 3; Chase F. Robinson, *Islamic Historiography* (Cambridge, 2003).

34. See al-Ṭabarī, *Ta'rīkh* I.2325-6, trans. Yohanan Friedmann, *The History of al-Ṭabarī* 12: *The Battle of al-Qādisiyyah and the Conquest of Syria and Palestine* (Albany, 1992), 114.

35. See David Brakke, "'Outside the Places, Within the Truth': Athanasius of Alexandria and the Localization of the Holy," in David Frankfurter (ed.), *Pilgrimage and Holy Space in Late Antique Egypt* (Leiden, 1998), 465–67; Goehring, "The Dark Side of Landscape." For the suggestion that Antony was also claimed by Arians, see Greg and Groh, *Early Arianism*. For the practice among the Donatist and Catholic Christian communities in North Africa of narrating communal histories describing the martyrdoms of the same figures, see Tilley, *Donatist Martyr Stories*, 1–3, 25–26.

36. Somers, "The Narrative Constitution of Identity." Narrative and its (contested) roles in the constitution of social reality has of course received much attention recently. For useful discussions of the recent career of narrative in humanities and social science disciplinary debates, see Kreisworth, "Merely Telling Stories?" and Wood (ed.), *On Paul Ricoeur*.

37. Somers "Narrative Constitution of Identity," 617.

38. Drake, *Constantine and the Bishops*, 91, 459–60, 463, 479.

39. See Ando, *Imperial Ideology and Provincial Loyalty in the Roman Empire*, esp. 336–405.

40. Drake, *Constantine and the Bishops*, 142–53, 346–483.

41. For the importance of stories about martyrs and ascetics in reckoning local identity, see Brown, "Enjoying the Saints in Late Antiquity."

42. Such recent contributions to the field of late antiquity as Drake, *Constantine and the Bishops*, and Van Dam, *Becoming Christian*, explore very profitably the role of narrative in the constitution of communal identities, although neither work explicitly theorizes the function of narrative in the processes each analyzes. See also Averil Cameron, *Christianity and the Rhetoric of Empire: The Development of Christian Discourse* (Berkeley, 1991).

43. For al-Ṭabarī, see Franz Rosenthal's long introductory essay in the first volume of *The History of al-Ṭabarī* (Albany, 1990), esp. 54: "The assumption that al-Ṭabarī's quotations can in general be relied upon as being accurate has not been disproved and, as mat-

ters stand, remains valid." For Ibn ʿAsākir, see James Lindsay (ed.), *Ibn ʿAsākir and Early Islamic History* (Princeton, 2001), passim. For al-Azdī, see Conrad, "Al-Azdī's History"; Mourad, "On Early Islamic Historiography."

44. Donner, *Narratives of Islamic Origins*, 204–14; Noth and Conrad, *Early Arabic Historical Tradition*, 111ff.; Cook, "Muslim Apocalyptic," 81.

45. See, for example, Theodoret of Cyr, *Historia Religiosa*, 2.16, ed. and French trans. Canivet and Leroy-Molinghen, 2.166–67, where Julian Saba becomes the object of a rumor campaign put forth by heretics suggesting that he accepts the teachings of Arius, where it is made plain that the prime danger here was that the local Christian community, accepting Julian's reputed discernment, would join the heretics. In the event, however, Julian confronts and bests the heretics. Cf. George of Sykeon, *Life of Theodore of Sykeon*, 42, where the great man "through his gift of discernment" recognizes recently acquired church vessels as having been crafted from silver which once served as a prostitute's chamber pot and thus inappropriate for use in church ritual. See also Besa, *Life of Shenoute*, 42–52, 80. See also Peter Brown, *The Making of Late Antiquity* (Cambridge, Mass., 1978); Brown, *Power and Persuasion*, ch. 3.

46. For a brief but thorough survey of the appearances of Baḥīrā in early Muslim texts connected with Muḥammad, see Rubin, *Eye of the Beholder*, 49–52. See also S. Gero, "The Legend of the Monk Baḥīra: The Cult of the Cross, and Iconoclasm," in Canivet and Rey-Coquais, *Syrie de Byzance à l'Islam*, 46–58, for a discussion of previous scholarship surrounding the Baḥīrā legend. For non-Muslim Baḥīrā stories, see Robert G. Hoyland, *Seeing Islam as Others Saw It: A Survey and Evaluation of Christian, Jewish and Zoroastrian Writings on Early Islam* (Princeton, 1997), 270–78, 476–79, 505–8, 538.

47. Muḥammad Ibn Isḥāq, *Sīrat rasūl Allāh*, ed. Ferdinand Wüstenfeld, 3 vols. (Frankfurt am Main, 1961), 115–8; English tr. Alfred Guillaume, *Life of Muhammad* (London, 1955), 79–82. See also al-Ṭabarī, *Taʾrīkh*, I. 1124–6; al-Balādhurī, *Ansāb al-ashrāf*, I, ed. Muḥammad Hamidullah (Cairo, 1959), 96. Cf. Ibn Manẓur, *Mukhtaṣar taʾrīkh dimashq li-Ibn ʿAsākir*, ed. Rūḥīyat al-Khās and Muḥammad Muṭīʿ al-Ḥāfiẓ, 29 vols. (Damascus, 1984–91), 5.154–55, which reports a similar tradition, although the threat to the young prophet here is posed by the Romans.

48. Elsewhere in the *Sīra* (119–20) Muḥammad is again recognized by a monk as a prophet when he sits under a tree which has only ever been a resting spot for prophets. Another narrative (136–44) details the process of conversion undergone by a pious young Zoroastrian, who is converted to Christianity and after a disappointing encounter with a greedy, corrupt bishop (representing another motif from Christian hagiography) becomes the disciple of a local monk. When the older monk is ready to die and the young man asks to be referred to another master, the monk tells him that there is no man as pious as himself but that a prophet will appear in Arabia who will only eat what is given to him but not what is given as alms and will bear between his shoulders the mark of prophecy. Sold to some Arabian Jews as a slave, the young man eventually meets the Prophet, recognizes the traits and mark of prophecy as the old monk described them. With the help of

Muḥammad's followers, he buys his freedom and becomes a warrior in Muḥammad's cause. For other appearances by monks in early Muḥammad legends, see Rubin, *The Eye of the Beholder*, 50–51; see also Muḥammad Ibn Saʿd, *Kitāb al-ṭabaqāt*, 8 vols. (Beirut, 1960), 1.153–55, cited by Rubin.

49. Rubin, *The Eye of the Beholder*, 72ff.

50. See also al-Balādhurī, *Ansāb al-ashrāf*, I, ed. Hamidullah, 281–82, for a description of one contemporary of Muḥammad, Abū ʿĀmr, who, in the days before the advent of Muḥammad as prophet, "was drawn to the *Ahl al-Kitāb*, and inclined toward Christianity, and followed the monks, and was on intimate terms with them, and frequently made trips to Syria, and was called 'the Monk.'" Abū ʿĀmr became "jealous" when Muḥammad's calling was made known, and he fought on the side of Quraysh, the elite Meccan oppressors of Muḥammad's fledgling community. One tradition reports that he was eventually miraculously killed while trying to attack Muḥammad (282).

51. Gordon Newby, "An Example of Coptic Literary Influence on Ibn Isḥāq's *Sīrah*," *JNES* 31 (1972): 22–28.

52. Al-Ṭabarī, *Taʾrīkh*, I. 919–25, trans. Bosworth, *The History of al-Ṭabarī* 5, 192–200.

53. Ibn Isḥāq, *Sīrat rasūl Allāh*, ed. Wüstenfeld, 20–25.

54. Al-Ṭabarī, *Taʾrīkh*, I. 915–25, trans. Bosworth, *The History of al-Ṭabarī* 5, 196–203. Eventually certain elements of the Faymiyūn story would find their way into the corpus of Muslim hagiography, describing there the "deeds" of the famous early Sufi Ibrāhīm b. Adham. See, for example, Abū Nuʿaym al-Iṣfahānī, *Ḥilyat al-awliyāʾ wa-ṭabaqāt al-aṣfiyāʾ*, 10 vols. (Cairo, 1967), 7.368–70. See also Ibn Manẓur, *Mukhtaṣar taʾrīkh dimashq li-Ibn ʿAsākir*, ed. Rūḥīyat al-Khās and Muḥammad Muṭīʿ al-Ḥāfiẓ, 29 vols. (Damascus, 1984–91), 4.22.

55. This according to al-Ṭabarī, *Taʾrīkh*, I. 925.

56. Newby, "An Example," 23–24; Ibn Isḥāq, *Sīrat rasūl Allāh*, ed. Wüstenfeld, 23–5; al-Ṭabarī, *Taʾrīkh* I. 924. ʿAbd Allāh's martyrdom is made by Ibn Isḥāq (and so by al-Ṭabarī) part of the sixth-century persecution of the Christian community of Najrān under the Ḥimyarite king Dhū Nuwās.

57. Al-Ṭabarī *Taʾrīkh* I. 794–811.

58. For this tendency generally, see Gaddis, *No Crime*, ch. 5, 92–95, 210.

59. See, for example, Peter Brown, *Authority and the Sacred*, ch. 2 and the reports in Socrates Scholasticus, *Historia Ecclesiastica*, 7.7, 7.14ff.; Sozomenos, *Historia Ecclesiastica*, 8.11; Theodoret, *Historia Ecclesiastica*, 5.29; Libanius, *Oratio* 30; Ambrose, *ep.* 40, 41, (ep. 1, 1.a), ed. Zelzer, CSEL 82.3: 145–77; John of Ephesus, *Lives of the Eastern Saints*, 5, ed. and trans. Brooks, 90–102; Besa, *Life of Shenoute*, 81–86. See also Gaddis, *No Crime*, passim; Daniel Caner, *Wandering, Begging Monks, Spiritual Authority and the Promotion of Monasticism in Late Antiquity* (Berkeley, 2002). For the anxiety inspired by some Christian ascetics among their Christian contemporaries, see Jerome, *ep.* 22, ed. Isidorus Hilberg, *Sancti Eusebii Hieronymi Epistulae, Pars I, Epistulae I–LXX*, CSEL 54 (Vienna, 1906 [1996]), 143–211, esp. 22.34, (196–97.); John Cassian, *Conferences*, 18.7–8, ed. and French trans. E.

Pichery, *Jean Cassien, Conférences*, 3 vols. (SC 42, 54, 64) (Paris, 1955–59), 3.18–22. Augustine, *De opere monachorum* 36, ed. Zycha, CSEL 41, 585–86; Synesius of Cyrene, *Dio* 12.

60. See Gregory, *Vox Populi*, 8–9, 46–47, 134–35, 149–51, 167–70, 185–90. See also Gaddis, *No Crime*.

61. Cited by Sara Sviri, "An Analysis of Traditions Concerning the Origin and Evolution of Christian Monasticism," *JSAI* 13 (1989): 195–208. See also Rubin, *Between Bible and Qur'ān*, 132–33.

62. Sviri, "Origin and Evolution," 195–208. The narrative describes accurately three sorts of ascetic—anchorites, stylites, and wandering monks. For affinities with late antique depictions of monasticism and its history among Christians, see Caner, *Wandering, Begging Monks*; James Goehring, "The Encroaching Desert: Literary Production and Ascetic Space in Early Christian Egypt," *JECS* 1 (1993): 281–96, reprinted in Goehring, *Ascetics, Society and the Desert*; E. A. Judge, "The Earliest Use of Monachos for 'Monk' (P. Coll. Youtie 77) and the Origins of Monasticism," *Jahrbuch für Antike und Christentum* 20 (1977): 72–89.

63. In a similar vein, Athanasius, when he wrote the foundational *Life of Saint Antony*, established early on that good ascetics, those who truly moved with God and could wield his might, were those who respected and obeyed their archimandrites and bishops. Those who did not were not real monks and ought to be shunned, or at the very least, ignored. See Brakke, *Athanasius and the Politics of Asceticism*; James Goehring, "Through a Glass Darkly: Diverse Images of the Apotaktikoi(ai) in Early Egyptian Monasticism," *Semeia* 58 (1992): 25–45; Caner, *Wandering, Begging Monks*. See also Gaddis, *No Crime*.

64. Sviri, "Origin and Evolution."

65. Ibn Qutayba, *ʿUyūn al-akhbār*, 4 vols. (Cairo, 1964), 4.297. Cited and translated by Suleiman A. Mourad, "Christian Monks in Islamic Literature: A Preliminary Report on Some Arabic *Apophthegmata Patrum*," *Bulletin of the Royal Institute for Inter-Faith Studies* 6 (2004): 90.

66. Al-Azdī, *Ta'rīkh futūḥ al-Shām*, 115–16. On the dating of this source, see Mourad, "On Early Islamic Historiography." See also Ibn ʿAsākir, *Ta'rīkh madīnat Dimashq*, ed. Ṣalāḥ al-Dīn al-Munajjid (Damascus, 1951), 1.477, where, in a cluster of traditions reporting that the *mujāhidūn* were "monks by day and horsemen by night" and that they "commanded the right and forbade the wrong." See also Ibn Qutayba, *ʿUyūn al-akhbār*, 1.127, where Ibn Qutayba gives very much the same *khabar* minus the comparison with monks.

67. See, for example, the role of Christian ascetics in the aftermath of the Riot of the Statues in fourth century Antioch, John Chrysostom, *Homily* XVII. For the stoning of Roman magistrates, see Socrates Scholasticus, *Historia Ecclesiastica*, 7.14 (ed. Hansen, 359–60) where a praetorian prefect is stoned by an Alexandrian monk. See also John of Ephesus, *Lives of the Eastern Saints*, 5, ed. and trans. Brooks, 102; Besa, *Life of Shenoute*, 81, 113. See also the Life of the eighth-century Syrian ascetic Timothy of Kākhushtā, in which the monk "reproves and forbids the adultery" of a Muslim neighbor, whom he later miraculously corrects. See *The Life of Timothy of Kākhushtā*, Saidnaya Version, 23.1–4, ed. and

trans. by Lamoreaux and Cairala, 558–59. For the tradition of "commanding the good and forbidding the wrong" (*al-amr bi-ʾl-maʿrūf waʾl-nahy ʿan al-munkar*) in Islamic society, see Cook, *Commanding Right and Forbidding Wrong*.

68. Al-Ṭabarī, *Taʾrīkh*, I. 2125–26, trans. Khalid Blankenship, *The History of al-Ṭabarī* 11: *The Challenge to the Empires* (Albany, 1993), 127; al-Ṭabarī, *Taʾrīkh*, I. 2395. Ibn ʿAsākir, *Taʾrīkh madīnat Dimashq*, ed. al-Munajjid, 1.474, 476–77. At al-Ṭabarī, *Taʾrīkh*, I. 2125–26, the *mujāhidūn* are described as men who would cut off their sons' hands for stealing or stone them for fornication. Intriguingly, the late eighth-century Christian Life of the Palestinian monk Stephan of Mar Sabas describes monks engaged in combat with demons as "like a brave horseman, who fights and is eager to conquer and not to be conquered, seeking thereby to receive a crown from the king" and "like a horseman brave and bold." See Leontius, *The Life of Stephen of Mar Sabas*, 11.11, 14.6. ed. and trans. John C. Lamoreaux, CSCO 579 (SA 51) (Louvain, 1999), 15, 22.

69. Leontius, *The Life of Stephen of Mar Sabas*, ed. and trans. Lamoreaux, 11.11, 14.6.

70. Ibn al-Mubārak, *Kitāb al-jihād*, ed. Ḥammād, 35–36, cited by Sviri, "Origin and Evolution" 200. See also Ibn al-Mubārak, *Kitāb al-zuhd* #840, where the same author, quoting the Prophet, writes "[A traditionalist] said, 'I prescribe for you that you should be strong in God, for he is the head of everything, and I prescribe for you *jihād*, for it is the monasticism of Islam. I prescribe for you the constant remembrance of God, and reading the Qurʾān . . . [and] I prescribe for you silence except [speaking] truthfully, and you shall vanquish Satan by means of it.'" See also Ibn al-Mubārak, *Kitāb al-zuhd* #845, "[It was said to the Prophet], 'O messenger of God, inform us about itinerant ascetics (*suyyāḥ*)!' And he said, 'The itinerant asceticism of my community is *jihād* on the path of God, (*siyāhāt ummatī al-jihād fī sabīl Allāh*).'"

71. See Ignaz Goldziher, *Introduction to Islamic Theology and Law* (Princeton, 1981), 131. See also Goldziher, *Muslim Studies*, 2.255–344.

72. Al-Ṭabarī, *Taʾrīkh*, I. 2220, trans. Friedmann, *The History of al-Ṭabarī* 12, 11–12. See Leah Kinberg, "What Is Meant by *Zuhd*?" *SI* 41 (1985): 27–44 for a worthy discussion of what the term *zuhd* meant to medieval Muslims.

73. Aḥmad b. Ḥanbal, *Kitāb al-zuhd* (Beirut, 1976), 114–15.

74. Al-Ṭabarī, *Taʾrīkh*, I. 2716–18. For salt and bread in the diet of monks, see, for example, Theodoret of Cyr, *Historia Religiosa*, 2.2, 11.1, 20.3, ed. and French trans. Canivet and Leroy-Molinghen, 1.196–97; 1.454–55; 2.244–45; Athanasius, *Vita Antonii*, 7.

75. Al-Azdī, *Futūḥ al-Shām*, 115–17. I am indebted to Nancy Khalek for pointing out problems in my initial interpretation of the Arabic in this passage.

76. For the prevalence of this "topos" in the early Islamic historiographic tradition, see Noth and Conrad, *Early Arabic Historical Tradition*, 94–95, 147, 153–54, 156, 206–8. For the importance of the battle at Qādisiyya, see Donner, *Early Islamic Conquests*, 204–5.

77. Al-Ṭabarī, *Taʾrīkh*, I. 2254, trans. Friedmann, *The History of al-Ṭabarī* 12, 50. See also al-Ṭabarī, *Taʾrīkh*, I. 2351.

78. Al-Ṭabarī, *Taʾrīkh*, I. 2271–73, trans. Friedmann, *The History of al-Ṭabarī* 12,

66–69. Such exchanges are common in early Muslim accounts of the conquests. In addition to the cited examples, see, as illustrations, Ibn ʿAsākir, *Taʾrīkh madīnat Dimashq*, ed. al-Munajjid, 1.461–62, 532–33; al-Azdī, *Futūḥ al-Shām*, 199–209, for Khālid b. Walīd's conference with the Roman commander Bāhān; Abū Muḥammad Aḥmad Ibn Aʿtham al-Kūfī, *Kitāb al-futūḥ*, 8 vols. (Hyderabad, 1968–75), 1.178–84. See also *Kitāb al-futūḥ*, 1.184–89; *Kitāb al-futūḥ*, 1.195–207, for a meeting between the last Persian shah Yazdgird III and a group of *mujāhidūn*; Abū al-Qāsim ʿAbd al-Raḥmān b. ʿAbd al-Ḥakam, *Futūḥ Miṣr wa-akhbāruhu*, ed. Charles C. Torrey (New Haven, 1922), 65–70, for ʿAmr b. al-ʿĀṣ's exchange with the Roman official "al-Muqawqis."

79. I am thinking here of the shared meaning of the Greek *martys/martyros*, the Coptic *martyros*, the Syriac *sāhdā*, and the Arabic *shahīd*, all of which are derived from roots signaling the act of bearing witness or testifying (Syriac *s*[e]*hed*, he witnessed, testified; Arabic *shahida*, he witnessed, testified). In the Christian experience, the Roman practice of prosecuting Christians as criminals within the Roman juridical system left as a trace the term "martyr," originally a legal term. Interestingly, the word used to signal the idea of dying for one's faith in early Islam retained the juridical sense acquired during the period of persecution undergone by Christians in the Roman world, despite the fact that the word did not precisely fit the experience of the Muslim community or the narratives that recalled it. This fact required explaining by later generations of Muslim scholars. See Keith Lewinstein, "The Revaluation of Martyrdom in Early Islam," in Margaret Cormack (ed.), *Sacrificing the Self: Perspectives on Martyrdom and Religion* (Oxford, 2001), 78–79. Lewinstein does not ask why this language was taken up by the early Muslim community (this is not the purpose of his article), nor what the adoption of this language might suggest about the evolution of early Muslim ideas of martyrdom and the pool of ideas and signs in dialogue with which those ideas might have been developed.

80. The offering of a bribe to the witness in question is a trope which occurs regularly in both Christian and Muslim narratives of this sort. See, for example, the Coptic martyrdom of Victor, where the martyr is offered great riches, a wife, and other rewards by his father if he will sacrifice to the pagan gods. *The Martyrdom of Saint Victor the General* in E. A. Wallis Budge (ed.), *Coptic Texts* IV (New York, 1977), 257. For the Coptic text, see *Coptic Texts* IV, 5. The rewards offered in this literature for apostasy could be less grand—in the story of the Najrān Martyrs, the wicked Jewish king offers nuts and figs as an enticement to a small child if he will renounce Christ. The child bites the king instead. *Zuqnīn Chronicle*, trans. Harrak (*The Chronicle of Zuqnīn: Parts III and IV A.D. 488–775*), 83–84. For the Najrān martyrs see Irfan Shahid, *The Martyrs of Najran: New Documents* (Bruxelles 1971). Compare this with the story from Ibn ʿAsākir's *Taʾrīkh madīnat Dimashq*, ed. al-Munajjid, 1.532–33 in which the famous Muslim warrior Khālid b. al-Walīd, in what reads as an instance of psychological warfare, rejects a Roman general's offer to send Khālid and his troops home with annually renewable gifts, and tells the Roman that he and his companions are in fact there not for a payoff but rather to taste the blood of the Romans, "than which [they] have heard there is none sweeter."

81. Donner, *Early Islamic Conquests*, 3: "The oldest view of the Islamic conquest is, of course, that of the Islamic community itself, which traditionally saw the conquest as the result of religious zeal for the new faith and as a truly miraculous demonstration of the favor that Islam is supposed to enjoy."

82. Brown, *Rise of Western Christendom*, 301.

83. Geertz, "The Growth of Culture and the Evolution of Mind," in Geertz, *Interpretation of Cultures*, and Geertz, "Religion as a Cultural System," in Geertz, *Interpretation of Cultures*, esp. 92. Cf. William H. Sewell Jr., "Geertz, Cultural Systems, and History: From Synchrony to Transformation," in Sherry B. Ortner (ed.), *The Fate of "Culture": Geertz and Beyond* (Berkeley, 1999).

84. See, among others, Muhammad Qasim Zaman, *Religion and Politics Under the Early ʿAbbāsids: The Emergence of the Proto-Sunnī Elite* (Leiden, 1997); Eerik Dickinson, *The Development of Early Sunnite Hadith Criticism: The Taqdima of Ibn Abī Ḥātim al-Rāzī (240/854–327/938)* (Leiden, 2001). For the evolution of a specifically Islamic theology and theological technologies see Josef van Ess, *Theologie und Gesellschaft in 2. und 3. Jahrhundert Hidschra. Eine Geschichte des religiösen Denkens im frühen Islam* 6 vols. (Berlin, 1991–97). See also the works cited notes 6–13 above.

85. See Bonner, *Aristocratic Violence and Holy War*, 119–34.

86. Ṣāliḥ b. Aḥmad b. Ḥanbal, *Sīrat al-imām Aḥmad b. Ḥanbal* (Beirut, 1997), 18. For the importance of such frontier warriors as Ibn al-Mubārak as models for communal self-fashioning among city-dwelling Muslims like Ibn Ḥanbal, see Cook, "Muslim Apocalyptic and Jihād," 102: "Clearly, at an early stage these bordermen acquired the aura of true Muslims, and could dictate their traditions of how Islam ought to look to their citified cousins."

87. For Muʿādh's *zuhd*, see Aḥmad b. Ḥanbal, *Kitāb al-zuhd*, 180–86. Ibn Ḥanbal's own ascetic practice was "mild," inclining toward a moderation that was consistent with the settled and socially active life he lived in Baghdād. Despite this, however, Ibn Ḥanbal still seems to have admired practitioners of extreme asceticism and understood his own ascetic ethos as kindred with theirs, as is made clear from an episode Ibn Ḥanbal's son reports that his father "frequently recalled." In that episode, a sun-scorched wandering ascetic, clad in skins and rags and without a single possession, called upon Ibn Ḥanbal for a brief discussion of the nature of *zuhd*, which they agree is the abandonment of desire in the present world. The encounter "gladdened [Ibn Ḥanbal's] heart." Interestingly, the confessional identity of this individual is never specified. Ṣāliḥ b. Aḥmad b. Ḥanbal, *Sīrat al-imām Aḥmad b. Ḥanbal*, 29–30. For the "mild" character of Ibn Ḥanbal's asceticism, see Hurvitz, "Biographies and Mild Asceticism"; Hurvitz, *The Formation of Hanbalism*.

88. Ṣāliḥ b. Aḥmad b. Ḥanbal, *Sīrat al-imām Aḥmad b. Ḥanbal*, esp. 27–31.

89. Hurvitz, "Mild Asceticism," esp. 44–50.

CHAPTER SIX

1. Cormac McCarthy, *Blood Meridian, or The Evening Redness in the West* (New York, 1992), 250.

2. For *jihād* waged on the frontiers of the early Islamic world in the moral imaginary of early Muslims, see Robinson, "Prophecy and Holy Man in Early Islam," 252–56; Michael Bonner, "Some Observations Concerning the Early Development of Jihad along the Arab-Byzantine Frontier," *SI* 75 (1992): 5–31; Cook, "Muslim Apocalyptic and *Jihād*." For *jihād* generally, see Reuven Firestone, *Jihād: The Origins of Holy War in Islam* (Oxford, 1999); Fred Donner, "The Sources of Islamic Conceptions of War," in John Kelsey and James Turner Johnson (eds.), *Just War and Jihad: Historical and Theoretical Perspectives on War and Peace in Western and Islamic Traditions* (New York, 1991), 31–70; Albrecht Noth, *Heiliger Krieg und heiliger Kampf in Islam und Christentum* (Bonn, 1966); Martin Hinds, "'Maghāzī' and 'Sīra' in Early Islamic Scholarship," in *Vie du Prophete Mahomet: Colloque de Strasburg, octobre 1980* (Paris, 1983), 57–66; Martin Hinds, "Al-Maghāzī," in EI², vol. 5, 1161–64; Blankinship, *The End of the Jihad State*; Knut Vikør, "*Jihad, ʿilm and taṣawwuf*—Two Justifications of Action from the Idrīsī Tradition," *SI* 91 (2000): 153–76; M. A. Shaban, *Islamic History, A.D. 600–750 (A.H. 132): A New Interpretation* (Cambridge, 1971); Bonner, *Aristocratic Violence and Holy War*.

3. The phrase "Islamic moral imagination" is from Hurvitz, "Biographies and Mild Asceticism." For the evolution of early and medieval Muslim asceticism and mysticism, see Jacqueline Chabbi, "Remarques sur le développement historique des mouvements ascétiques et mystiques au Ḫurasan," *SI* 46 (1977): 5–72; Jacqueline Chabbi, "Réflexions sur le sufisme iranien primatif," *Journal Asiatique* 266 (1978): 37–55; Michael Cooperson, "Ibn Hanbal and Bishr al-Hafi: A Case Study in Biographical Traditions," *SI* 86 (1997): 71–101; Ofer Livne-Kafri, "Early Muslim Ascetics and the World of Christian Monasticism," *JSAI* 20 (1996): 105–29; Kinberg, "What Is Meant by Zuhd?"; George Makdisi, "The Hanbali School and Sufism," in *Actas IV. Congresso de estudios arabes e islamicos* (Leiden, 1971), 71–84; Margaret Malamud, "Sufi Organizations and Structures of Authority in Medieval Nishapur," *IJMES* 26 (1994): 427–42; Louis Massignon, *Essay on the Origins of the Technical Language of Islamic Mysticism* (South Bend, 1998); Christopher Melchert, "The Transition from Asceticism at the Middle of the Ninth Century C.E.," *SI* 83 (1996): 51–70; Melchert, "The Hanabila and the Early Sufis"; R. A. Nicholson, *Studies in Islamic Mysticism* (Cambridge, 1921); Annemarie Schimmel, *Mystical Dimensions of Islam* (Chapel Hill, 1975); Sara Sviri, "*Wa-Rahbānīyatan Ibtadaʿūhū*: An Analysis of Traditions Concerning the Origin and Evaluation of Christian Monasticism," *JSAI* 13 (1990): 195–208; J. Spencer Trimingham, *The Sufi Orders of Islam* (Oxford, 1971).

4. See, for example, Hurvitz, "Biographies and Mild Asceticism." See also Chase F. Robinson, "Prophecy and Holy Man in Early Islam," in Howard-Johnston and Hayward, *The Cult of the Saints*, 241–62.

5. Barth, "Introduction."

6. See Barth, "Introduction."

7. See Bonner, *Aristocratic Violence and Holy War*, 125–30.

8. Abū Ḥatim Muḥammad al-Bustī Ibn Ḥibbān, *Kitāb mashāhīr ʿulamāʾ al-amṣār* (Cairo, 1959), 183. Cited by Bonner, *Aristocratic Violence and Holy War*, 126.

9. See Bonner, *Aristocratic Violence and Holy War*, 125–34; Arberry, *Sufism*, 36–38. For Ibn Adham in the imaginary of modern Muslims, see Fedwa Malti-Douglas, "Gender and Uses of the Ascetic in an Islamist Text," in Vincent Wimbush and Richard Valantasis (eds.), *Asceticism*, (Oxford, 1995), 395–411, esp. 400–405.

10. For Ibn Adham's penchant for miraculous encounters with supernatural figures, see, for example, Ibn Manẓur, *Mukhtaṣar taʾrīkh dimashq li-Ibn ʿAsākir*, ed. al-Khās and al-Ḥāfiẓ (hereafter Ibn ʿAsākir), 4.20–21. For Ibn ʿAsākir, see Lindsay, *Ibn ʿAsākir and Early Islamic History*. See also Ibn ʿAsākir 4.22. For Ibn Adham's concern for the poor and his compassion, see, for example, Ibn ʿAsākir 4.18. For Ibn Adham's expertise in fasting, see also al-Khaṭīb al-Baghdādī, *Taʾrīkh Baghdād*, 14 vols. (Cairo, 1931), 10.157. For the *TB*, see Fedwa Malti-Douglas, "Controversy and Its Effects in the Biographical Tradition of al-Khaṭīb al-Baghdādī," *SI* 46 (1977): 115–31.

11. Ibn ʿAsākir 4.19–20.

12. See *Life of St. Nino*, trans. D. Lang, in *Lives and Legends of the Georgian Saints* (1976, London). For the conversion of Iberia, see David Braund, *Georgia in Antiquity: A History of Colchis and Transcaucasian Iberia 550 BC–AD 562* (Oxford, 1994), 246–56, esp. 253. For Mar Qardagh, see Walker, *The Legend of Mar Qardagh*, 21–22, 131–39. For hunting as a mark of status among late Roman elites, see now Van Dam, *Kingdom of Snow*, 133–35.

13. See Paphnutius, *Life of Onnophrius* 28. For monks tending orchards, see Jerome, *Life of Paul*, 4–5. For theme of paradise regained in Christian ascetic thought, see Brown, *The Body and Society*, 218–24.

14. See, for example, Athanasius, *Life of Saint Antony*, 3 (PG 26:844). Even the *Life* of the seventh-century Syrian ascetic Mar Marouta, who seems to have been remarkable mostly for his administrative and literary activities, features this trope. See *Histoires d'Ahoudemmeh et de Marouta, métrepolitains jacobites de Tagrit et de l'Orient (VIe et VIIe siècles)*, Syriac text ed. and French trans. F. Nau, *PO* 3.1 (Paris, 1905), 53–96. For the topos of travel as a mark of holiness in late antiquity more generally, see J. Elsner, "Hagiographic Geography: Travel and Allegory in the Life of Apollonius of Tyana," *JHS* 117 (1997): 22–37. See also John Binns, *Ascetics as Ambassadors of Christ: The Monasteries of Palestine, 314–631* (Oxford, 1994), for an earlier period, see Graham Anderson, *Sage, Saint and Sophist: Holy Men and Their Associates in the Early Roman Empire* (London, 1994).

15. Ibn Isḥāq, *Sīrat rasūl Allāh*, ed. Wüstenfeld, 1.1.20–25, English trans. Guillaume, *Life of Muhammad*, 14–16. See also al-Ṭabarī, *Taʾrīkh*, I.920–25, trans. Bosworth, *The History of al-Ṭabarī* 5, 194–202; Newby, "An Example of Coptic Literary Influence on Ibn Isḥāq's *Sīrah*," 22–28.

16. See, for example, the Arabic version of the *Life of Saint Samuel*, text and transla-

tion in Alcock, "The Arabic Life of Anbā Samawī'l of Qalamūn," 327–31; Paphnutius, *Life of Onnophrius*, passim, Coptic text ed. and English trans. E. A. Wallis Budge, *Coptic Texts*, 5 vols. (London, 1914 [New York, 1977]), 4.205–24, 455–73; Leontius of Neapolis, *Life of Symeon the Fool* I–II, trans. Krueger, *Symeon the Holy Fool*, 134–48. Also see Krueger's ch. 3 for a discussion of late antique hagiographical topology. For the holy man in late antiquity more generally, see, among others, Brown, "Rise and Function of the Holy Man"; Brown, "The Rise and Function of the Holy Man in Late Antiquity, 1971–1997," *JECS* 6 (1998): 353–76; Peter Brown, "Holy Men," in *CAH* 14, 781–810; Fowden, "The Pagan Holy Man"; Averil Cameron, "On Defining the Holy Man," in Howard-Johnston and Hayward, 27–43; Averil Cameron, "Ascetic Closure and the End of Antiquity," in Vincent Wimbush and Richard Valantasis, *Asceticism* (Oxford, 1995), 147–62; Phillip Rousseau, "Ascetics as Mediators and Teachers," in Howard-Johnston and Hayward, 45–59.

17. Abū Nuʿaym al-Iṣfahānī, *Ḥilyat al-awliyāʾ wa-ṭabaqāt al-aṣfiyāʾ*, 8.29, cited by Bonner, *Aristocratic Violence and Jihād*, 128–29. See also Daniel the Stylite's council to the over-eager ascetic novice Titus in the *Life of Daniel the Stylite*, 62, trans. Dawes, and Baynes, 44–45. For Abū Nuʿaym, see Georges Raif Khouri, "Importance et authenticité des texts de *Ḥilyāt al-awliyāʾ wa-ṭabaqāt al-aṣfiyāʾ* d'Abū Nuʿaym al-Iṣbahānī," *SI* 46 (1977): 73–113. For *ṭabaqāt* literature more generally, see Chase F. Robinson, "Al-Muʿāfā b. ʿImrān and the Beginnings of the Ṭabaqāt Literature," *JAOS* 116 (1996): 114–20; Michael Cooperson, *Classical Arabic Biography: The Heirs of the Prophet in the Age of Maʾmūn* (Cambridge, 2000), 107–53, 154–87; Paul Auchterlonie, *Arabic Biographical Dictionaries: A Summary Guide and Bibliography* (Durham, 1987); Ibrahim Hafsi, "Recherches sur le genre 'ṭabaqāt' dans la littérature arabe," *Arabica* 23 (1976): 227–65; Hafsi, "Recherches sur le genre 'ṭabaqāt' dans la littérature arabe," *Arabica* 24.1 (1977): 1–41, Hafsi, "Recherches sur le genre 'ṭabaqāt' dans la littérature arabe," *Arabica* 24.3 (1977): 150–86; Bushra Hamad, "History and Biography," *Arabica* 45 (1998): 215–32; J. A. Mojaddedi, *The Biographical Tradition in Sufism: The Ṭabaqāt Genre from al-Sulamī to Jāmi* (Richmond, Surrey, 2001).

18. Abū Nuʿaym, *Ḥilyat al-awliyāʾ wa-ṭabaqāt al-aṣfiyāʾ*, 8.29–30. Livne-Kafri, "Early Muslim Ascetics and the World of Christian Monasticism," 108 n. 25, cites a passage at Abū Nuʿaym, *Ḥilyat al-awliyāʾ wa-ṭabaqāt al-aṣfiyāʾ* 2.365 in which the situation is reversed—a Muslim ascetic asks a Christian ascetic to teach him asceticism and the surprised monk asks him whether he is a Muslim. He says that he is but still wants to learn from the monk. Clearly, the kind of dislocation Ibn Adham feels in the above passage was understood to have the potential to affect persons on either side of a communal boundary.

19. For Alexandria, see Haas, *Alexandria in Late Antiquity*; Brakke, *Athanasius and the Politics of Asceticism*; Roger Bagnall, *Egypt in Late Antiquity* (Princeton, 1993); C. Kannengiesser, "Athanasius of Alexandria and the Ascetic Movement of His Time," in Wimbush and Valantasis, *Asceticism*, 479–92.

20. Abū l-Faraj ʿAbd al-Raḥmān Ibn al-Jawzī, *Ṣifat al-ṣafwa*, 4 vols. (Hyderabad, 1969–73), 4.321.

21. Keller, "Perceptions of Other Religions in Sufism," 183.

22. See for example, the long narrative from translated by Keller ("Perceptions of Other Religions in Sufism," 183) from Abū Nuʿaym, *Ḥilyat al-awliyāʾ wa-ṭabaqāt al-aṣfiyāʾ*, 9.356.

23. Goehring, "Monastic Diversity."

24. Fowden, *The Barbarian Plain*, 3.

25. Muhammad Qasim Zaman, "Death, Funeral Processions and the Articulation of Religious Authority in Early Islam," *SI* 89 (2001): 27–58. For shared holy sites in late antiquity and early Islam, see Elizabeth Key Fowden, "Sharing Holy Places," *Common Knowledge* 8.1 (2002): 124–46. For asceticism/martyrdom as a sign system recognized across a spectrum of late antique communities, see, for example, Susanna Elm, "Introduction," *JECS* 6 (1998): 343–51; W. H. C. Frend, *The Donatist Church: A Movement of Protest in Roman North Africa* (Oxford, 1952); Brown, "Religious Dissent/Coercion in the Later Roman Empire"; Peter Brown, "Christianity and Local Culture in Late Roman Africa," *JRS* 58 (1968): 85–95. See also Tilley "Sustaining a Donatist Self-Identity"; Boyarin, "Martyrdom and the Making of Christianity and Judaism."

26. Paulinus, *Vita Ambrosii* 48, ed. Kaniecka, 92: "exsequiarum turba innumerabilis . . . non solum christianorum, sed etiam Iudaeorum et paganorum."

27. Libanius, in particular, is renowned for interceding on behalf Christians and Jews, as well as pagans. See A. F. Norman, "Libanius: The Teacher in an Age of Violence," in Georgios Fatouros and Tilman Krischer (eds.), *Libanios* (Darmstadt, 1983), 150–72.

28. Zaman, "Death, Funeral Processions," 39. See also Hurvitz, "Biographies and Mild Asceticism."

29. See Abū Bakr al-Khallāl, *Ahl al-milal wa-ʾl-radda wa-ʾl-zanādiqa wa-ʾl-tārik al-ṣalāh wa-ʾl-farāʾiḍ min kitāb al-jāmiʿ li-ʾl-Khallāl*, ed. Ibrāhīm b. Muḥammad al-Sulṭān, 2 vols. (Riyadh, 1996).

30. A pious woman observes a group of ascetic youths and says, "ʿUmar, by God, made himself heard when he spoke, hurried along when he walked, and caused pain when he struck—he was truly a pious man (nāsik)." It should be noted that *nāsik* is also a term used to denote hermits, ascetics, and other kinds of monastic practitioners. Muḥammad Ibn Saʿd, *Kitab al-ṭabaqāt al-kabīr*, ed. Eduard Sachau et al., 9 vols. (Leiden, 1904–40), 3, pt. 1, 208. trans. Goldziher, *Introduction to Islamic Theology and Law*, 131. See also Goldziher, *Muslim Studies*, 2:255–344.

31. Muqātil Ibn Sulaymān al-Balkhī, *Tafsīr Muqātil Ibn Sulaymān*, ed. ʿAbd Allāh Maḥmūd Shiḥātah, 5 vols. (Cairo, 1969–2002), 1.336–37. See Sviri, "Analysis."

32. Ibn Qutayba, *ʿUyūn al-akhbār*, 4.18, cited by Goldziher, *Introduction*, 122–24.

33. Aḥmad Ibn Ḥanbal, *Musnad*, 6 vols. (Beirut, 1968), 5.163.

34. For the "paradoxical" tendency for those who reject the society of men to become exemplars for their religious community, see Brown, "The Saint as Exemplar in Late Antiquity."

35. This becomes especially visible around the questions of spiritual authority that gave birth to the Shīʿa and Kharijite sects. See Hinds, "Kufan Political Alignments";

Robinson, *Empire and Elites*; Crone, "Statement by the Najdiyya Kharijites"; Skladanek, "The Kharijites in Iran I"; Kenney, "The Emergence of the Khawarij"; Brunnow, *Die Charidschiten unter den ersten Omayyaden*; Julius Wellhausen, *The Religio-Political Factions in Early Islam*; Crone, "The First Century Concept of Hijra."

36. Ibn al-Mubārak, *Kitāb al-jihād*, ed. Ḥammād, #15; cf. #16.

37. *Kitāb al-jihād*, #17. Cf. Ibn al-Mubārak, *Kitāb al-zuhd*, #840, 845.

38. Bonner, *Aristocratic Violence and Holy War*, 119–25. See, for example, Ibn al-Jawzī, *Ṣifat al-ṣafwa*, 4.116 where Ibn al-Mubārak returns to Tarsus from a raiding expedition to find a young friend jailed over a debt. After intervening to free the young man, Ibn al-Mubārak makes the young man promise not to tell anyone until after his death. See also al-Khaṭib al-Baghdādī, *Ta'rīkh Baghdād*, 9.188–92. Ibn al-Mubārak was an especially noteworthy example of a much larger group of pious, ascetic Muslim warriors who assembled on the Syrian frontier. See, for example, Ibn al-Jawzī, *Ṣifat al-ṣafwa*, 4.250, where Abū Yūsuf al-Ghasūlī refuses on ascetic principle to partake in food captured in a raid on the Romans, even though he acknowledges that the food is *ḥalāl*. On this class of raiding Muslim border ascetics generally, see M. Bonner, "Some Observations Concerning the Early Development of Jihād on the Arabo-Byzantine Frontier."

39. For purity of intention as an aspect of Ibn al-Mubārak's thought, see Bonner, *Aristocratic Violence and Holy War*, ch. 4, esp. 123–24.

40. *Kitāb al-zuhd* #594.

41. Abū Nuʿaym, *Ḥilyat al-awliyā' wa-ṭabaqāt al-aṣfiyā'*, 8.167–68.

42. *Kitāb al-zuhd* #597; cf. #598: "The present world is as a prison for the faithful man and it subjects him to [its] customs, but when the present world is sundered so too will be the prison and [its] customs."

43. Ibn al-Jawzī, *Ṣifat al-ṣafwa*, 4.108.

44. Abu Nuʿaym, *Ḥilyat al-awliyā' wa-ṭabaqāt al-aṣfiyā'*, 8.164–65.

45. *Kitāb al-zuhd* #592.

46. So Abū Nuʿaym, *Ḥilyat al-awliyā' wa-ṭabaqāt al-aṣfiyā'*, 8.167: "[It was] said, 'Ibn al-Mubārak never broke his fast, but he was never seen fasting.'"

47. Abū Nuʿaym, *Ḥilyat al-awliyā' wa-ṭabaqāt al-aṣfiyā'*, 8:167.

48. See Bonner, *Aristocratic Violence and Holy War*, ch. 3, esp. 123–25.

49. *Kitāb al-jihād* #7, cited in Bonner, *Aristocratic Violence and Holy War*. Cf. *Kitāb al-jihād* #8, #47.

50. *Kitāb al-zuhd* #469.

51. For the Pachomian system, see Philip Rousseau, *Pachomius*; James Goehring, "New Frontiers in Pachomian Studies," in Pearson and Goehring (eds.), *The Roots of Egyptian Christianity*, 236–57.

52. See Owen Chadwick, *John Cassian* (Cambridge, 1968), 18–30 for a discussion of Cassian's effective use as a historical source, in which Chadwick concludes that "nothing about the *Conferences* suggests that they are not an authentic presentation of moral and ascetic ideals practiced in Egypt." See also Columba Stewart, *Cassian the Monk* (Oxford,

1998). See also Adalbert de Vogüé, *De Saint Pachṭme à Jean Cassien: études littéraires et doctrinales sur le monachisme égyptien à ses débutes* (Rome, 1996), 271–301; Rousseau, *Ascetics, Authority and the Church in the Age of Jerome and Cassian*, 169–234.

53. See Brown, *Body and Society*, 225–40.

54. John Cassian, *Institutes*, 4.8, ed. and French trans. Jean-Claude Guy, *Jean Cassien, Institutions Cénobitiques* (SC 109) (Paris, 1965), 130–33.

55. John Cassian, *Institutes*, 4.10, ed. and French trans. Guy, 132–34.

56. "The Rules for the Monophysite Monks in Persia," in Arthur Vööbus, *Syriac and Arabic Documents Regarding Legislation Relative to Syrian Asceticism* (Stockholm, 1960), 90. Another, later set of Persian rules, believed to date from the period after the Arab conquest, evinces especially tight control on those types of individuals allowed to enter monasteries. Potential monastic community members had to be approved by the bishop after an interview, free men, "a son of believers," and unencumbered with a wife and children, "for the care of his wife and children and his place among them is superior to the monastic life, and more acceptable to God. Whoever transgresses this rule shall be excommunicated." "Anonymous Rules for the Monks," Vööbus, *Syriac and Arabic Documents*, 110.

57. John Cassian, *Institutes*, 4.10, ed. and French trans. Guy, 132–35. Cf. Jerome, *ep.* 125.15, ed. and trans. F. A. Wright, *Select Letters of St. Jerome* (Cambridge, 1933 [1991]), 422–25; Vööbus, *Syriac and Arabic Documents*, 110.

58. See, for example, *Kitāb al-zuhd* #1465, where a monk pretends to gorge himself in order to disgrace himself and so avoid the admiration of a king and the crowd that follows him.

59. For the conquests and their miraculous interpretation in Muslim thought, see Robinson, *Empire and Elites*, 253–54 and Crone, "The First-Century Concept of Hijra." Interestingly, Ibn al-Mubārak was remembered as a figure in whom the numinous and the quotidian met and merged in small miracles, much as we find in late antique monastic literature. This is to be expected, perhaps, in Sufi *ṭabaqāt* literature (see Livne-Kafri, "Early Muslim Ascetics and the World of Christian Monasticism," passim), but in al-Khaṭīb al-Baghdādī's history of the city of Baghdād, for example, we encounter stories in which Ibn al-Mubārak restores a blind man's sight (*Ta'rākh Baghdād*, 10.167), predicts his own death (ibid., 10.168), visits his followers after his death to dispense wisdom (ibid., 10.168–69), and makes the pooled resources of a group of *mujāhidūn* last without decreasing the amount of money put into the pot, teasing his surprised companions gently, "Do you not know that God blesses the *ghāzī* in his provisioning?" (ibid., 10.157–58).

60. *Kitāb al-jihād*, #15, #16.

61. For the role of primordialist narratives in the construction of identities, see Suny, "Constructing Primordialism," 868: "Identities . . . are always formed within broad discourses, universes of available meanings, and are related to the historic positionings of the subjects involved, which are themselves constituted and given meanings by the identity markers." Cf. Suny, "Provisional Stabilities." For the role of narratives and various narra-

tive types in the construction of identities generally, see Somers, "The Narrative Constitution of Identity."

62. For the martyr and his relation to Roman rituals of truth making, see Gleason, "Truth Contests and Talking Corpses"; Paige duBois, *Truth and Torture* (New York, 1999). For the martyr as a resource for self-fashioning among late antique faith identities, see, among others, Clarysse, "The Coptic Martyr Cult"; Ross, "Dynamic Writing and Martyrs' Bodies"; Bailey, "Building Urban Christian Communities"; Trout, "Damasus and the Invention of Early Christian Rome"; Thacker, "*Loca Sanctorum*: The Significance of Place in the Study of the Saints"; Thacker, "The Making of a Local Saint"; Boyarin, *Dying for God.*

63. See Elm, *Virgins of God*; Brakke, *Athanasius and the Politics of Asceticism*; Goehring, *Ascetics, Society and the Desert: Studies in Egyptian Monasticism*; Harvey, *Asceticism and Society in Crisis.*

64. For flamboyant Christian ascetics as resources for communal self-fashioning, see Harvey, "The Stylite's Liturgy." For the "triumph" of the martyrs and their community over their persecutors see Drake, *Constantine and the Bishops*, 98–103, 402–40.

65. See ch. 5 and Sviri, "Analysis," 205.

66. Sviri, "Analysis," 201–8, esp. 203.

67. See Bonner's discussion in his *Aristocratic Violence and Holy War*, 119–34, esp. 120–21.

68. *Kitāb al-jihād* #151.

69. *Kitāb al-jihād* #154.

70. *Kitāb al-zuhd* #599. At *Kitāb al-zuhd* #600 a tradition is given in which man reports that he was once asked, "Does death delight you?" When he answered that in fact death did not delight him, his interlocutor sniffed, "I do not know anyone whom death does not delight except he who is inadequate."

71. *Kitāb al-jihād* #160.

72. Al-Ṭabarī, *Ta'rikh*, I.2270–71, trans. Friedmann, *The History of al-Ṭabarī* 12, 66–67. Elsewhere, al-Ṭabarī (I. 2351) has another Muslin readying himself to go and visit Rustam by arranging his hair into a similar style (trans. Friedmann, *The History of al-Ṭabarī* 12, 136–37).

73. See, for example, al-Ṭabarī *Ta'rīkh*, I. 2220, trans. Friedmann, *The History of al-Ṭabarī* 12, 11–12.

74. Al-Ṭabarī, I. 2716–18, trans. G.R. Smith, *The History of al-Tabari* 14: *The Conquest of Iran A.D. 641–643/A.H. 21–23* (Albany, 1994), 85–87. Cf. Ibn al-Mubārak, *Kitāb al-jihād* #164, where ʿUmar disputes a Bedouin's assertion that ʿUmar is the "best of the community" and insists that instead the best of the community is one who sells his property for funds with which to undertake *jihād* and who situates himself "between the Muslims and their enemies."

75. Robinson, *Empire and Elites*, ch. 5, esp. 109–16.

76. *The Epistle of Sālim Ibn Dhakwān*, trans. Patricia Crone and Fritz Zimmermann (Oxford, 2001), 1.

77. Donner, *Narratives of Islamic Origins*, 52–53, 149–54, 162–63.

78. See Sizgorich, "Narrative and Community in Islamic Late Antiquity," 28–41.

79. Al-Ṭabarī I. 2395, trans. Friedmann, *The History of al-Ṭabarī* 12, 181–82.

80. See Cook, "Muslim Apocalyptic and *Jihād*," 66–105.

81. See, for example, al-Khaṭīb al-Baghdādī, *Ta'rīkh Baghdād*, 9.188, where Sarī recalls raiding the lands of the Romans "on foot," an especially commendable way to practice *jihād*, according to Ibn al-Mubārak, *Kitāb al-jihād* #32, #33.

82. See, for example, al-Khaṭīb al-Baghdādī, *Ta'rīkh Baghdād*, 9.188–92. Cf. Abū Nuʿaym, *Ḥilyat al-awliyā' wa-ṭabaqāt al-aṣfiyā'*, 10.110ff.

83. Abā Nuʿaym *Ḥilyat al-awliyā' wa-ṭabaqāt al-aṣfiyā'*, 10:110. Cf. idem, 10:111.

84. Theodoret, *Historia Religiosa*, 2.2, cf. 9.1, 20.3, ed. and French trans. Canivet and Leroy-Molinghen, 1.196–97, 1.454–55, 2.66–67.

85. See Athanasius, *Vita Antonii*, 7.

86. Melchert, "Transition from Asceticism." For the end of late antiquity, see Clover and Humphreys, "Introduction," in Clover and Humphreys (eds.), *Tradition and Innovation.*

87. See, for example, Abu Nuʿaym, *Ḥilyat al-awliyā' wa-ṭabaqāt al-aṣfiyā'*, 10.126. Cf. *Ta'rīkh Baghdād* 9.188: [Al-Sarī said] "I raided on foot and we brought down destruction upon al-Rūm. And then I threw myself down on my back and raised my legs up on a wall, and a shout hailed me, 'O Sarī b. al-Mughalis, in this manner does the servant sit before his master?'"

88. *Ta'rīkh Baghdād* 9.188–92.

89. *Ta'rīkh Baghdād* 9.188.

90. *Ta'rīkh Baghdād* 9.188.

91. *Ta'rīkh Baghdād* 9.188.

92. See, for example, *Ta'rīkh Baghdād* 9.188–89 where Sarī plays the familiar holy man role of intercessor, intervening with local officials on behalf of a neighborhood woman and her son.

93. Ṣāliḥ b. Aḥmad b. Ḥanbal, *Sīrat al-imām Aḥmad b. Ḥanbal*, 18.

94. See Hurvitz, "Biographies and Mild Asceticism;" Hurvitz, *The Formation of Hanbalism.* Many later Muslims, especially but not only members of the Ḥanbalī school of jurisprudence, modeled themselves in turn after the figure of Aḥmad b. Ḥanbal. See, for example, the report of one follower of Ibn Ḥanbal who saw Aḥmad in a dream: "The Prophet . . . was walking on a path and he was holding the hand of Aḥmad b. Ḥanbal, and they were walking in an unhurried and gentle manner, and I was behind them, striving so that I might catch up with them, but I was not able." Ibn Abī Yaʿlā, *Ṭabaqāt al-fuqahā' al-Ḥanābila*, ed. ʿAlī Muḥammad ʿUmar, 1.34. For Ibn Ḥanbal, see below and Cooperson, *Classical Arabic Biography*, ch. 4.

CHAPTER SEVEN

1. Al-Balādhurī, *Ansāb al-ashrāf*, II 325–26 (#679).

2. Al-Balādhurī, *Ansāb al-ashrāf*, II 328 (#680). See al-Ṭabarī, *Ta'rīkh*, I. 3337–39,

trans. G. R. Hawting, *The History of al-Ṭabarī* 17: *The First Civil War* (Albany, 1996), 123–25; Abū l-ʿAbbās Muḥammad b. Yazīd al-Mubarrad, *Kamil fi al-lugha*, 560; al-Baghdādī, *Al-farq bayna al-firaq*, ed. Muḥammad Muḥī al-Dīn ʿAbd al-Ḥamīd, 76–77.

3. Al-Balādhurī, *Ansāb al-ashrāf*, II 324–26 (#679).

4. Al-Balādhurī, *Ansāb al-ashrāf*, II 324–27 (#679).

5. For the Khawārij, see Brünnow, *Die Charidschiten unter den ersten Omayyaden*; Wellhausen, *The Religio-Political Factions in Early Islam*; Crone, "The First Century Concept of Higra"; Hawting, "The Significance of the Slogan *Lā Ḥukma Illā Lillāh*"; Rubin, *Between Bible and Qur'ān*; Crone, "A Statement by the Najdiyya Kharijite"; Crone, "Even an Ethiopian Slave"; Crone, *God's Rule*, ch. 5; Cook, "Anan and Islam"; Skladanek "The Kharijites in Iran I"; Kenney, "The Emergence of the Khawarij"; Kenney, "Heterodoxy and Culture"; Lewinstein, "Making and Unmaking a Sect"; Lewinstein, "Notes on Eastern Hanafite Heresiography"; Lewinstein, "The Azariqa in Islamic Heresiography"; Blankinship, *The End of the Jihad State*; Hinds, "Kufan Political Alignments"; Shaban, *Islamic History*; Robinson, *Empire and Elites*, 114–26; Bosworth, *Sīstan Under the Arabs*, 37ff., 90; Morony, *Iraq after the Muslim Conquest*, 468–78.

6. See al-Ṭabarī, *Ta'rīkh*, I. 3329–55, trans. Hawting, *The History of al-Ṭabarī* 17, 78–104; al-Balādhurī, *Ansāb al-ashrāf*, II 248–316; al-Yaʿqūbī, *al-Ta'rīkh*, 2.219–23, al-Baghdādī, *Al-farq bayna al-firaq*, ed. ʿAbd al-Ḥamīd, 74–76. For ʿAlī's showdown with the Khawārij as Nahrawān, "The Battle of the Canal," see al-Ṭabarī, *Ta'rīkh*, I. 3376–90, trans. Hawting, *The History of al-Ṭabarī* 17, 126–40; al-Balādhurī, *Ansāb al-ashrāf*, 2.317–36.

7. Al-Ṭabarī, *Ta'rīkh*, I. 3333–34, trans. Hawting, *The History of al-Ṭabarī* 17, 82–83.

8. Al-Balādhurī, *Ansāb al-ashrāf*, 2.317 (#671); cf. al-Ṭabarī, *Ta'rīkh*, I. 3362–65, trans. Hawting, *The History of al-Ṭabarī* 17, 115.

9. Al-Balādhurī, *Ansāb al-ashrāf*, 2.326 (#679).

10. Al-Balādhurī, *Ansāb al-ashrāf*, 2.328 (#681).

11. Q:3.105.

12. Q:13.11.

13. For the difficulties associated with the term *maṣāḥif*, see Hawting, *The History of al-Ṭabarī* 17, 78, note 319.

14. Q:48.12

15. Al-Balādhurī, *Ansāb al-ashrāf*, II 329–30 (#681); cf. al-Ṭabarī, *Ta'rīkh*, I. 3376–77, trans. Hawting, *The History of al-Ṭabarī* 17, 126–27.

16. See Thomas Sizgorich, "'Become infidels or we will throw you into the fire': The Martyrs of Najran in Early Muslim Historiography, Hagiography and Qur'anic Exegesis," in Arietta Papaconstantinou (ed.), *Writing "True Stories": Historians and Hagiographers in the Late Antique and Mediaeval Near East* (Turnhout, forthcoming).

17. Al-Balādhurī, *Ansāb al-ashrāf*, 2.366 (#719). Cf. al-Ṭabarī, *Ta'rīkh*, I. 3418–19, trans. Hawting, *The History of al-Ṭabarī* 17, 172.

18. Al-Balādhurī, *Ansāb al-ashrāf*, 2.430 (#769).

19. See Hawting, "The Significance of the Slogan *Lā Ḥukma Illā Lillāh*," 453–58 for this failure of ʿUthmān to uphold "God's judgment" and its role in the rhetoric surrounding his murder.

20. Al-Balādhurī, *Ansāb al-ashrāf*, 2.329–30 (#681). Cf. al-Ṭabarī, *Ta'rīkh*, I. 3376–77, trans. Hawting, *The History of al-Ṭabarī* 17, 126–27.

21. Abū Bakr al-Khallāl, *Kitāb al-amr bi-'l-maʿrūf wa-'l-nahy ʿan al-munkar*, ed. ʿAbd al-Qādir Aḥmad ʿAṭā (Cairo, 1975), 95 (#31).

22. Cook, *Commanding Right and Forbidding Wrong*, passim.

23. Al-Azdī, *Ta'rīkh futūḥ al-Shām*, 211. Interestingly, in the *Futūh al-Jazīra* of pseudo-Wāqidi, which purports to date from the second or early third century A.H., but which is in fact believed to be the work of a later author, the Romans react to the Arab conquest of Syria and "much of Iraq" by going to a local stylite for answers. He tells them that the Muslims have come because of the loss of previous virtue. "You used to command right and forbid wrong," he tells them, "and you would refuse misdeeds and you spoke of the truth. And you kept your laws and you refrained yourselves from eating what was forbidden (*al-ḥarām*)." But the Romans had fallen away from the ways of their forebears, and the transgression of their previous behavioral norms had made the Romans vulnerable to the Muslim armies, the monk explained. Pseudo-Wāqidī, *Ta'rīkh futūḥ al-Jazīra wa-'l-khābūr wa-diyār bakr wa-'l-ʿIrāq*, ed. ʿAbd al-ʿAzīz Fayyāḍ Ḥarfūsh (Damascus, 1996), 90–91.

24. Abū Isḥāq al-Fazārī, *Kitāb al-siyar*, ed. Fārūk Ḥamād (Beirut, 1987), 316 (#610). For al-Fazārī's own commanding and forbidding, see Cook, *Commanding Right and Forbidding Wrong*, 60.

25. Yazīd Muḥammad al-Azdī, *Ta'rīkh Mūsil*, ed. ʿAlī Ḥabīb (Cairo, 1967), 104, cited by Patricia Crone and Martin Hinds, *God's Caliph: Religious Authority in the First Centuries of Islam* (Cambridge, 1986), 129. A version of this address, as it appears in the *Ansāb al-ashrāf* of al-Balādhurī, is translated by Crone and Hinds in Appendix III of their work. It also appears in other versions in a number of other texts, all cited by Crone and Hinds, 129. Cf. Sālim b. Dhakwān, *Sīrat Ibn Dhakwān*, 38, ed. and trans. Crone and Zimmermann, *The Epistle of Ibn Dhakwān*, 77. Even Syriac sources recall ʿUmar as a stern pietist, and one whose "zeal" prompted him to pressure Christians to convert. See *The Chronicle of Michael the Syrian*, ed. and trans. Chabot (*Chronique du Michel le Syrien patriarche jacobite d'Antioche [1166–1199]*), 4.488; 2.456.

26. Al-Balādhurī, *Ansāb al-ashrāf*, 2.320–21 (#674). Cf. al-Ṭabarī, *Ta'rīkh*, I. 3364–65.

27. Al-Khallāl, *Ahl al-milal*, ed. al-Sulṭān, 2.347 (#737, 738).

28. Al-Azdī, *Ta'rīkh futūḥ al-Shām*, 202.

29. Ibn al-Mubārak, *Kitāb al-jihād*, #154.

30. Ibn al-Mubārak, *Kitab al-jihād*, #45.

31. Ibn al-Mubārak, *Kitab al-jihād*, #47.

32. Ibn al-Mubārak, *Kitāb al-jihād* #164.

33. Al-Balādhurī, *Ansāb al-ashrāf*, IV/1, ed. Max Schloessinger and M. J. Kister (Jerusalem, 1971), 172 (#462).

34. Al-Azdī, *Ta'rīkh Mūsil*, ed. ʿAlī Ḥabīb, 70–71. For Ḍaḥḥāk b. Qays' rebellion, see also *ʿUyūn al-ḥadā'iq al-akhbār fī al-ḥaqā'q*, ed. M. J de Goeje (Leiden, 1871), 140, 157–64. Ḍaḥḥāk had conducted a strikingly Khārijī-style campaign while still under the command of Muʿāwiya, when he was dispatched against the Bedouin who supported ʿAlī, and "seized the property of the people and killed those Bedouin whom he met." See al-Ṭabarī, *Ta'rīkh*, I. 3447, trans. Hawting, *The History of al-Ṭabarī* 17, 201.

35. Al-Ṭabarī, *Ta'rīkh*, II.18–19, trans. Michael G. Morony, *The History of al-Ṭabarī 18: Between the Civil Wars: The Caliphate of Muʿāwiyah* (Albany, 1987), 22–23. Al-Balādhurī, *Ansāb al-ashrāf*, IV/1 168 (#460). For more examples of the Khārijī adoration of Khārijī martyrs in Khārijī poetry, see Ghada Bathish Hallaq, "Discourse Strategies: The Persuasive Power of Early Khārijī Poetry" (Ph.D. diss., University of Washington, 1988), esp. the examples of Khārijī poetry translated by Hallaq in his Appendix, pp. 130–51.

36. Al-Ṭabarī, *Ta'rīkh*, II. 20.

37. Al-Balādhurī, *Ansāb al-ashrāf*, 4.572.

38. Al-Balādhurī, *Ansāb al-ashrāf*, 4.581; al-Ṭabarī, *Ta'rīkh*, II. 900. See also Robinson, *Empire and Elites*, 113–12. For a brief account of Shabīb's rebellion, see al-Yaʿqūbī, *Ta'rīkh*, ed. Houtsma, 2.328.

39. Al-Baghdādī, *Al-farq bayna al-firaq*, ed. ʿAbd al-Ḥamīd, 91. For their deaths at Nahrawān, see al-Ṭabarī, *Ta'rīkh*, I. 3382.

40. See al-Baghdādī, *Kitāb al-milal wa-'l-niḥal*, ed. Albert N. Nader (Beirut, 1986), 75. Robinson, *Empire and Elites*, 113–14. Muḥammad Muḥī al-Dīn ʿAbd al-Ḥamīd's Cairo edition of al-Baghdādī lacks this passage.

41. al-Mubarrad, *Kamīl fī al-lugha*, ed. Wright, 584. See Wellhausen, *Religio-Political Factions*, 41–45.

42. Al-Ṭabarī, *Ta'rīkh*, II. 391.

43. Al-Mubarrad, *Kamīl fī al-lugha*, ed. Wright, 609. See Wellhausen, *Religio-Political Factions*, 41–45.

44. Isḥāq b. Ibrāhīm b. Hāni' al-Nīsābūrī, *Masā'il al-Imām Aḥmad Ibn Ḥanbal*, ed. Zuhayr al-Shāwīsh, 2 vols. (Cairo, 1980), 2.95 (#1587).

45. Al-Nīsābūrī, *Masā'il al-Imām Aḥmad Ibn Ḥanbal*, ed. al-Shāwīsh, 2.109 (#1638).

46. Al-Nīsābūrī, *Masā'il al-Imām Aḥmad Ibn Ḥanbal*, ed. al-Shāwīsh, 2.95–96 (#1588).

47. Al-Nīsābūrī, *Masā'il al-Imām Aḥmad Ibn Ḥanbal*, ed. al-Shāwīsh, 2.96 (#1590).

48. Q:9.123.

49. Al-Nīsābūrī, *Masā'il al-Imām Aḥmad Ibn Ḥanbal*, ed. al-Shāwīsh, 2.96–97 (#1592). Cf. #1595.

50. Al-Nīsābūrī, *Masā'il al-Imām Aḥmad Ibn Ḥanbal*, ed. al-Shāwīsh, 2.97. (#1594).

51. For Sāliḥ, see Chase Robinson, *Empire and Elites*, ch. 5, esp. 114–26; Morony, *Iraq after the Muslim Conquest*, 475–76.

52. Cf. Q:2.123, 146; 3.158.

53. Al-Ṭabarī, *Ta'rīkh*, II. 881–83. This passage of al-Ṭabarī is cited by Chase Robinson in his discussion of Ṣāliḥ's rebellion at Robinson, *Empire and Elites*, ch. 5, esp. 114–26. Cf. the passages on Muḥammad, Abū Bakr, ʿUmar, ʿUthmān and ʿAlī in the address attributed to Abū Ḥamza that appears in al-Balādhurī's *Ansāb al-ashrāf* and a number of other texts, and which is translated with comments in Appendix 3, Crone and Hinds, *God's Caliph*.

54. See Crone and Zimmermann, *The Epistle of Sālim Ibn Dhakwān*. For the Ibāḍī *madhhab*, see Ersilia Francesca, "The Formation and Early Development of the Ibāḍī Madhhab," *JSAI* 28 (2003): 260–77.

55. For Ṣāliḥ, see al-Balāduri, *Ansāb al-ashrāf*, VI, ed. Maḥmūd Firdaws al-ʿAẓm (Damascus, 1996), 572; cited by Robinson, *Empire and Elites*, 114–15. For Dhū al-Thafināt, see al-Balādhurī, *Ansāb al-ashrāf*, II 318 (#673) and above.

56. *Zuqnīn Chronicle*, trans. Harrak (*The Chronicle of Zuqnīn: Parts III and IV A.D. 488–775*), 164–65 [174–75].

57. In fact, some Khawārij took their wives with them, most notably Shabīb b. Yazīd. See below.

58. Q:9.6.

59. Al-Mubarrad, *Kamīl fī al-lugha*, ed. Wright, 528. See also al-Ṭabarī, *Ta'rīkh*, II. 895–96 for a slightly different version of this story. Rowson (*The History of al-Ṭabarī* 22, 47 n. 191) interprets the passage from al-Mubarrad's *Kamīl* to imply that Wāṣil b. ʿAṭāʾ and his companions decline to join the Khawārij (i.e., that they escort them back to their home community at the end of the conversation). This would seem to run contrary to the acceptance by the visitors to the Khawārij camp of the Khārijī *qawl*, however. Moreover, in the similar passage included in al-Ṭabarī's *Ta'rīkh*, the Muslims who insist upon Q: 9.6 and who hear out the views of the Khawārij also join the rebels.

60. Al-Balādurī, *Ansāb al-ashrāf*, 4.274. See also al-Baghdādī, *Al-farq bayna al-firaq*, ed. ʿAbd al-Ḥamīd, 77; al-Ṭabarī, *Ta'rīkh*, II. 754–57.

61. Muḥammad b. Aḥmad al-Malaṭī, *Kitāb al-tanbīh*, ed. Sven Dedering (Istanbul, 1936), 38, cited and translated by Crone and Zimmermann, 327.

62. Al-Ṭabarī, *Ta'rīkh*, II. 756, trans. Michael Fishbein, *The History of al-Ṭabarī* 21: *The Victory of the Marwanids* (Albany, 1990), 125.

63. Abū Isḥāq al-Fazārī, *Kitāb al-siyar*, ed. Ḥamād, 298 (#550). For al-Fazārī, see Bonner, "Some Observations," esp. 9–19.

64. Al-Balādhurī, *Ansāb al-ashrāf*, II 318 (#673). The ʿAlid deputy in question was ʿAbd Allāh b. al-ʿAbbās. He also asked the Khawārij if they really thought that the wrongs they were correcting was worth the spilling of the blood of Muslims.

65. For *istiʿrāḍ*, see the discussion of Crone and Zimmermann, *Epistle of Sālim Ibn Dhakwān*, 325–29, esp. 328. See al-Baghdādī, *Al-farq bayna al-firaq*, ed. ʿAbd al-Ḥamīd, 84

for the position the Azāriqa took with regard to the issue of killing women and children; 87 for the Najdāt; 91 for the Ṣufriyya.

66. Al-Balādhurī, *Ansāb al-ashrāf*, II 364–5 (#719). When ʿAlī's troops caught up with the murderers, their commanders asked the killers what had prompted them to do what they had done. Their leader, al-Khirrīt, simply said, "I was not pleased with your master, nor with his conduct, for I saw that he separated himself and was with those who agreed to arbitration." When asked to turn over those responsible for the murder, they refused, saying, "That is impossible. Has not your companion made peace with the killers of ʿUthmān?" The Kharijite then "summoned all of his companions, and [the ʿAlid troops and the Khawārij] fought one another fiercely until their spears were broken, and their swords were bent and all of their horses were wounded." Night then set in, and in the dark the Khawārij stole away toward Baṣra. Al-Balādhurī, *Ansāb al-ashrāf*, II 430 (#769).

67. Al-Balādhurī, *Ansāb al-ashrāf*, IV/1 172 (#462). Sahm was later crucified at his house when Umayyad authorities finally caught him.

68. For Bint Simāk b. Yazīd et al., see al-Ṭabarī, *Ta'rīkh*, II. 760, trans. Fishbein, *History of al-Ṭabarī*, 21, 129.

69. See Noth and Conrad, *The Early Arabic Historical Tradition*, ch. 3.

70. For violence against women, and women defying the Khawārij, see the following: Ibn Khabbāb's pregnant *umm walad* is disemboweled at al-Ṭabarī, *Ta'rīkh* I. 3375; al-Balādhurī, *Ansāb al-ashrāf*, 2.234–38; pregnant women are again reported to have been cut open by the Khawārij at al-Ṭabarī, *Ta'rīkh*, II. 755–56. The Khārijī leader Nāfiʿ b. al-Azraq is said to have made a practice of "ripping" women and killing children. See al-Balādhurī, *Ansāb al-ashrāf*, IV/2, ed. Max Schloessinger (Jerusalem, 1938), 414. Whether this refers to the practice of "ripping [open]" pregnant women is unclear, although the verb al-Balādhurī used to describe the act, *baqara*, is the same used to describe the opening of Ibn Khabbāb's *umm walad*'s belly (*Ansāb al-ashrāf*, 2.327,1; 328,9, where she is described as Ibn Khabbāb's "*umm walad*"). Al-Ṭabarī also uses *baqara* to describe the killing of Ibn Khabbāb's *umm walad* (*Ta'rīkh*, I. 3375.8). It may be significant here that while al-Balādhurī uses the verb *baqara* to denote the killing of women, in the same sentence he uses *qatala* to describe Nāfiʿ's tendency to kill children; it is this verb (*qatala*) that al-Ṭabarī and al-Balādhurī both use most frequently use to describe the act of killing men, women or children. Cf. al-Baghdādī, *Al-farq bayna al-firaq*, ed. ʿAbd al-Ḥamīd, 83–84, 87, where the permissibility of killing women and children among one particularly violent sect, the Azāriqa, is described, as is their view that wherever those who disagreed with them dwelled was to be considered the "abode of unbelief" and that within it women and children were to be killed; Rayṭa bint Yazīd scolds her Khārijī attackers before her murder, al-Ṭabarī, *Ta'rīkh* II. 756, trans. Fishbein, *History of al-Ṭabarī*, 21, 126; Bint Simāk b. Yazīd does the same, and tries to protect her father, who was mentally defective, al-Ṭabarī, *Ta'rīkh*, II. 760, trans. Fishbein, *History of al-Ṭabarī*, 21, 129; the wife of ʿAbd al-ʿAzīz b. ʿAbd Allāh was beheaded "out of zeal and indignation" by a Khārijī kinsman of hers, al-Ṭabarī, *Ta'rīkh*, II. 823, trans. Fishbein, *History of al-Ṭabarī*, 21, 200; for the "*umm walad*"

of Rabʿīa b. Nādj and the Khawārij, see al-Balādhurī, *Ansāb al-ashrāf*, VI/1. 274. Soon after the murder of ʿAlī, al-Balādhurī reports that a Khārijī named Shabīb "went out" and "he did not meet a child or a man or a woman on the road but that he killed them." *Ansāb al-ashrāf*, IV/1.166 (456).

71. For dialogues between Khawārij and caliphal officials, in addition to those cited above, see, among others, al-Ṭabarī, *Taʾrīkh*, I. 3360–64; al-Ṭabarī, *Taʾrīkh*, I. 3376–80; al-Ṭabarī, *Taʾrīkh*, II. 887–88; al-Mubarrad, *Kamīl*, 571 for an interview with a female Khārijī; al-Mubarrad, *Kamīl*, 572–73 for ʿAbd al-Malik's near conversion to Khārijī dogma; al-Balādhurī, *Ansāb al-ashrāf*, IV/1 166–67 (#456); Ibn Aʿtham, *Kitāb al-futūḥ*, 7.92–97. For Khārijī ascetic ideology and behavior, see, among others, the Khārijī leader Ḥayyān b. Ẓabyānʾs address to his colleagues, Ṭabarī, *Taʾrīkh*, II. 18–19. Shabīb b. Yazīd slits the saddle bags carrying captured tax receipts and lets the animal carrying them run through town, spilling the money as it goes. He instructs that if there is any money left when the animal reaches the river, it is to be thrown into the water,. For this episode, see Ṭabarī, *Taʾrīkh* II. 955–56. For a would-be Khārijī who borrows a hooded cloak called a "burnus," typically the garb of ascetics, as he prepares to "go out" with the Khawārij, see Ṭabarī, *Taʾrīkh* I. 3389, trans. Hawting, *The History of al-Ṭabarī* 17, 139 n. 580. For the Khārijī narrations of the recent Muslim past, see al-Balādhurī, *Ansāb al-ashrāf*, II. 329–3 (#681) and al-Ṭabarī, *Taʾrīkh*, II. 881–83.

72. See in particular the commentary sections in Crone and Zimmermann, *The Epistle of Sālim Ibn Dhakwān*, Parts II and III; Robinson, *Empire and Elites*, ch. 7. For a concise explication and deployment of this kind of methodology, see Robinson, "The Conquest of Khuzistan."

73. Al-Ṭabarī, *Taʾrīkh*, II. 737.

74. Abū Ḥanīfa Aḥmad b. Dāwūd al-Dīnawarī, *Kitab al-akhbār al-ṭiwāl*, ed. Ignace Kratchkovsky (Leiden, 1912), 313, cited and trans. Michael Fishbein, *The History of al-Ṭabarī* 21, 104 n. 387.

75. Al-Balādhurī, *Ansāb al-ashrāf*, IV/1 166–67 (#457).

76. ʿAbd Allāh b. Wahb b. Muslim al-Qurayshī Abū Muḥammad al-Miṣrī, *Kitāb al-Muḥāraba min al-Muwaṭṭāʾ* ed. Mīklūsh Mūrānī (Beirut, 2002), 44–46.

77. See Abū Jaʿfar Muḥammad b. Jarīr al-Ṭabarī, *Jāmiʿ al-bayān ʿan taʾwīl al-Qurʾān*, 30 vols. (Cairo, 1954), IX.220; Muqātil b. Sulaymān, *Tafsīr Muqātil b. Sulaymān*, ed. Aḥmad Farīd, 3 vols. (Beirut, 2003), II.12; Hūd b. Muḥakkam al-Hawwārī, *Tafsīr kitāb Allāh al-ʿazīz*, 4 vols., ed. Bālḥajj bin Saʿid Sharīfī (Beirut, 1990), II.83; ʿAbd al-Razzāq b. Hammām al-Ṣanʿānī [al-Ḥimyarī], *Tafsīr al-Qurʾān*, ed. Muṣṭafā Muslim Muḥammad, 4 vols. (Riyadh, 1989), IIb.257.

78. Al-Ṭabarī, *Taʾrīkh*, I. 3369–70, trans. Hawting, *The History of al-Ṭabarī* 17, 120.

79. Robinson, *Empire and Elites*, 124.

80. See Robinson, *Empire and Elites*, 124; Brünnow, *Die Charidschiten unter den ersten Omayyaden*, 10; Kenney, "The Emergence of the Khawarij: Religion and the Social

Order in Early Islam," 3. For the early Islamic narrative of betrayal and redemption, see Humphreys, "Qur'anic Myth and Narrative."

81. See Hawting, "The Significance of the Slogan *Lā Ḥukma Illā Lillāh*."

82. Cook, "Apocalyptic and Jihād," 102.

83. See Brünnow, *Die Charidschiten unter den ersten Omayyaden*, 10; Kenney, "The Emergence of the Khawarij," 3.

84. Al-Ṭabarī, *Ta'rīkh*, I. 3424, trans. Hawting, *The History of al-Ṭabarī* 17, 177.

85. Al-Ṭabarī, *Ta'rīkh*, I. 3460, trans. Hawting, *The History of al-Ṭabarī* 17, 217.

86. Abū Ḥanīfa al-Dīnawarī, *Kitāb akhbār al-ṭiwāl*, ed. Vladimir Guirgass (Leiden, 1888), 228.

87. See Skladanek, "The Kharijites in Iran I." For brief descriptions of the various Khārijī sects written by medieval Muslim heresiographers, see Muḥammad b. ʿAbd al-Karīm al-Shahrastānī, *Kitāb al-milal wa-'l-niḥal*, ed. William Cureton (London, 1846 [Piscataway, N.J., 2002]), 85–107.

88. For the Khawārij and *barā'a*, see Etan Kohlberg, "Barā'a in Shīʿī Doctrine," *JSAI* 7 (1986): 142–44. Cf. al-Baghdādī, *Al-farq bayna al-firaq*, ed. Muḥammad Muḥī al-Dīn ʿAbd al-Ḥamīd, 87. For the concept of *hijra* among the Khawārij, see Crone, "The First Century Concept of Higra."

89. *Sīrat Ibn Dhakwān*, 34, ed. and trans. Crone and Zimmermann, 75.

90. Cited and translated by Kohlberg, "Barā'a in Shīʿī Doctrine," 167.

91. See Khālid b. al-Walīd's dialogue with the Roman general Bāhān, al-Azdī, *Futūḥ al-Shām*, 205; and Mughīra b. Shuʿba's dialogue with the Persian shah at Ibn Aʿtham, *Kitāb al-futūḥ*, 1.195ff.

92. Translated by Charles Pellat, *The Life and Works of Jāḥiẓ* (Berkeley, 1969), 35.

93. Morony, *Iraq after the Muslim Conquest*, 475.

94. Morony, *Iraq after the Muslim Conquest*, 476–77.

95. Morony, *Iraq after the Muslim Conquest*, 477.

96. Robinson, *Empire and Elites*, 116–17.

97. Robinson, *Empire and Elites*, 117; on Shabīb, see Robinson, *Empire and Elites*, 119–21.

98. Al-Ṭabarī, *Ta'rīkh*, II. 885–980; al-Balādhurī, see Ibn Aʿtham, *Kitāb al-futūḥ*, VII 74–97. Wellhausen, *Religio-Political Factions*, ch. 10. As Chase Robinson notes (*Elites and Empire*, 120), Christian authors also took notice of Shabīb.

99. Al-Ṭabarī, *Ta'rīkh*, II. 864–73.

100. Al-Ṭabarī, *Ta'rīkh*, II. 976–78.

101. Al-Balādhurī, *Ansāb al-ashrāf*, VI.588. In al-Ṭabarī's version, she seems to have survived the collapse of her son's rebellion. See al-Ṭabarī, *Ta'rīkh*, II. 976–78.

102. The famous Khārijī motto and battle cry. See Hawting, "The Significance of the Slogan *Lā Ḥukma Illā Lillāh*."

103. Ibn Aʿtham, *Kitāb al-futūḥ*, 7.95–96. One version of al-Baghdādī (al-Baghdādī,

Al-farq bayna al-firaq, ed. ʿAbd al-Ḥamīd) reports that when Shabīb raided al-Kūfa, in addition to "a thousand of the Khawārij, with him were his mother Ghazāla and his wife Jahīra [sic] amongst two hundred of the women of the Khawārij who had taken up javelins and girded themselves with swords. And when they raided al-Kūfa by night, they made a beeline for the congregational mosque (*al-masjid al-jāmiʿ*) and killed the attendants (or guards "*ḥurrās*") of the mosque, and those who were busying themselves with prayer in it. And he set up his mother Ghazāla on the minbar so she could deliver a sermon." The edition of Albert N. Nader (al-Baghdādī, *Kitāb al-milal wa-ʾl-niḥal*, ed. Albert N. Nader [Beirut, 1986]), which is a version of an "unabridged" manuscript in the Bibliothèque des Waqfs à Bagdad (no. 6819/f.39), contains much the same report (p. 75) but leaves out the report of the killing of those praying in the mosque, and the number of Khārijī women is set at one hundred. In both texts it should be noted that the names of Shabīb's wife and mother are transposed.

104. Al-Mubarrad, *Kamīl fī al-lugha*, ed. Wright, 572.

105. Al-Mubarrad, *Kamīl fī al-lugha*, ed. Wright, 572–73.

106. Brown, *Rise of Western Christendom*, 301.

CHAPTER EIGHT

1. Thomas of Margā, *The Book of Governors*, ed. and trans. E. A. Wallis Budge, 2 vols. (London, 1893 [Piscataway, N.J., 2003]), 2.41.

2. Leontius, *The Life of Stephen of Mar Sabas*, ed. and trans. John C. Lamoreaux, CSCO 579 (Arab. 51) (Louvain, 1999), 52.3–10.

3. See Rabban Mār Simon, *The History of Rabban Hōrmīzd*, XI–XII, trans. E. A. Wallis Budge, *The Histories of Rabban Hōrmīzd the Persian and Rabban Bar-ʿIdtā* (London, 1902 [Piscataway, N.J., 2003]), 101–6; Ibn Abī Yaʿlā, *Ṭabaqāt al-fuqahāʾ al-Ḥanābila*, ed. ʿAlī Muḥammad ʿUmar, 1.268–69. Cf. *The Life of Timothy of Kākhushtā*, Saidnaya Version, 47.1–2, ed. and trans. Lamoreaux and Cairala, 611, where the Christian ascetic Timothy rides off on a lion.

4. *The Life of Timothy of Kākhushtā*, Saidnaya Version, 43.1–6, ed. and trans. Lamoreaux and Cairala, 599–603.

5. Al-Fazārī, *Kitāb al-siyar*, 334–35, Appendix I. #2, 3. Cf. *The Life of Timothy of Kākhushtā*, Saidnaya Version, 44.4, ed. and trans. Lamoreaux and Cairala, 603, where a Muslim *ghāzī* acknowledges that he is forbidden to kill monks but that he is considering making an exception in the case of a monk whose behavior confuses him.

6. Mēna of Nikiou, *The Life of Isaac of Alexandria*, ed. and French trans. E. Amélineau, *Histoire du patriarche Copte Isaac* (Paris, 1890), 67–71, trans. David N. Bell (Kalamazoo, 1988), 72. For ʿAbd al-ʿAzīz's gentle relationship with Isaac's predecessor John, and with Isaac himself, see Sāwirūs b. al-Muqaffaʿ, *History of the Patriarchs of Alexandria*, part

I, chapter xv, ed. and trans. B. Evetts, *PO* 5.1 (Paris, 1947), 16–18, 20. For ʿAbd al-ʿAzīz's career of cooperation with Isaac's successor, Simon, see *History of the Patriarchs of Alexandria*, part I, ch. xvi, 27–42.

7. Mēna of Nikiou, *The Life of Isaac of Alexandria*, trans. Bell, 63, 67–72.

8. We frequently find, for example, that in such texts as Sāwirūs b. al-Muqaffaʿ's *History of the Patriarchs of Alexandria*, even where brutal Muslim governors abuse the Christians of Egypt, this abuse is typically depicted as having been committed in the service of extortion rather than religious persecution and, notably, often at the behest of one Christian group acting against another via the power of the Egyptian *amīr*. Moreover, such brutal Muslim governors terrify Muslims as well as Christians. See, for example, Sāwirūs b. al-Muqaffaʿ, *History of the Patriarchs of Alexandria*, ed. and trans. B. Evetts, *PO* 5.1.68, where we hear of the fear shared in common between Muslims and Christians of a particularly rapacious and violent *amīr* in Egypt.

9. See, for example, see Sāwirūs b. al-Muqaffaʿ, *History of the Patriarchs of Alexandria*, part I, ch. xiv, ed. and trans. B. Evetts, *PO* 1.4 (Paris, 1948), 491. For the opinion of Heraclius among Syrians after the conquests, see John W. Watt, "The Portrayal of Heraclius in Syriac Historical Sources," in Gerrit J. Reinink and Bernard H. Stolte (eds.), *The Reign of Heraclius (610–641): Crisis and Confrontation* (Leiden, 2002), 63–80. These stand in stark contrast to the generally quite sympathetic views of Heraclius in Muslim literature. See Nadia Maria el-Cheikh, "Muḥammad and Heraclius: A Study in Legitimacy," *SI* 89 (1999): 5–21.

10. For the relative toleration of the early Islamic community toward its religious minorities, see Patricia Crone, *God's Rule*, 371–72, "Once the war was over, people received *dhimma* in return for the payment of *jizya* and were generally left in peace, again whether they were pagans or People of the Book." See also *God's Rule*, 373–82. For non-Muslims in Islamic holy texts, see Mahmoud Ayoub, "Dhimma in Qur'an and Hadith," in Robert Hoyland (ed.), *Muslims and Others in Early Islamic Society* (Aldershot, 2004), 27–35.

11. For Ibn Ḥanbal and the Ḥanbalīs, see Hurvitz, "From Scholarly Circles to Mass Movements"; Hurvitz, "Schools of Law and Historical Context"; Hurvitz, *The Formation of Ḥanbalism*, passim; Hurvitz, "Biographies and Mild Asceticism"; Laoust, "Le Hanbalisme sous le califat de Bagdad," esp. 69–74; Laoust, "Les premières professions de foi hanbalites," III.7–34; Laoust, *La profession de foi d'Ibn Baṭṭa*; Cooperson, *Classical Arabic Biography*, ch. 4. Christopher Melchert, *The Formation of the Sunni Schools of Law: 9th–10th Centuries C.E.* (Leiden, 1997), ch. 7; Melchert, "The Ḥanābila and the Early Sufis"; Spectorsky, "Aḥmad Ibn Ḥanbal's Fiqh"; Lapidus, "The Separation of State," esp. 378–85; Makdisi, "The Significance of the Sunni Schools of Law in Islamic Religious History"; Cook, *Commanding Right and Forbidding Wrong*, ch. 5. Lucas, *Constructive Critics*, passim and esp. 192–217. For the influence of Ḥanbalī thought as a basis for community in later medieval Islam, see Daniella Talmon Heller, "The Shaykh and the Community: Popular Hanbalite Islam in the 12–13th Century Jabal Nablus and Jabal Qasyūn," *SI* 79 (1994): 103–20.

12. *Madhāhib* were Islamic "schools of law." For a concise overview of their early growth and role within Islamic society, see Hurvitz, "From Scholarly Circles to Mass Movements."

13. Ibn Abī Yaʿlā, *Ṭabaqāt al-fuqahāʾ al-Ḥanābila*, ed. ʿAlī Muḥammad ʿUmar, 1.61–62.

14. For the uncreatedness of the Qurʾān, see Ibn Abī Yaʿlā, *Ṭabaqāt al-fuqahāʾ al-Ḥanābila*, ed. ʿUmar, 1.56: "The Qurʾān is the *kalām* of God; he uttered it. It is not created, and whoever maintains that it is created is a sullen unbeliever."

15. Ibn Abī Yaʿlā, *Ṭabaqāt al-fuqahāʾ al-Ḥanābila*, ed. ʿUmar, 1.39. See Cooperson, *Classical Arabic Biography*, 138–51 for a splendid discussion of the "cult of sanctity" that arose around the figure of Ibn Ḥanbal.

16. Ibn Abī Yaʿlā, *Ṭabaqāt al-fuqahāʾ al-Ḥanābila*, ed. ʿUmar, 1.40–41.

17. Ibn Abī Yaʿlā, *Ṭabaqāt al-fuqahāʾ al-Ḥanābila*, ed. ʿUmar, 1.39–40.

18. For the *miḥna*, see Walter M. Patton, *Aḥmed ibn Ḥanbal and the Miḥna* (Leiden, 1897); John A. Nawas, "The Miḥna of 218 A.H./833 A.D. Revisited: An Empirical Study," *JAOS* 116 (1996): 698–708; John A. Nawas, "A Reexamination of Three Current Explanations for al-Maʾmun's Introduction of the Miḥna," *IJMES* 26 (1994): 615–29; Nimrod Hurvitz, "Miḥna as Self-Defense," *SI* 92 (2001): 93–111; Hurvitz, *Formation of Ḥanbalism*, ch. 7–9; Lapidus, "Separation of State and Religion," 378–85; Crone and Hinds, *God's Caliph*, 94–97. For an outstanding narrative of Ibn Ḥanbal's role in the *miḥna*, crafted with superlative analysis of the sources, see Cooperson, *Classical Arabic Biography*, ch. 4, 117–28.

19. See al-Ṭabarī, *Taʾrīkh*, III. 1112–17, esp. 1116: "Begin by testing them out concerning what they say and by finding out from them their beliefs about God's creating and originating the Qurʾān in time." Trans. C. E. Bosworth, *The History of al-Ṭabarī* 32: *The Reunification of the ʿAbbāsid Caliphate* (Albany, 1987), 203.

20. See Hurvitz, *The Formation of Ḥanbalism*, ch. 7; Cooperson, *Classical Arabic Biography*, 138–40.

21. Ṣāliḥ b. Aḥmad b. Ḥanbal, *Sīrat al- imām Aḥmad Ibn Ḥanbal*; Ḥanbal b. Isḥāq b. Ḥanbal, *Dhikr miḥnat al-imām Aḥmad Ibn Ḥanbal*, ed. Muḥammad Naghsh (Cairo, 1977). For these men as biographers of Aḥmad b. Ḥanbal, see Cooperson, *Classical Arabic Biography*, 109–26.

22. For the Ḥanbalī origins of the *miḥna* grand narrative, see Cooperson, *Classical Arabic Biography*, 117–19; Hurvitz, *The Formation of Ḥanbalism*, see esp. 1–3, 13–21.

23. Ibn Abī Yaʿlā, *Ṭabaqāt al-fuqahāʾ al-Ḥanābila*, ed. ʿUmar, 1.33.

24. Ḥanbal b. Isḥāq b. Ḥanbal, *Dhikr miḥnat al-imām Aḥmad Ibn Ḥanbal*, ed. Naghsh, 60–61.

25. Ḥanbal b. Isḥāq b. Ḥanbal, *Dhikr miḥnat al-imām Aḥmad Ibn Ḥanbal*, ed. Naghsh, 61.

26. Ibn Abī Yaʿlā, *Ṭabaqāt al-fuqahāʾ al-Ḥanābila*, ed. ʿUmar, 1.37.

27. Ibn Abī Yaʿlā, *Ṭabaqāt al-fuqahāʾ al-Ḥanābila*, ed. ʿUmar, 1.33. For the *Ridda*

wars, see Ella Landau-Tasseron, "From Tribal Society to Centralized Polity: An Interpretation of Events and Anecdotes of the Formative Period of Islam," *JSAI* 24 (2000): 180–216.

28. See Cook, *Commanding Right and Forbidding Wrong*, 112.

29. Ibn Abī Yaʿlā, *Ṭabaqāt al-fuqahāʾ al-Ḥanābila*, ed. ʿUmar, 1.31–32. Ḥanbal b. Isḥāq b. Ḥanbal, *Dhikr miḥnat al-imām Aḥmad Ibn Ḥanbal*, ed. Naghsh, 102–5; Hurvitz, *Formation of Ḥanbalism*, 147–49.

30. Ibn Abī Yaʿlā, *Ṭabaqāt al-fuqahāʾ al-Ḥanābila*, ed. ʿUmar, 1.31; Ḥanbal b. Isḥāq b. Ḥanbal, *Dhikr miḥnat al-imām Aḥmad Ibn Ḥanbal*, ed. Naghsh, 104.

31. Sarī soon became the ascetic's student. The passage in which this story appears is as follows. "[Sarī said] I left Baghdad seeking a hospice for ascetics so that I might remain abstinent in it during Rajam, Shaʿbān and Ramadhān, and on my way I encountered ʿAlī al-Kharjānī and he was one of the great ascetics. When I ate my first meal at the end of Ramadhān, I had with me crushed salt and bread, and I said [to him], 'Come, may God have mercy upon you.' And he said, 'Your salt is ground and you have with you all sorts of food. You shall not pass through and you shall not enter the gardens of the beloved.' I looked at a provision sack he had with him in which was some barley mush. He ate from it, and I asked him, 'What introduced you to this?' He said, 'I count whatever is in the mouth against seventy hymns, and I have not tasted bread for forty years.' " Abū Nuʿaym al-Iṣfahānī, *Ḥilyat al-awliyāʾ wa-ṭabaqāt al-aṣfiyāʾ*, 10.110.

32. Abū l-Faraj al-Iṣfahānī (attributed), *Kitāb adab al-ghurabāʾ*, ed. Ṣāliḥ al-Dīn al-Munajjid (Beirut, 1972), trans. Patricia Crone and Shmuel Moreh, *The Book of Strangers: Medieval Arabic Graffiti on the Theme of Nostalgia* (Princeton, 2000).

33. Abū l-Faraj al-Iṣfahānī (attributed), *Kitāb adab al-ghurabāʾ*, ed. al-Munajjid, # 51 (pp. 64–68), trans. Patricia Crone and Shmuel Moreh, *The Book of Strangers*, 58–62.

34. For wine drinking and music as things forbidden to Muslims, see Cook, *Commanding Right and Forbidding Wrong*, 90–100. See also Néophyte Edelby, "The Legislative Autonomy of Christians in the Islamic World," in Hoyland, *Muslims and Others in Early Islamic Society*, 56, originally published as "L'autonomie législative des chrétiens en terre d'islam," *Archives d'histoire du droit oriental* 5 (1950–51): 307–51.

35. Ṣāliḥ b. Aḥmad b. Ḥanbal, *Sīrat Ibn Ḥanbal*, 60. This was a mode of reckoning community shared in common with other Muslim groups. See, for example, L. Clarke's fascinating study of early Shīʿī notions of community, which at first drew upon a extreme primordialist mythology that set "real" Shīʿa in opposition to all others, a division which was based in choices made by God before the creation of humans or the world. Later, Clarke demonstrates, this stridently rigorist view, which resulted in a Shīʿī-unbeliever binary ideal of social relations that was impractical for the realities of the Abbasid social and political world, was modified to include Shīʿa, who were a "chosen" people, "believers," who would accord roughly with those the Ḥanbalīs designated as "Muslims" and unbelievers. See L. Clarke, "Faith and Unfaith in Pre-Occultation Shīʿism: a Study in Theology and Social History," *Islam and Christian-Muslim Relations* 15 (2004): 109–23.

36. Ṣāliḥ b. Aḥmad b. Ḥanbal, *Sīrat Ibn Ḥanbal,* 60.

37. Ṣāliḥ b. Aḥmad b. Ḥanbal, *Sīrat Ibn Ḥanbal,* 63.

38. For the strain attempts at caliphal patronage put upon relations between Aḥmad and his family, see Hurvitz, *Formation of Ḥanbalism,* 36–40, 63–70.

39. See also Ḥanbal b. Isḥāq b. Ḥanbal, *Dhikr miḥnat al-imām Aḥmad Ibn Ḥanbal,* ed. Naghsh, 57–58; Ṣāliḥ b. Aḥmad b. Ḥanbal, *Sīrat Ibn Ḥanbal,* 60–62. See Cooperson, *Classical Arabic Biography,* 120–23.

40. For this "creed," see Cooperson, *Classical Arabic Biography,* 122.

41. Ḥanbal b. Isḥāq b. Ḥanbal, *Dhikr miḥnat al-imām Aḥmad Ibn Ḥanbal,* ed. Muḥammad Naghsh, 61. That is, they called for the "*ʿiqābān*" (literally "the eagle," the device to which one was tied in order to be flogged) and whips.

42. Steven Judd has demonstrated that two other very early *madhāhib,* those of ʿAbd al-Raḥmān b. ʿAmr al-Awzāʿī and Sufyān al-Thawrī, also depicted the founders of their communities as having stood up to Abbasid rulers under duress. In the narrative of al-Awzāʿī's *madhhab,* the founder endured a *miḥna* shortly after the Abbasid revolution because of his support for the previous regime. Similarly, the follower's of Sufyān's *madhhab* recalled that Sufyān had for his part confronted and spoken brazenly to the caliph al-Mahdī, even though most sources depict his behavior in the face of Abbasid hostility as having been much more timid than that of al-Awzāʿī. Indeed, Judd argues that it was precisely because the virtue of the founders of these rival communities depended upon the founder's willingness to confront bearers of worldly might that the largely legendary stories about Sufyān's *parrhesia* with regard to al-Mahdī became necessary additions to the biographical corpus recalling the life of the founder of the Sufyānī madhhab. See Steven C. Judd, "Competitive Hagiography in Biographies of al-Awzāʿī and Sufyān al-Thawrī," *JAOS* 122 (2002): 25–37. For the biographical strategies of other *madhāhib,* see, for example, Eerik Dickinson, "Aḥmad b. al-Ṣalt and His Biography of Abū Ḥanīfa," *JAOS* 116 (1996): 406–17.

43. Ibn Abī Yaʿlā, *Ṭabaqāt al-fuqahāʾ al-Ḥanābila,* ed. ʿUmar, 1.33.

44. al-Nīsābūrī, *Masāʾil al-Imām Aḥmad Ibn Ḥanbal,* ed. al-Shāwīsh, 2.175 (#1958). Cook interprets Ibn Ḥanbal's reaction as that of a man who has led a life "sheltered" from the evils of the world. One wonders whether he was not simply grossed out. See Cook, *Commanding Right and Forbidding Wrong,* 93.

45. Raiding with someone else's property, al-Nīsābūrī, *Masāʾil al-Imām Aḥmad Ibn Ḥanbal,* ed. al-Shāwīsh, 108–9. See, among others, #1632, 1633. Compulsion to wash, al-Khallāl, *Ahl al-milal,* ed. al-Sulṭān, 114–15 (#117, #119).

46. On matters relating to captives taken on raids, see al-Nīsābūrī, *Masāʾil al-Imām Aḥmad Ibn Ḥanbal,* ed. al-Shāwīsh, 2.97–98. For the use of captured booty, see ibid., 113–17, 119–23. For the sneezes of non-Muslims, see al-Khallāl, *Ahl al-milal,* ed. al-Sulṭān, 465 (#1123).

47. Al-Khallāl, *Ahl al-milal,* ed. al-Sulṭān, 55–57 (#1, 2, 4).

48. Or possibly "Who says the Christians and Jews?" al-Khallāl, *Ahl al-milal*, ed. al-Sulṭān, 59–60 (#6).

49. See Aḥmad Ziāuddin, "Abū Bakr al-Khallāl—the Compiler of the Teachings of Imām Aḥmad b. Ḥanbal," *Islamic Studies* 9 (1970): 245–54; Melchert, *Formation of the Sunni Schools of Law*, 143–55; Cooperson, *Classical Islamic Biography*, 109–10; Cook, *Commanding and Forbidding*, 88–90.

50. Michael Cook has recently used another collection of Ibn Ḥanbal's *responsa* compiled by al-Khallāl as a means of elucidating "everyday life" in Ibn Ḥanbal's world. See Cook, *Commanding and Forbidding*, 87–90.

51. Al-Khallāl, *Ahl al-milal*, ed. al-Sulṭān, 372–73 (#830–34). Ibn Ḥanbal draws a sharp distinction between a "prophet" (*nabī*) and a "messenger" (*rasūl*). A Jew, Magian, or Christian who called Muḥammad a "prophet" was still a Jew, Magian, or Christian. If, on the other hand, he said that Muḥammad was a "messenger" he had become a Muslim and could be compelled to take Islām as his religion. See also idem, #835, 836, 837. See Thomas of Margā, *The Book of Governors*, ed. and trans. Wallis Budge, 2.309–11 for a discussion of a "nominally Christian" community in Iraq that believed that Jesus was "an ordinary man, and said that 'he was one of the Prophets.'" For Muslim-Magian relations, see Jamsheed K. Choksy, "Conflict, Coexistence, and Cooperation: Muslims and Zoroastrians in Eastern Iran During the Medieval Period," *Muslim World* 80 (2001): 213–33.

52. Al-Khallāl, *Ahl al-milal*, ed. al-Sulṭān, 120 (#129).

53. Al-Khallāl, *Ahl al-milal*, ed. al-Sulṭān, 120–21 (#120, 121).

54. Al-Khallāl, *Ahl al-milal*, ed. al-Sulṭān, 341 (#731, 732).

55. Al-Khallāl, *Ahl al-milal*, ed. al-Sulṭān, 121 (#132).

56. The Prophet had done it, making it acceptable. See al-Khallāl, *Ahl al-milal*, ed. al-Sulṭān, 464–65 (#1116–22); al-Nīsābūrī, *Masā'il al-Imām Aḥmad Ibn Ḥanbal*, ed. al-Shāwīsh (#1981, 1982, 1983).

57. The act displeased Ibn Ḥanbal, although he admitted that there was disagreement about it. Others said one should beware of the act and that it was demeaning. See al-Khallāl, *Ahl al-milal*, ed. al-Sulṭān, 463–64 (#1113–15).

58. For early attempts at maintaining a distinct Muslim community through the imposition of rules and laws regarding Muslim and non-Muslim modes of dress, see Albrecht Noth, "Problems of Differentiation between Muslims and Non-Muslims: Re-Reading the 'Ordinances of ʿUmar' (*al-Shurūṭ al-ʿumariyya*)" = ch. 5 in Hoyland (ed.), *Muslims and Others in Early Islamic Society*, originally published as "Abgrenzungsprobleme zwischen Muslimen und Nicht-Muslimen. Die 'Bedingungen ʿUmars (*aš-Šurūṭ al-ʿumariyya*)' unter einem anderen Aspekt gelesen," *JSAI* 9 (1987): 290–315. See also M. J. Kister, "'Do Not Assimilate Yourselves . . .' *Lā tashabbahū* . . . ," *JSAI* 12 (1989): 321–53. For the Christian communities of Iraq immediately following Muslim conquests, see Morony, *Iraq after the Muslim Conquest*, ch. 12, esp. 343–46. For evidence of a semiotic vocabulary shared between early Muslims and some Christian communities, see ch. 5.

59. Ibn Abī Yaʿlā, *Ṭabaqāt al-fuqahā' al-Ḥanābila*, ed. ʿUmar, 1.37.

60. Leontius, *The Life of Stephen of Mar Sabas*, ed. and trans. Lamoreaux, 8.1–8.4.

61. See Hoyland, *Seeing Islam as Others Saw It*, 270–78, 476–79, 505–8, 538.

62. See Pierre Bourdieu, *Outline of a Theory of Practice*, translated by Richard Nice (Cambridge, 1977 [1999]), 164: "[W]hen there is a quasi-perfect correspondence between the objective order and the subjective principles of organization (as in ancient societies) the natural and social world appears as self-evident. This experience we shall call *doxa*."

63. Leontius, *The Life of Stephen of Mar Sabas*, ed. and trans. Lamoreaux, 11.11, 14.6. For the third/ninth-century relationship between Byzantium and the Abbasid empire, and their "increasingly shared culture of objects that included architectural concepts," see Hussein Keshani, "The ʿAbbāsid Palace of Theophilus: Byzantine Taste for the Arts of Islam," *al-Masāq* 16 (2004): 75–91. For the turning away of the monastic communities of Palestine from Byzantium and Europe and toward those with whom they shared the bonds of Arabic language, see Sidney H. Griffith, "Anthony David of Baghdad, Scribe and Monk of Mar Sabas: Arabic in the Monasteries of Palestine," *Church History* 58 (1989): 7–19.

64. Stephen, *The Life of Stephen of Mar Sabas*, ed. and trans. Lamoreaux, 23.4. On this particular occasion, however, he counseled another monk against traveling to Baghdād to confront the Muslim *amīr*.

65. For this text, see Ignace Dick, ed. and trans., "La passion arabe de S. Antione Ruwah néo-martyr de Damas (+ dec. 799)," *Le Muséon* 74 (1961): 109–33, cited by David Vila, "The Struggle over Arabisation in Medieval Arabic Christian Hagiography," *al-Masāq* 15 (2003): 35–46, esp. 38–44.

66. See, for example, al-Azdī, *Futūḥ al-Shām*, 203–4, in which Khālid b. al-Walīd and the Roman general "Bāhān" have a meeting: "[Bāhān said,] 'The struggle descended upon you from the dryness of the earth, and the want of rain, and you act wickedly in our lands, and you commit every depravity, and you mount our riding animals, and they are not like your riding animals, and you wear our clothes, and they are not like your clothes, for the clothes of the Romans are like sheets of silver, and you enjoy our food, and it is not like your food, and you cause us losses and you fill your hands with rosy gold and shining coins and the sumptuous objects and we have endured you now and all of that is ours, and it is in your hands. And we give it to you, so go and stay away from our lands. And if your souls insist that you covet and be greedy and desire that we give to you more from the houses of our estates what would make those weaker than you strong . . . [then] . . . we will order for your *amīr* 10,000 dīnārs, and we will order for you the same. And we shall order for your chieftains 1000 dīnārs and for the assembly of your companions 100 dīnārs on condition that you are faithful to us with regard to loyalty sworn by oath that you will not return to our lands.'" See also Ibn Aʿtham, *Kitāb al-futūḥ*, 1.195–96, in which the Muslim warrior al-Mughīra and the Persian king have a tête-à-tête: "[The Persian King said] 'But I am aware that what drove you to my land is that you are in a state of hunger, and suffering from misery and poverty. If it is like that, then just tell me so that I may be charitable to

you, and I will load these camels of yours which are with you with food and clothes and provisions and my power . . . will benefit you and you will go away to your lands peacefully.'"

67. See Michael Cooperson, "The Purported Biography of Ḥunayn ibn Isḥāq," *Edebiyāt* 7 (1997): 235–49.

68. Cooperson, "The Purported Biography of Ḥunayn ibn Isḥāq," 244.

69. Translated by Cooperson, "The Purported Biography of Ḥunayn ibn Isḥāq," 245.

70. Translated by Cooperson, "The Purported Biography of Ḥunayn ibn Isḥāq," 247.

71. Translated by Cooperson, "The Purported Biography of Ḥunayn ibn Isḥāq," 247.

72. *Al-Radd ʿalā al-naṣārā*, trans. Jim Colville, *Sobriety and Mirth: A Selection of the Shorter Writings of al-Jāhiz* (London, 2002), 70–93. For al-Jāḥiẓ, see Pellat, *Life and Work of al-Jāḥiẓ*, 3–9.

73. *Al-Radd ʿalā al-naṣārā*, trans. Colville, 74. Q:5.80–85, trans. Ali, 108–9.

74. *Al-Radd ʿalā al-naṣārā*, trans. Colville, 78.

75. *Al-Radd ʿalā al-naṣārā*, trans. Colville, 78.

76. *Al-Radd ʿalā al-naṣārā*, trans. Colville, 76.

77. *Al-Radd ʿalā al-naṣārā*, trans. Colville, 73–75.

78. *Al-Radd ʿalā al-naṣārā*, trans. Colville, 76.

79. *Al-Radd ʿalā al-naṣārā*, trans. Colville, 76. Christians are "secretaries to sultans, valets to princes, physicians to the court as well as parfumiers and bankers."

80. *Al-Radd ʿalā al-naṣārā*, trans. Colville, 75–76.

81. *Al-Radd ʿalā al-naṣārā*, trans. Colville, 77.

82. See Noth, "Problems of Differentiation between Muslims and Non-Muslims," passim.

83. Noth, "Problems of Differentiation between Muslims and Non-Muslims," 117–24.

84. Noth, "Problems of Differentiation between Muslims and Non-Muslims"; Kister, "'Do Not Assimilate Yourselves . . .' *Lā tashabbahū* . . ."

85. Noth, "Problems of Differentiation between Muslims and Non-Muslims," 115–24.

86. For the dyeing of beards and preservation of "traditional" modes of pre-Islamic dress, see Noth, "Problems of Differentiation between Muslims and Non-Muslims," 115–24.

87. Al-Khallāl, *Ahl al-milal*, ed. al-Sulṭān, 230 (#425).

88. Al-Khallāl, *Ahl al-milal*, ed. al-Sulṭān, 230 (#426, 427).

89. Al-Khallāl, *Ahl al-milal*, ed. al-Sulṭān, 230 (#429, 430, 431).

90. Al-Khallāl, *Ahl al-milal*, ed. al-Sulṭān, 317 (#668).

91. Al-Khallāl, *Ahl al-milal*, ed. al-Sulṭān, 317 (#663–65).

92. Q:2.256. See Crone, *God's Rule: Government and Islam*, 373–82.

93. A child's identity was determined by its parents, and it was not for others to interfere with this. See al-Khallāl, *Ahl al-milal*, ed. al-Sulṭān, 72–81 (multiple entries). This was a rule with many catches, however. A nursing infant was not to be left behind on a

raid, even if there was no one to nurse it with the raiding party. It should be fed and given drink, "and if it dies it dies, and if it lives it lives," and in either case it would be treated as a Muslim. The logic was that a child taken with no parent was a Muslim, and one would not leave a Muslim child with non-Muslims. Al-Khallāl, *Ahl al-milal*, ed. al-Sulṭān, 82 (#38, 39, 40). In contrast to adults, about whom see below, non-Muslim children who died without their parents were to be prayed over (p. 83, #42, 43, 45). Children with their parents were not to be compelled in matters of religion, Ibn Ḥanbal said, although the "frontier folk" are said in some traditions to have forced the conversion of children who were with their parents. Ibn Ḥanbal says that the frontier folk do things he does not know about (pp. 86–87, #49, 50). Elsewhere, he said, "I have heard that the frontier folk compel [children with their parents] to Islam, but I do not approve of compliance with [this]" (pp. 86–87, #50, cf. #51). A child without a parent could be compelled to Islam, however. If the child rejected Islam, Ibn Ḥanbal approved of compulsion involving the infliction physical pain and beating or torture (p. 85, #47, 48).

94. See, for example, what is to be done with the children of Christian slave girls who die with the Muslims, al-Khallāl, *Ahl al-milal*, ed. al-Sulṭān, 92 (#65, 66). For the religious identity of a child born to a Christian slave girl and a Christian slave who both belong to a Muslim, see al-Khallāl, *Ahl al-milal*, 92–93 (#71, 72, 73). Although once again the frontier folk disagree, the child's religious identity is held by Ibn Ḥanbal to follow that of his father.

95. Ibn Abī Yaʿlā, *Ṭabaqāt al-fuqahāʾ al-Ḥanābila*, ed. ʿUmar, 1.32.

96. Al-Khallāl, *Ahl al-milal*, ed. al-Sulṭān, 292, (#602,). See note 1, p. 292.

97. Al-Nīsābūrī, *Masāʾil al-Imām Aḥmad Ibn Ḥanbal*, ed. al-Shāwīsh, 2.180 (#1984, 1985). For contrary opinions, and other takes on the matter of greeting non-Muslims as well as a list of "others" that increased as time went on, see Kister, " 'Do Not Assimilate Yourselves . . .' *Lā tashabbahū . . .* ," 325–29.

98. Ibn Abī Yaʿlā, *Ṭabaqāt al-fuqahāʾ al-Ḥanābila*, ed. ʿUmar, 1.58. For Arab/non-Arab boundary issues and tensions, which are beyond the scope of this book, see, for example, Roy P. Mottahedeh, "The Shuʿūbīyah Controversy and the Social World of Early Islamic Iran," *IJMES* 7 (1976): 161–82.

99. For Muḥammad's refusal to sit with non-Muslims, his way of greeting them, and Ibn Ḥanbal's objection to visiting the houses of non-Muslims and nobles, see Ibn Abī Yaʿlā, *Ṭabaqāt al-fuqahāʾ al-Ḥanābila*, ed. ʿUmar, 1.92; al-Nīsābūrī, *Masāʾil al-Imām Aḥmad Ibn Ḥanbal*, ed. al-Shāwīsh, 2.180 (#1980). For Ibn Ḥanbal and the misrecognized *dhimmī*, see al-Nīsābūrī, *Masāʾil al-Imām Aḥmad Ibn Ḥanbal*, ed. al-Shāwīsh, 2.189 (#1980), cf. #1984. See also Kister, "'Do Not Assimilate Yourselves . . .' *Lā tashabbahū . . .* ," 328–29 for steps to be taken in the case of such misrecognition and the issuance of the "wrong" greeting.

100. Ṣāliḥ b. Aḥmad b. Ḥanbal, *Sīrat Ibn Ḥanbal*, 58.

101. Ibn Abī Yaʿlā, *Ṭabaqāt al-fuqahāʾ al-Ḥanābila*, ed. ʿAlī Muḥammad ʿUmar, 1.59. For the Murjiʾa, see Michael Cook, "Activism and Quietism in Islam: The Case of the Early Murjiʾa," in A. S. Cudsi and A. E. Hillal Dessouki (eds.), *Power and Islam* (Baltimore, 1982), 15–23.

102. *Sīra Ibn Dhakwān*, ed. and trans. Crone and Zimmermann, III.72.

103. Ṣāliḥ b. Aḥmad b. Ḥanbal, *Sīrat Ibn Ḥanbal*, 58.

104. Ṣāliḥ b. Aḥmad b. Ḥanbal, *Sīrat Ibn Ḥanbal*, 58. On Shīʿī views of the companions, see Etan Kohlberg, "Some Imāmī Shīʿī Views on the Ṣaḥāba," *JSAI* 5 (1984): 143–75, esp. 145–46; Etan Kohlberg, "Some Imāmī Shīʿī Interpretations of Umayyad History," in G. H. A. Juynboll (ed.), *Studies in the First Century of Islamic History* (Carbondale, 1982), 145–59, 249–54 [reprinted in Etan Kohlberg, *Belief and Law in Imāmī Shīʿism* (Hampshire, 1991), XII]. For the reclamation of the memory of the Umayyad caliphs under the Abbasids, see Tayeb el-Hibri, "The Redemption of Umayyad Memory by the ʿAbbāsids," *JNES* 61 (2002): 241–65. See also Abdelkader I. Tayob, "Ṭabarī on the Companions of the Prophet: Moral and Political Contours of Islamic Historical Writing," *JAOS* 119 (1999): 203–10; Josef van Ess, "Political Ideals in Early Islamic Religious Thought," *British Journal of Middle Eastern Studies* 28 (2001): 151–64, esp. 153–56.

105. Ibn Abī Yaʿlā, *Ṭabaqāt al-fuqahāʾ al-Ḥanābila*, ed. ʿUmar, 1.53. For the rejection and opposition to caliphal authority among radical Shīʿī groups, real or imagined, see R. P. Buckly, "The Early Shiite Ghulāh," *JSS* 42 (1997): 301–25. For Sunni obligation to obey the rulers of the *umma*, see Crone, "Even an Ethiopian Slave," passim.

106. Abū Bakr al-Khallāl, *Kitāb al-amr bi-ʾl-maʿrūf wa-ʾl-nahy ʿan al-munkar*, ed. ʿAbd al-Qādir Aḥmad ʿAṭā (Cairo, 1975), 95 (#31). For Ibn Ḥanbal's prescription of "gentleness," see #30. For late Ḥanbalī application of this principle, see Henri Laoust, *La profession de foi d'Ibn Baṭṭa* (Damascus, 1958), XLIX.

107. See, for example, the *Kitāb al-janāʾiz* in al-Nīsābūrī, *Masāʾil al-Imām Aḥmad Ibn Ḥanbal*, ed. al-Shāwīsh, 1.182–83.

108. See the excellent Zaman, "Death, Funeral Processions," 27–36. For a relevant anthropological study of the tensions inherent in the intersection of communal identity, tradition and death ritual, see Geertz, *The Interpretation of Cultures*, 153–69, cited by Zaman.

109. Al-Khallāl, *Ahl al-milal*, ed. al-Sulṭān, 291 (#600).

110. Al-Khallāl, *Ahl al-milal*, ed. al-Sulṭān, 291 (#602, 604, 605).

111. Al-Khallāl, *Ahl al-milal*, ed. al-Sulṭān, 291 (#603).

112. Al-Khallāl, *Ahl al-milal*, ed. al- Sulṭān, 291 (#602–5).

113. Al-Khallāl, *Ahl al-milal*, ed. al-Sulṭān, 294 (#612, 613).

114. Al-Khallāl, *Ahl al-milal*, ed. al-Sulṭān, 296–97 (#620, 621).

115. Al-Khallāl, *Ahl al-milal*, ed. al-Sulṭān, 297 (#622).

116. See Q:9.84. For this tradition, and al-Shāfiʿī's opinion that it was only the Prophet who was forbidden from praying over unbelievers, see Zaman, "Death, Funeral Processions," 30.

117. Al-Khallāl, *Ahl al-milal*, ed. al-Sulṭān, 297 (#623, 624).

118. See al-Khallāl, *Ahl al-milal*, ed. al-Sulṭān, 301 (#629, 630, 631, 632).

119. Al-Khallāl, *Ahl al-milal*, ed. al-Sulṭān, 298, (#625, 626).

120. Al-Khallāl, *Ahl al-milal*, ed. al-Sulṭān, 298 (#627). Here I am supplying the feminine noun *jināza*.

121. Al-Khallāl, *Ahl al-milal*, ed. al-Sulṭān, 300 (#628).

122. Al-Khallāl, *Ahl al-milal*, ed. al-Sulṭān, 301 (#628).

123. Al-Khallāl, *Kitāb al-amr bi-ʾl-maʿrūf wa-ʾl-nahy ʿan al-munkar*, ed. ʿAṭā, 106–7. For such behavior as a *jāhilī* practice, see p. 156 (#161); for forbidding such behavior, see 157 (#163).

124. Al-Khallāl, *Ahl al-milal*, ed. al-Sulṭān, 304–5 (#640, 641, 642).

125. Al-Khallāl, *Ahl al-milal*, ed. al-Sulṭān, 305 (#643).

126. Al-Nīsābūrī, *Masāʾil al-Imām Aḥmad Ibn Ḥanbal*, ed. al-Shāwīsh, 1.188 (#941).

127. See Cook, *Commanding Right and Forbidding Wrong*, passim, and esp. ch. 5. See also Hurvitz, "From Scholarly Circles to Mass Movements," 998–1002. For an intriguing discussion of the act of commanding and forbidding in the social and political milieu in which Ibn Ḥanbal came to prominence, see W. Madelung, "The Vigilante Movement of Sahl b. Salāma al-Khurāsānī and the Origins of Ḥanbalism Reconsidered," *Journal of Turkish Studies* 12 (1990): 331–37.

128. Kister, "'Do Not Assimilate Yourselves . . .' *Lā tashabbahū* . . . ," 335–49.

129. See Cook, *Commanding Right and Forbidding Wrong*, 101.

130. See Zaman "Death, Funeral Processions," 39 for the anxiety some Muslims experienced that participation in funerals of non-Muslims would "blur religious boundaries." Zaman discusses this danger on a grand scale, particularly as it applied to the burial of very prominent Muslims whose funerals were attended by non-Muslims. What I am suggesting here is that the practices prescribed by Ibn Ḥanbal had the effect of mitigating such anxieties as they related to much smaller, but also much more intimate, funeral rites.

131. Barth, "Boundaries and Connections," 28.

132. For bans on non-Muslims riding mounts like those of the Muslims, see Noth, "Problems of Differentiation between Muslims and Non-Muslims," 117.

133. For Muslim restrictions on "using the same patronymics (*kunya/kunan*)" (admittedly a slightly different phenomenon from that objected to by al-Jāḥiẓ) and "speaking like Muslims," see Noth, "Problems of Differentiation between Muslims and Non-Muslims," 117.

134. Al-Khallāl, *Ahl al-milal*, ed. al-Sulṭān, pp. 164–83 (multiple entries). For the *jizya*, see Morony, *Iraq after the Muslim Conquest*, 106–24.

135. See Noth, "Problems of Differentiation between Muslims and Non-Muslims," 113.

136. For the opposed religious views of al-Jāḥiẓ and Ibn Ḥanbal, see Cooperson, *Classical Arabic Biography*, 126–27.

137. See Crone and Moreh, *The Book of Strangers*, 150–52, esp. 151: "Monasteries . . . inspired poetry celebrating wine, love, and other worldly pleasures."

138. And with the transgression of other boundaries. See, for example, in his essay *Kitāb mufākhbarāt al-jawārī wa-ʾl-ghilmān*, a dialogue on the relative merits of boys and women as lovers (for men) al-Jāḥiẓ has "the Pederast" argue that it was a simple lack of refinement that led pre-Islamic poets to sing the praises of women rather than boys: "[Those poets were] nasty, brutish Bedouin who were raised in poverty and nourished on a diet of hardship, knowing nothing of life's comforts and its finer pleasures. They lived in the desert and avoided civilized society, just like wild animals. They ate hedgehogs and lizards,

for God's sake, and colocynth berries!" Had they known any better, he suggests, they would have preferred the pleasures of the refined and cultivated Arab gentlemen of his own day. See al-Jāḥiẓ, *Kitāb mufākhbarāt al-jawārī wa-ʾl-ghilmān*, trans. Colville, 209. A sense of what these pleasures will have entailed may be gained from the quite graphic poetic depiction of a back ally bout of boy-boy stranger sex in Baghdad. Abū l-Faraj al-Iṣfahānī (attributed), *Kitāb adab al-ghurabāʾ*, #62, trans. Crone and Moreh, 72–73.

139. Abū l-Faraj al-Iṣfahānī (attributed), *Kitāb adab al-ghurabāʾ*, ed. al-Munajjid, #13 (pp. 34–36), trans. Crone and Moreh, 32–34.

140. See Hurvitz, "Biographies and Mild Asceticism," 54–65 for an interpretation of the relationship between the Abbasid bon vivants known as *ẓurafāʾ*, against whom Hurvitz argues that Ibn Ḥanbal and other adherents of "mild asceticism" defined themselves. I am obviously suggesting the reverse process, that Ibn Ḥanbal and those like him established a kind of baseline Muslimness that could then be transgressed as a means of accumulating social capital.

141. Cook, *Commanding Right and Forbidding Wrong*, 112–13.

142. For the career of al-Barbahārī, see Simha Sabari, *Mouvments populaires à Bagdad à l'époque 'Abbasside, IXe-XIe siècles* (Paris, 1981), 104–6; Laoust, *La profession de foi d'Ibn Baṭṭa*, XXXIII-XLI; Laoust, "Le Hanbalisme sous le califat de Bagdad," 81–84; Cook, *Commanding Right and Forbidding Wrong*, 116–18; Hurvitz, "From Scholarly Circles to Mass Movements," 1002–5. Ibn Abī Yaʿlā, *Ṭabaqāt al-fuqahāʾ al-Ḥanābila*, ed. ʿUmar, 2.27–59 (#588).

143. For violence against those who disagreed with Ḥanbalī interpretations of the Qurʾān, see Laoust, *La profession de foi d'Ibn Baṭṭa*, XXXVII; For tension and popular violence against the Shīʿa, see Laoust, *La profession de foi d'Ibn Baṭṭa*, XCII–XCIII; Sabari, *Mouvments populaires à Bagdad*, 104–12. For attacks on Christians and Jews, apparently because they were thought to have benefited from Shīʿī patronage, see Laoust, *La profession de foi d'Ibn Baṭṭa*, XCII–XCIII. For Ḥanbalī antipathy and activism against the historian al-Ṭabarī, see Henri Laoust, *La profession de foi d'Ibn Baṭṭa*, XXXV–XXXVI; For ordinary sinners, see Sabari, *Mouvments populaires à Bagdad*, 105; Laoust, *La profession de foi d'Ibn Baṭṭa*, XXXIX–XXXX.

144. For the connection between the Ḥanbalīs and the Wahhābīs, see Cook, *Commanding Right and Forbidding Wrong*, ch. 8. For Wahhābī notions of proper relations with non-Muslims (and imperfect Muslims), see Elizabeth Sirriyeh, "Wahhābīs, Unbelievers and the Problems of Exclusivism," *Bulletin (British Society for Middle Eastern Studies)* 16 (1989): 123–32. See also Giles Keppel, *Jihad: The Trial of Political Islam*, trans. Anthony F. Roberts (Cambridge, Mass., 2002), 50–51, 72–75.

CONCLUSION

1. Michael the Syrian, *The Chronicle of Michael the Syrian*, ed. and trans. Chabot, *Chronique du Michel le Syrien patriarche jacobite d'Antioche (1166–99)*, II.494–96.

SELECT BIBLIOGRAPHY

PRIMARY SOURCES

ʿAbd Allāh b. Wahb b. Muslim al-Qurayshī Abū Muḥammad al-Miṣrī. *Kitāb al-Muḥāraba min al-Muwaṭṭāʾ*. Ed. Mīklūsh Mūrānī. Beirut, 2002.

ʿAbd al-Razzāq b. Hammām al-Ṣanʿānī [al-Ḥimyarī]. *Tafsīr al-Qurʾān*. Ed. Muṣṭafā Muslim Muḥamma. 4 vols. Riyadh, 1989.

Abū Bakr al-Khallāl. *Ahl al-milal wa-ʾl-radda wa-ʾl-zanādiqa wa-ʾl-tārik al-ṣalāh wa-ʾl-farāʾiḍ min kitāb al-jāmiʿ li-ʾl-Khallāl*. Ed. Ibrāhīm b. Muḥammad al-Sulṭān. 2 vols. Riyadh, 1996.

———. *Kitāb al-amr bi-ʾl-maʿrūf wa-ʾl-nahy ʿan al-munkar*. Ed. ʿAbd al-Qādir Aḥmad ʿAṭā. Cairo, 1975.

Abā l-Faraj ʿAlī b. al-Ḥusayn al-Iṣfahānī. *Kitāb al-aghānī*. 20 vols. Beirut, 1970.

Abū l-Faraj al-Iṣfahānī (attributed). *Kitāb adab al-ghurabāʾ*. Ed. Ṣāliḥ al-Dīn al-Mủnajjid. Beirut, 1972. Trans. Patricia Crone and Shmuel Moreh. *The Book of Strangers: Medieval Arabic Graffiti on the Theme of Nostalgia*. Princeton, 2000.

Abū Nuʿaym al-Iṣfahānī. *Ḥilyat al-awliyāʾ wa-ṭabaqāt al-aṣfiyāʾ*. 10 vols. Cairo, 1967.

Aḥmad b. Ḥanbal. *Kitāb al-zuhd*. Beirut, 1976.

Ambrose, *De obitu Theodosii* ed. and trans. Mary Dolorosa Mannix, *Sancti Ambrosii Oratio de Obitu Theodosii*. (Washington D.C., 1925.

———. *Epistulae*. Ed. Michaela Zelzer. *Sancti Ambrosi Opera, Pars X: Epistulae et Acta* CSEL 82. Vienna, 1990. English trans. H. de Romestin et al., NPNF, ser. 2, vol. 10.

Ammianus Marcellinus. *Res Gestae*. Ed. and trans. J. C. Rolfe, *Ammianus Marcellinus*. 3 vols. Cambridge, Mass., 1940 [1972].

Athanasius. *Vita Antonii*. PG 26:835-976. Ed. G. J. M. Bartelink, SC 400. Paris, 1994. English trans. Robert C. Gregg, *The Life of Antony and The Letter to Marcellinus*. New York, 1980.

Augustine of Hippo. *Contra litteras Petiliani*. Ed. M. Petschenig. CSEL 52. Leipzig, 1909.

———. *Contra Gaudentium*. Ed. M. Petschenig. CSEL 52. Leipzig, 1910.

———. *De oboedientia* = F. Dolbeau, "Nouveaux sermons du saint Augustin pour la

conversion des païens et des donatists (III)." *Revue des Études Augustiniennes* 32 (1992): 50–79.
———. *De opere monachorum*. Ed. Joseph Zycha. CSEL 41. Leipzig, 1906.
———. *Epistulae*. Ed. Al. Golbacher. CSEL 34-35, 44, 57-58. Vienna, 1895-1923. English trans. J. G. Cunningham, NPNF ser. 1, vol. 1.
al-Azdī al-Baṣrī, Muḥammad b. ʿAbd Allāh. *Taʾrīkh futūḥ al-Shām*. Ed. ʿAbd al-Munʿim ʿAbd Allāh ʿĀmir. Cairo, 1970.
al-Azdī, Yazīd Muḥammad. *Taʾrīkh Mūsil*. Ed. ʿAlī Ḥabīb. Cairo, 1967.
al-Baghdādī, ʿAbd al-Qahīr b. Ṭāhir. *Al-farq bayna al-firaq*, ed. Muḥammad Muḥī al-Dīn ʿAbd al-Ḥamīd, Cairo, n.d.
———. *Kitāb al-milal wal-niḥal*. Ed. Albert N. Nader. Beirut, 1986.
al-Balādhurī. *Ansāb al-ashrāf*, I. Ed. Muḥammad Hamīd Allāh. Cairo, 1959.
———. *Ansāb al-ashrāf*, II. Ed. Wilfred Madelung. Beirut, 2003.
———. *Ansāb al-ashrāf*, IV/1. Ed. Max Schloessinger and M. J. Kister. Jerusalem, 1971.
———. *Ansāb al-ashrāf*, IV/2. Ed. Max Schloessinger. Jerusalem, 1938.
———. *Ansāb al-ashrāf*, VI. Ed. Maḥmūd Firdaws al-ʿAẓm. Damascus, 1996.
Besa. *Letters and Sermons*. Ed. and trans. K. H. Kühn. 2 vols. CSCO 22. Louvain, 1956.
———. *Life of Shenoute*. Ed. J. Leipoldt and W. E. Crum. *Sinuthii Archimandritae Vita et Opera Omnia*, I. CSCO 4. Paris, 1906. English trans. David N. Bell. *The Life of Shenoute*. Kalamazoo, 1983.
Chronicle of 1234. Ed. and trans. Jean-Baptiste Chabot. [*Chronicon anonymum ad annum 1234*]. Syriac text CSCO 81 (Syr. 36) Louvain, 1953, CSCO 109 (Syr. 56) (Louvain, 1952).
Collectio Avellana. Ed. Otto Guenther. 2 vols. CSEL 35. Vienna, 1895.
al-Dīnawarī, Abū Ḥanīfa Aḥmad b. Dāwūd. *Kitāb akhbār al-ṭiwāl*. Ed. Vladimir Guirgass. Leiden, 1888.
———. *Kitab al-akhbār al-ṭiwāl*. Ed. Ignace Kratchkovsky. Leiden, 1912.
Dioscurus. *A Panegyric on Macarius, Bishop of Tkōw*. Ed. and trans. D. W. Johnson. CSCO 416 (Copt. 42), CSCO 415 (Copt. 41). (Louvain, 1980).
Doctrina Jacobi Nuper Baptizati. Ed. and French trans. Vincent Déroche. *Travaux et Mémoirés* 11 (1991): 70–223.
Eunapius. *Lives of the Philosophers*. Ed. and trans. Wilmer C. Wright, *Philostratus and Eunapius: Lives of the Sophists*. Cambridge, Mass., 1921 [1961].
Eusebius "Gallicanus." *Collectio homiliarum*. Ed. Fr. Glorie. CCSL 51a. Tournholt, 1971.
Eusebius. *Historia Ecclesiastica*. Ed. and trans. J. E. L. Oulton and H. J. Lawlor, *Eusebius: The Ecclesiastical History*. 2 vols. Cambridge, Mass., 1932 [2000].
———. *Opera*. Ed. Wilhelm Dindorf. *Eusebii Caesariensis Opera*. 4 vols. Leipzig, 1867–90.
Gregory Nazianzus. *Oratio* 4. Ed. and French trans. Jean Bernardi, *Grégoire de Nazianze, Discours 4-5 Contre Julien* (SC 309). Paris, 1983.
Ḥanbal b. Isḥāq b. Ḥanbal. *Dhikr miḥnat al-imām Aḥmad Ibn Ḥanbal*. Ed. Muḥammad Naghsh. Cairo, 1977.
Histoire de Barḥadbešabba ʿArbaïa. Ed. and French trans. F. Nau. *PO* 23.2. 1932.

Histoires d'Ahoudemmeh et de Marouta Metrepolitains Jacobites de Tagrit et de l'orient (VIe et VIIe siècles). Ed. and French trans. F. Nau. *PO* 3.1. Paris, 1905.

Ibn ʿAbd al-Ḥakam, Abū al-Qāsim ʿAbd al-Raḥmān. *Futūḥ Miṣr wa-akhbāruhu*. Ed. Charles C. Torrey. New Haven, 1922.

Ibn Abī Yaʿlā. *Ṭabaqāt al-fuqahāʾ al-Ḥanābila*. Ed. ʿAlī Muḥammad ʿUmar. 2 vols. Cairo, 1998.

Ibn ʿAsākir. *Taʾrīkh madīnat Dimashq*. Ed. ʿUmar b. Gharāma al-ʿAmrawī and ʿAlī Shīrī. 80 vols. Beirut, 1995–2001.

———. *Taʾrīkh madīnat Dimashq*. Vol. I. Ed. Ṣalāḥ al-Dīn al-Munajjid. Damascus, 1951.

Ibn Aʿtham al-Kūfī, Abū Muḥammad Aḥmad. *Kitāb al-futūḥ*. 8 vols. Hyderabad, 1968–75.

Ibn Ḥibbān, Abū Ḥatim Muḥammad al-Bustī. *Kitāb mashāhīr ʿulamāʾ al-amṣār*. Cairo, 1959.

Ibn Isḥāq, Muḥammad. *Sīrat rasūl Allāh*. Ed. Ferdinand Wüstenfeld. 3 vols. Frankfurt am Main, 1961. English trans. Alfred Guillaume, *Life of Muhammad*. London, 1955.

Ibn al-Jawzī, Abū l-Faraj ʿAbd al-Raḥmān. *Ṣifat al-ṣafwa*. 4 vols. Hyderabad, 1969–73.

Ibn Manẓur. *Mukhtaṣar taʾrīkh dimashq li-Ibn ʿAsākir*. Ed. Rūḥīyat al-Khās and Muḥammad Muṭīʿ al-Ḥāfiẓ. 29 vols. Damascus, 1984–91.

Ibn al-Mubārak, ʿAbd Allāh. *Kitab al-jihād*. Ed. Nazīh Ḥammād. Beirut, 1978.

———. *Kitāb al-zuhd wa-ʾl-raqāʾiq*. Ed. Ḥabīb al-Raḥmān al-Aʿzamī. Beirut, 1970.

Ibn Qutayba. *ʿUyūn al-akhbār*. Ed. Aḥmad Zakī ʿAdawī. 4 vols. Cairo, 1973 [1925].

———. *Kitāb al-maʿārif*. Ed. Tharwat ʿUkkāsha. Cairo, 1960.

Ibn Saʿd, Muḥammad. *Kitāb al-ṭabaqāt*. 8 vols. Beirut, 1960.

———. *Kitab al-ṭabaqāt al-kabīr*. Ed. Eduard Sachau et al. 8 vols. Leiden, 1904–40.

Isaac the Presbyter. *Life of Samuel of Kalamun*. Ed. and trans. Anthony Alcock, *The Life of Samuel of Kalamun by Isaac the Presbyter*. Warminster, England, 1983. Arabic Life, ed. and trans. A. Alcock. "The Arabic Life of Anbā Samawīʾl of Qalamūn." *Le Muséon* 109 (1996): 321–36.

Išōʿyahb Patriarch III. *Liber Epistularum*. Ed. and Latin trans. Rubens Duval. CSCO 11, CSCO 12. Paris, 1905.

Jacob of Serugh. *Homily* 5. Trans. C. Moss, "Jacob of Serugh's Homilies on the Spectacles of the Theater." *Le Muséon* 48 (1935): 87–112.

al-Jāḥiẓ. *al-Radd ʿalā al-naṣārā*. Trans. J. Colville, *Sobriety and Mirth: A Selection of the Shorter Writings of al-Jāhiz*. London, 2002.

al-Jāḥiẓ. *Kitāb mufākhbarāt al-jawārī wa-ʾl-ghilmān*. Trans. Colville, *Sobriety and Myth: A Selection of the Shorter Writings of al-Jāhiz*.

Jerome. *Epistulae*. Ed. Isidorus Hilberg. *Sancti Eusebii Hieronymi Epistulae, Pars I, Epistulae I–LXX*. CSEL 54. Vienna, 1906 [1996].

———. *Vita s. Hilarionis*. PL 23.55-54. English trans. R. J. Deferrari et al., *Fathers of the Church*, v. 15.

John Cassian. *Conferences*. Ed. and French trans. E. Pichery, *Jean Cassien, Conférences*, 3 vols. (SC 42, 54, 64). Paris, 1955–59.

———. *Institutes*. Ed. and French trans. Jean-Claude Guy, *Jean Cassien, Institutions Cénobitiques* (SC 109). Paris, 1965.

John Chrysostom. *Adversus Judaeos orationes*. PG 48:843–942. English trans. Paul W. Harkins, *Saint John Chrysostom: Discourses Against Judaizing Christians*. Washington, D.C., 1977.

———. "Against the Games and Theaters." PG 56:263-70. English trans. P. Allen and W. Mayer, *John Chrysostom*.

———. *17th Homily on the Statues*. PG 49:171-80. English trans. P. Allen and W. Mayer, *John Chrysostom*.

———. "Against the Opponents of the Monastic Life." Trans. D. Hunter, *A Comparison between a King and a Monk; Against the Opponents of the Monastic Life: Two Treatises*. Lewiston, N.Y., 1988.

John of Ephesus. *Lives of the Eastern Saints*. Ed. and trans. E. W. Brooks. *PO* 17, 18, 19. Paris, 1923-25 [Turnhout, 1974].

John of Nikiou. *Chronicle*. Trans. R. H. Charles. *The Chronicle of John, Bishp of Nikiu*. Oxford, 1916.

Julian. *Opera*. Ed. J. Bidez. *L'empereur Julien. Oeuvres Complètes*. 2 vols. in 4 parts. Paris, 1924. English trans. Julian, *Orations: The Works of the Emperor Julian*. Ed. and trans. W. C. Wright. 3 vols. Cambridge, Mass, 1912–23.

al-Khaṭīb al-Baghdādī. *Ta'rākh Baghdād*. 14 vols. Cairo, 1931.

Lactantius. *De mortibus persecutorum*. Ed. and trans. J. L. Creed, *Lactantius: De Mortibus Persecutorum*. Oxford, 1984.

Leontius. *The Life of Stephen of Mar Sabas*. Ed. and trans. John C. Lamoreaux. CSCO 579 (Arab. 51). Louvain, 1999.

Leontius of Neapolis. *Life of Symeon the Fool*. Trans. Derek Krueger, *Symeon the Holy Fool: Leontius' Life and the Late Antique City*. Berkeley, 1996.

Libanius. *Declamation* 1. Trans. D. A. Russell, *Libanius: Imaginary Speeches A Selection of Declamations*. London, 1996.

———. *Opera*. Ed. Richard Foerster, *Libanii Opera*. 12 vols. Leipzig, 1903–27 [1963].

———. *Oratio* 11. Trans. A. F. Norman, *Antioch as a Center of Hellenic Culture as Observed by Libanius*. Liverpool, 2000, 3–65.

Life of Ahoudemmeh. Ed. and French trans. F. Nau. *PO* 3.1. Paris, 1905.

Life of Daniel the Stylite. Trans. Elizabeth Dawes and Norman H. Baynes, in *Three Byzantine Saints: Contemporary Biographies Translated from the Greek*. Oxford, 1948 [Crestwood, N.Y., 1977, 1996].

Life of Nicholas. Ed. and trans. Ihor Ševčenko and Nancy Patterson Ševčenko, *The Life of Saint Nicholas of Sion*. Brookline, Mass., 1984.

Life of Symeon the Stylite the Younger. Ed. and trans. Paul van den Ven. 2 vols. Brussels, 1962.

The Life of Timothy of Kākhushtā. Ed. and trans. John C. Lamoreaux and Cyril Cairala. *PO* 48.4. Turnhout, 2000.

Livy. *Ab Urbe Condita*. Ed. Robert Seymour Conway, *Titi Livi ab urbe condita*. 5 vols. Oxford, 1914.

Mark the Deacon. *Life of Porphyry*. Ed. and French trans. Henri Gregoire and M. A. Kugener. Paris, 1930.

The Martyrdom and Miracles of Saint George of Cappadocia: Oriental Text Series I. Trans. E. A. Wallis Budge. London, 1888.

The Martyrdom of Anthony Ruwḥ. Ed. and trans. Ignace Dick, "La passion arabe de S. Antione Ruwah néo-martyr de Damas (+ dec. 799)." *Le Muséon* 74 (1961): 109–33.

The Martyrdom of Saint Theodore. Ed. Hippolyte Delehaye, *Les légends grecques des saints militaries*. New York, 1975.

The Martyrdom of Saint Victor the General. Ed. and English trans. in E. A. Wallis Budge, *Coptic Texts*. 5 vols. London, 1914 [New York, 1977].

Mēna of Nikiou. *The Life of Isaac of Alexandria*. Ed. and French trans. E. Amélineau, *Histoire du patriarche Copte Isaac*. Paris, 1890.

Michael the Syrian. *Chronicle*. Ed. and trans. Jean-Baptiste Chabot. [*Chronique du Michel le Syrien patriarche jacobite d'Antioche (1166–1199)*]. 4 vols. Paris, 1899–1924.

al-Mubarrad, Abū l-ʿAbbās Muḥammad b. Yazīd. *Kamīl fī al-lugha*. Ed. W. Wright. 2 vols. Leipzig, 1892 [Hildesheim, 1992].

Muqātil b. Sulaymān. *Tafsīr Muqātil Ibn Sulaymān*. Ed. ʿAbd Allāh Maḥmūd Shiḥātah. 5 vols. Cairo, 1969–2002.

———. *Tafsīr Muqātil b. Sulaymān*. Ed. Aḥmad Farīd. 3 vols. Beirut, 2003.

al-Nīsābūrī, Isḥāq b. Ibrāhīm b. Hāniʾ. *Masāʾil al-Imām Aḥmad Ibn Ḥanbal*. Ed. Zuhayr al-Shāwīsh. 2 vols. Cairo, 1980.

Pacatus. *Panegyricus*. Trans. and notes by C. E. V. Nixon, *Pacatus: Panegyric to the Emperor Theodosius*. Liverpool, 1987.

Paphnutius. *Life of Onnophrius*. Ed. and trans. E. A. Wallis Budge, *Coptic Texts*, 4.

Paulinus of Milan. *Vita Ambrosii*. Ed. and trans. Mary Simplicia Kaniecka, *Vita Sancti Ambrosii*. Washington, D.C., 1928.

Plutarch. *Moralia*. Ed. and trans. Frank Cole Babbitt, *Plutarch's Moralia*. 15 vols. Cambridge, Mass., 1936 [1962].

Polybius. *Historiae*. Ed. Theodore Buettner-Wobst, *Polybii Historiae*. 5 vols. Stuttgart, 1882.

Procopius. *Opera*. Ed. and trans. H. B. Dewing, *Procopius*. 7 vols. Cambridge, Mass., 1961 [1940].

al-Qurʾān: A Contemporary Translation. Trans. Ahmed Ali. Princeton, 1994.

Rabban Mār Simon. *The History of Rabban Hōrmīzd*. Trans. E. A. Wallis Budge, *The Histories of Rabban Hōrmīzd the Persian and Rabban Bar-ʿIdtā*. London, 1902 [Piscataway, N.J., 2003].

Ṣāliḥ b. Aḥmad b. Ḥanbal. *Sīrat al-imām Aḥmad b. Ḥanbal*. Beirut, 1997.

Sargis Istunaya de-Gusit. *The Disputation of Sergius the Stylite against a Jew*. Ed. and trans. Allison Peter Hayman. CSCO 338 (Syr 52) 73–4, CSCO 339 (Syr 153). Louvain, 1973.

Sāwirūs b. al-Muqaffaʿ. *History of the Patriarchs of Alexandria.* Ed. and trans. B. Evetts. *PO* 1.4., 5.1. Paris, 1947–48.

Severus of Antioch. *Homily* XVI. Ed. and French trans. Rubens Duval. *PO* 4.1. Paris, 1906.

al-Shahrastānī, Muḥammad b. ʿAbd al-Karīm. *Kitāb al-milal wa-ʾl-niḥal.* Ed. William Cureton. London, 1846 [Piscataway, N.J., 2002].

Sīrat Ibn Dhakwān. Ed. and trans. Patricia Crone and Fritz Zimmermann, *The Epistle of Sālim Ibn Dhakwān.* Oxford, 2001.

Socrates Scholasticus. *Historia Ecclesiastica.* Ed. Günther Christian Hansen, *Sokrates Kirchengeschichte.* Berlin, 1995. Ed. and French trans. Pierre Périchon and Pierre Maraval, *Socrate de Constantinople, Histoire Ecclésiastique.* 2 vols. (SC 477, 493). Paris, 2004-5. English trans. A. C. Zenos, NPNF ser. 2, vol. 2.

Sozomenos. *Historia Ecclesiastica.* Ed. J. Bidez and G. C. Hansen. Berlin, 1960. Trans. C. Hartranft, NPNF ser. 2, vol. 2.

Sulpicius Severus. *Vita s. Martini.* Ed. and French trans. J. Fontaine (SC 133-135). Paris, 1967–69. English trans. A. Roberts, NPNF ser. 2, vol. 11.

Synesius. *De Regno and Dion.* Trans. A. Fitzgerald, *The Essays and Hymns of Synesius.* 2 vols. London, 1930.

———. *Epistle* 43. Ed. and French trans. Antonio Garzya and Denis Roques, *Synésios de Cyrène, Correspondance: Lettres I–LXIII.* 3 vols. Paris, 2000.

al-Ṭabarī, Abū Jaʿfar Muḥammad b. Jarīr. *Jāmiʿ al-bayān ʿan taʾwīl al-Qurʾān.* 30 vols. Cairo, 1954.

———. *Taʾrīkh al-rasul wa-ʾl-mulūk.* Ed. M. J. de Goeje et al. 16 vols. Leiden, 1887–1901. English trans. C. E. Bosworth, *The History of al-Ṭabarī* 5: *The Sāsānids, the Byzantines, and Yemen.* Albany, 1999. English trans. Yohanan Friedmann, *The History of al-Ṭabarī* 12: *The Battle of al-Qādisiyyah and the Conquest of Syria and Palestine.* Albany, 1992. English trans. G. R. Hawting, *The History of al-Ṭabarī* 17: *The First Civil War.* Albany, 1996. English trans. Michael G. Morony, *The History of al-Ṭabarī* 18: *Between the Civil Wars: The Caliphate of Muʿāwiyah.* Albany, 1987. English trans. Michael Fishbein, *The History of al-Ṭabarī* 21: *The Victory of the Marwanids* Albany, 1990. English trans. E. K. Rowson, *The History of al-Ṭabarī* 22: *The Marwanid Restoration.* Albany, 1989.

Tacitus. *Annales.* Ed. and trans. J. Jackson. 3 vols. Cambridge, Mass., 1980.

Tertullian. *Apologia.* Ed. and trans. T. R. Glover. Cambridge, Mass, 1931.

Theodoret. *Historia Religiosa.* Ed. and French trans. Pierre Canivet and Alice Leroy-Molinghen, *Théodoret de Cyr, Histoire des Moines de Syrie: Histoire Philothée.* 2 vols. (SC 234 & 257). Paris, 1977–79. English trans. R. M. Price, *A History of the Monks of Syria.* Kalamazoo, 1985.

Theodoret of Cyr. *Historia Ecclesiastica.* Ed. F. Scheidweiler and L. Pamentier. Berlin, 1954. English trans. B. Jackson, NPNF ser. 2, vol. 3.

Theophylact Simocatta. *Historia Universalis.* Ed. C. de Boor, re-edited by P. Wirth. Stuttgart, 1972. Trans. Michael Whitby and Mary Whitby, *The History of Theophylact Simocatta.* Oxford, 1986.

Thomas of Margā. *The Book of Governors*. Ed. and trans. E. A. Wallis Budge. 2 vols. London, 1893 [Piscataway, N.J., 2003].

ʿUyūn al-ḥadāʾiq al-akhbār fī al-ḥaqāʿq. Ed. M. J de Goeje. Leiden, 1871.

Vincent of Lerins. *Commonitorium*. Ed. Adolph Jülicher, *Vincenz von Lerinum, Commonitorium pro Catholicae fidei antiquitate et universitate adversus profanas omnium haereticorum novitates*. Freiburg and Leipzig, 1895.

Vitruvius. *De Architectura*. Ed. Valentine Rose, *Vitruvii de architectura*. Leipzig, 1899.

al-Yaʿqūbī. *al-Taʾrīkh*. ed. M. Th. Houtsma. 2 vols. Leiden, 1883 [1969].

Zachariah. *Historia Ecclesiastica Zachariae Rhetori vulgo adscripta*. Ed. E. W. Brooks, CSCO 83–84, 87–88. Paris-Louvain 1919–24. Trans. F. J. Hamilton and E. W. Brooks, *The Syriac Chronicle*. London, 1899.

Zachariah Scholasticus. *Vie de Sévère par Zacharie le Scholastique*. Ed. and French trans. M.-A. Kugener. *PO* 2.1. Paris, 1903.

Zuqnīn Chronicle. Trans. Amir Harrak, *The Chronicle of Zuqnīn: Parts III and IV A.D. 488–775*. Toronto, 1999.

SECONDARY SOURCES

Ando, Clifford. *Imperial Ideology and Provincial Loyalty in the Roman Empire*. Berkeley, 2000.

———. "The Palladium and the Pentateuch: Towards a Sacred Topography of the Later Roman Empire." *Phoenix* 55 (2001): 369–406.

Bailey, Lisa. "Building Urban Christian Communities: Sermons on Local Saints in the Eusebius Gallicanus Collection." *Early Medieval Europe* 12 (2003): 1–24.

Barth, Fredrik. "Introduction." In Fredrik Barth (ed.), *Ethnic Groups and Boundaries: The Social Organization of Cultural Difference*, 15–38. Boston, 1969.

———. "Boundaries and Connections." In Anthony Cohen (ed.), *Signifying Identities: Anthropological Perspectives on Boundaries and Contested Values*, 17–36. London, 2001.

Bonner, Michael. *Aristocratic Violence and Holy War: Studies in the Jihad and the Arab-Byzantine Frontier*. New Haven, 1996.

Bourdieu, Pierre. *Outline of a Theory of Practice*. Translated by Richard Nice. Cambridge, 1977 [1999].

Bowersock, Glen W. "From Emperor to Bishop: The Self-Conscious Transformation of Political Power in the Fourth Century A.D." *Classical Philology* 81 (1986): 298–307.

———. *Martyrdom and Rome*. Cambridge, 1995.

Boyarin, Daniel. *Border Lines: The Partition of Judeo-Christianity*. Philadelphia, 2004.

———. *Dying for God: Martyrdom and the Making of Christianity and Judaism*. Stanford, 1999.

———. "'Semantic Differences,' or, 'Judaism'/'Christianity.'" In Adam H. Becker and Annette Yoshiko Reed (eds.), *The Ways That Never Parted: Jews and Christians in Late Antiquity and the Early Middle Ages*, 65–86. Tübingen, 2003.

Boyarin, Daniel and Virginia Burrus. "Hybridity as Subversion of Orthodoxy? Jews and Christians in Late Antiquity." *Social Compass* 52 (2005): 431–41.

Brakke, David. *Athanasius and the Politics of Asceticism*. Oxford, 1995.

———. "Origins and Authenticity: Studying the Reception of Greek and Roman Spiritual Traditions in Early Christian Monasticism." In David Brakke, Anders-Christian Jacobsen, and Jörg Ulrich (eds.), *Beyond Reception: Mutual Influence between Antique Religion, Judaism, and Early Christianity*, 175–89. Frankfurt am Main, 2006.

———. "'Outside the Places, Within the Truth': Athanasius of Alexandria and the Localization of the Holy." In David Frankfurter (ed.), *Pilgrimage and Holy Space in Late Antique Egypt*, 445–481. Leiden, 1998.

Brock, Sebastian. *Syriac Perspectives on Late Antiquity*. London, 1984.

Brown, Peter. *Augustine: A Biography*. Berkeley, 1967.

———. *Authority and the Sacred: Aspects of the Christianization of the Roman World*. Cambridge, 1995.

———. *The Body and Society: Men, Women and Sexual Renunciation in Early Christianity*. New York, 1988.

———. *The Cult of the Saints: Its Rise and Function in Latin Christianity*. Chicago, 1981.

———. "Enjoying the Saints in Late Antiquity." *Early Medieval Europe* 9 (2000): 1–19.

———. *The Making of Late Antiquity*. Cambridge, Mass., 1978.

———. *Power and Persuasion in Late Antiquity: Towards a Christian Empire*. Madison, 1992.

———. "The Rise and Function of the Holy Man in Late Antiquity." *JRS* 61 (1971): 80–101.

———. "The Rise and Function of the Holy Man in Late Antiquity. 1971–1997." *JECS* 6 (1998): 353–76.

———. *The Rise of Western Christendom: Triumph and Diversity, A.D. 200–1000*. 2nd ed. Oxford, 2003.

———. "The Saint as Exemplar in Late Antiquity." *Representations* 12 (1983): 1–25.

Bruner, Jerome. "The Narrative Construction of Reality." *Critical Inquiry* 18 (1991): 1–21.

Brünnow, Rudolf Ernst. *Die Charidschiten unter den ersten Omayyaden*. Leiden, 1884.

Castelli, Elizabeth A. *Martyrdom and Memory: Early Christian Culture Making*. New York, 2004.

Buell, Denise Kimber. *Making Christians: Clement of Alexandria and the Rhetoric of Legitimacy*. Princeton, 1999.

———. *Why This New Race: Ethnic Reasoning in Early Christianity*. New York, 2005.

Burrus, Virginia. *Begotten Not Made: Conceiving Manhood in Late Antiquity*. Stanford, 2000.

———. *The Making of a Heretic: Gender, Authority, and the Priscillianist Controversy*. Berkeley, 2005.

———. *The Sex Lives of Saints: An Erotics of Ancient Hagiography*. Philadelphia, 2004.

Cameron, Alan. "Paganism and Literature in Late Fourth Century Rome." In Alan

Cameron and Manfred Fuhrmann (eds.), *Christianisme et formes littéraires de l'antiquité tardive en Occident*,i., 1–40. Geneva, 1977.

Cameron, Averil. *Christianity and the Rhetoric of Empire: The Development of Christian Discourse*. Berkeley, 1991.

———. *Procopius and the Sixth Century*. London, 1985 [1996].

Cameron, Averil, and Lawrence I. Conrad (eds.). *The Byzantine and Early Islamic Near East: Problems in the Literary Source Material*. Princeton, 1992.

Caner, Daniel. *Wandering, Begging Monks, Spiritual Authority and the Promotion of Monasticism in Late Antiquity*. Berkeley, 2002.

Canivet, Pierre, and Jean-Paul Rey-Coquais (eds.). *La Syrie de Byzance à l'Islam VIIe—VIIIe siècles: Actes de colloque international Lyon-Maison de l'Orient méditerranéen Paris—Institut de monde arabe, 11–15 Septembre 1990*. Damascus, 1992.

Clark, Gillian. "Victricius of Rouen: *Praising the Saints*." *JECS* 7 (1999): 365–99.

———. "Translating Relics: Victricius of Rouen and Fourth Century Debate." *Early Medieval Europe* 10 (2001): 161–76.

Cohen, Jeffrey Jerome. "Introduction: Midcolonial," and "Hybrids, Monsters, Borderlands: The Bodies of Gerald of Wales." In Jeffrey Jerome Cohen (ed.), *The Postcolonial Middle Ages*, 1–17, 85–104. New York, 2000.

———. "Monster Theory: Seven Theses." In Jeffrey Jerome Cohen (ed.), *Monster Theory*, 3–25. Minneapolis, 1996.

———. *Of Giants: Sex, Monsters and the Middle Ages*. Minneapolis, 1999.

Cohen, Shaye J. D. *The Beginnings of Jewishness: Boundaries, Varieties, Uncertainties*. Berkeley, 1999.

Conrad, Lawrence I. "Al-Azdī's History of the Arab Conquests in Bilād al-Shām: Some Historiographical Observations." In Muḥammad Adnan Bakhit (ed.), *Proceedings of the Second Symposium on the History of Bilād al-Shām During the Early Islamic Period Up to 40 AH/640 AD*, 3 vols., 1.28–62. Amman, 1987.

Cook, David. "Muslim Apocalyptic and *Jihād*." *JSAI* 20 (1996): 66–105.

Cook, Michael. "The Opponents of Writing of Tradition in Early Islam." *Arabica* 44 (1997): 437–530.

———. *Commanding Right and Forbidding Wrong in Islamic Thought*. Cambridge, 2000.

Cooper, Kate. "Insinuations of Womanly Influence: An Aspect of the Christianization of the Roman Aristocracy." *JRS* 82 (1992): 150–64.

Cooperson, Michael. *Classical Arabic Biography: The Heirs of the Prophet in the Age of Ma'mūn*. Cambridge, 2000.

Crone, Patricia. "'Even an Ethiopian Slave': The Transformation of a Sunni Tradition." *BSOAS* 57 (1994): 59–67.

Crone, Patricia. "The First Century Concept of Higra." *Arabica* 41 (1994): 352–87.

———. *God's Rule: Government and Islam*. New York, 2004.

———. *Meccan Trade and the Rise of Islam*. Princeton, 1987.

———. *Slaves on Horses: the Evolution of the Islamic Polity*. Cambridge, 1980.

———. "A Statement by the Najdiyya Kharijites on the Dispensability of the Imamate." *SI* 88 (1998): 55–76.

Crone, Patricia and Martin Hinds. *God's Caliph: Religious Authority in the First Centuries of Islam*. Cambridge, 1986.

Crone, Patricia and Michael Cook. *Hagarism: The Making of the Islamic World*. Cambridge, 1977.

Curran, John. *Pagan City and Christian Capital: Rome in the Fourth Century*. Oxford, 2000.

Dagron, Gilbert. "Judaïser." *Travaux et Mémoirés* 11 (1991): 359–80.

Davis, Stephan J. "Crossed Texts, Crossed Sex: Intertextuality and Gender in Early Christian Legends of Holy Women Disguised as Men." *JECS* 10 (2002): 1–36.

de Goeje, M. J. *Mémoire sur la conquête de la Syrie*. Leiden, 1864.

Dickinson, Eerik. *The Development of Early Sunnite Hadith Criticism: The Taqdima of Ibn Abū Ḥātim al-Rāzī* (240/854–327/938). Leiden, 2001.

Donner, Fred McGraw. *The Early Islamic Conquests*. Princeton, 1981.

Donner, Fred M. *Narratives of Islamic Origins: The Beginnings of Islamic Historical Writing*. Princeton, 1998.

Donner, Fred M. "The Sources of Islamic Conceptions of War." In John Kelsey and James Turner Johnson, *Just War and Jihad: Historical and Theoretical Perspectives on War and Peace in Western and Islamic Traditions*, 31–70. New York, 1991.

Drake, H. A. *Constantine and the Bishops: The Politics of Intolerance*. Baltimore, 2000.

Dzielska, Maria. *Hypatia of Alexandria*. Trans. F. Lyra. Cambridge, Mass., 1995.

al-Duri, Abd al-Aziz. *Rise of Historical Writing among the Arabs*. Princeton, 1983.

Edelby, Néophyte. "L'autonomie législative des chrétiens en terre d'islam." *Archives d'histoire du droit oriental* 5 (1950–51): 307–51.

El Cheikh, Nadia Maria. *Byzantium Viewed by the Arabs*. Cambridge, 2004.

Elm, Susanna. *"Virgins of God": The Making of Asceticism in Late Antiquity*. Oxford, 1994.

Elsner, John. "Cult and Sculpture: Sacrifice in the *Ara Pacis Augustae*." *JRS* 81 (1991): 50–61.

Errington, R. Malcolm. "Christian Accounts of the Religious Legislation of Theodosius I." *Klio* 79 (1997): 398–443.

———. "Church and State in the First Years of Theodosius I." *Chiron* 29 (1998): 21–72.

Fatouros, Georgios and Tilman Krischer. *Libanios, Antiochikos (or. XI): Zur heidnischen Renaissance in der Spätantike*. Berlin, 1992.

Fonrobert, Charlotte Elisheva. "Jewish Christians, Judaizers, and Christian Anti-Judaism." In Virginia Burrus (ed.), *Late Ancient Christianity*, 234–54. Minneapolis, 2005.

Foucault, Michel. *Les anormaux: Cours au Collège de France (1974–1975)*. Paris, 1999.

Fowden, Elizabeth Key. *The Barbarian Plain: Saint Sergius Between Rome and Iran*. Berkeley, 1999.

———. "Sharing Holy Places." *Common Knowledge* 8.1 (2002): 124–46.

Fowden, Garth. "Bishops and Temples in the Eastern Roman Empire A.D. 320–435." *JTS* n.s. 29 (1979): 53–78.

———. *Empire to Commonwealth: Consequences of Monotheism in Late Antiquity*. Princeton, 1993.
———. "The Pagan Holy Man in Late Antique Society." *JHS* 102 (1982): 33–59.
Frankfurter, David. *Religion in Roman Egypt: Assimilation and Resistance*. Princeton, 1998.
———. "Syncretism and the Holy Man in Late Antique Egypt." *JECS* 11 (2003): 339–85.
———. "Things Unbefitting Christians: Violence and Christianization in Fifth-Century Panopolis." *JECS* 8 (2000): 273–95.
Frend, W. H. C. *The Rise of the Monophysite Movement: Chapters in the History of the Church in the Fifth and Sixth Centuries*. Cambridge, 1972.
Gaddis, Michael. *There Is No Crime for Those Who Have Christ: Religious Violence in the Christian Roman Empire*. Berkeley, 2005.
Garsoïan, Nina. *Armenia between Byzantium and the Sasanians*. Aldershot, 1985.
Geertz, Clifford. *The Interpretation of Cultures*. New York, 1973.
———. *Local Knowledge: Further Essays in Interpretive Anthropology*. New York, 1983.
Gleason, Maud. "Festive Satire: Julian's *Misopogon* and the New Year at Antioch." *JRS* 76 (1986): 106–19.
———. *Making Men: Sophists and Self-presentation in Ancient Rome*. Princeton, 1995.
———. "Truth Contests and Talking Corpses." In James I. Porter (ed.), *Constructions of the Classical Body*, 287–313. Ann Arbor, 1999.
Goehring, James. *Ascetics, Society and the Desert: Studies in Early Egyptian Monasticism*. Harrisburg, Pa., 1999.
———. "The Dark Side of Landscape: Ideology and Power in the Christian Myth of the Desert." *JMEMS* 33.3 (2003): 437–51.
———. "New Frontiers in Pachomian Studies." In Birger Albert Pearson and James E. Goehring (eds.), *The Roots of Egyptian Christianity*, 236–57. Philadelphia, 1986.
Goldziher, Ignaz. *Introduction to Islamic Theology and Law*. Princeton, 1981.
———. *Muhammedanische Studien*. 2 vols. Halle, 1889–90. Translated as *Muslim Studies*. 2 vols. Oxford, 1971.
Grabar, Oleg. *The Shape of the Holy: Early Islamic Jerusalem*. Princeton, 1997.
Gregg, Robert C. and Dennis Groh. *Early Arianism: A View of Salvation*. Philadelphia, 1981.
Gregory, Timothy. *Vox Populi: Popular Opinion and Violence in the Religious Controversies of the Fifth Century A.D.* Cincinnati, 1979.
Griffith, Sidney H. "Anthony David of Baghdad, Scribe and Monk of Mar Sabas: Arabic in the Monasteries of Palestine." *Church History* 58 (1989): 7–19.
Grig, Lucy. "Torture and Truth in Late Antique Martyrology." *Early Medieval Europe* 11 (2002): 321–36.
Groß-Albenhausen, Kirsten. *Imperator christianissimus: Der christliche Kaiser Bei Ambrosius und Johannes Chrysostomus*. Frankfurt am Main, 1999.
Haas, Christopher. *Alexandria in Late Antiquity: Topography and Social Conflict*. Baltimore, 1997.

Haldon, John. *Byzantium in the Seventh Century: The Transformation of a Culture*. Cambridge, 1997.

Hall, John. *Ethnic Identity in Greek Antiquity*. Cambridge, 2000.

Hallaq, Ghada Bathish. "Discourse Strategies: The Persuasive Power of Early Khārijī Poetry." Ph.D. diss., University of Washington, 1988.

Hamad, Bushra. "History and Biography." *Arabica* 45 (1998): 215–32.

Harvey, Susan Ashbrook. *Asceticism and Society in Crisis: John of Ephesus and the Lives of the Eastern Saints*. Berkeley, 1990.

Hawting, Gerald R. "The Significance of the Slogan *Lā Ḥukma Illā Lillāh* and the References to *Ḥudūd* in the Traditions About the Fitna and the Murder of *ʿUthmān*." *BSOAS* 41 (1978): 453–463.

Hinchman, Lewis P. and Sandra Hinchman. *Memory, Identity, Community: The Idea of Narrative in the Human Sciences*. Albany, 1997.

Hinds, Martin, Patricia Crone, Jere Bacherach, and Lawrence I. Conrad (eds.). *Studies in Early Islamic History*. Princeton, 1996.

Hoyland, Robert. "Arabic, Syriac and Greek Historiography in the First Abbasid Century: An Inquiry into Inter-Cultural Traffic." *ARAM Periodical* 3 (1991): 211–33.

———. "The Content and Context of Early Arabic Inscriptions." *JSAI* 21 (1997): 108–41.

———. *Seeing Islam as Others Saw It: A Survey and Evaluation of Christian, Jewish and Zoroastrian Writings on Early Islam*. Princeton, 1997.

Humphreys, R. Stephen. *Islamic History: A Framework for Inquiry*. Princeton, 1991.

———. "Qurʾanic Myth and Narrative Structure in Early Islamic Historiography." In Frank M. Clover and R. Stephen Humphreys (eds.), *Tradition and Innovation in Late Antiquity*, 271–90. Madison 1989.

Hunter, David G. "Vigilantius of Calagurris and Victricius of Rouen: Ascetics, Relics, and Clerics in Late Roman Gaul." *JECS* 7 (1999): 401–30.

Hurvitz, Nimrod. *The Formation of Hanbalism: Piety into Power*. London, 2002.

———. "From Scholarly Circles to Mass Movements: The Formation of Legal Communities in Islamic Societies." *American Historical Review* 103 (2003): 985–1008.

Jacobs, Andrew S. *Remains of the Jews: The Holy Land and Christian Empire in Late Antiquity*. Stanford, 2004.

Jameson, Fredric. *The Political Unconscious: Narrative as a Socially Symbolic Act*. Ithaca, 1981.

Johnson, Aaron P. *Ethnicity and Argument in Eusebius'* Praeparatio evangelica. Oxford, 2006.

Judd, Steven C. "Competitive Hagiography in Biographies of al-Awzāʿī and Sufyān al-Thawrī." *JAOS* 122 (2002): 25–37.

Judge, E. A. "The Earliest Use of Monachos for 'Monk' (P. Coll. Youtie 77) and the Origins of Monasticism." *Jahrbuch für Antike und Christentum* 20 (1977): 72–89.

Juynboll, G. H. A. *Muslim Tradition: Studies in Chronology, Provenance, and Authorship of Early Hadith*. Cambridge, 1983.

Kenney, Jeffrey T. "Heterodoxy and Culture: The Legacy of the Khawarij in Islamic History." Ph.D. diss. University of California, Santa Barbara, 1991.
Kinberg, Leah. "What is Meant by *Zuhd*?" *SI* 41 (1985): 27–44.
Khalidi, Tarif. *Arabic Historical Thought in the Classical Period*. Cambridge, 1994.
Khouri, Raif-Georges. "Importance et authenticité des texts de *Ḥilyāt al-awliyāʾ wa-ṭabaqāt al-aṣfiyāʾ* d'Abū Nuʿaym al-Iṣbahānī." *SI* 46 (1977): 73–113.
Kister, M. J. "'Do not Assimilate Yourselves . . .' *Lā tashabbahū* . . ." *JSAI* 12 (1989): 321–53.
———. *Society and Religion from Jāhiliyya to Islam*. London, 1990.
Lançon, Bertrand. *Rome in Late Antiquity: Everyday Life and Urban Change, A.D. 312–609*. Trans. Antonia Nevill. New York, 2000.
Landau-Tasseron, Ella. "Sayf Ibn ʿUmar in Medieval and Modern Scholarship." *Der Islam* 67 (1990): 1–26.
Laoust, Henri. "Le Hanbalisme sous le califat de Bagdad." *Revue des études islamiques* 27 (1959): 67–128.
———. *La profession de foi d'Ibn Baṭṭa*. Damascus, 1958.
Le Boulluec, Alain. *La notion d'hérésie dans la littérature grecque IIe–IIIe siècles*. 2 vols. Paris, 1985.
Levine, Lee I. (ed.). *The Synagogue in Late Antiquity*. Philadelphia, 1987.
Lewinstein, Keith. "The Azariqa in Islamic Heresiography." *BSOAS* 54 (1991): 251–68.
———. "The Revaluation of Martyrdom in Early Islam." In Margaret Cormack (ed.), *Sacrificing the Self: Perspectives on Martyrdom and Religion*. Oxford, 2001.
Lieu, Judith. "The Forging of Christian Identity." *JMA* 11 (1998): 71–82.
———. "'Impregnable Ramparts and Walls of Iron': Boundary and Identity in Early 'Judaism' and 'Christianity.'" *New Testament Studies* 48 (2002): 297–313.
Lim, Richard. "People as Power: Games, Munificence, and Contested Topography." In W. V. Harris and Javier Arce (eds.), *The Transformations of* Urbs Roma *in Late Antiquity*, 267–81. Portsmouth, R.I., 1999.
———. *Public Disputation, Power, and Social Order in Late Antiquity*. Berkeley, 1994.
———. "Religious and Social Disorder in Late Antiquity." *Historia* 44 (1995): 204–31.
Livne-Kafri, Ofer. "Early Muslim Ascetics and the World of Christian Monasticism." *JSAI* 20 (1996): 105–29.
Lyman, J. Rebecca. "Ascetics and Bishops: Epiphanius on Orthodoxy." In Susanna Elm, Éric Rebbillard, and Antonella Romano (eds.), *Orthodoxie, Christianisme, Histoire/Orthodoxy, Christianity, History*, 149–61. Rome, 2000.
———. "The Making of a Heretic: The Life of Origin in Epiphanius *Panarion* 64." *SP* 31 (1997): 445–51.
———. "2002 NAPS Presidential Address: Hellenism and Heresy." *JECS* 11 (2003): 209–222.
Maas, Michael. *Exegesis and Empire in the Early Byzantine Mediterranean*. Tübingen, 2003.
———. *John Lydus and the Roman Past: Antiquarianism in the Age of Justinian*. New York, 1992.

———. "Roman History and Christian Ideology in Justinianic Reform Legislation." *Dumbarton Oaks Papers* 40 (1986): 17–31.

MacCoull, L. S. B. "Prophethood, Texts, and Artifacts: The Monastery of Epiphanius." *GRBS* 39 (1998): 307–24.

MacMullen, Ramsay. "Judicial Savagery in the Roman Empire." *Chiron* 16 (1986): 147–66.

Madelung, W. "The Vigilante Movement of Sahl b. Salāma al-Khurāsānī and the Origins of Ḥanbalism Reconsidered." *Journal of Turkish Studies* 12 (1990): 331–37.

Maier, Harry O. "Private Space as the Social Context of Arianism in Ambrose's Milan." *JTS* 45 (1994): 72–93.

———. "Topography of Heresy and Dissent in Late Fourth Century Rome." *Historia* 44 (1995): 231–49.

McLynn, Neil. *Ambrose of Milan: Church and Court in a Christian Capital.* Berkeley, 1994.

———. "Christian Controversy and Violence in the Fourth Century." *Kodai* 3 (1992): 15–44.

Miles, Richard. "Introduction: Constructing Identities in Late Antiquity." In Richard Miles (ed.), *Constructing Identities in Late Antiquity*, 1–17. London, 1999.

Morony, Michael G. *Iraq after the Muslim Conquest.* Princeton, 1984.

Mourad, Suleiman. "On Early Islamic Historiography: Abu Ismāʿīl al-Azdī and His *Futūḥ al-Shām*." *JAOS* 120 (2000): 577–93.

Newby, Gordon. "An Example of Coptic Literary Influence on Ibn Isḥāq's Sīrah." *JNES* 31 (1972): 22–8.

Noth, Albrecht. "*Futūḥ*-history and *Futūḥ*-historiography: The Muslim Conquest of Damascus." *al-Qantara* 10 (1989): 453–62.

———. *Heiliger Krieg und heiliger Kampf in Islam und Christentum.* Bonn, 1966.

———. "Problems of Differentiation between Muslims and Non-Muslims: Re-Reading the 'Ordinances of ʿUmar' (*al-Shurūṭ al-ʿumariyya*)." = Chapter 5 in Robert Hoyland (ed.), *Muslims and Others in Early Islamic Society*, 103–24. Aldershot, 2004. Originally published as "Abgrenzungsprobleme zwischen Muslimen und Nicht-Muslimin, Die 'Bedingungen ʿUmars (*aš-šūrūṭ al-ʿumariyya*)' unter einem anderen Aspekt gelesen." *JSAI* 9 (1987): 290–315.

Noth, Albrecht and Lawrence I. Conrad. *The Early Arabic Historical Tradition.* Princeton, 1994.

Penn, Michael Philip. *Kissing Christians: Ritual and Community in the Late Ancient Church.* Philadelphia, 2005.

Polleta, Francesca. "Contending Stories: Narrative in Social Movements." *Qualitative Sociology* 21 (1998): 419–46.

———. " 'It was Like a Fever . . .': Narrative and Identity in Social Protest." *Social Problems* 45 (1998): 137–59.

Rajak, Tessa. "Dying for the Law: The Martyr's Portrait in Jewish-Greek Literature." In M. J. Edwards, and S. Swain (eds.), *Portraits: Biographical Representation in the Greek and Latin Literature of the Roman Empire*, 40–67. Oxford, 1997.

Ricoeur, Paul. *Time and Narrative.* 3 vols. Chicago, 1984.

Rippin, Andrew. "Literary Analysis of *Qur'ān, Tafsīr and Sīra*: The Methodologies of John Wansbrough." In Richard C. Martin (ed.), *Approaches to Islam in Religious Studies*, 151–63. Oxford, 2001.
Robinson, Chase F. "The Conquest of Khuzistan: A Historiographical Reassessment." *BSOAS* 67 (2004): 14–39.
———. *Empire and Elites after the Muslim Conquest: The Transformation of Northern Mesopotamia*. Cambridge, 2000.
———. *Islamic Historiography*. Cambridge, 2003.
Rousseau, Philip. *Ascetics, Authority and the Church*. Oxford, 1978.
———. "Orthodoxy and the Cenobite." *SP* 30 (1997): 239–56.
———. "The Spiritual Authority of the 'Monk-Bishop': Eastern Elements in Some Western Hagiography of the Fourth and Fifth Centuries." *JTS* 23 (1971): 381–419.
Rubin, Uri. *The Eye of the Beholder: The Life of Muḥammad as Viewed by the Early Muslims: A Textual Analysis*. Princeton, 1995.
Sāghy, M. "*Scinditur in partes populus*: Pope Damasus and the Martyrs of Rome." *Early Medieval Europe* 9 (2000): 273–87.
Schacht, Joseph. *The Origins of Muhammadan Jurisprudence*. Oxford, 1979.
Schoeler, G. "Writing and Publishing on the Use and Function of Writing in the First Centuries of Islam." *Arabica* 44 (1997): 423–35.
Serjeant, R. B. "Meccan Trade and the Rise of Islam: Misconceptions and Flawed Polemics." *JAOS* 110 (1990): 472–86.
Shaw, Brent D. "Body/Power/Identity: Passions of the Martyrs." *JECS* 4 (1996): 269–312.
———. "Judicial Nightmares and Christian Memory." *JECS* 11 (2003): 533–63.
Skladanek, Bogdan. "The Kharijites in Iran I: Division into Sects." *Rocznik Orientalistyczny* 44.1 (1985): 65–92.
Smith, Jonathan Z. *Map Is Not Territory: Studies in the History of Religion*. Chicago, 1993.
Somers, Margaret R. "The Narrative Constitution of Identity: A Relationship and Network Approach." *Theory and Society* 23.5 (1994): 605–60.
———."Narrativity, Narrative Identity and Social Action: Rethinking English Working-Class Formation." *Social Science History* 16 (1992): 591–629.
Sterk, Andrea. *Renouncing the World yet Leading the Church: The Monk Bishop in Late Antiquity*. Berkeley, 2004.
Stern, Sacha. *Jewish Identity in Early Rabbinic Writings*. Leiden, 1994.
Straw, Carole. "Settling Scores: Eschatology in the Church of the Martyrs." In Caroline Walker Bynum and Paul Freedman (eds.), *Last Things: Death and the Apocalypse in the Middle Ages*, 21–40. Philadelphia, 2000.
Strawson, Galen. "Against Narrativity." *Ratio* 17 (2004): 428–52.
Suny, Ronald Grigor. "Constructing Primordialism: Old Histories for New Nations." *The Journal of Modern History* 71 (2001): 862–96.
———. "Provisional Stabilities: The Politics of Identities in Post-Soviet Eurasia." *International Security* 24.3 (2000): 139–78.

Sviri, Sara. "*Wa-Rahbānīyatan Ibtadaʿūhū*: An Analysis of Traditions Concerning the Origin and Evaluation of Christian Monasticism." *JSAI* 13 (1990): 195–208.

Taussig, Michael. *Defacement: The Public Secret and the Labor of the Negative.* Stanford, 1999.

Thacker, Alan and Richard Sharpe (eds.). *Local Saints and Local Churches in the Early Medieval West.* Oxford, 2002.

Theuws, Frans, "Introduction: Rituals in Transforming Societies." In Frans Theuws and Janet Nelson (eds.), *Rituals of Power: From Late Antiquity to the Early Middle Ages*, 1–13. Leiden, 2000.

Tilley, Maureen A. *The Bible in Christian North Africa: The Donatist World.* Minneapolis, 1997.

———. *Donatist Martyr Stories: The Church in Conflict in Roman North Africa.* Liverpool, 1997.

Trout, Dennis. "Damasus and the Invention of Early Christian Rome." *JMEMS* 33 (2003): 517–36.

Van Dam, Raymond. *Becoming Christian: The Conversion of Roman Cappadocia.* Philadelphia, 2003.

———. *Empire of Snow: Roman Rule and Greek Culture in Cappadocia.* Philadelphia, 2002.

———. "From Paganism to Christianity in Late Antique Gaza." *Viator 16* (1985): 1–20.

van Ess, Josef. *Theologie und Gesellschaft in 2. und 3. Jahrhundert Hidschra. Eine Geschichte des religiösen Denkens im frühen Islam.* 6 vols. Berlin, 1991–97.

Vinson, M. "Gregory Nazianzen's *Homily 15* and the Genesis of the Christian Cult of the Maccabean Martyrs." *Byzantion* 64 (1994): 166–92.

Wansbrough, John. *The Sectarian Milieu: Content and Composition of Islamic Salvation History.* Oxford, 1978.

Wellhausen, Julius. *Das arabische Reich und sein Sturz.* Berlin, 1902. Translated as *The Arab Kingdom and Its Fall.* Calcutta, 1927.

———. *The Religio-Political Factions in Early Islam.* Trans. R. C. Ostle, and S. M. Walzer. Amsterdam, 1975.

White, Hayden. "The Value of Narrativity in the Representation of Reality." In W. J. Thomas Mitchell (ed.), *On Narrative*, 1–23. Chicago, 1981.

Wood, David (ed.). *On Paul Ricoeur: Narrative and Interpretation.* London, 1991.

Woolf, Greg. *Becoming Roman: The Origins of Provincial Civilization in Gaul.* Cambridge, 1998.

Zaman, Muhammad Qasim. *Religion and Politics Under the Early ʿAbbāsids: The Emergence of the Proto-Sunnī Elite.* Leiden, 1997.

Ziāuddin, Aḥmad. "Abū Bakr al-Khallāl—the Compiler of the Teachings of Imām Aḥmad b. Ḥanbal." *Islamic Studies* 9 (1970): 245–54.

INDEX

Aaron (Old Testament), priesthood of, 28
Abbasids: Christians under, 247–48, 250, 267–68; *madhāhib* on, 358n42; memory of Ummayad caliphs under, 363n104; pietist rebels against, 197; relations with Byzantium, 360n63; sociopolitical world of, 357n35; transgressive behavior by, 268–70, 365n140
Abbi (Syrian monk), 128
ʿAbd Allāh b. al-ʿAbbās, 350n64
ʿAbd Allāh b. al-Rābisī, 198, 200, 206, 213
ʿAbd Allāh b. Shajura, 200
ʿAbd al-ʿAzīz, relations with Christians, 232–33, 354n6
ʿAbd al-Malik, 151–52; and Kharijites, 229–30
ʿAbīda b. Hilāl, 210
Abraham b. Kayli (Chalcedonian bishop), 139
Abū ʿĀmr, 334n50
Abū Bakr, 237–38, 241; commanding and forbidding by, 206; embodiment of virtue, 204
Abū Bakr al-Khallāl, 271, 359n50; on consolation, 261; *Jāmiʿ*, 244; *Kitāb ahl al-milal*, 242–244, 253, 254; *Kitāb al-janāiz*, 258, 260, 262
Abū Bilāl Mirdās b. Udayya, 210
Abū l-Faraj al-Iṣfahānī, *Kitāb adab al-ghurabāʾ*, 238
Abu Ḥamza, 350n53; on ʿUmar, 206, 348n25
Abū Isḥāq al-Fazārī, 216; *Kitāb al-siyar*, 206; on protection of monks, 232
Abū al-Ṣahbā, two martyrdoms of, 188
Abū Simʿān, 174
Abū Ṭālib, 245
Abū Yūsuf al-Ghasūlī, 343n38
Acanthia (wife of Cynegius), 96, 312n45
Agnes (martyr), 72; tomb of, 309n87
Agricola (martyr), 59
Aḥmad b. Ḥanbal, 14, 18–20, 195; as arbiter, 242; asceticism of, 238, 338n87; behavior toward non-Muslims, 254–55; on belief, 239–40, 255; on boundary maintenance, 178, 237, 252, 256–59, 270–71, 277, 280–81; caliphal patronage of, 238, 240, 358n38; on captives, 362n93; on commanding and forbidding, 256, 263–64; communal life of, 194; on consolation, 261–62; funeral of, 177, 245; on funerals, 260–61, 263; *ghāzī* influence on, 239, 278; on *jihād*, 19, 211, 280; on Kharijites, 234–35, 255, 277; *Kitāb al-zuhd*, 162, 166; *madhhab* of, 230, 234, 235, 271; nonviolence of, 256, 280, 281, 363n106; on relations with non-Muslims, 242–43, 244, 280, 359nn50, 57; role in Muslim identity, 237, 241; torture of, 19, 236–38, 240, 248, 278, 279, 356n18, 358n42; on *zuhd*, 194, 338n87
akhbār (reports), 146; on caliph ʿUmar, 190; in communal narratives, 147; in *Kitāb al-jihād*, 187; on martyrs, 209; tribal, 153
ʿAkkāf b. Bashir al-Tammiyya, 179
Alcibiades, statue of, 100–101
Alexander (martyr), 58, 305n39
Alexander the Great, 101; as Roman archetype, 314n64
Alexandria, monastic violence in, 111
ʿAlī b. Abī Ṭālib (Prophet's son-in-law), 17, 196, 210; Ibn Ḥanbal on, 255; murder of, 257; relations with Kharijites, 197, 198–201, 203–4, 216, 221, 222, 351n66; struggle with Muʿāwiya, 16, 197–99
ʿAlī al-Kharjānī, 357n31

Altar of Victory, controversy over, 77–78
Ambrose (bishop of Milan): and Arian controversy, 60–62, 105; in Callinicum synagogue controversy, 81–84, 85, 88; *Epistle 72*, 77–78; excavation of martyrs, 59–60, 64; on Julian, 82–83, 84; on Magnus Maximus, 83; on martyrdom, 81–82; on Photinians, 105; on piety of emperors, 309n95; on Roman sovereignty, 104–5; and Theodosius, 3, 104, 105, 310n98; use of past narratives, 10, 79, 83, 104
ʿAmmār al-Baṣrī, critique of Islam, 1, 285n1
Ammianus Marcellinus: on Arab tribesmen, 141–42; on martyr adoration, 308n75
Ammonius (monk), 111
Anatolius (procurator), 325n124
Ando, Clifford, 92, 98, 102
Antioch: antipagan pogrom in, 317n10; banning of monks from, 103, 106; confessional identity of, 30–31, 111, 293n10; Judaizers of, 31, 37–38, 41, 170, 292n10; Libanius's panegyric to, 89–90; Riot of the Statues in, 335n67; Roman rule of, 90, 311n25
antiquity, late: communal boundaries of, 21–22, 24, 31, 201; confessional identity in, 21; *doxa* of, 246, 360n62; early Muslim tradition and, 153–56; fascination with zealotry, 4–5; fasting in, 25–26, 27; historiography of, 317n5; identity in, 7, 21, 22, 274, 292n3; influence on Muslim piety, 194; Islamic communities in, 158, 166–67, 328n8; in Islamic narratives, 201, 327n4; Islam in, 145, 153–56, 164, 166–67, 328n8; Jewish synagogues of, 294n25, 295n30, 296n36; *jihād* in, 187–88, 279; Kharijites in, 226; militant piety in, 3–5, 7; monotheism in, 147, 190, 203; monsters of, 141–42; narratives of, 86; public secrets in, 42–43; rituals of, 307n70; shared semiotic systems of, 34, 36, 43, 47–48, 99, 127, 147–49, 156, 169, 195, 275, 295n27, 301n5
Antony, Mark, feminine influence on, 313n46
Antony (saint), 124, 192; Arians and, 33, 297n46, 318n25; enforcement of boundaries, 33–34, 113; and heresy, 112–13
Apollinarii (elder and younger), 34
Arabs: conquest of Iberia, 144; conquest of Syria, 203; defense of Constantinople, 141–42; of Ḥijāz, 154; of Jazīra, 154; monotheism of, 144, 158
Arians, 105; Antony and, 33, 297n46, 318n25; martyrs, 60–62, 73; of Milan, 60–61, 306n53
Aristotle, al-Maʾmūn's dream of, 247
Armenia: genocide (1915), 49, 69, 308n79; past narratives of, 49, 50, 66–67
asceticism: imaginative power of, 180; and *jihād*, 182–85, 194, 211, 227; mentors in, 174; Muḥammad on, 178–79; semiotics of, 155–56, 171, 174, 176, 191; settings of, 322n82
ascetics, 181, 173, 192; confessional identities of, 170, 171–72, 175–76, 341n18; intercommunal contacts among, 176–77
ascetics, Christian, 108, 121, 142, 192; anxiety concerning, 334n59; bestial qualities of, 136; boundaries around, 118, 119; discernment of orthodoxy, 128, 160, 176; healing abilities of, 232; in Muslim tradition, 156–61, 341n18; as prophets, 321n65; self-mortification by, 126–27, 130, 322n77; types of, 35, 335n62; writings of, 119–20. *See also* monks
ascetics, Christian militant, 11–12, 108–9, 158, 226; boundary maintenance by, 111–16, 118–19, 161; among *mujāhidūn*, 161. *See also* monks, militant
ascetics, Islamic, 14–15, 180; Christian models of, 169, 341n18; in communal narratives, 192–93; concern for community, 171, 193–94, 276; diet of, 238, 357n31; Kharijites, 16–18; role in boundary maintenance, 178–80, 276; role in communal identity, 168, 170–71, 179, 190, 194, 214, 342n34; urban, 210–11; view of death, 188, 345n70
ascetics, Islamic militant, 5, 158–64; anxiety concerning, 169–70; at battle of Qādisiyya, 189–91; and caliphate, 197, 217–18, 220, 221; calls for *jihād*, 188–90; in *futūḥ*, 168, 212; narratives of, 146–47; and Persian luxury, 163, 189; raiders, 211–12; renunciation by, 211. *See also* Kharijites; *mujāhidūn*
Asclepius, statue of, 100–101
Athanasius (bishop of Alexandria), 72; on ascetics, 335n63; on Council of Nicaea, 303n10; Life of Antony, 112, 113, 124; and Melitians, 65, 112–13; and monasticism, 318n25
Augustine (saint): on Circumcellions, 307n64; *Epistle to Januarius*, 75; on

Manichaeans, 32; on martyrs, 62–65, 71, 73, 75–76, 309n84; *On the Works of Monks*, 35
Augustus (emperor), benefactions of, 91
al-Awzāʿī, ʿAbd al-Raḥmān b. ʿAmr, 358n42; funeral of, 177, 178
Azāriqa (Kharijite sect), 255, 351nn65, 70
al-Azdī al-Baṣrī, Muḥammad, 15, 156, 165; on asceticism, 162–63; on commanding and forbidding, 205–6, 207; *Taʾrīkh futūḥ al-Shām*, 160–61, 207, 289n35

Bāhān (Roman commander), 207, 353n91, 360n66
Baḥīrā (monk), 157, 245, 333n46
al-Balādhurī, 196, 206; *Ansāb al-ashrāf*, 197–98; on Jahīza, 228; on Kharijites, 199, 203, 208, 213–14, 217–21; on virtue, 204
baptism, true and false, 114–15
al-Barbaharī (Ḥanbalī), 271, 365n142
Barth, Fredrick, 172; on affordances, 280; on boundaries, 8, 266–67, 272–73, 291n2, 318n18
Basil of Caesarea, 57, 304n35
beards, dying of, 252, 361n86
Bedouins, 349n34; Symeon the Stylite and, 150–51; war narratives of, 165
Ben Dama, Elʿazar, 35–36, 120, 320n51
Besa (archimandrite), 119, 122; on intermingled communities, 320n54
Bonner, Michael, 182
borderlands: Anatolian, 168; cultural fusion in, 151–52; holy persons of, 150–51; Islamic, 149–59; monks in, 158; semiotics of, 152
boundary maintenance: Barth on, 266–67, 272–73, 291n3, 318n18; between Christians and Muslims, 223–24, 252–55; in late antiquity, 201; by monsters, 129, 130–31. *See also* communal boundaries; communities, intermingled
boundary maintenance, Christian, 11–12, 33–34; John Chrysostom on, 24, 31, 36–44, 46–47, 51, 111–12, 170, 251–52, 272, 279, 280, 293n10, 298n61; by martyrs, 15, 64, 275; by militant ascetics, 111–16, 118–19, 161; by monks, 44, 127, 137–38, 140, 159, 275; penalties for transgression, 120; at public games, 117. *See also* communal boundaries, Christian
boundary maintenance, Islamic, 234; asceticism and, 178–80, 276; commanding and forbidding in, 263; by Ḥanbalīs, 258, 260; Ibn Ḥanbal's role in, 178, 237, 252, 256–59, 270–71, 277, 280–81; by Kharijites, 213, 224–25, 226; among Muslims, 279–80, 281; peaceful, 18–20; *sunna* on, 179; violence in, 257. *See also* communal boundaries, Islamic
Bourdieu, Pierre, 98; on *habitus*, 99
Boyarin, Daniel, 35, 320n51; on Christian-Jewish boundaries, 31, 59, 293n10; on communal identity, 5, 11
Brakke, David, 33, 112, 318n25; on Shenoute, 115
Braund, David, 173
bribery, attempted: during *futūḥ*, 247, 360n66; in martyr narratives, 337n80
Brincus *(praepositus)*, 84
Brown, Peter, 65, 129, 243; on Arab past, 164; on the desert, 123; on martyrs, 125–26
Bruner, Jerome, 9
Buell, Denise Kimber, 6, 57, 292n9
Bunāna b. Abī b. ʿĀṣim al-Azdī, 215–16
Byzantium: martyr shrines of, 151; relations with Abbasids, 360n63

Callinicum (Syria), Christian violence at, 81–84, 85, 88, 106
Callinicus (hagiographer), 118
Cameron, Alan, 32
Cassian, John: on monasticism, 184; sources of, 343n52
Castelli, Elizabeth, 8
celibacy, Muḥammad on, 178–79
Chalcedon, monastic violence at, 131–33
children: of Christian slaves, 362n94; forced conversion of, 362n93; Islamic identity of, 361n93; monastic violence against, 136, 138; murder of, 4, 216, 351nn65, 70
Chosroes (Persian king), 221
Christianity, early: foundational traumas of, 52, 56, 61; organizing narratives of, 56; Others and, 6; primordial aspects of, 52, 55, 56, 59, 61, 74–75; and rabbinic Judaism, 5–6, 11, 24–32, 36–38; textual traditions of, 6; triumphal narratives of, 56, 57, 58, 103; use of Jewish past, 6. *See also* communities, Christian
Christians: in Abbasid society, 247–48, 250, 267–68; acceptance of Muḥammad, 160,

Christians (*cont.*)
245; assimilation into Roman society, 53; coexistence with pagans, 21, 291n1; false, 115; and Kharijites, 216, 217, 223; knowledge of Islam, 248–51, 267; Muslim anxiety concerning, 248–51, 253; under Muslim law, 251, 268; Muslim tolerance for, 231–33; nominal, 359n51; participation in Jewish festivals, 38, 41, 43, 293n13; recognition by Muslims, 251, 252, 267–68; suspicion of Ḥunayn b. Isḥāq, 247–48; teaching of pagan classics, 34, 134; use of magic, 33; use of Muslim semiotics, 245
Christopher (saint), 140–41, 326n130
Chrysostom, John: *Against the Games and Theatres*, 36–37, 116; on boundary maintenance, 24, 31, 36–44, 46–47, 51, 111–12, 170, 251–52, 272, 279, 280, 293n10, 298n61; on Council of Nicaea, 51, 53, 56; disciplining of community, 300n86; on fasting, 25–28, 31, 43, 46; female patrons of, 297n44; on martyrs, 45, 55, 75; on Matrona's Cave, 47; metaphors of, 37, 293n11, 299n68; orations against the Jews, 24–31, 37, 39–40, 47, 248, 292nn9–10
Cicero, 313n47; rhetoric against Antony, 313n46
Clark, Gilian, 58
Cohen, Jeffrey Jerome, 129
Collectio Avellana, 72, 73
commanding and forbidding, Christian, 272
commanding and forbidding, Islamic, 205–7, 364n127; among Ḥanbalīs, 264, 265; in boundary maintenance, 263; Ibn Ḥanbal on, 256, 263–64; violence following, 263
communal boundaries, 8, 21–22, 24, 31, 178, 201; ascetic practice across, 174; ascriptive and descriptive, 42, 43; belief systems of, 172; graves as, 305n44; individual adaptations to, 267; role in identity, 123–24, 273, 318n18; transgression of, 21, 27, 38, 40, 41, 43, 111, 119–21, 123, 275, 299n80. *See also* boundary maintenance
communal boundaries, Christian, 11–12, 54; Antony's enforcement of, 33–34, 113; Eusebius on, 53; with Jews, 31–32, 59, 293n10, 320n51; martyrs' defense of, 15, 64, 275; monastic, 120–21, 122; monks' defense of, 44, 127, 137–38, 140, 159; with pagans, 34–35; permeability of, 42; secrecy in violation of, 39–40, 42, 43; surveillance of, 34, 36–42, 44–48, 62, 111–12, 119, 120, 272, 298n61; transgression by monks, 119–21
communal boundaries, Islamic: Abbasid transgression of, 268–70; Ibn Ḥanbal's preservation of, 178, 237, 252, 256–62, 270–71, 277, 280–81; stability of, 230
communal narratives: of continuity, 287n20; Jewish, 70; Palestinian, 67–68; violence in, 68–69. *See also* foundation narratives; past narratives
communal narratives, Christian, 10–11, 48–49; ancestors in, 49; competing, 154; interpretation of Roman society, 86; martyrs in, 52–53, 57–58, 77; of past, 16, 70–72, 74–75, 78–79; persecution in, 87; postconquest, 156; Roman emperors in, 84; shared, 155
communal narratives, Islamic, 13; *akhbār* in, 147; ascetics in, 192–93; borderland aspects of, 149–59; conquest in, 164; foundational, 15–16, 168, 169; late antique context of, 327n4; mounted warriors in, 246; Muḥammad's revelation in, 166; origins in, 168; of past, 234; tribal elements in, 153, 332n33
communal narratives, Roman, 78; of elites, 86, 91–92; emperors in, 84
communities: Abrahamic monotheistic, 12; construction of reality, 65–66; foundation narratives of, 67; imagined pasts of, 9; membership in, 273; primordial foundations of, 23, 65–66; relations with Others, 6, 49; semiotic sharing among, 34, 36, 43, 47–48, 155, 301n5. *See also* boundary maintenance; identity, communal
communities, Christian: anti-Chalcedonian, 233; of Antioch, 30–31; ascetics' role in, 11–12, 185; and community of God, 155; conflict among, 72–75, 77, 79, 281–82; effect of persecution on, 53–55; imagined, 6; intermingling with non-Christians in, 109–10, 131–33, 137; kissing in, 6, 83, 292n9, 310n5; local traditions of, 79; markers of, 46; martyrs' redemption of, 55; monastic idea of, 123; monks and, 130, 134–40; past narratives of, 16, 70–72, 74–75, 78–79; place in Roman world, 106; possession of truth, 125; primordial past of, 59, 60,

74–75; primordial traumas of, 52, 56, 61; sacred space of, 78; of Syria, 108; violation of norms in, 38; violence among, 89; women's defense of, 297n44
communities, intermingled, 21–22; Christian and non-Christian, 31, 59, 109–10, 131–33, 137, 257, 293n10, 319n41, 320n54; coexistence within, 21, 232, 274; funerals in, 258, 260–61, 263, 265–66; Muslim and non-Muslim, 230, 231–34, 242–45, 247–48, 250, 256–62, 265–70, 279, 280, 355n10, 359n58; violence in, 86, 89, 112, 133
communities, Islamic: ascetic models for, 168, 171, 179, 190, 194, 214, 342n34; ascetics' concern for, 193–94, 276; claims concerning prophecy, 156; external relations of, 164–65; of *futūḥ*, 15, 17; Ḥanbalī, 19, 234–35, 355n11; heroes of, 246; individuals in, 181, 184; integrity of, 212; Kharijites role in, 214, 230; in late antiquity, 158, 166–67, 328n8; membership in, 204, 255; monks in, 169–70; Murjiʾa, 255; origin narratives of, 15–16, 169; primordial past of, 12–13, 189, 200–201, 213–14, 221–22, 224, 241; renunciation in, 187, 190; shared semiotics of, 145–46, 156, 195, 248, 276, 278–79; toleration within, 233, 355n10; tribal elements of, 152, 153, 332n33. See also *umma*, Islamic
consolation, between Muslim and non-Muslim, 261–62
Constantine (emperor): narratives of conversion, 305n42; temples under, 93; view of paganism, 312n38
Constantinople, Arab defense of, 141–42
Constantius II (emperor): condemnation of Athanasius, 72; power structure under, 95; wives of, 312n42
Cook, Michael, 148, 263, 264, 359n50
Cooper, Kate, 96
Cooperson, Michael, 240, 247, 248
Council of Chalcedon, 108
Council of Nicaea, 56, 303n10; on Pasch celebration, 51–52; survivors of persecution at, 51, 53, 75
Crone, Patricia, 148, 218
Cynegius, Maternus: female domination of, 95, 96; subversion of imperial authority, 96
Cynics, Julian and, 34–35
Cyril (bishop), 110–11

Ḍaḥḥāk b. Qays, 209; campaign against Bedouins, 349n34
Damasus (bishop of Rome): betrayal of community, 75; conflict with Ursinus, 72–75, 82, 85; excavation of martyrs, 58, 59; violence by, 72, 74, 75, 309n86
Daniel the Stylite, 140, 341n17; pre-Islamic Arab admirers of, 177; self-mortification of, 128, 185–86
death: Islamic ascetic view of, 188, 345n70; Muslim protocols for, 258, 260–61
Decius (emperor), 92
demons, 29: monks' conflict with, 336n68; revelation by, 299n78; Shenoute on, 115
Demosthenes, 313n46
Dhū al-Nūn (ascetic), 176
Dhū al-Thafināt, 214, 220, 222, 228
Dīnawarī, 219
Dolbeau, François, 62
Dome of the Rock, decorative elements of, 151, 158
Donatists: captives of, 306n56; Circumcellions, 307nn60, 64; martyrs of, 63–64, 76–77, 309n84; violence by, 75
Donner, Fred, 15, 152, 191, 275; *Narratives of Islamic Origins*, 148–49
Drake, Harold, 21–22, 78; on Christian rulership, 106; on Christian tolerance, 23–24

Eliade, Mircea, 65, 66, 74
elites, late Roman, 86, 100, 340n12; funeral customs of, 91–92; identity of, 32, 58, 99
Entrexios (prefect), 109
Epiphanius (monastery, Thebes), 234; magic at, 128; texts of, 121–22
Epipodius (martyr), 58, 305n39
Errington, R. Malcolm, 103
Eulalius (bishop), 117
Eulogius (archbishop of Alexandria), 325n124
Eunapius, on monsters, 142–43
Eurymedon, myth of, 142–43
Eusebius Gallicanus, sermons in, 57
Eusebius of Caesarea: *Ecclesiastical History*, 53; on martyrs, 54–55, 56, 57, 303n25; *Praeparatio Evangelica*, 6

families, Christian-Muslim, 252, 253–54; funeral protocols for, 258, 260–61, 265–66
fasting, 27, 46; boundary transgression through, 31, 38, 40, 41, 43; Ibn al-

fasting (*cont.*)
Mubārak's, 182, 343n46; proper and improper, 25, 26, 28, 115; among rabbinical Jews, 294n20
Faymiyūn (ascetic), 158, 159, 334n54
festivals: Jewish, 38–41, 43, 293n13; Roman, 58; true and false, 115
fetishes, and boundary transgression, 41, 299n79
Forty Martyrs of Sebasteia, 57, 304n35
Foucault, Michel, on monsters, 128–29
foundation narratives, Christian, 11, 52–53; violence in, 195, 223
foundation narratives, Islamic, 13, 146–47, 327n4; asceticism in, 180; communal, 15–16, 168, 169; *futūḥ* in, 191; *hijra* in, 230; *jihād* in, 171; of *umma*, 1–3, 14, 15–17, 145, 276, 279; violence in, 16–20, 195, 201
Fowden, Elizabeth Key, 150, 177
funerals: al-Awzāʿī's, 177, 178; and communal identity, 363n108, 364n120; Ibn Ḥanbal's, 177, 245; Muslim protocols for, 258, 260–61, 263, 265–66; Roman, 91–92
futūḥ , Islamic, 13, 15, 17; bribery attempts during, 247, 360n66; Christians following, 233; militant ascetics in, 168, 212; miraculous interpretations of, 185, 344n59; *mujāhidūn* of, 169, 220; narratives of, 146–47, 153, 164, 170, 191, 289n35, 338n81

Gabaditani, conversion to Christianity, 315n74
Gaddis, Michael, 124, 307n64, 309n89
games, public: boundary transgressions at, 117; injunctions against, 116–18
Geertz, Clifford, 9; on shared semiotics, 165, 279
Genesius (martyr), 304n35
George (martyr), 158
Gervasius (martyr), 60
Ghazāla (wife of Shabīb), 354n103
ghāzīs (raiders), 165, 169; ascetic piety of, 18, 191; belief in *jihād*, 210, 218; influence on Ibn Ḥanbal, 239; non-Muslims among, 253; view of monks, 354n5
Gnostics, ascetics among, 176
God, single community of, 33, 79, 119; and communal identity, 155; Ibn Ḥanbal on, 256; Kharijites and, 204, 205; primordial origins of, 235
Goehring, James, 121, 318n25; on ascetics, 128, 176, 322n82
Grabar, Oleg, 151, 152
Gregory (patriarch of Antioch), 325n124
Gregory Nazianzus, 295n27; and Emperor Julian, 71, 297n52; on Matrona's Cave, 47
Gregory of Neocaesarea, 319n41
Gregory of Nyssa, 58; on Forty Martyrs of Sebasteia, 57

habitus: Roman, 98–99; semiotic forms of, 102
ḥadīths: antimonastic, 178–80, 185, 187; on *jihād*, 15, 186, 187
al-Ḥajjāj, women captives of, 229
Ḥakīm al-Tirmidhī, *Nawādir al-uṣūl*, 160
Ḥanbalīs: boundary maintenance by, 19, 258, 260; communities of, 19, 234–35; community within a community of, 239, 255, 264–65, 277; following of *sunna*, 235; jurisprudence of, 346n94; militant, 271; relations with non-Muslims, 265; respect for caliphs, 255–56; violence against, 365n143; and Wahhābīs, 365n144
handshakes, with non-Muslims, 244, 359n57
Hārūn al-Rashīd, 246, 247
Ḥayyān b. Ẓabyān, 209
Helena (mother of Constantine), 104, 105
Heraclius (emperor), 221, 233; Syrian view of, 355n9
Ḥijāz, Arabs of, 154
hijra, 13, 144, 208; in formation narratives, 230; Kharijites and, 224; origin of, 327n1
Hilarion (ascetic), 114, 319n40
history, Islamic: inward-looking, 164–65; place of Kharijites in, 202–3; problems associated with, 218–19, 332n33; sources of, 148, 208, 218–19, 289n35, 329n12; traditionalist, 329n12; tribal elements in, 152
Honorius (emperor), 116
Hōrmīzd, Rabban, 114–15
Ḥunayn b. Isḥāq, 247–48
Ḥurqūs b. Zuhayr, 206
Hypatia of Alexandria, murder of, 110, 318n12
Hypatius (monk), 117–18

Ibāḍiyya (Khārijī sect), 216
Iberia, Arab conquest of, 144
Ibn Abī Yalʿlā, *Ṭabaqāt*, 234
Ibn ʿAsākir, 161

Ibn Dhakwān, *Sīra* of, 214, 225; *Sīra*, 224
Ibn Ḥibbān, 172
Ibn Isḥāq: martyr stories of, 158–59, 163; *Sīra*, 157, 245
Ibn Khabbāb, ʿAbd Allāh, 196; murder of, 197, 199, 216, 223
Ibn al-Mubārak, ʿAbd Allāh, 14–15, 18, 191, 222, 343n38; asceticism of, 166, 181–82; fasting by, 182, 343n46; as *ghāzī*, 165, 278; *Kitāb al-jihād*, 161, 166, 180, 182–83, 186–89, 208–9, 219, 227; *Kitāb al-zuhd*, 180–81, 183, 208; on martyrdom, 210; on miracles, 344n59; as model, 168, 338n86; on personal will, 182–84; practice of *jihād*, 180, 208, 211; purity of intention, 343n39
Ibn Muljam, 257, 258, 265
Ibn Qutayba, 227, 335n66; *ʿUyūn al-akhbār*, 160, 178
Ibn Saʿd, *Kitāb al-ṭabaqāt*, 178, 179
Ibrāhīm b. Adham, 172, 194, 334n54; ascetic praxis of, 173–76; conversion of, 173; encounters with ascetics, 176, 177–78, 192; encounters with supernatural, 173, 340n10; followers of, 191; mentors of, 174; in modern imaginary, 340n9; as new Adam, 174
identity: in antiquity, 7, 22, 274, 287n20, 292n3; constructedness of, 292n5; discourse of, 22; narrative in, 9–10, 48, 50, 87, 88, 287n20, 294n23, 344n61; Palestinian, 67–68; primordialist notions of, 22–23, 49–50, 66, 69–70, 344n61; Roman, 32, 58, 98, 99
identity, Christian: in Antioch, 43; Christological controversies over, 121; John Chrysostom on, 31; disciplining of, 11; Greek ethnicity in, 6; monks' role in, 136–38, 326n129; persecution in, 223, 274; role of martyrs in, 45, 71–72, 85, 274, 332n41; monastic violence and, 130–31; in Roman Empire, 6
identity, communal: boundaries in, 123–24, 273, 318n18; change processes of, 8–9; funerals and, 363n108, 364n120; and militant piety, 5; role of Islamic ascetics in, 168, 170–71, 179, 190, 194, 214, 342n34; role of narrative in, 7, 50, 273–74, 287n20, 332n42; role of suffering in, 8; semiotic elements of, 24; victimization narratives in, 69–70
identity, confessional: of Antioch, 30–31, 111, 293n10; of ascetics, 170, 171–72, 175–76, 341n18; in late antiquity, 21; in monasticism, 296n41; monks' disciplining of, 136–38
identity, Islamic, 13, 165, 222, 230, 361n93; authenticity in, 213, 214–15; Ibn Ḥanbal's role in, 237, 241; Kharijites' role in, 214–15, 223–24; militant piety in, 145, 201, 278; renunciation in, 214; role of ascetics in, 168, 170–71, 179, 190, 194, 214, 342n34
identity, Jewish: markers of, 295n36; primordial narratives of, 70
intolerance, Christian, 21–22, 95, 109–10; political process of, 23–24
Isaac (archbishop of Alexandria), relations with Muslims, 232–33
Isaac of Nineveh, 226
Islam: borderlands of, 149–59; Christians' knowledge of, 248–51, 267; early history of, 148, 164–65, 327n4; imagined past of, 15; in late antiquity, 145, 153–56, 164, 166–67, 328n8; moral imaginary of, 171, 339nn2–3; primordial, 12–13, 189, 200–201, 213–14, 221–22, 224, 226, 233–34, 240, 241, 270; recognition of Christian ascetics in, 156–58; revivalism in, 271. *See also* communities, Islamic
Īšōʿyahb (Nestorian bishop), 113

Jacob of Serugh, 117
Jacobs, Andrew, 6, 295n27
jāhiliyya (time of ignorance), 161, 225, 258
al-Jāḥiẓ, 225, 270; *al-Radd ʿalā al-naṣārā*, 248–51; on sexual mores, 364n138; on treatment of Christians, 267, 268
Jahīza (mother of Shabīb), 228, 353n101; militancy of, 229
Jameson, Fredric, 87–88
Jerome (saint), Life of Hilarion, 114
Jesus: celebration of Passover, 51, 302n16; dream visions of, 248
Jews: communal meals of, 25; conversions by, 114, 245; heretics, 11, 299n67; genealogies of, 303n19; in intermingled communities, 31, 59, 257, 293n10; Kharijites and, 216, 217, 223; Muslim dislike of, 250; narratives of, 70; sacred remains of, 59, 306n50; violence against, 81–84, 109; violence by, 82, 83
jihād, 14–15, 210, 279; and asceticism, 182–85,

jihād (*cont.*)
194, 211, 227; *ḥadīths* on, 15, 186; Ibn Ḥanbal on, 19, 211, 280; Ibn al-Mubārak on, 161, 166, 180, 182–83, 186–89, 208–9, 219, 227; and monasticism, 14, 15, 160, 161, 180, 185–87, 201, 227, 276, 336n70; in moral imaginary, 339n2; in past narratives, 171, 186–87
John of Ephesus, 110, 126, 330n20; *Lives of the Eastern Saints*, 131, 132, 135, 136
Johnson, Aaron, 6
Judaism, rabbinic: boundary transgression in, 26–27, 294n24; early Christianity and, 5–6, 11, 24–32, 36–38; fasting in, 294n20; priesthood of, 28; semiotics of, 27–30, 43, 295n27
Judaizing, 293n14; at Antioch, 31, 37–38, 41, 170, 292n10
judiciary, Roman: martyrs and, 45, 56, 74, 83–86, 125, 130, 155, 185, 337n79
Julian (emperor), 30; Christian subjects of, 34, 71, 84, 134, 297n52, 308n82; and Cynic philosophers, 34–35; and Gregory Nazianzus, 71, 297n52; tolerance of, 71, 82–83, 84
Julian Saba: diet of, 192; rumor campaigns against, 333n45
jurisprudence, Islamic, 14; Ḥanbalī, 346n94. See also *madhāhib*
Justinian (emperor): Christian sovereignty of, 106–7, 315n74; imperial ideology of, 80

Keller, C.-A., 176
Khālid b. al-Walīd, 207, 353n91, 360n66
Khalidi, Tarif, 152
Kharijites, 16–18, 19, 190, 197–98; ascetic ideology of, 352n71; ascetic influence on, 342n35; authenticity of, 208; availability of past for, 227; boundary maintenance by, 213, 224–25, 226; and caliphal power, 217–18, 220, 221, 352n71; child murder by, 216, 351nn65, 70; Christians and, 216, 217, 223; devotion to *sunna*, 219, 228; dissociation among, 225, 235; Ibn Ḥanbal's rejection of, 234–35, 277; and Jews, 216, 217, 223; martyrs, 209, 227, 349n35; militant piety of, 195, 206, 219, 220, 222; *mujāhidūn* and, 207–8, 213, 221–22, 277; murder of women, 215–16, 217, 223, 351n70; Muslim heresiographers on, 353n87; in Muslim imaginary, 228; on Muslim rulership, 207; and non-Kharijite Muslims, 215, 219; primordial aspects of, 200–201, 213–14, 221–22; purity of intention, 219; quietist, 216, 224; reading of past narratives, 202, 218, 222–34, 257, 276–77; rebellions of, 203, 218–20; relations with ʿAlī, 197–201, 203–4, 216, 221, 222, 351n66; renunciation by, 226; resonance for Muslims, 227–89; role in Islamic community, 214, 230; role in Islamic identity, 214–15, 223–24; romanticization of, 257; sects of, 224; self-renunciation by, 228; and single community of God, 204, 205; among Umayyads, 17; violence by, 212–25, 257, 277, 351n66; Wāṣil's rebuke to, 214–15; wives of, 214, 350n57; women's defiance of, 217, 351n66; women warriors among, 354n103; on worldly corruption, 203
Khirrīt b. Rāshīd (a Kharajite), 203–4, 351n66
Khusrau II (king of Persia), 150
kissing, in Christian communities, 6, 83, 292n9, 310n5
Kister, M. J., 251, 280
Kitāb adab al-ghurabāʾ, 268
Kristeva, Julia, 129

lamentation, as *jāhilī* practice, 261, 364n123
Lebanon: Israeli invasion (1982), 68; religious conflict in, 20
Leontius (prefect), 117, 118
Leo the Great, 32
lepers, violence by, 139–40
Libanius, 10; on Christian asceticism, 95, 142; on destruction of art, 100–101; oration to Theodosius, 86, 89, 90, 93–98, 101, 107, 108; panegyric to Antioch, 89–90; past narrative of, 79; on Roman sovereignty, 103
Liberius (bishop), 72, 309n89; as martyr, 73
Livy, on *decemvirs*, 313n47
Lyons, martyrs of, 57–58

Macarius of Tkōw: confessional cleansing by, 137–38; pogrom of, 4, 110, 139
madhāhib, 356n12; Abbasid rulers in, 358n42; Ibn Ḥanbal's, 230, 234, 235, 271
magic: monks' use of, 128, 296n43; Shenoute on, 115, 300n1; Syrian use of, 33

Magnus Maximus (emperor), 83, 310n6
al-Mahdī (caliph), 358n42
Maier, Harry, 32
al-Malaṭī, 215
al-Ma'mūn (caliph): *miḥna* of, 236, 238, 240, 248; patronage by, 247
Manichaeans, 155; ascetics among, 176; Augustine on, 32; Muslim involvement with, 249
Marcianus (monk), 114
Mare (wanderer), 126, 322n78
Mar Ḥnānīšōʿ, 113
Mark the Deacon, 110
Mar Marouta (ascetic), 340n14
Maro (Stylite), 113
marriages, Christian-Muslim, 253, 254
Martin of Tours, miracles of, 115
martyr narratives, Christian: archetypes of, 74; bribery in, 337n80; of Christian communities, 52–53, 57–58, 77; Eusebius's, 54–57, 303n25; Greek-language, 309n87; influence on *futūḥ* narratives, 247; North African, 332n35; pornographic detail in, 54–55, 124–26, 185, 304n29, 321n71; Roman judiciary in, 74; torture in, 124–27
martyr narratives, Islamic, 158–59, 163, 164; bribery in, 337n80
martyrs, Christian: Ambrose on, 81–82; anniversaries of, 58–59, 74, 306n45; in Arian controversy, 60–62, 73; Augustine on, 62–65, 73, 75–76, 309n84; availability of God through, 186; boundary maintenance by, 15, 64, 275; John Chrysostom on, 45, 75; in communal identity, 45, 55, 71–72, 85, 274, 332n41; in communal narratives, 52–53, 57–58, 77; Donatist, 63–64, 76–77, 309n84; intransigence of, 55, 73; local, 54, 57–58, 304n35; of Lyons, 57–58; of Matrona's Cave, 47; Melitian, 33, 64–65; of Milan, 59–62; as models, 202; monks and, 124–27, 186, 227; monstrous qualities of, 140; of Najrān, 201, 278, 337n80; *parrhesia* of, 85; in past narratives, 71–72, 75–76; role in Roman society, 310n9; and Roman judiciary, 45, 56, 74, 83–86, 130, 155, 185, 337n79; and Roman truth rituals, 185, 345n62; of Rome, 58–59; sacred space of, 65, 75; of Sebasteia, 57, 304n35; self-fashioning by, 345n62; torture of, 124–27; true and false, 62–64, 309n84; as witnesses, 337n79. *See also* persecution
martyrs, Islamic, 16, 158–59, 208–10, 337n79; *akhbār* on, 209; and ascetics, 158; Kharijites, 209, 227, 349n35
martyrs, Maccabean, 294n27
martyr shrines: Byzantine, 151; to Hebrew prophets, 295n27; monks' residence at, 124
Mary of Egypt (saint), 128
Matrona's Cave, 294n27; cures at, 47
Matthew (ascetic), 119
Maurice (emperor), persecution of pagans, 325n124
Mayrian (Georgian king), conversion of, 173
Melitian church (Egypt), 307n68; Athanasius and, 65, 112–13; martyrs of, 33, 64–65
Menouthis, monastic violence at, 109
Mercurius (saint), 140
Mesopotamia: Arab conquest of, 203; borderlands of, 149, 150, 151
miḥna: Ibn Ḥanbal during, 240, 248, 356n18, 358n42; al-Ma'mūn's, 236, 238, 240, 248; al-Muʿtaṣim's, 240, 248; narratives of, 356n22
Milan: Arians of, 60–61, 306n53; martyrs of, 59–62; primordial past of, 60
militants. *See* ascetics, Christian militant; ascetics, Islamic militant; piety, militant
Millar, Fergus, 91
miracles, 115; Ibn al-Mubārak on, 344n59; military, 189
monasticism: communal boundaries of, 120–21, 122; confessional identity in, 296n41; *ḥadīths* against, 178–80, 185, 187; *jihād* and, 14, 15, 160, 161, 180, 185–87, 201, 227, 276, 336n70; Pachomian, 343n51; Persian, 184, 344n56; primordial past of, 123
monks: black-robed, 97, 313n50; in borderlands, 158; during Christological controversies, 158, 275; coexistence with Muslims, 232; conflict with demons, 336n68; definition of Christian communities, 130; diet of, 162, 336n74; drunkenness of, 100, 314n59; as gatekeepers of truth, 157–58; healing abilities of, 232; as heretics, 128; individual will of, 184; Monophysite, 114–15; as monsters, 127–31; in Muslim communities, 169–70; Muslim tradition on, 156–61; Persian, 184; as plague carriers, 140; reproving of Muslims, 335n67; subversion of society by, 129–30; true and false, 335n63;

monks (*cont.*)
use of magic, 128, 296n43; wandering, 142, 313nn49–50, 335n62
monks, militant, 12, 143, 317n5; of Antioch, 103, 106; boundary maintenance by, 44, 127, 137–38, 140, 159, 275; disciplining of communities, 134–40; patrolling of Christian identity, 136–38, 326n129; and public games, 116, 117–18; relationship to martyrs, 124–27, 186, 227; Syrian, 97, 108, 313n50; transgression of boundaries by, 119–21
monotheism: aggressive, 107; Arab, 144, 158; of late antiquity, 147, 190, 203
monsters: at boundaries, 129, 130–31; defense from alterity, 141–43; monks as, 127–31
Morony, Michael, 226
Moses the Ethiopian, 128
Muʿādh b. Jabal, 15, 17, 162–63, 220
Muʿāwiya, war with ʿAlī, 16, 197, 198, 199
al-Mubarrad, *Kamīl*, 214–15
al-Mughīra, 360n66
Muḥammad: on asceticism, 178–79; behavior toward non-Muslims, 254–55, 359n56, 362n99; Christian view of, 2–3, 160, 245; on community, 212, 230; on *jihād*, 185; metanarratives of, 13; on monasticism, 180, 185; monks' recognition of, 157, 245, 333n48; prophetic authority of, 16, 152–53, 156, 276; responsibility to God, 204–5; Roman threat to, 333n47
mujāhidūn: caliph ʿUmar and, 162, 166, 189; Christian ascetics among, 161; commanding and forbidding by, 205; of *futūḥ* era, 169, 220; hybrid identity of, 220; Kharijites and, 207–8, 213, 221–22, 277; as models, 168–69; renunciation by, 167, 208; al-Ṭabari on, 336n68. *See also* ascetics, Islamic militant
al-Mukhtār, rebellion of, 219
Muqātil b. Sulaymān, *tafsīr* of, 178
Muslims: anxiety concerning Christians, 248–51, 253; Christian converts, 232; Christian slaves of, 231–32, 254; greeting of non-Muslims, 244, 254, 359n57, 362n97; monks and, 156–61, 169–70, 232, 335n67; recognition of Christians, 251, 252, 267–68; relations with Magians, 244, 359n51; tolerance for Christians, 231–33
al-Muʿtaṣim (caliph), torture of Ibn Ḥanbal, 240, 248
al-Mutawakkil (caliph): and Ibn Ḥanbal, 238, 240; transgressiveness of, 239, 268, 269

Najrān, Christian martyrs of, 201, 278, 337n80
names, Christian, Muslim restrictions on, 268, 364n134
narratives: and communal identity, 7, 50, 273–74, 287n20, 332n42; in constitution of reality, 332n36; emplotted, 48, 50–51, 67, 93, 202, 273; evaluation of, 67, 154–55; and identity formation, 9–10, 48, 50, 87, 88, 287n20, 294n23, 344n61; in integration of events, 305n42; Marxist, 87–88; in meaning of trauma, 304n26; of militant piety, 50–51; and perception, 87; and political praxis, 87; primordialist, 49, 50, 59, 74–75; selective appropriation in, 67, 155; of victimization, 81–82. *See also* communal narratives; foundation narratives; martyr narratives; past narratives
nationalism, ethnic, 69, 301nn6–10; Armenian, 66–67; Croatian, 50, 301n10; primordial, 49
Newby, Gordon, 158
Nilus of Ancyra, 142
al-Nīsābūrī, Isḥāq b. Ibrāhīm b. Hāniʾ, 262–63
Noth, Albrecht, 218, 251, 280

Orestes (prefect), stoning of, 110
Otto, Rudolph, 130

Pachomius, 343n51; vision of community, 121
paganism, 317n10; boundaries with Christianity, 34–35; Christian violence against, 10, 86, 92, 94, 97; Constantine on, 312n38; in Gaza, 297n44; semiotics of, 107; under Theodosius I, 93
paideia, imperial ideology of, 98, 99, 101–2
Palestine: communal narratives of, 67–68; Jewish narratives of, 70; monasticism in, 360n63
parrhesia (freedom of speech, behavior): of Jews, 133; of martyrs, 85
Pasch, celebration of, 51–52, 114
past narratives: Armenian, 49, 50, 66–67; communal, 23, 68; Roman, 76, 79–80, 96, 102; Serbian, 49–50, 69. *See also* foundation narratives; primordialism

past narratives, Christian, 16; Ambrose's use of, 10, 79, 83, 104; communal, 16, 70–72, 74–75, 78–79; martyrs in, 71–72, 75–76; primordial, 59, 60, 74–75
past narratives, Islamic, 148–49, 201, 202, 327n4; of *futūḥ*, 146–47, 153, 164, 170, 191, 289n35, 338n81; hybrid, 154, 156, 165, 169; *jihād* in, 171, 186–87; Kharijites reading of, 202, 218, 222–34, 257, 276–77; militant piety in, 167, 189, 191; Muḥammad in, 187; pious elements in, 153–54, 332n33; tribal, 153, 332n33
Paul (Novatian ascetic), 114
Paulinus of Milan, *Life of Ambrose*, 59, 61, 62
Paul of Antioch, 114
Pelagia (saint), 128
Penn, Michael Phillip, 6, 292n9
persecution, 51, 53, 55, 71, 155, 163; antipagan, 325n124; in Christian identity, 223, 274; effect on communities, 53–55, 87; of Jews, 81–84; tetrarchic, 82. *See also* martyrs
Persian empire: borderlands of, 150; Christian communities of, 3–4; hunting in, 173; Islamic conquest of, 1, 13, 144, 220, 221; Muslim ascetics and, 163, 189
Petit, Paul, 95
Pheidias, destruction of works of, 100
Philocrates, 96, 313n46
Phinehas (priest), murders by, 26–27, 294n24
Photinians, Ambrose on, 105
piety, Christian militant, 5, 50, 81–84, 102, 272; official interpretations of, 88–89; under Theodosius I, 3, 10, 79
piety, Islamic militant, 14, 201–2; among Kharijites, 195, 206, 219, 220, 222; in community formation, 12, 17–20, 201; *ghāzī*, 18, 191; Ibn al-Mubārak on, 166; in identity formation, 145, 201, 278; in past narratives, 167, 189, 191; in *umma*, 169–70
piety, militant, 3–5, 7; emplotted narratives of, 50–51; in communal identity, 5. *See also* ascetics, Christian militant; violence, Christian
Plutarch, 89
Poletta, Frances, 67
Polybius, on Roman character, 91–92
pornography: aesthetics of, 125; in martyr narratives, 54–55, 124–26, 185, 304n29, 321n71
Porphyry (monk), 110
Poseidon *(ducenarius)*, 84
primordialism, 9, 66–67, 69–70, 308n72; in community foundation, 23
Procopius, on Justinian, 106–7, 315n74
Protasius (martyr), 60
Prudentius, martyr narratives of, 124
public secrets, 42–43, 44, 300n81; in Roman Empire, 300n82

Qādisiyya, battle of, 161–62, 163; militant ascetics at, 189–91
Qays b. Saʿd b. ʿUbāda, 200
Quae gesta sunt inter Liberium et Felicem episcopos, 72, 73
Quraysh (Meccans), 334n50
Qur'ān, 148; createdness of, 235–36, 237, 356n14; *maṣāḥif* of, 200, 347n13

al-Rabīʿ b. Sulaymān, 241
raiding: captives taken in, 358n46; Ibn Ḥanbal on, 242; non-Muslim captives in, 253. See also *ghāzīs*; *mujāhidūn*
Rapaport, Era, 70
Rawḥ al-Qurayshī, martyrdom of, 246
Rayṭa bint Yazīd, 351n70
Ricoeur, Paul, 9
rituals, of late antiquity, 307n70; Jewish, 25; Roman, 77–78, 102, 314n65, 345n62
Robinson, Chase, 190, 210, 218, 226
Roman emperors: benefactions of, 91; in communal narratives, 84; historical station of, 103–5, 107, 312n35; images of, 92; models of rulership, 80, 106; in past narratives, 96, 102
Roman emperors, Christian: cultural symbolism of, 101; past narratives of, 96; protection of Roman ideals, 103; punishment under, 3; role in Roman world, 86, 102
Roman Empire: civilizing mission of, 89–93, 97, 98; cultural heroes of, 101; festivals of, 58; narratives of female domination in, 96; past narratives of, 79–80, 96, 102
Roman Empire, late: anti-Chalcedonian communities of, 233; Arab conquests in, 144; Christian identity in, 6; Christian militancy in, 5, 81–84; Christian violence in, 88–89, 274; common culture in, 99; eastern borderlands of, 149–50; militant piety in, 5, 81–84; Muslim conquest of, 1–3, 13, 15, 144, 220, 221; narratives of, 7–8,

Roman Empire, late (*cont.*)
10, 78, 86, 89; place of Christian communities in, 106; resistance to, 7–8, 10; social reality of, 78; tolerance in, 86; transgression of norms in, 348n23; truths of, 52. *See also* elites, late Roman; judiciary, Roman
romanitas: narrative-based, 92; role of temples in, 98, 99–100
Rome (city): martyrs of, 58–59; primordial past of, 58
Rousseau, Phillip, 124
Rustam (Persian commander), ascetic emissaries to, 163, 189, 345n72

Sághy, M., 59
Sahm b. Ghālib al-Hujaymī, 216
Said, Edward, 67–68
Ṣāliḥ b. Aḥmad b. Ḥanbal, 236, 239; on Ibn Ḥanbal's death, 245
Ṣāliḥ b. Musarriḥ, 209–10, 220, 222, 226, 349n35; asceticism of, 190, 214; insurgency of, 228, 350n53; on renunciation, 212–13
Samuel of Kalamun (martyr), 127; Life of, 340n15
Sarī al-Saqaṭī (mystic), 238; benevolence of, 193–94, 195, 279; *jihād* by, 193, 346nn81, 87; mentor of, 191–92, 357n31; social self of, 194
Sāwirūs b. al-Muqaffaʿ, 355n8
Sayf b. ʿUmar, 329n12
secrecy: concerning boundary transgression, 39–40, 42, 43; societal role of, 43–44
semiotics: of asceticism, 155–56, 171, 174, 176, 191; of borderlands, 152; of communal identity, 24; of fasting, 46; of Judaism, 27–30, 43, 295n27; of martyrdom, 155; in narratives, 93; social context of, 331n29
semiotics, shared: of Islamic communities, 145–46, 156, 195, 248, 276, 278–79; of late antiquity, 34, 36, 43, 47–48, 99, 127, 147–49, 156, 169, 195, 275, 295n27, 301n5
Serbs: fear of Croatian nationals, 301n10; past narratives of, 49–50, 69
Sergius (martyr saint), 150, 151, 154
Sergius (monk), violence by, 131–34
Sergius the Stylite, 32
Severus (zealot), antagonism of Jews, 133
Severus of Antioch, on games, 116–17
Shabīb b. Yazīd, 226, 350n57, 352n71; Christian authors on, 353n98; as exemplar of virtue, 228; raid on al-Kūfa, 354n103; rebellion of, 210, 349n38
al-Shāfiʿī, 241
Shenoute (archimandrite), 115, 123, 125–26, 300n1; on magic, 115, 300n1
Shīʿa, 225, 363n104; ascetic influence on, 342n35; idea of community, 357n35
Shils, Edward, 9
Simāk b. Yazīd, 217
Simeon (Syrian zealot), 257
Simeon the Mountaineer, 135–37; monstrous qualities of, 138
Smith, Jonathan Z., 65
Smith, R. R. R., 100
society, Roman: Christian narratives of, 86; Christians' assimilation into, 53; imaginative space of, 312n38; martyrs in, 310n9; monks' subversion of, 129–30; Theodosius I in, 102
Socrates Scholasticus, 111, 133; on ascetics, 114
Somers, Margaret, 8; on narrative, 9–10, 48, 67, 88, 154–55, 202, 273
sovereignty, Roman: Ambrose on, 104–5; Justinian's, 106–7, 315n74; Libanius on, 103
Sozomenos, on Theodosius, 103, 106
space, sacred, 65, 75, 78; in foundation narratives, 49; of late antiquity, 304n27
stele cults, Nabatean, 151, 331n27
Stephen of Mar Sabas, 161, 245, 246, 336n68, 360n64
Sufis, 171; *ṭabaqāt* literature of, 344n59
Ṣufriyyas (Kharijite sect), 210
Sufyān al-Thawrī, 358n42
Sulpicius Severus, *Life of Martin of Tours*, 115
sunna, Islamic: on boundary maintenance, 179; Ḥanbalī following of, 235; Ibn Ḥanbal on, 18–19; Kharijites' devotion to, 219, 228
Suny, Ronald Grigor, 8, 66–67; on identity, 22, 274; on primordialism, 9, 49, 50, 66
Sūrat al-Māʾida, 248–49
Sviri, Sara, 160
Symeon of Emesa, 115
Symeon the Stylite (the elder), 126
Symeon the Stylite (the younger), 127, 140; confrontation of heretics, 319n33; sanctuary of, 150–51; self-mortification of, 126, 128
synagogues, Jewish: of late antiquity, 294n25,

295n30, 296n36; power for Christians, 25, 27, 28, 30, 31, 36, 40; violence against, 12, 81–84, 85, 134
Synesius, on torture, 125
Syria: Arab conquest of, 203; borderlands of, 149–51; Chalcedonian creed in, 132; Christians of, 108, 134–40, 192; Islamic communities of, 146; pillar saints of, 154

al-Ṭabarī, Abū Jaʿfar, 156, 332n43, 329n12; on ascetics, 161–62; on battle of Qādisiyya, 163, 189; on Ibn Ḥanbal, 236; on Kharijites, 199, 203, 208, 212–13, 214, 217–21, 228; martyr stories of, 158–59; on *mujāhidūn*, 336n68; on Rustam, 345n72; *Taʾrīkh*, 158, 159, 212–13, 221
Taussig, Michael, 42, 43
Telemachus (monk), martyrdom of, 116
temples, pagan: imperial policy toward, 93–94; role in civic life, 90, 97, 102; role in *romanitas*, 98, 99–100; violence against, 86, 92, 97–102
Tertullian, on games, 116
al-Thaʿālib, monastery of, Muslims at, 269–70
Theodore (martyr), 124–27; militancy of, 246
Theodoret: on John Chrysostom, 300n86; on Julian Saba, 113
Theodore the Recruit (martyr), 84–85
Theodosius I (emperor): Ambrose and, 3, 102, 103–5, 310n98; in Callinicum controversy, 82, 83; defeat of Maximus, 310n6; Libanius's oration to, 86, 89, 93–98, 101, 107, 108; on monks, 312n41; zealotry under, 3, 10, 12, 79, 103, 105–6
Theophilus (bishop of Alexandria), 142
Theophylact Simocatta, 150
Timothy of Kākhushtā, 113
Trout, Dennis, 58
True Cross, discovery of, 104, 105
truth, transcendent, 29, 52, 56, 127; communities' possession of, 125; of Kharijites, 203

ʿUbayd Allāh Ziyād, 210
ʿUmar b. al-Khaṭṭāb (caliph), 166, 204, 241; asceticism of, 162, 189–90; Christians under, 251, 348n25; diet of, 192, 239; enforcement of communal norms, 205, 206; on funerals, 261; on *jihād*, 209, 345n74; and *mujāhidūn*, 162, 166, 189
ʿUmayya b. Abī al-Ṣalt, 157–58
Umayyads: Kharijites among, 17; Muslim identity under, 222; pietist rebels against, 197
umma, Islamic, 12–13; foundation narratives of, 1–3, 14–17, 145, 169, 276, 279; Ibn Ḥanbal and, 237; Kharijite influence on, 18; Kharijite threat to, 223; late antique semiotics in, 195; militant piety in, 169–70; monothestic, 158; non-Muslims in, 242–43, 250; primordial, 222, 227, 243, 254, 270, 277. *See also* communities, Islamic
Ursinus, conflict with Damasius, 72–75, 82, 85
ʿUthmān (caliph), 204, 205; Ibn Ḥanbal on, 255–56

Valens (emperor), sacrifice under, 93
Valentinian II, 93; in Altar of Victory controversy, 77–78; and martyrs, 308n75
Van Dam, Raymond, 57, 304n35
Victor (martyr), 337n80
Vincentius (martyr), 63
Vincent of Lérins, 55
Vinson, Martha, 47
violence: in communal narratives, 68–69; intercommunal, 86, 133, 201, 272
violence, Christian, 3–5, 195; at Callinicum, 81–85, 88, 106; by Damasus, 72, 74–75, 309n86; intercommunal, 89, 133; in late Roman Empire, 88–89, 272, 274; monastic, 97, 108–12, 130–40; against paganism, 10, 86, 92, 94, 97–102; against synagogues, 12, 81–84, 85, 134; under Theodosius I, 3, 10, 12, 79, 103, 105, 106. *See also* piety, militant
violence, Islamic, 1–2, 257, 263; in formation narratives, 16–20, 195, 201; imaginary of, 13–14; by Kharijites, 212–25, 257, 277, 351nn65–66, 70
Vitalis (martyr), 59

Wahhābīs, 271; Ḥanbalīs and, 365n144
Walker, Joel Thomas, 173
Wansbrough, John, 148
Wāqidī, pseudo-, *Futūḥ al-Jazīra*, 348n23
Wāṣil b. ʿAṭāʾ, 214–15, 350n59
White Monastery: boundaries of, 120; normative standards of, 122

will: annihilation of, 182; Ibn al-Mubārak on, 182–85; of monks, 184; purity of, 188
Williams, Linda, 124–25
women, Christian, 250; conversion to Islam, 252; defense of community, 297n44
women, Muslim, 354n103; Kharijite violence against, 215–16, 217, 223, 351nn65–66, 70
Woolf, Greg, 91

al-Yarmūk, battle of, 191
Yazīd b. Abī Muslim, 229

Zachariah (Christian apologist), 109
Zaman, Muhammad Qasim, 177, 364n130
Zimmermann, Fritz, 218
Zoroastrianism: Muslim involvement in, 249; Persian, 150; priests, 330n20
zuhd (asceticism), 162, 169; Ibn al-Mubārak on, 180–81, 183; Ibn Ḥanbal on, 194, 338n87. *See also* ascetics, Islamic militant
Zuqnīn Chronicle, 214

ACKNOWLEDGMENTS

I am fortunate enough to owe thanks to a great many friends, colleagues, and teachers. First among these are Hal Drake, R. Stephen Humphreys, James Brooks, Elizabeth Digeser, Clifford Ando, Michael Maas, Chase Robinson, Sharon Farmer, Nancy McLoughlin, John Lee, Cam Cocks, Dorothy Abrahamse, Conrad Barrett, Douglas Domingo-Forasté, David Hood, Karl Squitier, Timothy C. Graham, Jay Rubenstein, Justine Andrews, Charlie Steen, Tim Moy, Andrew Sandoval-Strausz, Cathleen Cahill, Liz Hutchison, Kym Gauderman, Sam Truett, and Patricia Risso, all of whom by their kindness, patience, and expertise have aided me immeasurably through the initial stages of my career, and contributed crucially to the evolution of this book. During the writing of this book itself, I benefited profoundly and ceaselessly from the wisdom, generosity, and love of Michael Proulx, David Torres-Rouff, Christina Torres-Rouff, Justin Stephens, Eric Fournier, Jonathan Sciarcon, Heidi Marx-Wolf, Monica Orozco, Tryntje Helfferich, Rachael Sizgorich, Cecily MacCaffrey, and Kathy Drake. I am also grateful for the generosity, encouragement, and advice of Suleiman Mourad, Nadia Maria El Cheikh, Ra'anan Boustan, Nimrod Hurvitz, Fred Donner, Cam Grey, Raymond Van Dam, Brent Shaw, Arietta Papaconstantinou, and Christopher Melchert. I am deeply indebted to the School of Advanced Research in Santa Fe, New Mexico, the Department of History at the University of New Mexico, the Department of History at Oregon State University in Corvallis, the Gorham Foundation, the National Endowment for the Humanities, and Claudia Rapp and the University of California Multi-Campus Research Group for their generous support and hospitality. I am grateful also for the permission granted by Johns Hopkins University Press and Cambridge University Press to reprint portions of articles that appeared initially in the *Journal of Early Christian Studies* and *Past & Present*. I also thank Edgar Kent Press and the

University of Toronto Press for their generous grant of permission to reprint sections of a chapter that first appeared in *Religious Identity in Late Antiquity* (2006). Finally, I feel particularly intense gratitude to Daniel Boyarin, Virginia Burrus, Derek Kreuger, and Jerry Singerman for all that they have done to bring this work from manuscript to book. Whatever errors, omissions, or inaccuracies this book still contains are of course my responsibility alone.